JUSTICE BEYOND ORWELL

Données de catalogage avant publication (Canada)

Vedette principale au titre

Justice beyond Orwell

2-89073-554-0

1. Justice, Administration of - Canada - Congresses. 2. Justice and politics - Canada - Congresses. 3. Civil rights - Canada - Congresses. 4. Orwell, George, 1903-1950. I. Abella, Rosalie S. (Rosalie Silberman). II. Rothman, Melvin L. III. Canadian Institute for the Administration of Justice.

KE8200.A66J87 1985   347.71   C86-096015-3

ISBN-2-89073-554-0

Legal Deposit
4th Trimester, 1985
National Library of Canada
Bibliothèque Nationale du Québec

JUSTICE BEYOND ORWELL

Edited by
Rosalie S. Abella and Melvin L. Rothman

Institut canadien d'administration de la justice
Canadian Institute for the Administration of Justice

LES ÉDITIONS
YVON BLAIS INC.
430, RUE ST-PIERRE
MONTRÉAL (QUÉ.)
H2Y 2M5
TÉL. 842-3937
TÉL. 1-800-363-3047

Remerciements

Comme toute entreprise de cette nature, celle-ci n'a été accomplie que grâce à la collaboration de plusieurs personnes. L'énergie intellectuelle de cette conférence a été fournie par les membres de son comité organisateur: M. le professeur Jean-Louis Baudouin, M. le juge Stephen Borins, M. le juge Marvin A. Catzman, Me Brian A. Crane, c.r., M. le juge Charles L. Dubin, M. le juge Jacques Dugas, Me L. Yves Fortier, c.r., M. le juge Charles D. Gonthier, Madame le juge Claire L'Heureux-Dubé, M. le juge John W. Morden, M. le juge en chef associé Lawrence A. Poitras, M. le professeur Ed Ratushny et M. le juge Claude Vallerand.

Le professionnalisme et l'efficacité de Me Yvon Blais et Me Johanne Forget, de la maison Les Éditions Yvon Blais Inc., ont été indispensables à la réalisation rapide de la publication de cette oeuvre. La compétence administrative de Gail Hill et de Jacqueline Grégoire a facilité le recueil et l'assemblage des documents de travail. Enfin, nous avons une dette énorme envers Mariette Dufresne, de l'Institut canadien d'administration de la justice, qui nous a aidés sans relâche à l'organisation de cette conférence.

La conférence n'aurait pas été possible sans l'aide financière du ministère de la Justice du Canada, du Conseil de recherches en sciences humaines du Canada, de la Commission de réforme du droit du Canada, des Fonds d'études juridiques du Barreau du Québec, du Secrétariat d'État, de la Province d'Ontario et de l'Ontario Law Foundation.

R.S. Abella
M.L. Rothman
Coprésidents de la Conférence

Preface

The 1984 Annual Conference of the Canadian Institute for the Administration of Justice was its 10th annual programme and the occasion was taken to look ahead — ahead to Law and Justice Beyond 1984.

The Conference, held in Ottawa from October 24th to 27th 1984 attracted over 250 conferees including judges, practising and academic lawyers, representatives of government and members of the public with interest in the administration of justice. The Conference was chaired by Judge Rosie Abella and Justice Mel Rothman. There were over 50 speakers and commentators.

This book represents a number of the principal papers which are thus maintained in a permanent form as a contribution to Canadian legal literature. The Conference on which these papers were based owed much of its success to the fact that those contributing papers were called upon not only to review past developments but to predict and suggest future ones. The approach was emphasized by constructing conference themes around quotations from George Orwell's ''1984''.

We are grateful that much of the work that provoked such useful discussion in the Conference can be made available in this form. The Department of Justice of Canada has provided financial support to this publication, and we are, again, indebted to Les Éditions Yvon Blais Inc. for undertaking the publication of annual conference papers.

W.A. Stevenson
President, C.I.A.J., 1984-5.

Introduction

Law has long occupied a position of intense curiosity and scrutiny for thoughtful observers of the human condition.

Through the centuries, as laws meandered through social and political institutions, philosophers of various ideologies have promoted their virtue, analyzed their impact, and denounced their inadequacies. They were defended as essential to public order, and decried as destructive of private initiative. They were alternately seen as maximizing civilized conduct, and as maximizing civilized chaos. But through the debate, their need was rarely questioned. Laws in their purest form regulate the permissible minimal standards below which behaviour is not tolerated, and so pronounce the character of the society which promulgates them. Their extent and intent may be questioned, but their existence as a body of social rules is not. At the very least, laws are seen as the midwife to justice, and as such their necessity is respected.

It is the notion of justice which attracts the wider controversy, not as a guiding principle, but as a concept of disputed definition. One person's justice is someone else's constraint. Because justice is an exalted but ineffable objective, and because it carries semantic baggage of different sizes, it is a magnet for all, a scapegoat to many, an anathema to few. It demands consistency only to the extent that public consensus permits, and since public consensus is itself an ineffable objective, it seemingly permits an incomprehensible inconsistency in methodology. To the extent that laws either promote or detract from the operative definition of justice, depending on the time and the issue, they bear the burden of justifying the means to the desired but undefined objective.

Law and justice intertwine inseparably but not necessarily harmoniously. These essential social tools cohabit naturally, invoking each other's morality and drawing nourishment from one another, but their union is not without tension. Laws make no sense without a just end; justice makes no sense without just means. When the ends are unclear, the means taunt irrelevancy; when the means are irrelevant, the ends are suspect.

The purpose of this Conference entitled "Law and Justice Beyond *1984*", was to isolate and assess the extent to which the fusion of law and justice has avoided this tension. George Orwell's novel *1984*, with its visionary horrors and its horrifying visions, set the thematic stage. A variety of members of the public and of the media, politicians, bureaucrats, academics, behavioural scientists, lawyers, and judges, were invited to express their views on how ably the legal system has struck or is likely to strike the balance between the public's right to order, predictability, and freedom from unwarranted intrusions, and the state's right to impose a collective judgment to achieve that order, predictability and freedom.

These papers explore the issues in their procedural as well as their substantive incarnations. They represent an attempt to isolate the layers of justice and to synthesize these layers with appropriate laws and their institutional settings. And they attempt where possible to replace the Orwellian stage with a legal millennium which strikes a more palatable balance.

R.S. Abella
M.L. Rothman
Conference Co-chairmen
September, 1985.

TABLE OF CONTENTS

PART II — THE ENFORCEMENT OF RIGHTS

Access to Law

Access to Justice

The Professionals in Justice

The Prospects for Justice

Justice in the Literary Tradition

*''… Nothing was illegal,
since there were no longer
any laws.''*

*''… Rien n'était illégal,
puisqu'il n'y avait
plus de lois.''*

George Orwell, *1984*

THE PURPOSE OF LAW

LES FINS DU DROIT

The Purpose of Law

Ronald Dworkin*

This text, reprinted with Professor Dworkin's permission, is a transcribed and edited version of his remarks. He delivered this lecture with the understanding that no printed paper would be required of him and he has not reviewed the following text.

The theme of this lecture is *"The Purpose of Law"*. But this is connected to issues both more abstract and more concrete even than that. In particular, problems about "the purpose of law", the central theme of this conference, in fact provide not only a very good understanding for certain classical jurisprudential disputes, but also have an important bearing on certain political problems. I am going to try to illustrate this by talking about a particular case decided in the Circuit Court of the District of Columbia.

Let me begin however by sketching what I think is the jurisprudential background of the most fruitful arguments about the purpose or function of law. I want to start with an antique idea, an idea now largely discredited, so thoroughly discredited that it is hard to remember the good effect that it once had on people, hard to remember that it remains alive, if at all, in a set of metaphors. I think that simply to repeat those metaphors is a reasonably good introduction to this way of thinking about law.

The law, lawyers once said, works itself pure. There is a law within and beyond, the hidden law, a higher law. Law has its own ambitions. There is a logic to the law, a dynamic of the law. These are, as I say, antique metaphors. They live only in a kind of citation of ridicule nowadays. One of the things that I hope to do in this lecture is to rehabilitate those metaphors, to try to offer a reading of them which will show them to be not only sensible but actually illuminating. These metaphors have to do with change in the law. They begin with the undoubted fact that judges are not simply passive purveyors of tradi-

* Professor, Oxford University and New York University. A fuller statement of his views on this lecture topic appears in "Law's Ambitions for Itself", 71 University of Virginia Law Review, 173-87 (March, 1985).

tion, that many changes in the law are in the hands of judges through their decisions. That is the undoubted fact.

The claim of these metaphors and the way of thinking about law that they represent is, I think, well put in the form of three mysteries about this process of change.

The first mystery is that in the process through which law changes while being applied through adjudication, law is the engine or motor or governor of its own change. Law as law personified is at work in changing law.

The second mystery is that when law is at work in changing itself, then the change is characteristically an improvement. It is not just a neutral kind of change which we judge to be good or bad by looking later to see its consequences. The fact that the change has been governed by law itself means that the situation has improved.

The third of the mysteries is the most mysterious of these, namely, that this changed law works, in itself, unfolding its internal ambitions for itself. This change is yet a deepening of law's identity. The change is on the surface, but the process is one through which the law becomes, through change, a more accurate representation of itself. The underlying result: law's internal ambitions are the real law; the law on the surface that has changed is less real.

That set of mysteries, of course, opened the way of looking at law unconventionally. It came to be called the *"natural law"* tradition. I think this is a marvellously inaccurate description of the tradition. But never mind that title. It was ridiculed savagely and finally, at least in jurisprudence texts, abandoned in the face of an onslaught that began in the middle of the 19th century through the brilliant work of Jeremy Bentham and the energetic proselytizing of his disciple, John Austin. It has been carried through by the great, largely English-speaking, positivists of present day. The attack was carried forward in North America in a tradition that came to be called *"legal realism"*, distinguished from *"positivism"* largely by the character of its rhetoric.

The attack took the following form: it said that this old way of looking upon the law as having an internal ambition, working itself through, rests on the silliest, most perverse kind of personification. It is nothing more than a figure of speech designed to keep from the public the truth, which is that the law on the surface, the law on the books, the law in the text of the statute, is all the law we have. The idea that there is something behind that law, something spooky inherent in it which can organize its own fulfillment, is the kind of mysticism, they said, which is present in obscurantism and will keep us from understanding what really goes on. Hence the titles "Positivism" and "Realism".

What interests me, particularly looking back on it now from the vantage point of this particular year, is the political alignment that was the companion to this jurisprudential dispute. In the first several decades of this century, it was reasonably clear that the people representing the old tradition, the tradition of mystery, the natural law tradition, were conservative on the whole. Using the term generously, these were the people who later were called formalists. They were said by some to be indifferent to the effect that law has on society, indifferent to the potentiality that law has, the working change. Some accusations went further. They said these conservatives were not simply blind formalists, more concerned with the niceties of legal logic than with social reality. On the contrary, the charge went, these people knew what they were doing, or at least their paymasters did, because the formalist legal tradition was nothing more, so Bentham charged, than a cloak of respectability draped around the excesses of capitalism. It was part of the superstructure, so Bentham charged, to stop people from realizing that the law is simply part of the myth through which they are kept in chains.

The remarkable thing to me about looking back on that period now, is that, though the battle continues, the political alignments have simply been reversed. This is particularly true now in the United States. As you all know, every four years attention is focussed upon the judicial process. Presidential elections have a way of focussing people's minds upon the courts. In the 1984 Presidential election, focus has been more intense. It is perfectly possible that with President Reagan's re-election, he will appoint four justices to the Supreme Court. These new appointments, together with those who are already on the conservative side, will change the character of the Court. There are candidates waiting in the wings for these appointments to the Supreme Court whose judicial philosophy is explicit and on the record. They were drawn from law schools and appointed by the President to important judicial positions, earning those positions, I think it is fair to say, by the character of their theoretical statements.

The people who now are worried, who are trying to save the achievements of judges in bringing a large measure of social justice into the law of the United States through the American Constitution, now express their concern in the language of mystery, in the language or natural law. The opponents, the people who say the Warren Court went much too far, who say that power must be given back to the people to govern themselves free from nosy interference by judges, those are the people who now claim themselves to be the inheritors of the legacy of Jeremy Bentham, the positivists and the legal realists.

But what interests me is an important question about the connection between abstract discussions of jurisprudence and the particular political issues of the day. What interests me is this remarkable reversal; now the conservatives, those on the right, are the people who are particularly anxious to salvage the way of looking at law, the so-called natural law tradition, that was once thought to be their natural legal philosophy. There are two explanations that might occur to you toward this remarkable reversal of political allegiance.

The first is one I do not like, largely because it threatens my job, which is jurisprudence, by suggesting that it has nothing at all to do with the real world. If you like the way things have been going rather recently you will talk about the laws in a dynamic manner; if you don't you will become a legal realist and say that it's all a myth. That is one explanation and nothing I say, I think, will talk you out of it if you are drawn to that.

One of the points I hope to make, however, is that there is some reason to reject that view of the connection of the jurisprudence and political reality in favour of one that I think has more merit; namely, that there is in fact a natural connection between the dynamic view, the idea that the law has its own internal ambitions, the so-called natural law tradition, and a concern for individual rights against the state. During a period in which a lively political issue is about individual rights, is about the dignity of the individual against the desires of the majority, and the left position is as it ought to be, one that stands in favour of protecting the individual, then the natural law position will seem particularly attractive to the left and will seem particularly repulsive to the right.

The key idea in this account is the idea of interpretation. My claim comes to this. The distinctive character of legal reasoning, the distinctive quality of the question, what is the law on this or that question, is that legal reasoning is interpretive. It falls under that kind of intellectual activity. That might seem reasonably commonplace to lawyers who are very familiar with the idea of interpretation of statutes. But I mean the claim to be much more general. I mean the claim to encompass not just statutes, constitutions, documents which were written at a particular time by people who might be thought to have had purposes in mind. I mean to embrace the law as a whole, the judge-made law, law stretching out into the past, and broadly to encompass a complex network of practices.

My suggestion is that it makes sense to think of interpreting legal practice as a whole, and the judicial technique (I don't mean as exercised only by judges, but I mean the technique addressed to the question of what is in fact the law) as principally interpretive of the entire canvas of legal practice. I therefore mean to include under this idea of interpretation a network of political and legal and judicial decisions made by a great many people. That may seem puzzling, but I want to speak of interpreting a network of decisions made by many different people at many different times.

It will seem bizarre if you have in mind interpretation after the model of most literary interpretation, which tells us that interpretation means discovering the intention of the author of some work. If that is what it means, then it would be silly to speak of discovering the intention of the author of the common law because no person or group could meet that description. But I think that is a mistake in, or rather an incomplete picture of, what interpretation is. It is perfectly true that there are many literary people who interpret a poem with the end in mind of retrieving what might be called the intention of the poet when he wrote it. But there are many literary people who do not think that that is the point of interpretation at all. That means simply that we need a general account of what interpretation is, sufficiently general, so that we can see the dispute amongst various people who interpret poems, some of whom seek after the intention of the author and others of whom pay more attention, for example, to how the poem strikes contemporary readers.

We want a description of interpretation sufficiently abstract so that it will encompass both of these activities. I am not going to repeat here the argument that I have elsewhere developed about what this general account of interpretation should be. I will simply report my conclusion and then apply it in the context I will describe.

My conclusion is this. Interpretation, as a general activity, is the enterprise of making the best of some material whatever the genre of that material may be. Interpretation of literature is an attempt to make of a poem or a play or a novel the best that can be of that genre, which means, of course, that people who have rather different theories about what the general point of literature is, will provide remarkably different interpretations. Those critics who think, even without being all that conscious of it, that the point of literature has to do with communication, will naturally be brought to seeking the point of a play in retrieving the intention of its author because an active communication has that intentional quality. Those who see the point of literature very differently will be led in other directions.

Now that, it seems to me, is something helpful to us as lawyers, because we can at once describe the activity that I call compendiously "the judicial activity", as an act of interpretation, while leaving open for argument more concrete questions about how exactly that should be carried out. Having agreed to the general characterization, it is important to consider too that interpreting the legal structure or some part of it, like the law of negligence for example, is at bottom an attempt to make the best of it — best from the standpoint of political morality.

That is my suggestion as to the unfolding of these old mysteries. It seems to me that they take on both meaning and indeed a large degree of accuracy once we redescribe them as appeals to this interpretive model.

If you are willing to think about the model that I describe, namely, thinking about the law as an interpretive exercise, then you will, I think, be led to see that any attempt to interpret a particular section or area of legal doctrine must be tested on two distinct dimensions. An interpretation must fit the range of both judicial and political decisions that it offers to interpret, otherwise it would be inventing rather than interpreting. Secondly, it must justify those decisions. It must justify and honour those decisions by showing them, to repeat the metaphor I have been using, in their best light.

The example I have chosen (perhaps I should apologize for this) is an American case, but I have done so because I want to connect this to the political dispute that I described a few moments ago about what the United States Supreme Court could be like in the next generation. The case that I have chosen is the *Dronenberg* case, decided in the District of Columbia by Judge Robert Bork last August (*Dronenberg v. Zech et al.,* U.S. Court of Appeals, D.C. Circuit, decided August 17, 1984). I will summarize the facts of it very briefly.

Dronenberg was a cryptographer and a linguist with the United States Navy. I think he served for nine years, had an excellent record and had been decorated several times. He was discharged from the Navy, however, once he had confessed that he was a homosexual, and had on several occasions committed, to use the phrase the Court used, "homosexual acts in the Navy barracks". The Navy had a regulation which said, straightforwardly, that anyone who is a homosexual and who commits homosexual acts can be discharged immediately. He was discharged. He appealed to the courts on the basis of both the due process clause and the equal protection clause of the United States Constitution. The case came before Judge Bork in the District of Columbia Circuit. Judge Bork decided that Dronenberg had no constitutional claim.

I want to use this case to illustrate the interpretive model that I have just described so abstractly. Somebody attracted to the old idea that the law has its own logic, that the law has ambitions that need to be worked out, would begin by asking for the material to be interpreted. What is the record that we find? The record consists (it is not a long record) in the text of the U.S. Constitution that commands due process of law. And it consists also in a string of recent Supreme Court decisions themselves interpreting that marvellously and fabulously vague language.

Here are the decisions that I think are important. The first is *Griswold v. Connecticut* (381 U.S. 479, 1965) in which the United States Supreme Court decided that the State of Connecticut could not constitutionally make it a crime for a married couple to use contraceptives. When that decision was first reached, several people thought that it was a decision about the sanctity of marriage. The Court said it would offend the due process clause to apply the Connecticut statute to a married couple. Several years later however, the Supreme Court decided in the case of *Eisenstad v. Baird* (405 U.S. 438, 1972) that it would be unconstitutional for a state to prohibit an unmarried couple from using contraceptives. Contraceptive cases concluded with a remarkable New York decision, *Carey v. Population Services International* (431 U.S. 678, 1977), in which the Supreme Court decided that the State of New York could not constitutionally require people to go to a drugstore to buy contraceptives and could not constitutionally forbid their sale even to children under sixteen years of age.

In the course of these several decisions, the Supreme Court used a word not to be found, I believe, in the Constitution. It said that the due process clause includes, when properly understood, a constitutional right to privacy, and then said that the right to privacy was infringed by these constraints in the use and sale of contraceptives. It used the same right to privacy, and an appeal to the contraceptive cases, to justify striking down a Virginia law that forbade inter-racial marriage. It said the state cannot intervene in the decision of people about whom to marry.

Finally, and of course most notoriously, the Supreme Court decided the abortion cases on the basis of the right to privacy as well. It decided that in the first trimester of pregnancy a state may not forbid abortion because that would be a violation of the right to privacy.

That is the record, or at least as much of it as we ought to consider. What interpretation fits? We must look, as I said, for an interpretation on two dimensions. We need to find a principle or set of principles, a vision, if you will, a tenet of justice, some piece of political morality, that fits these decisions. By that I mean simply such that a person or group required to enforce that particular vision, that section of political morality, would have reached just that decision. And secondly, because very likely we will find more than one such principle that fits in that sense, we need to find a principle that honours the decisions, that shows them as working out something that we ourselves, as interpreters, can accept as sound, not only as pieces of legal history, but as pieces of political philosophy as well.

What are the candidates? I can think of two and perhaps you can think of more. First, some version of Mill's principle seems to fit. Mill's principle, I think, comes to this. The state has no justification for constricting liberty and the only justification it might have is that the majority hates the conduct being constrained or thinks it wicked. That is the theory at least of Mill's principle and it seems to fit these decisions. What other principle might we find? We ought to have a list if we are engaged in interpretation theories. We might think of the following principle. The state has no business interfering with decisions that either aim at procreation or aim to prevent it. If these two principles both fit, and add whatever others we can think about, then the question for the interpreter becomes which of this set of decisions shows them in their most attractive way.

Everything turns on the choice between the two principles, assuming our list closed at those two. If Mill's principle provides, (in the terms I have described), the best interpretation of these cases, then surely Dronenberg cannot be fired because Mill's principle seems to hold, in my view much more plainly than in the abortion cases, against what the Navy did. But if the correct interpretation throws up the principle about procreation, then on the contrary, Dronenberg finds cover because only in the most Pickwickian sense can the *Dronenberg* decision be said to be a decision about procreation. I myself do not have much difficulty in choosing between these two.

It can be said, and I have deliberately not taken up this question in this lecture because I think it is both difficult and irrelevant, that interpretation is too subjective to be used in the judicial process. It can be argued that making something appear in the best light is to concede that there can be no objective truth about interpretation and, therefore, if we modelled the judicial process in this way, that there can be no right or wrong answer to a case. I think that is flatly wrong and the wrong conclusion to draw. But I do not press the argument here because the competitive way of deciding this case leans just as much on controversial positions and political morality as the interpretive model does.

If one is condemned as merely subjective and so is the other, then we are remitted to the only sensible question, which is: granted that judges will answer these questions differently, should we not at least be concerned to get straight which question it is we want them to answer.

It seems to me very plain which of these two principles provides the better interpretation. Mill's principle, while we can argue about its correct application, whether it really does fit the abortion cases, is one that pulls on our political instincts. It speaks for at least a strand of justice. It names a kind of concern for liberty which we all respect. The other principle I described is simply arbitrary. It draws a line around one kind of activity, namely procreation, which it does not even offer to explain in any larger vision of morality. It does not tell us what is special about procreation as distinct from homosexual conduct that would make it a firm barrier to state intervention in one case and not in the other.

If we started down the road of thinking of the judicial process as interpretive in that way, then I think that, at least in this particular case, there is no large problem about which of these principles is better. Dronenberg in short, wins on the old fashioned natural law.

Let us see how Judge Bork decided the case. He said that when the Supreme Court decided the contraception cases, the racial intermarriage case, the abortion cases, what it was doing was nothing more nor less than simply inventing new rights. It was not for Bork to say that they had invented the wrong rights, but it was clear to him and hardly needed argument that they had invented new rights. Now, says Bork, along comes this homosexual asking me to invent a new right for him. Notice that these are now thought to be discreet, independent pieces of legislation with no link between them. Bork said "I am simply a humble lower court judge. I cannot create new constitutional rights. I don't think anyone should". He said in a footnote: "It kind of compels me to say that if I were on the Supreme Court I would not have invented all those new rights, but in any case, sitting where I sit, there is no burden on me to create a new right".

What a remarkable contrast between these two styles of adjudication. For Bork, the new positivist, the realist, those who are minded to see in the law nothing but a series of discrete positive decisions so that each question is a fresh question, all the talk about the law having a logic that might itself compel a decision in favour of Dronenberg simply goes by the way. Every case is decided on its own and for the day.

I started by saying that I thought there was an important connection between the philosophical questions, about the character and fundamental nature of law, the sociological question about the function of law and the political question of what our jurisprudence should look like in practice in the next generation. I offer you the *Dronenberg* case and the contrast between these two ways of looking at it as an illustration of this.

I said, in the course of these remarks, that I would offer you my definition of what being philosophical is, and this seems to me as good a time as any to do it. When I first moved to England from America, I found myself sitting opposite two women on a train, one of whom who was extremely upset, obviously in great discomfort, and her friend said to her seeking to comfort her: "There, there, my dear, be philosophical. Don't think about it".

I have simply described to you two ways that we might think about law and offered in this case an example of why it makes a difference. How should we go about deciding? I have already said that I do not think that scepticism has anything to do with it, that is, if you find that one method is too subjective you would think about the other method. The idea that it's all new rights simply puts the question right at the front. Should we create a new right or not? Do you think that political morality is basically subjective or should you be neutral between the two methods?

One argument which one hears time and time again in the constitutional context seems to me so obviously circular as to raise some question as to how it can survive. But nevertheless it does. It is said on all sides that in the Warren Court judges asserted power, power that does not properly belong to judges, that the time has come for judicial constraint or restraint, that judges must be very careful about overstepping the bounds of their legitimacy.

But this is obviously a question begging argument, because if the interpretive model is right, Bork's decision in *Dronenberg* was itself illegitimate. If the interpretive model is right, according to it, Dronenberg had a constitutional right at the time the case arose to a decision in his favour. If that is the correct way to look at the Constitution of the United States, then Bork was amending the Constitution by judicial fiat in denying him recovery, and what could be more activist? What could be more usurpant? What could be more contemptuous of legitimacy? Of course, if Judge Bork is right, then what he did was legitimate, and people who would have found otherwise in the *Dronenberg* case would be the usurpers.

Yet I only mean that all the talk, familiar as it has become through decades now of constitutional theory, about ''usurpation'' and ''legitimacy'' — these are simply words to decorate the conclusion. They cannot provide argument, because whether they apply or not depends upon the argument and how they get in it. Then how can we choose between these two general ways of looking at things? There is no physical basis it seems to me. There is no basis in the virtues of judicial restraint or activism. All that is just silly talk, it seems to me.

It used to be thought that we could somehow decide this by semantic investigation, by thinking about how most people use the words of the law. But that plainly cannot be done. Issues of this magnitude are not going to be settled by how we all use the words of the law. How can we decide? It seems to me there is no blinking of the fact that the choice between these two ways of looking at the law is itself a question of political morality.

Our concept of law has got to be understood as a political concept. I think the best way to put the point across is perhaps this. The decision as to which way our court should approach the extraction and elaboration of our law is best seen as an interpretive problem itself. It is just interpretive at a higher level, but the same standards must be applied. In the end, we have to ask how the judicial office is best carried out. We have always to ask the question I described as the abstract form of the interpretive question. Looking at the entire practice of adjudication, thinking about the structures of law as a whole, which way of understanding them — on the interpretive model or on the positivist model — shows them in a better light? Which way fits and dignifies the process?

Comparison is difficult. It seems to me the first step is to try to find in these two methods a commitment to something else. So far, I have been treating these two as if they were just abstract descriptions, models that you could choose between. But surely they must stand for something deeper. The interpretive model I want to suggest, will appeal to us only if we see meaning and importance in a special political virtue. I say special because I think that it is useful to distinguish the virtue I am about to mention from canonical and familiar political virtues of justice and fairness. I think it is helpful to treat it as a separate virtue with its own competitive demands against those other virtues.

That separate virtue is political integrity. Political integrity is simply the idea that a community that is morally as well as in other ways a divided community can nevertheless commit itself to the general principle that any set of political decisions must be set beside other political decisions to see whether the whole is coherent. If the federal system, for example, protects people who want to use contraceptives and protects women who want abortions, and does so on the basis that could only be justified in a comprehensive way by appeal to something like a requirement that Mill's principle be respected to the boundaries of its natural dimension, then that is what the ideal of integrity requires.

It is an awesome ideal. It is an ideal in several ways; we cannot meet it fully and we cannot agree as to exactly when we do not meet it. But we can accept it. I believe we do accept it as an ideal, that is, as a critical standard. We can then argue about a question we have at least to face and answer.

Let us look for a moment to see whether we can find a similar virtue which we can take to be the nerve of this alternative way, this way now associated with the right wing attitude towards adjudication in the United States. I think we can. I think we can find another virtue to set beside the virtue of integrity to hold before us so that we can look at the two and perhaps choose. The second virtue is efficiency.

It is no accident that the people who are now the champions of judicial restraint in the Constitutional arena are exactly the people who are the champions of judicial activism in pursuit of what is called the economic analysis of law. They are all devotees of that way of looking at the common law often called the economic analysis.

If one finds dramatic appeal in this idea of efficiency, in this idea that the point of law is to give the people, so far as this can be done, what they want across the whole canvass of law from constitutional law, through criminal law, to the details of contract, then the most repulsive political virtue one could mention would be the idea of integrity, because integrity is a most inefficient idea. Thinking of efficiency in the way I just described it, as giving the people what they want, makes integrity a constraint. The force of this constraint, too, we can gauge quite quickly by looking at what we might call the phenomenology of preference in the various political issues I have so far mentioned — contraception, abortion, homosexuality. Each of these draws upon a different kind of emotional reaction from the majority. If we want to maximize the degree to which people as a whole have what they want, then it would be an extremely bad idea to impose any regime of consistency and coherence upon these desires because, as the simple phenomenological experiment will show, ideas are not expressed in that way. Preferences, desires and prejudices are not in themselves disciplined by any requirement of coherence.

I think it comes to this. If we set about making the choice, having rid ourselves of the idea that a kind of choice is to be made from the idea of legitimacy, rid ourselves of the idea that there is a linguistic way to make the choice, if we confront the fact that this is a choice between values, then I think we could do far worse than concentrate on the meanings, the social meanings, of the two ideas of *integrity* and *efficiency*. It seems to me they speak to two quite different views or pictures, models if you will, of how we relate to one another in the community, of what "community in diversity" can and should be like.

The idea of efficiency seems to me to suggest that we are resources and competitors for one another: resources insofar as our labours are a combination of our tastes and preferences, so as to make goods cheaper and more expensive; competitors because our preferences are not necessarily the same, particularly when these preferences are broadened so as to include political preferences, preferences about principle and prejudices about what our neighbor's sexual acts should be like. That is one picture of community I find distasteful.

Consider the picture of community that one could marshall behind the idea of integrity. It begins where I think any vision of community for us must begin — in abandoning the idea that it makes sense to think that we are tied together in community by a common commitment to what are often called shared values. If "shared values" means values about particular principles, about what counts as a decent life, about what counts as fairness and justice in politics, we are divided about that. We argue about that. We argue through modes of politics even though what those modes should be is part of the argument.

I think it would be a poorer community if we were much less divided about those issues than in fact we are. Nevertheless, I believe we can redeem the idea of community for ourselves through the virtue of integrity. We can achieve the idea of community in diversity if we accept something like this picture of our common situation. We will struggle in politics, but we will march forward towards a finer sense of fairness, towards the realization of the conditions for the flourishing of individual lives. We will march together, sometimes forward, sometimes back, but we hope more often forward than backward. We will struggle and compete, but as we go, we will be bound together by the principle that we are in the same boat, that we march together, and whatever we decide for one we decide for all, that we leave no wounded behind in our march towards justice.

Now that seems to me a more commendable picture of the character of community in diversity than the picture of resources and competition. And it does seem to me that that is the choice of judicial style, of our attitude towards the function and purpose of law. It is, I suppose, surprising that the philosophically correct attitude to take towards the ancient question, ''What is law?'', towards the more practical questions such as ''What investigations should a judge undertake?'', ''What should she or he ask himself or herself when faced with a case like *Dronenberg?*'', implicate these grand questions of political vision. The volumes of philosophy speak in the dissent of each judge's gavel. It sounds odd but I am sure it is true and may even be a little thrilling.

*"You are imagining that
there is something called
human nature which will
be outraged…"*

*"Vous vous imaginez qu'il y
a quelque chose qui
s'appelle la nature humaine
qui sera outragé…"*

George Orwell, *1984*

THE PUBLIC EXPECTATIONS OF JUSTICE

CE QUE LE PUBLIC ATTEND DE LA JUSTICE

The Politics of Justice

Dalton Camp*

I am not a lawyer. I did, however almost become a lawyer. I paid a $75.00 fee to the New Brunswick Lawyers' Association to allow me to article with a local law firm. I went to the London School of Economics, studied under Harold Laskie as much as I could. I returned to Canada and ended up in advertising. I never got my $75.00 back. But on the other hand I have since been told, and I am sure you know or have cause to know, that most lawyers would in any event rather have been accountants, except they lack the personality for it. By way of further introduction, I find myself, in Senator Marsden's phrase, a reductionist macro-manipulator, a handler.

I listened with rapt attention to Professor Dworkin and what struck me was, as David MacDonald said, there are differences in being an American in their legal system and being a Canadian in our own.

We don't elect any judges and we don't elect senators. All of our judges in the superior courts are appointed by Attorneys General and none of our Attorneys General have been anything else but pragmatists. I should say, of course, that judges are appointed by the Attorneys General in close consultation with the Canadian Bar — in most cases. There are these fundamental differences between the two systems. It reminds me of a statement made by a former member of Parliament, Robert Thomson. He said the Americans are our best friends whether we like it or not.

In any event, I have been listening to my companions on the panel with respect to the subject at hand and I felt that I must have, all my life, been tuned to another channel. Apart from being a reductionist, which is a way of making the world a manageable place, I am also one who believes in that American addage, if it ain't busted don't fix it. I think the justice system serves us very well. I have only been in court four times in my life. Twice as a character witness, if you can believe that; once, in order to strain your credulity further, as an expert witness, and, finally, in a divorce proceeding. I would rather go to the dentist.

---

* Journalist and author.

The courts to me are charismatic, as judges are charismatic, like University Presidents used to be. This may have something to do with the mystery of law to which Professor Dworkin referred. But I think I am the average citizen in the way in which, with respect to the judicial process, I have a respect that extends to the point of deference and a confidence that extends to the point of faith. I rather think my opinion is widely held. Not very many institutions in our society have survived in so robust a condition in terms of public opinion as has the justice system.

If you don't believe me, examine public opinion with respect to politicians, or with respect to Parliament, or the Senate, with respect to the church, or examine it with respect to the University. All these institutions have been subject to public scrutiny and public criticism and scepticism and a profound shift in public attitude. Less so, I think, the case of the justice system.

There must be reasons for that. Sometimes I think the principal reason has been in the growing mistrust of the political process as opposed to the judicial process. It doesn't seem to me an accident that when it came to the public question of whether we should have a written constitution and a Charter of Rights, the public was in favour. We are in favour of the Charter of Rights because I think it has been the experience of Canadians, and it would be a result of their observation of the American experience, that you cannot entrust rights to Parliaments. There is no evidence in this country of Parliament protecting minority rights and interests unless the minority is encapsuled in the majority. There is, in fact, evidence to the contrary.

I was always impressed, having been raised in my formative years in the United States, and having read the Constitution as we were all obliged to do, that were it not for the courts, minorities in the United States would still be in the back of the bus. There were 48 to 50 legislatures and there was a Congress. There is no evidence of any significant recognition of the constitutional rights of American minorities being protected by politicians.

The argument was made by my friend, Sterling Lyon, that civil rights are best safeguarded by not defining them. Yet those who consulted public opinion through the modern technique of polling discovered considerable majority public support for a Charter of Rights. You can ask Senator Kirby, you can ask Premier Davis, you can ask Premier Hatfield and learn that what finally turned the thing around was the gathering awareness of those who were opposed to the Charter of the broad public support for it.

I suppose if one is going to do justice to this subject, you could say we do have our complaints about the system. One of them is not, however, the mystique, the charisma, one finds in the system. I cannot think of anything we could do more damaging to the justice system than to open it to all the media, particularly to television. We are obviously going to have, in our time, 1,000 different television frequencies so that there would certainly be room to telecast court proceedings if one could find a sponsor. But it occurs to me that our American friends, who provide us with almost all of our violence and almost all of our pornography, could also provide us with our courtroom *cinema veritae*: We could poach on their system. But I think we have a system in our country which the public intuitively or historically respects and I can't believe we would improve that by using a medium invented and designed for the purposes of entertainment.

Having said that, it does seem to me the courts and the law do change and evolve - and for the better. There was a time when you could not buy a bottle of liquor; there was a time when you could only buy it if you had a doctor's prescription. Then there was a time when you could only buy it if you had a permit. Then there was a time when you could only buy it if you filled out the order and signed your name to it. Then there was a time when you could buy a drink providing you ate at the same time, and then a time when you couldn't buy one if you were standing up. Then there was a time when you couldn't buy one if you were outdoors.

Yet for a country as compassionate as Canadians generally are, and as clearminded and as sensible, for such a country to have a *Narcotics Control Act* which makes first possession of marijuana a criminal offence, is to me an intolerable oversight in the so-called justice system. But the complaint is not with the judicial process. The judges are sending signals ten, fifteen times a day by either throwing out the case or by imposing minimum fines. The politicians are responsible for the injustice in that legislation and also responsible for the public misunderstanding of the difference between decriminalization and whatever the opposite of decriminalization is.

One is also distressed by the snail's pace of family law reform. We have a system which is murderously expensive and lends itself to enormous personal strain and unnecessary suffering. But this is a system that the courts did not create. It is a system which the politicians have allowed even though I admit to some progress. So there are areas in the justice system which need attention.

To begin with, it is not the responsibility of those who administer the system. It is the responsibility of those who have responsibility for the system. After all, society does not make law in this country, Parliament makes law. What society does is determine which laws it will support and uphold. It is curious to me, with respect to some laws, such as prohibition, and possession of marijuana, that even though vast elements of society have at one time or another refused to support them, the legal system has been stuck with the problem. On the other hand,

La communication de la justice

Jean-Claude Delorme*

Il est particulièrement réconfortant de constater que l'Institut canadien d'administration de la justice ait voulu célébrer son dixième anniversaire en s'interrogeant sur le droit et la justice au-delà de 1984. En effet, il est opportun, alors que notre société est en mutation, qu'on examine le sens de la justice et le rôle de l'appareil judiciaire dans une perspective d'avenir.

On m'a fait l'honneur de m'inviter à exprimer mon point de vue sur ce que le public attend de la justice et plus particulièrement, sur la perception que se fait ce public de l'appareil judiciaire.

Les quelques heures de réflexion que j'ai pu consacrer à cette question m'ont amené rapidement à conclure que la réponse à cette question varierait énormément d'un groupe à un autre de notre société et que ce serait peine perdue de tenter de trouver une réponse universelle qui satisfasse tous les justiciables. En effet, suivant qu'on est plus ou moins près de l'appareil judiciaire et qu'on en connaît les possibilités autant que les limites, on en arrivera à une réponse plus ou moins positive et on sera plus ou moins indulgent pour ceux qui en font partie. Pour ma part, du fait que je sois membre du Barreau tout en exerçant des activités qui sont passablement éloignées de l'appareil judiciaire, je serais naturellement porté à donner une réponse plutôt positive et compréhensive à la question qui nous est posée et en ce faisant, j'accepterais volontiers de rationaliser les carences du système.

Cependant, et c'est là que se pose véritablement le problème, le public voit les choses d'un tout autre oeil et son opinion est généralement sans nuance; elle ne doit pas toutefois être pour autant rejetée. En effet, je ne vous surprendrai pas en affirmant que le public en général perçoit probablement le système et l'appareil judiciaire comme très imparfaits et vraisemblablement incapables de réaliser ses attentes en matière de justice.

* Président-directeur général de Téléglobe Canada.

Est-ce que ce public a raison de conclure ainsi? Est-ce que sa perception plutôt négative est fondée? Est-ce que les attentes et les espoirs qu'il entretient au sujet du système judiciaire sont réalistes et justifiables? Voilà autant de questions qu'on peut se poser devant l'attitude du public face aux lois et aux magistrats qui sont chargés de les appliquer. Pour ma part, je ne tenterai même pas d'y répondre car, en plus d'exiger une étude beaucoup plus exhaustive que celle qu'il m'a été possible de faire, répondre à ces questions reviendrait à éviter le véritable sujet à discuter aujourd'hui. En effet, la première démarche à entreprendre dans l'examen de ce sujet ne doit pas viser à déterminer qui du législateur, du magistrat ou du justiciable, a raison ou tort car même si on parvenait à démontrer que le public a tort, sa perception demeurerait la même tant et aussi longtemps que par des mesures appropriées on n'aura pas réussi à modifier l'opinion du public et surtout, à permettre à l'appareil judiciaire de se projeter sous un jour plus positif et je dirais même, plus conforme à la réalité telle que vous et moi la connaissons. Le problème à mon avis provient du fait que l'image perçue ne correspond pas à l'image réelle, ou encore à l'image qu'on voudrait projeter. A une époque où l'échelle des valeurs et les principes de justice sociale se transforment rapidement, il est de plus en plus essentiel de veiller à établir et maintenir une correspondance aussi parfaite que possible entre les attentes qu'on se fait de la justice dans le public, d'une part, et d'autre part les possibilités réelles de la justice objective. En effet, la crédibilité, toujours relative bien sûr, dont jouira le système judiciaire, sera proportionnelle à la concordance entre les attentes du public, et la réalité elle-même.

Voilà ma première observation. Avant de passer à la deuxième, je voudrais quand même préciser qu'on ne doit pas conclure de ce que je viens de dire que le problème serait réglé par la simple mise en oeuvre d'un programme d'information et de relations publiques. Plus d'information s'impose, sans doute, et j'y reviendrai, mais il faut se garder de croire sans réserve que la seule carence du système actuel est d'être perçu erronément ou d'être mal compris ou encore, qu'aucun changement ne pourrait réussir à satisfaire les attentes du justiciable de manière plus adéquate.

En effet, et j'en arrive à ma deuxième observation, les attentes du public vues dans une perspective d'avenir, sont susceptibles de devenir encore plus exigeantes et par voie de conséquence, les insatisfactions, fondées ou non, risquent de s'accentuer encore davantage.

En tentant de scruter l'avenir et de déterminer dans quel sens évoluera le droit et la perception que le public se fera de l'appareil judiciaire, on doit nécessairement tenir compte de deux facteurs principaux, soit d'une part, l'impact des médias sur l'opinion publique et d'autre part, les répercussions qu'auront certains textes de loi à caractère social, notamment la nouvelle Charte des droits et libertés.

Tout d'abord, quelques observations au sujet de l'impact des médias d'informations tant électroniques que conventionnels. Il est à peine nécessaire de rappeler, tant ce fait est universellement accepté, que les médias contribuent de manière importante et déterminante à former et à faire évoluer l'opinion publique sur quelque sujet que ce soit. Dans le domaine qui nous occupe, on constate régulièrement que les débats de nos tribunaux, en particulier de nos tribunaux de justice criminelle, ont leur écho dans la presse quotidienne et l'on ne peut donc se surprendre que le public se fasse une opinion sur la culpabilité de l'accusé au fur et à mesure que le procès se déroule et bien souvent avant qu'il ne soit terminé; en effet, on condamne ou on acquitte avant même que tous les faits ne soient connus et avant même que le verdict ou la sentence ne soient rendus. Par conséquent, suivant que l'issue du procès coïncidera avec l'opinion que s'est faite le public, ou en différera, la perception que se fera ce dernier de l'appareil judiciaire deviendra plus positive et confiante ou, alternativement, plus négative et sceptique.

En deuxième lieu, la Charte des droits et libertés a déjà provoqué plusieurs recours aux tribunaux sur des questions de nature sociale ou politique. En effet, les demandes ont été particulièrement nombreuses au cours des derniers mois où l'on a tenté d'obtenir le renversement d'une décision prise par des organismes privés ou publics, non pas parce que semblable décision contrevenait à une disposition spécifique de la loi mais parce qu'elle constituait, aux yeux du demandeur, une violation de ses droits ou une injustice sociale. Cette nouvelle Charte des droits et libertés a fait naître le juge interprète et arbitre des droits de la personne en conférant effectivement au magistrat la responsabilité de trancher ce type de débat et de statuer sur les droits de la personne en regard de l'intérêt public.

Qui plus est, on s'attend aussi à ce que la nouvelle jurisprudence soit le reflet fidèle et opportun de l'évolution socio-culturelle de notre société. Il s'agit là d'un développement majeur de notre droit que certains autres pays, comme les Etats-Unis en particulier, connaissent depuis plusieurs années. On peut difficilement préciser toutes les répercussions que ce développement aura sur l'orientation et l'administration de la justice mais on peut facilement prévoir que les jugements des cours qui seront rendus sur ces questions auront inévitablement un impact profond et déterminant sur la perception que le public se fera de la justice et de l'appareil judiciaire. Les décisions des magistrats seront donc davantage exposées à l'examen public, à la contestation, voire même à la critique. Dans cette perspective, comment éviter que le public ne perçoive la magistrature et l'appareil judiciaire comme devant jouer le rôle de ''conscience des autorités publiques'' ou de ''gardien'' ou ''fiduciaire de la morale publique'' pour reprendre une expression chère au droit constitutionnel d'inspiration britannique.

Considérant donc que l'intrusion des médias dans l'appareil judiciaire a eu pour effet de placer les magistrats dans une cage de verre et qu'au surplus, les litiges qui découleront de la Charte des droits et libertés donneront inévitablement naissance à des débats énergiques, pour ne pas dire passionnés, sur la place publique, on ne peut que conclure que la fonction judiciaire sera beaucoup plus visible, voire même exposée à la contestation, qu'auparavant et que par voie de conséquence, la perception que le public se fera de la justice sera vraisemblablement différente qu'elle ne l'a été jusqu'ici. Tous évidemment voudront que cette perception évolue dans un sens constructif et que l'intégrité et la crédibilité de l'appareil judiciaire ne soient d'aucune façon mises en cause. Comment y parvenir et, si l'on peut faire contrepoids aux autres influences, comment espérer que l'appareil judicaire soit perçu comme répondant fidèlement aux attentes du public?

Je voudrais pour ma part exprimer les plus grands espoirs en ce sens mais je dois dire que la situation actuelle m'inspire un certain scepticisme. En effet, traditionnellement, le rôle du magistrat consistait à interpréter et à appliquer les textes de loi à la lumière des faits en s'inspirant de l'intention du législateur, de la jurisprudence et de la doctrine. Les pouvoirs discrétionnaires du juge étaient limités et exceptionnels; au surplus, tout en étant public, le processus judiciaire était relativement à l'abri de la discussion publique et de la critique négative, d'autant plus que les principes et la doctrine de l'outrage au tribunal avaient pour effet de réduire plusieurs de ces critiques au silence. Dans un contexte où l'opinion publique, stimulée par les médias, se reconnaît le privilège de contester les décisions des tribunaux et ce, dans un contexte totalement nouveau où les tribunaux eux-mêmes sont appelés à trancher des débats à caractère socio-politique, on peut facilement prévoir que la situation sera dorénavant bien différente.

Quelle est donc la solution dans semblable conjoncture? Pour ma part, je vois mal, et c'est peut-être parce que mon optique est par trop influencée par la tradition, qu'un juge s'engage dans un débat sur la place publique pour expliquer sa décision, encore moins pour la justifier. Je crois qu'effectivement, le magistrat sera inévitablement condamné à continuer à oeuvrer dans la solitude, à rechercher malgré les assauts de l'opinion publique, l'objectivité la plus absolue et enfin, à faire preuve d'une abnégation exceptionnelle sans jamais attendre qu'on le félicite publiquement même pour une décision qui aura l'heur de satisfaire aux attentes du public. Il devra aussi, bien entendu, s'attendre à ce qu'on ne rate aucune occasion de mettre son jugement en cause si sa décision est contraire aux voeux de la population.

Dans ce contexte, quelques questions surgissent à l'esprit. D'une part, il me semble qu'il faudrait se demander si le législateur s'est préoccupé de donner aux magistrats les moyens et les outils qui leur sont nécessaires pour exercer les responsabilités accrues et les pouvoirs discrétionnaires que leur impartit la Charte des droits et libertés. Est-il raisonnable de s'attendre à ce que des juges, agissant seuls ou en groupe, et malgré toute leur formation et toute leur objectivité, puissent rendre des décisions objectivement acceptables dans des domaines aussi complexes que celui qui implique les droits de la personne et surtout, les rapports de la personne avec les pouvoirs publics; on semble, au contraire, s'attendre à ce que ce nouveau rôle puisse être assumé avec une compétence égale et comparable à celle qui a caractérisé l'appareil judiciaire traditionnel, alors que les règles et les responsabilités du magistrat étaient bien différentes.

C'est une responsabilité à laquelle la magistrature ne peut se soustraire mais qui, à mon avis, incombe en premier lieu aux gouvernements. En effet, j'estime que le scepticisme et les insatisfactions que le public entretient à l'endroit du système judiciaire, sont dirigés effectivement quoique inconsciemment, vers les autorités publiques plutôt que vers les juges. Je crois pour ma part que le public respecte la magistrature dans son ensemble et reconnaît que les juges sont prisonniers du système établi par le législateur et les gouvernements. C'est à ces derniers qu'il revient donc de donner aux juges les moyens d'action qui leur sont nécessaires pour assurer les lourdes responsabilités qu'on leur a confiées.

En deuxième lieu, si l'on ne peut s'attendre, encore moins justifier, qu'un magistrat vienne débattre sur la place publique le bien-fondé de ses décisions, n'y aurait-il pas d'autres moyens à envisager pour faire en sorte que le public ait une perception plus juste et des attentes plus réalistes de l'appareil judiciaire? En revanche, la magistrature a-t-elle les moyens de juger les attentes du public et a-t-elle suffisamment de liberté à l'intérieur du système actuel pour empêcher que l'écart entre l'image perçue et l'image réelle ne s'agrandisse encore davantage.

Ce sont là deux avenues qu'il conviendrait que la magistrature, mais avant tout le gouvernement, explorent en prévision de l'évolution à venir. Il est important qu'on s'y attarde car le pire danger qui guette notre société et notre régime démocratique est celui de voir s'amplifier les insatisfactions, le scepticisme, voire même le cynisme, qu'on entretient en plusieurs milieux à l'endroit de la justice. Par ailleurs, il faut bien reconnaître que s'il est inévitable que le justiciable ait toujours une perception incomplète et injuste de ses magistrats, il s'impose néanmoins de protéger la crédibilité de l'appareil judiciaire tout en cherchant à mettre en lumière, non seulement les grandeurs, mais également les servitudes de la justice humaine et ses limites intrinsèques.

The Sociology of Justice

Lorna R. Marsden*

The themes for this session are imaginatively drawn from the book for which this year was named. The book makes as good reading now as it must have when it was first published. The year, on the other hand, is not quite living up to those standards.

For the sociologist, it is not something called "human nature" about which one worries in relation to the expectations of our justice system, but the compelling forces of social structures and processes through which we create, affirm and express our expectations. The totalitarian vision of Orwell is not the only hostile environment for our concepts of justice. They must now thrive with different problems.

As sociologists contemplated the future in the post-war period, the theory of mass society was developed. Throughout the 1950's and 1960's they wrote about the breakdown of primary groups (or the ties of family and community), and the build up of a huge and concentrated mass of people in which individuals lived atomistically, anomically and in alienation from their work, their community and themselves - the "lonely crowd" as the popular Reisman book put it.

The deeper study of these issues, and especially the more recent theories of social networks, has revealed to us that the fears about the mass society or the effects of large, concentrated populations and isolating mass media are not well founded. Primary groups, families and communities are much changed, indeed transformed, in 1984 but social ties are not thereby necessarily diminished. In East York for example, studies by Barry Wellman and his colleagues from the University of Toronto have shown that the social existence of community and primary, helping networks remain strong outside geographical proximity. But mass society has other features useful to contemplate in this context.

In his book, *The Active Society*, Amitai Etzioni argues that "a society may show many of the symptoms usually associated with the concept of 'mass society' either because the micro-social units are dis-

* Senator and Professor of Sociology, University of Toronto.

integrating *or* because their ties to the society at large have been under-mined. In the first situation, if (societal) mobilization occurs, it is much more likely to be totalitarian; in the second, it is much more likely to be associated with a revival of some mode of democratic or authoritarian institutions''. (Etzioni, 1968:421).

In either case, the questions raised by Etzioni about the nature of our society are questions to be answered in relation to the public expectations of justice. In either case, the justice system is an intimate player in the social process. The people who compose the justice system need some understanding of the consensus in our society about what justice means and how that consensus is changing. They must know about the values of the majority and of the minorities. They must be insightful about how a consensus is formed and what role is played in that formation by elites, and by other social collectivities.

One aspect of the Etzioni view of mass society relates to the experience of individuals but the other aspect relates to the ties between primary social groups as such and the society as a whole. It is in this latter aspect that we find a contemporary problem for Canadians more difficult now than in the past. Modern society, Etzioni argues, set up the conditions of alienation of people - rampant bureaucracy, the intense division of labour in industrialization, and an overpowering belief in the legitimacy of rationality (i.e. in science and other social forms of such logic). But post-modern society goes one step further. It adds to that modern industrial base what Etzioni calls an "increased capacity for macroscopic manipulation, the generation of a *sense* of responsiveness where there is actually none. There have always been groups of men who were unaware of the basic facts of their socio-political lives and, thus, acted in opposition to their basic interests and private selves. It is the scope and depth of such false awareness and commitment that seem to be new". He calls his version of this problem "inauthenticity"[1] - a situation which exists if a relationship, an institution or a society "provides the appearance of responsiveness while the underlying condition is alienating". (Etzioni, 1968:619).

In Canada, at the present time, two significant events raise thoughts of Etzioni's analysis of post-modern times in relation to the theme for this panel - the public expectations of justice. The first event is our rapidly arriving reliance on the courts as a result of the Charter of Human Rigths and Freedoms, and in general the use of the courts to resolve disputes of a fundamental constitutional nature. While many of these

---

1. Etzioni's "inauthenticity" is not quite the same as Marx's "false consciousness" because each has a quite different theory of human nature, of the power of elites, and of the manner in which the social order changes. While quite similar, since I am not arguing the historical inevitability of changes in the marxian sense, I am using and explaining here the Etzioni term.

disputes, such as between governments, are not new, they are of renewed interest since our citizen rights are transparently involved. In any event, the links between the "micro-social unit", to use Etzioni's term for primary groups in which we live our daily lives, and the general values of our society will be mediated more visibly through the arguments of the courts and people in the justice system.

In itself this is a rather invigorating turn of events. Perhaps through the judges' decisions we will understand more about our civilization, gain a more sophisticated and loftier understanding of ourselves as a people and as a country. But the second event raises fears in the most optimistic among us that promise of self-knowledge and understanding may never be fulfilled.

This year we have been observers in two national elections - our own and that of the U.S.A. (in which we participate with such enthusiasm that I often think we ought to have the vote). I say we were observers because although many, many Canadians knocked on doors, made speeches, were candidates, donated money to candidates and worked in all phases of the election as Americans are doing now, the elections were going on, basically, elsewhere - principally on television. We went out and worked in our ridings and then we came home to see the "reality" on television. What we saw was just the tip of the iceberg, the bulk of the iceberg being the teams (or the "handlers" as they are called by the media) who put on the show.

These are not the first elections in which this has been the case, but perhaps in Canada the sense of inauthenticity was more marked this time. Inauthenticity, I remind you, is the "generation of a sense of responsiveness where there is actually none". The absence of understandable issues as the focal point in the struggle for one's vote in these campaigns raises a new unease. It is not a sense of personal powerlessness, because of course we have the vote. It is not alienation at that level we feel. But it is a sense of the powerlessness of the parties and the candidates at the macroscopic level that we sense. Committed activists are replaced by paid experts and pollsters and yet another small social unit which linked us as individuals to our parliament and our representatives is known only on television and through the other media. We can feel and authenticate our social experience in our family, our friendships, in our workplace and in our community associations but we cannot do so in the abstract world of giant corporations, enormous governments and media politics. In the latter, some intermediary group of people we neither know nor understand are having the social experience and interaction with the people who represent us in Parliament.

The fear which this represents for our society is at the opposite end of totalitarianism. It is a fear of authoritarianism. Etzioni describes this type of society as one in which a collectivity (such as a ruling family, occupational group or elite) and a state organization (such as parliament

or the courts) are closey interlinked, but the collectivity has an autonomous existence. This results in the government responding more to
the collectivity with which it is interwoven than to other collectivities.
It is a type of society which typically grows out of a democracy but in
which the "overlayer" of society is monopolized by one collectivity.
Pluralism is gone and the nature of the monopolizing collectivity is the
issue.

For most of us as individuals, notions of what constitutes justice
arise from our family and community experience in a democratic society. It is not problematic and not much understood. We leave corporate
and contract law to the experts. When forced to talk about it, we attempt
to extend by analogy our understanding of justice in daily life to those
quite different huge institutions and issues. This is simplistic, inadequate and a fatal weakness. It is also comforting.

Reductionism is our way of making the world a manageable place.
One doesn't really have to understand a great deal about our society in
order to get on with daily life. By such simplistic conveniences do we
contribute to the undermining of the ties between the micro-social units
in which we live and the larger society which contains them.

Television and the movies have been great simplifiers of complex
moral and emotional issues for most of our lives. The soaps, and the
doctor, police and newspaper serials give us a weekly occasion to feel
that we are confronting some issues. What they really do is to so reduce
and personalize the issues that the emergent problems of a real and
complex world are never revealed.

Now such simplifiers are incorporated into the daily news. Complex events with great historical dimensions come to us as fifteen seconds of the face of a starving child. The smiling face of the U.S. President belies the fact that he has big problems to solve. He doesn't have
to deny that big problems exist, just to hold the smile for thirty seconds
and we feel satisfied. It's called operant conditioning in learning theory.
Let me be clear. We, the great public, want it that way because we vote
the smilers into power. It is not on the electronic media that we, in
North America, find out whether or not the "basic facts of our socio-
political lives" are in accordance with, or in opposition to, our basic
interests, the consensus of our society, or the collectivities of which we
are members.

So it is difficult to escape the thought that the justice system may
be entrapped by the same processes which result in inauthenticity. Justice on television is so direct. We can pretend/feel that the past is back
with its values of order in a small society and with its good and bad
guys smiling at us from the screen. The great inner sense of justice
served which we learned on the playing fields and around the dinner
table is there. The civic values portrayed by the movie "Mr. Smith

Goes to Washington'', or Matt Dillon, are still around in new forms, and those electronic images push aside the necessity of examining as a public the society we have become.

Those who work in the justice system know quite well that the problems of today very seldom relate to such a simple view of the world (if indeed they ever did in reality). But they also know that much of what will happen is already captured by experts - by lawyers and the corporations and governments who are their patrons, by social workers and by interest groups. Since it is pointless to believe that individual citizens will ever understand what is happening, it is more sensible to work with and relate to these mediating groups. Let specially designed agencies work with the families, the work groups and the community associations.

But public unease and cynicism about the justice system and the simplistic answers which mobilize people to support simplistic solutions (such as hanging) require examination. Is the analysis put by Etzioni at the bottom of our disquiet? Are the members of the justice system captured by a monopolistic collectivity? Do we know that the mediating organizations between our world and the abstractions of court-room justice are serving our basic socio-political interests? Are Canadians equal before the law or do the big corporations, big governments, big unions and pressure groups interweave themselves so closely with the justice system that their interests are better served? Is there an appearance of justice because lawyers, judges and attorneys-general have ''handlers'' who make them appear so authentic that we are reassured and give up trying to understand?

Canadians are disturbed by a number of contradictions which remain unresolved. Why is sentencing and parole such that people who have offended against the community turn up back in the community so soon? Why do the police consistently complain about clogged court schedules and lawyers ''beating'' the system? How do we make sense of the DeLorean case as described to us in the papers? And why do foreign diplomats and so many rich and powerful seem to get off so easily? Why does the new technology seem to ferret out small tax avoiders and yet not allow single mothers to collect on court-ordered support payments? Just what rights are being protected and what now constitutes satisfactory justice?

We are not, after all, so far from the world in which the elders of the tribe talked out the problem and laid down the law before the community as a whole in a direct and understandable fashion. It is not that we would be prepared to accept that justice now, it is more that we have little grasp of how to come to terms with the meaning of justice in our world.

Daniel Bell and others view post-industrial society as containing new public expectations of justice. They argue that justice has now a new element concerned with "fairness" in it and that "representative" democracy is now to be understood as "participatory democracy". No longer equality of opportunity, it is now equality of result that interests us. The justice system is expected to go beyond its previous mandate and must do so if the public is to be satisfied.

The consensus in Canadian, and indeed North American, society has moved on to some logical extensions of our ideas of justice and of citizenship. Our mass society has added new players to the field - these macro-social units, or mediating collectivites, or big organizations - which are understood by only a small segment of the population.

"Human nature" is socially organized, institutionalized, differentiated into structured sets of social relationships. We are what we were but we are also collectively something new. The justice system has also changed, adapted and developed, but perhaps not sufficiently explained, its ways.

References

Daniel Bell, *The Cultural Contradictions of Capitalism*, New York, Basic Books, 1976.

Ralph Dahrendorf, *Life Chances, Approaches to Social and Political Theory*, Chicago, University of Chicago Press, 1979.

Amitai Etzioni, *The Active Society, A Theory of Societal and Political Processes*, New York, Free Press, 1968.

David Reisman, *The Lonely Crowd*, New Haven, Yale University Press, 1950.

The Morality of Justice

David MacDonald*

I am glad that I have had the opportunity of hearing Professor Dworkin because it confirms something that I have really only suspected but I think now has been stated with much greater clarity: that many of the attributes that have through the centuries been attributed to organized religion have found a new home. That is something that I do not say lightly or easily in this gathering but I think it must be stated. I also think that, particularly in response to Senator Marsden's remarks, that we all of us as Canadians are people without a home.

I think it is fascinating that we could be here discussing the public expectation of justice, listening in the first instance, and I do not mean this in any way disrespectfully, to a professor who really speaks to us from the kind of joint citizenship, if I can put it that way, of Anglo-American judicial experience. We can look at it from a sociological point of view and give it the kind of mid-Atlantic context which so far at least does not seem to recognize that Canada may have some rather unique fixtures and facets of its own. Some of you know that most of what I have done as an adult has been in aspects of public life and politics, and I would have to make here a kind of public confession. After almost twenty years of being involved in public policy in this country, I have discovered that the most difficult thing to understand is the country itself, and I suspect that is particularly true when it comes to dealing with something as complex and as mysterious as the legal justice system.

One of the things that I have discovered from people such as Dalton Camp who has been a kind of spiritual mentor in my political pilgrimage, is that if you really want to understand the political nature of the country, you really have to approach it from the stand-point of a mixture of kind of metaphysical analysis and the arts. What is so difficult in understanding our political life, is that it is so subtle. The really important things that are happening in this country are so difficult to get a handle on. If you ask what is politically significant in this country,

---

* Canadian Emergency Co-ordinator, African Famine.

I would say the really politically significant things are geography, the weather and occasionally a bit of history. I say that because I think that continues to impact upon the subject of the legal system. It is compounded no doubt by what has been referred to by both Jean-Claude Delorme and Lorna Marsden as the increasing interaction of the media and in particular the mass media.

And again I am struck by the unself-conscious attitude we take to media in this country. If there is anything that we have really gone to town on in Canada it is the media. We have it in just about every direction and every shape and fashion. We have almost all of what the Americans are able to unload on us plus all that we can produce by ourselves and we still want more. There must be something there that we like about it because we are so anxious just to keep producing it and to enjoy other people's mediating activity as it hits us.

That I think in some ways sets a sort of context for trying to get at the subject of this panel, because it is true that we do have a fair bit of media analysis of what our legal system is all about. One of the problems about much of the media analysis is that it uses a frame of reference and a value system that is only from time to time our own. We really have a great time sitting in the balcony of another country and occasionally, if we are lucky, we get down on the stage and do a little bit of acting ourselves. This of course has become increasingly complex and difficult for the average citizen, given the kind of constitutional roller coaster that we have been on for the last few years. We are still much too close to the recent constitutional developments with the entrenching of the Charter and all of its attendant political activity to really gauge the full aspect of the humourous quality of all this. I was constantly struck during the constitutional debate by the fact that only in Canada would we have had the kind of prolonged constitutional crisis about rescuing notions that were somehow sitting somewhere else, that needed to be made very much our own in order to become a fully self-respecting country at the ripe old age, depending on when you start counting, of 110 or 115 or 200 years. Those attitudes I think reflect in large measure the difficulty that we have in coming to grips with the Charter of Rights, and with the ways in which our constitution now guides and frames us in our relationship to the courts and to one another.

But I would like to come back to my original concern, the one that was properly raised by Professor Dworkin. I really felt for a while this evening that I had come into a restored cathedral of some wing of the Presbyterian Church. There is no doubt that the Presbyterians had a kind of par-excellence attitude about forms of predestination and natural law. I think that is where we are, except that the cathedral has changed, the canon is different, and those who are in holy orders behave somewhat differently, but basically we have established for ourselves a kind of framework which I think for the average citizen becomes a new holy of holies. To some degree the process that we have launched in this panel is at least an investigation if not a demystification of that holy of holies. Therefore I am grateful for Professor Dworkin's remarks because if he can take a position which attempts to raise some basic questions about those attitudes, then maybe those of us with much lesser experience and understanding can follow in his train.

I believe that the problem for the average citizen today is in fact the growing distance that exists, the sense in which there is a kind of otherness, a kind of removedness that makes it difficult for there to be the kind of respect, understanding and acceptance that at root must motivate and form the relationship of citizens to one another within their own legal system.

We in this country have in fact some very important traditions. One of the things I discovered during the last few months as we worked together on the Papal Visit was again the incredible tolerance, patience and respect that people have in this country. From my experience of Canadians over the course of the past few months, the kind of emergent course in Canadian society, we have this incredible sense of being respectful towards one another that surely in some way must inform the way in which we deal with one another, both in society generally and within various forms of legal confrontation or activity. I want to end these very informal remarks with a comment that in a sense goes to the heart of what Professor Dworkin was saying. Implicit and I think increasingly explicit in the way in which the legal system is developing in our society, are a series of basic assumptions that have really not been questioned. Whether we call this natural law, or whether we call it some form of jurisprudence, is not the issue. But there is no doubt in my mind that certain basic values that have been for many centuries the property of religious beliefs, have taken on new coinage within our legal system. They are so basic and so profound that they go to the heart of most of us who are active in politics on a daily basis. They have something to do with things such as the objectification of reality and increasingly its fragmentation. They go very much to the heart of notions of confrontation and in particular the weighing of questions of value which transend the importance and centrality of people as against their physical context. I realize that these are largely difficult and embarrassing questions to introduce at the end of these remarks and yet I would be less than frank if I did not put them on the table.

PART I

THE DEVELOPMENT OF RIGHTS

L'ÉVOLUTION DES DROITS

THE RIGHT TO SPEAK:
FREEDOM FROM EXPRESSION

LE DROIT DE S'EXPRIMER: LE DROIT DE NE PAS
SUBIR L'EXERCICE DU DROIT DE S'EXPRIMER

Le droit de s'exprimer

Michel Proulx*

INTRODUCTION

The time for defending freedom never goes by. Freedom is a habit that must be kept alive by use (F.R. Scott, 1933)

La *Charte canadienne des droits et libertés* garantit à l'article 2 (b) les ''libertés fondamentales de pensée, de croyance, d'opinion et d'expression, y compris la liberté de la presse et des autres moyens de communication.''

Toute société démocratique reconnaît la nécessité de certaines limitations à la liberté d'expression. (On peut voir à ce sujet, sur le droit américain, l'article de Paul Bender: ''The Canadian Charter of Rights and Freedoms and the United States Bill of Rights: A Comparison'', (1983) 28 *McGill L.J.* 858 et s.; voir aussi la *Convention européenne des droits de l'homme* et le *Pacte international relatif aux droits civils et politiques*). Au Canada, l'article 1 de la *Charte canadienne des droits et libertés* prévoit que les droits et libertés qui y sont énoncés peuvent être restreints par une règle de droit, dans des limites qui soient raisonnables et dont la justification puisse se démontrer dans le cadre d'une société libre et démocratique: ces mêmes droits et libertés peuvent être également restreints par le biais de l'article 33.

Le droit à la liberté d'expression n'est donc pas absolu. Dans certains cas, il entre en conflit avec celui de ne pas avoir à subir des paroles ou des images choquantes. Ceci est particulièrement vrai dans les secteurs qui nous sont proposés, à savoir: l'obscénité, la pornographie, la censure, les écrits haineux et la dissidence politique.

---

* Avocat et membre du Barreau du Québec.

Alors que nous entendons voir comment ces deux droits ont été conciliés par les tribunaux canadiens, il est important de noter que l'enchâssement des libertés fondamentales dans la Constitution du pays en 1982, devait nécessairement marquer le point de départ d'une nouvelle attitude de la part des tribunaux (Voir Clare Beckton, "Freedom of Expression" dans *The Canadian Charter of Rights and Freedoms, Commentary*, ed. by Tarnopolsky et Beaudoin, Toronto, Carswell, (1982) p. 80). Auparavant, malgré la *Déclaration canadienne des droits*, S.R.C. 1970, appendice III, laquelle en vertu du principe de la souveraineté parlementaire a été confinée, pour ainsi dire, dans le rôle d'une simple loi d'interprétation, et malgré aussi une certaine théorie dite du "Implied Bill of Rights", les tribunaux se fondaient sur le partage des compétences afin de limiter les entraves à la liberté d'expression (Voir *Switzman* c. *Elbling and A.G. Quebec*, [1957] S.C.R. 285; *A.G. Canada and Dupond* c. *City of Montreal*, [1978] 2 S.C.R. 770).

Ainsi qu'en concluait le professeur André Tremblay lors d'une conférence prononcée dans le cadre des Journées Strasbourgeoises en juillet dernier:

> Comme on peut le voir, les lois dérogatoires aux libertés que les tribunaux ont dû examiner avant avril 1982 s'analyseraient en termes de sujets ou de matières de compétences législatives et non pas en regard de limitations imposées aux corps législatifs en vue de protéger expressément une liberté fondamentale. La jurisprudence antérieure à l'entrée en vigueur de la *Charte canadienne* n'est pas devenue désuète: elle a le mérite d'avoir fixé, avec les moyens restreints dont elle disposait, des limitations à l'autorité publique et ces limitations demeurent.

Le statut et la lettre de la *Charte canadienne des droits et libertés* appellent une approche différente. De par son statut constitutionnel, elle exige des tribunaux qu'ils s'éloignent du principe de la souveraineté parlementaire pour se faire les véritables gardiens des droits et libertés fondamentaux. De par sa lettre, elle oblige les cours canadiennes à définir les libertés protégées et à tracer les limites à l'intérieur desquelles toutes restrictions à ces libertés seront raisonnables et dont on pourra démontrer qu'elles sont justifiables dans une société libre et démocratique.

Une attention toute particulière sera donc portée à l'examen des jugements dans lesquels les tribunaux canadiens, à travers ce nouveau prisme que leur impose la *Charte canadienne des droits et libertés*, ont tenté de concilier la liberté d'expression avec le droit de ne pas avoir à subir des paroles ou des images choquantes.

Auparavant, nous examinerons la portée et le contenu de l'article 2 (b) afin de préciser l'étendue de la protection constitutionnelle.

PORTÉE ET CONTENU DE L'ARTICLE 2 (b)

Dans les décisions judiciaires antérieures à la Charte canadienne, on retrouve plusieurs déclarations faites à propos de l'existence et de la nature de la liberté d'expression au Canada. Dans *Reference re: Alberta Legislation*, [1938] S.C.R. 100, l'honorable juge Cannon a souligné la nature fondamentale de cette liberté dans les termes suivants:

> Freedom of discussion is essential to enlighten public opinion in a democratic State; it cannot be curtailed without affecting the right of the people to be informed through sources independent of the Government concerning matters of public interest... As stated in the preamble of the *British North America Act*, our constitution is and will remain, unless radically changed, "similar in principle to that of the United Kingdom". At the time of Confederation, the United Kingdom was a democracy. Democracy cannot be maintained without its foundation: free public opinion and free discussion throughout the nation of all matters affecting the state within the limits set by the Criminal Code and the common law. (p. 145)

Cependant, comme le laissent deviner les derniers mots de la citation et comme l'expliquait l'honorable juge en chef Duff:

> The right of public discussion is of course, subject to legal restriction; those based upon considerations of decency and public order, and others conceived for the protection of various private and public interests with which, for example, the laws of defamation and sedition are concerned. In a word, freedom of discussion means, to quote the words of Lord Wright in *James* v. *Commonwealth of Australia*, [1936] A.C. at p. 627, "Freedom governed by law". (p. 133)

Puisque avant la Charte, la liberté d'expression qui existait au Canada en était une "governed by law", il est important comme point de départ de déterminer si c'est cette liberté qu'on a voulu enchâsser dans la constitution avec toutes les limites qu'elle comportait au 14 avril 1982. La question est importante car une réponse affirmative rend difficile, sinon impossible l'invalidation d'une disposition législative antérieure à la Charte.

Malgré quelques arrêts, cependant minoritaires sur ce point, qui concluent qu'il s'agissait toujours de cette liberté "governed by law" (*R. c. Reed*, (1984) 8 C.C.C. (3d) 153 (B.C. Co. Ct.); *R. c. McLachlan et al.*, 9:0867 W.C.B. 441, (Ont. Prov. Ct.), l'on peut conclure de l'ensemble des jugements que la seule règle d'interprétation valable et compatible avec la Charte est la suivante:

1°   qu'aucune présomption de constitutionnalité ne joue en faveur de la législation ou de la limite en litige;
2°   qu'il convient alors de déterminer si la limite répond au test de l'article 1.

Par conséquent, toute limite à la liberté d'expression, antérieure comme postérieure à la Charte, doit être appréciée par la cour en regard de l'article 1. L'honorable juge Smith dans *Re: Southam Inc. and R. (No. 1)*, (1983) 70 C.C.C. (2d) 257 (Ont. H.C.) (confirmée par la Cour d'appel dans *R. c. Southam*, (1984) 6 C.R.R. 1), jugement dans lequel il déclarait inconstitutionnel l'article 12(1) de la *Loi sur les jeunes délinquants*, S.R.C. 1970, c. J-3 qui imposait un procès "in camera", déclarait:

> Nor can I accept the statement made to this court that the Charter changes nothing; that it merely recognized existing rights. In my view, sovereignty of Parliament has been dealt a mid blow. The courts and Parliament are no longer the repositories of Constitution law rights. The Charter will prevail subject only to the "non-obstante" provisions embodied in s. 33 of the Charter. The desire expressed in the preamble to the *British North America Act*, 1867 (now the *Constitution Act*, 1867) to be federally united "with a Constitution similar in principle to that of the United Kingdom" is still a part of the Canadian Constitution. An important difference has been added which may be said to temper to some degree the sovereignty heretofore enjoyed by Parliament. With the advent of entrenchment of basic rights and freedoms, the court now has a constitutional responsibility to deny effect to a measure adopted by Parliament that contravenes the Charter. Such measure would very simply be unconstitutional and beyond its competence. (p. 263)

La Cour d'appel d'Ontario dans *Re Ontario Film and Video Appreciation Society and Ontario Board of Censors*, (1984) 5 D.L.R. (4th) 766, un arrêt qui portait sur la validité de l'article 3 (2)(a) du *Theatres Act*, R.S.O. 1980, c. 498, autorisant la censure du film, rejetait explicitement l'argument selon lequel cette limite à la liberté d'expression en étant une reconnue avant le 14 avril 1982, il n'était pas nécessaire de la justifier par l'article 1 (p. 767).

Enfin, sur le même point, il convient de souligner ce qu'en disait l'honorable juge Thorson dans *Re: SMITH; Global Communications Limited c. California and A.G. Ontario*, (1984) 38 C.R. (3d) 209, (C.A. Ont.):

> It must of course be acknowledged that it is no answer to the appellant's challenge to this legislation on the ground of s. 2 of the Charter that Parliament has or may have weighed the competing interests involved in cases of this kind and made a choice between them which operates in a way adverse to the interests of the appellant in this particular case. The new dimension is the Charter, and there can be no doubt that it is now given to the courts to determine whether or not the choice made by Parliament stands the test of the Charter. In that process, however, it would be wholly unwarranted, and in my opinion quite wrong, to conclude that the decision which Parliament has reached in the matter should be given no weight by the courts. (p. 223)
>
> In my opinion no useful purpose is served in this case by exploring whether or not "freedom of the press" ought to be given a meaning that recognizes the limitations which the law has previously placed on that

freedom and is thus not per se infringed by the order made in this case. (p. 224)

Peu importe la date d'entrée en vigueur de la limite à la liberté d'expression, il semble donc qu'il faille en tout temps appliquer le test de l'article 1 et que seules celles qui satisfont à ces critères seront valides. Il n'est plus suffisant non plus que le Parlement ait adopté, avant ou après la Charte, une mesure limitant la liberté d'expression pour que celle-ci soit automatiquement acceptée. Dans chaque cas, les tribunaux doivent déterminer si le choix du Parlement est conforme au test de l'article 1 (voir *Re: Smith; Global Communications Limited* c. *California and A.G. Ontario, op. cit.* et *R.* c. *Banville*, (1984) 5 C.R.R. 142, 3 C.C.C. (3d) 312 (N.B.Q.B.)).

Au plan des principes donc, les tribunaux acceptent de s'éloigner de la règle de la suprématie parlementaire. Cependant, au plan pratique comme nous le verrons plus loin (dans le domaine de l'obscénité principalement), cela se fait plus difficilement. Les tribunaux hésitent en effet à substituer à celle du Parlement leur conception de ce qui est raisonnable et justifiable dans le cadre d'une société libre et démocratique. Cela est particulièrement vrai dans les cas où, comme dans l'arrêt *Reed*, la mesure contestée est antérieure à la Charte.

- *Le contenu*

Une autre question se pose quant à la portée de la protection constitutionnelle de l'article 2 (b) de la Charte: il s'agit de savoir quelles formes d'expression sont incluses. Les tribunaux mettent à la charge de la partie qui conteste la validité de la législation le fardeau de démontrer une violation ''prima facie'' du droit ou de la liberté protégé avant que le fardeau de la justification sous l'article 1 ne passe à la partie qui invoque la validité de la législation (voir *Re: Ontario Film, op. cit.*; *R.* c. *Red Hot Video Limited*, (1984) 38 C.R. (3d) 275 (B.C. Co. Ct.); *Re: Federal Republic of Germany* c. *Rauca*, (1983) 4 C.C.C. (3d) 385 (Ont. C.A.). Dans cette optique procédurale, *le contenu de la liberté d'expression* a une importance considérable sur le déroulement du procès (voir Charter Beat, ''Court Upholds G String By-Law'', dans *The National*, Mars 1984).

Aux Etats-Unis, on reconnaissait que certaines catégories d'expressions étaient exclues du champ de la protection constitutionnelle. C'était le cas de l'obscénité, du libelle, de la profanation, du ''commercial speech'' et des ''fighting words'', (voir *Chaplinsky* c. *New Hampshire*, 315 U.S. 568 et *Valentine* c. *Chrestensen*, 316 U.S. 52). Cependant, la plupart de ces exclusions ont été éliminées dans des arrêts récents, (voir l'article de Paul Bender, *op. cit.*, p. 861). Seul le cas de l'obscénité laisse encore planer quelques doutes.

Au Canada, on retrouve dans les arrêts rendus à l'époque de la *Déclaration canadienne des droits*, certains passages qui tendent aussi à exclure certaines formes d'expression. Par exemple, dans *Re North American News and Deputy Minister of National Revenue for Customs and Excise*, (1974) 14 C.C.C. (2d) 63 (Ont. Co. Ct.):

> With respect to freedom of the press and freedom of speech, the right of free press and free speech does not include the right to distribute lewd, obscene, immoral and indecent publication... (p. 68)

Voir aussi *R. c. Prairie Schooner News Ltd. and Powers*, (1970) 1 C.C.C. (2d) 251 (Man. C.A.).

L'arrêt *Re Koumoudouros et al. and Municipality of Metropolitan Toronto, Re N.B. Theatrical Agencies and Municipalities of Metropolitan Toronto*, (1984) 6 D.L.R. (4th) 523 (Ont. Div. Ct.), rendu sous l'égide de la Charte, se situe dans cette ligne de pensée. On contestait, au nom de la liberté d'expression, la validité d'un règlement municipal qui obligeait les danseurs (burlesque entertainers) dans les ''adult entertainment parlors'' à porter des vêtements opaques couvrant la région pubienne.

L'''Ontario Divisional Court'', dans une décision majoritaire s'est refusée à considérer le règlement municipal comme une limite à la liberté d'expression. Après avoir exprimé des doutes sur la question de savoir si l'article 2 (b) couvrait plus que l'expression dans le domaine politique et gouvernemental, l'honorable juge Eberle exprimait ce qui suit:

> Therefore, assuming without deciding, that ''expression'' in the Charter includes ''artistic'' expression, the conclusion from the evidence is clear that the right claimed in these cases is not a right to freedom of artistic expression but the right to expose performers' pubic areas for the purpose of stimulating liquor sales... I am satisfied that ''freedom of expression'' guaranteed by the Charter does not include the public exposure of female pubic areas for the primary purpose of selling larger quantities of liquor. (p. 533)

L'honorable juge Osler, dissident, aurait quant à lui considéré le règlement municipal comme une entrave à la liberté d'expression mais justifiable par le biais de l'article 1. Plus libéral dans son interprétation de la portée de la protection constitutionnelle, il rejoint ainsi ce que nous croyons être l'interprétation majoritaire illustrée par le passage suivant de la Cour suprême de l'Ontario dans *Re Ontario Film and Video Appreciation Society and Ontario Board of Censors*, (1983) 34 C.R. (3d) 73 (Ont. Div. Ct.):

> It is clear to us that all forms of expression, whether they be oral, written, pictorial, sculpture, music, dance or film, are equally protected by the Charter. (p. 81)

Ce passage a été cité et approuvé dans *R. c. Red Hot Video Limited*, (1984) 38 C.R. (3d) 275 (B.C. Co. Ct., p. 279) portant sur la validité de l'article 159 du Code criminel et dans *Re: Luscher and Deputy*

Minister, Revenue Canada, Customs and Excise, (1983) 149 D.L.R. (3d) 243 (B.C. Co. Ct.), p. 249, portant sur l'article 14 du Customs Tariff Act, R.S.C. 1970, c. C-41 qui interdit l'importation de livres immoraux et indécents.

La Cour d'appel d'Ontario dans *R. c. Southam, op. cit.*, tout en reconnaissant que la liberté d'expression comprenait le droit d'accès du public aux cours de justice, prônait une interprétation large et libérale de la Charte des droits et libertés en ces termes:

> The Charter as part of a constitutional document should be given a large and liberal construction. The spirit of this new ''living tree'' planted in a friendly Canadian soil should not be stultified by narrow, technical, literal interpretations without regard to its background and purpose; capability for growth must be recognized. (p. 10)

C'est cette voie que semblent suivre les tribunaux canadiens relativement à la liberté d'expression, transportant le plus souvent le débat sur la question des limites raisonnables.

- Sur l'obscénité, outre les arrêts cités plus haut, voir: *Re Red Hot Video and City of Vancouver*, (1984) 5 D.L.R. (4th) 61 (B.C.S.C.); *Re University of Manitoba and Deputy Minister, Revenue Canada, Customs and Excise*, (1984) 4 D.L.R. (4th) 658 (Man. Co. Ct.).
- Sur l'expression en matière commerciale, voir *R. c. Halpert et al.*, (1984) 9 C.C.C. (3d) 411 (Ont. Prov. Ct.).
- Sur la liberté de presse et l'accès aux tribunaux, voir: *R. c. Southam, op. cit.*; *R. c. Banville, op. cit.*; *R. c. Robinson*, (1983) 34 C.R. (3d) 92 (Ont. H.C.); *Re Canadian Newspapers Co. Ltd. and The Queen*, (1984) 6 C.C.C. (3d) 488 (B.C.S.C.); *R. c. Sophonow*, (1984) 6 C.C.C. (3d) 396 (Man. C.A.).
- Sur la publicité (advertising), voir *Re Law Society of Manitoba and Savino*, (1981) 1 D.L.R. (4th) 285 (C.A. Man.).

Aussi, outre l'arrêt *Re Koumoudourous, op. cit.*, les arrêts *Re Edmonton Journal and A.G. Alta.*, (1983) 4 C.C.C. (3d) 59 (Alta. Q.B.) où on a refusé de voir dans l'article 2 (b) un droit d'accès du public aux tribunaux et l'arrêt *Source Perrier (Société Anonyme) c. Fira-Less Marketing Co. Ltd.*, (1983) 4 C.R.R. 317 (F.C.) nous apparaissent être quelque peu à contre-courant et d'une interprétation restrictive.

Dans *Source Perrier*, une compagnie de marketing avait mis sur le marché une bouteille d'eau portant le nom de ''Pierre Eh'', ressemblant grandement aux bouteilles d'eau minérale Perrier. C'était une satire politique destinée au premier ministre du Canada. L'honorable juge Dubé a refusé de voir une limitation quelconque à la liberté d'expression dans la demande de la compagnie Perrier. Celle-ci demandait que l'on cesse d'utiliser sa marque de commerce:

> In my view, the most liberal interpretation of ''freedom of expression'' does not embrace the freedom to depreciate the goodwill of registered trade marks, nor does it afford a licence to impair the business integrity of the owner of the marks merely to accommodate the creation of a spoof. (p. 322)

Il y aurait certes eu un avantage, au plan des principes, à définir plus largement la notion de liberté d'expression et à y inclure toute forme d'expression. Cela aurait imposé à la partie qui invoque la mesure susceptible d'entraver cette liberté, l'obligation de la justifier et au juge celle de soupeser les valeurs en jeu. Une telle approche empêche ainsi le plus possible l'effritement de la liberté d'expression (voir C. Beckton ''Freedom of expression in Canada - How free?'', (1983) *Man. L.J.* 583).

Ayant ainsi précisé la portée de la protection constitutionnelle accordée à la liberté d'expression, nous examinerons maintenant, à travers les domaines suivants, l'obscénité, la pornographie, la censure, la dissidence politique et la propagande haineuse, quelles sont les restrictions qui paraissent acceptables aux tribunaux canadiens. En bref, il s'agit de voir comment on interprète l'article 1 de la Charte et de préciser les tendances qui se dégagent pour l'avenir.

OBSCÉNITÉ - PORNOGRAPHIE

L'obscénité et la pornographie seront traitées sur le même pied. Quoique théoriquement il puisse y avoir une distinction entre les deux, on ne la rencontre pas dans la jurisprudence.

Outre les dispositions du Code criminel, certaines autres lois touchent le domaine de l'obscénité. C'est le cas notamment du *Customs Tariff Act*, R.S.C. 1970, c. C-41 permettant la saisie aux frontières de matériel jugé immoral ou indécent, des règlements du C.R.T.C. et de certaines lois et règlements provinciaux.

Notons que certaines de ces dispositions législatives peuvent aussi être vues sous l'angle de la censure; il en sera question plus loin dans l'étude distincte portant sur la censure.

Définition

On retrouve à l'article 159 (8) du Code criminel la définition suivante de l'obscénité:

> (8) Aux fins de la présente loi, est réputée obscène toute publication dont une caractéristique dominante est *l'exploitation indue* des choses sexuelles, ou de choses sexuelles et de l'un quelconque ou plusieurs des sujets suivants, savoir: le crime, l'horreur, la cruauté et la violence.

Cette définition de l'obscénité ne se retrouve au Code criminel que depuis 1959. Avant cette date, les tribunaux appliquaient un test d'obscénité proposé en Angleterre dans *R. c. Hicklin*. Celui-ci faisait l'objet de nombreuses critiques (voir C. Beckton, *The Law and the Media in Canada*, Toronto, Carswell, 1982, p. 146 et s.) et c'est dans le but de remédier à ces problèmes que la définition du Code criminel a été adoptée. Cependant, les difficultés d'application de cette nouvelle définition n'ont pas tardé à se soulever.

La première était celle de savoir si la définition du Code criminel était exhaustive ou si le test de l'arrêt *Hicklin* subsistait. Après de longs flottements jurisprudentiels, la Cour suprême du Canada trancha la question en 1977, décidant dans l'arrêt *Dechow* c. *R.*, (1977) 35 C.C.C. (2d) 22 que le critère de l'arrêt *Hicklin* était remplacé par l'article 159 (b) (voir C. Beckton, *The Law and the Media, op. cit.*, p. 149).

La principale difficulté vient de l'interprétation de la définition. La Cour suprême du Canada pour la première fois en 1962 dans la cause *Brodie, Dansky and Rubin* c. *The Queen*, [1962] R.C.S. 681 avait à se prononcer sur ce qui constitue ''une publication dont une caractéristique dominante est l'exploitation *indue* de choses sexuelles''. Certains principes furent dégagés de cette décision. Il semble qu'une publication puisse avoir plus d'une caractéristique dominante mais que si l'une d'entre elles est l'exploitation *indue* des choses sexuelles, les tribunaux doivent examiner la publication dans son ensemble et non pas en isolant certains passages. Il semble que ce ne soit pas le cas pour un magazine. Voir *R. c. Pink Triangle Press*, (1980) 51 C.C.C. (2d) 485 (Ont. Co. Ct.) et *R. c. Penthouse Int. Ltd.*, (1979) 46 C.C.C. (2d) 111 (Ont. C.A.) - permission d'appel refusée.

On devra tenir compte du but de l'auteur, du mérite artistique et littéraire de l'ouvrage et des normes d'acceptation de la collectivité (community standards of decency). A cette fin, les tribunaux n'ont pas hésité à permettre le témoignage d'experts.

Le critère essentiel tel qu'il se dégage de la jurisprudence apparaît être celui de la norme d'acceptation de la société ou ''Community standards of tolerance''. (Pour une bonne revue de la jurisprudence sur la question, voir *R. c. Doug Rankine Co. Ltd. and Act III Video Productions Ltd.*, (1984) 9 C.C.C. (3d) 53 (Ont. Co. Ct.). Un des arrêts importants sur cette question est *Dominion News and Gifts (1962) Ltd. c. The Queen*, [1964] 3 C.C.C. 1, dans lequel la Cour suprême adopte les motifs de l'honorable juge Freedman, dissident dans le jugement de la Cour d'appel du Manitoba, [1963] 2 C.C.C. 103.

Ce dernier mettait en garde les juges de ne pas transposer leurs goûts et préjugés en évaluant les normes d'acceptation de la société. Le test en est un objectif et qui doit tenir compte de l'évolution de la société. De plus:

> Those standards are not set by those of lowest taste or interest. Nor are
> they set exclusively by those of rigid, austere, conservative, or puritan

taste and habit of mind. Something approaching a general average of community thinking and feeling has to be discovered. (p. 116)

Plus loin il précisait:

I think I should add to my view that in cases close to the border line, tolerance is to be preferred to prescription. To strike at a publication which is not clearly obscene may have repercussions and implications beyond what is immediately visible. To suppress the bad is one thing; to suppress the not so bad, or even the possibly good is another. Unless it is confined to clear cases, suppression may tend to inhibit those creative impulses and endeavours which ought to be encouraged in a free society. (p. 117)

Il semble qu'il faille tenir compte de la façon dont est distribuée la publication, c'est-à-dire de la facilité avec laquelle on peut avoir accès à celle-ci. On peut voir *R. c. Sudbury News Service Ltd.*, (1978) 39 C.C.C. (2d) 1 (Ont. C.A.) et *R. c. Hawkshaw and R.*, (1983) 69 C.C.C. (2d) 503 (Ont. C.A.) (permission d'en appeler à la Cour suprême accordée - 69 C.C.C. (2d) 503n (S.C.C.)) dont nous citons l'extrait suivant:

The fact that the picture was intended solely for private viewing and was not intended to, and did not come into anyone's hands, other than those of the person who took the picture and the commercial establishment which developed it, may be very relevant in considering what the Canadian community would tolerate. A sketch or a model which is the product of the author's imagination and is only intended to be viewed privately might not be found by the trial judge to constitute an undue exploitation of sex. On the other hand, he might be driven to conclude that the community would not tolerate, even for private viewing, a photograph depicting the commission of an act of gross indecency where one of the participants is a minor. In short, publication is not a prerequisite to a determination that a picture is obscene, but it is a relevant circumstance to be weighed in making this determination. (p. 516)

L'article 159 (8) ne parle pas de publication; ce mot est toutefois interprété largement et peut comprendre une représentation cinématographique, une exposition etc. Ceci est démontré par l'opinion de l'honorable juge Ritchie (à laquelle ont souscrit quatre de ses collègues) dans l'arrêt *Deschow c. R., op. cit.*

En pratique, le test du "community standards of tolerance" est largement appliqué peu importe l'infraction reprochée.

Customs Tariff Act, R.S.C. 1970, c. C-41:
* *Minister of National Revenue for Customs and Excise* c. *Taché*, (1982) 40 N.R. 559 (F.C.A.);
* *Re Luscher and Dep. M.N.R.*, (1983) 149 D.L.R. (3d) 243 (B.C. Co. Ct.);
* *Re University of Manitoba and Deputy Minister, Revenue Canada, Customs and Excise*, (1984) 4 D.L.R. (4th) 658 (Man. Co. Ct.);

- Art. 163 (2) C.cr., spectacle théâtral, danse:
  - R. c. *MacLean and MacLean (No. 2)*, (1983) 1 C.C.C. (3d) 412 (Ont. C.A.);
  - R. c. *Charpentier*, [1982] R.L. 469;
- Art. 163 C.cr., représentation cinématographique:
  - R. c. *Towne Cinema Theatres (1975) Ltd.*, [1982] 1 W.W.R. 512 (Alta Q.B.)
  - R. c. *Les Cinémas Québécois Inc.*, [1982] R.L. 180;
  - R. c. *Lachapelle*, [1981] R.L. 133;
- Art. 159 C.cr.:
  - R. c. *Barr*, (1982) 16 Man. R. (2d) 1, (Man. Co. Ct.), macaron "Fuck Iran";
- Art. 170 C.cr., nudité, spectacle théâtral:
  - R. c. *Giambalvo*, (1983) 70 C.C.C. (2d) 324 (Ont. C.A.);
- Art. 164 C.cr., mise à la poste de choses obscènes, journal:
  - *Popert* c. *R.*, (1981) 19 C.R. (3d) 393 (Ont. C.A.).

Ce test est difficile d'application et pour une même publication peut donner des résultats différents. Par exemple, le numéro de décembre du magazine Penthouse a été considéré obscène par la Cour d'appel du Nouveau-Brunswick dans *R. c. Saint-John News*, (1976) 13 N.B.R. (2d) 564 alors que la Cour d'appel du Québec dans *Benjamin News* c. *R.*, (1978) 6 C.R. (3d) 281, décidait du contraire.

En définitive, comme le disait W.S. Tarnopolsky dans *The Canadian Bill of Rights*, 2° ed., Toronto, McClelland and Stewart Limited, (1975) p. 200, au sujet du rôle des juges:

> "As objective as this individual may try to be, it is he who will decide whether the "internal necessities" of the publication, or the "community standards", are such that "a dominant characteristic" of the work is the "undue exploitation of sex".

Sous la Charte

Depuis que la liberté d'expression est protégée dans un document constitutionnel, les cours canadiennes ont eu à se prononcer sur la raisonnabilité de quelques-unes des dispositions prohibant l'obscénité.

Dans *R. c. Doug Rankine Co. Ltd. and Act IV Video Production Ltd.*, (1984) 9 C.C.C. (3d) 53 (Ont. Co. Ct.), deux entreprises étaient accusées de distribution de publications obscènes, à savoir, la distribution de films enregistrés sur vidéo-cassettes. Alors que l'inconstitutionnalité de l'article 159 du Code criminel n'était pas plaidée, on soumettait que la protection accordée à la liberté d'expression par l'article 2 (b) obligeait les cours à réévaluer et à modifier le test jurisprudentiel du "community standards of tolerance" (page 65).

Les parties reconnaissaient que l'obscénité est exclue de la protection prévue à l'article 2 (b) et en regard de l'article 1.

Tout en reconnaissant qu'en évaluant la norme d'acceptation de la société, les tribunaux devaient tenir compte du "respect for freedom of expression" garanti par la constitution, l'honorable juge Borins rejeta l'argument des défendeurs. Le test reste donc le même. Il n'appartient pas aux tribunaux de réécrire le Code criminel. N'est-ce pas là ce qu'aurait fait le juge en changeant l'interprétation judiciaire de l'article 159 (8)? De plus, la question de la validité constitutionnelle de l'article 159 C.cr. reste entière malgré cette prise de position. C'est ce que reconnaît le juge en insistant sur le fait que l'inconstitutionnalité n'a pas été soulevée. A la page 66, il nous dit:

> ... I am not to be taken as expressing an opinion on whether or not obscenity should receive the absolute protection of s. 2 (b) free from such limits as may be demonstrated under s. 1. I have not, of course, directed my attention to such questions as whether the governmental interest served by the regulation of obscenity can only be reasonable and justifiable in a free and democratic society if the harm resulting from the failure to regulate overrides the harm caused by the regulation of freedom of expression. Nor is the court required to decide whether the values served by free expression should be subordinate to the values served by censorship.

Ce passage laisse entrevoir l'optique dans laquelle la question de limites raisonnables et justifiables dans le cadre d'une société libre et démocratique aurait été envisagée si elle avait été soulevée. Ces propos rejoignent d'assez près ceux du professeur Beckton dans *Freedom of Expression in Canada - How free, op. cit.*, et dans *Freedom of Expression - Commentary, op. cit.*

C'est toutefois d'une façon très sommaire que l'on a traité de la validité constitutionnelle de l'article 159 C.cr. dans *R. c. Red Hot Video Limited*, (1984) 38 C.R. (3d) 275 (B.C. Co. Ct.). Il faut dire, à la décharge du juge, que, dans la foulée de l'arrêt *Re Ontario Film and Video Appreciation Society and Ontario Board of Censors, op. cit.*, dont il sera question plus loin, l'inculpée avait surtout concentré son argumentation sur le caractère *"vague et incertain"* ("void for vagueness") de la disposition législative. Red Hot Video était accusée d'avoir en sa possession des vidéo-cassettes obscènes dans le but d'en faire la distribution. Elle concédait le caractère obscène de celles-ci, seule la validité constitutionnelle de l'article 159 était en jeu.

La cour, reconnaissant au départ que dans le cadre de l'article 1 de la Charte, l'article 159 constitue une *limite* à la liberté d'expression, s'est ainsi dirigée sur la question à trancher à partir de cette règle du "void for vagueness":

> In the case at bar the issue is whether or not the legislation passed by Parliament, insofar as it limits the guaranteed freedom of expression, is demonstrably justified in a free and democratic society. A consideration of the submissions of the appellant involve two questions: first, whether

or not a statute may be struck down on the basis that it is vague, undefined and totally discretionary (see Re Ont. Film & Video Appreciation Soc. and Ont. Bd. of Censors, *supra*) and when it conflicts with the guaranteed freedom; and second, whether or not s. 159 is vague and undefined. (p. 281)

Sans poursuivre davantage sur les composantes de la législation sur l'obscénité, la cour rejeta cet argument et conclut ainsi à la validité constitutionnelle de l'article 159.

Nous devons donc conclure de ce qui précède que le véritable débat sur la validité constitutionnelle de l'article 159 n'a pas encore été engagé.

D'autres décisions ont cependant suscité notre intérêt en ce qu'elles traitent de *conflits* entre des lois ou règlements relatifs à l'obscénité et la liberté d'expression. Examinons les solutions apportées par les tribunaux :

1° *Re Ontario Film and Video Appreciation Society and Ontario Board of Censors*, (1984) 5 D.L.R. (4th) 766 (Ont. C.A.):

Etait ici soulevée la constitutionnalité du pouvoir de censure accordé au Board of Censors de l'Ontario aux termes de l'article 3 (2) a) du *Theatres Act*, R.S.O. 1980, c. 498 qui était ainsi rédigé :

3(2) The Board has power,

a) to censor any film and, when authorized by the person who submits film to the Board for approval, remove by cutting or otherwise from the film any portion thereof that it does not approve of for exhibition in Ontario;

Ajoutons ici que la loi ne prévoyait aucun critère d'évaluation pour le bureau de censure.

Dans un arrêt confirmant le jugement très bien étoffé de la ''Divisional Court'' de la Cour suprême de l'Ontario, la Cour d'appel, composée de cinq juges, conclut sans équivoque à l'invalidité constitutionnelle du pouvoir de censure prévu à l'article 3 (2) a):

1. En soulignant que cette disposition constitue une entrave totale à la liberté d'expression dans ce domaine et n'impose aucune limite au pouvoir de censure, et

2. qu'ainsi on ne peut même pas s'interroger si des limites, en regard de l'article 1 de la Charte, sont raisonnables ou non, en l'absence de critères spécifiques de censure.

3. Notons que la Cour n'entendit pas se prononcer sur la question de savoir si des normes législatives imposées au bureau de censure constitueraient une limite raisonnable à la liberté d'expression, ou enfin si la censure, en soi, est justifiable.

4. En concluant que l'article 3 (2) a) ne constituait pas une limite raisonnable ''prescrite par la loi'', la Divisional Court s'était inspirée du concept ''void for vagueness'' qui s'énonce ainsi :

It is accepted that law cannot be vague, undefined, and totally discretionary; it must be ascertainable and understandable. Any limits placed on the freedom of expression cannot be left to the whim of an official; such limits must be articulated with some precision or they cannot be considered to be law.

Mais tout ce débat n'est pas clos puisque la Cour suprême du Canada a accepté d'entendre l'appel à l'encontre du jugement rendu par la Cour d'appel d'Ontario.

2° L'arrêt *Re Luscher and Deputy Minister, Revenue Canada Customs and Excise* (B.C. Co. Ct.) *op. cit.*, est un autre cas où, dans un contexte différent, une législation portant sur l'obscénité était contestée.

L'article 14 du *Customs Tariff Act*, R.S.C. 1970, c. C-41, prévoit que:

14. The importation into Canada of any goods enumerated, described or referred to in Schedule C is prohibited...

L'item 99201-1 de la Sch. C se lit comme suit:

Books, printed papers, drawings, paintings, prints, photographs or representations of any kind of .... immoral or indecent character.''

L'appelant contestait, comme la loi le lui permet, la décision du ministre qui avait confirmé la classification d'immoral et d'indécent d'un magazine, faite par l'officier de la douane. Selon lui, il s'agissait d'une restriction à la liberté d'expression, d'autant plus qu'il était admis que ce magazine devait servir à son usage personnel, cela constituant un facteur pertinent à la détermination des "community standards".

Ce jugement, tant au niveau de l'argumentation que de la justification ressemble grandement à celui dans *R. c. Red Hot Video, op. cit.* On reconnaît que la loi impose une restriction à la liberté d'expression et qu'il appartient à la couronne de démontrer que la restriction est une règle de droit, démonstrativement justifiable dans une société libre et démocratique et qu'il s'agit d'une limite raisonnable.

On invoquait encore ici, qu'étant donné le caractère vague et imprécis des mots "immoral" et "indécent", (obligeant même le ministre à émettre des directives d'interprétation aux officiers de douane), il ne pouvait s'agir de limites raisonnables et que ces limites ne constituaient pas une règle de droit.

Le juge distingue l'arrêt *Re Ontario Film and Video* en précisant qu'il ne s'agit pas ici d'un cas où la législation contestée ne contient aucune limite. Admettant que les directives d'interprétation fournies aux officiers ne peuvent être vues comme une règle de droit, il considère cependant que le *Customs Tariff* et la Sch. C., préparés sous l'autorité du Parlement, contiennent des limites qui sont prescrites par la loi.

La question de l'imprécision des termes est plutôt examinée sous l'angle des limites raisonnables. Le raisonnement est ici analogue à celui du juge Melvin dans *R. c. Red Hot Video*: la définition de ce qui est indécent ou immoral ne peut se retrouver que dans le concept large et évolutif du "community standards of tolerance". Plus la définition est précise, plus elle devient restrictive et difficile à changer. Il conclut que les limites imposées par la loi sont raisonnables.

Selon nous, ce jugement reconnaît la nature d'obiter du passage déjà cité du jugement de la "Divisional Court" dans *Re Ont. Film and Video*. On peut dire même qu'il rejette implicitement la théorie selon laquelle le caractère vague d'une législation l'empêcherait d'être une règle de droit au sens de la Charte. Faisant de l'imprécision d'un texte de loi une question de limites raisonnables, les difficultés d'interprétation de celui-ci ne seraient pas un motif d'invalidité constitutionnelle. Ce n'est que dans la mesure où l'imprécision de celui-ci risquerait de restreindre la liberté d'expression au-delà de ce qui est justifiable (overbreadth) qu'il serait invalidé.

Cela rejoint, croyons-nous, le raisonnement de la Cour d'appel d'Ontario dans *Re Ont. Film and Video, op. cit.*, qui a préféré faire porter sa décision sur le fait que la législation ne contenait aucune limite et permettait ainsi la négation complète de la liberté d'expression dans un domaine particulier.

3° La même disposition législative était contestée dans *Re University of Manitoba and Deputy Minister, Revenue Canada, Customs and Excise* (Man. Co. Ct.) *op. cit.* Ce n'est toutefois qu'en obiter que le juge s'est prononcé sur la validité constitutionnelle de cette loi puisqu'il était arrivé à la conclusion que le film "Male Masturbation", destiné à être visionné à la faculté de médecine du Manitoba, n'était pas obscène selon le degré de tolérance de la société canadienne. Au sujet de la Charte, il dit:

> I am not required to deal with the Canadian Charter of Rights and Freedoms argument. But were I to do so, I am satisfied that the Deputy Minister's actions are completely unwarranted invasions of the appellant's rights and a violation of the academic community's freedom of expression, as expressed and guaranteed in the Charter (s. 2). (p. 663)

4° L'article 2 (b) de la Charte a aussi été invoqué pour faire invalider certains règlements municipaux. L'arrêt *Re Koumoudouros, op. cit.*, en est un exemple infructueux. Nous en avons traité précédemment.

5° L'arrêt *Re Red Hot Video Ltd. and City of Vancouver*, (1984) 5 D.L.R. (4th) 61 (B.C.S.C.) en est un autre exemple. Le règlement de zonage contesté prohibait la vente ou la location de "sex-oriented products" dans toutes les zones de la ville.

Le règlement ne fut pas invalidé. Cet arrêt semble reconnaître comme applicable au Canada le principe selon lequel:

> ... statutory provisions which violate a freedom guaranteed by the Charter will be struck down as being too broad unless there are clear standards or criteria in the statutory provision by which it can be measured." (p. 65)

C'est encore une fois le principe du "void for vagueness" qui a connu son origine dans *Re Ont. Film and Video, op. cit.*, qui était invoqué. Le règlement qui visait deux types de produits, (1) "those products depicting a person or persons engaging in real or simulated sex acts" and (2) "items which simulate or are a reproduction of any human sex organ in any type of sexual activity", n'a pas été considéré imprécis. Malgré ses difficultés d'interprétation, le juge croit que toute personne raisonnable peut comprendre ce qu'est un "sex act" ou un "sexual activity" lorsqu'il en voit un. Par conséquent, les critères et les standards se retrouvent dans la loi.

Un argument de validité est tiré du fait que le règlement a une application limitée puisqu'en sont exclus les "sex-oriented products" qui ont une valeur éducative ou pharmaceutique; c'est un signe que la loi n'est pas trop vague et imprécise.

Appliquant les critères énoncés dans *Re Federal Republic of Germany and Rauca*, (1982) 141 D.L.R. (3d) 412 (Ont. H.C.), la cour considère la limite raisonnable puisque:

> ... I do not think that a fair-minded person accustomed to the norms of a free and democratic society would object to the limitation imposed on the freedom of expression by the by-law. (p. 66)

Enfin, malgré le fait que l'on n'ait pas démontré l'effet nuisible sur la société du commerce de Red Hot Video, la cour a pris connaissance d'office de son effet indésirable auquel toute personne raisonnable s'opposerait. Partant de là, la mesure apparaît justifiable dans le cadre d'une société libre et démocratique.

Conclusion

Il est certes trop tôt pour dresser un bilan susceptible de nous indiquer certains courants jurisprudentiels.

D'une part, il nous faudra attendre encore avant que la validité constitutionnelle de la législation sur l'obscénité soit attaquée en profondeur.

Quant à ces décisions où fut abordé le conflit entre une loi et la liberté d'expression, on ne peut que constater que dans l'ensemble les tribunaux n'ont pas renoncé à leur approche traditionnelle. Il nous faut ici rejoindre le professeur Clare F. Beckton dans un article qu'elle signait en 1983 dans le Manitoba Law Journal sous le titre "Obscenity and

Censorship Reexamined Under the Charter of Rights'', vol. 13, *Man. L.J.* p. 351, sur l'orientation souhaitable de nos tribunaux:

> Under the Charter, the Canadian courts must depart from their past approach in relation to obscenity . In this regard the American history will serve as a warning of the consequences of a failure to achieve a rational approach to morals problems. The Charter, by virtue of sections 1 and 2, requires a balancing of interests approach. The courts must start by enunciating first principles with respect to the section 2 guarantees of freedom of expression. This includes a theory of protection of freedom of expression which recognizes that it is valuable not only to the democratic process but as an end in itself.

> Freedom of expression is vital to the development of an individual who must be free to express himself or herself in both the political and social environment. If this is accepted then it becomes clear that limitations placed upon free expression are only justifiable when demonstrated societal or state rights override an indivual's right to liberty. There must be a demonstration that harm will result to society or the state if the limitation is not placed upon the right. No right is absolute but, without sufficient justification to abrogate or limit, it should be given full sway. (p. 362)

Dans aucun de ces jugements n'a-t-on évalué le tort que pouvait causer la prolifération de l'obscénité sur la société pour dans un deuxième temps voir si ce tort pouvait justifier une restriction à la liberté d'expression. Il n'a pas été question non plus de savoir s'il existait d'autres moyens tout aussi efficaces mais moins susceptibles de limiter la liberté d'expression dans cette lutte contre l'obscénité. La conception de ce qui est obscène étant loin d'être la même dans toutes les couches de la société, la définition du Code criminel de l'obscénité, interprétée comme signifiant ce qui va au-delà du degré de tolérance de la société canadienne ne risque-t-elle pas d'imposer la moralité de la majorité à celle des minorités? Espérons qu'à mesure que se développeront des critères précis d'évaluation de ce qui est une limite raisonnable et justifiable dans une société libre et démocratique, les tribunaux examineront avec plus d'attention la législation sur l'obscénité.

Pour l'instant, dans une attitude plutôt passive, les tribunaux semblent prendre pour acquis que les valeurs protégées par les législations sur l'obscénité justifient dans leur pleine mesure la restriction de la liberté d'expression.

CENSURE

Plusieurs dispositions législatives sont susceptibles d'être utilisées pour effectuer une censure des idées exprimées avant même que celles-ci aient reçu une diffusion. On peut citer l'article 160 du Code criminel qui permet la saisie de matériel obscène et l'article 281 (3) qui permet la saisie de matériel qui constitue de la propagande haineuse. Il y a aussi certaines dispositions du *Customs Tariff Act*, R.S.C. 1970, c. C-

41 qui permettent la saisie de matériel immoral et indécent et la *Loi sur les postes*, S.R.C. 1970, c. P-14 qui permet au maître de poste général de refuser de livrer le courrier s'il croit qu'une infraction est sur le point de se commettre, sans oublier cette législation qui prévoit la censure des films.

Dans le domaine de la liberté de presse, il y a tout le champ de la législation qui permet l'interdiction de publication de l'ensemble ou d'une partie de ce qui s'est dit au procès ou du nom des parties ou enfin de l'accès du public aux séances des tribunaux.

Au Canada, nous avons vu que les décisions portant sur la censure qui sont antérieures à la Charte ont été décidées en fonction du partage des compétences (voir *Les quotidiens et la loi*, Tarnopolsky, Wright, Beaudoin et Cody-Rice, Commission Royale sur les quotidiens, p. 11 et s., pour une revue de cette jurisprudence), et que la Charte introduit dans ce domaine une dimension nouvelle. Pour le professeur C. Beckton (''Freedom of Expression'', dans *C.C.R.F. Commentary, op. cit.*, p. 107):

> With the entrenchment of s. 2 (b) of the Charter, the Supreme Court will have to face squarely the limits of censorship. Clearly statutes which create censorship boards without specific criteria would be contrary to the guarantees of free expression, since no line is drawn between objectionable forms of expression. New standards will have to be created to measure the limits to which obscene expression may be regulated.

Le professeur Beckton suggère aux tribunaux l'application de la doctrine américaine ''d'overbreadth'' ou de celui du ''clear and present danger test'':

> Although the American approach does not offer much assistance to Canadian courts, it is submitted that the overbreadth approach or even a test similar to the clear and present danger standard should be used. It is not enough to say merely that moral standards are offended by the proliferation of obscene material, without demonstrating that harm is caused by the dissemination of objectionable material. If freedom of expression is to be a valuable right, a moral sense of indignity is not a sufficient reason for prohibiting access to allegedly obscene material. Any censorship which is not clearly justifiable interferes with the right of free expression. Clearly there are legitimate interests to be protected, particularly as they pertain to access by minors to material described as obscene or pornographic, but the danger is ever present from legislation that is overbroad, and from the lack of clear standards against which to measure the material. (p. 107)

On a vu que cette approche n'a pas été véritablement suivie en matière de législation sur l'obscénité. Dans le domaine de la censure toutefois l'attitude des tribunaux s'en rapproche plus, quoiqu'il faille distinguer entre la censure dirigée contre l'obscénité et celle dirigée contre la presse par exemple.

Comme prémisse, les tribunaux semblent accepter que la liberté d'expression a comme corollaire celle de recevoir et de conserver le produit de la libre expression des autres. Ceci est reconnu dans l'arrêt *Re Ont. Film and Video* (1° instance), *op. cit.*, p. 82:

> In addition, freedom of expression extends to those who wish to express someone else's ideas or show someone else's film. It also extends to the listener and to the viewer, whose freedom to receive communication is included in the guaranteed right.

Nous avons vu, dans le champ de l'obscénité, que les tribunaux n'ont pas reconnu comme limite raisonnable un régime de censure purement discrétionnaire; notons cependant qu'en obiter dictum et sans élaborer en profondeur, on a considéré que le principe de la censure pouvait être justifiable dans une société libre et démocratique et qu'est demeurée en suspens la question de savoir si des critères d'évaluation prévus par la loi pouvaient constituer une limite raisonnable.

L'acuité du débat portant sur l'opportunité de la censure face à la pornographie (particulièrement la violence sexuelle et les scènes qui mettent en évidence les enfants) ne laisse aucun citoyen indifférent et les tribunaux devront y apporter des solutions claires qui dissiperont la confusion.

- Les conflits avec la liberté de la presse

Avant l'adoption de la Charte, certaines contraintes préalables avaient été imposées à la presse par voie législative: ainsi en était-il des ordonnances de non-publication de la preuve à l'enquête préliminaire, des enquêtes portant sur la mise en liberté provisoire et du huis clos devant être ordonné par le juge dans certains cas, sans qu'il ne puisse exercer aucune discrétion.

Dès l'adoption de la Charte, la validité constitutionnelle de cette censure pouvait être attaquée par le biais de l'article 1. En nous référant à la règle d'interprétation élaborée ci-haut, les tribunaux avaient alors à résoudre la question suivante: ces dispositions entrent-elles en conflit avec la liberté d'expression ou la liberté de presse qui en est un dérivé et si oui, ces limites sont-elles raisonnables et peut-on en démontrer la justification dans le cadre d'une société libre et démocratique?

Voyons maintenant comment les tribunaux ont tranché cette question dans les cas qui leur furent soumis.

- Le huis clos

Depuis que la Cour suprême du Canada, dans l'arrêt *A.G. Nouvelle-Ecosse* c. *McIntyre*, [1982] 1 R.C.S. 175, avait sans équivoque exprimé cette idée que le huis clos des procédures, soit l'interdiction de l'accès du public aux cours de justice, ne se justifie que dans des circonstances très exceptionnelles (dans un litige précédant la Charte où l'on a permis à un journaliste de consulter le mandat de perquisition et la dénonciation s'y rapportant, après l'exécution), il ne fallait pas s'étonner que ce principe puisse servir de fondement à la discussion éventuelle lors de l'étude de ces dispositions qui prévoient le huis clos.

C'est ainsi que l'article 12(1) de la *Loi sur les jeunes délinquants*, S.R.C. 1970, c. J-3, qui stipule que le procès d'un enfant doit se dérouler à huis clos, a été jugé inconstitutionnel par la Cour d'appel d'Ontario dans *R. c. Southam Inc.*, (1984) 6 C.R.R. 1.

On a en effet considéré que le huis clos absolu ne constitue pas une limite raisonnable à la liberté d'expression, tenant compte de tous les objectifs poursuivis et des législations comparées et en concluant que la solution résiderait plutôt dans la discrétion qui devrait être laissée au juge du procès d'ordonner le huis clos.

Dans ce même arrêt, la Cour d'appel s'est appuyée sur le principe que le droit de l'accès du public aux tribunaux et à ses audiences, en plus de garantir la liberté d'expression, sert également à assurer la confiance que la société doit avoir dans l'intégrité de notre système judiciaire.

On s'inspirait ainsi de cette affaire *McIntyre* où l'honorable juge Dickson avait bien indiqué qu'on ne saurait restreindre cet accès au public ''que dans des affaires exceptionnelles où la présence du public rendrait l'administration de la justice impossible'' (p. 188).

D'autres arrêts ont subséquemment partagé la même conclusion que la Cour d'appel d'Ontario relativement à l'article 12 (1) L.J. Délinquants (*Re Can. Newspapers Co. c. The Queen*, (B.C. S.C.), *op. cit.*; *R. c. M.C.*, Ont. Prov. Ct. 22 juillet 1983).

Il est permis de s'interroger sur la validité de cette disposition de la *Charte québécoise des droits et libertés* qui impose le huis clos dans les audiences en matière familiale (article 23).

- *La publication restreinte*

Sur ce plan, les plaideurs ont voulu innover en cherchant à obtenir des tribunaux des mesures visant à réduire le tort causé par la publication du nom des accusés, ce à quoi la presse s'opposait fermement, ou encore en réclamant que soient déclarées *ultra vires* ces dispositions qui empêchent la diffusion de la preuve à certaines étapes des procédures.

Nous verrons que les tribunaux se sont montrés très réticents à agir comme censeurs et ont opté en faveur des principes du débat public sauf dans des circonstances exceptionnelles, ou lorsque d'autres valeurs tout aussi fondamentales (comme le droit à un procès juste et équitable devant un tribunal impartial) prédominent.

En premier lieu, l'article 467 du Code criminel qui prévoit l'ordonnance de non-publication de la preuve présentée à l'enquête préliminaire si le prévenu le requiert. En Cour du Banc de la Reine du Nouveau-Brunswick dans l'arrêt *R. c. Banville, op. cit.*, l'Honorable juge Hoyt, en se demandant si l'article 467 répondait au test de l'article 1 de la Charte, a conclu que cette disposition se justifiait au motif que la liberté de presse doit ici donner préséance pour assurer au prévenu un procès juste et équitable, d'autant plus que l'ordonnance n'empêche pas la tenue du procès en public et ne retarde que la publication de la preuve jusqu'au moment où le prévenu est libéré ou son procès est terminé.

C'est dans le même sens que la Cour d'appel d'Ontario en a conclu dans cet arrêt *Re: Smith, op. cit.*, en considérant raisonnable et justifiable la limite à la liberté d'expression contenue dans cet article 457.2 du Code criminel qui permet que ne soient pas publiées la preuve et les représentations faites lors d'une requête pour mise en liberté provisoire.

Dans un jugement fort étayé, la Cour d'appel, procédant à une étude comparée entre le système américain qui permet une diffusion plus large des débats judiciaires et le système canadien qui se traduit par une attitude beaucoup plus préventive, a conclu que nos traditions rendaient justifiable et raisonnable cette limite à la liberté de presse qui autrement mettrait en péril le droit au ''fair trial'' (328). Deux autres facteurs ont été considérés par la cour, à savoir que l'ordonnance n'empêche pas la présence du public (principe fondamental dont nous avons traité précédemment) et qu'elle est limitée dans le temps, par opposition à une mesure qui prohiberait la couverture d'un procès.

Toujours afin d'assurer que la présomption d'innocence et le droit à un procès juste et équitable ne soient battus en brèche, les tribunaux ont dans un cas permis que les motifs d'un jugement relatif à une demande de changement de venue ne soient pas publiés avant l'audition du procès (*Re Southam Inc. and The Queen no. 2*, (1982) 70 C.C.C. (2d) 264 (Ont. H.C.) et dans une autre instance (*R. c. Dolan*, inédit, 11 avril 1983, Co. Ct. Ottawa) prohibé la publication du plaidoyer de culpabilité d'un coaccusé tant que le procès de l'autre ne serait pas terminé.

Par contre, la Cour d'appel du Manitoba dans l'arrêt *R. c. Sophonow*, (1984) 6 C.C.C. (3d) 396, a rejeté la demande d'un appelant qui réclamait l'interdiction de la publication de commentaires pertinents à sa culpabilité ou à son innocence et particulièrement quant à une nouvelle preuve qu'il entendait soumettre à la cour, au motif que leur diffusion compromettait son droit à un procès juste et équitable s'il obtenait un nouveau procès. La cour n'a pas donné suite à cette requête en opinant qu'une telle mesure équivaudrait à une ''censure incompatible avec le principe d'une audition publique'' (p. 398 et 406); à cela la cour a ajouté que la présence de garanties procédurales et le recours à l'outrage au tribunal demeuraient des moyens qui, tout en protégeant l'accusé, limitaient le moins possible la liberté d'expression.

Qu'en est-il maintenant de la publication qui est susceptible d'entraîner des dommages irréparables à la réputation, soit, par exemple, la publication du nom de la victime ou de l'accusé (ou du prévenu)? Pourrait-on justifier, d'un point de vue constitutionnel, une ordonnance en interdisant la publication?

Dans *R. c. Robinson*, (1983) 34 C.R. (3d) 92 (Ont. H.C.), l'honorable juge Boland de la Cour suprême de l'Ontario a refusé de continuer une ordonnance temporaire qui permettait de ne pas publier le nom d'un inculpé de meurtre, au motif que le "prior restraint" à la liberté d'expression ne saurait être imposé sauf dans des circonstances exceptionnelles et qu'au surplus le droit accorde suffisamment de garanties à l'accusé pour qu'il obtienne un procès juste et équitable.

Ce sont sensiblement les mêmes motifs qui ont inspiré un collègue de la même cour dans l'arrêt *Re Regina and Several Unnamed Persons*, (1984) 8 C.C.C. (3d) 528 (Ont. H.C.), rejetant la requête de plusieurs inculpés de grossière indécence qui auraient souhaité éviter les inconvénients de la publication de leur nom à la comparution.

Cela contraste sans aucun doute avec l'arrêt *Southam Inc. c. De Bogyay* (C.S. Mtl, J.E. 83-1137) où il s'agissait d'une requête en révision d'une ordonnance de non-publication des noms des défendeurs et des témoins dans une cause civile de responsabilité médicale.

La cour a estimé que, malgré le droit à l'information et la liberté de presse, l'article quatre (4) de la *Charte québécoise des droits et libertés* qui prévoit le droit à la sauvegarde de la dignité et de sa réputation doit avoir préséance. Reconnaissant que la faute médicale fait scandale et que le récit d'un procès de cette nature avec noms à l'appui était donné dans les journaux, la cour en a conclu que *les dommages à la réputation sont irréparables et le jugement rendu ne pourra pas corriger cette situation*: elle a donc suspendu le droit à l'information jusqu'à ce que le jugement définitif soit rendu.

Commentant ce jugement, le professeur André Tremblay (dans sa conférence, voir ci-haut) met en doute la sagesse de cette décision et d'autres le suivraient, comme l'avocat M. David Lepofsky qui s'est fait le critique sévère des arrêts *Banville* et *Smith, op. cit.*, portant sur la validité constitutionnelle des articles 467 et 457.2 du Code criminel (voir M. David Lepofsky dans un article "Section 2 b) of the Charter and media coverage of criminal court proceedings", 34 *C.R. (3d)* 63).

Avec respect, je suis d'avis que ces mesures ou limites qui viennent en conflit avec la liberté de presse doivent, à regret, être maintenues au profit des principes plus fondamentaux que sont la présomption d'innocence et le droit à un procès juste et équitable: je dis "à regret" car je reconnais qu'un contrôle *a priori* (''prior restraint'') demeure toujours dangereux mais il faut reconnaître que la presse n'a pas exercé cette autocensure qui lui aurait évité ces mesures draconiennes.

Dans la même veine, les jugements qui ont refusé à des prévenus une ordonnance de non-publication de leur nom sont loin d'être convaincants et j'ajouterais que s'y retrouve une dichotomie entre les principes évoqués et le vécu. Je m'empresse de souligner que si ces jugements déçoivent, la responsabilité doit aussi en être partagée par les plaideurs qui ont peut-être manqué de créativité et surtout n'ont pas mis au dossier les éléments nécessaires qui leur auraient permis de faire la démonstration que requiert l'article 1, à savoir que l'expérience a démontré que la publication peut causer un préjudice irréparable qui doit être évité.

Tant sur le plan des principes que de l'expérience humaine, il me semble que la non-publication du nom est justifiable et ce, pour les raisons suivantes:

1° Qualifier d'''irréparable'' pour la présomption d'innocence et le droit à un procès juste le préjudice qu'entraîne la publication du nom n'est pas exagéré, si l'on s'en remet à l'expérience vécue: je pourrais en faire l'illustration par de nombreux cas que l'espace m'empêche de faire présentement.

2° Les garanties actuelles qui permettent d'assurer la présomption d'innocence et le procès équitable ne pourront jamais effacer les séquelles d'une publicité tapageuse, même après un acquittement (que les journaux relèvent généralement avec moins d'emphase).

Une poursuite en outrage au tribunal ne saurait aucunement modifier l'opinion des citoyens influencés.

3° S'impose donc l'établissement d'une mesure qui peut éviter ce préjudice, dans le même sens que le législateur l'a reconnu en adoptant les articles 467 et 457.2 du Code criminel. Il a fallu compiler plusieurs incidents regrettables pour amener le législateur à reconnaître que la trop grande publicité entourant l'enquête préliminaire doit être évitée et que la preuve étant faite du préjudice irréparable, la liberté de presse devait être ainsi restreinte.

4° Les principes invoqués par les tribunaux qui ont soutenu la validité constitutionnelle des articles 457.2 et 467 ne sont-ils pas les mêmes qui devraient militer en faveur de la non-publication du nom du prévenu?

5° Au surplus, demandons-nous pourquoi il serait nécessaire de publier le nom quand ''le droit de connaître'' du public pourrait très bien être respecté par la publication des faits pertinents sans les relier à un nom, comme cela se fait dans le cas où un individu de moins de dix-huit ans est concerné? De toute façon, le public peut toujours consulter le dossier à la cour, seul le droit de publier étant restreint.

A ce que je sache, nul n'a contesté la validité constitutionnelle de l'article 442(3) qui permet l'ordonnance de non-publication de *l'identité du plaignant* dans le cas des infractions sexuelles énumérées à l'article 246.4 du Code criminel.

N'y aurait-il pas lieu de s'inspirer de certaines restrictions au caractère public de l'enquête du coroner, telles que prévues à la nouvelle loi qui sera bientôt mise en vigueur au Québec et particulièrement à l'article 137 qui se lit comme suit:

> ''S'il l'estime nécessaire à l'intérêt public ou à la protection de la vie privée d'une personne, de sa réputation ou de son droit à un procès juste et équitable, le coroner peut, d'office ou sur demande, interdire la publication ou la diffusion de certaines informations relatées ou pouvant être relatées au cours de l'enquête.''

Enfin, pour démontrer comment la tendance actuelle est en faveur d'un contrôle de la presse dans ce cas où la présomption d'innocence est pratiquement illusoire, il est intéressant de noter que malgré la solution mise de l'avant par la Cour suprême du Canada dans l'arrêt *MacIntyre, op. cit.*, accordant à la presse le droit de publier le contenu du mandat de perquisition et la dénonciation qui l'accompagne, en autant que le mandat est exécuté, le ministre de la Justice déposa en 1983 un projet de loi qui aurait pour effet d'en interdire la publicité à moins qu'il n'en résulte des accusations. Il donnait ainsi suite aux représentations faites depuis longtemps par le Barreau et tous les représentants des procureurs généraux.

DISSIDENCE POLITIQUE

La liberté d'expression, en ce qu'elle a de pertinent face aux institutions politiques, a toujours été considérée comme essentielle au bon fonctionnement de celles-ci. A titre d'exemple, citons le passage suivant des motifs de l'Honorable juge Rand dans *Switzman* c. *Elbing, op. cit.*:

> ''Quelles que soient ses déficiences, le gouvernement au Canada est en fait l'émanation de la volonté de la majorité, exprimée directement ou indirectement par l'intermédiaire d'assemblées populaires. Cela correspond finalement à un gouvernement par le libre jeu de l'opinion publique dans une société libre, forme de gouvernement dont l'efficacité, comme les événements l'ont fréquemment démontré, est indiscutée.
>
> Toutefois, l'opinion publique, pour faire face à une telle responsabilité, exige comme conditions un accès à peu près libre aux idées et leur diffusion sans entraves. Le gouvernement parlementaire considère comme admise l'aptitude qu'a l'homme, agissant librement et sous son propre empire, à se gouverner lui-même. Ce progrès se réalise le mieux dans le degré de libération de l'homme de ses entraves, tant subjectives qu'objectives. Sous cette forme de gouvernement, la liberté de discussion au

Canada, comme sujet de législation, possède un intérêt et une importance qui s'étendent à tout le Dominion.'' (Traduction, p. 306)

On peut donc s'attendre à ce qu'au Canada, le droit à la dissidence politique soit amplement reconnu et même protégé. Cependant, lorsque cette dissidence prend des formes qui risquent de mettre en danger la sécurité de l'Etat, toute société démocratique accepte d'imposer des limites à la liberté d'expression. Celles-ci peuvent provenir de la criminalisation de la trahison (art. 46 C.cr.), de la sédition (art. 60 C.cr.) ou d'autres lois comme la *Loi sur les mesures de guerre*, S.R.C. 1970, c. W-2 ou la *Loi sur les secrets officiels*, S.R.C. 1970, c. O-3.

D'autres restrictions peuvent ainsi naître de la réglementation du processus électoral concernant les dépenses et le financement, la publicité et l'âge requis pour se présenter aux élections ou pour voter.

Il va sans dire que ce ne sont pas toutes ces restrictions qui peuvent être considérées comme déraisonnables. Certaines se justifient d'elles-mêmes et sont, dans un sens, nécessaires à l'exercice de nos droits politiques. D'autres sont toutefois plus problématiques.

Les infractions de trahison et de sédition sont plutôt rares. Il n'existe donc pas beaucoup d'arrêts sur la question. La définition de la sédition contenue au Code criminel a été interprétée dans l'arrêt important de la Cour suprême du Canada *Boucher* c. *Le Roi*, [1951] R.C.S. 265.

La sédition étant en quelque sorte la limite jusqu'à laquelle on peut critiquer le gouvernement, on comprendra l'importance de ce jugement. L'affaire est née du conflit entre les témoins de Jéhovah et le gouvernement du premier ministre Duplessis. La poursuite portait sur la distribution d'un pamphlet qui attaquait en des termes excessifs l'Eglise, le gouvernement et les tribunaux du Québec. L'accusé fut acquitté par une majorité de cinq juges contre quatre, en Cour suprême du Canada.

La Cour jugea que même des termes excessifs ou attisant la malveillance et l'hostilité entre les sujets, ne constituaient pas un motif suffisant de condamnation, comme le prévoyait la définition de la sédition qui existait alors en jurisprudence. On y exigea l'intention d'inciter les gens à la violence et de semer le désordre, ou d'avoir un comportement illégal contre Sa Majesté ou une institution publique.

Il semble donc qu'on puisse dire que toute opinion politique peut avoir libre cours au Canada à la condition qu'elle ne préconise pas le recours à des moyens illégaux, comme le meurtre ou l'enlèvement, pour effectuer un changement de gouvernement. Voir Baudouin, Fortin, Szabo, *Terrorisme et justice*, Montréal, Ed. du Jour, (1970) p. 106.

Pour C. Beckton, cette restriction à la liberté d'expression n'est pas justifiable au sens de l'article 1. Elle préconise l'approche américaine qui requiert que l'incitation à la violence ait des effets concrets et présente un danger réel et clair:

> The *Boucher* test contained no requirement that the language be likely to
> incite. It is submitted that the clear and present danger formulation is a
> better criteria since it protects the national interest without unduly limi-
> ting free expression. It is highly doubtful that the more stringent *Boucher*
> formulation is required in our democratic society. (p. 102, dans "Free-
> dom of Expression", *op. cit.*)

Il est pour le moins difficile de prévoir si ce raisonnement serait
reçu par les tribunaux canadiens. Cela nécessiterait une attitude plus
interventionniste des tribunaux à l'exemple des arrêts *National Citizens
Coalition Inc.* c. *P.G. Canada* (non rapporté) et *Collins c. R.*, (1983)
31 C.R. (3d) 283 (Ont. Co. Ct.), qui visaient des restrictions touchant
l'expression politique.

En premier lieu, dans *N.C.C.* c. *P.G. Canada*, il s'agissait
d'amendements apportés à la *Loi électorale canadienne*, S.R.C. 1970,
c. 14 (1er supp.) empêchant les groupes d'intérêts non affiliés aux parties et les simples citoyens à fournir des sommes qui serviraient à promouvoir ou à contester la candidature d'un parti ou d'un candidat à une
élection fédérale sans la permission d'un parti ou candidat enregistré.
Ces derniers devaient par la suite inclure cette somme dans leurs dépenses électorales. Nous citons les passages suivants du jugement (Alta
Q.B.) qui nous apparaissent fort intéressants (tels que rapportés dans
"The Globe and Mail", le 27 juin 1984):

> This involves a weighing of the individual right of freedom of expression
> in relation to society of an effective system for the selection of members
> of Parliament.
>
> In my opinion, the limitation must be considered for the protection of a
> real value to society and not simply to reduce or restraint criticism, no
> matter how unfair such criticism may be.
> ...
> Fears or concerns of mischief that may occur are not adequate reasons
> for imposing a limitation. There should be actual demonstration of harm,
> or a real likelihood of harm to a society value before a limitation can be
> said to be justified.
>
> In my view, it has not been established to the degree required that the
> fundamental freedom of expression need be limited. The limitation has
> not been shown to be reasonable or demonstrably justified in a free and
> democratic society.

Dans *Collins* c. *R.*, *op. cit.*, on demandait la révision de conditions
de la libération conditionnelle. L'accusé avait été arrêté lors d'une
manifestation contre le système de missile Cruise. Une des conditions
prévoyait que l'accusé ne devait encourager personne à manifester ou
manifester lui-même dans un rayon d'un demi-mille de l'endroit où il
avait été arrêté. L'honorable juge Hogg a jugé cette restriction incons-
titutionnelle. Il a énoncé certains principes à partir desquels une restriction à la liberté d'expression et d'association pourra être imposée (p.
285):

These rights cannot be restricted on a speculative concern of danger. Such is too easy to so make.

For the court to justify an interference with these rights, the prosecution must show that the restriction furthers an important or substantial state interest unrelated to the suppression of expression, and the limitation sought on this basis freedom is no greater than is necessary or essential for the protection of the public.

It must, in the words of an American judge "reach the magnitude of a compelling state interest". The restrictions or freedoms sought by the prosecution must be tested by the court with stringent standards and subject to vigorous scrutiny.

Infringement of protected freedoms by the State in the public interest must be precisely drawn without any unnecessary erosion of rights.

Apparemment, les tribunaux accordent une place de choix à la diffusion des idées politiques. Nulle part dans les autres secteurs que nous avons étudiés, ne retrouve-t-on aussi clairement l'exigence de restreindre le moins possible la liberté d'expression. Pour nous, au plan des principes, ces deux arrêts sont un exemple à suivre. Ils permettent le moins possible l'érosion de la liberté d'expression en exigeant d'une part que l'on démontre l'effet nuisible du comportement que l'on veut prohiber ou restreindre et d'autre part qu'on le fasse selon des moyens qui n'entraveront pas cette liberté au-delà de ce qui est nécessaire.

PROPAGANDE HAINEUSE

Le Code criminel traite de la propagande haineuse aux articles 281.1 et 281.3. Pour une étude de ces articles, on peut lire W.S. Tarnopolsky, *The Canadian Bill of Rights*, 2e édition, *op. cit.*, p. 185 et s.

L'article 281.1 interdit de préconiser le génocide. Cet article apparaît clairement justifiable.

L'article 281.2 interdit l'incitation publique à la haine ainsi que la publication de déclarations qui fomentent la haine, alors que l'article 281.3 prévoit la saisie et la confiscation de propagande haineuse définie comme étant "tout écrit, signe ou représentation visible qui préconise ou fomente le génocide ou dont la communication par toute personne constitue une infraction aux termes de l'article 281.2."

Le seul arrêt publié sur ce sujet est l'affaire *R.* c. *Buzzanga et Durocher*, (1979) 101 D.L.R. (3d) 488 (C.A. Ont.) où les deux prévenus, deux canadiens français, étaient accusés d'avoir volontairement fomenté la haine contre un groupe identifiable (281-2(2)). Ce groupe était la population canadienne française du comté d'Essex en Ontario. Les deux accusés ont expressément nié avoir eu quelque intention d'inciter à la haine puisque le pamphlet qu'ils avaient publié était une satire dans le but de soulever l'apathie de leurs compatriotes afin que ceux-ci forcent le gouvernement à agir et à faire construire une école française.

La Cour d'appel d'Ontario précisait, lors de sa décision que le terme ''volontairement'' signifiait l'incitation consciente et intentionnelle à la haine contre un groupe identifiable ou, au plus, si les déclarations avaient été diffusées dans un autre but, alors, au moins le fait de prévoir que l'incitation à la haine contre un groupe identifiable était certaine d'aboutir à un résultat.

Ces articles n'ont pas encore été testés sous les nouvelles dispositions constitutionnelles. Nous ne pouvons donc faire que des hypothèses quant à leur validité constitutionnelle.

L'article 281.3 est le plus susceptible d'invalidation étant donné qu'il permet la censure sans qu'aucun critère d'évaluation de ce qui constitue de la propagande haineuse n'y soit précisé.

L'article 281.2, lorsque interprété comme l'a fait la Cour d'appel d'Ontario, pourrait être validé. Toutefois, cela n'apparaît pas certain si les tribunaux adoptent le test américain du ''clear and present danger''.

Certes la lutte contre la propagande haineuse représente un intérêt suffisant qui justifie une restriction à la liberté d'expression. La question principale est celle de savoir si les dispositions du Code criminel risquent d'empêcher la propagation d'idées qui ne constituent pas de la propagande haineuse. De l'avis de W.S. Tarnoposlky, op. cit., d'autres moyens tout aussi efficaces risqueraient moins d'entraver la liberté d'expression (p. 194).

Outre les interdictions prévues au Code criminel en matière de propagande haineuse, plusieurs lois canadiennes sur les droits de la personne prévoient l'interdiction de la publication, de l'exposition ou de la radiodiffusion d'images ou de symboles exprimant toute forme de discrimination ou l'intention de commettre des actes discriminatoires. Ces lois sont donc susceptibles d'application dans les cas d'écrits haineux.

La plupart de celles-ci, sinon toutes, énoncent expressément que cette interdiction n'a pas pour effet de limiter le droit à la libre expression des opinions sur n'importe quel sujet. L'article de E.H. Lipsett, ''Freedom of expression and Human Rights Legislation: A Critical Analysis of s.2 of the Manitoba Human Rights Act'', (1983) 12 *Man. L.J.* 285, nous convaincra que, selon l'interprétation qui en est faite, cela n'est pas toujours le cas.

L'auteur critique sévèrement trois décisions qui illustrent particulièrement le danger de ces législations pour la liberté d'expression: *Singer* c. *Iwasyk and Perrywise Foods Ltd.*, Saskatchewan Human Rights Commission, non rapporté, 5/11/76, *Rasheed* c. *Bramhill*, (1980) 2 C.H.R.R. D/249 (Nova Scotia Board of Inquiry; *McKinlay* c. *Cranfield and Dial Agencies*, (1980) 1 C.H. R.R. D/246 (Saskatchewan Board of Inquiry).

Principalement, en ne faisant pas de l'intention de promouvoir la haine un élément de responsabilité (*cf.* arrêt *Singer* et *Rasheed (op. cit.)*, ces lois accordent en définitive moins de protection que n'en accorde l'article 281.2 (2) C.cr.

Telles qu'interprétées, il y a fort à parier que ces dispositions soient considérées non raisonnables en vertu de l'article 1 de la Charte. Non pas que leur but ne constitue pas un objectif et un intérêt suffisants, mais parce que leur champ d'application est trop large (overbreadth).

L'ironie de l'histoire, c'est que ces lois que l'on veut réparatrices et que l'on interprète libéralement risquent fort d'entraver la liberté d'expression. Peut-être, comme le souhaite Lipsett, s'agit-il d'un cas où on devrait déroger à la règle d'interprétation? Il ne faudrait surtout pas que le remède apporte plus de mal que le mal lui-même.

Dans son article, tout comme le faisait Tarnopolsky, Lipsett met en doute l'efficacité de ces dispositions. Il va même jusqu'à émettre l'hypothèse que celles-ci ont un effet contraire aux objectifs poursuivis (p. 309). Nous concluons en citant le passage suivant qui résume assez bien la pensée de l'auteur:

> I must re-emphasize that I can appreciate and support the aims of such provisions and decisions to promote equal opportunity, and to encourage compliance with the ''letter and spirit'' of human legislation. I recognize the need to overcome stereotypical thinking and prejudice. But, as has often been pointed out, educational and persuasive means, by human rights commissions, and other official agencies, private groups and concerned private citizens are more appropriate methods towards achieving those goals in a democratic society. Legal sanctions should be provided only for unlawful actions, e.g. denials of discriminatory treatment concerning jobs and other benefits on prohibited grounds, or direct incitement to such unlawful conduct.

> Although respect for the dignity of all individuals and groups is certainly highly desirable and to be encouraged, these are particularly inappropriate values to be enforced through legal sanctions. These are matters largely related to attitudes, interpersonal and intergroup relationships, and even personal characteristics such as consideration, politeness, and fairmindedness. In such matters, creation of an unduly controlled society, can unacceptably limit individual freedom. (p. 308)

CONCLUSION

La jurisprudence étudiée laisse voir l'importance du rôle des tribunaux dans la recherche d'un équilibre entre le droit à libre expression et le droit de ne pas avoir à subir des paroles ou des images choquantes. Ce rôle est issu de la volonté politique des gouvernements qui ont entendu faire des tribunaux les gardiens des libertés fondamentales au Canada. Ceux-ci doivent invalider toute législation qui limite le droit à la libre expression et qui ne peut se justifier dans le cadre d'une société libre et démocratique.

L'enchâssement des libertés fondamentales dans la constitution du pays devait marquer le point de départ d'une nouvelle attitude de la part des tribunaux canadiens (*supra*). Qu'en est-il advenu? Les traditions judiciaires ont cette particularité d'être difficiles et longues à changer. A cet égard, quelque deux années et demie de jurisprudence, ce n'est pas énorme. Aussi peut-on s'attendre à ce que tant que la plus haute cour de ce pays ne se sera pas prononcée sur les dispositions constitutionnelles pertinentes, il régnera une certaine incertitude et peut-être même un certain conservatisme dans ce domaine.

Quoi qu'il en soit, certaines tendances se dégagent et se précisent. On a vu qu'en général on interprète libéralement la portée de la protection constitutionnelle. Mais en définitive, c'est dans l'interprétation de l'article 1 de la Charte que se traceront les confins de la liberté d'expression.

Nous avons noté les différences qui pouvaient exister à ce niveau selon les domaines visés par les législations. Celles-ci ne se justifient nullement par le texte de l'article 1 qui propose un test unique et uniforme. Les tribunaux ne devraient pas, non plus, hésiter à déclarer une législation non raisonnable. Comme le mentionnait la Cour d'appel d'Ontario dans *Re Ont. Film and Video, op. cit.*, il n'y a pas de présomption pour ou contre la validité constitutionnelle d'une loi.

A notre avis, une restriction à la liberté d'expression ne devrait être justifiable que lorsque l'on démontre un réel préjudice causé à une autre valeur importante pour la société (voir *Collins* c. *R.* et *N.C.C.* c. *A.G. Canada, op. cit.*). Il n'y a aucune raison pour que ce raisonnement ne s'applique pas dans tous les secteurs.

BIBLIOGRAPHIE

BAUDOUIN, J.L., FORTIN, J., SZABO, D., *Terrorisme et justice*, Montréal, Ed. du Jour, (1970).

BECKTON, C.F., "Freedom of Expression", dans BEAUDOIN, G.A., TARNOPOLSKY, W.S. (ed.), *The Canadian Charter of Rights and Freedoms - Commentary*, Toronto, Carswell, (1982), p. 75.

BEKCTON, C.F., "Freedom of Expression - Access to the Courts", (1983) 61 *Can. Bar. Rev.* 101.

BECKTON, C.F., "Freedom of Expression in Canada - How Free?" (1983) 13 *Man. L.J.* 583.

BECKTON, C.F., "Obscenity and Censorship Re-Examined Under the Charter of Rights", (1983) 13 *Man. L.J.* 351.

BECKTON, C.F., *The Law and the Media in Canada*, Toronto, Carswell, (1982).

BENDER, P., "The Canadian Charter of Rights and Freedoms and the United States Bill of Rights: A Comparison", (1983) 28 *McGill L.J.* 857.

BUSHNELL, S.I., ''Freedom of Expression - The First Step'', (1977) 15 *Alta L.R.* 93.

HAGE, R.E., ''The Hate Propaganda Amendment to the Criminal Code'', (1970) 28 *U.T. Fac. L. Rev.* 63.

HOGG, P.W., *Canada Act 1982 Annotated*, Toronto, Carswell, (1982).

LEPOFSKY, D., ''Constitutional Right to Attend and Speak About Criminal Court Proceedings - An Emerging Liberty'', (1983) 30 *C.R. (3d)* 87.

LEPOFSKY, D., ''Section 2 (b) of the Charter and Media Coverage of Criminal Court Proceedings'', (1983) 34 *C.R. (3d)* 63.

LIPSETT, E.H., ''Freedom of Expression and Human Rights Legislation: A Critical Analysis of s. 2 of the Manitoba Human Rights Act'', (1983) 12 *Man. L.J.* 285.

MANNING, M., *Rights, Freedoms and the Courts: A Practical Analysis of the Constitution Act, 1982*, Toronto, Emond-Montgomery Limited, (1983).

NIZER, L., ''In Camera - An Interview with Louis Nizer'', (1978) Vol. 2, no. 4 *Canadian Lawyer* 30.

PEMBER, D.R., ''Does Pretrial Publicity Really Hurt?'' *Columbia Journalism Review*, Septembre/octobre 1984, p. 16.

SWAN, K., ''Court Upholds G String By-Law'', *The National*, Mars 1984.

SWAN, K., SWINTON, K., ''How has Freedom of Expression Fared so Far?'' Mars 1984, *The National*, p. 7.

TARNOPOLSKY, W.S., *The Canadian Bill of Rights*, 2e édition, Toronto, McClelland and Stewart Limited, (1975).

TARNOPOLSKY, W.S., ''La liberté de la presse'', dans *Les quotidiens et la loi*, Commission royale sur les quotidiens, publications de recherche, vol. 3, Approvisionnements et Services Canada, Ottawa, 1981.

TREMBLAY, A., ''De la liberté d'expression au Canada: Le cheminement vers le marché libre des idées'', texte d'une conférence donnée aux Journées Strasbourgeoises, Juillet 1984.

JURISPRUDENCE CITÉE

A.G. Canada and Dupond c. City of Montreal, [1978] 2 S.C.R. 770.

A.G. Nouvelle-Ecosse c. McIntyre, [1982] 1 R.C.S. 175.

Benjamin News c. R., (1979) 6 C.R. (3d) 281 (C.A. Qué.).

Boucher c. Le Roi, [1951] R.C.S. 265.

Brodie, Dansky and Rubin c. The Queen, [1962] R.C.S. 681.

Chaplinsky c. New Hampshire, 315 U.S. 568.

Collins c. R., (1983) 31 C.R. (3d) 283 (Ont. Co. Ct.).

Dechow c. R., (1977) 35 C.C.C. (2d) 22 (C.S.C.).

Dominion News and Gifts (1962) Ltd. c. The Queen, [1963] 2 C.C.C. 103 (Man. C.A.).

Dominion News and Gifts (1962) Ltd. c. The Queen, [1964] 3 C.C.C. 1 (C.S.C.).

McKinlay c. Cranfield and Dial Agencies, (1980) 1 C.H.R.R. D/246 (Saskatchewan Board of Inquiry).

Minister of National Revenue for Customs and Excise c. Taché, (1982) 40 N.R. 559 (F.C.A.).

National Citizens Coalition Inc. c. P.G. Canada, (non rapporté) (Alta Q.B.), 26 juin 1984.

R. c. Banville, (1984) 5 C.R.R. 142 (N.B.Q.B.).

R. c. Barr, (1982) 16 Man. R. (2d) 1 (Man. Co. Ct.).

R. c. Buzzanga et Durocher, (1979) 101 D.L.R. (3d) 488 (C.A. Ont.).

R. c. Charpentier, [1982] R.L. 469.

R. c. Dolan, Ont. Co. Ct., 11 avril 1983.

R. c. Doug Rankine Co. Ltd. and Act III Video Productions Ltd., (1984) 9 C.C.C. (3d) 53 (Ont. Co. Ct.).

R. c. Giambalvo, (1983) 70 C.C.C (2d) 324 (Ont. C.A.).

R. c. Halpert et al., (1984) 9 C.C.C. (3d) 411 (Ont. Prov. Ct.).

R. c. Hawkshaw and R., (1983) 69 C.C.C. (2d) 503 (Ont. C.A.).

R. c. Lachapelle, [1981] R.L. 133.

R. c. Les Cinémas Québécois Inc., [1982] R.L. 180.

R. c. M.C., Ont. Prov. Ct. 22 juillet 1983.

R. c. MacLean and MacLean (No. 2), (1983) 1 C.C.C. (3d) 412 (Ont. C.A.).

R. c. McLachlan et al., 9:0867 W.C.B. 441 (Ont. Prov. Ct.).

R. c. Penthouse Int. Ltd., (1979) 46 C.C.C. (2d) 111 (Ont. C.A.).

R. c. Pink Triangle Press, (1980) 51 C.C.C. (2d) 485 (Ont. Co. Ct.).

R. c. Prairie Schooner News Ltd. and Powers, (1970) 1 C.C.C. (2d) 251 (Man. C.A.).

R. c. Red Hot Video Limited, (1984) 38 C.R. (3d) 275 (B.C. Co. Ct.).

R. c. Reed, (1984) 8 C.C.C. (3d) 153 (B.C. Co. Ct.).

R. c. Robinson, (1983) 34 C.R. (3d) 92 (Ont. H.C.).

R. c. Saint-John News, (1976) 13 N.B.R. (2d) 564 (N.B.C.A.).

R. c. Sophonow, (1984) 6 C.C.C. (3d) 396 (Man. C.A.).

R. c. Southam, (1984) 6 C.R.R. 1 (Ont. C.A.).

R. c. Sudbury News Service Ltd., (1983) 69 C.C.C. (2d) 503 (Ont. C.A.).

R. c. Towne Cinema Theatres (1975) Ltd., [1982] 1 W.W.R. 512 (Alta Q.B.).

Re Canadian Newspapers Co. Ltd. and The Queen, (1984) 6 C.C.C. (3d) 488 (B.C.S.C.).

Re Edmonton Journal and A.G. Alta, (1983) 4 C.C.C. (3d) 59 (Alta Q.B.).

Re Federal Republic of Germany c. Rauca, (1983) 4 C.C.C. (3d) 385 (Ont. C.A.).

Re Federal Republic of Germany and Rauca, (1982) 141 D.L.R. (3d) 412 (Ont. H.C.).

Re Koumoudouros et al. and Municipality of Metropolitan Toronto, Re N.B. Theatrical Agencies and Municipalities of Metropolitan Toronto, (1984) 6 D.L.R. (4th) 523 (Ont. Div. Ct.).

Re Law Society of Manitoba and Savino, [1984] 1 D.L.R. (4th) 285 (Man. C.A.).

Re Luscher and Deputy Minister, Revenue Canada, Customs and Excise, (1983) 149 D.L.R. (3rd) 243 (B.C. Co. Ct.).

Re North American News and Deputy Minister of National Revenue for Customs and Excise, (1974) 14 C.C.C. (2d) 63 (Ont. Co. Ct.).

Re Ontario Film and Video Appreciation Society and Ontario Board of Censors, (1984) 5 D.L.R. (4th) 766 (Ont. C.A.).

Re Ontario Film and Video Appreciation Society and Ontario Board of Censors, (1983) 34 C.R. (3d) 73 (Ont. Div. Ct.).

Re Red Hot Video and City of Vancouver, (1984) 5 D.L.R. (4th) 61 (B.C.S.C.).

Re Regina and Several Unnamed Persons, (1984) 8 C.C.C. (3d) 528 (Ont. H.C.).

Re Smith, Global Communications Limited c. California and A.G. Ontario, (1984) 38 C.R. (3d) 209 (Ont. C.A.).

Re Southam Inc. and R. (No. 1), (1983) 70 C.C.C. (2d) 257 (Ont. H.C.), confirmé à (1984) 6 C.R.R. 1 (Ont. C.A.).

Re Southam Inc. and The Queen No. 2, (1983) 70 C.C.C. (2d) 264 (Ont. H.C.).

Re University of Manitoba and Deputy Minister, Revenue Canada, Customs and Excise, (1984) 4 D.L.R. (4th) 658 (Man. Co. Ct.).

Reference re: Alberta Legislation, [1938] S.C.R. 100.

Popert c. R., (1981) 19 C.R. (3d) 393 (Ont. C.A.).

Rasheed c. Bramhill, (1980) 2 C.H.R.R. D/249 (Nova Scotia Board of Inquiry).

Singer c. Iwasyk and Perrywise Foods Ltd., Sask. Human Rights Commission, non rapporté, 5/11/76.

Source Perrier (S.A.) v. Fira-Less Marketing Co. Ltd., (1983) 4 C.R.R. 317 (F.C.).

Southam Inc. c. De Bogyay, C.S. Mtl, J.E. 83-1137.

Switzman c. Elbing and A.G. Quebec, [1957] S.C.R. 285.

Valentine c. Chrestensen, 316 U.S. 52.

Obscenity, Morals and the Law: Challenging Basic Assumptions

Kathleen E. Mahoney*

INTRODUCTION

The question of obscenity, morals and the role of law has been debated for hundreds of years, largely by men. Women have been conspicuous by their absence in decisions regarding the definition of obscenity and the characterizations of its harms. Feminist Elizabeth Cady Stanton commented in 1853:

> Thus far women have been the mere echoes of men. Our laws and constitutions, our creeds and codes, and the customs of social life are all of masculine origin. The true woman is as yet a dream of the future.[1]

It is trite to say that no man understands what it is like to be a woman, and that no woman knows what it is like to be a man. Men and women, no matter how closely they live and work together, live in different perceptual worlds. Yet laws have traditionally been interpreted and enforced by men.[2] These laws embody and reinforce an essentially male conception of human interaction. The laws relating to marriage, marital property, divorce, control over children, illegitimacy, abortion, contraception, prostitution and rape[3] are good examples of how men have defined ''women's place'' by controlling their

---

* Faculty of Law, University of Calgary.

1. Elizabeth Cady Stanton in a letter to Susan B. Anthony, cited in *Take Back the Night: Women on Pornography*, ed. L. Lederer (1980).
2. For a discussion, see S. Dranoff, *Women in Canadian Law*, Toronto (1977). For an historical account in greater detail, see L.M. Glanz, *The Legal Position of English Women Under the Early Stuart Kings and the Interregnum, 1603-1660*, Loyola University of Chicago (1973).
3. Many laws dealing with morality set one standard for men and another for women. For example, the law has treated prostitutes as deviant, labeling them criminals but has considered male customers of female prostitutes to be ''normal'', indulging a natural urge. Similarly, laws have treated adultery as a serious offence when committed by women yet not so when committed by men. Under Victorian divorce laws, men could sue their wives for divorce on adultery grounds alone but women were required to prove adultery along with bigamy, cruelty, desertion, incest or other ''unnatural'' offences if they were to get a divorce.

financial independence, their physical integrity, their sexuality and their actual and potential maternity.[4] When those laws were combined with the private sanctions that ostracized women who left male protection, a "woman's place" became the home. The definition of a woman's role as submissive and domestic was reflected in legal constructs that both assumed and guaranteed her dependence on men.

"Being female" has always interfered with the recognition of women as complete and independent individuals. A legal system that gives unequal legal rights to men and women reinforces the latter's status as dependents. Traditionally, women were placed in the same "protected" category as lunatics, drunkards and children,[5] and were denied access to the political means available to change that categorization. It was, unbelievably, as late as 1928 before women became legal "persons" in Canada. That year marked a turning point of sorts; the Judicial Committee of the Privy Council overruled the Supreme Court of Canada and held that women were "persons" within the meaning of s. 24 of the *BNA Act* and, thus, were eligible for appointment to the Canadian Senate.[6] Since that decision, some progress has been made in changing the traditional role assigned to women, both in society's attitudes generally and in those embodied in legislation.[7] However, change has come about slowly. This is in part because of a lack of information as the different perceptions that women have. Any inroads made have been mere revisionist incursions into a male-defined legal construct. To date the feminist fight has been to obtain an equal place within the present legal system[8] by lobbying for legislation to secure what women now define as their "rights". In the future women can be expected to do more than ask for rights: they will begin to define rights in their own way, in accordance with their own understanding of justice and morality. In this respect our society must make an effort to try to outline and account for the different moral perceptions of men and women.

---

4. In recent years, most universities have instituted Women's Studies Programs, an academic discipline which is devoted to defining women's own realities, examining the contradictions between them and the social or cultural "givens" that generally have been structured by men, in their own interest. This re-evaluation of widespread assumptions is dealt with extensively in a Women's Studies textbook, *Women's Realities, Women's Choices*, Hunter College Women's Studies Collective (1983).

5. See Dranoff, *op. cit.* and Dept. of Labour Canada, *Legal Status of Women in Canada*, Ottawa (1924). For the situation of American women, see K. DeCrow, *Sexist Justice*, New York (1974).

6. *"Persons" Reference re Meaning of Word, in s. 24 of the B.N.A. Act*, [1929] S.C.R. 276.

7. The inclusion of s. 28 in the Charter of Rights and Freedoms guaranteeing rights equally to male and female persons has been the most significant victory to date, although it remains to be seen how this section will be interpreted.

8. K.G. Banting, R. Simeon, ed., *And No-One cheered: Federalism, Democracy and the Constitution Act*, Methuen, Toronto (1983).

It is only recently that any significant body of literature has developed on men's and women's different moral perceptions. In 1949, Simone de Beauvoir's classic work, *The Second Sex*,[9] illuminated some of these differences and provided a challenge to many feminist writers who followed. Now a rich and sophisticated literature exists that provides a philosophical, sociological and scientific framework for the investigation of gender-related biases in fundamental social assumptions.[10] One of the most recent contributions is a book by psychologist Carol Gilligan, exploring male/female differences in moral values.[11] Through experiments, Professor Gilligan analyzed the responses to classic moral dilemmas of a sample of males and females, ranging in age from 6 to 60 years. In outlining the responses, she highlighted the different conceptions that men and women have about justice and morality.[12] These conceptions cannot help but shape how men and women view the nature of the legal system and the purpose and content of legal rules. She used two contrasting metaphors to describe men and women. The metaphor for men is the ladder, and for women, the web. Men and women have a different moral perspective that can be traced to a different sense of self.

For men, moral development consists largely of a process of individuation.[13] As adolescents, boys must try to separate themselves from the women who are primarily responsible for their care. A male child knows that he is different and seeks to carve out a separate, workable identity. He is more prepared to abstract his situation into rules that will help confirm and preserve this identity.[14] The resulting morality of the ladder is a morality of rights and a hierarchy of rules that regulate the contest between highly competitive, independent individuals. It is a morality based on principles of non-interference with the rights of others. From the male perspective justice is best served by the least interference with the autonomy of others. Men view rights as personal zones of non-interference.

---

9. Trans. and ed. H.M. Parshley. N.Y. Alfred A. Knopf (1952).
10. An example of the many bibliographies now available is the Selected Accessions List, Office of Equal Opportunities for Women, Public Service Commission.
11. C. Gilligan, *In a Different Voice, Psychological Theory and Women's Development*, Harvard Univ. Press (1982).
12. Gilligan demonstrates that gender is the one determinant which explains the different responses.
13. This is a steady theme in the literature on human development. Freud's psychoanalytic theory depended upon it. See *Three Essays on the Theory of Sexuality* (1905), Vol. VII, Hogarth Riers, London, (1961). He concluded that women's superego was... "never so inexorable, so impersonal, so independent of its emotional origins as we require it to be in men... For women the level of what is ethically normal is different from what it is in men."
14. N. Chodrow, *The Reproduction of Mothering*, Univ. of California Press, 1978, cited in Gilligan, *op. cit.* at p. 7 and 8.

By contrast, the perception of morality expressed by the web is one of individuals "connecting" with one another.[15] No process of individuation or separation is required between a female adolescent and her mother. The female child, therefore, focuses on and learns to define herself and her moral judgments in terms of her relationship to others. Morality for her consists of fulfilling responsibilities to other people in particular circumstances, and justice becomes a contextual concept. Professor Gilligan found that females have a sense of justice that prefers equitable solutions to the problems that real people experience in their everyday lives, as opposed to a concept of justice based on a hierarchy of abstract rules. She pointed out that all human beings, male or female, share some of these moralities. Nevertheless, our institutions, including the law, are largely systems of the ladder and for the ladder.[16]

For purposes of this article, I have described the differing moralities as male/female to highlight the distinctions between the two modes of thought and to emphasize the feminist analysis as a fresh appraisal. The association with gender is not absolute. Gilligan makes the point that while gender characteristics are based on empirical observations the differences between the sexes are best characterized by theme. The importance of making the distinctions is to make it possible to focus on the problem of interpretation and to present another option.

By asking for social change, women are in fact saying that it is now time for the law to recognize the need to protect the web. To do this, the law must broaden its limits. It will be necessary for the courts to expand their inquiry, look beyond zones of personal non-interference and autonomy and to recognize the value of interdependence and concern for real harms to real people. There is much to be gained from a system of laws that takes into account a view of life, self and morality that represents the thoughts of the female half of the population. To illustrate the advantages of such a system I will use the law of obscenity as a case in point. This article will demonstrate how two conflicting moralities, both originating from the ladder, have dominated the development of the law of obscenity. The result is a quagmire of precedent that fails to satisfy either side. This article points out a third perspective

---

15. Virigina Woolf made a similar observation about values after studying 19th century literature. She concluded, "It is obvious that the values of women differ very often from the values which have been made by the other sex, (yet) it is the masculine values that prevail." *A Room of One's Own*, New York, Brace & World (1929).

16. John Stuart Mill recognized this in 1859, when he wrote in *On Liberty* (1859) ed., A. Castell (1949), p. 6:
"Wherever there is an ascendant class, a large portion of the morality of the country emanates from its class interests, and its feelings of class superiority. The morality between ... men and women, has been for the most part the creation of these class interests and feelings: and the sentiments thus generated, react in turn upon the moral feeling of the members of the ascendant class, in their relations among themselves."

- a perspective from the web - with the hope that it may provide some new solutions to an old and vexing problem.

The three perspectives on the issue of obscenity translate into three political philosophies: liberalism, conservatism and feminism. While it is true that feminism has its early roots in liberal philosophy,[17] major components of liberal tradition have been rejected by feminist analysts.[18] Particularly in the area of sexual expression, feminism has outgrown its liberal roots.[19]

This article begins with a discussion of the traditional liberal and conservative analysis of morality, neither of which incorporates web morality. Harm, the vital ingredient in the differing moral constructs, is then examined in terms of the values the two traditional philosophies seek to protect. It is suggested that both the traditional philosophies emanate from the ladder. The third section of the article presents an analysis of female or web morality, which is discussed in terms of feminist definitions of pornography and feminist perceptions of the harm inherent in pornographic expression. The traditional view of morality and harm is critically analyzed and the beneficial consequences that would flow from a web interpretation of morality are discussed.

The final section of the article deals with the response of the courts to the problem of obscenity. Courts have generally fluctuated between the two traditional views discussed in the first section of the article, but there is some evidence that the feminist voice is beginning to be heard.

The article concludes with some thoughts on the judicial interpretation of fundamental freedoms, particularly the right to be free from certain forms of expression.

THE TRADITIONAL ANALYSIS OF MORALITY

Morality and Law

Two conflicting moralities, both originating from the ladder, have dominated the development of the law of obscenity. They can be labelled "conservative" and "liberal" moralities. Under the conservative morality, obscenity is judged from the point of view of the intrinsic wickedness or virtue of the material in question. Underlying a determination of wickedness is an assessment of whether or not the material

---

17. This is evident in the writings of early feminists like Mary Wollstonecraft and John Stuart Mill.

18. *See* A. Jaggar & P. Rothenberg-Struhl, *Feminist Frame Works,* (1978) et A. Jaggar, *Feminist Politics and Human Nature,* (1983).

19. *See, e.g.,* S. WENDELL, A (Qualified) Defense of Liberal Feminism (unpublished paper presented at the Annual Conference for the Canadian Society for Women in Philosophy, 9-11 Nov. 1984, Concordia University, Montreal, P.Q.).

poses a threat to the organizational structure of society and its institutions. If it is found to pose a threat, there is sufficient reason for the material to be banned.

In contrast, the liberal morality is not concerned with the material's inherent character, but rather asks whether more harm will be caused by banning it than by permitting its publication. The suppression of material is regarded as harmful since it is believed to erode the fundamental freedoms upon which a democratic society is based. Individual freedom of expression is regarded as a moral right that should be upheld, however personally distasteful one may find the material, as long as the material does not result in direct harm. In essence, the conservative morality gives priority to institutional integrity, whereas the liberal morality emphasizes individual expression.[20]

These divergent points of view were recognizable as early as 1727, in the first reported successful common law prosecution for publishing an obscene libel.[21] The charge was brought against the publisher[22] of "Venus in the Cloister or the Nun in her Smock", a book about lesbian love in the convent. The differences between the conservative morality and the liberal morality are reflected in the legal arguments submitted to the court as well as in the majority and minority judgments. The majority of the court accepted the argument made by the Attorney-General, based on a conservative morality, that morality was an area of expression subject to the restrictions of the common law. The majority held that the publication:

> [was] an offence at common law as it tends to corrupt the morals of the King's subjects and is against the peace of the King. Peace includes good government and order and thus peace may be broken without actual force... if [it be] against morality.[23]

In dissent, Mr. Justice Fortescue was strongly of the opinion that an actual breach of the peace was required before the law could impose restrictions on expression. This limitation, based on the liberal view that direct harm was necessary, was specifically rejected by the majority.

This early case had two important consequences: it introduced the concept of obscenity as a punishable offence, and it placed the responsibility for public morality in the hands of the judiciary. In fulfilling that responsibility, the courts were forced to address the critical issue

---

20. For a discussion on a variety of views on censorship held by pressure groups, lawyers, judges and Parliament and the social background that moulded the formation of such opinions: *see* Davies, "How our Rulers Argue About Censorship", in *Censorship and Obscenity*, eds. R. Dhavan and C. Davies, (1978).

21. *R. v. Curl* (1727), 2 Strange 788; 93 E.R. 849 (K.B. 1727).

22. An account of the exploits of Edmund Curl can be found in A. Craig, *Suppressed Books 20* (1963), Chapter 2.

23. *Id.*, p. 789; 93 E.R. p. 850.

of when and under what circumstances they should involve themselves in questions of public morality.

The Question of Harm

Both conservatives and liberals agree that some type of harm is required before the legal system should intervene in the sphere of public morality, but their perceptions of what constitutes harm are very different. Originally, the law defined morality in terms of the individual, but its perspective was religious.[24]

Prior to the *Curl*[25] case, offences relating to morality were dealt with by the ecclesiastical courts. The purpose of those courts was to protect a person's soul, and thus they dealt with moral issues as those issues applied to the individual. By extending regulations beyond their religious base in *Curl*, conservatives came to believe that obscenity had political ramifications and could cause harm not only to the individual, but to society generally.[26]

Although obscenity prosecutions were relatively rare throughout the 18th century, by the 19th century there were about three prosecutions each year. Charges were laid against works that were purely sexual in content, largely because of the activism of the Society for the Suppression of Vice, founded in 1802. Byron's *Don Juan* and Shelley's *Queen Mab* were both found to be obscene along with 152 other publications, out of 159 prosecuted. The decisions almost always supported the conservative view.[27] The apprehension of conservatives that obscene publications could undermine the structure of society is evident in the writings of Ernst and Segal:

> It is important to understand that sex radicalism in modern life is the best general index of radicalism in other spheres. The man who publically upholds birth control, the single standard, free love, companionate marriage, easy divorce, and legitimization, is a man prone to play with subversive ideas on private property, to be attracted to criminal syndicalism, to be dubious about the House of Lords, or about the fitness of the republican party to govern, and to question the general efficacy of prayer.

24. *See* A. Gerber, "The Real Reason We Have Obscenity Legislation", *Sex, Pornography and Justice*, New York (1965), p. 213-217.
25. *Supra* note 21.
26. Obscenity paralleled the offence of blasphemy in this regard. In *R. v. Williams* (1797), 26 St. Tr. 653 at 716-717, Ashhurst J. said blasphemy was "[n]ot only [an offence] to God but [a crime] against the government ... as [it] tend [s] to destroy those bonds and obligations whereby Civil Society" is bound together.
27. J. Schauer, *The Law of Obscenity* (1976). In his book, Mr Schauer describes how the efforts of the Society for the Suppression of Vice resulted in obscenity prosecutions emphasizing works that were purely sexual in context without the necessity of political or religious implications. Women have taken part in a number of anti-pornography social movements, many of them opposed to any form of social change. Their ideology, however, echoed the male moralist view.

When such an individual is attacked under sex censorships it is assumed that no very great tenderness for his rights need be shown.[28]

More recently, former President Nixon gave expression to this approach when he said, "if an attitude of permissiveness were to be adopted... this would contribute to an atmosphere condoning anarchy in every other field and would increase the threat to our social order as well as our moral principles."[29]

The conservative and liberal positions were defined and debated in the Devlin-Hart exchange on the role of law in the enforcement of morals, which took place in print between 1959 and 1963.[30] Lord Devlin, speaking from the conservative position, maintained that society was justified in prohibiting any form of action or speech that invoked feelings of intolerance, indignation and disgust.[31] He relied heavily on notions of good and evil, suggesting that there were absolutes that right-thinking persons could discern. He maintained that demonstrable harm to society need not be shown in order to restrict individual freedom because society must protect itself from moral disintegration.[32]

Professor Hart maintained that not only is the preservation of society not dependent upon enforcement of morality, but that the enforcement of morality brings about other evils, such as human misery and the restriction of individual freedoms, that outweigh any benefit derived from the preservation of social morality.[33] He disagreed with the idea that there are ascertainable, eternal truths and said that Lord Devlin's approach would allow the state to define sexual norms. Hart stated that, in order to justify state incursions on liberty, harm must be demonstrated and attempts to change sexual norms would not in themselves constitute harm.[34] The liberal approach thus requires a direct harm before the state is justified in intervening. Those advocating any restriction on free expression are called upon to prove the existence of an immediate threat that will cause direct harm to an individual. Unless a causal connection can be made between the material sought to be restricted and the harm, the restriction cannot be justified. Hart was no doubt encouraged by the Wolfenden Committee's Report emphasizing "the importance which society and the laws ought to give to individual freedom of choice and action in matters of private morality" and that "there

---

28. M.L. Ernst and W.L. Segal, *To the Pure - A Study of Obscenity and the Censor*, 176 (1928).
29. Cited in P.R. MacMillan, *Censorship and Public Morality*, Gower Pub. (1983), p. x.
30. Lord Devlin's argument appears in *The Enforcement of Morals* (1965), and H.L.A. Hart's position can be found in Hart, *Law, Liberty and Morality* (1963).
31. Lord Patrick Devlin, *id.*, p. 17.
32. *Id.*, p. 18.
33. H.L.A. Hart, *supra* note 31, *id.*, p. 83.
34. *Id.*, p. 52.

must remain a realm of private morality which is, in brief and crude terms, not the law's business."[35]

Conclusion

Both the conservative and liberal approaches to obscenity can be traced to a male-defined concept of justice and individual rights. Each focuses on the "rights" of the individual, although different tests are used to determine when the state is justified in infringing those rights. It is noteworthy that both approaches share an underlying belief in the unhindered freedom of expression, despite its effects on others. This is consistent with the ladder theory of morality that emphasizes recognized zones of non-interference as the basis of morality and human interaction. Conservatives justify intervention into these private zones if the material is inherently bad. Liberals, on the other hand, require proof of a clear and present danger before any limits on the freedom of expression can be justified. This appeal to human freedom, made in terms of relative consequences, explains the great interest that liberals have in scientific research on the effects of pornography on human behavior.[36] Until a direct link between obscene material and physical harm can be proven, they insist that no infringement on expression can be justified.[37]

THE FEMINIST ANALYSIS OF MORALITY AND OBSCENITY

In this section, the feminist approach to pornography and Professor Gilligan's web theory are linked. A selection of feminist definitions of pornography are analyzed and their common characteristics identified. All of the definitions exhibit Gilligan's defining characteristics of web morality, requiring respect for women's freedom and privacy, and a conception of individuals in their social circumstances. The underlying rationale of feminist morality is utterly different from that of liberals or conservatives. The traditional analyses of morality are criticized on the grounds that they fail to address either the concerns raised by the morality of the web or the realities of twentieth-century technology. The "clear and present danger" test is criticized in terms of its applic-

---

35. United Kingdom Parliament *Report of the Committee on Homosexual Offences and Prostitution* (1957), Cmnd. 247 (Sir John Wolfenden C.B.E.).

36. For example, millions of dollars were spent by the American Commission on Obscenity and Pornography to investigate causalist questions. Large amounts are being spent on causalist research today by the Canadian government.

37. See Canadian Civil Liberties Association, "Pornography and the Law", *Submissions to the Special Committee on Pornography and Prostitution*, April 6, 1984 and C. Beckton, "Obscenity and Censorship Re-examined Under the Charter of Rights" (1983), 13 *Man. Law. J* 351 at 361.

ability both in law and in fact. The section concludes with the feminist analysis of harm, the manner in which it relates to the subject of pornography and why the law should take that analysis into account.

The feminist analysis of morality is critical of both the conservative and liberal approaches, but on different grounds. Rather than focusing on the morality of sexual expression within established, male-defined norms as conservatives do, the feminist analysis concentrates on non-violence, responsibility and caring that goes beyond individualism. Rather than focusing on direct harm as liberals do in order to justify limits on expression, feminists focus on generalized harm to others in the social context. They make a distinction between sexual mores and questions of morality. They argue that harm to others is the defining characteristic of immorality,[38] but they disagree with the liberal view that sexual chastity must be completely detached from moral virtue. Where a liberal view insists that no matter how offensive the material may be, it must be tolerated in the name of freedom of expression, the web theory examines the psychological and social consequences of material and thereby recognizes the reality of peoples' lives in a historical world.[39]

Definitions of Pornography[40]

The feminist definitions of pornography differ markedly from those in the *Criminal Code*[41] or in the common law.[42] Distinctions are made between pornography and erotica, pornography and sex education and pornography and moral realism. Helen Longino, a feminist philosopher, defines pornography as:

> [v]erbal or pictorial material which represents or describes sexual behavior that is degrading and abusive to one or more of the participants *in such a way as to endorse the degradation.*[43]

---

38. Helen E. Longino, ''Pornography, Oppression and Freedom: A Closer Look'' in Laura Lederer, ed., *Take Back the Night: Women on Pornography*, 40 New York (1980).
39. C. Gilligan, *op. cit., supra* note 12, ''Concepts of Self and Morality'', p. 64-105.
40. Feminists prefer the word ''pornography'' to ''obscenity'' because of its etymology and original meaning. Pornography is defined in Volume VII of the *Oxford English Dictionary* 1131 (3d ed. 1970) as ''description of the life, manners, etc. of prostitutes and their patrons [from the greek *porne* meaning ''harlot'' and *grapho* meaning ''to write'']; hence the expression or suggestion of obscene or unchaste subjects in literature or art.'' The term ''obscenity'' comes from the Latin phrase *ob cenum*, meaning ''about filth'' and is defined as material which is ''offensive to modesty or decency, lewd; causing or intending to cause sexual excitement or lust''. Feminists prefer the word ''pornography'' because it more clearly defines what is objectionable: treatment of women as a commodity whose purpose is the sexual pleasure of men.
41. R.S.C. 1970, c. C-34, s. 159.
42. See notes 102-29 and accompanying text *infra*.
43. *Supra* note 38, at 43.

Debra Lewis, a feminist criminologist, defines pornography as material that:

> [d]epicts, condones and encourages acts of domination, degradation and violence towards women.[44]

The National Action Committee on the Status of Women has defined pornography as:

> [a]ny printed, visual, audio or otherwise represented presentation, or part thereof, which seeks to sexually stimulate the viewer or consumer by the depiction of violence, including but not limited to, the depiction of submission, coercion, lack of consent, or debasement of any human being.[45]

The Canadian Advisory Council on the Status of Women defines pornography as:

> a presentation, whether live, simulated, verbal, pictorial, filmed or videotaped, or otherwise represented, of sexual behavior in which one or more participants are coerced overtly or implicitly, into participation; or are injured or abused physically or psychologically; or in which an imbalance of power is obvious, or implied by virtue of the immature age of any participant or by contextual aspects of the presentation, and in which such behavior can be taken to be advocated or endorsed.[46]

All these definitions reflect Professor Gilligan's web theory of morality. They are typical of the feminist view of pornography, in that they emphasize that whether or not a work is pornographic depends upon the context within which it is presented. Explicit depictions of sex, simple representations of degrading behavior or descriptions or representations of rape will not be pornographic unless they are advocated, endorsed or designed to sexually stimulate the viewer. Feminists say that such subject matters can be highly moral when the consequences of the acts are explored and the victim's dignity is acknowledged and reaffirmed.[47] Sex education materials, artistic material, and erotic sexual material that have often been improperly repressed in times when all non-procreative sex was considered immoral, are not caught by feminist definitions.

---

44. Report of the standing committee on justice and legal affairs, no. 12 at 4 (1978).
45. Cited in the Canadian Civil Liberties Association, *op. cit.*, p. 5. See also, Municipality of Metropolitan Toronto, Task Force in Public Violence Against Women and Children, *Final Report* (1984), p. 27, which adopted a similar definition.
46. Canadian Advisory Council on the Status of Women, *Brief to the Special Committee on Pornography and Prostitution*, April 6, 1984.
47. For example, the National Film Board production, ''Not a Love Story: A Film About Pornography'', contained explicit, degrading and violent sexual depictions and was banned from commercial theatres in Ontario for this reason. If the film had been scrutinized under any of the feminist definitions cited above, it would not have been banned, because the context would have been examined. The depictions, although offensive when taken out of context, provided a powerful medium for a highly moral film affirming women's dignity and worth.

All the feminist definitions have in common the theme of non-violence and equality. "[A] film showing two people making love is much different from one portraying the rape and murder of women for male sexual stimulation".[48] Unlike traditional moralists, feminists believe that erotica is not destructive and harmful and should be freely available to those who wish to obtain it.

The fundamental distinction between pornography and erotica is central to the feminist viewpoint. The word "erotica" derives from the word "eros" which means passionate love. Gloria Steinem defines erotic sex as:

> a mutually pleasurable, sexual expression between people who have enough power to be there by positive choice.[49]

The message of pornography, she says, is:

> violence, dominance, and conquest. It is being used to reinforce some inequality, or to create one, or to tell us that pain and humiliation (ours or someone else's) are really the same as pleasure...

> Perhaps one could simply say that erotica is about sexuality, but pornography is about power and sex-as-weapon in the same way we have come to understand that rape is about violence, and not really about sexuality at all.[50]

Feminist Critique of the Traditional Analysis of Morality

In this section I will analyze the deficiencies in the conservative and liberal approaches to obscenity.

Conservative Morality

The feminist morality largely disagrees with the assumptions, application and consequences of the conservative morality as it is applied to obscenity.

First, the conservative morality creates and advocates what is to many an unacceptable sexual ethic, one that asks the law to subordinate sex to procreation and condemn all sexual interaction outside marriage. Sexual morality is seen by conservatives as the "glue" holding together the rest of the structure of society. Integral to that notion of morality is the concept of the dependent and virtuous woman, without access to birth control, without access to divorce, without access to a single life or to any of the benefits the law generally confers upon men. The "ladder" is well protected by this philosophy since men are free to pursue

---

48. Dr. Pauline Bart & Dr. Margaret Jozsa, "Dirty Books, Dirty Films and Dirty Data", Laura Lederer, ed., *op. cit.*, p. 204 at 207 (1980).

49. G. Steinem, "Erotica and Pornography: A Clear and Present Difference", Lederer ed., *op. cit.*, p. 37.

50. *Ibid.*, at 37-38.

their lives within a society where inequality is rationalized by theories explaining the need for its continuation.

Second, conservatives, with their blanket emphasis on all sexual interaction, fail to distinguish between the different ways in which sexual interaction can be depicted. They simply condemn it all. They catch in their net materials dealing with sex education, erotica and moral realism. Under the feminist analysis only something qualifying as "pornography" is considered obscene and worthy of condemnation and censorship.

Liberal Morality

Feminists criticize the liberal approach to morality because of what they see as its improper insistence on proof of a clear and present danger before state intervention is justified and because it stresses the rights of individuals apart from their social context, to the point where the welfare of women and children are compromised. There are two grounds for this criticism: the test has no legal foundation in the law of obscenity and it is based on a theory that does not translate well into twentieth-century capitalism and technology.

Some of the more extreme liberal causalists argue that the test for any infringement on expression, including obscenity, should be the clear and present danger test.[51] They urge its adoption if and when the current obscenity provisions are challenged under the Canadian Charter of Rights and Freedoms.[52] However, their approach is misconceived since that test does not properly apply to cases of obscenity.

The "clear and present danger" standard was originally formulated to review government repression of political speech. In order to prove a clear and present danger in law, a compelling and overwhelming threat of harm that is tangible and immediate and that can only be avoided by suppressing speech must be shown. The example usually cited to demonstrate the concept is someone falsely shouting "Fire!" in a crowded theatre. In a democratic society the importance of an individual's right to comment on the activities of his government was said to justify this stringent standard. Political speech constituted a clear and present danger only if it presented an immediate threat to national security. This test was adopted in 1919 in the sedition case of *Schenck* v. *United States*,[53] which involved the distribution of pamphlets that opposed the military draft. It has been most recently applied in the United States where the government, in its role of guardian of national

---

51. See Canadian Civil Liberties Association, *op. cit.* and C. Beckton, "Obscenity and Censorship Re-examined Under the Charter of Rights", *op. cit.*, p. 368.
52. *Constitution Act, 1982*, Part. I, enacted by the *Canada Act, 1982*, U.K. 1982, c. 11.
53. 249 U.S. 47 (1919).

security, attempted to suppress publication of the Pentagon Papers.[54] Although this test applies to restrictions on the freedom of political speech, it has not been successfully upheld in Canada or in the U.S. as an appropriate test for obscene publications.[55]

To suggest that the clear and present danger standard should be adopted in the case of violent pornography is to improperly imply that pornography is a form of protected political speech. The Manitoba Court of Appeal in *R. v. Prairie Schooner News Ltd.* made it clear that obscene material is not protected speech:

> Freedom of speech is not unfettered either in criminal law or in civil law. The *Canadian Bill of Rights* was intended to protect, and does protect, basic freedoms of vital importance to all Canadians. It does not serve as a shield behind which obscene matter may be disseminated without concern for criminal consequences.[56]

The Court further commented on the question of harm, that

> [I]t is not for the Court to determine whether publications of this kind hurt anyone or do any demonstrable harm. Parliament has already made that determination.[57]

Although the *Prairie Schooner* case was decided pursuant to the Canadian Bill of Rights,[58] the same result seems inevitable under the Canadian Charter of Rights and Freedoms. A challenge to the current obscenity provisions under the Charter would require the courts to determine whether or not the provisions "unreasonably" infringe upon freedom of expression. The reasonable limitation clause in section 1 of the *Charter* makes it clear that none of the fundamental freedoms are absolute. The High Court of Ontario addressed this question in *Re Ontario Film and Video Appreciation Soc'y and Ontario Board of Censors*.[59] It held that some prior censorship of films was demonstrably justifiable in a free and democratic society in order to prevent sexually offensive films from being shown. However, it held that although the Ontario Censor Board's authority was constitutional, its guidelines were

---

54. *New York Times Co. v. United States*, 403 U.S. 713 (1971).
55. In *Commonwealth v. Gordon*, 66 Pa. D. and C. 101 (1949), Justice Bok sought to establish the principle that no book should be suppressed unless it could be shown that there was a clear and present danger of the commission of a crime as a result of its publication. This reasoning was not upheld in the Appeal Court. In *Miller v. California,* 413 U.S. 15, 93 S. Ct. 2607, 37 L. Ed. 2d 111 9 (1973), Mr. Justice Burger held that, "to equate the full and robust exchange of ideas and political debate with commercial exploitation of obscene material demeans the grand conception of the First Amendment and its high purposes in the historic struggle for freedom. It is a misuse of the great guarantees of free speech and free press."
56. 1 C.C.C. (2d) 251, at 271, 75 W.W.R. 585, at 604 (Man. C.A. 1970).
57. *Id.,* at 254, 75 W.W.R. 585, at. 588.
58. R.C.S. (1970), (App. III).
59. 41 O.R. (2d) 583, 157 D.L.R. (3d) 58 (H.C. 1983).

not: they were not definite and precise enough to meet the "prescribed by law" requirement in the Charter.

The British Columbia County Court in *R. v. Red Hot Video Ltd.*[60] held that subsections 159(1) and (8) of the *Criminal Code*,[61] which make it an offence to distribute obscene material and which define obscenity, do not offend the guarantee of freedom of expression in subsection 2(b) of the *Charter*. The Court further held that section 159 could not be said to be vague, broad or unreasonable. More recently, the Manitoba Court of Queen's Bench in *R. v. Ramsingh*[62] held that section 159 of the *Criminal Code* represents a reasonable limitation prescribed by law that can be demonstrably justified in a free and democratic society within the meaning of section 1 of the *Charter*. The Court said that the purpose of section 159 is to protect society generally and that it is not unreasonable for a democratic society to impose some limits on what can be viewed, such as child pornography or sex with violence or horror.[63]

The constitutionality of the *Customs Tariff*[64] was challenged in *Re Luscher and Deputy Minister, Revenue Canada*.[65] It was held to be a demonstrably justifiable and reasonable limit on freedom of expression to prevent "socially offensive material" from entering Canada. The judge held that the words "immoral" and "indecent" were a sufficiently precise limit to be properly prescribed by law as required under the *Charter*.

In an appeal to the Federal Court of Appeal,[66] the decision of the lower court was reversed on the grounds that the words "immoral and indecent" in section 14 of the *Customs Tariff* are not sufficiently "prescribed by law" to satisfy section 1 of the *Charter*. The Court made the observation that the words "immoral and indecent" were not defined in the legislation, thus distinguishing *Customs Tariff* provisions from the obscenity provisions of the *Criminal Code*. Further, the Court commented that the words "immoral" and "indecent" are highly subjective and emotional in their content and thus are too uncertain to meet the degree of predictability of legal consequences the *Charter* requires. Within a matter of days, the Federal Court of Appeal decision was effectively overruled when Parliament passed temporary emergency legislation restoring powers of customs officials to prohibit materials

---

60. 38 C.R. (3d) 275, 11 C.C.C. (3d) 389 (B.C. Cty. Ct. 1984).
61. R.S.C. 1970, c. C-34, subs. 159(1) and (8).
62. 14 C.C.C. (3d) 230 (Man. Q.B. 1984).
63. *Id.*, at 244.
64. R.S.C. 1970, c. C-14.
65. 149 D.L.R. (3d) 243 (B.C. Cty. Ct. 1983).
66. *Luscher v. Deputy Minister, Revenue Canada, Customs and Excise* (unreported, F.C. App. D., 7 Mar. 1985).

from entering Canada.[67] The legislation redefined prohibited material as:

> 1. Books, printed paper, drawings, paintings, prints, photographs or representations of any kind...
>> (ii) that are deemed to be "obscene" under s. 159(8) of the *Criminal Code*...

The United States Supreme Court has taken the position that the first Amendment's[68] protection of speech does not extend to obscene material. Such material is not "speech" in a constitutional sense, because it lacks communicative content.[69] Obscene material could, therefore, be suppressed without showing the circumstances that amount to a "clear and present danger".[70]

The second criticism is that the clear and present danger standard is based upon a political theory that is no longer applicable in the context of obscenity. Liberals argue that John Stuart Mill's "marketplace of truth" theory[71] applies to obscenity.[72] For example, the American Civil Liberties Union has stated that any restrictions, including the restriction of a juvenile's access to obscene material, inhibit both the creative artist's free expression of ideas and the individual parent's freedom to choose what his or her children will read.[73] The Union states:

> Obscenity statutes which punish the distribution of material purchased or view [sic] by minors violate the First Amendment, and inevitably restrict the right to publish and distribute such material to adults.[74]

Mill posited that the only way that truth can emerge is through a form of natural selection in a "free market" of ideas: if all ideas are allowed expression, good ideas will multiply and bad ideas die out. Mill hoped that this theory would help to further "[t]he permanent interests of man as a progressive being".[75] The implication of the American Civil Liberties Union's approach is that if the messages con-

---

67. Bill C-38, 33rd Parl., lst sess., 1984-85 (proclaimed in force 2 Apr. 1985).
68. U.S. Const.
69. See *Roth* v. *United States,* 354 U.S. 476 (1957). See also F. Schauer, "Speech and "Speech" - Obscenity and "Obscenity"": An Exercise in the Interpretation of Constitutional Language, 67 *Georgetown Law Journal* 899-933 (1979).
70. *Ginsberg* v. *New York,* 390 U.S. 629 (1968), U.S.S.C. *per* Brennan J.
71. *Supra,* note 16, at 15-54.
72. It is interesting that the proponents of the clear and present danger test for obscenity rely so heavily on Mill's reasoning to justify their stand when a sequel to *On Liberty* was an eloquent protest against the manner in which women's freedoms have been subjected to irrational limitations: J. Mill, "The Subjection of Women" (1869). Social science studies indicate that pornography perpetuates those irrational limitations: see notes 86-110 and accompanying text *infra*.
73. American Civil Liberties Union Policy Guide, No. 5, p. 8 (1981).
74. *Id.,* No. 4, p. 5.
75. *Supra,* note 17, at 33.

tained in pornography are bad, they will die out and be replaced by good ones. Therefore, the view that women are equal to men, and that children have dignity and deserve to be treated with respect, will prevail. The messages in pornography that women and children are sex objects, available to be violated, subjugated and coerced at the will of men, will disappear. In fact, however, one only needs to observe the modern marketplace to know that the "marketplace of truth" cannot be advanced as the governing approach to the modern genre of pornography. Pornographic images proliferate virtually everywhere[76] and statistics of rape,[77] wife battering[78] and sexual abuse of children[79] indicate that egalitarian ideals are far from being universally accepted. Modern methods of mass media communication, unanticipated by Mill, make it difficult to see how his argument can include all forms of publication, especially pornographic photographs, which are largely devoid of any expression at all. Marshall McLuhan analyzed the difference between print and photographic images. He said that

> [t]he logic of the photograph is neither verbal nor syntactical, a condition which renders literary culture quite helpless to cope with the photograph.[80]

Further, it can be argued that it is naive to transpose nineteenth-century laissez-faire notions on to the multi-million dollar pornography market. A "free market of ideas" implies equal, unhindered access to the marketplace and an opportunity for all citizens to communicate and to be heard. The reality of today is that the mass media own the skills and language techniques necessary to address the citizenry. The marketplace of truth - if it ever did exist - has long ago given way in the face of technological and social change. In today's world, untruths can certainly prevail if powerful agencies with enough profit motive behind them gain a hold on the market.[81] The ninety-eighth Congress of the United States recently enacted the *Child Protection Act* of 1984[82] which has taken the true marketplace into account. Section 2 of that Act states:

---

76. See Department of Justice, Special Committee on Pornography and Prostitution, *Issues Paper* (Nov. 1983), p. 11.
77. See Clark and Lewis, *Rape: The Price of Coercive Sexuality*, Toronto (1977), p. 61. They state that the incidences of rape increased by 174% between 1961 and 1971. In the period 1969-1973 it increased 76%.
78. S. Armstrong, "Wife Beating: "Let's Stop it Now"", *Canadian Living* (1984), p. 89, states that one woman in every ten is beaten by her husband or common-law mate.
79. Report of the Committee on Sexual Offences Against Children and Youths (1984), p. 180-83, states, among other staggering statistics of abuse, that 50 percent of women and 30 percent of men have been victims of unwanted sexual acts, the majority of these occurring before they were legal adults.
80. M. McLuhan, *Understanding Media: The Extensions of Man*, 197 (1964).
81. See note 86, *infra*, where the extent of the pornography market is discussed.
82. *Child Protection Act*, of 1984, P.L. no. 98-292, 98 Stat. 204.

The Congress finds that -
(1) child pornography has developed into a highly organized, multi-million dollar industry which operates on a nationwide scale;
(2) thousands of children including large numbers of runaway and homeless youth are exploited in the production and distribution of pornographic materials; and
(3) the use of children as subjects of pornographic materials is harmful to the physiological, emotional, and mental health of the individual child and to society.

Gresham's Law, that bad money drives out good, would be a more sensible rule of thumb in the commercial world of pornography.[83] It has also been persuasively argued that Mill, if he were living today, would interpret his words so as to include the requirements of social justice.[84]

For these two reasons then, the liberal approach is flawed. Its insistence on direct harm is not sound in law and its underlying rationale cannot be literally transposed into twentieth-century society where modern communication techniques have facilitated the growth of a multi-million dollar pornography industry.

The Question of Harm

''Harm'' in the feminist analysis of pornography differs from both the liberal and the conservative concepts. The conservative view that obscenity is harmful because it causes the erosion of the social order, and the liberal view that obscenity is harmful if it constitutes a direct injury to individuals, both fail to take into account the harms perceived by feminists.

---

83. This point is made in ACTRA *Policy Statement on Censorship and Pornography*. *ACTRA SCOPE*, Vol. 13, No. 6, May, 1984, p. 14-16. It states that
''... members who refuse to participate in such productions [of material which is sexually violent and indicates harm to other people] find that the small amount of work available becomes smaller.''
National Committee on Women's Issues, Submission on Pornography and Censorship to the ACTRA Board of Directors makes the point more clearly:
''Canada, unlike America, is the only country we know of where the pornography industry and the mainstream film industry are inextricably combined. Opportunities in the film industry here mean work in the porn industry... The combination of these two industries in Canada seriously limits the artistic development of writers and performers, in that porn production insists on formula films, i.e. ''T. & A.'', ''Chop'em Ups'', etc. The porn and mainstream cross-over seriously bleeds legitimate films of funds they need to be made, and lowers the general quality of all film.''
84. J. Humphrey, ''The Just Requirements of Morality, Public Order and General Welfare in a Democratic Society'', *The Practice of Freedom*, ed. R. MacDonald and Humphrey, Toronto (1979).

The feminist analysis of harm starts with the premise that to understand the harm caused by pornography, the full implications of violence against women in contemporary society must be examined. Feminists point out that, for many years, women have been unable to walk the streets after dark without male protection. Women routinely protect themselves with mace, whistles, extra keys, dead-bolt locks, security buildings and peep holes.[85] Rape crisis centers, battered wives' shelters, and child abuse and incest counselling centers are considered social necessities in many Canadian cities and towns. Sexual harassment has become so common that guidelines to deal with it have been legislated or bargained for in most places of employment.

At the same time, debasement of women in pornographic magazines, books, movies, films, and television, on street corner newsstands, on covers of record albums and in shop windows has steadily increased. Three recent surveys indicate that sales of pornographic magazines in Canada increased by 326.7 percent between 1965 and 1980. This represents an increase of at least fourteen times the growth of the Canadian population during the same period.[86] Content analysis studies on "soft-core" pornographic magazines indicate that depictions of sexual violence increased steadily in the five year period between 1973 and 1977.[87]

The Report of the House of Commons Standing Committee on Justice and Legal Affairs commented on the image that pornography presents of women:

> This material is exploitive of women - they are portrayed as passive victims who derive limitless pleasure from inflicted pain, and from subjugation to acts of violence, humiliation, and degradation. Women are depicted as sexual objects whose only redeeming features are their genital and erotic zones which are prominently displayed in minute detail... The effect of this type of material is to reinforce male-female stereotypes to the detriment of both sexes. It attempts to make degradation, humiliation, victimization, and violence in human relationships appear normal and acceptable.[88]

---

85. For a thorough discussion about rape and the fear of rape in Canada, see Clark and Lewis, *Rape: The Price of Coercive Sexuality, op. cit.,* note 77.

86. *Supra,* note 79 at 1267. It is estimated by the Committee that the gross revenue of pornographic magazines is at least $100 million annually in Canada. This figure would not include pornographic pocket books, films, "sex aids", and admission fees charged for commercially exhibited motion pictures.

87. N. Malamuth, B. Spinner, "A Longitudinal Content Analysis of Sexual Violence in the Best-selling Erotic Magazines", *Journal of Sex Research,* Vol. 16, No. 3 (Aug. 1980) p. 226-237. Similar results were reported by Dietz and Evans in a more recent study in 139 Am. J. Psych. 1493-95 (1982).

88. Report of the Standing Committee on Justice and Legal Affairs, No. 3, 1978, p. 3-4.

The Committee concluded that pornography "promotes values and behavior which are unacceptable in a society committed to egalitarian, consensual, mutual and non-violent human relationships".[89]

Harm to Women Generally

Feminists argue that one of the harms of pornography is that it provides a framework that encourages a whole range of violent, coercive and exploitive acts against women. They claim that the sheer volume of pornography requires that the moral issue be expanded to include not only the assessment of individual works, but also the meaning and force of the mass production of pornography.[90] If allowed to continue unabated, the pornographic image of women will foster oppression by further entrenching sexist attitudes.

Feminists are of the view that, unlike rape, wife battering and incest aggression where the victims are individuals, pornography's victims are women in general. The harm it causes is public, generalized harm - the degradation of women as a class, resulting in assaults on institutions, values and practices relating to marriage, privacy, employment and the family, in a way not envisioned by male moralists. Many women's goals, such as greater participation in public life, equal pay for work of equal value and daycare are that much more difficult to achieve when female credibility is assaulted on such a massive scale.[91]

Social scientific research over the last fifteen years clearly supports the feminist stand. It has been demonstrated in context analytic research that violent and degrading pornography can have a number of harmful effects. Subjects exposed to pornography demonstrate an increased acceptance of rape myths, increased aggressive behaviour toward women in a laboratory setting, decreased future perceptions of rape victim suffering, a future desensitization to sexual violence and an increased reported willingness to rape.[92]

In their book, *Sex, Violence and the Media*, H.J. Eysenck and D.K. Nias undertook an extensive review of the literature on violence and pornography and concluded that:

> [w]here the context is hostile to women, as most pornographic films are, we feel that such films should fall under the category of "incitement to violence towards minority groups" - even though women are not a

---

89. *Ibid*, at 7.
90. *Supra*, note 38 at 46.
91. T. McCormick, *Making Sense of Research on Pornography*, Department of Sociology, York University, p. 37.
92. Check & Malamuth, *Pornography and Sexual Aggression : A Social Learning Theory Analysis* in Communication Yearbook 9 (M. McLaughlin ed. 1985). See also *Pornography and Sexual Aggression* (N. Malamuth & E. Donnerstein eds. 1984).

minority group. Nevertheless such films do constitute a clear case of incitement to maltreat women, downgrade them to a lower status, regard them as mere sex objects, and elevate male "machismo" to a superior position on the scale of values. Evaluative conditioning, modeling, and desensitization all point to the same conclusion, namely that such presentations have effects on men's attitudes which are detrimental to women; in fairness to more than one half of the population, such incitements should be proscribed.[93]

In another summary of research, psychologist Edward Donnerstein concluded:

> Given the increase in sexual and other forms of violence against women depicted in the media, a concern over such presentations seems warranted. There is ample evidence that the observation of violent forms of media can facilitate aggressive response.[94]

In its recent report, the "Badgley Committee"[95] also came to the conclusion that pornography is harmful because it corrupts moral and social values and alters personal values and behavior.[96] There is also some support in American case law for the view that pornography is related to actual harm. In *Miller* v. *California*[97] the U.S. Supreme Court held that the states, in determining whether or not something was obscene, had the right to assume that there was a causal connection between pornography and crime or other anti-social behavior. In *Paris Adult Theatre I* v. *Slaton*,[98] the court said there was "at least an arguable correlation between obscene material and crime".[99] Feminists argue that if, as the researchers say, pornography promotes the view that women are less equal, less valuable and less worthy than men, allowing pornography to proliferate will create a culture of perpetual inequity. This argument remains valid even where physical aggression or direct harm cannot be proved in individual cases.

Harm to Children

The Badgley Committee also found a link between direct harm to children and pornography. Its Report states:

> The graphic accounts given, when taken in conjunction with cases investigated by the police, leave no doubt that incidents of unwanted exposure of children to pornography occur, and that in some of these situations,

---

93. H.J. Gysenck, D.K. Nias, "Sex, Violence and the Media" (1978), p. 259.
94. E. Donnerstein, "Pornography and Violence Against Women: Experimental Studies" (1980), 347 *Annals of the New York Academy of Science* 277 at 287.
95. *Op. cit.*, note 79.
96. *Id.*, p. 1274.
97. *Supra*, note 55.
98. 413 U.S. 49 (1973).
99. *Id.*, at 98.

such exposures are associated with children having been sexually assaulted.[100]

These findings are strikingly different from those of the Committee on Obscenity and Film Censorship in England in 1979 and the U.S. Commission on Obscenity and Pornography in 1970. The British Committee was reluctant to confirm any link between pornography and harm, because the studies placed before it contained conflicting evidence:

> It seemed to us right to be sceptical about attempts to apply the lessons of these laboratory experiments to real life and we therefore preferred the more noncommittal view.... . We consider that the only objective verdict must be one of ''not proven.''[101]

The U.S. Commission concluded that exposure to pornography does not seriously promote anti-social behavior. The Commission stated:

> In sum, empirical research designed to clarify the question has found no evidence to date that exposure to explicit sexual materials plays a significant role in the causation of delinquent or criminal behavior among youth or adults.[102]

A minority of that Commission called for removal of all restrictions, noting that there was no evidence that pornography was harmful even to juveniles. The findings of both the British and American Committees have been severely criticized on the grounds of faulty methodological approach, the type of data examined,[103] and inherent sexual bias.[104]

Harm to Participants

Another harm that feminists consider significant is that suffered by those involved in the production of pornography. Lederer's research confirms that many runaway girls are used in the production of pornography because they have no other means of livelihood. She notes the coercion used to secure their participation and the evidence of venereal disease and psychological damage that results from employment as a pornographic model.[105] Similar findings appear in other research on adult participants in pornography.[106]

---

100. *Op. cit.,* p. 1275, *supra,* note 79.
101. Report of the Committee on Obscenity and Film Censorship, Home Office, 1979, p. 68.
102. Report of the Presidential Commission on Obscenity and Pornography (Washington, D.C.: U.S. Government Printing Office (1971), p. 32.)
103. For example, see Bart and Jozsa (1980), *supra,* note 48 and Donnerstein (1983), *supra,* note 94.
104. McCormick, ''Machismo in Media Research: A Critical Review of Research on Violence and Pornography'', *Social Problems,* Vol. 25, No. 5, June (1978) p. 544.
105. L. Lederer, ''An Interview with a Former Pornography Model'', *op. cit.,* p. 57-70.
106. K. Barry, Femal Sexual Slavery (1979); Crimes Against Women: Proceedings of the International Tribunal (D. Russell & N. Van de Ven eds. 1976).

In summary, the feminist contention that pornography causes harm is supported by three arguments:

(1)　Oppression and exploitation of women and children is reinforced by the dissemination of distorted perceptions about female nature.

(2)　Some women and children become real-life victims of crimes of violence in which pornography is implicated.[107]

(3)　Women and children who participate in the production of pornography are degraded and abused.

Harm to Society

A fourth argument advanced by feminists is that pornography harms society because it is a form of hate propaganda.[108] Society suffers harm because hatred contributes to the destruction of a free and democratic society. When members of a society are encouraged to hate each other, democracy disintegrates.

Conclusion

If the "clear and present danger" test were used for obscenity, a kind of pornographic anarchy with complete freedom of expression for pornographic materials would be the inevitable result. Sociological and psychological studies are not capable of making the necessary connection between pornography and direct harm to satisfy the test, other than in child pornography or in violent pornography where it can be proven that actual harm occurs. In order to establish a "clear and present danger", the Crown would have to show that watching a pornographic video or movie would cause people to rush from the theatres to rape or murder. This is ludicrous. Any examination of the scientific data makes it clear that pornography's effects are far more subtle. The effects discussed earlier in this article,[109] and supported by scientific evidence, are the promotion of an ideology that fosters and supports sexual aggression. This helps to create and maintain a climate that is more likely to tolerate the actual physical abuse of women, and in which opportunities for women are limited.

The concept of pornography as sexual discrimination was accepted in the recent case of *Saskatchewan Human Rights Commission* v. *Engineering Students' Soc'y*.[110]

107.　D.E.H. Russell, "Pornography and Violence: What Does the New Research Say?", L. Lederer ed., *op. cit.* 218.

108.　For example, see, J. Riddington, *Discussion Paper on Pornography*, prepared for National Action Committee on the Status of Women, March 1983; E. Wachtel, "Our Newest Battleground: Pornography" (1979), 63 *Branching Out* 33, at p. 35; A. Dworkin, *Women Hating* (1976).

109.　See notes 85-107 and accompanying text *supra*.

110.　5 C.H.R.R. p. 2074 (Sask. Human Rights Code Bd. of Inquiry 1984).

The Human Rights Commission alleged that a newspaper regularly published by the student Engineering Society ridiculed, belittled and affronted the dignity of women contrary to s. 14 of the *Saskatchewan Human Rights Code*.[111] The Board held that the publication, which promoted violent and demeaning treatment of women, contravened the *Code* because it interfered with women's rights to equal enjoyment of education, employment and security of the person. The Board further held that the protection of women's equality rights outweighed the right to freedom of expression, guaranteed in the *Canadian Charter of Rights and Freedoms* and in the *Saskatchewan Human Rights Code*.[112]

This decision clearly reflects a concept of rights not as absolutes, but as reciprocal and proportionate to other rights. The liberal approach tends to view freedom of expression as an absolute right that is a function of each individual rather than of a reciprocal relationship between individuals. The feminist concept of the equal value of all human beings requires that limits be placed on freedom of expression with respect to pornography. The real evil of pornography is not that it violates chastity but that it portrays women and children simply as instruments of pleasure for men, thereby denying their value as individual human beings.[113]

THE RESPONSE OF THE COURTS

In this section, obscenity cases are examined in light of underlying moral rationales. Do the courts protect the liberal, conservative or feminist moralities or have they adopted a morality of their own? Common law definitions of obscenity and pornography are examined and compared to the feminist definitions. The failure of the courts to acknowledge violence as a component of the obscenity definition is examined. Finally, the community standards test is explained and criticized as being both conceptually unsound and unfairly applied.

Definitions of Pornography

From time to time, judges have attempted to distinguish between ''pornography'' and ''obscenity''. The majority of the Manitoba Court of Appeal in *R*. v. *Dominion News and Gifts (1962) Ltd.*[114] in *obiter*

---

111. S.S. 1979, c. S-24.1, s. 14.
112. A similar approach was taken in *Rasheed and Black United Front* v. *Bramhill* (1980), 2 C.H.R.R. 249 at 252 (N.S. Human Rights Act Bd. of Inquiry 1980), a case where racial depictions on a badge were found to offend the *Human Rights Act*, S.N.S. 1969, c. 11. The Board said:
    ''In particular cases, the right of free speech may have to give way to other human rights, such as the right not to be discriminated against...''
113. For a discussion of value reciprocity, see R.J. Henle & A. Rosenbaum, *The Philosophy of Human Rights: International Perspectives*, p. 87-93 (1980).
114. [1963] 2 C.C.C. 103, 42 W.W.R. 65 (Man. C.A.).

dicta said a publication did not have to be pornographic to be obscene, and that sex in itself was not obscene. Unfortunately the Court did not elaborate on its concept of "pornography". However, it appeared to indicate that pornography is something worse than obscenity. In *R. v. Odeon Morton Theatres Ltd. et al.* Provincial Court Judge Enns defined pornography as:

> [t]hat complete depiction of every conceivable kind of carnal connection between humans or humans and animals vividly portrayed in close-up views.[115]

On appeal, the Manitoba Court of Appeal did not dispute this definition.

Another definition of "hard-core" pornography is cited by Professor Charles in *Obscene Literature and the Legal Process in Canada*:

> ...[H]ard core pornography does not usually have much of a story line, and insofar as it does, this only serves as a flimsy frame on which to hang a series of erotic incidents. Hard core pornography also either neglects altogether or underplays characterization of the persons in the story, descriptions of surrounding, philosophical or political discussions, and so forth. This is done to provide for maximum erotic concentration in the story.[116]

In *R. v. Prairie Schooner News Ltd. et al.*; Freedman C.J.M., in finding the publications before him to be obscene, cited the above definition and held that the books in the case before him conformed to the "standard formula of hard core pornography".[117] It is evident that Chief Justice Freedman was also of the view that erotic depictions could amount to hard-core pornography.

In the United States, as in Canada, attempts by judges to define pornography have not met with much success. In *Jacobellis* v. *Ohio*, Mr. Justice Stewart, in referring to "hard-core" pornography, said:

> I shall not today attempt further to define the kinds of material I understand to be embraced within that shorthand description; and perhaps I can never succeed in intelligibly doing so. But I know it when I see it...[118]

Definitions attempted by the various courts have considered pornography from the female perspective only very recently. They most often fail to consider the context within which pornography is shown or what it means to women generally. Instead, they examine each depiction on the basis of offence to the sensibilities of the viewer. The degree of explicitness is usually the ultimate criterion in determining

---

115. 16 C.C.C. (2d) 185, at 198, [1974] 3 W.W.R. 304 at 316 (Man. C.A.), citing the unreported provincial court decision.

116. Charles, "Obscene Literature and the Legal Process in Canada", 44 *Can. B. Rev.* 243, at. 277 (1966).

117. *Supra,* note 56, at 258, 75 W.W.R. at 592.

118. 378 U.S. 184, at 197 (1964).

whether a depiction is "pornographic" or unduly exploitive. The endorsement of violence, coercion and degradation, the critical elements of the feminist definition, has rarely been considered in judicial attempts to define pornography.

Definitions of Obscenity

Both liberal and conservative arguments have been heard in courts of law for more than 250 years so it is not surprising that their views are reflected in the legal decisions. The traditional demarcation between the two was noted as early as the eighteenth century decision in *R. v. Curl*.[119] However, a legal definition of obscenity was not established until 1868, in the case of *Regina v. Hicklin*.[120] One can only presume that up until that time the meaning of obscenity was universally agreed upon, and thus the need for a legal definition was not apparent. The publication found to be obscene in *Hicklin* was an anti-Catholic pamphlet that suggested illicit sexual behavior between priests and female parishioners. In his decision, Cockburn, C.J. defined obscenity as:

> the tendency of the matter charged... to deprave and corrupt those whose minds are open to such immoral influences and into whose hands a publication of this sort may fall.[121]

The *Hicklin* test of obscenity survived in England until 1954[122] and in Canada until 1959, when the Parliament of Canada enacted its own definition.[123] The present Canadian definition of criminally obscene material provides that:

> Any publication, a dominant characteristic of which is the undue exploitation of sex, or of sex and any one or more of the following subjects, namely, crime, horror, cruelty and violence, shall be deemed to be obscene.[124]

By enacting the legislation, Parliament appeared to depart from the traditional emphasis on the immorality of explicit sex. Parliament enlarged the definition of obscenity to include the portrayal of certain forms of violence if accompanied by the undue exploitation of sex. Violence could not by itself be obscene. This became known as the "sex plus" requirement and its effect was to limit the reach of the obscenity law to sexual depictions.[125]

---

119. *Supra*, note 21.

120. L.R. 3 Q.B. 360 (1868).

121. *Id.*, at 371.

122. *R. v. Martin Secker Warburg*, [1954] 2 All E.R. 683, [1954] 1 W.L.R. 1138 (Cent. Crim. Ct.).

123. *An Act to Amend the Criminal Code*, S.C. 1959, c. 40, s. 11.

124. R.C.S. 1970, c. C-34, sub. 159(8).

125. In England this is not the case. In *John Calder (Publications) Ltd. v. Powell*, [1965] 1 Q.B. 509, [1965] 1 All E.R. 159 (1964), it was held that a book advocating drug use had the tendency to deprave and corrupt and was, therefore,

In 1962, the majority of the Supreme Court of Canada held that the new definition was the exclusive test of obscenity, thereby rendering the *Hicklin* test obsolete.[126] The cornerstone of the definition of obscenity became the "undue exploitation of sex" rather than the "tendency to deprave and corrupt". Community standards were to determine whether or not the exploitation of sex was "undue", but because the crown was not required to adduce evidence of community standards, this determination was often made by the judge based on his understanding and appreciation of community levels of tolerance. It is apparent from a review of the case law that the term "undue exploitation of sex" in the new definition came to be interpreted as nothing more than the degree of explicitness of sexual depiction. The definition's additional categories of sex combined with cruelty, violence, horror and crime were largely ignored by the courts. Certainly the impact of sexual depictions on equality was not analyzed or commented upon. It is also apparent that in recent obscenity cases, the courts have shifted from a conservative to a liberal approach. This has, by and large, resulted in greater permissiveness.

The liberal view was emphasized in *R. v. C. Coles Co. Ltd.*, a case involving the book *Fanny Hill, Memoirs of a Woman of Pleasure*, which described the activities of a prostitute[127]. Chief Justice Porter stated that the freedom to describe human life with complete candor is fundamental to the progress of a free society and should not be curtailed unless "extreme circumstances" exist. The majority of the Court was of the view that the book had historical and literary merit and lacked the degree of pruriency required to render it obscene. Roach, J.A., in dissent, adopted the classic conservative view. In his judgment he said the book in question "descends to the lowest possible level of impurity or lust in that it is a deification of the phallus.... It is plain, unvarnished dirt for dirt's sake."[128]

Mr. Justice Roach Further stated that:

[s]adism, beastiality, cruelty and crime are not necessary ingredients of pornography if that term is to be equated with obscenity.[129]

Similar emphasis on the degree of sexual explicitness as the critical factor of illegality is evident in cases decided pursuant to customs legislation. Section 14 of the *Customs Tariff* reads:

---

obscene. Later, in *R. v. Calder & Boyars Ltd.*, [1969] 1 Q.B. 151, [1968] 3 All E.R. 644 (C.A. 1968), it was held that violence *per se* was obscene, a finding similar to that in *D.P.P. v. A. & B.C. Chewing Gum Ltd.*, [1968] 1 Q.B. 159, [1967] 2 All E.R. 504 (1967).

126. *Brodie* v. *The Queen*, [1962] S.C.R. 681, 32 D.L.R. (3d) 507.

127. [1965] 1 O.R. 557, [1965] 2 C.C.C. 304 (C.A. 1964).

128. *Id.*, at 573, [1965] 2 C.C.C. at 322-323.

129. *Id.*, at 572, [1965] 2 C.C.C. at 322.

The importation into Canada of any goods enumerated, described or referred to in Schedule C is prohibited... .[130]

The provisions of tariff item 99201-1 of Schedule C (prohibited goods) reads as follows:

Books, printed papers, drawings, paintings, prints, photographs or representations of any kind of ... an immoral or indecent character.[131]

This section was recently challenged in the case of *Re Luscher and Deputy Minister, Revenue Canada.*[132] A magazine, brought from the U.S. into Canada, was wholly concerned with sexual activity between a man and a woman. The Lower Court found that, although the actions contained in the magazine were in no way unnatural or unlawful and were a common part of the lives of Canadian men and women, they were immoral and indecent. He gave immoral and indecent their dictionary definitions of "morally evil", "dissolute", "wicked", "lewd", "unchaste", "in extremely bad taste", "suggestive or tending to obscenity", "disgusting" and "obscene", saying that these words must be applied in light of contemporary moral or ethical standards. Similar magazines were presented to the judge as evidence of contemporary community standards in British Columbia. The judge found all the exhibits tasteless but said that:

[n]one of them feature such explicit sexual activity as the magazine in question.[133]

Although violence was not an issue in the case, the Court was clearly deciding whether the material was obscene on the basis of the degree of sexual explicitness in the magazine.[134]

A suggestion that something other than explicit sex could be obscene (and therefore harmful) was finally discussed in the case of *Delorme* v. *The Queen,*[135] which involved the book, *Histoire d'O.* The majority of the Court held that the book was obscene because it contained repeated descriptions of sexual acts - both normal and anormal - accompanied by acts of extreme brutality. The defence of public good failed even though the Court felt that the book might have been of some literary or scientific value in psychology or sexology courses. The fact that it was made available to the general public eliminated any defence

---

130. R.S.C. 1970, c. C-14, s. 14.
131. R.S.C. 1970, c. C-14, sched. C.
132. *Supra*, note 65.
133. *Id.*, at 247.
134. The decision was reversed on other grounds: see note 66 and accompanying text *supra*.
135. 21 C.R.N.S. 305, 15 C.C.C. 350 (Que. C.A. 1973). The Ontario Court of Appeal in *Re Gordon Magazine Enterprises Ltd.*, 46 C.R. 313 (Ont. C.A. 1965), on an appeal from a forfeiture order, held that in the pocket novels seized, sex was a dominant characteristic associated in varying degrees with crime, horror, cruelty and violence. No further analysis was offered by the Court.

of "public good" because the average reader, unsophisticated in psychology or sexology, would derive no "advantage" from the book. The Court's analysis of the defence of "public good" did not consider any negative impact that the book might have on women or on equality between the sexes.

A different approach to violent content was taken in the case of *R. v. Odeon Morton Theatres*.[136] This case concerned the movie "Last Tango in Paris". At trial, the defence called a number of film critics, two professors of English, a stage director and the chairmen of the Manitoba and Ontario film classification boards. None of the experts found the movie to be obscene, but a dissenting judge in the Court of Appeal, Mr. Justice Monnin, found that the most surprising aspect of the expert testimony at trial was the opinion that no violence occurred in the film. He quoted from the transcript:

Q	Did you find a combination of - we will just say the exploitation of sex, we won't say "undue", but did you see in your assessment of "Tango" an exploitation of sex in conjunction with violence?
A	First, I see no violence in "Last Tango". Secondly, I see no exploitation of sex. I don't like the word "exploitation".
Q	Do I understand, Father Pungente, that you saw no violence in the film?
A	No.
Q	Do I understand then that in your view the simulated anal intercourse scene did not have any element of violence whatsoever?
A	I don't see that as violence, no.
THE COURT:	I have listened for a long time; are you seriously suggesting that scene, no matter if it is symbolic, or what symbolic means, then suggests nothing of violence at all? It suggested no protesting, screaming, almost shrieking, hurt her, of this brutal pinning of her down, holding her arms down? Do you suggest that is all nothing, is not suggestive of violence; is that sincerely your view?
THE WITNESS:	No, when you explain it like that, your honour, that I understand, yes. Well, I'm sorry, what I was understanding Mr. Montgomery to mean is the type of violence in films today.
THE COURT:	You are talking of sub machine guns and -
THE WITNESS:	Pulling people's stomachs apart, ripping them open, burning them alive.

---

136. *Supra*, note 115.

THE COURT: I see. With a strong force of violence.
THE WITNESS: With a force such as you express it, I understand it
                  better, yes.[137]

This exchange is a good example of how certain male perceptions of violence can exclude the consideration of female reality. Thelma McCormick describes this recurring phenomenon as "machismo". She says,

> Machismo refers to an attitude of male pride in sexual virility, a form of narcissism that condones the sexual use and abuse of women, and, in the extreme, violence as a dimension of sexual gratification or instrumental to sexual goals.[138]

In the foregoing example, "machismo" is arguably occurring at two levels - in the movie itself, and in the witness box. Mr. Justice Monnin disagreed with the experts when he concluded that:

> [O]n the basis of the transcript as it appears, the exhibits as I have read or seen, the film is unduly exploitive of sex and that by virtue of this undue exploitation, coupled with a degree of violence in language and in acts which can be seen or heard through the 129 minutes of it, the film is deemed to be obscene pursuant to s. 159(8).[139]

Even though Monnin and Guy JJ.A. thought the violence was obscene, the majority of the Court dismissed the appeal and concluded that there was no error of law on the face of the record. However, Chief Justice Freedman, in *obiter dicta,* commented on the merits of the Crown's Appeal. Violence was not specifically considered in his analysis; it merely became part of the sexual activity in the film. He looked at the "internal necessities" of the film and found that the sexual scenes were justified. He also compared the degree of sexual explicitness in *Last Tango in Paris* with "skin-flicks" and found that there were far more explicit films being shown in various parts of Canada and that, therefore, it would be "particularly unfair" to find *Last Tango in Paris* obscene.

In recent lower court decisions, more attention has been directed toward depictions that combine sex and violence. In *R.* v. *McCormick*,[140] where homosexual acts were depicted in photographs showing juvenile boys engaged in fellatio and sadomasochistic activities, the Court said that the depictions combined sex with cruelty and violence and were thus obscene.

Degradation and dehumanization in the context of sexual depictions were specifically discussed for the first time in the case of *R.* v.

---

137. *Id.,* at 205, [1974] 3 W.W.R. at 323-24.
138. *Supra,* note 104, at 545.
139. *Supra,* note 115, at 208, [1974] 3 W.W.R. at 327.
140. Unreported, Ont. Cty. Ct., 10 Jan. 1980.

Doug Rankine Co. Ltd. et al.[141] Mr. Justice Borins of the Ontario County Court held that videotapes for private home use were obscene when they consisted:

> [s]ubstantially or partially of scenes which portray violence and cruelty in conjunction with sex, particularly where the performance of indignities degrade and dehumanize the people upon whom they are performed...[142]

The *Rankine* case represents the first time a Canadian Court has examined an allegedly obscene depiction specifically from the point of view of the victims of the sexual abuse, rather than of the sensibilities of the observers. Mr. Justice Borins, however, still maintained that a high degree of explicit sex is obscene. He stated that:

> As for the other films which I am satisfied are obscene and which do not contain scenes of sex and violence and cruelty, it is the degree of explicitness of the sexual act which leads me to the conclusion that they exceed community standards.[143]

In *R. v. Ramsingh*,[144] another case involving home video cassettes, the Manitoba Court of Queen's Bench appears to have taken Mr. Justice Borins' analysis one step further. While Borins J. would require that sex and violence be accompanied by degradation and dehumanization in order to find depictions obscene, Ferg J. in *Ramsingh* suggested that degradation and dehumanization alone could be obscene. He commented:

> As well, I think that where violence is portrayed with sex, *or* where there are people, particularly women, subjected to any thing which degrades or dehumanizes them, the community standard is exceeded, even when the viewing may occur in one's private home.[145]

In a recent landmark decision in Alberta,[146] the feminist analysis of obscenity laws and morality seems to have been adopted. The general principles set forth in *Rankine*[147] and *Ramsingh*[148] were applied in the case, but several new approaches were taken as well. In his analysis of the meaning of "undue exploitation of sex", Shannon J. of the Alberta Court of Queen's Bench distinguished three different types of sexually explicit material: violent, non-violent but degrading and dehumanizing, and erotica. He described the three categories in detail, providing exam-

---

141. 9 C.C.C. (3d) 53 (Ont. Cty. Ct., Jul., (1983). In *R. v. Intercity News Co.* (unreported, Ont. Prov. Ct., 1982), a magazine was found to be obscene where the Court found an article "display[ing] violent and abnormal sex in an objectionable and repulsive manner."
142. *Id.*, at 70.
143. *Id.*
144. *Supra*, note 62.
145. *Id.*, at 240.
146. *R. v. Wagner* (1985), 43 C.R. (3d) 318, 36 Alta L.R. (2d) 301 (Q.B.).
147. *Supra*, note 141.
148. *Supra*, note 62.

ples of each, and held that the Canadian community will tolerate erotica, but not material falling into the other two categories. Unlike Borins J. in *Rankine,* Shannon J. was of the opinion that explicit sex *per
se* is not obscene. He said that "[i]t is the message that counts, not the
degree of explicitness".[149] By emphasizing "the message", the Court
is saying that the context of the sexual depictions is the paramount
consideration.

With the exception of the recent trial court decisions and dissenting
opinions cited above, judicial acknowledgement of violence in obscenity is rare. At the Appeal Court level, the degree of explicitness of a
sexual depiction is still the most important factor in deciding whether
or not an obscenity finding will be made. It remains to be seen whether
or not appeal courts will change their view that the "harm" of obscene
depictions lies, by and large, in their explicitness. Mr. Justice Shannon's decision has provided the courts with the opportunity of assessing
the social harm caused by pornography.[150] In dealing with the *Charter*
argument that subsection 159(8) of the *Criminal Code*[151] is an unwarranted infringement on the freedom of expression, Shannon J. held[152]
that the obscenity section came within the saving provision of section I
of the *Charter* because of the social harm that results from viewing
obscenity. He held that sexually violent or degrading and dehumanizing
pornography causes social harm to women. He accepted evidence that
men repeatedly exposed to such depictions become calloused towards
women and are less receptive to their claims for equality. By relying
on social science evidence and by identifying social harm as a justification for infringements of subsection 2(b) of the *Charter*, Shannon J.
added a new dimension to the type of evidence usually heard in obscenity cases. This development is very much in line with the view that
courts should, in interpreting the *Charter*, consider the social, economic and political context of Canadian Society.[153]

The Community Standards Test

Its Development[154]

In 1964, the Supreme Court of Canada adopted Manitoba Chief
Justice Freedman's dissenting opinion on the question of community

---

149. *Supra,* note 146.
150. The B.C.C.A. in *Red Hot Video* v. *The Queen* (1985), 45 C.R. (3d) 36 (B.C.C.A.)
     adopted the Shannon approach and found that violent and degrading depictions
     in pornography adversely affect women's right to equality.
151. R.S.C. 1970, c. C-34, sub. 159(8).
152. *Supra,* note 146.
153. Gibson, *Interpretation of the Canadian Charter of Rights and Freedoms: Some
     General Considerations,* in *Canadian Charter of Rights and Freedoms* 25, at 27
     (W. Tarnopolsky & G. Beaudoin eds. 1982).
154. For a thorough discussion on the recent developments of obscenity law in Canada,
     see M. Manning, *Rights, Freedoms and the Courts* 1983.

standards in the case of *Dominion News and Gifts (1962) Ltd.* v. *The Queen.*[155] These standards were not to be set by those individuals of lowest taste or interest. Nor were they to be set exclusively by those of rigid, austere, conservative or puritan taste and habit of mind. In stating that the general average of community thinking was to be the standard, Freedman, C.J.M. also held that in borderline cases, tolerance was to be preferred to proscription because to do otherwise might inhibit creative endeavors.[156] This decision marked a significant departure from the conservative espousing of a single moral ethic, in favor of the liberal view of free expression, using the community standards test as the vehicle of change.

The *Coles*[157] case established that the literary purpose and merit of a publication, viewed as a whole, was to be considered, as was its author's or creator's motive. The Supreme Court of Canada in *Dechow* v. *The Queen*[158] added that the test of "undueness" was to be the objective standard of the contemporary Canadian community as a whole. In *R.* v. *Prairie Schooner News Ltd.* the Manitoba Court of Appeal said that expert testimony regarding community attitudes was admissible and desirable, as were public opinion surveys, as long as proper methods were used and the materials were introduced through an expert in the field of opinion research.[159] In *R.* v. *Sudbury News Service Ltd.* the Ontario Court of Appeal said that the manner and circumstances in which printed material were also relevant to the community level of tolerance.[160] In *R.* v. *Times Square Cinema Ltd.,*[161] the community standard was described as the instinctive sense of decency of the average contemporary Canadian. The Court in *R.* v. *MacLean and MacLean (No. 2)* identified the relevant factors to be taken into account where theatrical performances are challenged:

> (1) the locale of the performance; (2) the forewarning of the public of the nature of the performance; (3) the condition of admission; (4) the size and nature and the extent of the reception of the audience to the particular performance and to similar performances.[162]

The Court added that the performer's purpose in giving the performance should also be considered.

155. [1964] S.C.R. 251, [1964] 3 C.C.C.1, *Rev'g. Dominion News, supra,* note 114.
156. *Supra,* note 114, at 116-17, 42 W.W.R. at 79-80.
157. *Supra,* note 127.
158. [1978] 1 S.C.R. 951, 76 D.L.R. (3d) 1.
159. *Supra,* note 56, at 265, 75 W.W.R. at 599.
160. 18 O.R. (2d) 428, at 435, 39 C.C.C. (2d) 1, at 8 (C.A. 1978).
161. [1971] 3 O.R. 688, 4 C.C.C. (2d) 229 (C.A.).
162. 1 C.C.C. (3d) 412, at 414-15 (Ont. C.A. 1982), *leave to appeal denied,* [1982] 2 S.C.R. x, 1 C.C.C. (2d) at 412n-13n.

A Feminist Critique of the Community Standards Test

The community standards criterion appears, at first blush, to fulfill the requirement of the web. Judicial analysis of the impact of obscene material on the community seems to address women's need to have the court look beyond the narrow confines of strict legal interpretation at evidence of real harm to real people. However, the test has not in fact fulfilled this function.[163] It has resulted in a downward spiral of increasing permissiveness because the only evidence actually considered comes from the side of the ladder. As support for the liberal ideology grows, it has become increasingly difficult for the courts to find material "obscene" on the basis of the old-fashioned conservative view. When the view from the web is not heard,[164] there is very little, in permissive society, that can be found to be obscene.

Experts often testify to the community's increasing tolerance of sexual material by referring to its widespread availability. For example, in *R. v. Campbell*, the judge commented that:

> [t]he evidence of Professor Haines was to the effect that all of these periodicals were acceptable to the community and that their availability on the newsstands indicated such.[165]

Chief Justice Freedman also used widespread availability as one of his reasons for judgment:

> In a situation where films of the "skin-flick" character are being shown in various parts of Canada with the apparent acquiescence of the agencies of prosecution it would be particularly unfair to proscribe "Last Tango" as obscene.[166]

This method of analysis is circular. Offending material cannot be taken off the streets until it is deemed obscene, but if it is on the streets it cannot be obscene because its presence indicates that the community accepts it. Since most pornography is imported[167] into Canada and because the standards applied under the *Customs Tariff*[168] were less stringent than those in the *Criminal Code*,[169] standards are constantly lowered and foreign pornographers were provided with an incentive to flood the Canadian market with increasingly "harder-core" material. When acceptance into the marketplace is the admissible evidence of

---

163. However, the new development in the case of *R. v. Wagner, supra,* note 147 is encouraging.
164. Except in *Pei-Yuan v. The Queen,* 8 C.C.C. (3d) 399, 30 D.L.R. (3d) 57 (B.C. Cty. Ct. 1972).
165. 17 C.C.C. (2d) 130, at 135 (Ont. Cty. Ct. 1974) Fogarty J.
166. *Supra,* note 115, at 197, [1974] 3 W.W.R. at 315.
167. Fox, "Obscenity", 12 *Alta L. Rev.* 172, at 212-13 (1974).
168. R.S.C. 1970, c. C-14. The standard of "indecent and immoral", having been struck down by the Federal Court of Appeal in *Luscher, supra,* note 66, was recently replaced by the *Criminal Code* standard discussed at note 67 and accompanying text, *supra.*
169. R.S.C. 1970, c. C-34. *See supra,* note 164.

community standards, a two-way relationship develops between the judiciary or other censoring bodies on the one hand, and authors, publishers and producers on the other. What "just makes it" today is the standard fare tomorrow, which in turn will be used to determine what can "just make it" the day after tomorrow.

Another aspect of the pornography trade that the "marketplace" analysis overlooks is the fact that large quantities of pornography are smuggled into the country.[170] Often numerous copies are made for distribution and sale.[171] These materials then circulate in the community. To use the mere presence of these materials as evidence of community standards is to abdicate the responsibility of applying any standards at all.

The trial court judge in *R. v. Odeon Morton Theatres Ltd.* recognized the problem of the downward spiral of standards. He said:

> What must surely be the concern of the judiciary is that wittingly or not, by being the final arbiter in the assessing of prevailing community standards of acceptance with each decision, in a sense, a new level of acceptance, is, so to speak, officially sanctioned; which then in turn encourages even further degrees of permissiveness to evolve. While the law simply demands that courts mirror the prevailing community standards, by this argument they indeed become allies to the cause of increasing and legal exploitation of sex.[172]

The Court of Appeal disagreed, stating there were at least as many convictions for obscenity as there were acquittals.[173] The Court failed to recognize that the number of convictions does not necessarily address the issue of lowering standards of permissiveness.

In obscenity cases involving theatrical performances, judges often look to audience reaction as a measure of community standards. In *R. v. Kleppe*, the Court held that:

> The law now seems to say that if a performance does not offend the audience that chooses to watch it, it is not obscene. Is simulated sexual intercourse before an uncomplaining audience obscene? Who is being offended? Is it as bad and as offensive as a man who, much to the displeasure of those around him on a bus, insists on smoking a very cheap and foul-smelling cigar?[174]

In *R. v. Heathcote et al.*[175] the judge dismissed charges against participants in a performance because the 26 men who attended the

---

170. *Supra,* note 79, at 1168-69.

171. J. Riddington, *supra,* note 108, at 19.

172. *Supra* note 115, at 198, [1974] 3 W.W.R. at 316 (Monnin J.A.), *citing* the unreported provincial court decision.

173. *Id.,* at 189, [1974] 3 W.W.R. at 308 (Freedman C.J.M.).

174. 35 C.C.C. (2d) 168, at 174 (Ont. Prov. Ct. 1977).

175. Unreported Ont. Prov. Ct., Jul. 1982.

show did not seem offended in the least by the women's actions. In *R.* v. *Gray*[176] a case involving a charge of public nudity, the judge found that there was evidence to indicate that the appellant's performance did not offend public decency , that it was tolerated "in the milieu in which it occurred" and that none of the spectators showed any disapproval of it.

When this evidence is used to determine community standards, the standards of those who would not attend such performances are ignored.[177] Studies indicate that pornography is produced for, and caters to, the male consumer.[178] It is also true that most of those involved in the manufacture and control of pornography are male. The manufacturers, the police, the expert witnesses, the prosecutors and the judges, are key participants in the determination of community standards. Women are not heard when it is decided whether or not there has been "undue" exploitation of the female body.[179] By applying the community standards test in the manner described above, judges are imposing the standard of the man in the Clapham omnibus, but not that of the woman sitting beside him. Women are forced to accept a standard that does not consider their views, but victimizes and exploits them instead.

In a recent case where women were called upon to testify as to community standards, defence counsel argued that their evidence should be disregarded because they were presenting a "fashionable notion of militant feminism".[180] To his credit, Mr. Justice Borins responded:

> A woman does not have to be a "militant feminist" to be intolerant of what is portrayed in many of the films before the court. Nor does a woman have to be a "militant feminist", or any other type of feminist, to believe that the distribution of such films would be unacceptable on the basis of current community standards. She need only be a person who respects the dignity of life and rejects those who seek to degrade it.[181]

---

176. 65 C.C.C. (2d) 353 (Ont. H.C. 1982).
177. In most of the leading cases on obscenity, evidence of community standards put before the courts has been from male expert witnesses. *See* e.g.; *Coles, supra,* note 127; *Prairie Schooner, supra,* note 56; *Brodie* v. *The Queen, supra,* note 126; *Delorme* v. *The Queen, supra,* note 134; *R.* v. *Great West News Ltd.,* [1970] 4 C.C.C. 307, 72 W.W.R. 354 (Man. C.A.); *Dominion News, supra* note 114.
178. Berl Kutchinsky, *Pornography in Denmark - A General Survey of Censorship and Obscenity* in *Censorship and Obscenity*, eds. Rajeev Dhavan and Christie Davies, *op. cit.,* p. 76.
179. There are some exceptions to this approach. In *R.* v. *Campbell* (1974), 17 C.C.C. (2d) 130, the Ontario County Court agreed that those who voluntarily attend performances do not set community standards. The Ontario Provincial Court in *R.* v. *Giambalvo* (1981), 63 C.C.C. (2d) 122, rev'd 39 O.R. (2d) 588, 70 C.C.C. (2d) 324 (C.A. 1982), also held that generally accepted standards of modesty and decency could not be set aside merely to pander to the tastes of people who attended the performance.
180. *Supra,* note 141, at 56.
181. *Id.*

Another problem associated with the community standards test is that the Crown is not required to adduce evidence of community standards.[182] In light of the lack of sensitivity and awareness sometimes displayed by witnesses and judges to the views that women generally hold, it would be preferable if the Crown was required to adduce evidence of community standards, provided that the evidence adduced represented the whole community and not just the male portion of it. As Mr. Justice Dickson (as he then was) stated, "[t]he area is treacherously subjective."[183].

Mr. Justice Shannon in the *Wagner*[184] case identified an inherent weakness in the community standards test when it is used to describe the general attitudes of Canadians to obscenity. An expert witness for the defence testified that Canadians generally are very liberal when it comes to judging what sexual materials their neighbours can consume. However, he also admitted that most Canadians are unaware of the content of modern pornography. Mr. Justice Shannon concluded from this admission that, if most Canadians are unaware of what they profess to tolerate, such uninformed attitudes have little value as indicators of community standards. By using this mode of analysis, Shannon J. seems to be questioning the "presence in the market place" criterion as an indicator of community acceptance. Arguably, he is suggesting that in the future, the evidence of informed citizens or citizens' groups be treated as more accurately reflective of community standards than the evidence that traditionally has been relied upon. If this analysis is followed in future cases it will encourage the Crown to call evidence of community standards from informed sources.

Conclusion

If the community standards test is to be used to determine what will or will not be banned, a greater effort should be made to determine what the standards are in the real community, one composed of both men and women. Otherwise, the *laissez-faire* attitude toward community standards, where men generally establish what is acceptable, assumes that there is only one kind of social experience and interpretation. The morality of the web, which abhors violence, coercion, degradation and child abuse, is not adequately reflected in the community standards that so far have been defined in the case law. Susan Brownmiller succinctly states the feminist standard:

---

182. *See, e.g., Coles, supra,* note 127; *Brodie* v. *The Queen, supra,* 126; *Great West, supra,* note 177.
183. *R.* v. *Great West News Ltd., id.,* at 309, 72 W.W.R. at 355.
184. *Supra,* note 146.

... We are unalterably opposed to the presentation of the female body being stripped, bound, raped, tortured, mutilated and murdered in the name of commercial entertainment and free speech.[185]

If evidence were required from a truly representative sample of the community in order to determine the community standard, the courts would arrive at a more complex construction of human experience. The moralities of both separation and attachment would be brought to bear on the obscenity issue and, more important, the courts would recognize the integrity of two separate approaches to existence that represent equally valuable truths.

To continue to emphasize explicit sex as the governing criterion for "undue exploitation of sex" in the definition of obscenity, is to use a consideration that is irrelevant in light of modern pornography and modern morality. The elements of crime, horror, cruelty and violence in the sexual context are of far greater importance. Two alternative interpretations of subsection 159(8) are possible. First, "undue exploitation" in subsection 159(8) could be interpreted as applying only to "undue exploitation of sex". The remainder of the section, which reads,

...[o]r of sex and any one or more of the following subjects, namely, crime, horror, cruelty and violence, shall be deemed to be obscene.[186]

could be interpreted as not requiring "undue exploitation". This interpretation makes sense because if undue exploitation of sex (*i.e.* explicit sex) is the governing factor for an obscenity ruling, then the words following "or" are superfluous. Furthermore, it is arguable that if the drafters of the legislation intended to have the words "undue exploitation" modify all the subsequent words, they would have put a colon after the words "exploitation of" and then listed the proscribed grounds. The difficulty with this interpretation, however, is the presence of the word "of", before the words "sex and any one or more of the following." Grammatically, "of" properly refers to "undue exploitation."

Furthermore, to eliminate the words "undue exploitation" as a modifier would be to eliminate the community standards test from the latter half of the definition. This result could create more problems than it would solve.

A second, and perhaps more workable solution would be to consider material containing sex and violence or any one of the other enumerated criteria, as a different kind of obscenity in which the "undueness" requirement could be satisfied by something less than explicit sex. Arguably, the presence of the other elements of violence, crime, horror, and cruelty, add a different meaning to the words "undue exploitation". This argument is particularly persuasive when one considers scientific evidence that certain depictions of violence in a

185. Brownmiller, *Let's Put Pornography Back in the Closet,* in Take Back the Night: Women on Pornography, p. 254 (L. Lederer ed. 1980).
186. Criminal Code, R.S.C. 1970, c. C-34, sub. 159(8).

non-explicit sexual context can be harmful.[187] Through this interpretation, depictions that do not include explicit sex, but which are nevertheless violent, degrading or dehumanizing could be found to be obscene.

The approach taken by Borins, Ferg and Shannon JJ. and now the British Columbia Court of Appeal is a step in the right direction.[188] By focusing on the degradation and dehumanization of those portrayed in pornography they have added an important element of context that goes some way to protect the interests of women.

The *Wagner*[189] decision has future ramifications for films shown in commercial theatres. While the Court dealt only with highly sexually explicit films, of a type not usually shown in commercial theatres, it is arguable that its reasoning could be applied to less explicit commercial films that degrade and dehumanize people. By stressing context rather than explicitness, Mr. Justice Shannon gave the impression that he would have found the videos obscene even if they had not contained explicit sex. At one point in his judgement he commented on *The Story of O*, a commercial film offered by the defence as evidence of community standards because it had been approved by the Alberta Board of Censors.

Mr. Justice Shannon in describing the film adopted the words of an expert witness: "It's one of the most violent and degrading films that I have come accross in a long time because the woman submits to incredible brutality and abuse".[190] Although it was not necessary for him to pass judgement on *The Story of O*, his statements, when read with his general comments regarding the context, indicate that he would have found such a film obscene.

CONCLUSION

The concepts of separation and attachment to a great extent shape the pattern of our lives. Professor Gilligan describes their part in reproduction and human development. Because of the different roles that separation and attachment play in the formation of their sexual identity, men and women embody different truths. For the former, separation defines and empowers the self; for the latter, the ongoing process of attachment creates and sustains the human community.[191] The egalitarian principles of the *Canadian Charter of Rights and Freedoms* guarantee equal citizenship for all Canadians. The idea of citizenship that emerges from our present obscenity laws, however, confirms the citizenship of men at the expense of women. The male view, which values separateness and non-interference, is the one that enjoys the most pro-

---

187. *See* notes 89-109 and accompanying text *supra*.
188. *See* notes 136-38, 150, and accompanying text *supra*.
189. *Supra*, note 146.
190. *Id*.
191. *Supra*, note 11, at 156.

tection in the law of obscenity. Individual rights and zones of personal non-interference are assiduously but narrowly protected. Cultural harms are largely ignored, with the result that the integrity of the female experience and female morality is not recognized.

Short of amending the present obscenity provisions in the *Criminal Code*,[192] any significant and meaningful change must come from the courts. To make the "clear and present danger" test the determining factor in deciding whether limits on freedom of expression in pornography are justified would be to ignore the changing role of women in society as well as their perception of justice and morality. Use of this test would ignore precedent and would set a standard that cannot address the very significant social harms scientifically determined and accepted by several government commissions.

The community standards test should be abolished in its present form. As it is applied now, it rarely represents the community standards of people who do not consume pornography, nor does it reflect the standards of web morality. It fails to address the concept of harm articulated by feminist philosophers and commentators and demonstrated by social scientific research. Furthermore, evidence of availability in the marketplace, admissible as evidence of community standards, encourages proliferation of increasingly "harder-core" material in Canadian society. Prevalence in the community should not be considered a relevant factor in identifying community standards.

A number of laws have been altered in recent years in recognition of the fact that the law has not recognized women's interests fairly in the past. Obscenity laws should also change, for in their present state they are outdated and unacceptable. The *Canadian Charter of Rights and Freedoms* is a new legal instrument that provides courts with an opportunity to create new precedent. The act of judging always requires choices among competing interests. In making these choices, judges and legislators should take into account moral conflict in its particular context. This could lead to a changed understanding of human development and to a more generalized view of human life. The association of gender with the web and the ladder is not absolute. The views presented in this article have been described as male/female only to highlight a distinction between the two modes of thought. The focus, regardless of gender, should be on the problem of interpretation, rather than on a generalization about either sex. The ability to discover new approaches to the law is the essence of the "living tree" doctrine often ascribed to constitutional law.

Fear of the unknown often prevents action, yet once changes are made, it is not very long before those changes become a natural and inevitable part of life.

---

192. R.S.C. 1970, c. C-34.

Hate Literature

Irwin Cotler*

John Stuart Mill's essay *On Liberty*,[1] as Dean Harry Wellington reminds us in his seminal article on "Freedom of Expression"[2], begins with an introduction that ends with an apology. As Mill approaches his famous chapter on the liberty of thought and discussion, he writes: "Those to whom nothing which I am about to say will be new, may I hope excuse me if on a subject which for three centuries has been discussed, I venture on one discussion more."[3] One hundred and twenty years later, as Wellington put it in his introduction to his own article, "I too apologize for venturing on one more discussion."[4]

Speaking now five years after Wellington, and one hundred and twenty-five years after Mill, "one discussion more" may well evoke from you the audience — and perhaps validate the subject-matter of this panel — a plea for freedom from expression, or for freedom from more expression on what is freedom of expression. And so if I venture one discussion more it is because I suspect that the presumed antimony of freedom of expression and freedom from expression may really be more dialectical than real.

In a word, and this is the burden of my remarks today, protecting freedom from certain forms of expression, may well be the basis of, and indeed involve fidelity to freedom of expression itself, as both principle and reality. I do not propose — and in any case Alan Borovoy has sought polemically to preempt the attempt — to base my argument on the theory that freedom of expression is not absolute (I will add to Alan Borovoy's characterizations of this argument as banal or trite the reminder that the fact that something is banal does not mean that it is thereby invalid); nor will I regale you with statutory or common law limitations on freedom of expression, so that freedom of expression appears almost as a network of limitations rather than a rights theory.

---

* Faculty of Law, McGill University.
1. J.S. Mill, "On Liberty", in R. McCallum, ed., *On Liberty and Representative Government* (1946).
2. H. Wellington, "On Freedom of Expression" (1979), 88 Yale L.J. 1105.
3. *Supra,* note 1 at 13.
4. *Supra,* note 2 at 1105.

On the contrary, I happen to be one of those who argued on behalf of a *Charter* — and a notion of fundamental freedoms as the most "fundamental" of all freedoms — in order to supplant the prevailing pre-Charter sense of freedom of expression as a theory or ideology of "limitations". It seemed to me that only an entrenched notion of freedom of expression in a charter of rights could supplant the notion of freedom of expression as a "legislative adjunct" of legal federalism, a by-product of a legal culture whose organizing idiom for one hundred and fifteen years was parliamentary sovereignty.

Accordingly, I not only acknowledge Alan Borovoy's characterization of freedom of expression as the "lifeblood of democracy" but I happily embrace it. Indeed, I would venture to refine this rationale, if not go beyond it, to argue that freedom of expression is as much a means of assuring individual self-fulfillment and spiritual liberty as it is a means of safeguarding the democratic process. The rights set forth in s. 2 are not only "fundamental freedoms", but may very well be the condition of all other rights. As a corollary, as Wellington put it, freedom of expression should enjoy greater immunity from government regulation than most forms of human conduct; or, in *Charter* terms, that limitations on freedom of expression should be subject to "strict scrutiny" as suspect prohibitions.

Yet, as Wellington himself acknowledges, though the notion of freedom of expression as a "preferred right" may be an important "first step"[5] towards articulating freedom of expression as a rights theory, it remains only a first step. For a theory of freedom of expression, and that of freedom from expression — which I suggest it otherwise comprehends — must confront the essential question: how do we distinguish protected speech from unprotected speech? What criteria, if any, do we have or can we discern?

Nor is this a matter of "sticks and stones can break my bones but words will never hurt me". We know that speech can hurt. We have learned that words can maim. We have felt the pain as individuals, as vilified members of an identifiable group, of what it means to be the victim of this kind of group vilification. We know, as Wellington put it, that "words can offend, injure reputation, fan prejudice or passion and, regrettably, ignite the world".[6] How then can we determine, for juridical if not also existential purposes, what is to be regarded as protected speech, or, more particularly, how can we distinguish protected from unprotected speech?

Three years ago, shortly after the Proclamation of the *Charter,* groups of civil liberties lawyers and representatives from visible minorities gathered in Vancouver for a Conference on "Race Relations and

---

5. *Supra,* note 2 at 1105.
6. *Supra,* note 2 at 1106.

the Law''. In the course of a discussion on free speech and hate propaganda, some of the civil liberties lawyers advanced the view that the Criminal Code provisions respecting hate propaganda[7] were an infringement of *Charter* provisions respecting freedom of expression, and that, as a result of the *Charter,* may well be unconstitutional.

The reaction of the representatives of the visible minorities was one of shock if not anguish. Their response was immediate: ''We saw the Charter as a protection of our fundamental freedoms... now you tell us that it may be a shield for racists — that it may in fact protect the dissemination of hate propaganda rather than protect us against hate propaganda.'' Added another: ''We've been had... if we had known that this would be the effect of the *Charter,* we never would have lobbied for it... it is disturbing to think that such hate propaganda will now enjoy constitutional protection, and that were it not for the *Charter,* this racism would not be protected at all.''

The anguish — and apprehension — of the representatives of the visible minorities were understandable. As targets for hate propaganda many of them had actually made representations before the Joint House — Senate Committee on the Constitution[8] in support of a *Charter*. They saw in the *Charter* not only a notion of human dignity and, of equality rights, but a protection — a guarantee — against the violation of these rights. For them and indeed for myself — and I found myself at this Conference characterized as both a civil liberties lawyer and a representative from the visible minorities — the *Charter* was a statement of values, an expression of hope, an instrument of redress. Many, including groups on whose behalf I acted and who sought a specific prohibition against hate propaganda written into the *Charter* itself, were assured by its drafters, including the Minister of Justice at the time, that the *Charter* was in effect a manifesto for minority rights.

The position of the civil liberties lawyers, while not unsympathetic to the concerns of the representatives from the visible minorities, was one of overriding concern for freedom of speech. They argued — and it is a position which, as I've said earlier, I not only share but have advocated — that freedom of speech is one of the most fundamental of all rights and titled, appropriately enough, ''fundamental freedoms''; that it is at the foundation of individual liberty and the democratic process; that what was needed was ''more speech, and not less speech''.

My own position, as it evolved then and since, is that there is no necessary contradiction between the civil liberties position and that of the visible minorities. Hate propaganda represents a fundamental assault on human rights and fundamental freedoms. Hate propaganda does not belong to or qualify as protected speech — it gives free speech a bad

---

7. *Criminal Code,* R.S.C. 1970, c. C-34, s.s. 281.1 ff.
8. Special Joint Committee of the Senate and the House of Commons of Canada.

name. Legislation against hate propaganda can be characterized, in effect, as legislation protective of human rights — of human rights law.

Accordingly, I would like to focus on the Criminal Code provisions respecting the dissemination of hate propaganda, not only because I was invited to address this particular issue as a case study in freedom *from* expression, but also because it serves as a case-study in the articulation of the very values that underlie the justification for freedom of expression itself. To put the matter another way, it may serve not only as a case-study of a section 1 limitation on the freedoms set forth in s. 2 of the *Charter*, but as a means of determining or identifying section 2 protected freedoms, and distinguishing thereby protected speech from unprotected speech.

My thesis is this: that there exists a "genre" of expression which lies outside the protection of s. 2, and that this "genre" of expression shares common characteristics that account for and justify that non-protected status. As the United States Supreme Court in the *Chaplinsky*[9] case put it: "There are certain well-defined and narrowly limited classes of speech whose prevention and punishment have never been thought to be raising any constitutional problem". I would suggest, therefore, that there is a discernible category of group vilifying speech that typifies this "genre", the prohibition of which would not breach a s. 2 freedom since it is not protected speech to begin with; however, should this "genre" of speech be somehow characterized *prima facie* as a s. 2 freedom, then I would suggest that the Criminal Code provisions respecting the dissemination of hate propaganda are otherwise "reasonable limitations, prescribed by law, demonstrably justified in a free and democratic society."

How then, does one characterize this "genre"? Is it enough to say that "there are certain well-defined... classes of speech... whose prevention and punishment have never been thought to raise any constitutional problems"? Or that these classes of speech are "limited" to libel, obscenity and fighting words? Are there any identifiable features or criteria that can assist us in recognizing these "well-defined catagories"?

May I submit the following questions or criteria as a normative and juridical framework for identifying the "genre" of this non-protected speech, or distinguishing protected from non-protected speech; or, at the very least, providing us with a means of determining whether these are reasonable limitations demonstrably justified on the expression itself.

1. Does the speech threaten harm to some substantial public interest, i.e. the inherent dignity and worth of the human person, itself a rationale or justification for freedom of expression? I would submit that

---

9. *Chaplinsky* v. *New Hampshire*, 315 U.S. 568 (1942).

the finding by the recent Special Parliamentary Committee on Visible Minorities of a "critical mass" of racist propaganda being disseminated in Canada today constitutes a serious assault on the inherent dignity and worth of the human person. In a word, holding up the target of vilification to public contempt, hatred or disgrace, or causing the target group or its members to be shunned, avoided or abandoned may be as injurious to the community as it is to the target group.

Moreover, the harm caused is not only to the specific target of group vilification, but there is also general demonstrable harm caused in the creation and maintenance of discriminatory attitudes and practices throughout society. The continued vilification of a group combined with the ensuing discrimination may cause members of the target group to have lowered self esteem and have raised levels of responsive aggressiveness which would have the effect of damaging their participation in the political process.

This exercise, then, in the debasement and degradation of the human person — and the target group of which he or she is a member is prejudicial to the very dignity and self-worth of the individual person, the very self-government and democratic process that is the very rationale and justification for freedom of expression itself; and that is why I say that there is no inherent contradiction in freedom from certain forms of expression on the one hand and the freedom of expression itself on the other.

2. Does the speech go beyond, as the courts have put it, the cautious faculties of the hearer, as, for example, when speech become obscene because it appeals to the "prurient interest"; or becomes "fighting words" when it incites a breach of the peace; or incitement to racial hatred when it promotes hatred or contempt of an identifiable group?

Again, this "genre" of speech is a denial of the very deliberative or "political public speech" which First Amendment commentators have stated is the basis for that speech.

3. Does the speech threaten not only the inherent dignity and worth of the human person, but the equal worth of all human beings in society? I would submit that the dissemination of hate propaganda is not simply a free speech issue but also an equality issue; for the systematic dissemination of hate propaganda over time against an identifiable target group has the effect of reducing the standing and respect of that group in society thereby creating an equality issue.

Moreover, the notion of "Equality Rights" is itself an organizing idiom of the *Charter,* not only as an abstract principle but as a clear statement of law in Section 15(1) of the *Charter.*

> Every individual is equal before and under the law and has the right to the equal protection and equal benefit of the law without discrimination

and, in particular, without discrimination based on race, national or ethnic origin, colour, religion, sex, age or mental or physical desirability.

4. Does the speech undermine or prejudice the constitutional norm of multiculturalism set forth in s. 27 of the Charter and which reads as follows:

This Charter shall be interpreted in a manner consistent with the preservation and enhancement of the multicultural heritage of Canadians.

In interpreting the *Charter of Rights,* as the former Minister of Justice, Mark MacGuigan, said in testimony to the Parliamentary Committee on Visible Minorities, s. 27 will have an important role to play with regard to the interpretation of s. 2 freedoms, including, in consequence thereof, the validation of restrictions respecting the dissemination of hate propaganda.

5. Does this speech result in Canada being in breach of our international obligations as set forth in international treaties such as the International Covenant on Civil and Political Rights or the International Convention on the Elimination of Racial Discrimination?

Both these Treaties call upon state parties to the convention, including Canada as a state party, to prohibit, as a matter of law, the dissemination of hate propaganda. Accordingly, the Criminal Code restrictions respecting hate propaganda are an effective domestic implementation of our international obligations under these Treaties, and in full conformity with "protected speech" as defined by these Treaties. Indeed, if we had not enacted these provisions it would be incumbent upon us to do so as a signatory of these Treaties.

6. Does this speech violate Canadian constitutional values developed over time — a kind of domestic *jus gentium* — as found in what the Canadian Bar Association's Special Committee on Hate Propaganda called "The Generation of Recommendations and Legislative Responses Argument",[10] from the Special Committee on Hate Propaganda in 1966, to the recent judgment of the Federal Court in the *Taylor case*. In the words of the court: "It is Canadian policy that individuals under the guise of freedom of speech cannot say things or take steps to incite or advocate the destruction of freedoms which all of us enjoy"; these freedoms have emerged, in effect, as constitutional norms.

7. Is this speech in accordance with or does it violate constitutional norms of protected speech as defined in other free and democratic societies. While time does not permit going into the specifics of comparative legislation in these jurisdictions, a survey would show that such legislation is on the statute books in the following countries: Australia, Austria, Denmark, Federal Republic of Germany, France, Greece, Italy, Netherlands, New Zealand, Norway, Sweden, Switzerland and

---

10. *Report of the Special Committee on Hate Propaganda,* Ottawa, (1966).

the United Kingdom. Where tested, such legislation has been upheld in the courts. For example in Sweden a person was sentenced to 10 months for publishing hate propaganda. In France a historian was found criminally liable for disseminating hate propaganda. In 1979 the European Commission of Human Rights upheld the Netherlands anti-hate law in a ruling which said that the distribution of ideas encouraging racial discrimination and violation of the rights and freedoms of others was not "protected speech" under article 10 of the European Convention on Human Rights, and which European Convention has a limitation clause similar to that which has been imported into s. 1 of the Canadian Charter of Rights and Freedoms.

8. Is the speech an essential part of the exploration of ideas, or is it of such slight social value that any benefit is clearly outweighed by the public interest in both the inherent dignity and worth of the human being and the equal worth of all human beings in our society?

Finally, I would submit that even if one were to accept this "genre" of speech as *prime facie* protected speech, a legislative restraint nonetheless would be characterized as a reasonable limitation demonstrably justified in a free and democratic society. In a word, the foregoing evidence of what is transpiring in other free and democratic societies, the evidence respecting the growing incidence of racial propaganda and its effect on both the inherent dignity and worth of the human person as well as on the equal worth of all persons, the conformity with our international treaty obligations, the fact that the restrictions are proportionate to the objectives sought to be secured taken together, this would likely validate a restriction under Section 1.

In conclusion, we have arrived at a moment in our constitutional life where the entrenched fundamental freedoms in s. 2 of the *Charter* brush up against the hate propaganda provisions of the Criminal Code; and brush up against the attempts, which have achieved a very large and significant consensus throughout our society, to even strengthen the provisions of the Criminal Code, on the grounds that it is not "free speech" that is being threatened at this point but in fact the human dignity of the victims through the weakness of the enforceability of these provisions themselves. Indeed we run the risk of exposing ourselves to a certain kind of legal and cultural dissonance at this point. For the very people amongst the visible minorities who advocated the adoption of a Canadian Charter of Rights and Freedoms now see the possibility that the *Charter* will be used not as a shield to protect them from racial discrimination but as a shield to protect the racism. The contradiction between "freedom from expression" and "freedom of expression" is, in fact, more apparent than real. Protecting ourselves from hate propaganda will enable us to practice fidelity to freedom of expression itself, as we protect the inherent dignity and worth of human beings in our society.

Freedom of Expression:
Some Recurring Impediments

A. Alan Borovoy*

INTRODUCTION

It is trite law and even more trite philosophy to acknowledge that freedom of expression is not and cannot be an absolute. Nevertheless, this "penetrating glimpse into the obvious" is trotted out virtually every time there is a proposed encroachment on this freedom. Indeed, on many occasions it is the *only* justification which is offered. In beginning this paper by acknowledging the non-absoluteness of this value, my aim is not simply to disarm my adversaries; it is also to force them to produce more compelling justifications for the measures they advocate.

In return, I ask them to acknowledge that, while freedom of expression is not absolute, it is nevertheless the lifeblood of the democratic system. Freedom of expression entails the right to attempt persuasion, the opportunity to marshall the support of others in the quest for the redress of our grievances. In this sense, it is what American philosopher Sidney Hook called a "strategic" freedom. It is a freedom on which so many other freedoms depend. In the words of a wise old trade unionist, freedom of expression is the "grievance procedure" of democratic society.

But freedom of expression is even more. It is the vehicle through which the quest for truth may be pursued. In science and technology, for example, a plurality of theories and methods may openly compete in order to demonstrate their respective validity. The same in religion and philosophy. Ultimate questions concerning the nature and meaning of life are settled, not by governmental fiat, but by individual choice. And the ability to choose is enhanced by the right to explore contesting ideas and experiment with alternative approaches.

And, in culture and the arts, freedom of expression provides the prerequisite for enrichment. To the extent that all persons have the right

---

* General Counsel, Canadian Civil Liberties Association.

to produce and consume as they are moved to do - in literature, films, art, music, dance, - they have the opportunity to enrich their own lives and those of others.

Inevitably, such vast freedom carries with it enormous risks. Freedom of expression can be used to propagate lies as well as truths, wrongs as well as rights, injustice as well as justice, and junk as well as art. On the basis of maximum possible exposure, the people are entitled to choose for themselves.

The central question is: where are we prepared to put our trust? In dictatorships, governments arrogate to themselves rather wide powers to decide how far people may express themselves and be exposed to the expressions of others. The assumption is that those in power are sufficiently wise and benevolent to make such decisions on behalf of everybody. Democracies, on the other hand, are fearful of reposing so much trust in their leaders. It's not that democratic societies necessarily have blind faith that the masses of people will always choose wisely. It's that they have considerably *less* faith in anyone else.

Indeed, the power to encroach on public communication carries with it a substantial risk of tyranny. The exercise of such power can decide the outcome of almost any conflict. Deny tenants the right to distribute their leaflets and you ensure victory for their landlords. Stop employees from picketing and you guarantee the domination of their employers. Take opposition viewpoints off television and you hand the next election to the government.

In science, philosophy, and culture, the exercise of comparable tyranny is likely to abort creativity. To the extent that government asserts a power to determine orthodoxy in those fields, scientific innovations will decline, intellectual activity will atrophy, and the arts will wither. This is not to argue that openness is a guarantee of vitality. It is simply to maintain that repression is a guarantee of aridity.

Democracies prefer to run the risk of error through the free competition of viewpoints than to run the risk of tyranny through curtailing what the people may say, see, and hear. If there be error, the answer to it generally is not less communication but more communication.

Inevitably, however, there are pressures to encroach on this vital freedom. In democracies like Canada, the problem with encroachments on freedom of expression is not wholesale invasion; it's piecemeal erosion. The danger here is that an accumulation of legislative enactments and judicial pronouncements will serve, not to eradicate, but to emasculate freedom of expression. In a number of key areas, we can see disquieting signs. While freedom of expression receives homage in our constitutional documents and official rhetoric, it is beset by a host of impediments to its practical realization. What follows is an attempt to identify some of the more important of these impediments and the fundamental fallacies that lie behind them.

It's too early to tell, of course, how far, if at all, these problems are likely to be influenced by our new Charter of Rights and Freedoms. Since the jurisprudence on the Charter is in such an embryonic state, this is the time for a less inhibited exploration of the policy choices in our law making. Hopefully, such an exercise can help to persuade judges as well as politicians.

THE DEMAND FOR APPEALS TO REASON

In the course of upholding the validity of an anti demonstration by-law enacted by the City of Montreal, the Supreme Court of Canada made a rather remarkable statement.

> Demonstrations are not a form of speech but of collective action. They are of the nature of a display of force rather than of that of an appeal to reason...[1]

Why does free speech have to appeal to reason? While the Court used the word "speech" and the Charter uses the word "expression", there is some suggestion from other cases that, as regards demonstrations, this distinction may not matter.[2] Indeed, even the Charter protection for "assembly" may receive similar treatment.[3] If that turns out to be so, it would be most unfortunate.

People in the real world are persuaded most often, not by reason, but by pressure. Politicians hungering for position will respond more to political tension than to logical syllogism. In order to extract higher wages from a tight-fisted employer, it will usually be more effective to threaten him with a strike than subject him to a sermon.

Of course, this is not to justify the abandonment of reason in social affairs. It is simply to recognize its limitations. Pressure without reason may be irresponsible but reason without pressure will be ineffectual. To be sure, the range of acceptable pressure cannot include the commission or threat of physical violence. But it must be able to entail varying levels of political, economic, and social injury. And freedom of expression, to be effective, must be able to include, therefore, the threat to inflict such injury and the attempt to recruit the support of others for it.

---

1. A.G. Can. v. *Dupond*, [1978] 2 S.C.R. 770, at 797.
2. In one of the first Charter cases on the subject, (see *infra*, fn. 8) the lack of rational appeal was a factor in depriving labour picketing of Charter protection as "freedom of expression". Since picket lines, like demonstrations, might also qualify as an "assembly", it is curious that "freedom of assembly" did not emerge as an issue in this case. For a pre Charter example of a similar phenomenon, see *infra* fn. 4.
3. *Ibid.*

Consider, for example, the demonstration of 100,000 people who gathered in Ottawa during the fall of 1981 to protest the federal budget of former Finance Minister Allan MacEachen. When such a large, representative, and angry crowd is prepared to incur the inconvenience of travelling to Ottawa on a stormy November Saturday, a pointed message is conveyed to the government in power. Let us make no mistake about it. This was not primarily "an appeal to reason". Mr. MacEachen already knew and had rejected the arguments of his critics. The demonstration was essentially a dramatized threat to deprive the government of the votes it needed for re-election. Where argument had failed, the protesters were hoping that pressure would succeed. They were effectively saying, "accommodate our interests or we'll vote you out of power". Why can't *that* qualify as an exercise in expression?

In short, to confine the right of free expression to appeals to reason is to load the dice against the "have-nots" of society. The "haves" use the pressure of money to advance their interests. They grant and withhold economic benefits. Why can't the "have-nots" use the pressure of numbers to advance *their* interests? By assembling in the streets, they threaten to grant and withhold political benefits.

This is not to suggest that such expression must always be unfettered. Remember, I have already acknowledged that freedom of expression is not an absolute. The Charter does say that the rights and freedoms which it contains are to be subject to "such reasonable limits as can be demonstrably justified". Even freedoms as fundamental as expression must be susceptible to certain trade offs. The problem, however, is that the Supreme Court of Canada might not even put demonstrations into the hopper. For the Court, this necessary weapon of the disadvantaged might simply be defined as something beyond the range of the Charter's protections.

Unfortunately, this unreality about freedom of expression appears rather well ingrained in Canadian judicial thinking. Thirty years ago, the late Mr. Justice Ivan Rand attempted to set out the limits of permissible behaviour for lawful picket lines.

> ... there is a difference between watching and besetting for the purpose of coercing either workmen or employer by presence, demeanor, argumentative and rancorous badgering or importunity, and unexpressed, sinister suggestiveness, felt rather than perceived in a vague or ill defined fear or apprehension on the one hand; and attempting to communicate information for the purpose of persuasion by the *force of a rational appeal*, on the other.[4] (emphasis added).

The judge was attempting to construe the Criminal Code section on "watching and besetting". To the extent that these remarks are

---

4. *Williams* v. *Aristocratic Restaurants*, [1951] S.C.R. 762, at 784.

considered a valid interpretation, the law itself should be changed. Why should "argumentative and rancorous badgering" be proscribed? Of course pickets should not be able to employ or threaten physical violence or obstruction. But why shouldn't they be able to use unpleasant social pressure? In short, why shouldn't they be free to embarrass and censure those employees and customers who enter the impugned premises? Suppose, for example, picket line interlopers were greeted with epithets such as "scabs", "finks", or "traitors"? Since the proprietor is free to use economic benefit to entice people across the picket line, pickets should be free to use social pressure to try and keep them away. To restrict the pickets to rational persuasion is to bias the rules in favour of the proprietor.

This demand for appeals to reason has already produced some questionable practices in this country. When courts have faced evidence of violence or disorder on labour picket lines, they have frequently issued injunctions restricting the number of pickets to not more than three or four at a gate.[5] What might have begun as a powerful expression of vital grievances often wound up looking like a pathetic advertisement for "Eat at Joe's". According to the judges, such emasculation of picket line potency could be justified on the basis that greater numbers are not necessary for the purpose of communicating information i.e. for appeals to reason. Such judgments revealed a striking insensitivity to the realities of the social conflicts at issue. Large demonstrations happen to carry greater moral weight in our community than do small ones. Token picketing tends to convey an appearance of half-hearted or non existent support. Unfortunately, it was not until the advent of legislative intervention at least in certain jurisdictions that the courts stopped perpetrating these unacceptable inequities. To their credit, some of the provincial legislatures now require a demonstration of both danger and a police inability to handle it before they will permit the courts to undermine by injunction the integrity of a labour picket line.[6]

But, even in those jurisdictions that have such legislation, certain picket lines are not safe from such judicial interference. Indeed, apart from very few places, a picket line that is perceived as "secondary" will likely be enjoined in its entirety. No question of reducing the numbers; secondary picketing in most jurisdictions is considered illegal *per se*.[7]

---

5. See, for example: *Lever Brothers* v. *Briggs et al.*, 57 C.L.L.C., par. 15,336; *Tilco Plastics Limited* v. *Skurjat et al.*, [1966] O.R. 547; *Weyerhausur* v. *Renaud, et al.*, Ont. High Ct., No. 103/64, March 12, 1964.
6. See, for example: *Judicature Act*, R.S.O. 1980, c. 223, s. 20.
7. *Darrigo's Grape Juice Ltd.* v. *Masterton*, [1971] 3 O.R. 772. See also *Hersees Ltd.* v. *Goldstein*, [1963] 2 O.R. 81 (C.A.). The situation appears to be different, however, in Manitoba. See *Channel Seven Television Ltd.* v. *NABET*, 21 D.L.R. (3d) 424.

Recently, for example, the British Columbia Supreme Court held that secondary picketing could not even claim Charter protection as "freedom of expression". In the course of issuing an injunction against all of the picketing at issue, the majority of the Court quoted with approval the following statement of an American writer.

> A labour picket line is thus not so much a *rational appeal* to persuasion as a signal for the application of immediate and enormous economic leverage, based upon an already prepared position. As such it must, under ordinary circumstances, be classified as action, rather than expression.[8] (emphasis added)

Once more, we are told that the prerequisite for free expression is an appeal to reason. But, even if we were to agree (as I do not) that picket lines lose their character as "expression" when they can effectively trigger a work stoppage, not all picket lines called "secondary" have enjoyed such prowess. Yet that didn't stop *them* from being declared illegal.

Such was the fate of a few attempts by Canadian sympathizers of the California farm workers. On a number of occasions, picket lines were set up in order to discourage the purchase of California grapes at large Canadian retail stores. While there was some indication that customer patronage did decline, there was little indication that employees of the stores stopped working. Indeed, it was the express policy of the farm workers and their supporters that work stoppages in Canada should be avoided. Notwithstanding this solicitude a number of the picket lines in question were prohibited by injunction.

Admittedly, these injunctions preceded the era of the Charter. In consequence, the issue of free expression was not specifically addressed in the judgments. There are clues, however, that the judiciary was unable to perceive the implications for freedom of expression in such picket lines.

Consider, for example, the comments of the Quebec Superior Court when it issued an injunction against farm workers picketing at Montreal's Dominion Stores.

> If the respondents had limited their campaign to a plea to the public to support the boycott of California grapes... without centering their activities at or near petitioner's stores, and without assailing petitioner for refusing to support the boycott, petitioner might not have grounds for complaint.[9]

---

8. *Dolphin Delivery Ltd.* v. *Retail, Wholesale and Department Store Union, Local 50, et al.*, 84 C.L.L.C., par. 14,036, at 12,146.
9. *Dominion Stores Limited* v. *United Farm Workers, et al.*, unreported decision of the Quebec Superior Ct., May 30, 1975. In an unreported judgment, this case was dismissed on appeal.

The implication is clear. Of course, the pickets were entitled to freedom of expression to make their case. No problem. They could have published an ad, purchased radio or television time, even hired a hall. What they couldn't do, in the words of the Court, was "picket petitioner's stores in order to alienate or estrange petitioner's customers". In short, the supporters of the grape boycott could do all sorts of things to advance their cause, *except what might be effective*.

It's of some interest that the Quebec Court did not once refer to this picketing as "secondary". A similar case which produced an injunction in Toronto did refer to the farm workers picketing as "secondary".[10] Indeed, the Ontario Supreme Court judge in the case pointed out "that secondary picketing is prohibited and for very sound social reasons... to do otherwise is simply to import into our province the social and economic battles of other people, the end of which one could not possibly foresee".[11]

It's one thing to prohibit secondary picketing of the kind that was involved in the above British Columbia case. In that situation, a union having a dispute with one employer attempted to bring pressure upon him by picketing one of his customers, a stranger to the dispute. One need not approve the social policy at work in this situation in order to recognize the difference in the two cases. The B.C. case might be seen as an attempt to limit the ambit of industrial conflict to the primary parties. Perhaps the court was simply trying to establish what it believed to be fair ground rules for the waging of disputes in the province.

But no such considerations were involved in the Ontario case. The primary dispute was not in Ontario but in California. Of course, the court might have wished to immunize Ontario residents from the impact of foreign struggles. But the implications of such an approach appear far reaching. On the basis of the court's reasoning, would injunctions issue against those who picket premises because they are selling South African wine or Soviet-made cars? Would a picket line in such a situation also be perceived or defined as devoid of implications for freedom of expression?

This denigration of picket lines has emerged in completely non labour contexts as well. In November of 1982, for example, a planned peace demonstration was undermined by certain actions of law enforcement authorities. The Metro Toronto police established a blockade so as to prevent demonstrators from coming within a half mile of Litton Industries, a company which manufactures guidance systems for the cruise missile. Presumably, this action was influenced by a bombing which had occurred there a few weeks earlier.

---

10. *Darrigo's, supra*, fn. 7.
11. *Id.*, at 774.

Lacking access to the specific information which triggered this police action, I am in no position to pass judgment on whatever justification may be offered for it. But what is susceptible of judgment at this point is the lack of adequate legal machinery for adjusting such conflicts between demonstrators and police. The problem is that the police had been given the legal power unilaterally to adopt this extraordinary measure. Moreover, both police and government appeared to be quite insensitive to the important interests they had jeopardized in the process. As far as they were concerned, a demonstration half a mile from the impugned premises was quite capable of conveying its message to the public. In short, it could still appeal to reason.

Unfortunately, however, it could not exert all of the pressures that had been contemplated. In order to be minimally effective, certain kinds of demonstrations must have some opportunity to confront those who are engaged in the process under attack. In the case of places like Litton Industries, the people to be confronted would include the management, the employees, and even the customers whose activity or patronage helped to bolster the cruise missile production at issue. One of the objects of such a demonstration is to generate an atmosphere of social pressure on those who are going in and out of the premises. The idea is to create in these people a sense of guilt, shame, or at least a feeling of censure. While the demonstrators must not be allowed to use or threaten physical violence, they must be as free as possible to inflict such social pressures. It is obvious that this cannot be done from a distance of half a mile away.

While I acknowledge the possibility that there may be some situations where the interests of public safety might require the separation of demonstrators from the premises at issue, it is not proper to repose in the police the unilateral power to make such decisions. The police interest in the conduct of demonstrations is to keep the peace and to ensure an orderly flow of traffic. But such functions, as important as they are, must be weighed against the interests of the demonstrators. As indicated, effective demonstrations often require greater physical proximity to the premises under attack.

To allow the police the power of unilaterally imposing such limits on the demonstrators is to make the police the umpires of their own ball game. No matter how fair their decisions may be in fact, they may well not *appear* fair. Indeed, they will often provoke suspicion that the restrictions they impose are motivated less by the objective needs of the situation than by the desire to ease the burdens of their job. In consequence, I believe such decisions should be made by the courts of law, on application from the police.[12] It is obvious, however, that the polit-

---

12. For an indication of how this might work, see letter from Canadian Civil Liberties Association to Ontario Attorney General re police blockade of demonstration at Litton Systems, dated April 19, 1983.

ical prerequisite for such a transfer of power is the recognition that the existing arrangements are unfair. So long as the only demonstrations and picket lines which are seen as worthy of protection are those that appeal to reason, there will be no incentive to change the law. There will not be a sufficient appreciation of the fact that a Litton type of blockade represents a substantial encroachment on the *effective* freedom of expression.

For the sake of perspective, it is worth mentioning once more that the foregoing comments do not seek an unlimited right to demonstrate or to picket. Unquestionably, there may be a number of regulations and controls over these activities. Such restrictions may serve the interests of public order, traffic, and perhaps even equity. For example, a picket line which is established to promote a racial boycott might be prohibited because of the illegality of its purpose. There might even be some argument that, in view of the other levers of pressure available to unions, they shouldn't be allowed to engage in certain forms of secondary picketing. While I have some difficulty with such reasoning, my thesis here does not require me to resolve this issue.

All I am seeking at this point is some minimal understanding about demonstrations and picket lines. Even if such activities don't appeal to reason and even if their prime function is to exert unpleasant pressure, they may nevertheless lay claim to be instruments of expression. As such, they are entitled, presumptively at least, to constitutional protection. But since freedom of expression is not an absolute, they may sometimes have to be modified in order to accommodate certain other values and interests. That's not now in issue. What is now in issue, however, is the dismissal of so many demonstrations and picket lines as something other than expression. Once that is done, there will be no need to examine and weigh the competing values at issue. The stage will have been set for the unwarranted suppression of one of the most valid and vital vehicles through which disadvantaged people can impress their interests on the general community.

THE EFFORT TO BAN OFFENSIVE MATERIAL

To a great extent, offensive material undermines our sense of dignity. People will go to great lengths, therefore, to immunize themselves from the impact of what offends. They will even seek resort to the power of legal prohibition.

On the other hand, freedom of expression must include the right to say not only nice but also nasty things. Since one of the pragmatic functions of free expression is to create the conditions by which we can redress our grievances, we must have the right to condemn as well as to approve. At what point does one person's right to utter nasty criticisms outweigh another person's right to be immunized from offensiveness?

Similar considerations apply to cultural matters. Often the same material will produce opposite impacts - some will be pleased, others will be hurt. There has even been material which has had the ability both to enrich and outrage. Should the law protect the higher or the lower tolerance level?

The ensuing remarks attempt to examine these conflicts in the light of certain restrictions against offensive speech which our law has enacted to protect the administration of justice, individual reputation, racial harmony, and sexual dignity. In my view, it is rarely possible to express, for legal purposes, the relevant distinctions - between acceptable criticism and unredeemed offensiveness, between the worthwhile and the worthless. I conclude, therefore, that in general the law should avoid the attempt. Subject to few exceptions, it is better to risk exposure to insult than to allow an interference with society's "grievance procedure". By the same token, it is usually better to permit a piece of trash than to suppress a work of art.

Scandalizing the Courts

In the spring of 1969, a young student in the Maritimes spent 10 days in jail for having written in a university student publication that a certain trial was a "mockery of justice" and that the courts were "instruments of the corporate elite".[13] His offence? Scandalizing the courts and particularly the presiding judge by bringing the court, the judge, and the proceedings of the trial into "public hatred, contempt, and ridicule".

This offence, a hold-over relic from the British common law of contempt of court, was designed to protect the administration of justice. According to the theory, judicial authority in the community could be undermined by intemperate public criticism. Indeed, the fear of a hostile public opinion was so great that the courts were able to send offenders to jail until the judges were satisfied that the contempts had been purged.

But this power was spawned in another era, before the evolution of democracy as we know it. How in the world can such power be squared with modern notions of free speech? After all, freedom of expression includes nastiness as well as niceties. In fact, according to democratic beliefs, our institutions are supposed to function best in an atmosphere of free public criticism.

The courts nowadays are quick to point out that they too believe in freedom of expression. It's all right, they say, to knock the courts. But such sniping should avoid "invective and abuse, and the imputation of... corrupt... motives"[14] to the judges. The only problem with this is

---

13. *R. v. Murphy* [1969], 4 C.C.C. 147 (N.B.S.C. App. Div.).
14. *R. v. Amos Rowe* (1880), Man. R. Temp. Wood 309, at p. 322, 323.

that a publication devoid of invective is likely also to be a publication devoid of readers. When, for example, was the last time you saw a line-up to buy the Canadian Bar Review? That august journal has rarely qualified as a runaway best seller. In the real world, verbal vinegar is often necessary for social impact.

This is not necessarily to defend all the abusive language which could be directed at judges or anyone else. To be sure, there are times when such invective would be unfair and irresponsible. But there are also times when it would be completely justified. Former law Dean Harry Arthurs summarized the problem succinctly:

> Unless you assume that judges can't be venal or biased, there must be a right to say so.

So the problem is: how far should the targets of criticism be allowed to set the limits of that criticism? Just about everywhere else in the law, the courts are impartial referees. Not so in the scandalizing contempt situation. They have the power to punish what they see as undue injury to their own institutional reputations. Those accused of contempt are not even entitled to a trial by jury.

Consider, for example, the case of a man named DeCastro in 1873 England. During the course of a public speech in which he was attempting to raise money for a friend who was facing a perjury charge, DeCastro had some nasty things to say about the impartiality of the judge who was slated to preside at his friend's trial. So nasty were his remarks that DeCastro found *himself* in court charged with contempt. At his own trial, DeCastro asked the panel of judges to have a jury hear the charge against him. ''I am charged with contempt of court for complaining of the Lord Chief Justice and you are his colleagues'', he said, ''it is not fair that you should try it without a jury''. In response, one of the judges declared that DeCastro's argument would be ''without avail''.

Small wonder that, at the turn of the century, the British House of Commons passed a resolution describing the contempt power of the judges as ''practically arbitrary''.[17] Yet those same ''arbitrary'' powers were adopted by the Canadian Parliament and applied by the Canadian courts. What we don't yet know, of course, is how far they will survive a challenge under the new Charter of Rights and Freedoms.

As we have seen, I am not just talking theory. On a number of occasions, the court's actual use of these powers has revealed a remarkable touchiness. In 1954, for example, journalist Eric Nicol wrote a bitter article against capital punishment in the Vancouver Province newspaper. In allegorical style, he portrayed all society as the accused before the Bar of Heaven for allowing legal executions. In making his point, he described the jury in a recent B.C. capital trial as ''the people

---

17. House of Commons resolution 1906.

who planned the murder'' and the judge as the one who "chose the time and the place and caused the victim to suffer the exquisite torture of anticipation''.[18]

It is clear that Nicol's scorn was directed not against the judge or jury in that particular case but against capital punishment in general. Despite the fact that the references to judge and jury were obviously allegorical, Eric Nicol and the Province newspaper were convicted of scandalizing the administration of justice. Although writer and newspaper were fined only $250. and $2500. respectively, the judge pointed out that, had it not been for the apology tendered and the newspaper's respected record, he would have imposed "severe penalties''.[19]

Such thin-skinned judgments can only erode our faith in the courts' ability to draw the line when *they* are the ones under attack. As I have indicated, the laws we support depend upon the risks we would take. On balance, I would prefer to allow a lot more anti judicial invective than permit the muzzling of Eric Nicol's eloquence.

To be fair, there are many cases in which the courts have resisted the impulse to punish their detractors. But that just confuses the issue. Since the courts have been both tolerant *and* intolerant about attacks on their reputations, it becomes harder to know where you stand. Consider, for example, the following statement which was made about a judge in another case.

> ... Mr. Justice Higgins is, we believe, what is called a political judge, that is, he was appointed because he had well served a political party. He, moreover, seems to know his position, and does not mean to allow any reflection on those to whom he may be said to be indebted for his judgeship.[20]

Remarkably, in this case, the court *acquitted* the writer of scandalizing contempt of court. Yet, how can any rational person say that this comment was *less* offensive than what Eric Nicol wrote? The inconsistency and confusion in the cases contribute little to the protection of freedom of speech. The consequence of the confusion is that lawyers who wish to advise their clients how to stay out of trouble will urge caution when it comes to criticism of the courts. In the result, we can expect an excess of unwarranted *self* censorship.

Some people say that curtailing this contempt power would trigger the decline, perhaps even the collapse of our judicial system. On the contrary, I think the *use* of such power is much more likely to impair the prestige of the courts.

---

18. *R. v. Nicol*, [1954] 3 D.L.R. 690 (B.C.S.C.), at 692. f19. *Id.*, at 700.
19. *Id.*, at 700.
20. *R. v. Nicholls* (1911), 12 C.L.R. 280 (Aus. H.C.).

Besides, the courts may be the only institution in our society still protected in this way. Barring an incitement to violence, it is generally not unlawful to speak such ill of any other government agency. This may even be true of the many administrative tribunals - such as the provincial labour relations boards, liquor licencing boards, and welfare appeal boards - which, like the courts, exercise a wide range of judicial functions. If such a contempt power has ever been used to protect their reputations, you would have to turn the law books upside down to find an example of it. Yet there isn't the slightest sign that our system of administrative justice is crumbling. So what, then, entitles the courts to this special coddling?

The courts are different, say some people, because the judges can't protect themselves. Their tradition and position make it improper for them to answer attacks or to sue for defamation. But why shouldn't the same restraints apply to administrative adjudicators? Indeed, it would be a rare event to see one of *them* answer abuse with a lawsuit or a polemic. And it is fair to say that these adjudicators have been known to suffer barbs.

Remember too that judges are already protected more than most people. They enjoy a unique kind of job security. Until they die or reach a ripe old age, it would take a virtual cyclone to remove them from office.

In any event, however, this contempt power was never designed for the personal reputations of the judges. It has to stand or fall on whether it's a necessary safeguard for the judicial system itself.

It is worth noting that the administration of justice in the United States does not appear to have suffered any significant erosion of its authority despite the lack of comparable contempt powers in that country. In this connection, I remember well the sight of large billboards so conspicuously posted during the 1960's in the south. The billboards carried signs reading "impeach Earl Warren". Moreover, there was an abundance of literature suggesting that the late former U.S. Chief Justice was a dupe of the Communist Party. Somehow, both Earl Warren and the court over which he presided managed to survive intact.

For these purposes, I can think of no better authority than a much neglected court judgment from the turn of the century. The highest appeal court in the British Empire, the Judicial Committee of the Privy Council, declared that contempt of court convictions for "scandalizing the court... (had) become obsolete" and that the courts could "leave to public opinion attacks or comments derogatory or scandalous to them".[21] This expresses the essence of our society's commitment to

---

21. *McLeod* v. *St. Aubyn*, [1899] A.C. 549 (P.C.), at p. 552.

freedom of expression. At base, there must be a willingness to trust the people or at least mistrust them less than the elites. Surely, it's more democratic for our courts and judges to preserve the respect they enjoy, not through the awesomeness of their powers, but through the quality of their justice.

Defamation

During the winter of 1969, an underground newspaper in British Columbia sustained a criminal conviction for publishing an article which awarded "the Pontius Pilate Certificate of Justice" to a named Vancouver magistrate.[22] This case resurrected the criminal offence of defamatory libel from the grave of obscurity in which it had been languishing for a generation. The offence inflicts the punishment of the criminal law upon a person for making a statement "that is likely to injure the reputation of any person (not only a judge) by exposing him to hatred, contempt, or ridicule".

The original rationale for this offence grew out of the danger that "libellous" statements could provoke breaches of the peace. By now, however, the Criminal Code is overflowing with offences which incite or tend to incite breaches of the peace - counselling the commission of an offence, attempting to commit an offence, causing a disturbance, watching and besetting, obstructing, etc. In view of the multiplicity of prohibitions against behaviour which could cause breaches of the peace, there is very little role for defamatory libel to play in that area. Its role has been virtually confined to the protection of injured reputations.

But why should there be *prosecutions* to vindicate reputations? Why does the state have a greater interest in the reputation of A than in the free speech of B? It is one thing for A to launch a civil action for damages if B has libelled him. But it is quite another matter to threaten B with prosecution, conviction, and possible imprisonment. The vindication of personal reputation hardly warrants the awesome power of incarceration. The section ought to be repealed.[23]

But even civil defamation creates some unwarranted risks to legitimate freedom of expression. In the late 1970's, for example, the British Columbia Cabinet Minister responsible for administering public welfare successfully sued a newspaper for publishing a cartoon which portrayed him gleefully tearing the wings off a fly. While the court of appeal subsequently overturned the judgment, the case illustrates the lengths to which the law might go to vindicate a fragile ego.[24]

---

22. *R.* v. *Georgia Straight Publishing Co. et al.*, [1970] 1 C.C.C. 94 (B.C. Co. Ct.).
23. A similar conclusion has been reached in a working paper produced by the Canada Law Reform Commission. See Defamatory Libel. Working Paper 35, Ottawa: Queen's Printer, 1984.
24. *VanderZalm* v. *Times Publishers*, [1980] 4 W.W.R. 259 (B.C.C.A.).

At the very least, the litigation rights of public personalities should be reassessed. The viability of the democratic processes requires a very broad right to challenge, criticize, and even satirize the wielders of power and influence. The thin skin of a leader should not be able to impair the free speech of a critic. As I indicated above, the standards of Emily Post can dilute the impact of freedom of speech.

Moreover, the effective right to criticize stands to be jeopardized if, in the midst of a heated issue, the fear of a lawsuit fetters the spontaneity of debate or muzzles the utterance of what is reasonably believed. In general, this has to give supporters of the status quo a considerable advantage over dissenters. As a practical matter, not everything that emerges in public debate can be exhaustively researched beforehand. Thus, there is an argument for restricting the defamation claims of public personalities.

Besides, involvement in public life is usually a matter of voluntary choice. As Harry Truman once warned, "if you can't stand the heat, stay out of the kitchen". It should also be noted that those in public life can often command access to the media in order to reply to any attacks they may have sustained. For all of these reasons, we should consider amending these features of the law on civil defamation. In this regard, the American experience would be instructive. In that country, public personalities have to prove malice in order to recover damages.[25]

Civil defamation disputes periodically produce another device which is excessively threatening to freedom of communication. I refer to the court injunction which restrains people from saying what they had intended. A few years ago, a company suspected of polluting the atmosphere persuaded a court to restrain the CBC from showing a certain film which attempted to document the pollution allegations.[26] In my view, the injunction power should not extend this far. The case represented, in effect, a form of prior restraint censorship. It's one thing to exact punishment or order compensation *after* there is a contentious communication. It's another thing entirely to prohibit the communication in the first place.

Prior restraint inhibits timely debate; it prevents information and ideas from circulating at the point when they could be most influential. Moreover, injunctions in such circumstances are designed usually to maintain the equities between the parties *pending* a proper determination of the merits of the case. So, when an injunction issues against a

---

25. *New York Times* v. *Sullivan*, 84 S.Ct. 710.
26. See: *Canada Metal Co. Ltd. et al.* v. *Canadian Broadcasting Corp. et al.* (1974), 3 O.R. (2d) 1 (Ont. H.C.); *Canada Metal Co. Ltd. et al.* v. *Canadian Broadcasting Corp. et al.* (1974), 3 O.R. (2d) 65 (Ont. H.C.); *Canada Metal Co. Ltd. et al.* v. *Canadian Broadcasting Corp. et al.* (1975), 7 O.R. (2d) 261 (Ont. Div. Ct.).

communication in such circumstances, it is likely that the merits of the defamation will not have been determined. This, of course, simply exacerbates the impropriety.

Moreover, in a case such as the one involving the CBC, there is no need for injunctive restraint. The CBC was a highly solvent defendent; it was not likely to go out of business or leave town. If it published anything defamatory, its substantial treasury was available to pay the damage claim. In my view, these considerations should have loaded the merits against issuing an injunction. I think our defamation laws should be amended accordingly.

Hate Propaganda

In the mid 1960's, a mere 20 years after the end of World War II, North Americans were shocked by the emergence of new political groups which called themselves Nazis. Donning uniforms and displaying swastikas, the emblem of our World War II enemies, these fledgling groups began to resurrect the anti-Semitic and racist invective of the Hitler era. Once again, the social climate was contaminated by shrill mindless racism. White Christians were admonished to be on guard against mongrelization by inferior Blacks and subversion by an international Zionist-Communist-banker-Jewish conspiracy.

The brazen chutzpah of this propaganda provoked widespread revulsion. In Canada, the revulsion found further expression in demands that new laws be enacted to stop the propagation of racial hatred. The demands came from Jews who had survived the horrors of Nazi concentration camps, Blacks whose memories embraced the lynch mobs of the Ku Klux Klan, veterans of World War II, and many many others who sought simply to maintain racial and inter group harmony in their communities. By the end of the 1960's, the Parliament of Canada had enacted an amendment to the Criminal Code making it illegal to espouse certain forms of racial, religious, and ethnic hatred.

The theoretical arguments for such legislation are rather alluring. Racists would not allow free speech for others, why should they enjoy it; it's one thing to tolerate legitimate differences of opinion on racial matters, there is no need to tolerate outbursts of sheer hatred; after the holocaust, racism is simply beyond the pale. Problems arise, however, when the focus shifts from theoretical considerations to practical ones. At that point, the question is how to articulate a prohibition which is precise enough to curb this neo Nazi propaganda without running a terrific risk of catching in the same net a lot of other material which it would be unconscionable for a democratic society to suppress. The value at risk, of course, is freedom of expression.

The Canadian law prohibits the public communication of statements "which wilfully promote hatred" against people distinguished by race, religion, and ethnicity. I could see no objection to a law which purported to prohibit the incitement of racial *violence* in situations where there was an imminent peril that the violence would occur.[27] But "hatred" is a much more nebulous and, therefore, dangerous concept. Our experience tells us that freedom of speech is often most necessary when it creates some level of tension or unrest. The late Martin Luther King Jr., for example, referred to the upshot of his tactics as "creative tension". The problem, then, is how to distinguish destructive hatred from constructive tension. And who can we trust to do it?

Indeed, the section has already been used against people other than its intended racist targets. During the 1975 Shriner's Parade in Toronto, the police used the anti-hate law to arrest some young people who had been distributing leaflets bearing the words "Yankee Go Home".[28] Although the Crown Attorney had the good sense subsequently to withdraw the charge, these young activists suffered the suppression of their free speech rights and some of them spent up to two days in jail. In the late 1970's, there was a bizarre anti-hate case in Windsor against French Canadians who distributed anti-French leaflets in order to create pro-French sympathy. In that case, there was a conviction at trial which was overturned on appeal. Despite the ultimate results, there was in both cases legal harassment against people quite different from the anti-Semites and racists for whom the law was designed.

As will be noted from the comments above, the similar wording of our laws on criminal defamation and scandalizing contempt of court produced some rather dubious consequences there too. Remember again the criminal convictions that were registered for the "Pontius Pilate Award for Justice", the allegorical references to the role of a judge and jury in planning the "murder" of a condemned man, and the denunciation in a campus newspaper column of the courts as "instruments of the corporate elite". All this was made possible by legal prohibitions against "hatred, contempt, and ridicule".

---

27. Another part of the hate propanganda law (s. 281.2(1)) makes it an offence to incite hatred in any public place "where such incitement is likely to lead to a breach of the peace". The problem with this provision is that it can be read so as to make a violent heckler the effective censor of certain public statements. In order to avoid this problem, the law should make it clear that a speaker would be punishable, not for attracting the violence of antagonists to himself, but for inciting the violence of his followers against others.

28. See newspaper reports of this incident: Editorial, *Globe and Mail*, Wednesday, July 2, 1975; Article, *Globe and Mail*, Friday, July 4, 1975.

And, if certain people have their way, an even greater variety of people could be imperilled. There are attempts afoot to remove from the anti hate law a number of provisions that had been inserted there as special protections for freedom of expression. While I never believed that those safeguards were adequate, I think their removal would be downright dangerous.

Understandably frustrated over the failure of the existing law to convict at least one genuine racist, numbers of people are calling for the deletion of the "wilful" requirement. This change is designed to eliminate the need to prove a "specific intention to promote hatred".[29] But that requirement is there in order to reduce the risk that this law might be used against over-eager speakers in the context of an otherwise legitimate polemic. Suppose, for example, in a fit of anger over a land claims dispute, a native spokesman blamed Canadian whites in general for the poverty of the Indian people. While such a statement would arguably be improper, it should certainly not be unlawful. Democratic debate cannot coexist with such a demanding obligation to bite one's tongue.

Indeed, such an amendment might well imperil communications media such as the CBC for including, in a newscast film, footage of a hate monger making a speech. Without a requirement of wilfulness, such a film showing might make the CBC liable to a conviction for "communicating" the hate monger's message.[30]

There is some indication also of an attempt to remove the safe-guards for certain religious discussions. While this change might make it easier to take action against the racist sermonizing which periodically occurs, there is also a serious downside risk. How far, for example, would such a deletion render vulnerable a group like Quebec's Jeho-vah's Witnesses for the kind of nasty things they said about the Roman Catholic Church during the late 1940's and early 1950's? Believing as they did that the Church hierarchy was behind the persecution they suffered at the hands of the Duplessis regime, the Witnesses published a stream of anti Catholic material. The response of the Duplessis gov-ernment was to charge the group's leaders with seditious libel.

The Supreme Court of Canada was widely praised for dismissing the charge on the grounds that, by itself, the creation of inter group ill-will was not an offence.[31] Ironically, some of the very constituencies

---

29. *R. v. Buzzanga and Durocher* (1979), 49 C.C.C. (2d) 369 (Ont. C.A.).
30. Perhaps it might be argued that, in such a situation, the media might be able to invoke the defense that, in good faith, they "intended to point out, for the purpose of removal, matters producing or tending to produce feelings of hatred..." s. 281.2(3)(d). It's not at all clear, however, that this would apply where the ostensible goal is simply to report.
31. *Boucher v. The King* (1950), 99 C.C.C. 1 (S.C.C.).

which hailed that judgment as a landmark protection for civil liberties are now advocating legislative change that could undo its effect.

There is also a proposal to delete the requirement that certain prosecutions must have the consent of the attorney general in the affected province. Again, this would expose a lot more people, not just genuine racists, to the ordeal of prosecution. The consent requirement acts as a potential buffer against the abuse of these awesome powers.[32]

A further irony is that there may be a real danger here to one of the groups which has been campaigning for many of these changes - the Jewish community. There is a good chance, for example, that Canadian sympathizers of the Palestine Liberation Organization might lay anti hate charges against Canadian Zionists on the basis of the PLO's fatuous slogan that Zionism equals racism. Even if a conviction were very unlikely, the prosecution itself would cause enormous distress.

To what end are we asked to incur all these risks? In order to nail a miniscule group of pathetic peripheral creeps whose constituencies could not fill a telephone booth. Despite its recommendation in favour of the anti hate law which was finally enacted, the government-appointed Cohen Committee admitted that our hate mongering problem could not be described "as one of crisis or near crisis proportions".[33] Moreover, Daniel G. Hill, the first Director of the first Human Right Commission in Canada, declared that "the Canadian public is relatively immune to extremist anti Semitic, and other 'hate' materials".[34]

In this regard, it is worth examining the condition of Alberta's Social Credit Party, the political party that accepted James Keegstra as a candidate despite the reports of his anti Semitic activities. In the last federal election, that party contested 15 ridings. It ran last in 11. Where it didn't run last, it was rescued from such disgrace by its success in nosing out some other aspirants to oblivion - the Libertarians, the Communists, the Rhinoceros Party etc. Indeed, the Alberta Social Credit Party polled only .6% of the total vote. At that, it just squeezed by the official practical jokers, the Rhinoceros Party. It had .4%

While there are serious racial problems in this country, they do not emanate from the extremists. Nevertheless, I don't suggest that we should ignore the fringe fascists in our midst. Of course, they bear watching lest they begin at some point to acquire more serious dimensions. Even at that, however, we might not have to choose between criminal prosecution or doing nothing.

---

32. Of course, the Attorneys General would nevertheless retain their power to stay prosecutions. But if Parliament were to abolish the need for their consent, they might find this a politically difficult power to exercise.
33. Department of Justice, Report of the Special Committee on Hate Propaganda in Canada, Ottawa: Queen's Printer, at p. 59.
34. Id., at p. 27.

Consider again the case of Alberta's James Keegstra. After the revelation of the sorts of things he was reportedly teaching to his students, his Board of Education deprived him of his teaching position and the voters deprived him of his mayoralty position. After all that, prosecution is a monumental anti climax.

Nor should we forget that the Weimar Republic of pre Hitler Germany had criminal legislation similar in some respects to our anti hate laws.[35] Indeed, in the fifteen years or so of the Weimar Republic, some 200 court cases were activated because of anti Semitic speech. In the opinion of the leading Jewish organization of that time, no more than 10% of the court cases between anti Semites and Jews were mishandled by the authorities.[36] As subsequent history so painfully testifies, this type of legislation produced virtually nothing on the one occasion when there was a real argument for it.

In my view, the most sensible response to hate mongering in today's Canada is to raise political hell whenever racist utterances emanate from people of authority or social standing. The goal should be to drive them out of their relevant positions of influence unless or until they make an adequate public apology for their objectionable statements. As for the more peripheral racists, I think our public response should generally be indirect. We should continue to strengthen our laws against racially discriminatory behaviour - in jobs, housing, public accommodations, etc. The fallout from a stronger program against racist *deeds* is likely to weaken further the impact of racist *words*.

I realize, of course, that such suggestions represent an inadequate response to the phenomenon of hate propaganda. On balance, however, I believe it is the *least* inadequate of the available alternatives. In the real world, there is no more compelling measure of good sense.

Pornography

I have seen... women's naked and mutilated bodies suspended upside down on barbed wire fences, a woman spread-eagled and forced to have relations with a dog, brutal and sadistic gang rapes... spikes hammered

---

35. The German Criminal Code made it unlawful to insult in public "a Christian church or any religious community with incorporated rights". During the Weimar period, there were some forty cases involving insults to the Hebrew religion. The other relevant section was one on criminal defamation which was similar to our defamatory libel. The difference, however, is that, during the Weimar period, Nazis frequently defamed identifiable Jewish individuals. And there were many prosecutions brought under this section - during the period in question, one hundred and sixty-three. Ambrose Doskow and Sidney Jacoby, "Anti-Semitism and the Law in Pre-Nazi Germany", (1940) *Contemporary Jewish Record* 498-509.
36. Donald Niewyk, "Jews and the Courts in Weimar Germany", (1975) *Jewish Social Studies* 99-113.

into vaginas, nipples hacked from the breasts of a woman pinioned with a leather bit in her mouth.[37]

These are examples of the "entertainment" which is reportedly provided by certain modern films. As a consequence, the power of legal suppression has acquired a new respectability. A number of feminists as well as fundamentalists are demanding that such material be banned. It's hard not to sympathize. How can the celebration of sexual abuse elicit a reaction more positive than revulsion?

We are obliged to distinguish, however, between moral condemnation and legal prohibition. The former is easy; the latter is fraught with difficulty. Again, the legal problem is one essentially of definition. How is the law to formulate a standard which will prohibit this vile pornography without simultaneously catching in the same net a lot of other material which it would be unconscionable to suppress? So often, our obscenity laws have wound up nailing the wrong material.

Within the last decade, for example, arguably artistic and educational works such as the film "Last Tango in Paris"[38] and the book "Show Me"[39] had to undergo prolonged and expensive court battles before they were ultimately vindicated. In the opinion at least of a number of prosecutors and police, these works fell within the Criminal Code definition of obscenity - "the undue exploitation of sex". But what in the world is an "undue" exploitation? Indeed, what is a "due" exploitation? The answer, we are told, is to be found in community standards. But how are they to be discerned? Not infrequently, numbers of experts have offered conflicting opinions as to whether a particular work violated community standards. How are the triers of fact supposed to choose? Indeed our judges have often been at diametric odds with each other over the interpretation and application of this terminology.

Consider these cases. One trial judge, three appeal court judges, and four judges of the Supreme Court of Canada found that "Lady Chatterly's Lover"[40] was obscene within the above definition. However, five judges of the Supreme Court of Canada carried the day in a declaration that the book was not obscene. Despite the acquittal, the judicial head count was 8 to 5 in favour of a conviction. The book "Fanny Hill" was found to be obscene by a trial judge and two appeal court judges and not obscene by three other appeal court judges.[41] Here the judicial head count wound up in a three-all tie. In a case involving

37. *Globe and Mail*, Monday, February 7, 1983, p. A5 from the report of a speech by Ontario Film Censorship Board Chairman Mary Brown.

38. *R. v. Odeon Morton Theatres Ltd. and United Artists Corp* (1974), 16 C.C.C. (2d) 185 (Man. C.A.).

39. *R. v. MacMillan of Canada Ltd.* (1977), 13 O.R. (2d) 630 (Co. Ct.).

40. *R. v. Brodie; R. v. Dansky; R. v. Rubin* (1962), 132 C.C.L. 161 (S.C.C.).

41. *R. v. Coles Co. Ltd.* [1965] 1 O.R. 557.

an art gallery,[42] the trial judge and four appeal court judges held that the impugned pictures were obscene but one appeal court judge went the other way. While the judicial head count was five to one in favour of the conviction that was ultimately imposed, it is interesting that the dissenting judge, the late Bora Laskin, subsequently became the Chief Justice of the Supreme Court of Canada.

If the most eminent legal experts in the community disagree so sharply about what constitutes an "undue exploitation of sex", how is the lay citizen supposed to make such judgments? Unlike the situation with most other criminal laws, those who may be violating this one often have no way of determining in advance that they are doing so. A person who picks up a gun to rob a bank knows in advance that his conduct will run afoul of the criminal law. But a person who writes, publishes, or distributes a particular book may not know that the book in question will ultimately be considered an "undue exploitation of sex". Thus, unless they were virtually to avoid material with realistic sexual content, publishers, film makers, authors, and booksellers would be in a state of constant insecurity as to whether they were in compliance with the obscenity laws.

Moreover, as a practical matter, it is often the *police*, not the courts, who make the effective judgments as to what is obscene. Faced with the possible threat of prosecution or arrest, few publishers, theatre owners, distributors, and booksellers are likely to defy police instructions to discontinue a film showing or remove certain literature. Thus, in great numbers of cases, decisions are made without the courts ever considering the matter. There are times also when the distributors of material feel obliged to withhold it even without the involvement of the police. This works an unfairness especially in the case of large scale magazine distributors. Although they bear no responsibility for what has been published, they may become criminally responsible if they are involved in the distribution. This has imposed upon innocent third parties an obligation to act as censors. The hardships are exacerbated by the difficulties in interpreting what is essentially such a vague and subjective definition.

One flawed definition, of course, does not invalidate the exercise. But there is reason to fear that dangerous imprecision is inherent in the very attempt to define pornography. It would be useful, therefore, to examine some of the more important of the latest proposals in this area.

The last initiative in this area by the last Federal Government of the Liberal Party would have defined obscenity as "the undue exploitation of... sex, violence, crime, horror or cruelty, through degrading representations of a male or female person or in any other manner".

---

42. *R. v. Cameron* (1966), 58 D.L.R. (2d) 486 (Ont. C.A.).

The essence of this proposal was to move the definition of obscenity beyond the subject matter of sex. I think it would be likely to *increase* the dangers to legitimate communication. Indeed, this definition might be broad enough to suppress the 11 o'clock news. To what extent, for example, might pictures of Viet Nam war casualties and cult suicides be considered "undue" exploitation of violence or horror? How far might descriptions or commentary concerning executions, kidnappings, floggings, and gas chambers be construed as "degrading representations of a male or female person"? To what extent, therefore, might editors and commentators be subject to legal sanctions for the realistic portrayal of the news? Even if charges are not laid, such an enactment could create an apprehension that the coercive power of the state might intimidate our various media of communications.

Significantly, the National Action Committee on the Status of Women has proposed a narrower definition - "any printed, visual, audio or otherwise represented presentation, or part thereof, which seeks to sexually stimulate the viewer or consumer by the depiction of violence, including, but not limited to, the depiction of submission, coercion, lack of consent, or debasement of any human being".[43] And, for the purpose of this definition, NAC would make the depiction of anyone as being under the age of sixteen as sufficient to stigmatize the material as pornographic.

While the NAC approach contains fewer of the dangers than some of the others, it is nevertheless unduly flawed. If enacted into law, it could wind up suppressing a work of art such as the famous rape scene in Ingmar Bergman's classic "The Virgin Spring". Indeed, it might even prohibit important political commentary. Suppose, for example, that a film maker wished to dramatize some of the sexual horrors which occurred at Auschwitz? It is conceivable that such a portrayal would be very much in the public interest. By reviving and making vivid this despicable epoch in human history, it could help psychologically to fortify the viewer against the evils of racism. Yet, such a film arguably could fall within the NAC definition.

Indeed, the history of literature is full of material which might fit the NAC definition. In Robert Browning's classic poem, "My Last Duchess", a man's ownership of a woman is so complete that he murders her out of sexual jealousy. Notwithstanding his evil deed, he retains his social position and acquires another desirable woman as his next duchess. In Greek mythology, the God Zeus, appearing in the form of a swan, rapes the beautiful Leda. The progeny of this coerced union is the even more beautiful Helen of Troy. In Ayn Rand's "The Fountainhead", the protagonist is represented as a hero partly because of his

---

43. National Action Committee and the Status of Women, Brief to the Special Committee on Pornography and Prostitution, February 1984.

wilful character which results in the rape of the heroine. This is depicted by the author, without apology, as an expression of his admirable individuality.

Undoubtedly, partisans of the NAC approach could be expected to argue that none of this material seeks "to sexually stimulate"; therefore, none of it would be prohibited. It's not so clear, however, that such a finding would be made. To whatever extent the material did in fact cause sexual stimulation, there might well be an inference that this was intended. The law already contains a presumption that people intend the natural consequences of their acts. This would be rendered all the more likely to whatever extent the material were accompanied by pictures or expressed in film.

Moreover, the NAC argument has to rely primarily on the literary and cinematic judgment of the courts. It reveals no disrespect for our judges to point out that in matters of art, literature, and films, everyone's power of discernment is infected with subjectivity. What could appear to be a serious political or psychological statement to one viewer could well look like sexual exploitation to another. Remember, how diametrically our judges have already disagreed with one another about such matters. And, even if some of the NAC leaders were disposed to place a higher level of trust in the courts on this subject, would they feel the same way about the police who, as I have indicated, are most often the effective decision makers on issues of obscenity?

Considerations of space preclude an exhaustive examination of the definitions which have surfaced on this subject. Suffice it for now to indicate that I have never seen one which is devoid of the kind of difficulties I have been describing. Indeed, I don't think such a definition is possible. I suspect that our language simply lacks the precision to make the requisite distinctions. Thus, the key question is which of the competing risks is the least dangerous to incur. Is it better (or less bad) to risk the suppression of works of art and important political statements? Or is it better (or less bad) to risk the greater proliferation of material depicting unredeemed decadence and sadism?

At this stage of history, I believe it is more sensible to opt for the latter danger over the former one. In part, of course, this preference is based upon the desire to protect, as much as possible, the concomitants of freedom of expression. In part, also, my position is based upon some considerable doubt about the harm which flows from even the vilest forms of pornography.

A word about the contemplated dangers to women and children. Many of the current claims are based upon recent laboratory research in which men who have been exposed to certain kinds of violent pornography respond more aggressively to women than do those men who have not been so exposed.[44] The problem with such research is that the comparisons are necessarily confined to the socially approved aggression which the experiment subjects have been specifically invited to commit in the laboratory setting. There is a world of difference, however, between socially approved aggression in the laboratory and socially *disapproved* aggression in society. There have been many cases, for example, where violent football and hockey players were nevertheless gentle in "real life". Moreover, there has been little measurement of the cathartic effects of exposure to pornography. For how many men does such material serve as an instrument to sublimate their aggressive propensities?

On the basis of his review of the research literature, Professor Jonathan Freedman, Chairman of the Psychology Department at the University of Toronto, made the following statement.

> ... the particular work that has been done on the effects of pornography is fraught with problems and, in my opinion, tells us little about how exposure to pornography affects aggression or sexual crimes in the world outside the laboratory... The basic situation is that we do not have sufficient scientific evidence to draw any clear conclusions... there is no evidence that pornography is harmful to women or to our society.[45]

What about the suggestion of a long-term link between pornography and the subordination, even exploitation, of women? It has been argued, for example, that exposure to such material could fortify the male domination of our culture and render equality for females more difficult, even impossible, to achieve. Some commentators have gone even further and argued that exposure to pornography will gradually erode the taboos against sexual aggression.

Even if all this were true, legal prohibition need not follow. There are all kinds of influences which in time could create harm. But they don't operate in a vacuum. They are subject to counter influences. Indeed, couldn't it similarly be said that exposure to communist propaganda will gradually erode the taboos against totalitarianism and that exposure to films about adultery will gradually erode our commitment to the family? Aren't such risks inherent in the very exercise of the democratic system? In general, the democratic antidote to harmful material is not censorship but helpful material.

---

44. See, for example: Edward Donnerstein, "Aggressive Erotica and Violence Against Women", *Journal of Personality and Social Psychology* 39 (1980) 269-277; Neil Malamuth and James Check, "The Effects of Mass Media Exposure on Acceptance of Violence Against Women: A Field Experiment", *Journal of Research in Personality* 15 (1981) 436-446; Neil Malamuth and Edward Donnerstein, "The Effects of Aggressive-Pornographic Mass-Media Stimuli", in *Advances in Experimental Social Psychology*, ed. L. Berkowitz, N.Y.: Academic Press, 1982, p. 129.

45. Canadian Civil Liberties Association, Pornography and the Law, Special Committee on Pornography and Prostitution, April 6, 1984, at p. 19.

Indeed, in the case of women, there is growing evidence that this response is actually working. Despite what has been described as a proliferation of pornography in today's society, women have made more rapid progress than ever before in history. Within the past few years alone, the number of women entering male dominated occupations has increased very substantially. Certain faculties are reporting unprecedentedly high female enrolments. In some law classes, for example, at least 50% of the students are reportedly women. Moreover, every jurisdiction in this country contains a legal prohibition against sexual discrimination on the public market. No political leader of any stature or significance has suggested that such laws be repealed or even weakened. The arguments among the political leaders focus on how to *strengthen* such statutes.

This is not to suggest, of course, that the millennium for sexual equality has arrived. It is simply to observe that the publication of pornography has not necessarily undermined the quest for social progress.

The most compelling basis for encroaching on freedom of expression remains the clear and present danger. When someone falsely shouts ''fire'' in a crowded theatre, there is no opportunity for conflicting messages to be evaluated. There is likely to be an *immediate* panic. That is why such shouting can attract a legal sanction in those circumstances. On the basis of the research literature, however, aggressive pornography cannot be designated as a clear and present danger.

While much of this material cannot be categorized as physically injurious, there is no difficulty describing it as aesthetically offensive. We know, of course, that many people are repelled by sexually explicit material. Since they have just as much right to use the streets as those with stronger stomachs, the law might consider some measures to protect their sensibilities. In this connection, we should examine the distinction between public and private obscenity which was recommended by the Law Reform Commission of Canada.[46] It suggested that the law might regulate what sellers could display in public but not what adults could consume in private. One of the most eloquent explications of this distinction emerged in an essay by U.S. literary critic Irving Howe.

> If you want to go into one of those joints for five dollars and see what you see and do what you do there, I don't propose to stop you. But I see no reason why I or my kids should be *forced* to look, when we walk along the streets, at the stuff which delights you and disgusts me. Go to the porn movie but don't oblige me to look at its stills just because I'm walking by. Get your *Hustler* in a brown paper wrapper, but don't oblige me to be hustled by it just because there is a news stand around my corner.[47]

46. Canada. Law Reform Commission, The Limits of the Criminal Law Obscenity: A Test Case, Ottawa: Queen's Printers, 1979.
47. Irving Howe, ''The Problem of Pornography'', Dissent 25, Spring 1978, 193-208, p. 205.

It is significant that, in the same essay, Professor Howe makes the following statement.

> At this point in history, after all we have tasted of the age of totalitari-anism, how can anyone suppose that the possible benefits of censorship could outweigh the probable dangers?[48]

Thus far, I have dealt with material in which there is *simulated* sexual abuse. The films or books simply depict the offensive behaviour. In recent years, however, an even newer form of pornography has emerged which reportedly involves the actual, not simulated, abuse of real people. The "snuff" films are said to feature real tortures and killings. Some "kiddie porn" is supposed to involve real children in actual sexual encounters.

To the extent that certain particularly repugnant crimes are com-mitted for the purpose of titillating a potential audience or readership, there is an arguable case for a legal prohibition against the resulting film or literature. Indeed, this may be a variant of the "clear and present danger" exception. The knowledge that the films or pictures will enjoy a legally accessible market might serve as an incentive to the commis-sion of the initial crime. In that sense, there could be a direct relation-ship between the distribution of the material and the criminal assault on the particular individuals. When such assaults are committed *for the purpose* of producing distributable material, there is an argument for making it unlawful knowingly to engage in such distribution.

But, for the reasons indicated, it would be more dangerous to prohibit than to permit material involving *simulated* sexual abuse. Where such material is concerned, therefore, legal prohibition should not be attempted.

In any event, one practice which should be eliminated forthwith is film censorship. Prior restraint is a more pervasive intrusion even than subsequent prosecution. It is one thing to render people accountable for the things they publish and show. But it is quite another matter to require that they have their material cleared before they are allowed to convey it. Nor is there a need for such prior restraint. The power of subsequent prosecution is a potent weapon. Its mere existence is likely to deter the greatest number of potential offenders. Anyone who is not so deterred is not likely to be significantly more deterred by the need to go to a censorship board. In short, there is little difference in the enforcement coverage. But prior restraint exacts a greater level of intrusion on free-dom.

In this regard, the situation in Canada is absurdly anomalous. The disclosure of the most delicate of defence secrets is subject only to criminal prosecution. There is no obligation on any of the media to

---

48. *Ibid.*

clear such material with a censor before publishing it. Yet, in some places, sex-related films can be pre-censored. Conclusion: sex is potentially more dangerous than a breach of national security.

Apart from legal weapons, governments should explore alternate mechanisms for reducing the influence of pornography. If pornography can be seen as weakening the taboos on violence against women, there are certain activities which can be seen as strengthening such taboos. In this regard, consider the myriad of feminist activities in our society - the counselling of rape victims to charge their assailants, the provision of shelter and assistance for battered women, the campaigns for laws against sexual discrimination, the lobbies for improved daycare facilities, etc. The combined effect of all this is to impress the dignity of women on the psyche of society. Government should undertake, therefore, to increase its support of such activities.

THE PROPENSITY TO OVER PROHIBIT

It has to be acknowledged, of course, that there are a number of areas in which it is legitimate to impose some restrictions on freedom of expression. The problem in Canada, however, is that many of these restrictions are greater than the situation warrants.

These excesses are perpetrated, not by malevolent autocrats who seek to do evil, but by "tunnel visioned" bureaucrats who seek to do good. The fixation with their good goals often makes them obliviously insensitive to the other interests that they affect. Fearing most of all being caught out on a limb, such bureaucrats take no chances. They engage in what I call "power-hoarding".

In order to avoid even the remotest possibility of failure, they seek an expanding level of power to accomplish their objectives. Such power is designed to cover every hypothetical scenario that the bureaucratic imagination can conjure. The problem is that each additional grant of power for the bureaucrats is often acquired at the cost of commensurately less freedom for the citizenry.

The result is a host of needless restrictions on our fundamental freedom of expression. What follows is an examination of some of the more glaring examples.

Official Secrets

Because of the dangers in the world around us, it would be hard to object to a legal prohibition against the disclosure of our nation's vital secrets. Indeed, since the advent of the nation state, espionage has been almost universally prohibited. But our *Official Secrets Act*, like some of its counterparts elsewhere, goes even further. It prohibits not only spying but also "leaking". Conceivably, some well-motivated leaks to the media could cause as much damage as some ill-motivated tips to our enemies. Thus, I cannot object in principle to an anti-leakage prohibition.

But, instead of defining as narrowly as possible the kind of material which should be barred from publication, the *Official Secrets Act* in Canada goes almost to the other extreme. It renders unlawful virtually *any* unauthorized disclosure of government information. Indeed, the prohibition is so wide that a former British Attorney General said, about the similar provisions of his country's statute, that a person could go to jail for doing nothing more than reporting "the number of cups of tea consumed per week in a government department".[49]

The problem is that it is the government that must authorize a disclosure. And it is the government that reviews the validity of such government decisions. And the government, of course, has partisan political, as well as national security, interests to protect. Thus, on the basis of a unilateral, unreviewable, and potentially self-serving decision of the government, the press may not be free to publish and the public may lose its right to know.

There is simply no valid basis for an encroachment on freedom of expression which is at once so broad in its scope and so devoid of adequate safeguards. While this country has not suffered a plethora of official secrets prosecutions, some disquieting trials have nevertheless occurred within the past few years. Charges were brought against Peter Treu for unlawful retention of government information even though his authorization to have the material had been revoked without his knowledge.[50] Charges were also brought against the Toronto Sun newspaper even though much of the government information it published had already been disclosed in another public medium.[51] Although both accused were ultimately acquitted, they paid a high price in terms of time, money, and tension. Moreover, the problem with the *Official Secrets Act* is not only the prosecutions that have been launched but also the ones that can be threatened. After all, the precious freedom of expression can be diminished as much by the fear, as the reality, of prosecution.

Nothing short of a statutory overhaul will suffice. In my view, the offence should be narrowed to the point where the only state secrets which it is criminally unlawful to disclose are those that could reasonably be expected to cause serious injury to the physical safety and defence of Canada. As far as the disclosure of other vital government

---

49. *Sir Lionel Heald, Q.C., in The Times, March 20, 1970, p. 13, cited in David Williams, "Official Secrecy and the Courts" in P.R. Glazebrook (ed.), Reshaping the Criminal Law, London, 1978, at p. 160-1.*

50. *R. v. Treu* (1979), 49 C.C.C. (2d) 222 (Que. C.A.).

51. *R. v. Toronto Sun Publishing Ltd.* (1979), 24 O.R. (2d) 621 (Prov. Ct.).

secrets are concerned - cabinet documents, inter provincial negotiations, etc. - the need for the criminal sanction has not been demonstrated.

In the first place, we are told by experts such as William Clark
that, to a great extent in the Anglo American democracies, "secrecy is
maintained by tradition rather than by laws or rules".[52] In the second
place, most civil servants who leak government information are likely
to be vulnerable to various forms of employment discipline. In the third
place, it should be possible to create or enforce a variety of civil remedies for at least some of the damage that is sustained as a result of a
breach of a secrecy oath.

In short, it should suffice to invoke a mix of tradition, discipline,
and civil liability on those who breach their employment or contractual
oaths of secrecy. But, apart from vital defence secrets, the criminal
sanction need not and should not be used on them or anyone else. This
means that very little would get out that shouldn't and most of what did
could safely be published. By and large, this would strike about the
right balance.

I am bolstered in this approach by the fact that its general direction,
if not its specific details, has been adopted by a number of major inquiries into the subject which have been conducted in the United Kingdom
and Canada in recent years.[53] The consensus of all these efforts is that
the role of the criminal sanction should be substantially reduced.

In some respects, the American experience might be even more
persuasive. A number of experts believe that, apart from a narrow range
of cryptographical material and espionage, it may not be unlawful to

---

52. William Clark, at p. 12 of a paper prepared for the Conference on Secrecy, Democ-
    racy, and Foreign Policy held at New York University in February, 1973. The
    papers presented at the Conference were subsequently published under the title
    Secrecy and Foreign Policy, ed. Thomas M. Franck and Edward Weisband, New
    York, Oxford University Press, 1974.
53. Great Britain, Report of the Departmental Committee on Section 2 of the *Official
    Secrets Act* 1911, Cmnd. 5104, London, 1972 (the Franks Report).
    Great Britain. Reform of Section 2 of the *Official Secrets Act* 1911, Cmnd. 7285,
    July 1978.
    Canada. Commission of Inquiry Concerning Certain Activities of the Royal Cana-
    dian Mounted Police, First Report, Security and Information Ottawa, Queen's
    Printer, 1979.
    Many of my detailed disagreements with these inquiries can be found in the fol-
    lowing:
       Canadian Civil Liberties Association, Public Disclosure and the *Official Secrets
       Act*, Submission to the MacDonald Commission, October 3, 1979.
       Canadian Civil Liberties Association, Brief: Bill C-43 The Accessibility of Gov-
       ernment Information and the Protection of Personal Information. Presented to
       the House of Commons Standing Committee on Justice and Legal Affairs, March
       26, 1981.

publish even defence information in the United States.[54] There is much agreement with the expert who argued that no criminal sanction could have applied to a U.S. newspaper for accurately publishing the headline, "Normandy to be Invaded", where the purpose was simply to appease reader curiosity.[55] While this issue has created some controversy in that country, it is significant that there has never been a *conviction* for the mere leakage of defence information. It isn't necessary to urge the replication of this liberalism in Canada in order to appreciate how the American experience dramatizes the unwarrantedly draconian nature of the Canadian law.

The adequate protection for freedom of expression in this area will require also an improvement in the procedures for prosecution. Under the current *Official Secrets Act*, it is difficult for an accused to challenge the government's classification of whatever documents may have been leaked. While I have been associated elsewhere with some detailed proposals to address this problem,[56] it will suffice for the moment to indicate the importance of *independent review* of such governmental decisions. At the very least, a court should be required to conduct an *in camera* examination of the contested documents. Before a conviction could be registered, the court should be required to find that the government's classification decisions satisfied the statutory criteria. In this way, the law would reduce the risk that anyone could be muzzled or jailed on the basis of a self-serving governmental fiat.

Sedition

The existence of this offence owes its origins to the fear of revolutionary violence. Why should the power of the state languish in helpless paralysis until the violence actually occurs? Shouldn't our law enforcement authorities have some power of prevention?

As a consequence, our law prohibits not only the acts of violence but also a certain amount of the speech which precedes them. The sedition section renders punishable a person who "teaches or advocates... the use, without the authority of law, of force as a means to accomplish a governmental change within Canada".

---

54. Benno C. Schmidt, Jr., "The Espionage Statutes and Publication of Defense Information", p. 36, Conference on Secrecy, Democracy and Foreign Policy.
   As the Ellsberg and recent Morrison cases make clear, this interpretation is not shared by the U.S. Justice Department. Significantly, however, until the abortive attempt to prosecute Ellsberg, every U.S. indictment for the unlawful disclosure of defence information since the amendments of 1950 contained a specific allegation that the accused intended to injure the United States or assist a foreign power. See Boudin on the Ellsberg case, Conference on Secrecy, Democracy and Foreign Policy, at p. 17.
55. See *Schmidt, supra*, fn. 54, at p. 19.
56. See CCLA Brief on the *Official Secrets Act, supra*, fn. 53.

Again, I believe the law goes further than necessary. The issue is at what point in the continuum between the thought and the deed is it appropriate for the law to intervene. Speech which is likely to result in imminent violence is arguably dangerous enough to warrant legal intervention. On the other hand, speech which is not likely to culminate in this way does not warrant such intervention.

The risk which is created in the sedition offences is that mere teaching and advocacy are sufficiently wide and vague to encompass the soapbox orator who has no followers and the theoretician who seeks no followers. A person who expresses the desirability of overthrowing the government by force is not necessarily a threat. A person who philosophically justifies revolution or violence is not necessarily a threat. The threat is the call to action by someone who has followers. The law properly intervenes at the point where speech is likely to precipitate immediate action.

On this basis, the sedition sections should prohibit not the mere teaching or advocacy of the violent overthrow of government, but rather the *incitement* to such action. To leave the law in its current state is to run the risk of punishing the impotent preacher along with the dangerous demagogue. Canadian criminal law should be amended to confine the offence of sedition to the incitement of violence against government in situations where there is a clear and present danger that the incitement will be acted upon.

Sub Judice Contempt of Court

"Trial by media" has become a pejorative epithet in our society. The feeling is that adjudication must occur in the dignified setting of a courtroom, not in the sensationalized representations of the media. One of the most important instruments for obtaining this objective is the legal concept known as "sub judice". Under our law, certain public statements about pending court cases are subject to punishment for contempt of court. The ostensible goal is to protect the right to a fair hearing.

Again, there is certainly a plausible basis for the existence of such a restriction on freedom of expression. The right to a fair trial has to enjoy a very high priority in a society like ours and so there is an understandable desire to suppress whatever speech might interfere with it. Once more, however, I believe that the legal prohibition (or at least the general understanding of it) may well go too far.

During the fall of 1983, alone, there were three separate incidents in which the "sub judice" prohibition became the basis for some very questionable attempts to intrude on freedom of expression.

In December of that year, the Chief Justice of Canada rebuked Ottawa lawyer Lawrence Greenspon for arguing his impending cruise missile case outside of court before arguing it inside. According to the judge, the lawyer's behaviour had come "close to contempt of court".[57]

It's hard to fathom why it was wrong for Greenspon to grant media interviews about his Charter challenge of the government's proposed cruise missile tests. Indeed, in the circumstances, his interviews might have made a positive contribution to the public interest. They could have helped to inform the public about the rather complicated issues in the case. Thus, members of the public would have been more likely to be able to follow what happened when the matter got to court. To restrict such pre-hearing commentary is to make the public excessively dependent on press reports of the incomprehensible legalisms which are uttered in court.

In any event, how could Greenspon's public pronouncements possibly undermine the court processes? In no way was he dealing with matters of evidence the disclosure of which could prejudice a potential jury. He was dealing essentially with legal and policy issues which were slated for consideration by professionally trained judges. When such issues are involved, the adjudicators are not confined, as they may be on questions of evidence, to what they hear in the courtroom. They are clearly entitled to seek help outside. What harm was therefore caused?

Indeed, I question how far such pre-trial restrictions should apply even to evidentiary questions.

In October of 1983, for example, the panelists at an Ontario Press Council forum were circulated with a lawyer's letter cautioning them about any statements they might wish to make on the subject of the controversial Susan Nelles case.[58] Since Nelles had begun a lawsuit against certain law enforcement officials, the panelists were warned to be careful not to say anything which could influence a potential member of the jury. If it were alleged, for example, that the police had been out to "get" the young nurse, the speaker might be found in contempt of court.

As important as it is to protect the right of a fair trial for all parties who are involved in court cases, should it really operate as such a broad restriction on freedom of speech and the press? Why should a private lawsuit of the kind Nelles launched deprive the public of an important and timely debate about the police handling of her case? The entire public had an interest in determining at the earliest possible moment whether the police had misbehaved at that time.

It simply will not suffice to tell the public, as some courts periodically have done, that freedom of speech on such matters is not being

---

57. See newspaper reports, December 23, 1983.
58. See commentary in Trial by Media, A Report on an Open Forum sponsored by the Ontario Press Council, Ottawa, 1984, at p. 6-7.

denied, it is simply being delayed - until the end of the trial. Such replies are hardly consoling. This kind of litigation could go on for years. Is the public supposed to rest content all that time? If there was indeed misconduct in the police investigation, might it not be repeated against other people? Moreover, several years from the time at issue, there will be a lot less inclination for a vigorous debate. The passage of time has a way of eroding political enthusiasm.

Where issues of such public importance are concerned, why can't the legal and political processes run concurrently? Why should the courts be allowed to exercise this kind of monopoly over whatever issues are brought before them? In short, I question why the judicial process should enjoy such an automatic priority over all of the other processes in our society.

In any event, if the chief harm is the undue influencing of potential jurors, this might be addressed in the jury selection process. Or, we might even ask the provinces to modify the right to trial by jury in some affected civil cases.

I assume that our society would be prepared to trust its judges to resist the influence of a public debate. Indeed, this is the kind of trust we repose in them all the time.

Judges are often expected, for example, to exclude from their consideration some evidence which they may have ruled inadmissible. If we depend on our judges to disabuse themselves of something they may have heard within the last two minutes, why can't that apply to something that they may have read within the last two months? Despite the importance we attach to trial by jury, its preservation in civil disputes cannot outweigh the right of the public to a full and timely scrutiny of its vital institutions.

I have more sympathy with the attempt to curtail certain press comment about pending *criminal* trials. This is designed to reduce the risk that innocent people will be railroaded into jail as a consequence of sensationalizing by the media. Yet, even in criminal matters, the law of contempt may go too far.

In September of the same year, for example, a former Toronto alderman, accused of indecently assaulting a juvenile, convened a press conference to answer the charges against him. The Toronto Star report of the press conference omitted some of the alderman's most crucial arguments. Perhaps the omission was explained by the Star's rather remarkable comment that much of what the accused and his supporters had to say could well be a contempt of court?[59] How bizarre! A law whose prime function is to protect the accused winds up suppressing what he says in his own defence.

---

59. *Toronto Star*, September 20, 1983.

It is not clear, how far, if at all, any of the above matters would actually have been found in contempt of court. But, when the Toronto Star, an eminent press council lawyer, and the Chief Justice of Canada raise the contempt issue in relation to such matters, it becomes apparent that the law itself has to undergo a substantial change. A viable democracy cannot afford to create such an aura of doubt about the legality of legitimate debate.

A PERSPECTIVE

The Joint Parliamentary hearings on Canada's Constitution (1980-81) generated great expectations for our new Charter of Rights and Freedoms. The resulting document is very much a synthesis of the many suggestions that were made, particularly by the host of voluntary citizen groups that went to Ottawa to testify on it. For this reason, the development and evolution of the Charter have a special importance. To whatever extent the reality fails to fulfill the expectations, cynicism is likely to ensue.

It's not without significance that "freedom of expression" is found among the first cluster of freedoms which appear in the Charter. No doubt, this is some reflection of the central role which this freedom was designed to play in our kind of society. Of no less significance is the fact that our Charter uses the word "expression" rather than simply "speech" as is the case in the U.S. Bill of Rights which so heavily influenced the Canadian debates. Moreover, we should take note also of the fact that the guarantee for "freedom of expression" is augmented by a number of other guarantees which have no apparent counterpart in the U.S. Bill of Rights - "freedom of thought, belief, (and) opinion".

All this suggests that those who enacted the Canadian Charter intended to expand this range of protections beyond what is contained in the U.S. Constitution. That's why it's particularly disquieting to face the possibility that demonstrations and picket lines may be defined as something beyond the reach of this provision. And that's why we should be particularly wary of those American cases which hold that certain kinds of speech such as obscenity fall outside of the constitutional protection. But it's also why we have to be somewhat cheered by the remarks of the Ontario Supreme Court to the effect that art, music, and dance are, for such purposes, forms of "expression".

While we must spare no effort to persuade the courts to adopt a liberal construction of this freedom, we would be unwise to put all of our eggs in the judicial basket. The history of Canadian jurisprudence reveals an unacceptable conservatism on such matters. The trends since the Charter's proclamation are too mixed for comfort. Moreover, so much will depend on matters beyond logic and our control, for example, the cosmic coincidence of what judges happen to sit on any given case. In any event, since reform by the judiciary can only develop on a case by case basis, even the most liberal judges are not likely to produce anything more than a piecemeal patchwork of inadequate responses.

That's why so many of the foregoing comments explicitly seek a legislative solution to the problems they address. This is not to exaggerate legislative solutions either. It is simply to recognize that legislation can usually provide a more comprehensive way of dealing with problems than can adjudication. In any event, we are likely to achieve more by moving on all fronts. Thus, we must be prepared to continue the quest for freedom of expression not only in the judicial but also in the political arena. This means what it has always meant - testifying before Parliamentary Committees, lobbying politicians, courting the media, and, yes, even demonstrating and picketing.

Finally, we must resist the use of unrealistic criteria to measure the validity of our efforts. No matter how robust the protections for freedom of expression may become, our society is not likely to undergo any early or utopian transformation. Indeed, some of our disagreements could well be rather unpleasant. We might well have an increase in disruption - demonstrating, picketing, offensive speaking, etc. Hardly an idyllic situation.

To put these matters in perspective, I am reminded of a comment which was made by John Turner during the 1974 federal election campaign. In response to attacks on the Prime Minister, Mr. Turner said, ''don't compare the Prime Minister to the Almighty, compare him to the alternative''.

While it must be acknowledged that strong protections for freedom of expression cannot promise to make life lovely, weak protections can promise to make it intolerable. That remains the most sensible basis for action in the real world.

"Ignorance is strength."

"L'ignorance c'est la force."

George Orwell, *1984*

THE RIGHT TO PRIVACY: FREEDOM FROM INFORMATION

LE DROIT À L'INTIMITÉ: LE DROIT DE NE PAS ÊTRE CONTRAINT DE SUBIR L'INFORMATION

The Protection of Privacy: The Judicial Role

John D. McCamus*

INTRODUCTION

Privacy is a much cherished value in our society. A number of explanations for this may be offered. Invasions of one's privacy disrupt one's peace of mind. As well, depending on their nature and severity, they may inflict serious mental distress and substantial pecuniary loss. A moment's reflection will suggest that the preservation of a realm for private thought and private action is conducive, not merely to the preservation of one's mental health, but to the preservation of other valued features of our social and political lives. As Alan Westin argued in his influential study, *Privacy and Freedom*,[1] some measure of freedom from surveillance of one's activities by others is a necessary condition for the exercise of moral choice. To the extent that one conforms with social norms because of the presence of surveillance rather than on the basis of independent assessment of their moral worth, one's autonomy is obviously diminished.

Moral autonomy is not desirable solely as an instrument of personal fulfillment. It is an essential condition for meaningful participation in democratic government. A society which forbade the free association of individuals and ideas, refused to utilise the secret ballot or in other ways constrained the formulation or expression of political views, would be thought by many to be, to this degree, undemocratic by reason of its unwarranted invasions of personal privacy. One would expect, then, that democratic societies would be particularly anxious to avoid inhibiting personal autonomy through the use of excessive surveillance, especially surveillance deployed by the state.

As others have pointed out, the ability to control the kinds of disclosures that are made to another also plays an important role in the development of personal relations of various kinds. If we were, for example, to develop a public register of all available medical information concerning individuals, there would be a number of reasons for

* Dean, Osgoode Hall Law School, York University.
1. Alan F. Westin, *Privacy and Freedom* (Atheneum, N.Y., 1967).

lamenting this invasion of individual privacy. Not the least of them, however, would be that it would deprive individuals suffering from medical difficulties of one sort or another of the ability to engage in the process of deciding whether or not and when to disclose information of this kind to another individual. The capacity to make such determinations plays an important part in defining one's personal relations with others.[2] Indeed, if one could routinely discover the intimate details of others' lives, social interaction as we understand it at the present time would be drastically altered in ways which we would no doubt find rather unpleasant.

This much has been evident, at least since Orwell,[3] and it is no doubt for reasons such as these that historians and anthropologists have been able to identify the protection of privacy as a concern in earlier times and in societies very unlike our own.[4] It is also evident that there is a widespread perception that in our own time, privacy values are threatened as never before.[5] Some may find this surprising. Contemporary life, especially in large urban settings, appears to offer opportunities for anonymity, isolation and secrecy[6] which were unavailable to our ancestors. I share the view, however, that privacy values are under increasing pressure and that their protection requires renewed legislative and judicial effort.

There are a variety of sources of this pressure. Tradition requires that at least some of the blame be laid at the feet of the media. Indeed, the influential 1890 law review article of Warren and Brandeis[7] is said to have been provoked by press coverage of the wedding of the daughter of Mr. Warren.[8] Certainly, the evolving practices of the print and electronic media in the ensuing ninety-odd years have done little to under-

---

2. C. Fried, *An Anatomy of Values* (Harvard University Press, Cambridge, 1970) c. 9.
3. George Orwell, *1984* (Signet, N.Y., 1950). And see, I. Howe (ed.), *1984 Revisited: Totalitarianism in our Century* (Harper & Rowe, N.Y., 1984).
4. See, generally, Westin, *op. cit., supra*, note 1 at pp. 8-18; J.M. Roberts and T. Gregor, *Privacy: A Cultural View*, in J.R. Pennock and J.W. Chapman (eds.) *Privacy* (Atherton Press, N.Y.; 1971) at pp. 199-225; P.H. Klopfer and D.I. Rubenstein, *Privacy and its Biological Basis* (1977), Journal of Social Issues 52.
5. N. Vidmar & D. Flaherty, "Concern for Personal Privacy in an Electronic Age", *Journal of Communication* (in press). A more detailed version of this study is to be found in N. Vidmar, *Privacy and Two-Way Cable Television: Public Opinion* (Ont. Min. of Trans. and Comm., Downsview, 1983).
6. These having been identified, in a persuasive article, as the three irreducible elements of "privacy". See, R. Gavison, "Privacy and the Limits of Law" (1980), 89 *Yale L.J.* 421 ("Our interest in privacy, I argue, is related to our concern over accessibility to others: the extent to which we are known to others, the extent to which others have physical access to us, and the extent to which we are the subjects of others' attention." at p. 423).
7. C. Warren and L.D. Brandeis, "The Right to Privacy" (1890), 4 *Harv. L. Rev.* 92.
8. H. Kalven Jr., "Privacy in Tort Law - Were Warren and Brandeis Wrong?" (1966), 31 *Law and Cont. Problems* 326 at 329, n. 22.

mine legitimate concern of this kind. Nevertheless, there appear to be more important causal factors linked to the emergence of modern technologies of various kinds and to the growth of the modern state.

The importance of technological innovation is most easily seen in the context of surveillance technologies. Indeed, the central diagnosis of the privacy problem set forth in Westin's *Privacy and Freedom*[9] was that technological innovation of this kind had outstripped the capacity of the legal system to protect privacy values. Whereas the American legal system in the late eighteenth and nineteenth centuries had successfully protected privacy through laws relating to trespass, privacy of the mails and the like, the modern legal system had not yet developped responses to such developments as the invention of optical and acoustical "bugging" devices, the growing use of the polygraph and other psychological testing devices and the increasing use of computer technology in the collection and manipulation of personal information concerning individuals.[10] In the decade and a half since the publication of Westin's book, innovation in surveillance technology has, of course, continued and, notwithstanding some adaptation of the legal system, its use remains largely unregulated at the present time. In recent years, the principal contribution of technological change has been to produce unanticipated economies in what are now familiar modes of surveillance. Surveillance in the work place has surfaced as an issue in recent years not long after monitoring devices became inexpensive and their utilisation by management became an economically sound proposition.

It is not only the surveillance technologies, however, that appear to carry with them a capacity to reduce the quality of our private lives. We live in an era in which technological change is a pervasive reality. Modern technologies are not only enormously powerful but carry with them very considerable risks of injury through misuse, either intended or accidental. This has led, in turn, for an increased appetite for the kinds of social control which we can purchase, or think we can purchase, through increased use of surveillance techniques. Powerful and risky technologies of whatever type thus generate an apparent need for more effective surveillance and create serious risks for the protection of personal privacy. Nuclear energy is perhaps the most obvious illustration of a technology of this kind and it would appear that we are only just beginning to appreciate some of the risks to our civil liberties inherent in the utilisation of this technology.[11]

For the average citizen, it may be that the most important source of the pressure to invade personal privacy arises from the growth of the

---

9. *Supra*, n. 1.
10. *Id.*, p. 98.
11. See, generally, "Symposium: The Civil Liberties Implications of Nuclear Power Development" (1980-81), 10 *N.Y.U. Rev. L. & Soc. Change* 183.

modern state. The latter is not a phenomenon unrelated to the growth of technology, of course, inasmuch as the enormous growth in the size of the state reflects, in part, a series of decisions to harness some of these modern technologies through public institutions. But more importantly, the enormous range and complexity of the tasks we have assigned to the state in recent history has generated an ever increasing need for the collection and manipulation of personal information - indeed, often quite intimate personal information. Public institutions simply know much more about the individuals with whom they have contact than they did in the past.

It must be conceded, then, that the recent and remarkable increase in the handling of personal data by government is, in part, at least, an unavoidable consequence of asking the state to undertake the range of services it now provides. And yet, the highly sensitive nature and the amount of much of the information that is gathered appears to reflect as well an insensitivity to the implications for privacy protection of the design of systems of eligibility and entitlement.[12] Be that as it may, this growth in data gathering and manipulation or ''data surveillance'' as Westin called it,[13] generates a number of privacy ''costs''. Being required to yield sensitive information is viewed by many as an invasion of their privacy. Secondly, the now rather remarkable documentation of our lives creates the risk that people will ''behave for the record'' rather than in accord with their own best lights. People are deprived of the opportunity to put the past behind them. (How curious that we recognise so clearly the need for this in the context of records of criminal convictions,[14] but not with respect to lesser misdeeds and embarrassments.)

Thirdly, the collection of sensitive information also creates the risk that such information will be misused either within the public authorities themselves or through inappropriate transfer of the information beyond their boundaries. It is for reasons such as these that the need for extensive regulation of the operation of government personal data banks has come to the top of most privacy reform agendas.

There are other features of modern life that are conducive to the gathering and circulation of personal information. Mention has not been made of the impact of politically motivated violence on the escalation of surveillance by the state for security purposes nor of the extensive use of computerised information systems by the private sector. Perhaps enough has been said, however, to substantiate the general proposition that privacy values are under intense pressure at the present time. Sup-

---

12. This view is developed in J. Rule, *The Politics of Privacy* (New American Library, New York, 1980).

13. *The Criminal Records Act*, R.S.C. 1970, 1st Supp., c. 12.

14. *Supra*, note 1 at pp. 158 et seq.

port for these broader propositions may be found in the reports of two recent Royal Commissions, the Commission of Inquiry Concerning Certain Activities of the Royal Canadian Mounted Police (The McDonald Commission) and the Commission of Inquiry into the Confidentiality of Health Information (The Krever Commission). The McDonald Commission Report[15] chronicles and usefully analyses the dangers of overzealous surveillance and disruptive tactics with respect to national security matters. It also demonstrates that surveillance undertaken for reasons of national security is remarkably extensive and, in certain instances at least, remarkably insensitive to privacy protection concerns.[16] The findings of the Krever Commission are, however, perhaps of greater significance for the broad propositions set forth above. As is well known, the provinces have created massive data banks to facilitate the operation of medicare schemes. These computerised systems contain basic information, including diagnostic data, pertaining to every visit made to a physician whose services are covered by the scheme. It could not be more obvious that this information is, in many cases, highly sensitive. One would expect that the precautions taken against improper disclosure would be as extensive as possible, and one would expect, further, as was the case, the disclosure would be prohibited by the statute under which the information is collected.[17] And yet, the Krever Report[18] informs us that sensitive medical information was frequently obtained from the Ontario OHIP data bank by law enforcement officials, by private investigative firms and by others for a variety of uses. The fact that a particular individual had visited a psychiatrist and received a particular diagnosis was utilised by a law enforcement agency in its attempts to disrupt the activities of a political group.[19] Medical histories were made available to private sector parties interested in them for such purposes as preparation for litigation and investigations by employers of prospective employees.

The lessons that can be drawn from the Krever Report are many. I will confine myself to a few general points. First, the Krever experience suggests that if sensitive personal information has sufficient value in the marketplace, its improper disclosure is likely to occur, notwithstanding the presence of measures taken to ensure the physical security of the data and notwithstanding the existence of criminal prohibitions

---

15. Commission of Inquiry Concerning Certain Activities of the Royal Canadian Mounted Police, *Second Report, Volume 1, Freedom and Security Under Law* (Supply and Services Canada, Ottawa, 1981).

16. As, for example, in the context of surveillance of the activities of political parties. *Id.*, at pp. 445 et seq.

17. *The Health Insurance Act 1972*, S.O. 1972, c. 91, as am. S.O. 1974, c. 60 and c. 86, secs. 44 and 50.

18. Commission of Inquiry into the Confidentiality of Health Information, *The Report*, 3 Volumes, (Queen's Printer, Ontario, 1980).

19. *Id.*, vol. 2, pp. 38 et seq.

against disclosure. Second, the privacy concern with respect to personal autonomy and ''behaviour for the record'' is highlighted by the Krever revelations. Would a young person at the beginning of a professional career be likely to, or perhaps be wise to, consider the implications of the Krever Report before visiting a psychiatrist, for example?

Third, the potential for misuse of sensitive data by public authorities is apparently not a phenomenon restricted to the United States of the Watergate era. Fourth, the diminution in privacy effected by the scheme affects, to some extent at least, the population generally. Finally, as is too often the case, these privacy ''costs'' of the medicare scheme are the incidental and presumably unintended effect of a scheme that perhaps most would find desirable in all other respects.

The privacy protection problem, in my view, is a large and growing one. A comprehensive strategy for addressing this problem must find its major focus in the legislative and executive branches of government. There are, however, a number of areas in which a constructive and appropriate contribution can be made by the judiciary. I propose to touch briefly on three areas of interest, the recognition of a tort of invasion of privacy, the interpretation of the new federal *Privacy Act*,[20] and the protection of privacy values under the *Canadian Charter of Rights and Freedoms*.[21]

THE TORT OF INVASION OF PRIVACY

American courts, building on the work of Warren and Brandeis,[22] and the later work of Prosser,[23] have given explicit recognition to a tort of invasion of privacy.[24] No similar development has occurred in common law Canada[25] or, and this is not an unrelated fact of course, in England.[26] The reasons for this are perhaps not abundantly clear. Judicial conservatism may play a role, but the law of torts has been a rather fertile, occasionally even volatile, area of doctrinal growth. Further,

---

20. See, text, *infra*, at n. 64.
21. See, text, *infra*, at n. 76.
22. *Supra*, n. 7.
23. W. Prosser, ''Privacy'' (1960), 48 *Cal. L. Rev.* 383.
24. Indeed, it is Prosser's view that the tort is not one, but a complex of four linked by a common concern with the ''right to be let alone'', intrusion upon the plaintiff's physical solitude or seclusion, public disclosure of private facts, appropriation of the plaintiff's name or likeness for the defendant's benefit and publicity placing the plaintiff in a false light in the public eye. See, W. Prosser, *Torts* (4th ed., 1971) p. 804 et seq.
25. See, e.g., *Re Zaduk* v. *The Queen* (1979), 98 D.L.R. (3d) 133 at pp. 142-143, per Weatherston J.A. (*dictum* to this effect in a dissenting judgment).
26. See, e.g., *dicta* in *Malone* v. *Metropolitan Police Commissioner*, [1979] 2 All E.R. 620 at p. 644 *per* Megarry V.-C.; *Re X*, [1973] 1 All E.R. 697 et 704 *per* Lord Denning M.R. See, generally, J.G. Fleming, *The Law of Torts* (6th ed., 1983) c. 25.

although it is no doubt true that plaintiffs whose privacy has been invaded are not likely to wish to compound their injury through the publicity that might be associated with a lawsuit, it is nonetheless true that many plaintiffs have been willing to come forward in the United States.[27]

As one who, for obvious professional reasons, chooses to believe that law review articles are of some influence, I like to think that it is significant that Canadian and English authors of law review articles on the general subject of privacy in recent years appear to be unfavourably disposed to the idea that recognition of the privacy tort would be a desirable innovation.[28] At the risk of considerable over-simplification, it may be said that there are essentially two schools of thought underlying these views. First, there is a body of opinion which suggests that the existing nominate torts, including trespass, battery, nuisance, defamation, intentional infliction of nervous shock, breach of confidence and, possibly, passing off, often have the effect of protecting privacy values and, indeed, substantially occupy the field.[29] Thus, recognition of a privacy tort is thought to be an unnecessary step or an undesirable source of potential confusion.[30] This view also attracted the support of the distinguished Younger Committee in England, which suggested that the claim for breach of confidence could "turn out to be a practical instrument for dealing with many complaints in the privacy field".[31]

The second school of thought rejects this sort of suggestion and adopts the view that there are important gaps in the treatment of privacy problems by the existing common law. This group suggests that the

---

27. In 1971, Prosser observed that there were more than four hundred reported cases. See, Prosser, *op. cit.*, n. 24, p. 804.

28. A noteworthy exception, from which I have profited, is S. Stoljar, "A Re-examination of Privacy" (1984), 4 *Leg. Stud.* 67.

29. It may be that one should now tentatively add conversion to this list. The Ontario Court of Appeal, in *R.* v. *Stewart* (1983), 149 D.L.R. (3d) 583 held that confidential information concerning certain employees could be the subject of theft within the meaning of the Criminal Code. The decision has been severely criticized, however, and is under appeal to the Supreme Court of Canada. See R.G. Hammond, "Theft of Information" (1984), 100 L.Q.R. 252 for an extended critique of Stewart.

30. See, for example, J. Irvine, "The Invasion of Privacy in Ontario - A 1983 Survey", in *Law Society of Upper Canada, Special Lectures, Torts in the '80s* (1983) 25-58; R. Wacks, "The Property of Privacy" (1980), 96 *L.Q.R.* 73. And see, D. Gibson, "Common Law Protection of Privacy: What to do Until the Legislators Arrive", in L. Klar (ed.), *Studies in Canadian Tort Law* (1977) 343 at 376, suggesting that "even in provinces lacking general privacy legislation, common law principles offer reasonably satisfactory protection of privacy" and further, that recognition of a general principle of protecting privacy through tort law is likely to be articulated in the future. Nonetheless, the author appears to favour the enactment of privacy legislation.

31. *Report of the Committee on Privacy*, 1982, Cmnd. 5012 at p. 204 (Chmn., The Rt. Hon. Kenneth Younger).

courts ought not to be encouraged to develop new doctrine in this, or indeed in other areas, inasmuch as they are ill-equipped to decide important questions of public policy. Such writers note that a privacy tort has been established by legislative enactment in four Canadian provinces[32] and suggest that this is the appropriate forum for reform of this kind.[33]

As it is my view that judicial recognition of a privacy tort would be an appropriate innovation, it follows that I must suppress my reverence for law reviews and suggest that both schools of thought are misconceived. I offer two responses. With respect to the first point of view, I argue that obvious and compelling cases of privacy invasion are currently not remedied by the existing common law torts, thus rendering recognition of the privacy tort a useful step. My response to the second point of view is that such writers fail to acknowledge the existence of the law-making role confided to the judiciary by our constitutional system and, in so doing, pander to that strain of judicial thought which seeks to abdicate this responsibility. As a preliminary point, I should note that on both fronts I draw strength from the basic thesis of the first school which holds that existing tort principle now occupies much of the privacy field. As this is indeed the case, it is but a short step to the recognition of a privacy tort and for this reason alone, an appropriate one for the courts themselves to take without awaiting legislative instruction to do so.

In developing a concise but, hopefully, persuasive statement of the view that there are important gaps in the current treatment of privacy problems at common law, I propose to deal with two different categories of privacy invasion - intrusions, that is to say actions invading an individual's physical isolation or realm of secrecy, and secondly, unwanted publicity, that is, actions involving an invasion of an individual's desire for anonymity.[34] The first category, intrusions, is best illustrated by the activities of those who engage in prying and spying - that is, eavesdroppers and those who have been so colourfully described

---

32. British Columbia, Manitoba, Saskatchewan and Newfoundland. See, generally, P.H. Osborne, "The Privacy Acts of British Columbia, Manitoba and Saskatchewan" in D. Gibson (ed.), *Aspects of Privacy Law* (Butterworths, Toronto, 1980) at pp. 73-110.

33. See, e.g., H.J. Glasbeek, "Limitations of the Action of Breach of Confidence" in D. Gibson (ed.), *op. cit., supra*, note 32, 217 at pp. 217-223.

34. Two of Prosser's categories are thus not the subject of discussion here, cases of "false light" and "appropriation of personality". See, *supra*, n. 24. The rationale for this is not merely the need for brevity. "False light" cases appear to have more in common with defamation cases than with the notion of personal privacy. The appropriation cases appear to represent the appropriation of a commercial opportunity that properly belongs to the plaintiff rather than a privacy invasion. With respect to the latter category, see J. Irvine, "The Appropriation of Personality" in D. Gibson (ed.), *op. cit., supra*, n. 32 at pp. 163-216.

in the title of an American law review article as "Peeping Toms and Other Men of Vision".[35] The category extends, however, to all other kinds of unauthorised and unwanted forms of surveillance or interruption. The second category draws attention to the activities of the media in generating unwanted publicity but embraces, of course, the activities of others who create publicity of this kind.

The existing treatment of intrusions at common law is found principally in the torts of trespass and nuisance, and it is true that both of these torts carry with them the possibility of awarding compensation in many cases of prying and spying. I wish to suggest, however, that the theory of liability underlying both torts is not directly linked with the concept of privacy protection and accordingly, that a successful attempt to meet the privacy protection issue with tort law must involve the recognition of a new category of tortious liability.

Many intrusive acts will, of course, involve trespass to the land or chattels of another and will give rise to claims in trespass. Moreover, in dealing with such claims, the courts have been willing to award compensation for injuries to the dignity of the person whose proprietary interest has been invaded.[36] Further, it appears that if one is permitted to use the land of another for one purpose and then, in abuse of this permission, uses the land for the purpose of invading the landowner's privacy, an action in trespass will be successful.[37] Trespass does, however, appear to be limited to cases where proprietary interests have been invaded. Thus, if one merely observes the landowner's activities from a neighbouring property, there would be no trespass to land.[38] Or, if one merely observed and memorised the private papers of another without touching them, there would be no trespass to chattels.[39] Thus, trespass appears to be quite incapable of dealing with the modern devices for surveillance which were so much the focus for concern in Westin's *Privacy and Freedom*.[40]

The tort of nuisance is subject to similar restrictions inasmuch as the "gist of private nuisance is interference with an occupier's interest in the beneficial use of his land".[41] To be sure, Canadian and English courts have been inclined to innovative extension of the categories of private nuisance. Thus, in *Motherwell* v. *Motherwell*,[42] the Alberta

---

35. Note, "Crimination of Peeping Toms and Other Men of Vision" (1951), 5 *Ark. L. Rev.* 388, nominated by Prosser for the "all-time prize law review title", in *op. cit., supra*, n. 24, 808.
36. *Greig* v. *Greig*, [1966] V.R. 376.
37. See, *Hickman* v. *Maisey*, [1900] 1 Q.B. 752.
38. *Victoria Park Racing and Recreation Grounds Company Limited* v. *Taylor* (1937), 58 C.L.R. 479.
39. See J. Irvine, *supra*, n. 30 at p. 37.
40. *Op. cit., supra*, n. 1.
41. Fleming, *op. cit., supra*, n. 26 at p. 384.
42. *Motherwell* v. *Motherwell* (1976), 73 D.L.R. (3d) 62 (Alta C.A.).

Court of Appeal adopted the view that persistent harassment of the plaintiffs by telephone calls, as many as sixty calls in one day, over a period of some years, should be held to constitute a private nuisance. In reaching this conclusion, the court specifically indicated the need to expand the nuisance doctrine in this fashion so as to embrace the invasion of privacy resulting from this abuse of the telephone system. In so doing, however, the Alberta court was careful to note the nature of the plaintiffs' proprietary interest and the fact that their use and enjoyment of the property was seriously affected by this form of harassment.

It may well be that invasion of privacy could be recognised as a tort indirectly, through expansion of the categories of private nuisance. Surely, at some point, however, we will have lost contact with the underlying rationale of nuisance relief and it will conduce to confusion of thought to continue calling it "private nuisance". Electronic surveillance, for example, might be a likely candidate for indirect recognition through an extension of nuisance liability. It is of some interest that in the context of a "bugging" case, *Malone* v. *Commissioner of Police*,[43] Megarry V.-C. expressed the view that there was no general right of privacy known to English law and suggested that the problem of privacy protection was too complex for judicial law-making. Nonetheless, it is at least conceivable that in cases where the target of the surveillance is located in premises in which he or she has a proprietary interest, courts might consider an expansion of liability for private nuisance to be a satisfactory doctrinal vehicle for the imposition of liability.

A much clearer view of the problem, from my perspective at least, was adopted by an Ontario County Court judge in *Saccone* v. *Orr*.[44] In that case, a municipal councillor, anxiously in need of evidence which would dispel certain rumours of wrongdoing, took the extraordinary measure of tape-recording a telephone conversation with a fellow councillor and playing the tape at a council meeting. The County Court judge, without much doctrinal ado, awarded compensation in a modest amount for this "invasion of privacy". No doubt the plaintiff would have a difficult time saying with a straight face, that his claim should lie in private nuisance because his enjoyment of the use of his home was significantly undermined by the defendant's actions. In such cases, it is the covert gathering of private information that is offensive, not any interference with the pleasant enjoyment of residing in one's own premises. Indeed, in *Saccone* it might be said that no interference of this kind was occasioned inasmuch as the plaintiff was quite unaware of the surveillance undertaken by the defendant.

---

43. [1979] 2 All E.R. 620.
44. (1981), 34 O.R. (2d) 317.

Even if nuisance could be stretched to capture situations of this kind, there would remain many cases in which the factual circumstances are so different from traditional trespass and nuisance cases that it would be pointless to describe them in these terms. Consider, for example, the invasion of privacy that might result from snooping in records held by third parties. Thus, if a curious person were able to gain information from an individual's banking records or health records, there would either be a cause of action for invasion of privacy or, I suggest, no cause of action at all. Unsurprisingly, there is an American privacy case in which unauthorised snooping in the plaintiff's bank records was held actionable.[45] Further, if the intrusion is one of observation of the plaintiff in premises other than those owned or occupied by the plaintiff, there would appear to be no basis for engaging traditional tort doctrine. In *Bolduc and Bird* v. *The Queen*,[46] a physician had obtained his patient's consent to allow a friend to observe a vaginal examination on the pretext that his friend was a medical colleague. When the patient discovered the truth, a prosecution for assault was launched. The prosecution was unsuccessful on the ground that the consent was held, by the Supreme Court of Canada, to be a sufficient basis for exempting this invasion of privacy from criminal liability. Whether or not the physician might himself have been liable in tort for battery, there would appear to be no basis, on existing principle, for the imposition of independent liability in tort on his friend. Can it be seriously maintained that there should not be an action of some kind on these facts? Recognition of a privacy tort would supply a needed analytical framework.

Turning to unwanted publicity, the invasion of privacy in such circumstances results from the public disclosure of true but embarrassing information about previously private lives. The existing body of tort doctrine which appears the most likely source of redress on the basis of existing principle is the action for breach of confidence. Indeed, some of the recent breach of confidence cases cast the breach of confidence principle in very broad terms and, in so doing, offer some encouragement to those who think that unwanted publicity problems

---

45. *Brex* v. *Smith* (1929), 146 A. 34 (N.J.); *Zimmerman* v. *Wilson* (1936), 81 F. 2d 847 (3rd Cir.).

46. (1967), 63 D.L.R. (2d) 82 (S.C.C.), for discussion of which, see H.J. Glasbeek, "Outraged Dignity - Do We Need a New Tort?" (1968), 6 *Alta L. Rev.* 77 at pp. 91-92. For an American authority allowing relief in such circumstances, see *DeMay* v. *Roberts* (1881), 40 Mich. 160, 9 N.W. 146 (assault, consent vitiated by deceit). In the absence of touching, however, liability would have to be based on a privacy theory. This type of injury to dignity or feelings would not normally be compensable in deceit. See *Wilkinson* v. *Downton*, [1897] 2 Q.B. 57. *Graham* v. *Saville*, [1945] O.R. 301 (C.A.) may be read as suggesting the contrary, but see *Smythe* v. *Reardon*, [1948] Q.S.R. 74. Moreover, it is not difficult to imagine similar situations in which no fraudulent statement is made.

can be solved in large measure under existing tort law. In *Coco* v. *Clark*,[47] Megarry J. offered the following generalisation:

> It seems to me that if the circumstances are such that any reasonable man standing in the shoes of the recipient of the information would have realised that upon reasonable grounds information was being given to him in confidence, then this should suffice to impose upon him the equitable obligation of confidence.[48]

The principle thus seems to be that whenever someone communicates information to another and has a reasonable expectation of privacy with respect to the information, the confidence must be observed. The reality, however, is less encouraging than this. A recent and careful examination of the breach of confidence cases demonstrates that they are of essentially two kinds.[49] The first and larger category consists of cases in which the breach of confidence has a distinctly commercial character and value. Thus, breach of confidence claims are often brought by employers against employees who leave their employment and then seek to utilise for their own benefit information originally acquired from the employer. This is not, of course, a privacy problem. The issue at stake in such cases is the familiar tension between a concern to protect the value of the initiatives and investment of the entrepreneur by constraining disclosure of his confidential information and, on the other hand, the concern to enable former employees to compete vigorously in the marketplace with their former employers. Where breach of confidence claims of this kind succeed, the balance is obviously struck in favour of the former interest. Claims of this type are not restricted to the employment context. Indeed, *Coco* v. *Clark* itself is a case in which an inventor of a design for a moped who attempted to interest the defendent in its commercial exploitation discovered that after the defendant rejected his own design, he marketed a product which was similar in material respects. Again, it could not be more obvious that the problem is not one of privacy protection.

The other kind of breach of confidence case which surfaces in the reported case law involves the protection of certain kinds of confidential relationships. To choose an obvious case, there is no doubt that a lawyer who breached a client's confidence would be exposed to a breach of confidence claim. This is much closer to a true privacy problem inasmuch as it would appear that the legal principle is designed to ensure that there is a realm of privacy within which legal advice can be solicited and obtained. If such confidences were not respected, people would presumably be more reluctant to seek legal advice in many instances. The point of the rule, then, is to encourage the creation of professional

---

47. *Coco* v. *A.N. Clark (Engineers) Ltd.*, [1969] R.T.C. 41.
48. *Id.*, at p. 58.
49. H.J. Glasbeek, "Limitations on the Action of Breach of Confidence" in D. Gibson (ed.), *op. cit., supra*, n. 32.

relationships of this kind. This reason for protecting confidences has been applied in non-professional relationships as well. In *Argyll* v. *Argyll*,[50] a husband was restrained from publishing confidential information concerning his wife which was communicated to him by her in confidence during the subsistence of their marriage. The reasoning of the court is very much rooted in a concern that the protection of marital confidences would foster the socially valuable institution of marriage. Disclosure of colourful information concerning the plaintiff's past immorality was restrained, therefore, not because the invasion of her privacy would cause her humiliation and embarrassment, but rather because disclosures of this kind would tend to undermine the institution of marriage by discouraging marital partners from making such disclosures.

The famous case of *Prince Albert* v. *Strange*[51] appears to straddle these two categories of commercially valuable confidences and the fostering of important relationships. As is well known, in that case Prince Albert and his wife, having made a number of etchings, engaged a printer to make copies of them for their own private enjoyment. An employee of the printer, without authority to do so, made copies of the prints available to a third party who announced a public sale and exhibition of the prints and, in collaboration with Mr. Strange, produced a catalogue concerning the exhibit. When the facts were revealed to the parties, Mr. Strange indicated an intention to publish the catalogue and was restrained from so doing in this action. This case is often relied upon by those who assert that breach of confidence claims can become a satisfactory vehicle for compensation of injuries resulting from unwanted publicity. The language of the decision suggests, however, that the court was as much concerned to protect the ability of the plaintiff to determine when and in what manner to exploit this valuable artistic commodity as it was to protect the privacy of the monarch and her consort. To the extent that the latter point was a matter of serious concern, however, it is evident that the decision in *Prince Albert* v. *Strange* is not a substantial extension of the proposition advanced in *Argyll* v. *Argyll* that confidences exchanged between spouses should be protected by the law of tort in order to foster marital relationships.

Thus far in its evolution, then, the breach of confidence claim appears to be deployed by the courts in aid of two different objectives - first, protecting the capacity of the original source of the information in question to exploit commercial opportunities for its sale or use and secondly, fostering the successful creation of relationships such as solicitor and client and husband and wife, which are thought to have significant social value. To some extent, especially in the second category of claims, breach of confidence actions obviously preserve privacy val-

---

50. *The Duchess of Argyll* v. *The Duke of Argyll*, [1965] 1 All E.R. 611 (Ch.).
51. (1849), 1 Mac. & G. 25, 41 E.R. 1171.

ues. They do, however, require something in the nature of an initial relationship between two parties in which the disclosure of information *inter se* carries with it a reasonable expectation of confidentiality. A cause of action premised on this initial source of the obligation cannot, in my view, be effectively generalised to meet all meritorious privacy claims of the unwanted publicity variety. Consider, for example, the famous California case, *Melvin* v. *Reid*.[52] The plaintiff in this case was a woman who had at one time been a prostitute but, at the time of the events in question had put her past behind her, married, and was living what the trial judge described as "an exemplary, virtuous, honourable and righteous life".[53] The plaintiff's past came back to haunt her, however, when the defendant decided to make a film, "The Red Kimono", based on various incidents in her earlier life. The plaintiff's claim for invasion of privacy was successful. It is of interest to note that no breach of confidence action should lie in such circumstances. The story of the plaintiff's career as a prostitute was described in great detail in the transcript of a trial and had thus become part of the public record. The offensive aspect of the defendant's conduct was the refusal to let this woman "continue in the path of rectitude"[54] free from unwanted publicity of this kind. The trial judge described the defendant's conduct as a "willful and wanton disregard of that charity which should actuate us in our social intercourse, and which should keep us from unnecessarily holding another up to the scorn and contempt of upright members of society".[55] Mrs. Melvin would appear to have no claim under existing Canadian law for injuries inflicted in this manner.[56]

In sum, then, whether one considers the problem of intrusions or the problem of unwanted publicity, the existing common law remedies

---

52. (1931) 297 P. 91 (D.C.A. Cal.).
53. *Id.*, 91.
54. *Id.*, 93.
55. *Id.*, 93.
56. Cf. *Re X (a minor)*, [1975] 1 All E.R. 679 (C.A.) in which a claim was brought on behalf of a psychologically fragile 14-year-old girl to restrain publication of a book describing the depraved sexual activities of her late father. The plaintiff had asked the author and publisher to revise the manuscript, and upon their refusal to do so, sought an injunction. An injunction allowed at trial was discharged by the Court of Appeal. Lord Denning noted that there was "as yet no general remedy for infringement of privacy" and explained the basis for the decision in the following terms (at p. 704):

    The reason why in these cases the law gives no remedy is because of the importance it attaches to the freedom of the press; or, better put, the importance in a free society of the circulation of true information. The metes and bounds of this were already staked out by the rules of law. The law of libel stops that which is untrue of a living person. The law of contempt stops that which is prejudicial to a fair trial. The law of obscenity stops that which tends to deprave and corrupt. It would be a mistake to extend these so as to give the judges a power to stop publication of true matter whenever the judges - or any particular judge - thought that it was in the interests of a child to do so.

are inadequate to effect compensation for injuries inflicted through the invasion of privacy. Although it is often suggested that what is needed is a gradual extension of the existing causes of action to capture some of these situations, the better view, I suggest, is that the underlying theories of obligation of these causes of action are not capable of addressing these problems and that an explicit recognition of invasion of privacy as a cause of action would therefore be a fruitful evolution of common law doctrine. This would be, however, merely an evolution of doctrine. It is abundantly clear that a concern to protect privacy can be seen to underlie remedies made available in many situations under the traditional headings of tort liability. It is not an unfamiliar path of doctrinal growth for the courts to grant explicit recognition to interests protected by or principles underlying the application of existing rules where those rules are shown to be an inadequate expression of or protection of the principle or interest in question.

The second line of attack on the notion that recognition of the existence of a privacy tort would be a valuable initiative, to which I earlier referred, shares the view that a privacy tort should be recognised but suggests that this should only be done by the legislature inasmuch as the courts are poorly designed to engage in law-making of this kind. This argument has a familiar form. Courts cannot undertake the kinds of enquiries that might be useful before making public policy decisions, limited as they are by the circumstances of the case before them. Judicial law-making requires individuals to gamble resources on being able to persuade a particular judge to seize the initiative. To leave issues of this kind to the happenstance of judicial creativity results in a patchwork approach to reform. Courts are not democratically elected and therefore do not enjoy a mandate for law-making.[57]

My response to this school of thought is essentially two-fold. First, this approach fails to recognise the inherent instability and uncertainty of legal doctrine, whether that doctrine is of common law origin or arises from the interpretation of statutes. Some measure of judicial law-making is simply unavoidable, and we must turn our attention to the question of what a reasonable division of responsibility between the judiciary and the legislature would be.

More particularly, we must ask what the appropriate division of responsibility is in an area of this kind, a relatively minor adjustment of the principles of tortious liability. Traditionally, of course, this particular law-making task has been assumed by the courts. This is, in my view, a tradition grounded in common sense. Those who believe that matters of this kind should be handled only by the legislature rather substantially exaggerate the capacity of the legislature to undertake systematic reform of this kind and encourage the courts to ignore their

---

57. See, e.g., Glasbeek, *loc. cit.*, *supra*, note 33.

responsibility for adjustment and reshaping of the private law of obligations. Although I share the respect demonstrated by these writers for democratic institutions, it is not my view that the legislators are at their best trying to, for example, fashion new rules on the doctrine of promissory estoppel in the law of contract[58] or other similarly *recherché* problems of our private law. It is not surprising that the legislature should have difficulty in dealing with matters of this kind. The problems involve subtle matters of legal analysis on which the average legislator will not have an informed opinion. Further, it is a more manageable task to decide cases on an individual basis than to formulate and anticipate the application of legislation of general application. One of the attractions of the common law method of reform is the very particularity and tentativeness of the process that its critics decry.

More importantly, the agenda of the typical modern legislature is very full indeed and ought not be needlessly complicated by detailed supervision of the adjustment of common law doctrine. At the risk of overstating the point, there is something to be said for the view that the courts, given this historical constitutional role, should not put legislatures in the position of having to solve problems of this kind through legislative enactment. On the other hand, this is not to deny that there may be questions of private law which raise such serious questions concerning the allocation of public or private resources that they ought normally to be addressed only through legislative enactment. Even in such cases, it may sometimes be the case, as Chief Justice Laskin said in his dissenting judgment in *Murdoch* v. *Murdoch*, that "the better way is not the only way".[59] Substantial change has been effected through the common law method of judicial law-making. Recognition of the tort of privacy would not require this sort of initiative, however. The shift from the current rag-bag of tort remedies for privacy invasions to an explicit privacy tort would be much less dramatic and more clearly within the range of the traditional role the courts have taken in crafting adjustments to the law of obligations. It is of interest that the provincial privacy tort statutes seem to do nothing more than briefly reiterate the basic principles of the American case law.[60] The courts are given no statutory guidance as to how to apply these vague general principles to typical factual patterns. In short, the matter is legislatively remitted to the common law method. Recognition of a common law tort invasion of privacy is long overdue.

---

58. The Canadian Statutory overruling of *Foakes* v. *Beer*, (1889) 9 App. Cas. 605 (H.L.) is notoriously unsuccessful. See S.M. Waddams, *The Law of Contract* (2nd ed., 1984) pp. 107-108.

59. (1973), 41 D.L.R. (3d) 367 at 385, *per* Laskin J.

60. See, *supra*, n. 32.

THE CANADIAN PRIVACY ACT

In the introductory section of this paper, I identified the collection, use and dissemination of vast amounts of personal data by government agencies as an important threat to the value of personal privacy in modern social conditions. Recognition of a privacy tort would not, in itself, solve many of the problems associated with this phenomenon. To be sure, an unwanted publicity tort might provide a useful means of compensating the victims of improper disclosure from such data banks, but it is not likely that tort alone would make a significant contribution to the regulation of the establishment and administration of such data banks where they are utilised for authorised purposes. Many jurisdictions in the United States and continental Europe have attempted to address these problems by the enactment of so-called "fair information practices" laws. Such statutes normally attempt to minimise the intrusiveness of government data collection and handling by adopting some or, more typically, all of the following devices:

.   public information concerning the existence and nature of information holdings through the publication of catalogues or registers of data banks

.   controls on the nature of the data that can be collected and its manner of collection

.   the conferral of rights of access to data concerning oneself, together with the right to amend or file corrections with respect to information alleged to be erroneous

.   control over the transfer of personal data within government and its dissemination to parties outside government

.   supervision of the arrangements for storage, the period of retention and the destruction of personal data.

It is a lamentable fact that only Quebec[61] among the Canadian provinces has enacted legislation of this kind. At the federal level, however, legislation of this kind was enacted as Part IV of the *Canadian Human Rights Act*.[62] Part IV required the publication of a catalogue of federal data banks containing personal information, granted access and correction rights to individual citizens concerning personal data held by the government, and subjected a number of tasks relating to the establishment and operation of data banks to supervision by the Treasury Board of Canada. The rights of access and correction conferred by the statute were not enforceable at law. Complaints concerning denial of access or refusal to correct were to be referred to an ombudsman, the

---

61. *An Act Respecting Access to Documents Held by Public Bodies and the Protection of Personal Information*, R.S.Q., c. A-2.1 (1982).

62. S.C. 1966-67, c. 33, as am. 1977-78, c. 22, s. 5. For a description of the Act and its implementation, see I. Hansen, "The Canadian Human Rights Act", Part IV, in J.D. McCamus (ed.), *Freedom of Information: A Canadian Perspective* (1981) at pp. 249-259.

Privacy Commissioner.[63] Although favourable assessments of the work of the Treasury Board in administering federal data banks have been made, it is of interest that notwithstanding the ostensible purposes of the statute, control over the collection, storage and dissemination of personal data remained completely within the control of public authorities. The government obviously has a strong interest in maintaining control over its capacity to invade privacy through the collection, use and dissemination of personal information and is apparently reluctant to confine its ability to do so through the enactment of vigorous regulatory schemes.

In 1982, however, an improved version of Part IV, now renamed *The Privacy Act*, was enacted as part of a legislative package that also included the new *Access to Information Act*.[64] In the new *Privacy Act*, the rights of access and correction were made subject to judicial review. Thus, a broad right of access to records concerning personal information is conferred upon individuals by the statute, together with a right to request correction or note on the record "corrections requested but not made".[65] The statute then goes on to articulate a number of exceptions to the general principle of access.[66] Thus, for example, access is not permitted to information relating to certain aspects of law enforcement investigations, various corrections matters, international affairs, national defence, federal-provincial affairs, and so on. On the vexatious question of access to medical records, the government retains a discretion to refuse disclosure where disclosure would be "contrary to the best interests of the individual".[67] In the interpretation of these provisions, of course, the courts will play an important role in defining the structure of these access rights. It would be inappropriate within the confines of the present paper to attempt to identify a number of the difficult points of interpretation that are likely to arise. I would like to suggest, however, that as a general matter courts ought to adopt an approach to the interpretation of these provisions which favours, in

---

63. See, e.g., D.H. Flaherty, "Comment", in McCamus (ed.), *op. cit., supra*, n. 62 at pp. 260-265.
64. Parl. 1st Sess., 32nd Parl. 1980, House of Commons, Bill C-43, "An Act to Enact the Access to Information Act and the Privacy Act, to Amend the Federal Court Act and the Canada Evidence Act and to Amend Certain Other Acts in Consequence Thereof" as passed by the House of Commons, June 28, 1982, Schedule I ("The Access to Information Act") and Schedule II ("The Privacy Act").
65. *Privacy Act*, Section 12. The data may be located either in a "personal information bank" or in another document "with respect to which an individual is able to provide sufficiently specific information... as to render it reasonably retrievable..."
66. The Governor-in-Council may exempt entire data banks where the information contained therein relates principally to law enforcement or international affairs and defence. *Id.*, s. 18. Exemptions pertaining to particular types of information are set forth in ss. 19-28.
67. *Id.*, sec. 28.

cases of ambiguity, the extension of access rights. The preamble of the statute indicates that the purpose of the Act is "to extend the present laws of Canada protecting the privacy of individuals..."[68] Further, there is now a Federal Court decision interpreting parallel provisions of the *Access to Information Act* in which it is held that "public access ought not to be frustrated by the Courts except upon the clearest grounds so that doubt ought to be resolved in favour of disclosure." Further, the Court held that "the burden of persuasion must rest upon the party resisting disclosure", that is to say, the government.[69]

In the context of both statutes, for obvious reasons, the government may be perceived to have a strong interest in resisting disclosure which is inconsistent with the general purpose of the statutory scheme in each case. The approach to interpretation advocated by the Federal Court in the context of the Access Act should be adopted in the context of the Privacy Act as well.

Apart from the enforcement of access rights, however, direct appeals to the intervention of the judiciary are not invited by the statute. Thus, such difficult questions as whether to establish data banks, how much information they are to collect and retain, who is to be granted access to the data, whether from within or without government, and so on, are confided to the discretion of the government. The second point I wish to make with respect to this legislative scheme, however, is that the courts could usefully keep an open mind on the question of whether or not judicial supervision of the administration of the Act may not be warranted, in particular circumstances, by general principles of administrative law. Consider, for example, the general question of whether personal information concerning individuals should be disclosed on request to third parties outside government such as academic researchers, public interest groups or journalists. This is surely one of the most important problems in the privacy constellation. The approach taken by the Act is to stipulate that government institutions shall refuse to disclose personal information for any purpose unless it is "the opinion of the head of the institution (that) the public interest in disclosure clearly outweighs any invasion of privacy that could result from the disclosure".[70] This vitally important question, then, is simply confided to

---

68. *Id.*, sec. 2.
69. *Maislin Industries Limited* v. *The Minister for Industry, Trade and Commerce, Regional Economic Expansion* (1984), 10 D.L.R. (4th) 417, *per* Jerome A.C.J.

   It is true that the preamble to the Access Act may be thought to lend greater support to such interpretation as it explicitly states that "necessary exceptions to the right of access should be limited and specific" but, as the exempting provisions in both statutes are in some instances worded in precisely the same manner, it would be a surprising interpretation of the two statutes which would allow greater access to the public at large than to individuals seeking access to data concerning themselves.

70. *Privacy Act*, Sec. 8(2)(m).

administrative discretion. By way of contrast, it is interesting to note that under parallel American legislation, third parties of this kind have an enforceable legal right to personal information unless disclosure would constitute, in the opinion of a court, a "clearly unwarranted invasion of privacy".[71] In the U.S., then, a substantial body of jurisprudence has developed from which general principles for balancing these competing interests may be derived.

In the Canadian context, however, it is not only the case that the matter has been confided to administrative discretion but, as well, there does not as yet appear to be any evidence of a willingness on the part of the government to develop internal guidelines for structuring this important discretionary power. The question that I wish to raise, then, is whether the courts do not have an appropriate role in encouraging the executive branch to develop a principled and reasoned approach to the exercise of very broad and very important discretions of this kind. At the very least, it is established that the courts will intervene where the exercise of discretion is perceived to be "arbitrary or capricious".[72] Thus, one might ask, for example, whether it is a proper exercise of statutory discretion of this kind to refuse disclosure so as to avoid providing a basis for criticism of the actions of a governmental institution. My own view, certainly, is that when one reads the Access to Information and Privacy Acts together, it becomes apparent that any such purpose would be improper and, arguably therefore, reviewable by the courts.

More than this, however, the present context might be thought to demonstrate a need for greater sensitivity than has occasionally been evidenced in the past[73] to the desirability of internal guidelines adopted for the purpose of structuring and confining the discretion of officials exercising statutory discretionary powers. As I have argued elsewhere,[74] it is possible to articulate a number of factors which could reasonably be weighed in exercising this discretion (pro: will disclosure conduce to effective scrutiny of government activity, will it promote public health or safety or informed choice in the purchase of goods and services, will access benefit the subject of the information; con: will

---

71. *Freedom of Information Act*, 5 U.S.C. s. 552 (b)(6).

72. See, generally, J.M. Evans et al., *Administrative Law* (2nd ed., 1984) c. 13 "Confining and Structuring Discretion"; J.M. Evans (ed.), *deSmith's Judicial Review of Administrative Action* (4th ed., 1980) pp. 322-354.

73. See, e.g., *E.W. Bickle Limited* v. *M.N.R.*, [1979] 2 F.C. 448, 100 D.L.R. (3d) 55 (F.C.A.), in which it is suggested that the Minister might be on safe ground in relying on a dictionary definition of the term in dispute, but was not so when relying on internal guidelines which purported to offer a definition of the term in question.

74. J.D. McCamus, "The Delicate Balance: Reconciling Privacy Protection with the Freedom of Information Principle", in *Conference on Privacy: Initiatives for 1984* (Queen's Printer, Ontario, 1984) pp. 51-61.

access frustrate the objectives of the statutory scheme under which the data was collected, is the information especially sensitive, is it unlikely to be accurate or reliable, will the data subject suffer harm, was it submitted on the assumption that it would be treated confidentially, and so on). It would be undesirable, in my view, to hold that a public agency that articulated such guidelines and attempted to follow them had, in some sense, "fettered" its discretion in a way which exposed its decisions to reversal.

A further possibility might be considered. Canadian courts have been very reluctant to impose a duty on public authorities to articulate guidelines for the exercise of discretionary powers conferred upon them. Although there does appear to be at least one decision in which this has been attempted,[75] the case law does not disclose any enthusiasm for intervention of this kind. Although I share the view that the courts ought to be reluctant to intervene in this manner, there may well be cases in which the supervision of public authorities of this kind is appropriate and it may be that the present context - a broad discretionary power conferred on the vast majority of governmental institutions - is one within which the imposition of such a requirement deserves serious consideration.

In sum, then, the privacy protection problems inherent in the establishment and operation of large holdings of personal information have been subjected to regulation, albeit somewhat half-hearted regulation, by the federal Privacy Act. There are, however, important opportunities for the courts to attempt to ensure that the fundamental purposes of the statute are not frustrated by narrow construction or by the arbitrary exercise of discretionary power.

THE CANADIAN CHARTER OF RIGHTS AND FREEDOMS[76]

One might expect the new Canadian *Charter of Rights and Freedoms* to be a fertile source of privacy protection law in securing constitutional protection for "freedom of conscience and religion", "freedom of thought, belief, opinion and expression", "freedom of association", (Section 1), "the right to life, liberty and security of the person and the right not to be deprived thereof except in accordance with the principles of fundamental justice" (Section 7), and "the right to be secure against unreasonable search or seizure" (Section 8). The Charter clearly establishes a number of safeguards which will, at the very least, indirectly serve to protect privacy values. What is less clear, however, is whether the Charter should properly be construed so as to grant constitutional protection to privacy values in a more general way.

---

75. *Garden of the Gulf Court and Motel Inc.* v. *Island Telephone Co. Ltd.* (1981), 126 D.L.R. (3d) 281 (P.E.I. S.C., in banco).

76. *Constitution Act*, 1982, Part I, s.s. 1-34, as enacted by the *Canada Act*, 1982, c. 11 (U.K.).

In order to provide some focus for an unduly concise discussion of this question, I would suggest that the possible application of the Charter to a particular fact situation be considered - the establishment of a privacy invasive data bank by a public authority. Assume, for the purposes of this example, that a province chooses to establish a data bank which collects sensitive medical information from health care professionals for purposes of medical research and further, proposes to allow access to the data bank to law enforcement officials. Would the Charter constrain the province in its establishment of this data bank or in its dissemination of personal information from the bank?

The answers to these questions must turn, to some extent, on whether Canadian courts will follow the lead of the American constitutional privacy jurisprudence in two important respects. First, consideration must be given to the transportability of the reasoning of the U.S. Supreme Court in *Griswold* v. *Connecticut*.[77] In *Griswold*, the Court held that a number of the specific guarantees in the Bill of Rights have "penumbras, formed by emanations from those guarantees that help give them life and substance" and that the cumulative effect of these emanations was to establish a constitutionally protected "right to privacy". Secondly, the growth of a privacy jurisprudence under the Charter will depend very considerably on the outcome of the important question of whether Section 7 offers constitutional guarantees which are substantive in nature or merely procedural.

With respect to the first point, it must first be noted that there are very close parallels between the provisions of the American Bill relied on by the Court in *Griswold* and the provisions of the Canadian Charter.[78] Moreover, Justice Douglas placed particular emphasis on the fact that U.S. case law had treated the Fourth Amendment's protection against unreasonable search and seizure as creating a "right to privacy",[79] and this, too, has a Canadian parallel in the recent decision of the Supreme Court of Canada in *Hunter et al.* v. *Southam Inc.*[80] In *Southam*, the Court held that the Section 8 protection against unreasonable search and seizure has as its underlying purpose the protection of "individuals from unjustified State intrusions upon their privacy".[81] More important than the parallelism of *Griswold*, I would suggest, is the congeniality

---

77. (1965), 381 U.S. 479, 85 S. Ct. 1678.
78. It may be thought that the American Ninth Amendment ("The enumeration in the Constitution, of certain rights, shall not be construed to deny or disparage others retained by the people") is more hospitable to the *Griswold* style analysis than our own Section 26 ("the guarantee in this Charter of certain freedoms shall not be construed as denying the existence of any other rights or freedoms that exist in Canada"). On the other hand, reliance on the Ninth Amendment does not appear to be an indispensable part of the reasoning in *Griswold*.
79. *Mapp* v. *Ohio* (1961), 367 U.S. 643.
80. Unrep., September 17, 1984.
81. *Id.*, p. 21 per Dickson C.J.C.

of Section 7's language to a right of privacy. If one returns to philo-sophical analysis of the nature and importance of privacy, it becomes difficult to think of a constitutional guarantee of the right to "life, liberty and security of the person" that would not carry with it a broad protection of the citizen's right "to be let alone".

Assuming, then, that the Charter is properly construed to include a right to privacy, we must turn to consider the nature of the protection afforded. Section 24, of course, confers on the courts a broad remedial power which would enable the courts, for example, to award compen-sation when constitutional rights of privacy are invaded. But the more difficult question is whether the protection afforded by Section 7 is merely procedural rather than substantive in character. Does Section 7 allow invasions of privacy as long as proper procedures are followed? Or, does Section 7 confine the ability of public authorities to invade privacy?

Assuming that the protection is procedural only, Section 7 would nonetheless retain some significance. Returning to our medical data bank example, it may well be that a search of records held by third party institutions such as banks or public authorities would be outside the scope of the protection against "unreasonable search or seizure" afforded by Section 8. The data subject, the patient, does not own or indeed have access to the records which law enforcement authorities may wish to search. Canadian courts may take the view that in such cases the data subject is not subject to a "search" in the requisite sense.[82] If Section 8 does not cover searches of this kind, Section 7 would stand as a procedural safeguard against fishing expeditions which would be unduly invasive of personal privacy.

Obviously, however, more effective privacy protection would be secured by the Charter if Section 7 were interpreted to permit substan-tive review of government conduct. American courts have held that such review is possible under roughly equivalent American constitu-tional provisions. Thus, in *Whalen* v. *Roe*,[83] the U.S. Supreme Court indicated that it would be prepared, in appropriate circumstances, to strike down state legislation authorising the establishment of a data bank containing sensitive medical information. In the particular facts of the case, the Court was satisfied that there was, given the purpose of the legislative scheme, a genuine need for the data in question and that adequate safeguards were in place to protect its confidentiality. In other circumstances, however, the establishment of such a data bank might well be held to invade the constitutionally protected zone of privacy.

I am reluctant to enter the lists in the debate on the difficult ques-tion of whether Section 7 of the Canadian Charter should be construed

---

82. *Cf. Miller* v. *U.S.* (1976), 425 U.S. 435.
83. (1977), 97 S. Ct. 369.

to permit substantive review of this kind.[84] Courts are, thus far, divided on the question.[85] However this matter is resolved in the immediate future, it does seem to me likely that in the fullness of time, some substantive review is likely to occur under Section 7. The significance of the legislative history, whatever its purport may be, is likely to fade with the passage of time. Moreover, as Chief Justice Laskin once observed, the line between procedural and substantive review is not a clear one.[86] Further, the existence of the legislative override power in Section 33 is an invitation to a more vigorous reading of the Charter than might otherwise be appropriate. The most forceful argument against substantive review in the United States is, surely, its finality. Under the Canadian Charter, the legislature can correct overly adventuresome judicial initiatives. No doubt substantive review would be looked upon as a mixed blessing in many quarters. On balance, I am persuaded that it is likely to be a positive development. The shift brought about by the Charter of important decision-making concerning civil liberties to the judicial system from the legislature has been viewed by many as undesirable. Surely the worst of all possible worlds would be to have this shift occur, as it has done, and then find that the courts were not responsive to depradations of the values which appear to be enshrined in the provisions of the Charter.

Personal privacy, like other values enshrined in the Charter, is placed at particular risk by the actions of public authorities. The legislatures, acknowledging this peril, have directed the courts to safeguard liberties from depradations arising from their own legislative activity. An appropriate balance between undue timidity and overly zealous application of the Charter will not be easily struck. In interpreting Section 7, however, it would not seem wise to strike the balance invariably and (inevitably) arbitrarily on the basis of some perceived, perhaps mythical, dividing line between substance and procedure.[87]

---

84. See, generally, J. White, "Fundamental Justice: The Scope and Application of Section 7 of the Charter" (1983), 13 *Man. L.J.* 455.

85. Compare *R.* v. *Stevens*, [1983] 3 C.C.C. (3d) 198 (Ont. C.A.) with *Reference re Motor Vehicle Act s. 94(2)* (1983), 4 C.C.C. (3d) 243, (B.C.C.A.), the latter decision currently under appeal to the Supreme Court of Canada.

86. *Morgentaler* v. *R.*, [1976] 1 S.C.R. 616 at p. 633:

    I am not, however, prepared to say, in this early period of the elaboration of the impact of the Canadian Bill of Rights upon federal legislation, that the prescriptions of s. 1(a) must be rigidly confined to procedural matters. There is often an interaction of means and ends, and it may be that there can be a proper invocation of due process of law in respect of federal legislation as improperly abridging a person's right to life, liberty, security and enjoyment of property.

87. It will be argued, no doubt, that the decision of the Supreme Court of Canada in *Duke* v. *The Queen*, [1972] S.C.R. 917 has, in the context in that *Canadian Bill of Rights* (1960), 8-9 Eliz. II, c. 44, sec. 2 determined that the phrase "fundamental justice" adverts to procedural protections only. See P.W. Hogg, *Canada Act 1982 Annotated* (Carswell, 1982) at pp. 26-27 for this point. To this it may be

Certainly, American courts have exercised the jurisdiction they have assumed for substantive review vigorously in the area of privacy protection. The privacy jurisprudence has, indeed, become quite controversial in its protection of personal and family autonomy. Thus, American courts have struck down as unconstitutional legislation authorising the sterilization of felons,[88] restricting the right of married couples to use contraceptive devices (these, indeed, were the facts of *Griswold*), prohibiting the distribution of contraceptives to unmarried persons,[89] laws restricting freedom of choice in marriage relationships, such as statutes barring inter-racial marriage,[90] and, of course, in the famous decision in *Roe* v. *Wade*,[91] a statute prescribing abortion in circumstances other than where it is necessary to save the life of the mother. The extent to which American courts will develop this jurisprudence in such a way as to protect personal decision-making with respect to such difficult matters as sexual orientation or the right to forego lifesaving medical treatment remains very much an open question.[92]

I am not attempting to argue that some or all of the American jurisprudence on these difficult issues should be unquestioningly accepted by Canadian courts. On the contrary, these are issues which call for wisdom rather than precedent. On the other hand, it would seem to be most unfortunate indeed if Canadian anxiety about such decisions as *Roe* v. *Wade* would lead us to reject the very principle of substantive review and deprive Canadians of the protection afforded by decisions like *Whalen* v. *Roe*.

In conclusion, then, there appear to me to be a number of areas in which the creative powers of the judiciary can make a valuable contribution to the protection of personal privacy or, as Mr. Justice Brandeis described it, "the right to be let alone - the most comprehensive of rights and the right most valued by civilized men".[93]

---

answered that the language of sec. 2 ("deprive a person of *the right to a fair hearing* in accordance with the principles of fundamental justice") commands such a result and that this language is not present in sec. 7 of the Charter. Moreover, the phrase "fundamental justice" does appear more hospitable to substantive review than the American "due process".

88. *Skinner* v. *Oklahoma* (1942), 316 U.S. 535.
89. *Eisenstadt* v. *Baird* (1972), 405 U.S. 438.
90. *Loving* v. *Virginia* (1967), 388 U.S. 182.
91. *Roe* v. *Wade* (1973), 410 U.S. 113.
92. See, generally, J.E. Nowak et al., *Constitutional Law* (2d ed., 1983) at pp. 758 et seq. And see, generally, L. Tribe, *American Constitutional Law* (1978), c. 15.
93. *Olmstead* v. *United States* (1928), 277 U.S. 438 at p. 478.

Information, Privacy and the Press

Mark Harrison*

I have no difficulty in determining the point at which the public's right to know overrides the government's right to withhold disclosure of information. As a newspaper editor, I believe the public's right to know is almost absolute in the area of government activity. My role is to tell the public as much as I possibly can about what government is doing. A major exception must, of course, be made on matters of national security, although too often I think that term is used as a shield to conceal information for no rational reason. Even when national security is invoked legitimately, it seems to me it can be argued that there are times when the public interest might be better served by disclosure. An unusual example of this was the Bay of Pigs incident some twenty years ago when the New York Times, while aware of the impending assault, chose, on the grounds of national security and in response to pressure from the Kennedy administration, to keep silent. After the event, of course, there was some rueful public comment by members of the Kennedy administration, including the President himself, speculating on what might have occurred if the story had indeed been published and whether perhaps in the long run the public interest might not have been better served by disclosure.

Much is to be said for the Swedish system whereby almost all government documents are open to public scrutiny unless specifically prohibited. We tend in this country to lean in the other direction, towards the British custom which often seems based on the notion that the public has no right necessarily to know what the people who are conducting the public's business are doing. I say that despite the recent passage in a variety of jurisdictions of freedom of information legislation whose value has yet to be demonstrated. One of the best examples of the scepticism this breeds can be found in this morning's edition, [October 1984] of my own newspaper in referring to civil service salaries in the City of Montreal. Until this year, those salaries were all on the public record. Now that we have a Freedom of Information Act in Quebec,

---

* Editor, Montreal Gazette.

explained the Chairman of the City's executive Committee this week, those salaries are classified information. I fail to follow the logic.

We have in this country, it seems to me, an inordinate respect for government confidentiality over public disclosure. I suspect the Watergate disclosures could never have occurred in Canada because our public servants too often tend to regard journalists as intruders rather than as surrogates of the public. Perhaps that is why the relationship between government and the press will continue to be one of creative tension, as James Reston of the New York Times refers to it.

I find myself much more concerned on a daily basis as a newspaper editor with privacy as it relates to the individual, in trying to determine the point at which the public's right to know may outweigh the individual's right to privacy. The judgments which must be made every day in Canadian newsrooms are often very difficult.

In preparation for this presentation I was looking at a reference in the Harvard Law Review and came across this passage in an article entitled ''The Right to Privacy'':

> Photographs and newspaper enterprise have invaded the sacred precincts of private and domestic life and numerous mechanical devices threaten to make good the prediction that what is whispered in the closet shall be proclaimed from the housetops. The press is overstepping in every direction the bounds of propriety and of decency.

That passage has a contemporary ring but it was, of course, written ninety-four years ago by two young Boston lawyers, one of whom, Louis Brandeis, was later to become a distinguished member of the American Supreme Court. In that article, he argued the case for recognition of a general right to privacy to protect individuals against public exposure of their private affairs without their consent. He argued in essence for the right to be left alone.

I find myself, however, inclined to agree with those who argue that merely to live in a society implies a willingness not to be left entirely alone. I understand that there are at least thirty-three states in the American union which have enacted privacy legislation since 1903 and in this country we have federal legislation and legislation in British Columbia, Manitoba and Saskatchewan which assert a form of protection for privacy. But nowhere, as I understand it, in the Commonwealth is there any legislation which asserts a general right of privacy. In my own province of Quebec there have been at least two judicial decisions which have suggested that the reporting of news and discussion of public issues and public figures were situations in which the public interest may override public rights. And in commenting on these decisions I note an article in the Canadian Bar Review 1974, Vol. 52 by Patrick Glen of the McGill Faculty of Law which suggests that the public interest extends not only to what might be considered the public interest but also to that which is simply newsworthy and of interest to the public. The author states:

> The individuals private life may therefore be publicly exposed if it is deemed newsworthy. Such a definition of the public interest places severe limitations on the right to privacy since news reporters are in large measure responsible for defining what is newsworthy. By the act of reporting they may thus secure a shield from the consequence of that same reporting.

As an editor I have no difficulty in accepting that concept, though I suspect it may offer a greater degree of latitude to journalists than this audience may find acceptable. Certainly I would not argue for the relatively unlimited journalistic freedom which appears to prevail south of the border particularly since the U.S. Supreme Court decision in *The New York Times* v. *Sullivan*, which appears to permit the press to invade the privacy of anyone whose privacy they choose to invade. I find myself more in agreement with the views expressed some years ago by the Younger Committee on Privacy in Britain which weighed the arguments for and against state intervention in protecting the privacy of the individual against what was perceived in 1972 as a growing threat from new technology. That Committee reported in July 1972 and concluded that the case for government intervention was strongest in the field of new technology. But as for the media, it concluded "that the standards of both the press and the broadcasting agencies have been rising and that the threat to privacy, far from growing, may even have been diminishing". The Committee considered that statute law or even case law was a clumsy instrument for the handling of breaches of privacy. It said, "It is questionable whether a topic which is subject to such rapid change in social convention as privacy can suitably be regulated on the basis of case law, slowly built up, which would tend to reflect the values of an earlier period rather than of contemporary society. We have concluded that on balance there is no need for a general law of privacy". But it added "we conclude that because it is impossible to devise any satisfactory yardstick by which to judge, in case of doubt, whether the importance of a public story should override the privacy of the people and personal information involved, the decision on this point can be made only in the light of the circumstances of each case. The question we have to answer therefore is who should make that decision". And it added, "The initial decision can only be made by those responsible for the publication, that is by the press themselves".

I think that was a prudent and a realistic conclusion and it appeared to have influenced the British Press Council which four years later, in 1976, issued a Declaration on Privacy with which I agree totally. It upheld the right of individuals to be protected against unwarranted intrusion into their private lives or affairs and it added, "The Council is convinced that the right of privacy is incapable of satisfactory definition by statute law and that any attempt to legislate on privacy would be contrary to the public interest.'' No statutory enactment on privacy it said could secure adequate protection ''without at the same time curtailing the right of the public at large to be informed about matters of public concern. Any such enactment would make it more difficult for the press to carry out those duties of vigilance, inquiry and disclosure which are appropriate to a healthy democracy''. The Council also issued a statement of policy which read in part, ''The publication of information about the private lives or concerns of individuals without their consent is only acceptable if there is legitimate public interest overriding the right of privacy''.

On this issue I suspect there will always be argument, and Canadian editors generally stake out a position somewhere between the American and the British practice. In the United States, you may recall, during the Eisenhower Presidency it was considered, for example, entirely appropriate for newspapers to publish details of the President's bowel movements when he was ill. Indeed the presidential press secretary would solemnly each day announce the details to a waiting world, firm in the belief that the American public was entitled to know such things about its chief executive. The British sometimes are inclined toward the other extreme and I recall that shortly after Sir Winston Churchill's funeral some years ago, the British Press Council seriously pondered a complaint from an irate citizen who was appalled that the London Sunday Times had the temerity to publish a photo of the funeral showing members of the Churchill family following the coffin. It was a state funeral of a public figure of world renown, the most admired Briton of his time, watched on television by millions of people around the world. The complainant, however, felt that the newspaper had no right to intrude on the private grief of Lady Churchill. The Press Council in its infinite wisdom, I am pleased to report, rejected the complaint.

Privacy and the Criminal Process

David C. McDonald*

I propose to discuss three distinct ways in which, in the real Canadian society of 1984, there is a threat to the privacy of individuals and of their minds and therefore a threat to their volitional autonomy.

ELECTRONIC SURVEILLANCE IN CRIMINAL INVESTIGATIONS

More than a decade has passed since the passage of the *Protection of Privacy Act*, the purpose of which was to protect communications from electronic interception by anyone, when the parties to the communication have a reasonable expectation of privacy. Onto this general rule a major exception was grafted: judicially authorized electronic interception in criminal investigations.

What is known of the procedure by which such interceptions are authorized is limited because of the secrecy of the procedure. Perhaps the most useful information about the procedure is found in "Freedom and Security under the Law" (Second Report of the Commission of Inquiry concerning Certain Activities of the R.C.M.P.), Vol. 2, p. 1021-1022:

> 12. Results of our research, based on a broad survey of experience gained in administering the application procedure, raise issues which a more extensive review process might study thoroughly. These issues are of a kind that a yearly statistical summary cannot answer. Some of our research results are as follows:
>
> > (a) Applications to a judge are usually completed in less than half an hour - in many cases in less than 15 minutes.
> >
> > (b) Frequently, but far from always, when the application is made privately to the judge, the agent of the Solicitor General of Canada or of the provincial attorney general is accompanied by the police officer who swore the affidavit.

---

* Justice of the Court of Queen's Bench of Alberta.

(c) In order to supplement the information contained in the affidavit, many judges question the policemen. Some judges receive this additional information under oath, but most do not. Some judges require the additional information in writing, some do not.

(d) There is evidence that the applications are well prepared, but the fact that they lack detail about a variety of matters is a ground for some degree of dissatisfaction.

(e) There is substantial evidence that the fact that almost all applications are successful is due to the efforts of police forces and Crown agents to submit only those applications that have been well prepared and are likely not to encounter difficulty.

(f) Although, as has been disclosed by the Annual Reports of both the Solicitor General of Canada and the provincial attorneys general, very few applications have been refused by judges, there is some evidence that this information is somewhat misleading. It appears that applications are frequently withdrawn when the judge points to inadequacies in the affidavit. Thus the official statistics are misleading because they do not record the number of applications which are made but withdrawn.

(g) Some judges attach a condition to the authorization that there be periodic progress reports to the judge.

(h) In the several provinces in which research was conducted, there was evidence that the system adopted by each Court for determining which judge received applications has reduced but not eliminated "judge-shopping" by the Crown - i.e. the selection of judges more likely to be amenable to such applications. Despite the minimization of this undesirable risk, it may be that, wherever possible, instead of all the judges in the court being entitled to receive applications, there should be a limited number of designated judges who would be so entitled. This would reduce the possibility of "judge-shopping" and at the same time develop a number of judges who have a certain expertise in analysing the quality of the applications.

In the Report certain recommendations were made, which have perhaps been lost sight of because public interest has focussed on those aspects of the Report that relate to security intelligence matters. The Report said (at p. 1019-1020):

8. ... we are confident that electronic surveillance is a valuable and necessary tool in the investigation of crime and the prosecution of offenders...

10. We think that there should be a mechanism to facilitate an effective review of the use of electronic surveillance. The yearly statistical reports of the provincial attorneys general and the Solicitor General of Canada to provincial legislatures and Parliament, while more useful than the yearly report on the Security Service's use of electronic surveillance, does not provide for an extensive enough review of this investigative method. In Part III, Chapter 3, we explained the constraints that make it

difficult for a Commission of Inquiry to review thoroughly the manner in which the process of applying for authorization under section 178 is working. Any other government body would face at least equal difficulty in doing so. If our proposal for a more thorough review of the use of electronic surveillance in criminal investigations by all police forces in Canada is adopted, section 178 would have to be amended to allow access to sealed packets and to the product of interception. Presumably this access could be limited to certain federal Commissioners appointed under Part I of the Inquiries Act.

11. One means of improving the safeguards, both with regard to electronic surveillance and with regard to the search of mail for illicit drugs or narcotics, would be the creation of a committee appointed jointly by federal and provincial governments to review the exercise of these powers by peace officers across Canada. This committee, consisting of two judges, two lawyers, and two citizens (one of whom might, for example, be a person active in a civil liberties organization) could review the documents filed in support of applications for judicial authorization, the orders themselves, the alternatives available to the police, the results of the investigative work to the extent that it was aided by the means authorized by the judicial authorizations, and so on. In addition this committee could sponsor sessions in which judges from across the country could compare experiences and seek to arrive at high standards by which applications for authorization orders should be judged. Moreover, the committee could report annually to Parliament, taking care to keep its comments on specific cases at a general level so as not to prejudice the rights of individuals or the techniques and circumstances of past and continuing police investigative operations.

I do not intend to comment on this further. My former fellow Commissioners and I have, by agreement, remained silent on all matters dealt with in our Reports. Certainly, as a judge, I cannot comment further on matters that are in the political domain. This issue has not been the subject of any public discussion; nevertheless it is just as well that I do no more than quote from the Report, as I have done, and thus remind you, or inform you for the first time, of what we proposed.

THE PUBLIC INQUIRY AS AN INSTRUMENT OF THE INVASION OF PRIVACY

As a former chairman of a Commission of Inquiry, I have some experience that enables me to raise, as an issue, whether federal Royal Commissions, Commissions of Inquiry, or provincial Public Inquiries, while they may be instruments of beneficial purpose, may nonetheless in certain circumstances unfairly and undesirably operate against the interests of an individual who is compelled to testify in public. Whether or not the terms of reference of the Commission permit the Commissioners, in their report, to make any findings or express any opinions as to the legal culpability of a certain individual, the very fact that he must testify in public may colour the rest of his life: his reputation, his career, and his self-confidence may be affected adversely. If he is already a public figure, in the sense that he has attained or even sought the limelight, perhaps the price he is asked to pay is not disproportionate, given the benefit that is expected to accrue to the state - that is, to the public - in terms of public exposition of the problems or abuses of a public institution. If he is not in the public eye, but is nevertheless a public servant, the proportionality of the price he has to pay is less clear but still arguable. If he is neither a public figure nor a public servant, it is hard to justify the invasion of his privacy, and I find it difficult to do so.

This is an issue separate and apart from the issue of whether it is appropriate to have a public inquiry into possible offences by an individual, and whether it is appropriate to require that individual to testify before the public inquiry, where the prosecuting authorities have not undertaken not to proceed against that individual in a court of law. That is an issue which our Commission discussed in reasons for a decision we gave on May 22, 1980. We then pointed out that in England, the Royal Commission on Tribunals of Inquiry (chaired by Lord Salmon), reporting in 1966, said:

> The publicity... which such hearings usually attract is so wide and so overwhelming that it would be virtually impossible for any person against whom an adverse finding was made to obtain a fair trial afterwards. So far no such person has ever been prosecuted. This again may be justified in the public interest because Parliament having decided to set up an inquiry under the Act has already considered whether or not civil or criminal proceedings would resolve the matter and has decided that they would not.

We continued:

> 4. The risk of prejudicing the right to a fair trial was recognized by one observer of the Report of an earlier Royal Commission - the Taschereau-Kellock Commission on Espionage. In a dispatch to the Dominions Secretary dated August 22, 1946, the British High Commissioner to Canada, Sir Alexander Clutterbuck, said:
>
> > "It must be recognized, too, that the Commissioners were placed in a dilemma by having a dual task thrust upon them. According to their terms of appointment, their primary duty was to report on who, in the public service, was involved: but they also had the wider function of investigating the whole espionage system. But this inevitably means that their Report takes on two self-contradictory qualities - it is not only a commission appointed to report to Parliament on a general question, but also it inevitably constituted itself a judicial tribunal, in effect, to try certain persons of suspected illegal activities, without any actual charge being laid against them. It is fair to the Commissioners to say that this difficulty was inherent in the problem and was an insuperable one. But it has led them to make comments in a public document which cannot fail

to be prejudicial to the individual if and when proper judicial proceedings are taken. In certain cases, for example, the Commissioners frankly state that the person questioned was furtive and evasive and that they did not accept his answers.''

5. The English attitude is illustrated by a statement made by the Attorney General of England, Mr. Samuel Silkin, explaining why it was undesirable to appoint a tribunal of inquiry:

"It is absolutely essential, in the interests of justice, that the trial of a person charged with a criminal offence should proceed without any taint being cast on the defendant before the proceedings commence. Indeed, the task of the police in carrying out their investigation would be made impossible by a concurrent inquiry into the very same matters.''

Our Commission commented:

Such consideration does not appear so clearly to be given by the Governments of Canada or of the provinces when they appoint commissions of inquiry. In England a commission of inquiry, at least if it is to sit in public, is a mechanism of investigation that should be used only if the decision has been made not to prosecute the individuals whose conduct the Commission is bound to investigate if it is to carry out its mandate.

In the Third Report of our Commission, where these passages are found, we then added:

that the problem is complicated in Canada, for the federal government, when it appoints a commission of inquiry, has no means of undertaking that a provincial attorney general will not prosecute.

Of course, that observation does not apply to a provincially-appointed inquiry. In those cases, the issue of fairness in requiring the individual to testify, and of whether a fair trial can ever be obtained in a case of notoriety, should be addressed by those concerned with the relationship between the individual and the state.

This issue is discussed more fully in Professor Ratushny's book, "Self-Incrimination in Canada''.

As I have said, this second issue is not one so much giving rise to concerns about privacy as it is about fairness, although it can be said that the very basis of the broader principle of not requiring a person to condemn himself out of his own mouth is that that principle guards the privacy of the mind.

SAFEGUARDING THE ACCUSED AGAINST MEDIA DISCUSSION OF THE FACTS OF THE CASE OR HIS CHARACTER AFTER CHARGES ARE LAID AND BEFORE TRIAL

This is an issue which is ordinarily cast in terms of the right to a fair trial, but I think that it can also be seen as an aspect of the privacy of a person, which is entitled to protection.

The accused has a right to a fair trial. It follows that there should not be public discussion of the facts of the case, or disclosure of his character, before his trial. Such discussion may constitute contempt of court. For example, publication of his criminal record, or even of the fact that he has previously been convicted of a criminal offence, might prejudice a fair trial. Even publication of his good qualities might do so, for the trial must be fair to the prosecution as well as to the accused, and as such evidence would not generally be admissible at trial, it should not be published before trial.

The media in Canada, no doubt under the mistaken impression that the law here is the same as in the United States, often ignore these rules in notorious cases.

Recently the Attorney General of Alberta wrote to the media to remind them of their responsibilities in this regard. He is to be commended for doing so. I hope that his example will be followed, and that, if necessary, prosecutions for contempt will be undertaken in the future to drive the point home.

I also hope that police forces and the Parole authorities will cease feeding such information to the media, if they have done so. Their doing so would be an abuse of power.

THE PUBLIC'S RIGHT TO HAVE ACCESS TO CONFIDENTIAL INFORMATION POSSESSED BY A NON-GOVERNMENTAL ENTITY, AND THE EXTENT TO WHICH THE LAW PROTECTS SUCH CONFIDENTIAL INFORMATION

This point is relevant to Dean McCamus' skepticism about the efficacy of an action based on breach of confidence as a means of protecting privacy.

A great deal of attention is directed toward the competing claims of disclosure to the public of information in the hands of government, and the individual's right to have his privacy protected by non-disclosure of such information about him.

It should not be forgotten that there may be circumstances when the public's "right to know" should take priority over the privacy of an individual when the issue concerns confidential information about that individual which has fallen into the hands of another person.

Two recent English cases illustrate the problem: In *Francome* v. *Mirror Group*, [1984] W.L.R. 892, the Court of Appeal granted an interlocutory injunction restraining the defendant newspaper from publishing information concerning alleged breaches by the plaintiff of rules of the Jockey Club. Not to grant the injunction would result in publication of an article which might prejudice the plaintiff's rights such that "he could not be adequately compensated in damages for any wrong done thereby to him whatever the result of subsequent proceedings''. But in *Lion Laboratories Ltd.* v. *Evans*, [1984] 2 All E.R. 417, the Court of Appeal discharged an interlocutory injunction that had been granted. The defendant newspaper, this time the *Daily Express*, sought to prevent publication of information contained in confidential internal documents of the plaintiff company, taken by ex-employees. The documents cast doubt upon the reliability and accuracy of intoximeters (what we would call breathalyzers) which were manufactured by the plaintiff. Seven hundred of these intoximeters were used as one of the two devices approved by the Home Office for use by the police. The plaintiff was the sole manufacturer of this particular instrument. Despite the fact that the newspaper's possession of the documents originated in a breach of confidentiality, the Court of Appeal held that it was in the public interest that information which showed that such an instrument was not reliable should be made public because otherwise it was possible that there might be wrongful convictions for a serious criminal offence.

These cases illustrate that the courts will generally protect the right to privacy relating to information of a confidential nature, even commercial information, but that there may be exceptions in which such protection will not be granted: where, in the words of Lord Wilberforce in *British Steel Corp.* v. *Granada Television Ltd.*, [1981] A.C. 1096 at p. 1168, the matter is not merely "interesting to the public" but one that "is in the public interest to make known".

The criminal law has also met the need to protect confidential information, as is dramatically illustrated by the decisions of the Ontario Court of Appeal in *R.* v. *Kirkwood* (1983), 35 C.R. (3d) 97, and *R.* v. *Stewart* (1983), 35 C.R. (3d) 105.

In *Kirkwood* the court held that the offence of fraud (s. 338 C.C.) could be committed by selling and renting videotapes which were copies made by the accused from legitimate tapes, even though there was no deceit practised upon the real owner of the distribution rights and copyright. It is sufficient for a conviction that the accused be aware of a risk of prejudice to the economic interests of the owner. Dishonesty is the key.

In *Stewart*, the accused was charged with counselling a hotel employee to commit fraud and theft of confidential information, namely, the names, addresses and telephone numbers of the hotel's employees contained in the employees' personnel files on a computer printout. The accused desired the information which was sought by a union seeking to form a bargaining unit in the hotel. He offered to pay the employee for the information and suggested that he make a copy of the records surreptitiously without removing them. The majority of the court held that what the employee was asked to do constituted both theft and fraud. It would be theft because the confidential lists were included in "anything animate or inanimate'' (s. 283(1) C.C.) and were indeed property. Houlden J.A. rejected the view of the English Divisional Court in *Oxford v. Moss* (1978), 68 Cr. App. R. 183, in which it was held that the accused could not be convicted of theft when he obtained examination questions. He said:

> The last half of the 20th Century has seen an exponential growth in the development and improvement of methods of storing and distributing information. I believe that s. 283(1) of the Code is wide enough to protect the interests of those who compile and store such information and to restrain the activities of those who wrongfully seek to misappropriate it.

As for fraud, he found that the confidential information was ''property'' (s. 283 C.C.) and that the element of deprivation, which the Supreme Court of Canada in *R. v. Olan*, [1978] 2 S.C.R. 1175, 86 D.L.R. (3d) 212 had held was sufficient to support conviction (as compared with actual economic loss), was present. Cory J.A., the other member of the majority, also held that such confidential information is ''property'', and is within the meaning of ''anything''. His judgment contains the following striking passage:

> Information and its collection, collation and interpretation are vital to most modern commercial enterprises. Compilations of information are often of such importance to the business community that they are securely kept to ensure their confidentiality. The collated, confidential information may be found in many forms covering a wide variety of topics. It may include: painstakingly-prepared computer programs pertaining to all aspects of the firm's business; meticulously-indexed lists of suppliers, with comments as to their efficiency, reliability and time required for delivery; laboriously-compiled lists of customers and their needs; instructions as to manufacturing processes learned from months of experimentation and trial; or lists of employees, including reference to their physical well-being and disciplinary history, that may be required to be kept confidential in compliance with the terms of a collective bargaining agreement. For many businessmen their confidential lists may well be the most valuable asset of their company. Their security will be of utmost importance to the firm.

> If questioned, a businessman would unhesitatingly state that the confidential lists were the ''property'' of his firm. If they were surreptitiously copied by a competitor or outsider, he would consider his confidential data to have been stolen. The importance of confidential information will increase with the growth of high technology industry. Its protection will be of paramount concern to members of industry and the public as a whole.

He also held that, even if confidential information *per se* is not property, there is a *right of property* in confidential information which falls within the meaning of ''property'' in s. 283(1). He noted that the author of compiled information or his employer has a property interest which the common law and the *Copyright Act* have protected and regarded as ''property''.

Statistics, Privacy and the Public Interest

Martin B. Wilk*

This area is of intense interest to statisticians. After all, the entire raison d'être of Statistics Canada is to provide an Information Service to serve the public interest.

My comments will be from the perspective of a statistical agency, specifically Statistics Canada.

I will start by addressing two topics which are closely related to information and privacy — namely, statistical information and confidentiality. The distinctions may be subtle but are extremely important.

Statistical information is always concerned with the characteristics of Aggregates. Examples are items such as:

- The growth rate of the Canadian economy;
- The longevity of Canadian women;
- The rate of unemployment;
- The Canadian balance of payments;
- The distribution of income;
- The average number of years of post-secondary education;
- The rate of increase of prices;
- The distribution of population;
- The aggregate investment in new housing;
- The divorce rates for each of the Provinces.

I hope these examples serve both to illustrate the definition of statistical information, as well as to indicate the importance of statistical information to our society.

Now how does one develop such statistical information? In general, the answer is that one obtains data from individuals who constitute the aggregate of interest, and from the analyses of that individual data, one establishes estimates of the statistical information respecting the aggregate.

* Chief Statistician of Canada.

In order to produce statistical information, one needs to have individual data. What comes in is individual, what goes out is statistical.

The mandate and mission of Statistics Canada is to produce statistical information. The *Statistics Act* specifies that Statistics Canada shall:

> Collect, compile, analyze, abstract and publish statistical information relating to the commercial, industrial, financial, social, economic and general activities and condition of the people.

This activity, of course, is under the direction of a minister responsible.

The Act also requires that there should be no disclosure of "any information... in such a manner that it is possible from any such disclosure to relate the particulars... to any identifiable individual person, business or organization."

Now a word about confidentiality. The *Statistics Act* provides for an absolute assurance of confidentiality for any identifiable information collected under the *Statistics Act*.

First, such information cannot be accessed by anyone outside Statistics Canada at any time under any conditions or under any authority, including judicial authority.

Second, such information cannot be employed, directly or indirectly, in any proceedings.

Third, Statistics Canada employees are required to take an oath of confidentiality, and would be subject to severe penalties if they broke that oath.

Fourth, in the 66 year history of Statistics Canada there has never been a case of a breach of confidentiality.

Lastly, the commitment to confidentiality is the cornerstone of the professional culture of Statistics Canada and indeed of statisticians practically everywhere in the world.

This is not a claim of the moral superiority of statisticians. Rather, this is a consequence of the reality that "Reliability, Objectivity and Confidentiality" are all essential, and mutually supportive, in the functioning of the profession of statistics and the operation of a statistical agency .

The concept of privacy is basically a form of Restriction of Information.

The mandate of Statistics Canada, to produce *only* statistical information, under conditions of absolutely assured confidentiality of individual information, *also* involves a stringent restriction of information.

We say to the public and individual respondents:

> Help us to develop publically necessary or useful statistical information. What you provide about yourself will be held strictly confidential.

We need your help in the public interest. We will not do anything with your data which will relate to you or affect you directly.

Despite this compelling commitment and logic, that Statistics Canada activities constitute only a very very limited threat to individual privacy, there are residual matters of concern.

First, respondents resist the imposition of the physical burden of providing data.

Second, there is the psychic objection occasionally to answering certain questions, despite confidentiality provisions.

Third, there is concern from time to time that the confidentiality assurances may not be respected.

Fourth, there are some few respondents who object to the intrusions, via telephone or interviewer visit, which may be necessary to access the respondent.

(The questions of the cost/benefit of developing the statistical information is a separate matter from privacy and is not part of the present topic).

Thus, despite the fact that Statistics Canada produces only statistical information under assurances of absolute confidentiality of individual data, there remains a *tension* between the public value of statistical information and the respondent's resentment of the overall burden of supplying data, including privacy concerns.

The balance of that tension changes over time, with changing values, needs, attitudes and technology.

The statistical programs of Statistics Canada have evolved over decades in response to the needs and expectations of Canadian society. At any point in time, the balance is determined by what I will term the market place equilibration of supply and demand.

Statistical programs evolve not only in response to changing public information requirements but also in response to respondent's attitudes, behaviour and complaints, guided always by political judgments of elected representatives.

In Japan, the Statistical Bureau carries out a very large and very expensive Family Budget Survey every month. This is one of their most important vehicles for guiding economic policy and programs. Respondents are cooperative and supportive for this Survey.

In Canada, Statistics Canada carries out a Family Expenditure Survey only once every two years. The Survey is usually resented and publicly criticized, sometimes by public officials. More frequent and reliable Family Expenditure data would be no less valuable in Canada than in Japan, but public attitudes have dictated different current practices.

*"So long as human beings
stay human, death and life
are the same thing."*

*"Aussi longtemps que nous
serons humains, la vie et
la mort seront la même
chose."*

George Orwell, *1984*

THE RIGHT TO LIFE AND DEATH:
FREEDOM FROM TREATMENT

LE DROIT À LA VIE ET À LA MORT:
LE DROIT DE REFUSER D'ÊTRE TRAITÉ

Le droit de refuser d'être traité

Jean-Louis Baudouin*

Dans la perspective de George Orwell, en 1984, vie et mort devaient être confondues au sein d'une seule et même réalité. Heureusement pour nous, il n'en est pas ainsi. Toutefois, alors qu'au moment où Orwell a écrit son roman, les frontières de la vie et de la mort étaient relativement faciles à tracer, la réalité n'est pas aussi simple de nos jours. Le débat entourant, par exemple, les critères mêmes de détermination de la mort, à la suite des premières greffes cardiaques à la fin des années 60, n'est pas encore éteint[1].

Dans un siècle, on caractérisera notre époque d'une façon qui ne ressemblera probablement que très peu à notre propre perception de cette réalité. Toutefois, une constatation restera, à notre avis, objectivement vraie. Cette seconde moitié du XXe siècle, aura été marquée, entre autres, par deux phénomènes importants. Le premier et le plus général, est l'adaptation, parfois fort difficile, à laquelle la science juridique législative et jurisprudentielle, aura eu à faire face, pour répondre adéquatement aux nouveaux défis de la technologie, de la médecine et de la biologie. Le second, plus spécifique, est la tendance constante vers un accroissement du pouvoir et du contrôle de l'être humain, sur sa vie, sur sa destinée et sur sa mort.

George Orwell avait le génie du paradoxe ou du *"double talk"*. Pourtant, la réalité de 1984 lui donne raison jusqu'à un certain point, puisque l'on parle couramment aujourd'hui de *"droit de ne pas être traité"*, de *"droit de mourir"*, de *"liberté face au traitement et à la mort"*.

---

* Professeur à la Faculté de droit de l'Université de Montréal.
1. Voir: *Les critères de détermination de la mort*, Document de travail no 23, Commission de réforme du droit, Ottawa, 1979; Rapport au Parlement no 15, Commission de réforme du droit, Ottawa, 1981; L. KUSNIR, "Bridging the Gap: the Discrepancy Between the Medical and Legal Definitions of Death", (1976) *U. of T. Fac. L.R.* 199; R. FREEMAN, "New Reflections on Organ Transplantation and the Definition of Death in Canada", (1982) 3 *Health Law in Can.* 3; H. EMSON et E. KEYSERLINGK, "Exchange of Correspondance", (1982) 3 *Health Law in Canada* 85; R. KOURI, "Réflexions sur la nécessité d'une définition de la mort", (1983) 13 *R.D.U.S.* 447.

Les progrès de la technologie médicale sont tels qu'il est désormais possible d'entretenir ou de simplement soutenir des vies humaines d'une façon artificielle. L'acharnement thérapeutique, suite logique sur le plan médical de la doctrine philosophique et théologique du vitalisme[2], dispose désormais de nouveaux moyens qui ont souvent pour effet de déshumaniser la mort[3], d'accroître les souffrances physiques et morales et d'enlever à l'homme le pouvoir de contrôler sur son propre corps. Il n'est donc pas étonnant d'assister, depuis quelques années, à l'éclosion de divers mouvements revendiquant qui, le droit de mourir dans la dignité, qui, le droit de se faire aider en cas de suicide, qui, même le droit à l'euthanasie active volontaire.

Nous avons pensé, dans les quelques pages qui suivent, tenter de faire le point sur l'état actuel du droit et indiquer brièvement les principaux axes de solutions qui émergent comme éléments de réponses à ces nouveaux défis. Pour plus de clarté, et surtout pour permettre une meilleure identification de certains particularismes éthiques et juridiques, nous avons choisi de regrouper nos observations autour de trois cas précis: le patient adulte et capable, le patient psychiatrique et l'enfant.

Existe-t-il un droit à la mort, un droit de ne pas être traité? Si oui, quelles en sont les limites?

LE TRAITEMENT DU PATIENT ADULTE ET CAPABLE

Le premier cas, qui fera l'objet de notre étude, est celui du patient adulte, pleinement capable en droit et en fait, de prendre une décision libre et éclairée sur son propre sort. Nous examinerons successivement l'état du droit actuel sur la question, les problèmes qui se posent et les solutions qui peuvent être envisagées.

L'état du droit

Le fait, pour une personne adulte et capable, de prendre elle-même les décisions sur son propre corps, est l'expression juridique du principe de l'autonomie de la volonté et du droit à l'autodétermination.

---

2. Sur le courant vitaliste voir: E. SHILS, ''The Sanctity of Life'' dans D. LABBY, *Life or Death: Ethics and Options*, Seattle, U. of Wash. Press 1968, p. 12 et s.; E. KEYSERLINGK, *Le caractère sacré de la vie*, Commission de réforme du droit du Canada, Ottawa, 1979; R. VEATCH, *Life Span; Values and Life Extending Technologies*, Hastings Center, 1979.
3. C'est de là d'ailleurs qu'est venue l'expression ''mourir dans la dignité''. Voir: P.A. CRÉPEAU, ''Prolonger le mourir: qui décide?, (1979) 46 *Assurances* 279; B. DICKENS, ''The Right to Natural Death'', (1981) 26 *McGill L.J.* 847; aussi: J. FLETCHER, ''The Right to Live and the Right to Die'', (1974) 34 *The Humanist* 13; R. VEATCH, ''Prolonging Living and Prolonging Dying: A Distinction That is Not Decisive'' dans *Genetics and the Law*, New York, Plenum Press 1980, p. 182.

La pensée et le système juridique ont évolué, au cours des ans, sur cette question. A une certaine période de l'histoire, on niait en effet, à l'être humain le pouvoir de décider de sa vie et de sa mort. La vie était considérée comme simplement prêtée par Dieu et non comme donnée à l'homme. Celui-ci devant rendre ce prêt, n'était donc pas libre d'en disposer comme il l'entendait[4].

De nos jours, le droit canadien, comme la plupart des droits modernes, s'est éloigné de cette conception et reconnaît l'autonomie de la personne à plusieurs niveaux. Au niveau constitutionnel tout d'abord, de façon indirecte. L'article 7 de la *Charte canadienne* protège le citoyen contre les atteintes à sa vie, à sa liberté et à sa sécurité et l'article 12 défend de le soumettre à un traitement cruel ou inusité. Même si ce dernier texte n'a pas encore fait l'objet d'interprétation dans le contexte médical, il nous semble admettre implicitement, le respect du droit à l'autodétermination individuelle. Si, de plus, le mot "traitement" est large et ne couvre sûrement pas le seul concept de "thérapie", il ne nous paraît pas l'exclure pour autant.

En droit québécois, la *Charte des droits et libertés de la personne*[5] sanctionne le droit à la vie, à la sûreté, à l'intégrité et à la liberté de la personne, de même qu'au respect de la vie privée. De plus, l'article 18 du Code civil consacre de façon très explicite la reconnaissance de l'autonomie de la personne, en rendant celle-ci inviolable sans son consentement ou l'autorisation de la loi. Le consentement de l'individu étant nécessaire, on doit conclure que celui-ci est seul maître, hors les exceptions spécifiquement prévues par la loi[6], de toute décision portant sur l'administration du traitement médical.

On retrouve une conception semblable en droit criminel, puisque l'atteinte non librement consentie ou autorisée par la loi à l'intégrité physique est constitutive de voies de fait[7]. Ainsi, le médecin qui traite un patient sans son assentiment, ou sans prendre la peine de s'assurer que son consentement est libre et éclairé, commet un acte criminel. C'est d'ailleurs la même perspective que l'on retrouve à l'article 45 qui considère le traitement médical comme constituant une voie de fait, soumise toutefois à la triple justification prévue par le texte soit: le caractère raisonnable de l'acte, le fait qu'il soit accompli pour le bien

---

4. Voir: E. KEYSERLINGK, *op. cit., supra*, note 2 et D. CALLAHAN, *The Roots of Ethics: Science, Religion and Values*, Hastings Center, 1981.
5. *Charte des droits et libertés de la personne*, L.R.Q. 1977, c. C-12, art. 1 et 5.
6. Il arrive quelquefois, mais rarement, que le législateur impose un traitement. Voir: *Loi sur la protection et la santé publique*, L.R.Q. 1977, c. P-35.
7. Art. 244 C.cr.

du patient et avec une habileté raisonnable[8]. Certes, les poursuites pénales dirigées contre des médecins et fondées sur le seul défaut d'obtenir le consentement sont rares et il faut admettre que les textes du Code criminel ont, en droit médical, davantage une valeur préventive. Par contre, les poursuites civiles sont fréquentes. De plus, les nouvelles exigences posées par la Cour suprême en matière de contenu de l'obligation de renseignement sont telles qu'elles ont considérablement renforcé la protection juridique de l'autonomie du patient[9].

Le pouvoir du consentement n'est cependant pas absolu, mais conditionné d'une double façon. D'abord, par les droits correspondants des autres. Ainsi, l'individu ne peut disposer de son corps d'une façon qui aurait pour effet de mettre en péril la vie ou la santé des autres. Ensuite, par l'ordre public. La loi impose parfois une limite au droit de libre disposition. Ainsi, elle ne permet pas l'aliénation entre vifs d'une partie du corps non susceptible de régénération ou d'un organe vital[10]. Sous réserve de cette double limite, on peut considérer cependant comme absolu le droit à l'autonomie et à l'autodétermination.

La réalité quotidienne, dans les hôpitaux, met cependant celui-ci parfois à rude épreuve pour plusieurs raisons. La première est la peur de la part des praticiens de poursuites civiles et pénales par leurs patients. Le nombre des actions en responsabilité civile contre les médecins a beaucoup augmenté au cours des dernières années et les tribunaux se montrent de plus en plus généreux dans l'octroi des compensations. Il est donc logique pour un médecin, en cas de doute, de favoriser l'administration d'un traitement, plutôt qu'une abstention. La seconde est qu'une interprétation stricte et littérale de l'article 199 du Code criminel laisse penser que le droit actuel consacre l'acharnement thérapeutique[11]. Ce texte crée une infraction de cesser d'accomplir un acte déjà entrepris, si cette cessation peut mettre la vie humaine en danger. Lu en conjonction avec l'article 198 qui définit les devoirs de ceux qui prati-

---

8. J. FORTIN, A. JODOIN et A. POPOVICI, ''Sanctions et réparation des atteintes au corps humain en droit québécois'', (1975) 6 *R.D.U.S.* 150; M. SOMMER-VILLE, ''Medical Interventions and the Criminal Law: Lawful or Excusable Wounding?'' (1981) 26 *McGill L.J.* 82; B. STARKMAN, ''A Defence to Criminal Responsibility for Performing Surgical Operations: Section 45 of the Criminal Code'', (1981) 26 *McGill L.J.* 1048; R. KOURI, ''Reflexions sur les interventions chirurgicales et la défense de l'article 45 du Code criminel'', (1982) 12 *R.D.U.S.* 499.

9. *Hopp* c. *Lepp*, [1980] 2 R.C.S. 192; *Reibl* c. *Hughes*, [1980] 2 R.C.S. 880; S. RODGERS-MAGNET, ''Recent Developments in the Doctrine of Informed Consent to Medical Treatment'', (1980) 14 *C.L.L.T.* 61, commentaires M. GOCHNOVER et D. FLEMING, (1981) 15 *U. of B.C.L. Rev.* 475.

10. Art. 20 C.c.; A. MAYRAND, *L'inviolabilité de la personne humaine*, Montréal, Wilson et Lafleur, 1975, p. 80 et s.

11. Voir: *Le traitement médical et le droit criminel*, Commission de réforme du droit du Canada, Document de travail no 26, Ottawa, 1980.

quent des opérations dangereuses, il signifierait, littéralement interprété, qu'une fois un traitement entrepris (par exemple le patient placé
sur respirateur), le médecin ne serait plus libre de l'interrompre (de
débrancher l'appareil), lors même qu'il est devenu médicalement inutile.

Cette interprétation doit être rejetée. La philosophie de notre droit
pénal n'est pas aussi pointilleuse et formaliste. Le législateur entend
pénaliser seulement les actes de négligence inacceptables, qui mettent
la vie ou la santé d'autrui en danger. Interrompre un respirateur parce
que le patient est en état de coma dépassé n'est pas un acte de négligence. Cesser un traitement parce qu'il n'a plus aucune valeur thérapeutique n'est pas une faute, mais relève au contraire d'une saine pratique médicale.

La seconde réalité, qui constitue parfois un obstacle au libre exercice du droit du patient, est le jugement que peut porter le médecin sur
les motifs du refus de traitement. Il ne faut pas oublier, en effet, que le
rôle principal de la médecine est de combattre la mort et de rétablir la
santé. On ne saurait donc s'étonner des réactions négatives du théra-
peute, face à un patient qui, pour des raisons personnelles, religieuses,
culturelles ou autres, refuse un traitement qui peut empêcher sa mort,
ou exige l'interruption d'un traitement déjà entrepris qui va, à coup sûr,
avoir pour effet de l'entraîner. La récente affaire *Bouvia*[12] aux Etats-
Unis est là pour le rappeler, de même que le cas encore fréquent du
témoin de Jéhovah qui refuse une transfusion sanguine[13]. Pourtant,
même si le devoir moral du médecin est probablement de tenter de
convaincre son patient de changer d'avis, il doit accepter et respecter
celui-ci, quel qu'il soit, même s'il lui paraît irrationnel et qu'il n'aurait
pas, lui-même, pris une décision identique: le respect de l'autonomie
passe par là!

Les problèmes actuels

Pour les fins du présent document, nous éliminerons la discussion
touchant la reconnaissance par la loi de l'euthanasie active et volontaire
et la décriminalisation du meurtre par compassion. Cette controverse
existe depuis plusieurs années[14]. L'euthanasie active n'a cependant

---

12. Elizabeth Bouvia s'est en effet adressée à un tribunal américain au début de 1984
    pour obtenir de ne plus être artificiellement nourrie. Le tribunal a cependant décidé
    qu'on ne pouvait obliger les autorités hospitalières à fournir de l'aide à un suicide.
    Voir à cet égard les recommandations de la "President's Commission for the Study
    of Ethical Problems in Medicine and Biomedical and Behavioral Research", *Deci-
    ding to Forego Life-Sustaining Treatment*, Washington, 1983.
13. R. KOURI, "Blood Transfusions, Jehovah's Witnesses and the Rule of Inviola-
    bility of the Human Body", (1974) 5 *R.D.U.S.* 156.
14. H. TROWELL, *The Unfinished Debate on Euthanasia*, Londres, S.C.M. Press,
    1973; A. DOWNING, *Euthanasia and the Right to Death*, Londres, Orwen, 1977.

jamais reçu un endossement favorable de la part des juristes, à de très rares exceptions près[15]. Un document récent de la Commission de réforme du droit du Canada la condamne explicitement[16]. Nous nous attacherons, par contre, à deux problèmes principaux. Le premier est celui du devoir du médecin, lorsque son patient est incapable de manifester son consentement. Le second porte sur le droit éventuel du patient à exiger du médecin ou d'un tiers une aide dans la réalisation de son suicide.

Lorsqu'il s'agit d'un patient inconscient et pour lequel le prognostic est défavorable, le médecin doit-il traiter, alors même que, d'après lui, la continuation ou l'initiation du traitement est inutile et ne fera que retarder l'issue fatale? C'est le cas du cancéreux en phase terminale, qui développe une infection pulmonaire. En pratique, dans ce genre de situation, la décision est prise par le médecin en conjonction avec les proches ou avec la famille, donc la plupart du temps de façon commune et collective. Parfois, au contraire, une divergence de vues surgit. Dans ce cas, la crainte de poursuites judiciaires motive en général le médecin à poursuivre le traitement et, en fin de compte, si la divergence persiste c'est le tribunal qui devra trancher.

Le second problème est celui de l'aide au suicide. De nombreux groupes revendiquent une décriminalisation de l'aide au suicide. Si, prétendent-ils, la liberté de l'homme sur sa vie n'est pas un vain concept, l'exercice de cette liberté passe par son droit de demander de l'aide lorsqu'il entend mettre fin à ses jours et est physiquement incapable de le faire seul. La loi ne devrait donc pas pénaliser le médecin ou le proche qui fournit au patient en phase terminale un produit lui permettant de mourir au moment choisi et d'une manière douce.

Des groupes comme Exit en Angleterre, Hemlock aux Etats-Unis, ou Death Dignity au Canada préconisent cette modification aux lois et ont reçu une audience parfois sympathique de la part du public et de certains juristes[16a]. Ici aussi, nous semble-t-il, le droit se doit, d'une façon ou d'une autre, de réagir et de préciser si l'autonomie et le droit à l'autodétermination de l'individu va jusqu'à lui permettre d'exiger une aide des autres.

---

15. Glanville WILLIAMS, ''Euthanasia'', (1973) 41 *Med. Leg. J.* 14 et *The Sanctity of Life and the Criminal Law*, Londres, Faber, 1958. C'est le juriste américain Y. KAMISAR qui, adversaire de l'euthanasie répondit sur ce point à Glanville Williams: ''Some Non Religious Views against Proposed Mercy Killing Legislation'', (1958) 42 *Min. Law Rev.* 969. Aussi G. WILLIAMS, ''Mercy Killing Legislation: A Rejoinder'', (1958) 42 *Min. Law Rev.* 1.

16. *Euthanasie, aide au suicide et interruption de traitement*, Commission de réforme du droit du Canada, Document de travail no 28, Ottawa, 1982; Rapport au Parlement no 20, 1982.

16a. Voir T. ENGELHARDT et M. MALLOY, ''Suicide and Assisting Suicide: A Critique of Legal Sanctions'', (1982) 36 *Southwestern L.J.* 1003.

Les solutions possibles

Il faut tout d'abord admettre qu'il n'existe pas de solution miracle à la plupart de ces problèmes. Ce n'est pas, en effet, une modification ponctuelle aux lois existantes qui peut, d'un seul coup, trancher la majorité de ces débats, car c'est aussi les mentalités, les attitudes, les conduites qu'il importe de modifier.

Le droit actuel, tout du moins dans les textes, contient implicitement les éléments nécessaires pour apporter réponse aux interrogations que nous avons posées sur le plan de la reconnaissance du droit à l'autonomie. Par contre, il reste ambigu sur les limites de l'imposition du traitement au patient inconscient ou en phase terminale, d'une part, et contesté, d'autre part, sur l'aide au suicide.

L'interruption de traitement

Le problème du traitement du patient inconscient peut être résolu d'une double façon. On peut tout d'abord, à l'exemple de certains pays, donner plein effet juridique à une expression écrite et formalisée de la volonté du patient, avant qu'il ne sombre dans l'inconscience. C'est l'option utilisée aux Etats-Unis et connue sous le nom de *"Living will"* (*"testament de vie"*)[17]. Plusieurs états américains ont effectivement adopté un *"Natural Death Act"*[18]. Ces lois reconnaissent pleine valeur légale à un document signé par le patient et dans lequel il demande à ce que des moyens "exceptionnels" ou "extraordinaires" ne soient pas entrepris advenant la situation où il se trouverait dans la phase terminale d'une maladie mortelle. Cette démarche législative a été rendue nécessaire, aux Etats-Unis, par l'augmentation des recours en dommages contre les médecins et par les montants parfois astronomiques accordés par les jurés. Le testament de vie entend donc remédier à une situation anormale et aberrante, qui a conditionné de façon négative une partie de la pratique médicale. Certains ont préconisé son adoption au Canada, jusqu'ici, sans succès[19]. Il ne nous est pas possible de discuter ici en

---

17. M. GARLAND, "Politics, Legislation and Natural Death", (1976) 6 *Hastings Center Reports* 5; "The Living Will: the Right to Death with Dignity", (1976) 26 *Case W. Res. L. Rev.* 485; R. VEATCH, "Death with Dignity: the Legislative Options", (1977) 7 *Hastings Center Reports* 5; E. KEYSERLINGK, "Le testament de vie", (1979) 14 *Le Médecin du Québec* 16; B. DICKENS, "The Right to Natural Death", (1981) 26 *McGill L.J.* 847.

18. La Californie, par exemple: "Health and Safety Code", Stat. of Cal. 1976, c. 1439, Sect. 3, 9; M. STEINBERG, "The California Natural Death Act: a Failure to Provide for Adequate Patients Safeguards and Individual Autonomy", (1977) 9 *Conn. Law Rev.* 203.

19. En Ontario: Private Member's Bill no 3, *An Act Respecting the Withholding or Withdrawal of Treatment where Death is Inevitable*, 4e Session de la 30e Législature de l'Ontario (1977). En Alberta: Private Member's Bill no 220, *An Act Respecting the Withholding or Withdrawal of Treatment where Death is Inevitable*, 1ère Session de la 19e Législature (1979).

détail de la valeur de cette première option. A notre avis cependant, elle a pour effet de consacrer et de légitimer ce que nous devrions tous considérer comme une mauvaise pratique de la médecine, c'est-à-dire une médecine défensive basée sur la crainte des poursuites judiciaires, imprégnée d'acharnement thérapeutique et où même les moyens extraordinaires sont appliqués de façon routinière à tous les patients. Accepter cette première option équivaut à admettre l'existence d'une obligation légale de traiter, lors même que le traitement est devenu inutile ou n'est plus raisonnable dans les circonstances particulières de l'espèce. Elle nous paraît donc inutile et non souhaitable dans le cadre d'une pratique normale et raisonnable de l'art médical. Elle est, en outre, dangereuse puisque basée sur une formule qui contredit la réalité. Pour que le patient ''échappe'' aux soins extraordinaires et inutiles et donc se réinsère dans un processus de pratique médicale normale, il doit, en effet, manifester sa volonté de le faire (système du *''opting out''*). On impute donc à celui qui ne l'a pas fait, le désir de vivre à tout prix, quelles que soient les souffrances à endurer et la qualité de sa vie future ou, au moins, celui de recevoir dans tous les cas les soins exceptionnels. Enfin, on peut se demander si, malgré toutes les précautions dont s'entoure en général l'établissement d'un testament de vie, les tentatives de définir un champ précis d'application, notamment ce que constitue, par exemple, ''la maladie terminale'' sont bien réalistes.

Il est possible de remédier au problème d'une autre façon[20]. C'est celle que préconise la Commission de réforme du droit du Canada dans son Rapport No 20. Elle consiste tout simplement à lever les ambiguïtés qui subsistent encore en droit criminel actuel en raison de l'inadaptation des textes provenant du siècle dernier à la réalité de la pratique médicale moderne. Cette option part du principe fondamental que le respect du caractère sacré de la vie ne doit pas empêcher de prendre en considération des éléments de qualité de vie, et que la préservation de la vie n'est donc pas chose souhaitable en toutes circonstances. Tout jugement à la base de la décision de laisser vivre ou de permettre de mourir en paix doit prendre en considération un ensemble de facteurs touchant non seulement le prognostic, mais aussi les souffrances auxquelles s'exposera le patient, la conscience qu'il gardera, etc. Ce jugement relève en principe du patient lui-même. Lorsqu'il est inconscient ou incapable de le formuler, le médecin doit intervenir, et décider en fonction des informations qu'il possède et des expressions antérieures de la volonté du patient, sans toutefois qu'il soit nécessaire, pour avoir le droit de ne plus appliquer un traitement inutile ou extraordinaire, d'un écrit formalisé. Il suffirait donc, pour lever toute ambiguïté, de quelques

---

20. Voir S. PHILLIPS-NOOTENS, ''Face à la maladie mortelle, deux décisions possibles et leurs implications juridiques'', (1982) 12 *R.D.U.S.* 432.

modifications au code actuel, énonçant notamment qu'un médecin n'a pas d'obligation de continuer à traiter un patient lorsque le traitement est devenu inutile, sauf si son patient le requiert. La décision de traiter ou de ne pas traiter serait prise par le médecin sur la base de son expérience, en tenant compte de la volonté expresse ou présumée de son patient, de toutes les circonstances et de l'utilité ou de la non-utilité de la thérapie. Le droit criminel, comme le droit civil, reste cependant là pour réprimer les abus qui pourraient se manifester dans l'exercice de ce pouvoir.

Il conviendrait ensuite, pour éliminer tout doute sur la légalité des soins palliatifs, de prévoir qu'il est parfaitement légal pour le médecin d'administrer des drogues anti-douleur à son patient pour le soulager, même si ce geste a pour effet de raccourcir son expectative de vie.

A notre avis, le législateur devra avant longtemps, prendre position parce que l'ambiguïté actuelle est génératrice d'abus potentiels non nécessairement sanctionnés et, dans la pratique hospitalière, d'une incertitude parfois angoissante dont les patients sont les premières victimes.

L'aide au suicide

Le législateur canadien, en 1973, a, pour des motifs humanitaires, décriminalisé la tentative de suicide. Il a cependant conservé à l'article 224 l'infraction d'aide au suicide, la punissant sévèrement d'un maximum de 14 ans de prison.

Est-il opportun de décriminaliser l'aide au suicide, du moins celle apportée à un malade en phase terminale? Malgré les pressions mises sur les législateurs américain et canadien au nom du droit à la mort dans la dignité, ceux-ci jusqu'ici ont fait la sourde oreille. La Commission de réforme du droit, pour sa part, après un long examen du problème, s'est prononcée contre, principalement en raison des abus qu'un tel geste est susceptible d'entraîner. Sur le plan humain[21], il est vrai, la différence entre absoudre le patient encore capable d'avaler un poison mortel et traiter comme un criminel le conjoint qui, à sa demande et parce qu'il est paralysé, lui tient le verre, est fort mince. Par contre, tout juriste comprendra aisément les difficultés pratiques de la décriminalisation, notamment celle de distinguer l'aide au suicide authentique et véritable de l'homicide pur et simple. Dans certains cas, il n'y a en effet qu'un pas à franchir entre l'aide au suicide et le meurtre ou, du moins, l'euthanasie active.

---

21. Voir D. HUMPHRY, *Jean's Way*, New Edition, Los Angeles, Hemlock Society 1983, et *Let Me Die Before I Wake*, Los Angeles, Hemlock Society 1982.

Il est difficile de prédire si le droit du futur se laissera convaincre ou non. A l'heure actuelle, cependant, il faut bien dire que la situation ne cause pas de difficultés majeures, puisque les poursuites fondées sur l'article 244 sont inexistantes.

Sur cette première question, une conclusion s'impose à notre avis. Le droit actuel reconnaît l'autonomie et la liberté de l'individu sur sa vie et sa santé et donc son droit de refuser ou d'interrompre un traitement médical. Il ne sanctionne pas, pour autant, un droit à la mort véritable qui lui permettrait soit d'exiger un acte d'euthanasie active, soit de bénéficier d'une aide au suicide.

LE TRAITEMENT DU PATIENT PSYCHIATRIQUE

La façon dont le droit aborde les effets de la maladie mentale a considérablement évolué en raison du changement des attitudes de la société et du développement de nouvelles techniques (notamment la chimiothérapie) qui ont permis de démarginaliser les malades. Alors qu'antérieurement l'interdiction civile entraînait pratiquement une perte totale du pouvoir décisionnel pour celui qui en faisait l'objet, les solutions de nos jours sont plus nuancées et tendent à conserver au malade une certaine marge de participation, au moins aux décisions concernant sa santé et sa vie. Le problème actuel est de tracer les limites de cette participation et de déterminer si certains patients psychiatriques conservent malgré tout le droit de refuser un traitement.

L'état du droit

Le patient psychiatrique, comme tout autre patient, est d'abord protégé par les textes fondamentaux de droit constitutionnel, de droit pénal et de droit civil. Nous ne reviendrons pas sur cette analyse. En outre, les législateurs provinciaux ont tous aménagé un régime juridique particulier de protection du malade mental. Ce régime varie de province à province, même si l'on retrouve, à travers le Canada, un certain nombre de points communs caractéristiques.

Avant d'entrer dans le vif du sujet, quelques brèves remarques s'imposent. En premier lieu, notre discussion ici ne porte que sur l'administration d'un authentique traitement psychiatrique, c'est-à-dire d'un acte thérapeutique appliqué dans le but de guérir ou de soulager l'affection psychologique dont souffre un patient. Toute autre est la question de savoir si, pour des raisons d'ordre social, l'Etat peut s'arroger le droit d'utiliser les techniques psychiatriques dans un but de contrôle social, comme la chose se fait d'ailleurs, à l'heure actuelle, dans certains pays. Autre chose est aussi de décider s'il est légitime pour l'Etat de confondre traitement psychiatrique et sanction pénale et, par exemple, de condamner celui qui a transgressé la loi à une thérapie plutôt qu'à une peine classique. Nous n'aborderons ni l'une ni l'autre de ces questions[22] dans le cadre de cette étude[23].

En second lieu, il faut être conscient qu'à certains niveaux rien ne singularise le patient psychiatrique par rapport au patient ordinaire. Un médecin, par exemple, a, à notre avis, le droit de soigner un malade mental sans obtenir son consentement, en situation d'urgence lorsque le défaut de prodiguer les soins requis risquerait de constituer un danger immédiat pour le patient ou pour son entourage. La doctrine de l'état de nécessité suffit alors à justifier l'intervention.

En troisième lieu, le droit ne connaît pas qu'une seule catégorie de malade mental. Les lois provinciales classent en effet ceux-ci en divers groupes et appliquent à chacun un régime juridique particulier[24]. On trouve, tout d'abord celui que l'on désigne parfois sous le nom de ''patient volontaire''. Il s'agit de la personne qui, atteinte par certains problèmes d'ordre mental ou émotif, consulte un spécialiste pour obtenir de l'aide. Le droit présume alors sa capacité juridique et la traite comme toute autre personne qui s'engage dans un processus thérapeutique quelconque. Le médecin n'a aucun pouvoir de lui imposer un traitement. Le patient a toute liberté de continuer celui-ci ou d'y mettre fin de façon provisoire ou définitive.

Une seconde catégorie est constituée par ceux qui, en raison d'une décision judiciaire ou quasi-judiciaire, ont été déclarés juridiquement incapables de prendre soin de leurs affaires. Les interdits du Code civil

---

22. R. ERICSON, ''Penal Psychiatry in Canada: the Method of our Madness'', (1976) 26 *U. of T. L.J.* 25; M. SCHIFFER, ''Psychiatric Treatment of Mentally Disordered Offenders: the Canadian Cuckoo's Nest'', (1977) 41 *Sask. L. Rev.* 269; *Mental Disorder and the Criminal Trial Process*, Toronto, Butterworths, 1978; *Psychiatry Behind Bars: A Legal Perspective*, Toronto, Butterworths, 1982; B. SWADRON, *Detention of the Mentally Disordered*, Toronto, Butterworths, 1964; aussi: R. SPEECE, ''Conditioning and Other Technologies Used to Treat? Rehabilitate? Demolish? Prisoners and Mental Patients'', (1972) 45 *So. Cal. Law Rev.* 615; G. TRASLER et D. FARRINGTON, *Behavior Modification with Offenders: A Criminological Symposium*, Cambridge Institute of Criminology, Cambridge, 1979: L. SELVA, ''Treatment as Punishment'', (1980) 6 *New Eng. J. Pres. L.* 265, 325; B. WINICK, ''Legal Limitations on Correctional Therapy and Research'', (1981) 65 *Min. Law Rev.* 331. Notons aussi le récent projet du ministère de la justice fédérale intitulé: ''Projet sur le désordre mental, Révision du droit pénal'', dirigé par G. SHARPE.

23. Nous n'aborderons pas non plus ici le problème illustré aux U.S.A. par l'affaire Saikewicz: *Superintendent of Belchertown State School* c. *Saikewicz*, 370 N.E. 2d 417 (1977) sur la cessation de traitement chez l'aliéné. Voir G. ANNAS, ''The Incompetent's Right to Die: the Case of Joseph Saikewicz'', (1978) 8 *Hastings Center Reports* 21.

24. Pour le Québec voir: V. BERGERON, *L'attribution d'une protection légale aux malades mentaux''*, *Montréal, Editions Yvon Blais Inc., 1981; B. HILL*, ''Civil Rights of the Psychiatric Patient in Quebec'', (1977) 12 *R.J.T.* 503. Voir aussi: M.P. CHAMPENOIS-MARMIER, *Droit, folie et liberté*, Paris, P.U.F. 1983.

en sont un exemple au Québec[25]. La loi leur nomme alors un curateur qui les représente dans les actes de la vie civile et prend soin de leur personne. Ce représentant, lorsque la loi lui confère un pouvoir sur la personne et pas seulement sur les biens, peut alors autoriser le traitement de l'incapable, en prenant pour base le meilleur intérêt de celui-ci.

Une troisième catégorie est celle de l'interné involontaire, non pourvu d'un représentant et placé en institution. Il peut s'agir, par exemple, d'une personne détenue en vertu d'un mandat du lieutenant-gouverneur[26] ou de quelqu'un qui a été placé en "cure fermée"[27] parce que constituant un danger pour elle-même ou pour les autres. Deux questions se posent alors. Ce patient, en premier lieu, conserve-t-il le droit de s'opposer au traitement? Peut-il être traité malgré lui? Ce patient, en second lieu, garde-t-il une liberté dans le choix du traitement auquel il est soumis[28]?

Les divers droits provinciaux ne fournissent pas une réponse unanime[29]. Ils se divisent, au contraire, en trois grandes catégories. Pour certains, Terre-Neuve par exemple, la loi mentionne expressément que le patient peut être traité sans son consentement[30]. Les autorités de l'hôpital ou de l'institution ont donc une complète latitude. Pour d'autres, qui représentent à l'heure actuelle la majorité, il semble, avec toutefois des nuances considérables, que le patient ne soit pas en mesure

---

25. Art. 325 et s. C.c.; A. MAYRAND, *L'inviolabilité de la personne humaine*, Montréal, Wilson et Lafleur, 1975, p. 50 et s.

26. Art. 542 et s. C.cr.

27. Voir *Loi sur la protection du malade mental*, L.R.Q. 1977, c. P-41.

28. Sur le sujet voir: J. JACOB, "The Right of the Mental Patient to his Psychosis", (1976) 39 *Mod. L. Rev.* 40; J. COCCOZA et M. MELICK, "The Right to Refuse Treatment: a Broad View", (1977) 5 *Bull. of Am. Acad. of Psy. and Law* 7; N. RHODEN, "The Right to Refuse Psychotropic Drugs", (1980) 15 *Harv. L. Rev.* 362; M. MILLS, "The Rights of Involuntary Patients to Refuse Pharmacotherapy: What is Reasonable?, (1980) 8 *Bull. of Am. Acad. of Psy. and Law* 313; A. REISER, "Refusing Treatment for Mental Illness", (1980) 137 *Am. J. of Psy*, 329; E. TANAY, "The Right to Refuse Treatment and the Abolition of Involuntary Hospitalization of the Mentally Ill", (1980) 8 *Bull. of Am. Acad. of Psy. and Law* 1; J. HENEBERY, "The Right of the Psychiatric Patient to Refuse Treatment", dans WECHT, *Legal Medecine*, Philadelphia Saunders, 1982, p. 138 et s.; A. BROOKS, "The Constitutional Right to Refuse Antipsychotic Medication", (1980) 9 *Bull. of Am. Acad. of Psy. and Law* 179; H. ARKIN, "Forcible Administration of Antipsychotic Medication", (1983) 249 *J.A.M.A.* 2784; T. WELLSCH, "The Right of the Civilly Committed Mental Patient to Refuse Treatment", (1984) 48 *Sask. L. Rev.* 269.

29. Voir: R. GORDON, "Comparative Study of Mental Health Legislation in the Commonwealth", (1983) *Int. J. of Law and Psychiatry* 5.

30. *Mental Health Act*, St. Nfld, 1971, no 870, art. 6(1).

de refuser un traitement ou que son droit soit fort limité[31]. Cette règle cependant, résulte d'une déduction faite à partir de la lecture de l'ensemble des lois et non d'une disposition expresse. Enfin, l'Ontario[32] et la Nouvelle-Ecosse[33] ont mis sur pied un régime différent. Ces deux provinces se prononcent en principe contre le traitement imposé. Le patient se voit clairement accorder le droit de refuser un traitement. Si les autorités jugent que, malgré tout, il devrait le recevoir pour son bien et est vraiment incapable de décider pour lui-même, une procédure spéciale, respectueuse de ses droits fondamentaux, permet d'en autoriser l'administration. Récemment, au Québec, la question s'est posée à propos d'un individu interné à la suite de menaces proférées contre le premier ministre et qui refusait de se laisser soigner. La Cour supérieure autorisa l'intervention en se fondant sur son pouvoir de *parens patriae*[34]. La cause est maintenant en appel et soulève des questions complexes et intéressantes. Il n'est pas certain, en effet, que le pouvoir de *parens patriae*, réservé par le common law aux seuls tribunaux d'équité, ait été reçu en droit québécois d'une part et ressortisse, d'autre part, à la Cour supérieure.

Qu'en est-il, en second lieu, du droit du patient de choisir son traitement ou, tout en acceptant des soins en général, de refuser une forme particulière de thérapie? La réponse à cette seconde question est intimement liée à la première et a d'ailleurs fait l'objet de quelques décisions jurisprudentielles récentes. Dans l'affaire *Carsley* c. *Douglas General Hospital*[35], un père de famille contestait la thérapie utilisée par les médecins sur sa fille internée. Le tribunal rejeta l'action du père, qui se faisait le porte-parole de son enfant, avalisant ainsi en quelque sorte l'idée que le médecin, sauf cas d'abus manifeste, est réellement maître de la thérapie.

En Ontario, l'affaire *T.* c. *Board of Review for the Western Region*[36] a également touché ce problème. Une personne internée s'opposait à ce qu'on lui applique l'électrochoc. Pour ce faire, elle argumentait que ce traitement était l'équivalent de la psychochirurgie parce qu'il avait pour effet de détruire ou d'interrompre au sens de l'article 35(1) du *"Mental*

---

31. *Mental Health Act*, Rev. St. B.C. 1979, c. 256, art. 25(2); *Mental Health Act*, Rev. St. Man. 1970, c. M-110, art. 8(4); *Mental Health Act*, Rev. St. Sask. 1978, c. M-13, art. 25(a) et 26; *Mental Health Act*, Rev. St. Alta 1980, c. M-13, art. 13, 15 et 19. Voir T. WELLSCH, "The Right of the Civilly Committed Mental Patient to Refuse Treatment", (1984) 48 *Sask. L.R.* 369.

32. *Mental Health Act*, Rev. St. Ont. 1980, c. 262, art. 35.

33. *Hospitals Act*, Cons. St. N.S. 1979, c. H-19, art. 43 et s.

34. *Institut Philippe Pinel* c. *Dion*, [1983] C.S. 438; voir D. WEISSTUB, *Law and Psychiatry in a Canadian Context*, Toronto, Pergaman Press, 1980, p. 325 et s.

35. *Carsley* c. *Douglas General Hospital*, C.S. Mtl, no 500-05-008783-837, 27 juillet 1983.

36. *T.* c. *Board of Review for the Western Region*, (1983) 44 O.R. (2d) 153.

Health Act"[37] la continuité histologique du tissu cérébral. La cour, se fondant sur la preuve d'expertise, conclut que ce traitement ne constituait pas une véritable psychochirurgie, procédure formellement défendue aux termes de la loi.

Les problèmes actuels

Le principal problème pour le droit actuel est de trouver un équilibre acceptable entre les droits du patient psychiatrique interné et l'intérêt évident qu'il y a parfois à le traiter sans son consentement ou en dépit de son opposition, de manière à tenter de lui rendre la véritable autonomie décisionnelle dont il est privé. Le mouvement antipsychiatrie aux Etats-Unis a fait beaucoup pour contester l'autorité suprême des psychiatres et pour forcer l'Etat à reconnaître aux patients des droits fondamentaux et le bénéfice d'une procédure adéquate pour les faire valoir. Ce mouvement existe aussi au Canada et l'avènement de la Charte canadienne va sans doute lui fournir des arguments de poids. Un problème secondaire, mais non moins réel, est posé par le défaut d'harmonisation, pourtant souhaitable, entre les différentes législations provinciales, face aux droits fondamentaux qui sont les mêmes pour tous les citoyens canadiens.

Les solutions possibles

L'administration du traitement psychiatrique à un patient interné non volontairement soulève, comme nous venons de le voir, des problèmes fort complexes. Plusieurs provinces, notamment l'Ontario[38] et le Québec[39], se sont penchées sur la question et ont soit adapté leur législation actuelle aux nouvelles exigences, soit proposé de nouveaux textes sur le sujet. Eu égard à la Charte, et considérant les abus inévitables qui ont été commis en la matière, il nous semble y avoir effectivement place pour une réforme en profondeur. La Commission de réforme du droit du Canada publiera d'ailleurs bientôt un document de travail constituant, au moins une réflexion critique sur ces problèmes. A notre avis, on doit admettre que, dans certains cas, il est légitime de passer outre le refus d'un patient psychiatrique d'être traité, lorsque son refus est le fruit d'un consentement inexistant parce qu'atteint par la maladie. Par contre, on doit aussi éviter de tomber dans l'excès contraire et, parce qu'un patient a été déclaré juridiquement incapable, le priver systématiquement de tout contrôle sur les décisions de ce genre.

---

37. Précité note 32.
38. Pour l'Ontario, voir: *Mental Health Act*, précité note 32.
39. Au Québec, voir les nouvelles dispositions du projet de loi no 106 portant réforme du Code civil du Québec sur le droit des personnes qui reconnaît trois régimes de protection pour le majeur (art. 197 et s.).

Il convient donc tout d'abord de maintenir et même de renforcer la règle traditionnelle selon laquelle la capacité se présume toujours. Il faut admettre ensuite qu'une personne internée, et donc cataloguée par le système juridique comme inapte à prendre des décisions légales valables, doit, au moins en matière de traitement médical, conserver un certain droit de regard sur son administration et bénéficier d'un système de contrôle assurant le respect de ses droits fondamentaux et la poursuite de ses intérêts véritables.

LE TRAITEMENT DE L'ENFANT

L'administration de soins médicaux à l'enfant pose aussi des problèmes complexes. Comme pour le patient psychiatrique, la difficulté vient du fait que, là aussi, le droit doit prévoir un système de consentement substitué et identifier les critères dont on doit tenir compte dans la prise de décision.

L'état du droit

Le droit criminel, comme le droit civil, impose aux parents un certain nombre de devoirs à l'égard de leurs enfants. Le Code criminel sanctionne sévèrement le défaut de fournir les choses essentielles à la vie[40]. Le droit civil, de son côté, les oblige à nourrir, à élever, à éduquer et à entretenir l'enfant[41]. Dans les deux cas, la loi, avec raison, fait confiance aux parents pour décider en lieu et place de l'enfant. Les liens affectifs sont, en effet, une garantie que les décisions parentales seront prises dans le meilleur intérêt de celui-ci. Comme cependant les abus sont toujours possibles et qu'il faut donc une protection pour l'incapable, le droit retire parfois, pour des motifs particulièrement graves, ce pouvoir au père et à la mère en prononçant la déchéance de la puissance parentale[42]. En outre, le législateur provincial, sur une plus vaste échelle, a mis sur pied un système général de protection de la jeunesse contre les mauvais traitements[43].

En matière de traitement médical, ce sont donc, en principe et en règle générale, les parents qui prennent les décisions pour l'enfant. Toutefois, pour prévenir certains abus, le droit permet l'intervention des tiers. Un médecin peut aussi traiter un enfant, sans requérir l'autorisation des parents en cas d'urgence[44]. De plus, la loi favorise le déve-

---

40. Art. 197 C.cr.
41. Art. 647 et s. C.C.Q.
42. Art. 654 et s. C.C.Q.; voir *A. c. L.*, [1982] C.S. 964; *Sabourin c. Laframboise*, J.E. 82-476; R. JOYAL-POUPART, ''La loi 89 et l'autorité parentale'', (1982) 13 *R.G.D.* 97.
43. *Loi sur la protection de la jeunesse*, L.R.Q. 1977, c. P-34.1.
44. *Loi sur la protection de la santé publique*, L.R.Q. 1977, c. P-35, art. 43.

loppement rapide de l'autonomie décisionnelle de l'enfant. Au Québec, par exemple, un médecin peut fournir des soins au mineur de plus de 14 ans sans obtenir le consentement du titulaire de l'autorité parentale, à moins que le cas ne nécessite un hébergement supérieur à 12 heures ou un traitement prolongé[45]. Enfin, en cas de conflit entre le médecin et les parents ou d'impossibilité d'obtenir l'autorisation nécessaire, il est possible de s'adresser à un juge de la Cour supérieure. Plusieurs affaires canadiennes, dont l'affaire *Dawson*[46] en Colombie britannique et l'affaire *Goyette*[47] au Québec, ont récemment illustré ce type de conflit.

La protection de l'enfant en matière de traitement médical est donc assurée à la fois par les textes généraux que nous avons déjà examinés et par l'ensemble de la législation pénale, civile et administrative touchant la protection de l'enfance. Cet ensemble, non seulement sanctionne les abus, mais prévoit aussi, grâce à la multiplication des mécanismes de prévention, un contrôle a priori sur l'exercice du pouvoir décisionnel en matière de traitement.

Les problèmes actuels

Le problème majeur en matière de traitement des enfants est celui des nouveaux-nés atteints de malformations congénitales graves. Les progrès de la néonatologie font que, de nos jours, il est possible de sauver des enfants qui, en d'autre temps, n'auraient jamais survécu plus que quelques heures ou quelques jours[48]. Comme pour l'adulte inconscient, la question se pose donc de savoir quand faire vivre et quand laisser mourir.

Ce dilemme n'est évidemment pas spécifique au Canada. Ainsi, en 1981 un tribunal d'appel anglais ordonnait de procéder à une opé-

---

45. *Loi sur la protection de la santé publique*, L.R.Q. 1977, c. P-35, art. 42.

46. *In the matter of Stephen Dawson*, [1983] 3 W.W.R. 597; (1983) 42 B.C.L.A. 173.

47. *Goyette* c. *Centre des services sociaux du Montréal métropolitain*, [1983] C.S. 424.

48. La littérature juridique sur le sujet est extrêmement nombreuse. Nous nous contenterons donc de citer ici quelques textes seulement: J. MAGNET, ''Withholding Treatment from Defective Newborns: a Description of Canada Practise'', (1980) 4 *Legal Med. J.* 271; ''Withholding Treatment from Defective Newborns: Legal Aspects'', (1982) 42 *R. du B.* 187; E. KLUGE, ''The Euthanasia of Radically Defective Neonates; Some Statutory Considerations'', (1980) 6 *Dalhousie* (.). 229; B. DICKENS, ''The Right to Natural Death'', (1981) 26 *McGill L.J.* 847. Pour le droit américain, voir: J. ROBERTSON, ''Involuntary Euthanasia of Defective Newborns: A Legal Analysis'', (1975) 27 *Stan. L. Rev.* 213; ''Legal Aspects of Withholding Medical Treatment from Handicapped Children'', dans *Legal and Ethical Aspects of Treating Critically and Terminally Ill Patients*, A. Doudera ed., Ann Arbor Aupha Press, 1982, p. 213.

ration chirurgicale correctrice chez un nouveau-né atteint du syndrôme de Down[49]. Aux Etats-Unis, plus récemment, le cas *"Baby Doe"*[50] a fait couler beaucoup d'encre, puisqu'il a incité l'administration américaine à mettre sur pied un véritable système de délation organisée et à adopter une politique qui a fait l'objet d'une réprobation quasi unanime[51].

L'une des difficultés supplémentaires en matière de traitement du nouveau-né, vient du fait que dès sa naissance, celui-ci est déjà engagé dans un processus de mortalité. N'ayant, à la différence de l'adulte, jamais donc eu le loisir d'exprimer une volonté quelconque face à la vie ou à la mort, la décision le concernant va devoir être entièrement prise par d'autres, à l'aide de critères dont aucun ne peut se fonder sur la volonté présumée du patient. Les parents devront donc, à l'aide de l'information fournie par les médecins, décider s'il faut faire vivre ou laisser mourir leur enfant, en tenant compte de divers facteurs dont sa future qualité de vie. Le plus grand défi au droit, à l'heure actuelle, est de concevoir un système efficace d'identification et de contrôle des critères décisionnels, séparant ceux qu'il convient de retenir de ceux, au contraire, qu'il faut écarter. Ainsi, tous, je pense, sont d'accord pour affirmer que la souffrance de l'enfant, le nombre et le genre d'interventions médicales qu'il devra subir, le prognostic sur son expectative de vie, la qualité de la vie relationnelle qu'il peut envisager sont autant de facteurs qui doivent être pris en considération. Par contre, d'autres facteurs soulèvent de sérieuses interrogations tant sur le plan éthique que sur le plan juridique. Ainsi, s'il est établi que l'enfant va nécessiter des soins constants de la part de ses parents, faut-il tenir compte de la résistance émotive et psychologique et de l'aptitude personnelle de ceux-ci à faire face au problème? Faut-il également, si l'état de l'enfant va obliger à des dépenses considérables, prendre en considération la situation économique des parents et leur capacité de payer[52]?

Un second problème, qui touche plus directement le pouvoir judiciaire, est celui du genre de forum qui est le mieux adapté au contrôle de ce genre de décision. A l'heure actuelle, en cas de divergence de vues entre les parents et le médecin, c'est aux tribunaux qu'il appartient de trancher. Les affaires *Dawson* et *Goyette*[53] en constituent deux exemples. La tradition fait confiance au système judiciaire, parce que

---

49. *In re B.*, [1981] 1 W.R.L. 1421.
50. Voir "The Case of Baby Jane Doe", dans (1984) 14 *Hastings Center Report*, p. 10 et s.
51. R. SHAPIRO, "Medical Treatment of Defective Newborns: An Answer to the Baby Doe Dilemna", (1982) 20 *Harv. J. Leg.* 137; M. COSBY, "The Legacy of Infant Doe", (1982) 34 *Baylor L. Rev.* 699; G. ANNAS, "Baby Doe Redux: Doctors as Child Abusers", (1983) 13 *Hastings Center Report* 26.
52. Voir J. ARRAS, "On the Case of Imperiled Newborns: Toward an Ethic of Ambiguity", (1984) 14 *Hastings Center Report* 24.
53. *Supra*, notes 46 et 47.

l'indépendance, la neutralité et le prestige dont il jouit constituent une garantie sérieuse. Pourtant, on doit, à notre avis, se poser la question de savoir si le système judiciaire est bien le meilleur instrument décisionnel dans ce cas. Notre système de résolution des conflits est en effet basé sur la confrontation de deux vérités et sur l'identification, en fin de compte, d'un gagnant et d'un perdant. Or, lorsqu'il s'agit de décider de la vie ou de la mort d'un nouveau-né, ce processus n'est peut-être pas celui qui convient le mieux. En effet, il n'y a place ici ni pour un gagnant, ni pour un perdant. Le conflit reste en plus artificiel, puisque d'un côté comme de l'autre, on recherche, en fin de compte, l'intérêt de l'enfant et non la défense d'intérêts égoïstes.

En outre, notre système est essentiellement contradictoire. Chaque côté présente au juge, dans les limites fixées par la loi, une preuve au soutien de ses prétentions, preuve nécessairement partisane. Le juge n'a que très rarement le pouvoir d'aller lui-même rechercher les faits et recueillir la preuve de sa propre initiative. Il doit se fier à celle que les parties lui présentent. Il n'est pas sûr, qu'en matière de traitement médical de l'enfant, ce système soit le meilleur pour permettre la découverte de la vérité.

Enfin, décider de la vie ou de la mort est une responsabilité morale sérieuse. Il y a quelque chose d'injuste, pour un juge, à être saisi d'un problème aussi considérable, de la même façon que d'une requête en injonction, d'une demande de saisie-arrêt ou en cautionnement. Il y aurait donc probablement lieu d'envisager une certaine spécialisation du pouvoir judiciaire.

Les solutions possibles

Les solutions possibles au problème du traitement du nouveau-né sont de deux ordres. Les premières touchent le fond du problème; les secondes les mécanismes d'adjudication.

A l'heure actuelle, dans tous les pays, on constate de la part des médecins, des juristes et des éthiciens[54], un travail de réflexion considérable sur les critères qui peuvent ou doivent entrer en ligne de compte dans la prise de décision. Jamais ne sera-t-il possible, probablement, de développer des critères entièrement objectifs. La chose n'est d'ailleurs probablement pas souhaitable de toute façon. Toutefois, il est permis d'espérer que notre société réussisse à faire l'unanimité autour d'un certain consensus de base. Les disparités entre provinces, entre

---

54. Voir D. ROY, *Medical Wisdom and Ethics in the Treatment of Severelly Defective Newborns and Young Children''*, *Montreal Eden Press, 1978; A. JONSEN, ''Critical Issues in Newborn Intensive Care: A Conference Report and Policy Proposal''*, *(1975) 55 Ped.* 756; ''Ethics the Law and the Treatment of Seriously Ill Newborns'', dans DOUDERA, *Legal and Ethical Aspects of Treating Critically and Terminally Ill Patients*, Ann Arbor, Aupha Press, 1982, p. 236.

régions, et même entre centres hospitaliers ne sont sûrement pas souhaitables, même si, pour être réaliste, elles sont probablement inévitables jusqu'à un certain point[55]. Il faut admettre ouvertement et clairement que, sur la base de certains critères, l'intérêt même de l'enfant exige parfois que l'on n'intervienne pas dans un processus de mortalité déjà engagé. Il faut admettre que certains impératifs de qualité de vie doivent entrer en ligne de compte, pour le nouveau-né comme pour l'adulte.

Le second axe de réforme touche le processus décisionnel lui-même. Comme nous l'avons déjà dit, le modèle judiciaire contradictoire ne nous paraît pas personnellement bien adapté à la résolution harmonieuse de ce type de conflit. C'est, en effet, un modèle basé davantage sur le consensus que sur la confrontation qui serait souhaitable. Le juge doit toutefois rester présent, mais à un autre niveau. Nul ne saurait, en effet, se dispenser d'un contrôle judiciaire et de la répression des abus et le juge doit donc conserver son rôle de défenseur et de protecteur ultime des droits de l'enfant. Toutefois, ni les règles traditionnelles de la procédure classique, ni celles de la preuve ne nous paraissent adaptées à ce type de prise de décision. Il y a là matière à plus ample réflexion.

Dans l'un des Rapports du Parlement, la Commission de réforme du droit du Canada a opté pour une sorte de *statu quo*, et en même temps plaidé pour une plus grande transparence au niveau des critères décisionnels[56]. La réforme en l'espèce est toutefois, à notre avis, beaucoup plus un problème de changement des attitudes et des comportements, que de modification des règles juridiques.

Comme on peut donc le constater, le droit actuel est en pleine mutation en raison des changements d'attitude de la société face à la vie et face à la mort et des impératifs nouveaux de la médecine moderne.

Ces bouleversements entraînent inévitablement des situations conflictuelles qui sont d'autant plus importantes qu'elles touchent à des valeurs fondamentales. Il appartient donc au législateur et aux tribunaux de faire oeuvre créatrice et, à partir des postulats fondamentaux et des principes sur lesquels notre société est fondée, de dégager les solutions qui s'imposent.

Il reste à espérer que celles-ci n'amèneront pas un monde Orwellien où vie et mort sont confondues et où les valeurs humaines fonda-

---

55. J. MAGNET, ''Withholding Treatment from Defective Newborns: A Description of Canadian Practices'', (1980) 4 *Leg. Med. Q.* 271.
56. *Euthanasie, aide au suicide et interruption de traitement*, Commission de Réforme du droit du Canada, Document de travail no 28, Ottawa, 1982; Rapport au Parlement 1983. Voir aussi pour les Etats-Unis les recommandations de la ''Commission for the Study of Ethical Problems in Medicine and Biomedical Research'', Washington 1983, *Deciding to Forego Life - Sustaining Treatment*.

mentales sont ignorées et manipulées par un Etat tout puissant. En matière de décisions sur la vie ou sur la mort des individus, il n'appartient pas à l'Etat de se substituer aux désirs et aux libertés individuelles. Contrairement au monde clos de Georges Orwell, c'est en effet le pouvoir individuel qui doit être le centre de l'exercice de cette liberté. L'Etat, par le biais de ses institutions et de ses règles juridiques, ne doit fixer que des paramètres très larges à cette liberté et ne réprimer que les abus les plus grossiers. En aucun cas il ne doit s'accaparer le droit de prendre ou d'imposer ce genre de décision, même sous le couvert, parfois fallacieux, du meilleur intérêt de l'individu.

The Right to Die: Moral Considerations

David J. Roy*

INTRODUCTION

"Dying with dignity" is little more than a slogan until its meaning is spelled out in guidelines facilitating medical decisions that honor a patient's needs and wishes. The attempt to do this shifts "dying with dignity" to the center of a debate, as yet unfinished, on a series of issues.

When should efforts to prolong or save a patient's life be stopped? On what moral basis should these decisions be made? How is the responsibility to take such decisions to be shared? If it is morally justifiable to let a patient die, why is it not morally justifiable to hasten a patient's death?

These and other related questions are still challenging society and professional communities to work out a defensible consensus to resolve difficult moral dilemmas in medicine today.

DYING WITH DIGNITY: AN UNFINISHED CONTROVERSY

"Dying with dignity" has dominated the last ten years of medical practice, medical ethics, and medical law. It is often far from clear what that slogan should mean in hospitals that have become theatres for the deployment of a complex life-prolonging technology needing the services of many specialized persons. The sick and possibly dying person represents a cluster of clinical challenges woven into the pattern of a unique personal history. That history of desires, plans, achievements, loves and hopes, not just health and biological survival, are thrown into question when devastating illness strikes and death threatens. That unique person, certainly weak and possibly frightened and confused, should be not only the object of the clinical decisions that have to be made but also the norm of the fundamental human choices

* Director, Center for Bioethics Clinical Research Institute of Montreal.

that define the meaning of clinical activity at the extremes of life. How-ever, who is to make these choices and how are they to be made in a highly pluralistic society and highly specialized hospitals?

Theatre, television and film have recognized the deep concerns carried by the phrase "dying with dignity" and are responding to it with moving dramatizations of real-life stories, both personal and professional, that occur nearly on a daily basis in intensive care units and hospitals today. Some of these stories have become court cases and some initial decisions have gone through several appeals. The Quinlan, Saikewicz, Dinnerstein, Becker, Fox, Storar and Spring cases, to name a few of the better known among many North American cases, docu-ment our unfinished confusion and lack of societal consensus about what dying with dignity means today. The reappearance of groups pro-moting active euthanasia and "rational" suicide reveals levels of des-peration that mark profound societal discord about important matters. The ways we deal with the dying, the terminally ill, and with those whom medicine can save but not cure are in question. The unfinished controversy is about life, not just about ideas.

Dying with dignity: the problem

People rarely die alone today, even if many may die lonely.

People used to die at home, in the midst of their families, sur-rounded by all of the objects and memories which captured and kept a life history alive and present to dying persons during their last days, hours and moments. Most frequently people die in hospitals today, in places that are strange and sterile, places that bear no mark or memory of how one has lived, of those with whom one has lived.

People today die in places usually equipped with a massive and complex technology capable of supporting and prolonging life, fre-quently only biological life, when cures and returns to health and vital-ity are no longer possible. Terminally ill and dying patients may be technologically bound to biological existence beyond the moments when they could have died conscious and in mastery of their ultimate moments of life. Philippe Ariès has described the situation that has arisen because of our new life-prolonging technologies and our uncertainty about when this technology is out of place.

> Death has been dissected, cut to bits by a series of little steps, which finally makes it impossible to know which step was the real death, the one in which consciousness was lost, or the one in which breathing stopped. All these little silent deaths have replaced and erased the great dramatic act of death, and no one any longer has the strength or patience to wait over a period of weeks for a moment which has lost part of its meaning. [Philippe Ariès, *Western Attitudes toward Death: From the Middle Ages to the Present.* Baltimore: The John Hopkins University Press, 1974, p. 88-89]

Dying today means dying with medicine's complex technology and with its technologists. One rarely dies on one's own. Dying has almost become a team activity, an interdisciplinary performance. People do not simply die, nor do they die simply. Their dying calls for decisions. However, the dying person is often not the central action, nor the decision-maker, but an object of custody about whom others decide.

As dying patient, one may be easily separated from one's own dying. This process of alienation has a long history.

> From the end of the eighteenth century we had been impressed by a sentimental landslide which was causing the initiative to pass from the dying man himself to his family — a family in which henceforth he would have complete confidence. Today the initiative has passed from the family, as much an outsider as the dying person, to the doctor and the hospital team. They are the masters of death — of the moment as well as of the circumstances of death —... [Philippe Ariès, op. cit., p. 89]

The kinds of decisions that have to be taken for and with dying persons are not purely technical. They become an intrinsic component of the event of dying. Depending on the content and mode of these decisions, some people will have the chance to die well, masters of their dying, not alone and not lonely. Others may die before their time, without a chance to live their dying through. Others may die too late, reduced to biological systems that have to be tended. Some may die uninformed and unenlightened, caught trying to play Scene One when the drama is about to close. Still others may die, who could have lived.

Decisions with such consequences are eminently moral. They cannot be made without calling upon and expressing our deepest values and beliefs about what is truly worthwhile in life. People may differ profoundly on such matters. Consequently, even once we move beyond negligence, insensitivity, incompetent pain control, mindless medical intervention, reflex applications of medical technology, and medical paternalism, "dying with dignity" remains as a plea for compassionate understanding as a category of controversy, and as a symbol of quest for a moral and societal consensus. The consensus, not to be identified with uniformity, is growing and includes space for those who differ from established views.

Dying With Dignity: A Model

Dying with dignity has become a slogan of opposition to degrading and useless technological prolongations of biological life when a patient's organism, though still minimally functional, no longer supports or permits the exercise of intelligent and personal control over the events of his life. All would agree that it is an appalling degradation of human dignity to treat a person as a mere object. We readily accept this as a moral basis of our dealings with one another in all phases of life. The slogan, ''dying with dignity'', is a call to respect this moral foundation in our relationship to those who are dying.

Blaise Pascal has said that a human being, even when subjected to the laws of nature that dictate descent into death, remains superior to the entire universe. This is so, because a human being can know that he dies, while the universe knows nothing about what it does. Though the dignity of a human being does not consist in thought alone, how can one's dying be an expression of human and personal dignity if it has no chance to be the final expression of the meaning one has given to life and to love?

In a *first* sense, dying with dignity means dying without a frantic technical fuss and bother to squeeze out a few more moments or hours of biological life, when the important thing is to live out one's last moments as fully, consciously, and courageously as possible. Helping people to die with dignity means recognizing that biological life is not an absolute, not the highest value. It means recognizing that a moment arrives when technological attempts to prolong biological life may interfere with higher personal values and should give way to other forms of care.

Second, dying with dignity means dying without that twisting, racking pain that totally ties up a person's consciousness and leaves one free for nothing and for no one else. Methods exist today to control pain while maintaining patient consciousness. Yet, a wide gap still exists between what can be done and what is in fact achieved. Many patients still suffer high enough levels of pain to make pain the dominant experience during their final period of life. Their consciousness becomes shriveled down to the level of that experience. This is degrading, particularly so, when it can be avoided, but is not avoided because of physician ignorance or insensitivity. In her review of this program, carrying the title ''The Quality of Mercy'', Dr. Marcia Angell reports:

> Few things a doctor does are more important than relieving pain. Yet the treatment of severe pain in hospitalized patients is regularly and systematically inadequate. One study showed that 73 per cent of patients undergoing treatment for pain continued to experience moderate to severe discomfort. This is not for want of tools. It is generally agreed that most pain, no matter how severe, can be effectively relieved by narcotic analgesics. Why this inconsistency between what is practiced and what is possible? [Marcia Angell, ''The Quality of Mercy'', New England Journal of Medicine, 1982; 306:98]

Third, dying with dignity means dying in surroundings that are worthy of a human being who is about to live what should be one's ''finest hour''. When our bodies, that mirror the world to us, are in a phase of final collapse, we are not helped to rise to the pitch of our dignity when we are placed in sterile rooms devoid of art and all the objects that carry the rich memories of our lives. Matters are worse if our last days of consciousness and relationship with those who contributed to the meaning of our lives are dominated by the intrusive apparatus of life-prolonging technology. The environment of a dying patient should clearly say: the technical drama of medicine has receded to the background to give way to the central human drama, the drama as the poet would say, of a unique human being "wrestling with his God".

Fourth, dying with dignity means that people meet one another simply and richly as human beings. In extreme situations, in situations of war, catastrophe and death, our common humanity comes to the fore and levels the importance of the many differences that distinguish us from one another and place us in classes of various kinds. Professional roles, attitudes, and masks are a necessary part of life at various times for diverse relationships and occasions of human contact. Dying, however, is that very unique moment of living that calls for genuine person to person contact, for communication that expresses the unique person one is, not just the trained professional one happens to have become.

Dying cannot be done well without genuine human encounters. Dying is not meant to be just "passing away". Achieving these encounters is an integral part of what dying means. Dying is meant to be a very unique kind of living. This is the privileged moment to move beyond all pretense, beyond the fragmented refractions of ourselves that we project through our roles, professional or other, through our biases and all the other cramping restrictions that may have imprisoned the open freedom of our spirit.

Fifth to die with dignity is an art. The ancients spoke of the *ars moriendi*, that art of dying. Dying is one of the performing arts. Dying can be something that one does, not simply is called to do with one's own personal style. How could it be otherwise, if the performance called for is a final integration of one's life. Life, however, is an ongoing process and pattern of communication. So this integration has to be also an integration of one's relationships. Indeed, dying is a high and difficult achievement. This is why a moment arrives when open, genuine communication is the only last thing that really matters.

Sixth, dying with dignity means dying with one's eyes open. When we die with our eyes open, we don't play games. We don't pretend. We find and give to one another the courage to admit what is happening. We face the fact of having to die and, as well, the possible confusion, deep frustration, and experience of emptiness at the fact of having to die now. We look this reality in the face. A human being who can do this is already ahead of dying and superior to death.

Seventh, dying with dignity means dying with one's mind open. The really hard questions that go to the core of our dreams and hopes will face us unanswered at the time of dying. To die firmly holding on to these questions, to refuse to latch on to some little myth that will reduce the questions to harmlessness and rob them of their power to echo through the soul, is what dying with one's mind open demands.

I once saw an old man do this. He went raging into the night with a fierce desire to know. He also went with a smile. He was already ahead of his questions.

Eighth, to die with dignity means dying with one's heart open. We might think that concern for others, living beyond self-centeredness, is the way to be when we are young, strong alive with our future all in front of us. But when we are dying? This surely, is the time to be centered on ourselves.

Perhaps. Dying can bring one to varying degrees of fear and anxiety. Both can narrow one's concerns and constrict the reach of one's heart to others. But I've seen a young woman master the fear and anxiety. She died with her heart turned towards her loved ones and towards those who had cared for her during her terminal cancer. It was a very odd experience. We usually feel great pity for a young person dying in this way. She seemed to feel a great sadness for us, a sadness filled with understanding.

Because her heart was open to us in her most difficult hour. She opened our hearts to one another and gave us a bond of trust. She gave us something of herself that reached beyond her death and that her death could not take away. She made us want to live courageously and to live for others.

Dying is meant to be an act of life, an act of integration, and an act of communication. Professional skills are there to serve the achievement of these acts. At this moment, professional authority gives way to the new authority that appears in a person who rises to the demands of dying with unique and personal dignity.

Dying With Dignity: Uncertainties and Controversies

Reality is always too varied and complex to fit neatly into any one model of what dying with dignity means. The model may work well for a conscious and competent patient. However, how do we respect the dignity of an unconscious or incompetent patient? What do we do when a fully conscious and reasonable patient refuses treatment that would definitely prolong life? What does respect for dignity mean when the patient is a severely defective newborn child who, with treatment, will live severely handicapped mentally and physically? What does respect for dignity demand or permit when patients are young and in deep, irreversible coma or are old and are in deep, irreversible senility? These and many other situations today place doctors, nurses, and families square in the center of a swirl of uncertainties and the heat of controversy.

● *The Refusal of Life-Prolonging Treatment*

Many today experience little difficulty with abandoning life-prolonging treatment when a patient's brain is so damaged that consciousness is irretrievably lost. The very same persons may find it most difficult to collaborate with patients who refuse life-prolonging treatment because their bodies are severely damaged.

The Cartesian "cogito" defines a dominant value, even a moral norm of our culture. However, for many patients — quadraplegics, severe burn victims — only to think is not really to live. In the play "Quelle Vie", based on Brian Clark's original "Whose Life Is It Anyway?", Joncas, the sculptor left quadraplegic after an automobile accident, refuses catheterization, though he absolutely needs this procedure to live. Joncas' refusal is a rejection of the thesis that a human being is at bottom just a functioning brain.

We find it impossible to accept that a bright, intelligent person would refuse to live, even a life of major handicap, when life can be medically and technically sustained. We have all been very eloquent in recent years about patient autonomy. We marshall increasing legal support for our public moral claims that it is a patient's right to refuse life-prolonging treatment if and when that treatment conflicts with personal beliefs about how one's life is to be lived.

However, we do not always find it easy to live in the same categories in which we think. We publicly think about patients in the categories of autonomy and rights to self-determination. We frequently live in the categories of paternalistic protection.

● *Patients in Coma: The Imperative of the Rare Exception*

Some rare individuals have emerged out of a state of prolonged coma to vigorous, conscious life. The temptations for families and for some doctors is strong to turn these exceptional cases into the general rule: never abandon hope or treatment. Patients suffering from major neurological deficit usually need major life-support measures. The following dilemma arises: if we aggressively treat a neurologically deficient patient, we may well stabilize the patient's vital functions, fail to bring the patient back to conscious life and confine that person to prolonged, irreversible vegetative and purely biological existence. In such cases, the "success" of aggressive treatment consists in a stabilization of the patient's vital functions. The "failure" of this treatment is obvious: an irreversibly comatose patient, stable now in this coma because of the very success of our treatment. We passed by the opportunity of allowing the patient to die peacefully and quietly.

Only the working out of more precise criteria, to distinguish patients who have a chance to awake from coma from those who do not, will reduce the uncertainty that surrounds decisions in this area of human tragedy.

● *Advanced Senility: What Can Be Done Should Be Done?*

Biological existence in human beings is a condition for higher levels of development and achievement. Bernard Lonergan has expressed this point as follows:

> Man develops biologically to develop psychically, and he develops psychically to develop intellectually and rationally. The higher integrations suffer the disadvantage of emerging later. They are the demands of finality upon us before they are realities in us. [Bernard Lonergan, Insight. A Study of Human Understanding. New York: Longmans, 1957, p. 625]

When an old person is in an irreversible state of advanced senility we witness development in reverse. The "higher integrations" to which Lonergan refers are no longer possible. They have disappeared. These persons cannot think, reason, decide choose, speak, communicate, or maintain an interpersonal relationship. If these higher, distinctively human activities can never again be a reality in these older persons, how can they exert a moral force of finality of developmental direction, upon our moral decisions in medicine? The question may be phrased more sharply: if biological existence in these older persons cannot achieve its higher human purposes, need we make major medical efforts to maintain this biological existence? Need we give antibiotics to cure pneumonia in a patient now fallen into a state of irreversible advanced senility? Should we do this?

● *The Severely Defective Newborn Child: Allowing To Die or Helping to Die Quickly?*

Neonatal intensive care centers set the scene for one of today's most intensive debates. The issue, in its crudest and most unqualified form, is: to treat or not to treat seriously defective newborn babies. At an earlier period, many or even most of these babies would simply have died, indeed, quite quickly. Because little could then be done for these babies, little had to be decided.

Things have changed. Medicine has advanced. Many of these babies now need not die as a direct and quick result of their defects at birth. Their lives can now be "saved" or at least prolonged for a very significant period.

In some cases, the prolongation resulting from medical treatment amounts to little more than an extension of the dying process. The anencephalic and hydranencephalic child, the child with major neurological and multi-system defects are examples.

In other cases, vigorous and prolonged medical treatment will save the baby's life. The child, later, the teenager and young adult will be handicapped, more or less severely. Depending on the circumstances, the handicap will be both physical and mental. Babies born with spina bifida and myelomeningocele are examples.

In a third set of cases, babies are born with a physical defect that can be treated successfully and is lethal if left untreated. These babies, however, are also marked by other sorts of defects that are not lethal but very handicapping and untreatable. Such, frequently, are babies with Down's syndrome, the babies formerly called mongol.

These cases raise a host of questions about treating, prolonging life, or allowing to die. These questions merit a complete discussion, too lengthy for this article. If we assume that it is medically and morally justifiable to withhold treatment from some of these babies, need we then just allow them to die or may we help them to die quickly?

Recent cases in England and the United States have provoked passionate discussions on whether this practice is any more justifiable than a direct, painless killing of these babies. If allowing these babies to die, and this frequently means without food as well as medical treatment, is justifiable, why should painlessly killing them be unjustifiable? The end result is the same and painless killing seems more merciful and compassionate than allowing a baby to linger for days or weeks in the agony of dying.

This position is hotly contested. The counter-position holds that doctors do not have a mandate of total responsibility to relieve suffering and certainly not the authority to kill when they cannot cure.

- *The Incompetent Patient: Who Decides?*

Who really does have the ultimate competence, responsibility, and authority to decide whether a patient, unable to form or express his own will, is to receive life-prolonging treatment or is to be left without this treatment and allowed to die? If the patient, unlike Brother Charles Fox in the famous Fox case, has never or has never been able to express a personal will in this matter before becoming unconscious, who decides whether life-prolonging treatment will be withheld or discontinued? The doctor? The family? The Court? An ethics committee?

All of these suggestions have been offered as answers to our central question. Neither answer alone is adequate, realistic, or justifiable. Wise and prudent decision on behalf of incompetent or unconscious patients call for a community or care and cooperation that unites family, physician, and nursing staff together building the decision that best protects the patient and honors his dignity.

Conclusion

Decisions in extreme situations appeal necessarily to our deepest principles and beliefs. Moreover, though we share a common humanity, persons are unique, often remarkably different in what they value most highly in life. As we strive to build a medical ethics on the basis of our common humanity, the danger to be avoided is the production of an establishment ethics that leaves little freedom for moral minorities. As we strive to build an ethics capable of respecting personal originality, the danger to be noticed is the seduction of a facile relativism that ignores the bonds and the possibilities of our shared humanity.

The Right to Live: Philosophical Considerations

Charles Taylor*

I feel very much like an interloper on this panel because there are two kinds of expertise which you need to discuss this question - medical and legal; I have neither. What can I offer? I think nevertheless I can do something to help clarify one side of this issue, strictly from a philosophical point of view.

What can a philosopher contribute?

In each one of the cases Dr. Roy discussed in his paper my moral intuitions went hundred percent along with his and with the decisions he was reporting in those cases. But I wonder about the framing of some of the principles that he put forward, particularly the one where he said the patient's will should be taken as ultimate.

Underlying this way of putting it are actually two very different principles that, I think, are kicking around in our civilization at the moment and that, in a confused way, we all draw on when we make these decisions. But they are actually incompatible in their ultimate consequences. It is worth while seeing this because sometimes the force of logic, which in a way we all live under, even though we don't always want or respect it, can push us into directions we don't want to go if we find one of these principles taking over as the justification we live by.

One of them is the basic principle Professor Dworkin put forward in his lecture. He quoted John Stuart Mill, and this is a principle that we ought to accord everybody: full autonomy to do what they want to do with their lives as long as they don't in the course of doing that override autonomy for others. This is the famous distinction between self-regarding and other-regarding actions that Mill makes. In self-regarding actions you should be unrestrained. It is not a sufficient ground to interfere in someone's life that one do so for his or her own good. Or, as Dworkin put it, the simple fact that the way of life I choose for myself is repugnant to the majority, is not a good ground for anyone stopping me.

---

* Professor of Philosophy and Political Science, McGill University.

If you look at the kinds of reactions that Dr. Roy was describing to certain cases where laymen like myself feel the medical profession sometimes goes on too long or feels an obligation to go on too long in treating people, they are really attacking this question from the standpoint of this principle. This is the kind of principle that I think a lot of us would perhaps more easily accept in areas like sexual behavior, questions like homosexuality. I think the decriminalization of homosexuality in almost all western countries responds to this Millian principle and probably almost everyone in the room would agree with that. Basically on the Millian grounds, this same way of thinking is just carried over into the right to die as another way of living life, or, in this case, ending it. If that suits you, no one else should interfere with it just because they find it repugnant.

There is another line of thought, however, which I think a lot of people share which could lead to a quite different approach but which might also converge in supporting the actual cases Dr. Roy mentioned. What is interesting in these particular cases is that these two lines of thought can converge, but nevertheless diverge in other important cases. Let me try very quickly to articulate a set of feelings or intuitions we would all have now, not about public policy, of course, but just about how to live your life: the moral feelings which probably everybody in this room has in some way or other and which come from the Jewish and Christian tradition, although they have secularized variants.

Life ought to be affirmed. That means that people always do struggle to make their life meaningful, partly by changing bits of their life in order to make it meet their standards of meaningfulness, partly by struggling to see as meaningful what cannot be changed in life. These two things are always going on. This drive of human beings goes right up to the moment or the event of dying. In a sense this is not just one among other events in life but, from the point of view of making one's life meaningful, it has a special place, perhaps a unique place. This affirmation of life is successfully done when you can carry it through to the moment of death. In some way, coming to terms with death or coming to terms with that ending, as a closure to your life, means that at that moment of closure you can say, as it were, ''yes'' to that whole life so that it then becomes a unity, a closed unity at the moment of death.

This is obviously an ideal but it is something that is entailed in the notion of affirming life. It is an extremely important part of it, an extremely important crux in an extremely important moment in it. The wonderful paper that Dr. Roy read about dying with dignity I think really calls on these intuitions very powerfully.

Here we have a moral view about life which probably in some way or other everybody in this room shares. And here is where these two philosophies, the Millian and this philosophy, can come into conflict. In the Millian philosophy, particularly as Ronald Dworkin has very well reconstructed it in the 20th century, the fundamental principle is: there should not be a public philosophy. That is, there should not be, in a society's legal system, a publicly accepted ideal about what a good life is. The state, the government and the law should be neutral between such views and should allow everyone to have their own and make sure they do not interfere with others or prevent others from fulfilling theirs. But there should not be a public state philosophy about what a good life is.

I just articulated one such bit of philosophy about affirming life. If you follow through on this Millian principle, the idea should be that even this should not be part of the public philosophy. By analogy to our believing that the state shouldn't be in favour either of heterosexuality or homosexuality in sexual life, or in favour of formal marriage or co-habitation in heterosexual life, neither should it be in favour of this philosophy of affirming life, or in favour of other kinds of philosophy which take a very different view about the whole of life, and toward somebody who desired to end their life out of despair in a moment when, because of pain or deprivation, they do not wish to affirm their life. The Millian philosophy would allow this as something perfectly permissible. It would be accepted just as well as the philosophy of affirming life on the basis that, as a public philosophy, our society ought not to take a stand for one role or the other.

Let me just try to bring together the point where these two attitudes to life - let me call one the affirming one and let us call the other one the Epicurean one - would come into conflict. I am not going to give you a distinction which is tied down to legal norms since I do not know how to do that, but rather in terms of the moral choice that you might face as an individual, either as a member of the medical profession or as a non-medical friend, or relation.

It seems to me that there are two quite different kinds of cases. In one kind, where either the person concerned has come to terms with his or her death, or where something medically has happened which brings that person beyond or below the capacity to go on making further decisions, those who accept the life-affirming philosophy will agree that it does not make sense to go on to try and keep the person alive.

But that is a quite different philosophical justification for turning off the respirator, if I can use it as an example, from the justification of someone who says the will of the person concerned, no matter what it is based on, even if it is based on a moment of black despair or hatred or what have you, must be unconditionally respected by other people -

the medical profession, friends and so on. Here we do not look to the motivation. We do not look to the spirit in which it is done, we take the same kind of stand in these cases as we do in other spheres, like sexual behavior. With the modern conception of the state, what the person says goes. And that should be the norm for friends, for relations, for the medical profession and so on.

I think here you see that the two philosophies which converge on the first kind of case I have been talking about and the cases that Dr. Roy mentioned, do not converge on other kinds of cases. I can almost feel or imagine the waves of apprehension that arise in a legally trained audience when I make this kind of distinction on moral terms ultimately on the basis of what is moving the patient or what his or her motives are. How can you ever translate this into legal norms? Probably you cannot.

But that is not my purpose in raising this. My purpose in raising this is to ask the question "which of these two philosophies ought we to accept?" Or, put another way, because we all to some extent accept the Millian philosophy for a lot of contexts in life, particularly things like sexual behavior, do we have to accept the Millian philosophy as our justification for the kinds of cases that Dr. Roy presented? My answer to this is no.

What makes the question of life or death different from the question of, for example, sexual preference when it comes to applying the Millian principle? It seems to me that the very case for believing in human freedom and autonomy as an extremely supremely important value depends on a philosophy of affirming life. Here we are in a kind of limit situation and a limit set of issues which are quite different from the kinds of views of how you should lead your life in the sexual sphere or any other spheres. And therefore I think that, morally, I would not feel myself bound as a friend or a relation to go along with the wishes of somebody who was close to me who asked me to help him die if I judged that that simply came out of a mood of black despair. I would feel bound to resist that even though in other kinds of spheres I would, as a respector of his autonomy, feel bound to go along with him.

If we move the question, just a bit further, we ask the question which is the interesting question for us here: Ought the whole society, the state, to have this much public philosophy that it stands as a basis of the legal system that one ought not to help or go along with the person's wishes in the kind of case? I would also say yes, because, it seems to me, if there is a strong case in morals for separating this issue of the right to die from, for example, the right to live in one or another sexual manner, then there is a strong case for separating it in the sphere of political philosophy as well.

I think it can be useful to make this kind of distinction that I have tried to make today because if we get ourselves a little bit panicked and pushed into putting all our justifications for these very good points that Dr. Roy has made in terms of the Millian philosophy, we will find ourselves sometimes pushed by a false logic into going beyond where we want to go and taking positions we may not want to take.

The Doctrine of "Informed Consent": Informed Choice in Medical Care

Bernard M. Dickens*

The amplification of principles of legally effective consent into the doctrine of medical "informed consent" is a product of United States' jurisprudence the origin of which is conventionally attributed to the judgment of Cardozo J. in the 1914 case of *Schloendorff* v. *Society of New York Hospital*.[1] United States' jurisdictions have consolidated the doctrine during recent decades, for instance through such cases[2] as *Natanson* v. *Kline*,[3] which was the first to assess the adequacy of disclosure by the physician prior to the patient giving consent, and *Canterbury* v. *Spence*.[4] Early Canadian decisions on informed consent include that given in *Kenny* v. *Lockwood*,[5] but it has only been in quite recent years that Canadian doctrine has been advanced, through the Supreme Court of Canada judgments in *Hopp* v. *Lepp*[6] and particularly *Reibl* v. *Hughes*.[7] Since Canadian courts are still labouring to clarify the doctrine of "informed consent",[8] and since English courts have specifically rejected the doctrine,[9] it may still be appropriate in Canada

---

* Professor, Faculty of Law and Faculty of Medicine, University of Toronto.
1. (1914), 105 NE. 92 (N.Y.C.A.). The most celebrated observation is that "every human being of adult years and sound mind has a right to determine what shall be done with own body", at p. 93. This paper addresses only decisions of adults of sound mind, made in the context of proposed therapy or cosmetic treatment, as opposed to the context of research or experimental treatment.
2. Developments in United States' jurisdicitions are not based only upon judicial initiatives; see L.B. Andrews, "Informed Consent Statutes and the Decisionmaking Process" (1984), 5 *J. Legal Medicine* 163.
3. (1960), 350 P.2d 1093 (Kan. S.C.), clarified at 354 P.2d 670.
4. (1972), 464 F.2d 772, (U.S.C.A., D.C.) cert. denied 409 U.S. 1064n.
5. [1932] 1 D.L.R. 507 (Ont. C.A.).
6. (1980), 112 D.L.R. (3d) 67.
7. (1980), 114 D.L.R. (3d) 1.
8. See M.A. Somerville, "Structuring the Issues in Informed Consent" (1981), 26 *McGill L.J.* 740.
9. *Sidaway* v. *Bethlem Royal Hospital Governors*, [1984] 1 All E.R. 1018 (C.A.), aff'd. [1985] 1 All E.R. 643 (H.L.). See the critical discussion in I. Kennedy, "Notes of Cases: The Patient on the Clapham Omnibus" (1984), 47 *Modern L.R.* 454.

to hope and urge that the expression "informed consent" itself will be displaced by the preferable expression "informed decision-making" or "informed choice".[10]

The expression "informed consent" is misleading and dysfunctional to describe the physician-patient interaction. The expression "fully informed consent" is even more unsound; the most demanding requirement anywhere is that information be adequate. The words "informed consent" incorrectly suggest, to physicians and others, that:

(i)   patients are not informed if they decline to consent to a proposal for medical treatment;

(ii)   the purpose of giving information is to gain consent, and

(iii) refusals of consent to treatment need not be informed, or need not be as well informed as decisions to accept treatment.

It is important that physicians and other health professionals not be induced to believe that they may or should use information simply for the purpose of persuading patients to agree to treatments or to medical goals the professionals have determined to be in patients' best interests. Using information for manipulative purposes or, for instance, for self-protective purposes is legally risk-laden, not least because over-informing a patient may be no less malpractice than giving inadequate information.[11] The true role of information is to serve patients' autonomy, permitting them to exercise choices which accord with their own wishes. Autonomous persons are governed by their wishes even when these may conflict with their apparent interests; they do not live in a Therapeutic State in which cadres of medical or other professionals determine and impose upon them their "best interests". Most people wish, of course, that their best interests be served, and seek medical and scientific information in order that they may realize their best interests, as they themselves perceive them. When conflicts may appear between wishes and interests, however, autonomous people are governed by what they wish. They are in control of the commanding heights of decisions which affect them and determine the goals of their medical care even when they yield to health professionals the choice of technical means for pursuing those goals. The function of professionals possessing special knowledge is to provide information which individuals consider material to their exercise of choice.[12]

---

10. Laskin C.J.C. has used the expression "an informed choice of submitting to or refusing recommended and appropriate treatment"; see *Reibl* v. *Hughes*, note 7 above, at 11.

11. See *Natanson* v. *Kline*, note 3 above.

12. Generally, the physician who proposes treatment bears the duty of disclosure, but the courts have not fully explained who bears the duty, and the issue is not pursued here; see D.S. Ferguson, "Informed Consent to Medical Treatment" (1984), 5 *Advocates' Quarterly* 165 at 187.

The decision to decline treatment is no different from the decision to accept treatment. Insofar as the law of battery is concerned, of course, the difference between not touching a person and touching that person without legally effective consent is significant, reflecting historical distinctions between nonfeasance and misfeasance. The modern law of medical informing for consent has come to rest, however, upon the law of negligence,[13] in that the duty of making appropriate disclosure to permit a patient to exercise autonomous choice is recognized as an element of the duty of care owed by a health professional to a patient for whom that professional has a legal responsibility.[14] Accordingly, choices both to accept treatment and to refuse treatment must be adequately informed, and the legal doctrine of informed medical choice embraces concepts both of informed consent and informed dissent.[15]

This may be illustrated by reference to terminal patients' legal right to decline aggressive artificial life-sustaining care;[16] it also appeared, in more routine circumstances, in the 1980 California Supreme Court case of *Truman* v. *Thomas*.[17] That decision applied the reasoning of *Cobbs* v. *Grant*[18] and *Canterbury* v. *Spence*[19] which the Supreme Court of Canada endorsed in *Reibl* v. *Hughes*. The case concerned a family physician's failure specifically to inform a patient of the risks of not having a routine pap smear test for detection of cervical cancer. The defendant physician claimed that he had told the patient of the desirability of having the test, but that she had declined it on the ground that she could not afford the cost. In holding the defendant to have breached his duty of care to the patient, the court applied the reasoning of *Cobbs* v. *Grant*,[20] which it interpreted to include the propositions that:

> If a patient indicates that he or she is going to *decline* the risk-free test or treatment, then the doctor has the additional duty of advising of all material risks of which a reasonable person would want to be informed before

---

13. See *Reibl* v. *Hughes*, note 7 above: "unless there has been misrepresentation or fraud to secure consent to the treatment, a failure to disclose the attendant risks, however serious, should go to negligence rather than to battery", *per* Laskin C.J.C. at 11.
14. *Id.*: "Although such a failure [of disclosure] relates to an informed choice of submitting to or refusing recommended and appropriate treatment, it arises as the breach of an anterior duty of due care, comparable in legal obligation to the duty of due care in carrying out the particular treatment to which the patient has consented."
15. See D. Friedman, "Informed Dissent: A New Corollary to the Informed Consent Doctrine?" (1981), 57 *Chicago Kent L.R.* 1119.
16. See B.M. Dickens, "The Right to Natural Death" (1981), 26 *McGill L.J.* 847.
17. (1980), 611 P.2d 902 (Cal. S.C.). For a case of liability of a surgeon for failure to explain risks involved if his recommendation for treatment was not followed, see *Chisher* v. *Spak* (1983), 471 N.Y.S. 2d 741 (N.Y.S.C.).
18. (1972), 502 P.2d 1 (Cal. S.C.).
19. See note 4 above.
20. Note 18 above.

deciding not to undergo the procedure. On the other hand, if the recommended test or treatment is itself risky, then the physician should always explain the potential consequences of declining to follow the recommended course of action.[21]

This language is applicable to informed medical choice in modern Canadian law, but appreciation of its special significance requires explanation of key legal principles established in *Reibl* v. *Hughes.*

In *Reibl* v. *Hughes*, the plaintiff was aged 44 when in 1970 he underwent surgery for removal of a blockage in a carotid artery which had been associated in his understanding with the onset of his severe headaches. A conscientious family man with four children, he had worked for the Ford Motor Company for almost eight and a half years, and, upon achieving ten years' employment, would have become entitled to a life-time retirement pension and to certain extended disability benefits. The defendant surgeon had informed him of his medical condition and that, without surgery, he would in several years' time become highly likely to suffer a severely disabling or fatal stroke. The defendant had not been very explicit about the fact that the indicated surgery itself presented irreducible risks of causing a stroke or death, if a flake from the artery lining came loose in the bloodstream and entered the brain. The plaintiff was given to understand little more than that he would be better off to have the operation than not to have it, and that the operation would alleviate his headaches and hypertension so that he could continue comfortably in his job. Presented with the choice of having the operation, which the defendant recommended, or not having it, the plaintiff consented to have the surgery to be performed within the next few days. During or immediately following surgery, the plaintiff suffered a massive stroke which paralysed the right side of his body and left him impotent. It was accepted that the surgery had not been negligently performed, the stroke being an unavoidable risk of undergoing the operation.

The plaintiff's claims that his consent to the surgery had not been adequately informed due to the defendant's negligent non-disclosure of material information, and that this breach of duty caused his injury since he would not have consented to run the risks of surgery at that time had he been adequately informed, succeeded at trial.[22] The Ontario Court of Appeal considered that the trial judge did not examine the issue of causation appropriately and ordered a new trial,[23] but the Supreme Court of Canada, recognizing the parties' mutual wish to have the issue of liability resolved without more,[24] restored the trial court's

---

21. Note 17 above, at 906, emphasis in original.
22. (1977), 78 D.L.R. (3d) 35 (Ont. H.C.).
23. (1978), 89 D.L.R. (3d) 112 (Ont. C.A.).
24. See note 7 above, at 5.

finding of negligence, consisting in the defendant's failure to make adequate disclosure of material information.[25]

In explaining how the defendant's insufficient disclosure of information material to the plaintiff's choice to accept or decline surgery caused the plaintiff's injury as a matter of law, Laskin C.J.C. observed for the Court that:

> Relevant in this case to the issue whether a reasonable person in the plaintiff's position would have declined surgery at the particular time is the fact that he was within about one and one-half years of earning pension benefits if he continued at his job; that there was no neurological deficit then apparent; that there was no immediate emergency making the surgery imperative; that there was a grave risk of a stroke or worse during or as a result of the operation, while the risk of a stroke without it was in the future, with no precise time fixed or which could be fixed except as a guess of three or more years ahead. Since, on the trial Judge's finding, the plaintiff was under the mistaken impression, as a result of the defendant's breach of the duty of disclosure, that the surgery would relieve his continuing headaches, this would in the opinion of a reasonable person in the plaintiff's position, also weigh against submitting to the surgery at the particular time.[26]

In requiring that information be pitched at the level of "a reasonable person in the plaintiff's position", the Supreme Court adopted a significant principle which has found favour in the case law of a number of United States' jurisdictions and in academic commentary, which the Supreme Court cited with approval. There are in principle three standards, orientations or levels by reference to which appropriate disclosure of information may be determined, and the Supreme Court selected one of them both by elimination and by virtue of the positive merits of the selection made. The standards are:

(i)   the medical professional standard, determined by the level of disclosure which would have been met by a reasonable medical professional practicing in the specialty of the professional in question;

(ii) the "subjective patient" standard, determined by the informational needs the specific plaintiff-patient can demonstrate he or she required at the time of decision-making, and

(iii) the "objective patient" or "reasonable patient" standard, determined by the material information which would have been required by a reasonable person in the plaintiff-patient's position.

The Supreme Court had addressed the medical professional standard of disclosure a few months before its decision in *Reibl* v. *Hughes*,

---

25. The trial court's finding of liability in battery was rejected; see note 13 above.
26. See note 7 above, at 35.

in the case of *Hopp* v. *Lepp*.[27] In a judgment which anticipated *Reibl* v. *Hughes*, the Supreme Court comprehensively reviewed developments in Canadian and American jurisprudence on medical disclosure, and rejected applicability of the medical professional standard of disclosure. Laskin C.J.C. for the Court stated that:

> since a particular patient is involved upon whom particular surgery is to be performed or particular therapy administered, and it is a duty of disclosure to him that affects the validity of his consent, evidence of medical experts of custom or general practice as to the scope of disclosure cannot be decisive, but at most a factor to be considered.[28]

In *Reibl* v. *Hughes*, the Supreme Court was critical of the Ontario Court of Appeal's approach for similar reasons. Laskin C.J.C. observed that:

> I think the Ontario Court of Appeal went too far, when dealing with the standard of disclosure of risks, in saying ... that 'the manner in which the nature and degree of risk is explained to a particular patient is better left to the judgment of the doctor in dealing with the man before him'... The Ontario Court of Appeal appears to have adopted a professional medical standard, not only for determining what are the material risks that should be disclosed but also, and concurrently, for determining whether there has been a breach of the duty of disclosure... To allow expert medical evidence to determine what risks are material and, hence, should be disclosed and, correlatively, what risks are not material is to hand over to the medical profession the entire question of the scope of the duty of disclosure, including the question whether there has been a breach of that duty.[29]

Rejection of the decisiveness of the medical professional standard of disclosure, which had previously been applied in Canada[30] and has been upheld in England,[31] is reinforced by the policy consideration that if legal negligence consists in failure to satisfy a professionally determined standard, the profession might subconsciously be inclined to set a standard lower than might serve patients' interests and reasonable expectations. The courts have always reserved the power to set required legal standards of medical care, through tort law[32] and implied terms of physician-patient contracts,[33] although recent employment of this

---

27. See note 6 above.
28. *Id.*, at 80.
29. Note 7 above, at 12-13.
30. *Per* Linden J. in *White* v. *Turner*, note 44 below: "in analysing the quality and quantity of the information given to a patient under negligence principles, the test to be employed is no longer the professional medical standard, heretofore used by our Courts, but rather the reasonable patient standard. This is a major shift heralded by the Supreme Court of Canada in *Reibl* v. *Hughes*," at 283.
31. See note 9 above.
32. See A.M. Linden, "The Negligent Doctor" (1973) 11 *Osgoode Hall L.J.* 31.
33. Early litigation against physicians was based upon contractual claims; see, for instance, *Slater* v. *Baker* (1767), 2 Wils. (K.B.) 359, 95 Eng. Rep. 860.

power in the Unites States[34] has provoked a reactionary legislative back-lash in favour of the decisiveness of professional custom and practice.[35]

The Supreme Court of Canada in *Reibl* v. *Hughes* required that a patient-oriented approach be taken to the question of disclosure of infor-mation, but found that the subjective patient standard of disclosure pre-sented an excessive possibility and risk of working injustice. The Court adopted the reasoning appearing in an academic commentary[36] that:

> Since proximate causation exists only if disclosure would have resulted in the patient's foregoing the proposed treatment, a standard must be developed to determine whether the patient would have decided against the treatment had he been informed of its risks. Two possible standards exist: whether, if informed, the particular patient would have foregone treatment (subjective view); or whether the average prudent person in plaintiff's position, informed of all material risks, would have foregone treatment (objective view). The objective standard is preferable, since the subjective standard has a gross defect: it depends on the plaintiff's testimony as to his state of mind, thereby exposing the physician to the patient's hindsight and bitterness.[37]

It appears persuasive that the defendant physician's fate should not be decided by the quadriplegic or otherwise severely injured plaintiff's answer to the question ''Had you known then what you know now about the risks of the medical procedure, would you have consented to it?'' The ''bitter hindsight'' test compels rejection of the subjective patient standard.

The objective patient standard appears appropriate not simply by elimination, however, but also because it is more practically operable. The formula of ''a reasonable person in the patient's position'' presents considerable difficulty in psychiatric and related fields, however, where a person in the patient's position may by definition not be reasonable. In working through this difficulty, it must be remembered that patients in principle are entitled to be respected so long as they are competent by cognitive standards to exercise choice,[38] even when their decisions are emotional and sentimental rather than strictly rational. Laskin C.J.C. favoured in general the objective standard, but immediately added that:

> In saying that the test is based on the decision that a reasonable person in the patient's position would have made, I should make it clear that the

---

34. Notably in *Helling* v. *Carey* (1974), 519 P.2d 981 (Wash. S.C.).

35. See L.B. Andrews, note 2 above.

36. ''Informed Consent - A Proposed Standard for Medical Disclosure'' (1973), 48 *New York Univ. L.R.* 548.

37. *Id.*, at 550.

38. Even incompetent patients are entitled to the respect, of course, of not having imposed upon them treatments to which, or to consequences of which, they are emotionally or otherwise opposed, except perhaps for the purpose of saving their lives or permanent health; see J. Jacob, ''The Right of the Mental Patient to his Psychosis'' (1976), 39 *Modern L.R.* 17.

patient's particular concerns must also be reasonably based; otherwise, there would be more subjectivity than would be warranted under an objective test. Thus, for example, fears which are not related to the material risks which should have been but were not disclosed would not be causative factors. However, economic considerations could reasonably go to causation where, for example, the loss of an eye as a result of nondisclosure of a material risk brings about the loss of a job for which good eyesight is required. In short, although account must be taken of a patient's particular position, a position which will vary with the patient, it must be objectively assessed in terms of reasonableness.[39]

Accordingly, information given to be the patient must initially be designed to serve a reasonable person in the position of the patient. The patient's position can be understood, of course, with different degrees of specificity, although the more specific the position becomes, the more it may approach the subjective standard rejected in *Reibl* v. *Hughes*. If the individual patient asks a question which demonstrates a special interest, however, the concern underlying the question shows the position of the patient appraised objectively. Further, sufficient must be known about the patient's circumstances in life to indicate the patient's position, and if information is not available from the patient's record, family or conversation, it must be sought by the physician asking appropriate questions, and giving proper attention to the patient's responses.

This points to a further inadequacy in the expression "informed consent". The phrase suggests that the physician's function is simply to inform, and that the patient responds simply by giving (or at least considering giving) consent. The true requirement, however, is that the physician learn enough about the patient reasonably to know what information is material to the patient. This may require the physician to become reasonably informed, and to ask questions and initiate a dialogue, directed perhaps less to the means of prospective treatment than to its goals. Means of treatment concern biological, physiological and, for instance, pharmacological matters in which the patient may not be educated. Goals of treatment, on the other hand, concern questions of preferred lifestyle, the patient's perception of his or her best interests, individual physical and emotional tolerances and sensitivities, and preferred means to resolve incompatible interests in future opportunities and relationships. The dialogue thus centres upon issues initially known to the patient and not necessarily to the physician, and aids the patient's autonomy by disclosing the range of certain and possible consequences of different potential treatments, permitting the patient to exercise maximum control of choice.

Control by patients may be maximized through the realization that patients usually wish to be responsible for the overall design and intended effect of their management, although they may be prepared to leave

---

39. Note 7 above, at 17.

details of finer tuning to physicians. Accordingly, the patient who says "I leave it to you, doctor" (and who may not be as common as many physicians believe) is not surrendering his or her entire human destiny to the physician. The patient assumes the physician's awareness of and sympathy to the patient's goals,[40] and cedes control only of the means of pursuing those goals. Surgery may be undertaken by one technique or another, or a drug may be used of one pharmacological operation or another, provided always, however, that the detailed option applied by the physician is not incompatible with the patient's goals in consenting to treatment.[41] In case of doubt, the physician should seek further information from the patient about the patient's preferences regarding intended and possible outcomes of treatment choices.

The aim of informing is to give the patient the means not only to know and control the degree of pain he or she may experience (in accepting one treatment as opposed to another or in deciding to decline treatment and endure a medical condition and its untreated prognosis) but also to know and control his or her suffering. Emotional and intellectual responses to pain involve the phenomenon of suffering, but pain does not necessarily cause suffering; social, philosophical, religious and other of the patient's convictions or preferences may make pain acceptable, and avoidance of pain at a cost borne by others for whom the patient cares may render the avoidance of pain unacceptable. The interaction of pain and suffering is subtle and individual. The function of informing the patient is to afford the patient means to determine this interaction, and to resolve it to maximum satisfaction.[42]

This is not to say, however, that the physician is compelled to seek out special features of the patient's character, temperament and philosophy.[43] The reasoning in *Reibl* v. *Hughes* establishes not only an objective standard to determine disclosure, but also an objective test of

---

40. The Canadian Medical Association's *Code of Ethics* accordingly provides that "An Ethical Physician ... when his morality or religious conscience alone prevents him from recommending some form of therapy, [he] will so acquaint the patient" (Responsibilities to the Patient, para. 16). There may be a positive duty to refer the patient elsewhere for appropriate care, for instance, where therapeutic abortion is an option; see *Zimmer* v. *Ringrose* (1981), 124 D.L.R. (3d) 215 (Alta. C.A.).

41. Any untoward consequence of such treatment would not leave the physician vulnerable to suit, because the legal doctrine of *volenti non fit injuria* or assumption of risk shows that the patient has accepted any risk of treatment which the physician observed a legal duty to disclose; see text below and note 48.

42. See M.A. Somerville, "Pain and Suffering at Interfaces of Medicine and Law" (1984), 10 *Jus Medium* 133.

43. For instance, in *Videto* v. *Kennedy* (1981), 125 D.L.R. (3d) 127 (Ont. C.A.), judgment for a plaintiff was reversed on appeal since she had not shown that a physician performing a contraceptive sterilization should have known that disclosure of its risks would have caused her to decline to have it, since her commitment to the procedure was uncertain due to her Roman Catholic faith and wish not to risk unsightly extensive scarring which might result.

causation of damage. A physician aware of a patient's peculiarities must accommodate them, but there is no duty to explore for unusual characteristics. Patients no less than physicians are required to be reasonable, and a patient who has not disclosed an unusual preference cannot complain because it was not accommodated. A judgment applying *Reibl* v. *Hughes* has observed that:[44]

> It is not enough, therefore, for the Court to be convinced that the plaintiff would have refused the treatment if he had been fully informed: the Court must *also* be satisfied that a reasonable patient, in the same situation, would have done so... Consequently, a patient who says he would have forgone life-saving treatment because it might have caused a rash or a headache, cannot recover on the basis of inadequate disclosure, even if he is believed, because a reasonable patient would have gone ahead.[45]

In *Reibl* v. *Hughes*, negligence was found where the defendant denied the plaintiff the opportunity to protect his family's financial welfare, an important consideration in the life of this conscientious family man anxious to be able to stay in his job. In offering only the choice to have the surgical procedure or not, the defendant did not explore the option of postponing surgery for eighteen months or so. The surgical risk would not have been reduced by delay, but the risk of the patient's condition would not have significantly increased either. The advantage of the delay would have been to the patient's preferred lifestyle and sense of welfare — in the form of improved pension and disability benefits — rather than to this narrowly assessed health. The Supreme Court observed that:

> In the present case, the anticipation of a full pension would be a special consideration, and, while it would have to be viewed objectively, it emerges from the patient's particular circumstances.[46]

Again, in addressing inadequate disclosure as the cause of the patient's injuries, the Court noted that:

> Relevant in this case to the issue whether a reasonable person in the plaintiff's position would have declined surgery at the particular time is that fact that he was within about one and one-half years of earning

---

44. Linden J. in *White* v. *Turner* (1981), 120 D.L.R. (3d) 269 (Ont. S.C.) at 286-7.

45. In *Buchan* v. *Ortho Pharmaceutical (Canada) Ltd.* (1984), 46 O.R. (2d) 113 (Ont. S.C.), it was questioned whether the causation test in *Reibl* v. *Hughes* applies to a products liability case. Holland J. observed that: ''If it were to be strictly applied in the case of the sale of oral contraceptives and if the judge came to the conclusion that a reasonable person, in the plaintiff's position, because of the very small absolute risk of harm compared to the highly effective method of contraception, would have accepted the risk, then it would render the duty to warn meaningless. It appears to me that a proper test for the plaintiff to meet is, on a balance of probabilities, was there a reasonable likelihood that a reasonable person in the plaintiff's particular position, if fully informed, would not have taken the drug?''; at 147.

46. Note 7 above, at 16.

pension benefits if he continued at his job; that there was no neurological deficit then apparent; that there was no immediate emergency making the surgery imperative; that there was a grave risk of a stroke or worse during or as a result of the operation, while the risk of a stroke without it was in the future, with no precise time fixed or which could be fixed except as a guess of three or more years ahead.[47]

The Court also noted the significance of the plaintiff's mistaken belief, based upon inadequate disclosure, that the surgery would relieve his continuing headaches, a reasonable person aware that the surgery did not present that prospect would not have accepted the irreducible risks of the procedure at that time. The patient's voluntary assumption of risk, the legal doctrine of *volenti non fit injuria*, is, of course, the key principle of the law on consent; the corollary is that the physician bears the financial risk of any consequence the possibility of which was improperly not disclosed.[48]

Reibl v. *Hughes* makes clear that decisions about whether or not to have medical treatment are not only medical decisions. A patient requires medical and scientific information in order to make a decision, but the critical choice is based upon considerations arising out of the patient's circumstances in life, including personal philosophy, domestic and economic situation and, for instance, ambitions. The significance of the patient's lifestyle is shown in applications of *Reibl* v. *Hughes*. In *White* v. *Turner*,[49] for instance, a patient was not informed that her primarily cosmetic breast reduction by plastic surgery might result in bad scarring and mis-shaping. It was held that the physician had been negligent in not disclosing the risk of serious scarring. The Court observed of the plaintiff that:

> For her to make a considered choice she, as a reasonable patient, was entitled to have information about the appearance of her breasts following the surgery. Because of the well-known public misconception that plastic surgery is scarless surgery, this was especially necessary.[50]

The judge concluded that:

> I cannot find that Mrs. White, acting reasonably, would have gone ahead with this operation, if given the full picture of the material and special risks involved. On the contrary, I find that a reasonable person, in the position of Mrs. White, if she were shown the photographs of what her breasts looked like following the first operation and were told that this

---

47. *Id.*, at 35.
48. See J.G. Fleming, *Law of Torts* (6th ed., 1983), at 264-278. Comprehensive self-protective disclosure is not an appropriate response, since it has been seen that over-informing may be no less malpractice than under-informing; see *Natanson* v. *Kline*, note 3 above, and text at note 11 above.
49. See note 44, above.
50. *Id.*, at 289.

was a possible result of the surgery, would probably not have undergone the operation, except perhaps in rare circumstances.[51]

The judgment referred to the earlier case of *Petty* v. *MacKay*[52] as an application of *Reibl* v. *Hughes*, although that case was decided before the Supreme Court handed down its decision. It involved an exotic dancer who sought cosmetic surgery to perfect and reduce her stomach size in order to maintain employment. She was not informed of the risk of unsightly scarring, and sued when it resulted. She failed in the action, however, because she could not show that a reasonable person in her position would have declined the procedure upon disclosure of such information. It was accepted that an exotic dancer might be distinguishable from a woman whose primary goal was to look attractive in a bikini swimming suit.[53] The Court found that:

> ... a reasonable and prudent person, in the circumstances of the plaintiff, including the knowledge and experience of the plaintiff and her desire to attain a state of cosmetic perfection or near-perfection, would have gone ahead with this operation even if the risks involved had been fully discussed with that reasonable and prudent person prior to the operation.[54]

Various formulations of the different items legally required for disclosure have been proposed, most dating from the time when the standard of disclosure was the now abandoned medical professional standard. Further, they arose in the belief that failure to observe them rendered treatment actionable as a battery. Under modern negligence theory, of course, failure of disclosure is actionable only if the plaintiff can show that the failure caused the injury in law. Specific disclosure requirements may be derived from recent decisions,[55] and may be summarized in the tabulation that a physician must consider disclosure of:

(i)   the prognosis if the patient remains untreated;[56]
(ii)   reasonably accessible treatment alternatives and their benefits, including alternative goals of treatment and alternative means of pursuing such goals;[57]
(iii)   success and failure rates of different means of treatment;
(iv)   known irreversible and other effects and risks, discomforts and side-effects of different means of treatment and the likelihood of occurrence, even when treatment is successfully undertaken;

---

51. *Id.*, at 290.
52. (1979), 14 B.C.L.R. 382 (B.C.S.C.).
53. But see *Videto* v. *Kennedy*, note 43 above, where a plaintiff failed to show that unsightly scarring has to be disclosed as a risk of contraceptive sterilization because the risk of scarring would be liable to deter consent to the procedure.
54. Note 52 above, at 388.
55. See D.S. Ferguson, note 12 above, at 178-9.
56. This should show whether the treatment is necessary or elective; see *Reibl* v. *Hughes*, note 7 above, at 6, and *Zamparo* v. *Brisson* (1981), 120 D.L.R. (3d) 545 (Ont. C.A.).
57. See *Ferguson* v. *Hamilton Civil Hospital* (1983), 144 D.L.R. (3d) 214 (Ont. S.C.).

(v)   the limits of relevant knowledge, and the areas in which it appears
       that more needs to be learned;
(vi)   the patient's means of asking (further) questions;
(vii) matters concerning which the patient specifically enquires,[58] and
(viii) the physician's recommendation about whether treatment should
       be undertaken.

Although this agenda may appear to require comprehensive disclosure (and cosmetic surgery for instance, may indeed require "complete disclosure of risks"[59]), it must be remembered that disclosure of
risk centres upon "material risks" and "special or unusual risks".[60]
The meaning of these terms is not defined beyond doubt, but a risk
appears to be "material" when it frequently materializes; in *White* v.
Turner, for instance, Linden J. observed that:

> Mrs. White should have been told about the possibility that her scars
> might open up and that there might be a need for corrective surgery to
> repair a bad result. These two risks, I find, may not be 'material', because
> they are so rare, but they must be classified as 'special or unusual risks',
> as this term is used in *Reibl* v. *Hughes*... They do occur periodically and
> they are not insignificant. A reasonable patient would want to know about
> them. Hence, they are special or unusual risks that should be disclosed
> before proceeding with an operation such as this.[61]

The distinction between a "material" risk and a "special or unusual" risk may be drawn in terms of a "material" risk being relatively
common, while a "special or unusual risk" is rare, with the addition
that a rare risk must be disclosed only when it is of serious effect. The
distinction is confounded in that the Supreme Court in *Reibl* v. *Hughes*
observed of its earlier decision that:

> The Court in *Hopp* v. *Lepp* also pointed out that even if a certain risk is
> a mere possibility which ordinarily need not be disclosed, yet if its occur-
> rence carries serious consequences, as for example, paralysis or even
> death, it should be regarded as a material risk requiring disclosure.[62]

Distinguishing "material" from "special or unusual" risks may
be an interesting exercise,[63] but it may also be of limited consequence
since both categories of risks must be disclosed.[64] Accordingly, it

---

58. See *Hopp* v. *Lepp*, note 6 above, at 81, and *Reibl* v. *Hughes*, note 7 above, at 12.
59. *White* v. *Turner*, note 44 above, at 289; see also *Zamparo* v. *Brisson*, note 56
    above, where the Court dealt with elective surgery which was "almost in the
    cosmetic category", at 554.
60. See *White* v. *Turner*, note 44 above, at 289.
61. *Id.*
62. Note 7 above, at 5.
63. Further categories of risks are discussed in Somerville, note 8 above, at 760.
64. In *White* v. *Turner*, Linden J. recognized that there may be an overlap between
    "material" and "unusual or special" risk, but observed that "material risks are
    significant risks that pose a real threat to the patient's life, health or comfort... if
    there is a significant chance of slight injury this too may be held to be material...

appears that risks must be disclosed when they are common and significant even though not necessarily grave in effect, and when they are rare but particularly serious in effect. There is, of course, a continuum from a common to a rare risk, and from a mild to a serious effect. The courts and the underlying jurisprudence can say little more about this than that physicians must act reasonably, and that patients must also be reasonable[65] and be expected to understand that all medical procedures bear some risk of adverse effects. Physicians should understand that, the more serious the consequences and the higher their probability, the more likely it is that the reasonable patient will want to be informed of them.

The doctrine outlined above in the context of the patient's consent to therapeutic procedures is applicable, of course, both to a decision to decline treatment and to acceptance and refusal of diagnostic tests.[66] Further, it is applicable, with appropriate adjustments, to health professionals other than physicians reflecting the manner in which reasonable patients may expect to be informed by them.

The Ontario Court of Appeal in *Videto* v. *Kennedy*[67] has summarized the Supreme Court of Canada's conclusions on disclosure following *Reibl* v. *Hughes* in the following eight principles. These are expressed in terms limited to the particular case, but may be projected *mutatis mutandis* into other medical treatments and other health professions, and indeed to a person's decision not to become or remain a patient. (1) The questions of whether a risk is material and whether there has been a breach of the duty of disclosure are not to be determined solely by the professional standards of the medical profession at the time. The professional standards are a factor to be considered. (2) The duty of disclosure also embraces what the surgeon knows or should know that the patient deems relevant to the patient's decision whether or not to undergo the operation. If the patient asks specific questions about the operation, then the patient is entitled to be given reasonable answers to such questions. In addition to expert medical evidence, other evidence, including evidence from the patient or from members of the patient's family, is to be considered. In *Reibl* v. *Hughes*,[68] Laskin C.J.C. stated:

As for 'unusual or special risks', these are those that are not ordinary, common, everyday matters. These are risks that are somewhat extraordinary, uncommon and not encountered every day, but they are known to occur occasionally. Though rare occurrences, because of their unusual or special character, the Supreme Court has declared that they should be described to a reasonable patient, even though they may not be 'material' ''; note 44 above, at 284-5.

65. See text above, at note 39.
66. See *Truman* v. *Thomas*, note 17 above.
67. Note 43 above, at 133-4.
68. Note 7 above, at 12.

The patient may have expressed certain concerns to the doctor and the latter is obliged to meet them in a reasonable way. What the doctor knows or should know that the particular patient deems relevant to a decision whether to undergo prescribed treatment goes equally to his duty of disclosure as do the material risks recognized as a matter of required medical knowledge.

(3) A risk which is a mere possibility ordinarily does not have to be disclosed, but if its occurrence may result in serious consequences, such as paralysis or even death, then it should be treated as a material risk and should be disclosed. (4) The patient is entitled to be given an explanation as to the nature of the operation and its gravity. (5) Subject to the above requirements, the dangers inherent in any operation, such as the dangers of anesthetic or the risks of infection, do not have to be disclosed. (6) The scope of the duty of disclosure and whether it has been breached must be decided in relation to the circumstances of each case. (7) The emotional condition of the patient and the patient's apprehension and reluctance to undergo the operation may in certain cases justify the surgeon in withholding or generalizing information as to which the surgeon would otherwise be required to be more specific. (8) The question of whether a particular risk is a material risk is a matter for the trier of fact. It is also for the trier of fact to determine whether there has been a breach of the duty of disclosure.

Against the patient's right to know may be set the physician's right of non-disclosure, which is divisible into general non-disclosure and special non-disclosure, often described as the physician's "therapeutic privilege". The right of general non-disclosure is based upon the common knowledge the ordinary reasonable patient is expected to possess. This "right" is not a privilege of the physician's, but a recognition that, as a matter of common sense, patients understand the general medical context of their decisions. It has been observed, for instance, that:

> ... there are some common, everyday risks that exist in all surgery, which everyone is expected to know about. Doctors need not warn about them, since they are obvious to everyone. Consequently, just as one need not warn that a match will burn or that a knife will cut, because that would be redundant, one need not warn that, if an incision is made, there will normally be some bleeding, some pain and a scar will remain when the cut has healed. So too, everyone is expected to know that there is a chance of infection in any surgical procedure. There may be other minor discomforts following most surgical treatment, which need not be disclosed to patients...[69]

This observation reflects the legal approach to all medical treatments, whether surgical or non-surgical. It is expected to be known, for instance, that proposed treatments may fail, and physicians are not

---

69. *White* v. *Turner*, note 44 above, at 285.

taken to guarantee the success of their treatments unless they do so by an express or necessarily implied contractual undertaking.[70] Where treatment failure may be material in relation to the risks of treatment, of course, disclosure may be required. For ordinary or routine medical care, however, assessed by reference not to a physician's experience but to the community and experience of the prospective patient, disclosure is not required of what is taken to be obvious, nor of what is too remote a possibility to affect decision-making. Blood sampling by venepuncture, for instance, for diagnostic or monitoring purposes, carries risks which are not normally required to be disclosed beyond perhaps risk of bruising, soreness and easily controlled infection. When certain that the patient is not a hemophiliac, the physician need not relate anecdotal incidents known to have resulted from routine venepuncture, because they are not material.[71] They include hematoma, dermatitis, cellulitis, abscess, osteomyelitis, septicemia, endocarditis, thrombophlebitis, pulmonary embolism and death.[72]

It has been seen that low risk of serious harm or death may constitute a "special or unusual risk" which should be disclosed. Indeed, the Supreme Court has observed of a possible risk that "if its occurrence carries serious consequences, as for example, paralysis or even death, it should be regarded as a material risk requiring disclosure".[73] It must be remembered, however, that the objective patient is reasonable, so that even when a court accepts that a particular plaintiff would in fact have refused a treatment had an item of information about it been given, for liability to follow according to causation principles of negligence law "the Court must *also* be satisfied that a reasonable patient, in the same situation, would have done so."[74] Courts do not require a relation of anecdotal horrors when a patient routinely considers venepuncture,[75] nor, for instance, disclosure of the risk of contracting hepatitis B from transfused blood.[76] Ordinarily intelligent and reasonable persons are not influenced in their decisions by the rare risks of venepuncture, blood transfusion or comparable procedures when they are part of reasonably indicated medical treatment. Blood transfusion, for instance, is recommended only for good cause, and then the risk of contracting hepatitis will be unlikely to dissuade the reasonable patient.

---

70. See the full discussion in R.A. Epstein, "Medical Malpractice: The Case for Contract" (1976), 1 *American Bar Foundation Research J.* 87.
71. It may be contended, however, that because of their seriousness they approach the "special or unusual risks" category of required disclosure, and in experimentation their disclosure may be advisable; see *Halushka* v. *University of Saskatchewan* (1965), 53 D.L.R. (2d) 436 (Sask. C.A.).
72. See *Cobbs* v. *Grant*, note 18 above, at 1 (note).
73. Note 62 above.
74. Note 44 above.
75. See *Cobbs* v. *Grant*, note 18 above.
76. See *Perlmutter* v. *Beth David Hospital* (1954), 123 N.E. 2d 792 (N.Y.C.A.).

It follows from the approach taken in *Reibl* v. *Hughes* to the duty of disclosure that established areas of medical knowledge exist which a physician or other health professional is not required to disclose before a patient makes a decision to accept or reject proposed treatment. Information will be assessed according to the objective patient standard, and if it is not required to be disclosed by that standard, a plaintiff claiming that the information should have been given in his or her case bears the burden of proving that the defendant had been placed on special notice of the plaintiff's circumstances, for instance through questions asked by the plaintiff, to recognize that in the particular circumstances the information was of "material" or "special or unusual" risks. The plaintiff cannot claim a right to have been treated according to a purely subjective test, but may be able to show that enough was known or should have been known of his or the circumstances and characteristics that assessment of the informational needs of an objectively perceived patient in a like position should have been adequately sensitive to include that information.

Once it is determined that information should be disclosed according to an objective patient standard, a physician may nevertheless decide by way of an exception to the general rule of disclosure that it should be withheld from a particular patient. The burden of proving the propriety of that exception will rest upon the physician when sued by the uninformed patient, but the physician may invoke the therapeutic privilege of nondisclosure, exercised upon grounds of clinical judgment. The courts have noted that "The physician's privilege to withhold information for therapeutic reasons must be carefully circumscribed, however, for otherwise it might devour the disclosure rule itself."[77] Information which would be countertherapeutic, dysfunctional or distorting for a specific patient to receive in the particular circumstances may legally be withheld under this principle. The physician must be able to show that, although the information might not have unduly affected the objective patient, it would have affected the plaintiff.

The doctrine of therapeutic privilege is beset by conceptual contradictions,[78] although its claimed application in individual cases may be hard to assail. The privilege is expected to be consciously applied at the time of critical informing of a patient, not to be raised after the event to rationalize or excuse oversight or thoughtlessness of disclosure; such oversight or lack of attention may escape sanction, however, when it appears that the information would not have influenced the plaintiff's choice or that of a reasonable person, and was not therefore legally

---

77. See *Canterbury* v. *Spence*, note 4 above, at 789.
78. See L.B. Andrews, note 2 above, at 211.

causative of injury following its omission.[79] The difficulty of challenging a positive decision of non-disclosure consists in the special sanctity
courts often attach to clinical judgment, for instance on the existence
of emergency, when it is conscientiously exercised in full awareness of
the risks entailed in the decision.[80]

Therapeutic privilege is sometimes regarded as an application of
the defence of necessity.[81] Necessity to act to save human life may
clearly justify disregard of the process of deliberation and counselling
implicit in doctrine on informed medical decision-making, although it
may be considered not to displace the law on medical consent, but
rather to illustrate implied consent.[82] The setting of necessity may explain
why no therapeutic privilege can be invoked outside a therapeutic setting, notably in pure experimentation,[83] and why a higher level of disclosure may be expected for more cosmetic procedures.[84] The conceptual contradictions found in acceptance of the doctrine of therapeutic
privilege centre upon its tolerance of paternalistic attitudes and its legal
approval of limitation of a competent patient's autonomy, which legal
principles of informed medical choice claim to protect.[85] Such paternalism has been defined or described as "interference with a person's
freedom of action or freedom of information, or the deliberate dissemination of misinformation, where the alleged justification of interfering
or misinforming is that it is for the good of the person who is interfered
with or misinformed."[86]

In *Hopp* v. *Lepp* the Supreme Court of Canada recognized therapeutic privilege in conditions of surgical necessity when a patient is

---

79. See text at note 44 above.
80. See *Whitehouse* v. *Jordan*, [1981] 1 All E.R. 267 (H.L.). In *Reibl* v. *Hughes* it
     was suggested, however, that expert testimony must be called to show the exis-
     tence of such emergency; see note 7 above, at 13, and note 89 below.
81. See Somerville, note 8 above, at 770.
82. Implied consent may relate to unconscious or incompetent patients, however, rather
     than to competent patients prone to respond emotionally to information. See how-
     ever *Male* v. *Hopmans* (1965), 54 D.L.R. (2d) 592 (Ont. S.C.), where Gale C.
     J.H.C. recognized the implied consent of a competent patient unable to compre-
     hend the nature and risks of treatment alternatives: approved on appeal (1967), 64
     D.L.R. (2d) 105 (Ont. C.A.) at 113.
83. See B.M. Dickens, "What Is A Medical Experiment?" (1975), 113 *Can. Med.
     Assn. J.* 635.
84. See the approach taken, for instance, in *White* v. *Turner*, in text above between
     notes 49 and 51. Risk of scarring from surgery need not normally be disclosed (see
     note 69 above) but disclosure was expected in this case. See also *Zamparo* v.
     Brisson, note 56 above, at 554.
85. Another way to deny a patient's autonomy is to assert incompetence; see G.J.
     Annas and J.E. Densberger, "Competence to Refuse Medical Treatment: Auto-
     nomy vs. Paternalism" (1984), 15 *Toledo L. Rev.* 561.
86. A. Buchanan, "Medical Paternalism" (1978), 7 *Philosophy and Public Affairs*
     370 at 372.

liable to make an emotional response to information. The Court observed that:

> No doubt, a surgeon has some leeway in assessing the emotional condition of the patient and how the prospect of an operation weighs upon him; the apprehension, if any, of the patient, which may require placating; his reluctance, if any, to submit to an operation, which, if the surgeon honestly believes that the operation is necessary for the preservation of the patient's life or health, may demand a detailed explanation of why it is necessary.[87]

In *Reibl* v. *Hughes*, the Supreme Court expressed the matter more generally as to treatments, which were not confined to surgery, but more specifically as to the patient. The Court acknowledged that:

> ... it may be the case that a particular patient may, because of emotional factors, be unable to cope with facts relevant to recommended surgery or treatment and the doctor may, in such a case, be justified in withholding or generalizing information as to which he would otherwise be required to be more specific.[88]

While the principle is accordingly clearly recognized to exist, its application turns upon the facts of each case and is not amenable to determination by precedent. This is consistent both with the clinical nature of the judgment involved and with the preference expressed by the courts to limit availability of the right of non-disclosure. In *Hopp* v. *Lepp*, Laskin C.J.C., speaking for the Court, noted that he was "far from persuaded that the surgeon should decide on his own not to warn of a probable risk... It should not be for that physician to decide that the patient will be unable to make a choice and, in consequence, omit to warn him of risks."[89] In *Videto* v. *Kennedy*, for instance, the Court dismissed the possibility of entitlement to therapeutic privilege (which was not claimed) in the sentence:

> The elective surgery which was undertaken did not fall in the category where the surgeon was justified in withholding or generalizing information because of the patient's emotional condition or apprehension.[90]

It has been proposed that the proper approach to determining the scope of the duty of disclosure and the therapeutic privilege of non-disclosure is "to test the plaintiff's case objectively before proceeding

---

87. Note 6 above, at 77.
88. Note 7 above, at 13, repeated in *Videto* v. *Kennedy* in point 7 of its summary; see text above following note 67.
89. Note 6 above at 79-80. This may hint at a need either for having a second opinion at the time of (non-)informing, which may be inconsistent with the necessity of the circumstances, or for requiring expert testimony at trial to confirm the necessity and the harmful impact of disclosure. The latter seems more likely, in view of *Reibl* v. *Hughes*, note 7 above, at 13, quoting with approval "Comment, New Trends in Informed Consent" (1975), 54 *Nebraska L.R.* 66 at 90.
90. Note 43 above, at 136.

to consider it subjectively.''[91] Accordingly, if information is required to be given under the objective patient test, the physician may then consider whether it should be given to the individual patient in his or her circumstances.[92] It follows that ''The subjective test thus determines whether or not therapeutic privilege justifies a particular non-disclosure.''[93]

The emotional condition or apprehension of the patient which may justify application of the therapeutic privilege must be of an exceptional order and be of severe if not actually pathological extent. Information must be disclosed according to the standard of the objective patient, but the patient's responding decision is not required to conform to objective or rational principles of reasoning in order to be competent and authentic. Patients may decide upon the basis of their subjective perceptions of suffering, rather than upon the basis of physicians' perceptions of pain.[94] Many personal decisions are based upon emotion and sentiment rather than upon objectively or rationally defensible thought processes or data-based considerations, including the most important decisions in individual lives, such as whom to marry and where to live. Medical decisions are similarly not required to be rational in order to be respected and effective. Medical treatment can be sought or rejected upon sincerely held grounds of emotion and apprehension. The justification for withholding or generalizing information may be the patient's likely emotional and apprehensive response not to prospective treatment, but to the actual content of the information which is proposed to be withheld or generalized.

This may be the significance of the expression approving therapeutic privilege that ''a particular patient may, because of emotional factors, *be unable to cope with facts* relevant to recommended surgery or treatment.''[95] Accordingly, outside cases of emergency, a physician may have to consider alternative means of effective communication in order to make appropriate disclosure to the patient in a manner which will not find the patient unable to cope with the information. A physician will be entitled to invoke therapeutic privilege only upon concluding after due consideration of alternative means and in good faith that the information cannot be presented in a way which would not harm the patient. While this interpretation has found academic favour, how-

---

91. *Per* Brooke J.A. in *Reibl* v. *Hughes* (1978), 89 D.L.R. (3d) 112 (Ont. C.A.) at 125. See also Somerville, note 8 above, at 769-770.
92. The Supreme Court rejected the converse proposition, that if disclosure is not required by the objective test it may nevertheless be required according to a subjective test based upon the individual patient; see note 7 above, at 15-16, and the ''bitter hindsight'' factor, considered in the text above, below note 37.
93. Somerville, note 8 above, at 770.
94. See note 42 above.
95. *Reibl* v. *Hughes*, note 7 above, at 13, emphasis added.

ever,[96] it is not consistently supported by judgments. A number suggest, although without consideration of the narrower interpretation outlined above, that the privilege may be invoked simply upon a physician's fear that the patient's response to information would be to reject a treatment the physician considers necessary, even when receipt of the information itself would not be a source of distress.

Remaining uncertainty as to the basis, operation and focus of therapeutic privilege shows that there is still room for judicial clarification of the legal principles of informed choice in medical care. Recent decisions have advanced patients' interests in autonomy, however, while affording health professionals an objective basis upon which to design their information practices and protection against being at the mercy of the individual plaintiff's subjective view, formed after injury, of whether prior disclosure of its risks would have caused the treatment to be rejected. Patients are required and enabled to act as "intelligent", mature and rational individuals";[97] health professionals are required to approach them as such, and are protected when they do.

---

96. See Somerville, note 8 above, at 767: "It is submitted, however, that a preferable approach is that the physician may rely on therapeutic privilege to justify non-disclosure of risks where ... the disclosure, *in itself*, would physically or mentally harm the patient to some significant degree."

97. *Per* Linden J. in *White* v. *Turner*, note 44 above, at 290.

*"Inequality (is) the price
of civilization."*

*"L'inégalité (est) le prix
de la civilisation."*

George Orwell, *1984*

THE RIGHT TO EQUALITY:
FREEDOM FROM MAJORITIES

LE DROIT À L'ÉGALITÉ:
LA LIBERTÉ À L'ENCONTRE DES MAJORITÉS

Equality and Discrimination

Walter S. Tarnopolsky*

DISCRIMINATION AND THE LAW BEFORE THE CONSTITUTION ACT, 1982

The Constitutional Position

Although the *British North America Act* (now *Constitution Act, 1867*) does not include a bill of rights, it does contain provisions protecting certain minority rights. Thus, section 93 protects certain collective religious rights to the establishment of separate schools, even though it does not apply to all religious groups nor, to the same extent, to all provinces. Section 133 protects Canadians' rights to the use of the English and French languages in judicial and legislative institutions at the federal level and in Quebec and section 23 of the Manitoba Act makes the same provisions for Manitoba, although these provisions, too, do not apply equally to all Canadians since they touch only Quebec and Manitoba.[1]

Apart from these provisions the *Constitution Act, 1867* makes no reference to individual equality rights. More importantly, the Judicial Committee of the Privy Council decided early in our constitutional history that discrimination on racial grounds was not a basis for invalidating provincial legislation. In *Union Colliery* v. *Bryden*,[2] the court dealt with a challenge to British Columbia legislation forbidding "Chinamen" from working underground in mines. The Judicial Committee made it clear that it was not concerned whether the exercise of legislative power was "discreet", and that "courts of law have no right whatever to inquire whether [the] jurisdiction has been exercised wisely or not". Similarly, in *Cunningham* v. *Tomey Homma*,[3] the Judicial Committee was faced with a provision in the British Columbia Elections Act

---

* Justice, Ontario Court of Appeal.
1. For the application to Quebec of s. 133 of the B.N.A. Act, see *Attorney-General of Quebec* v. *Blaikie et al.*, [1979] 2 S.C.R. 1016. For the application of s. 23 of the Manitoba Act, see *Attorney-General of Manitoba* v. *Forest*, [1979] 2 S.C.R. 1032.
2. [1899] A.C. 580.
3. [1903] A.C. 151.

denying the franchise to "Chinamen, Japanese and Indians". The court declared that "the policy or impolicy of such an enactment as that which excludes a particular race from the franchise is not a topic upon which their Lordships are entitled to consider". Although in the former case the legislation was held invalid on the ground that it infringed federal jurisdiction over "naturalization and aliens", it is quite clear from both cases that as long as provincial legislation was not beyond the jurisdiction of the province, it was valid, even though it discriminated on racial or any other grounds.

It is not surprising, therefore, that in 1914 the Supreme Court of Canada, in the case of *Quong-Wing* v. *The King*,[4] upheld the validity of a Saskatchewan Act prohibiting white women from residing or working in "any restaurant, laundry or other place of business or amusement owned, kept or managed by any Chinaman". As long as Parliament and the provincial legislatures did not exceed their legislative jurisdiction as set out in the *British North America Act*, racially discriminatory legislation would not be challenged on grounds of constitutionality.

Nevertheless, one should point out that federalism can provide protection for minority and equality rights in at least three different ways. In the first place, it can do so by giving large minorities control of regions. The French language is protected in Canada, not so much by the Constitution, as by the existence of the Province of Quebec, where a French-speaking majority dominates. Moreover the very necessity of dealing with the government and people of a French-speaking province enforces at least a certain minimum of bilingualism on the federal Parliament and the federal public service.

Second, since in a federal state every person is at the same time a citizen of a province and of the country as a whole, and since legislative jurisdiction relating to the various human rights is divided between the two orders of government, neither order alone can totally determine the limits on rights. Third, it is not easy for any one government, even when acting within its jurisdiction, to be more restrictive of civil liberties than another, because there is the ever present possibility of comparing the status of civil liberties within one province with that in another. Moreover, with eleven governments and First Ministers, even if the same political party were dominant in each province, the rivalry between these heads of government provides a certain check on the oppressiveness or arbitrariness of any one government.

---

4. (1914), 49 S.C.R. 440.

Racial Discrimination under the Common Law and the Civil Law

The leading decision is that of the Supreme Court of Canada, given in 1939, in the case of *Christie* v. *York Corporation*.[5] Christie was a black man who was a season subscriber to hockey games in the Montreal Forum, where the respondent operated a beer tavern. Although the appellant had previously bought beer in the tavern, on the evening in question the waiter declined to serve him and stated that he was instructed ''not to serve coloured people''. When the manager affirmed the refusal, the appellant sued for damages. Four of the five judges of the Supreme Court held that the respondent could refuse service on the ground that ''the general principle of the law of Quebec was that of complete freedom of commerce'', and that it could not be argued ''that the rule adopted by the respondent in the conduct of its establishment was contrary to good morals or public order''.

A year later the British Columbia Court of Appeal held that the principles established by the Supreme Court of Canada in the *Christie* case were not confined to Quebec, but were applicable in the common law provinces as well.[6] Similarly, in 1961 the Alberta Court of Appeal, without written reasons, upheld a lower court decision that the plaintiff was not a ''traveller'' and the motel, which did not serve food, was not an ''inn'' and so was not bound by the principle of English common law applicable to inns.[7]

At the end of World War II a decision concerning a racially restrictive covenant not to resell land to ''Jews, or to persons of objectionable nationality'', gave an Ontario judge the opportunity to hold that such racially based grounds were contrary to public policy. The judge also held the covenant to be void for uncertainty and for being a restraint upon alienation.[8] Subsequently, however, another restrictive covenant, prohibiting the sale of land to any person of ''Jewish, Hebrew, Semitic, Negro, or coloured race or blood'', was upheld as valid by a lower court and by the Ontario Court of Appeal. The Court of Appeal did not agree that there was a ground of public policy to render such covenants void. Before the case reached the Supreme Court of Canada, the legislatures of both Ontario and Manitoba passed amendments to their property legislation providing that such covenants were invalid. Despite this further evidence of the view of legislatures about public policy on racial discrimination and restrictive covenants, the Supreme Court did not choose the egalitarian route, bur rather held the covenant invalid

---

5. [1940] S.C.R. 139.
6. *Rogers* v. *Clarence Hotel* [1940] 3 D.L.R. 538 (B.C.C.A.).
7. *King* v. *Barclay and Barclay's Motel* (1961), 35 W.W.R. (N.S.) 240.
8. *Re Drummond Wren* [1945] O.R. 778, 4 D.L.R. 674.

because it did not relate to the use of land. The Court also held that it was void for uncertainty.[9]

In the absence of judicially developed protection of equality rights, the provincial legislatures moved into the field and started to enact antidiscrimination legislation, the administration and application of which has largely been taken out of the courts.

The Rise and Spread of Human Rights Legislation

For almost a century after the *British Emancipation Act* of 1833, the trend in Canada was to enact discriminatory legislation. The first minor changes came during the 1930's,[10] but it was not until near the end of World War II that modern human rights legislation started to spread. In 1944 the Province of Ontario enacted the Racial Discrimination Act, which prohibited the publication or displaying of signs, symbols, or other representations expressing racial or religious discrimination.[11] The Act was brief, and limited to one specific purpose, and it was not until 1947 that the first detailed and comprehensive statute was enacted: The Saskatchewan Bill of Rights Act.[12]

The Saskatchewan Bill did not deal only with antidiscrimination legislation, but with the fundamental freedoms as well. Moreover, it purported to bind the Crown and every servant and agent of the Crown. Enforcement of this legislation was through penal sanctions: the imposition of fines, perhaps injunctive proceedings, and imprisonment. There was no provision for any special agency charged with administration and enforcement of the Act; that was left to the regular enforcement of police and courts as would apply with respect to any other provincial statute that include prohibitory provisions, such as the liquor or vehicles Acts.

Both the Saskatchewan Bill of Rights and the Ontario Racial Discrimination Act were quasi-criminal statutes in that certain practices were declared illegal and sanctions were set out. But experience soon showed, as it had in the United States, that this form of protection — although better than none, and having a certain usefulness by way of indicating a government's declaration of public policy — was subject to a number of weaknesses. First, there was a reluctance on the part of the victim of discrimination to initiate the criminal action if complaint to the police had failed to result in a prosecution and it always appeared that the police did not act. Second, there were all the difficulties of

---

9. *Noble and Wolf* v. *Alley* [1951] S.C.R. 64, 1 D.L.R. 321.
10. For example, the Ontario *Insurance Act* was amended to forbid discrimination in assessing risks (S.O. 1932, c. 24); the Manitoba *Libel Act* was amended to prohibit group libel (S.M. 1934, c. 23).
11. S.O. 1944, c. 51.
12. S.S. 1947, c. 35.

proving the offence according to the criminal standard of proof, i.e. beyond a reasonable doubt (and it is extremely difficult to prove that a person has not been denied access for some reason other than a discriminatory one). Third, there was reluctance on the part of the judiciary to convict — a reluctance probably based upon a feeling that some of the prohibitions impinged upon the traditional freedom of contract and upon the right to dispose of one's property as one chose. Fourth, without extensive publicity and education, most people were unaware that such legislation existed for their protection. Members of minority groups, who were the frequent victims of discrimination, tended to be somewhat sceptical as to whether the legislation was anything more than a sop to the conscience of the majority. Fifth, and this was as important a factor as any, the sanction (in the form of a fine or even if it were imprisonment) did not help the person discriminated against in obtaining a job, a home, or service in a restaurant, hotel, or barbershop.

To overcome the weaknesses of quasi-criminal legislation, Fair Accommodation and Fair Employment Practices Acts were enacted. These new types of human rights provisions were copied from the legislative scheme first introduced on this continent in 1945 in the State of New York.[13] The New York legislation was an adaptation of the methods and procedures that had proved effective in labour relations. These Acts provided for assessments of complaints, for investigation and conciliation, for the setting up of commissions or boards of inquiry where conciliation proved unsuccessful and — but only as a last resort — prosecution and the application of sanctions. The first of this new legislation, the *Fair Employment Practices Act*, was passed in Ontario in 1951,[14] and within the next decade and a half, most of the provinces enacted similar statutes. The first Fair Accommodation Practices Act was enacted by the Province of Ontario in 1954,[15] and again most of the other provinces followed within the decade.[16]

The Fair Employment and Accommodation Practices Acts were an improvement over the quasi-criminal approach, but they still continued to place the whole emphasis in promoting antidiscrimination legislation on the victims, who were obviously in the least advantageous position to help themselves, as if discrimination were solely their problem and responsibility. The result was that very few complaints were made and very little enforcement was achieved.

The next major step was taken by Ontario in 1962 with the consolidation of all human rights legislation into the Ontario Human Rights

---

13. N.Y. Public Laws of 1945, c. 118, added to Article 12 of Executive Law 1909; now see Art. 15 of Executive Law of 1951.
14. S.O. 1951, c. 24.
15. S.O. 1954, c. 28.
16. For more details see my book *Discrimination and the Law*, Toronto: De Boo, 1982, c. 2.

Code,[17] to be administered by the Ontario Human Rights Commission, which had been established a year earlier. By 1975, every province in Canada had established a Human Rights Commission to administer antidiscrimination legislation and, in 1977, the Canadian Human Rights Act established a federal commission.[18] With minor variations, all the legislation is similar except that Saskatchewan and Quebec have additional protections. Saskatchewan has continued the protection for fundamental freedoms introduced in its 1947 Bill of Rights.[19] Quebec, in its Charter of Human Rights and Freedoms, has enacted a comprehensive Bill of Rights which proclaims fundamental freedoms, legal civil liberties, egalitarian rights, and even economic and social rights.[20]

The consolidation of human rights legislation into a code to be enforced by administrative commissions was intended to ensure community vindication of the person discriminated against. Without active community involvement, people who suffer from discrimination may lack knowledge of the purpose and scope of the legislation, or may feel that the costs of vindication (in money and embarrassment) would be too great, or they may fear that the proclamation of human rights is not intended to produce tangible results but merely to soothe the consciences of the majority. The objects and purposes of Human Rights Commissions in administering human rights codes could not be better described than in the words of Dr. Daniel Hill, former director, then chairman, of the Ontario Human Rights Commission:

> Modern day human rights legislation is predicated on the theory that the actions of prejudiced people and their attitudes can be changed and influenced by the process of free education, discussion, and the presentation of socio-scientific materials that are used to challenge popular myths and stereotypes about people... Human rights on this Continent is a skillful blend of educational and legal techniques in the pursuit of social justice.[21]

The Scope of Human Rights Legislation

All of the human rights acts in Canada prohibit discrimination on racial grounds, in the wide sense of "racial" defined in the *United Nations Convention on the Elimination of all Forms of Racial Discrim-*

---

17. S.O. 1960-61, c. 92.
18. S.C. 1976-77, c. 33.
19. The Saskatchewan Human Rights Code, R.S.S. 1978, c. S-21.1.
20. S.Q. 1975, c. 6.
21. *Human Relations*, Ontario Human Rights Commission, June, 1965, 4. For further articles on the Codes and Commissions see I. A. Hunter, "Human Rights Legislation in Canada" (1976), 15 *U. of Western Ontario L. Rev.* 21. A.W. Mackay "Equality of Opportunity: Recent Developments in the field of Human Rights in Nova Scotia" (1967), 17 *U. of Toronto L. J.* 176; D. Proulx, "Egalité et discrimination dans la charte des droits et libertés de la personne: étude comparative" (1980), 10 *Revue du Droit* 381.

ination. Thus, both ''race'' and ''colour'' are referred to in all the acts. Other terms relating to one's ancestry or racial origin include: ''national extraction'', ''national origin'', ''place of birth'', ''place of origin'', ''ancestry'', ''ethnic origin'', and ''nationality'', with the last term used only in Manitoba, Ontario and Saskatchewan.

In addition to the racial grounds, all jurisdictions have legislation prohibiting discrimination on grounds of ''sex'' and ''marital status'' or ''family status'' or ''civil status''; all of them prohibit discrimination on the ground of ''age'', and five — British Columbia, Manitoba, Newfoundland, Prince Edward Island and Quebec — prohibit discrimination on the basis of ''political opinion'', ''belief'' or ''convictions''. In addition, the Quebec Act adds ''language'', ''social condition'' and ''sexual orientation'' as prohibited grounds of discrimination, while the Manitoba legislation adds ''source of income''. The federal act includes, as prohibited grounds of discrimination, ''a conviction for which a pardon has been granted''. Discrimination on the ground of ''physical handicap'' is found in the acts of Manitoba and Nova Scotia, while New Brunswick, Prince Edward Island and Saskatchewan adopt the term ''physical disability'', and Alberta the term ''physical characteristics''. In the federal act, as well as those of British Columbia, Ontario and Quebec, protection is provided for ''handicapped'' persons, which includes both ''physical'' and ''mental'' handicap.

The acts address themselves to equality of access to places, activities, and opportunities. All acts prohibit discrimination in employment; in the rental of dwelling and commercial accommodation; in accommodations, services, and facilities customarily open to the public; and in the publishing and/or displaying of discriminatory notices, signs, symbols, emblems or other representations. In addition, New Brunswick, Nova Scotia, British Columbia, Manitoba, and Saskatchewan prohibit discrimination in the selling of real property. The Quebec Act appears to be the most comprehensive:

12. No one may, through discrimination, refuse to make a juridical act concerning goods or services ordinarily offered to the public.

13. No one may in a juridical act stipulate a clause involving discrimination.

Discrimination

All the Acts (except Quebec's) prohibit not only specific acts of denial of access, but also the act of ''discrimination'' as such, where these are based on one of the prohibited grounds. However, none of these statutes, except the Quebec Charter, provides a definition of the term ''discrimination''. The *Oxford English Dictionary* defines ''to discriminate against'' as: ''to make an adverse distinction with regard to; to distinguish unfavourably from others''.

The American definition of the word "discrimination" (as provided by *Webster's New World Dictionary of the American Language*) includes "A. showing of partiality or prejudice in treatment, specific actions or policies directed against the welfare of minority groups". The term "discrimination" as used in human rights legislation in Canada is intended to mean: an action or policy showing partiality or prejudice in treatment directed *against* members of certain specific groups. Furthermore, although human rights legislation may be concerned with the motive or intent of the individual who has performed a specific, prohibited act, it is the overt action, not the thought, which is prohibited. And if the *effect* of an action is discriminatory, that action could be contrary to human rights legislation, even in the absence of discriminatory intent.

It is important, however, to look closely at two comments frequently made regarding antidiscrimination legislation. First, it is claimed that such legislation attempts to change thoughts, views, or attitudes. Though such changes may be desirable, and in fact may be the very object of human rights legislation, it is the overt act that the legislation prohibits. Second, it is sometimes argued that every action undertaken in favour of one group thereby indicates partiality or prejudice against another. Although this may be true in specific instances, it poses no problem in the overwhelming majority of cases, where the action can be proved to be "directed against" a person or a group "because of" membership in one of the groups specified in the legislation.

Although it is clear that the "discrimination" prohibited in the various human rights Acts in Canada is the kind of action that involves adverse or unfavourable distinction, no specific definition of the term is provided except in s. 10 of the Quebec Charter of Human Rights and Freedoms:

> Every person has a right to full and equal recognition and exercise of his human rights and freedoms, without distinction, exclusion or preference based on race, colour, sex, civil status, religion, political convictions, language, ethnic or national origin or social condition.
>
> Discrimination exists where such a distinction, exclusion or preference has the effect of nullifying or impairing such a right.

Discrimination then, in the Quebec Charter, is: a distinction, exclusion, or preference, which is based on one of a number of specified grounds, and which has the effect of nullifying or impairing the right of every person to full and equal recognition and exercise of human rights and freedoms. Obviously, the human rights and freedoms referred to are those proclaimed in ss. 10 to 19 of the Quebec Charter — the accommodations, goods, services, facilities, employment, and so on — to which a person must have right of access, or from which he must have equality of opportunity to benefit.

This definition accords very closely with the one provided in the International Convention on the Elimination of Racial Discrimination, which has been ratified by Canada. The reference is to "any distinction, exclusion, restriction or preference... which has the purpose or effect of nullifying or impairing the recognition, enjoyment or exercise, on an equal footing, of human rights and fundamental freedoms".

EQUALITY RIGHTS, MINORITY RIGHTS AND THE CONSTITUTION ACT, 1982

The Equality Rights

There are three equality rights provisions in the Canadian Charter of Rights and Freedoms — ss. 15, 27 and 18. These are the provisions that probably received the greatest attention from lobbying groups, particularly women and associations of handicapped persons. In addition, if the experience in Canada since 1960, under the Canadian Bill of Rights, and in the United States since 1954, under the Fourteenth Amendment, are any guide, these are the provisions that are likely to be raised most frequently in litigation under the new Charter. This prediction, however, cannot be tested until after April 17, 1985 because, by section 32(2) of the Charter, section 15, the foundation provision, does not come into effect until three years after the Charter came into force. Although there is no similar delay with respect to sections 27 and 28, most of the impact of these sections will be determined within the context of the equality rights in section 15. Further, since sections 15 and 28 are individual rights provisions, while section 27 is a group rights provision, section 27 will be dealt with separately after a discussion of the other two.

Although section 15(1) may seem to be the camel that a committee produces when attempting to design a horse, the provision is understandable in light of the restricted effect given by the Supreme Court of Canada to the "equality before the law" clause in section 1(b) of the Canadian Bill of Rights. First, in response to Mr. Justice Ritchie's judgment in the *Lavell* case,[22] wherein he implied a distinction between the "equality before the law" clause, and unequal treatment "*under the law*", section 15(1) includes protection for equality "under the law". Second, because majorities on the Supreme Court of Canada have rejected any adoption of the "egalitarian conception" set forth in the American Fourteenth Amendment,[23] the legislative draftsmen added a counterpart to the American "equal protection" clause. Third, because

---

22. *A.G. Canada* v. *Lavell et al.* [1974] S.C.R. 1349, 1365-67 and 1372-73.
23. *Lavell* case, *ibid.*, 1365. Also see Fauteux, C.J.C., on behalf of the majority in *Smythe* v. *The Queen* [1971] S.C.R. 680, 687.

in a case[24] dealing with unemployment insurance benefits, Mr. Justice Ritchie rejected a contention that distinctions made with respect to pregnant women constituted discrimination on the basis of sex, on the ground that such distinctions "involved a definition of the qualifications required for entitlement to *benefits*", section 15(1) also includes a clause providing for "equal *benefit* of the law."

Thus, it is clear that section 15(1) governs every possible application of the law to individuals, although it should be expected that *some* distinctions will be permitted. The section 1 "reasonable limitations" provision applies. As a result, some distinctions will fall while others will be upheld. Along these lines, it might be useful to consider the way that the U.S. Supreme Court has applied the equal protection clause of the Fourteenth Amendment. The Court applies three levels of "scrutiny".[25] The highest, strict scrutiny, applies to race, color, and religion. Distinctions made on these grounds are considered inherently suspect. As a result, unless the government can show "an overriding state purpose, which could not be achieved in a less prejudicial manner", the distinction will fall.[26] Probably because the U.S. Supreme Court has had to consider statutes which were intended to protect women from turn-of-century working conditions, sex was not included as an inherently suspect basis of distinction; hence the U.S. Equal Rights Amendment proposal. In Canada, given modern conditions and section 28 of the Charter, sex must be considered to be inherently suspect. Also, because for many years various Human Rights Codes have included these as prohibited grounds of discrimination and because of section 27 of the Charter, national and ethnic origin must also be included as such a proscribed criterion.

At the opposite end of the scale from strict scrutiny, the U.S. Supreme Court has applied minimal scrutiny to distinctions made on such ground as indigence, residence, ability to pay taxes, and similar

24. *Bliss* v. *A.G. Canada* [1979] 1 S.C.R. 183. The other ground for rejecting the challenge was that the distinction was between pregnant women and everyone else: not a distinction on the basis of sex.

25. For some of the numerous recent articles discussing current interpretation and suggesting new approaches, see J.A. Hughes, "Equal Protection and Due Process: Contrasting Methods of Review Under Fourteenth Amendment Doctrine" (1979), 14 *Harv. C.R.-C.L.L. Rev.* 529; M.J. Perry, "Modern Equal Protection: A Conceptualization and Appraisal" (1979), 79 *Col. L. Rev.* 1023; L.A. Alexander, "Modern Equal Protection Theories: A Metatheoretical Taxonomy and Critique" (1981), 42 *Ohio St. L.J.* 3; J. Ely, *Democracy and Distrust* (Cambridge, Mass.: Harvard University Press, 1980); Symposium on "Equal Protection, The Standards of Review: The Path Taken and The Road Beyond" (1980), 57 *U. of D. J. of Urban Law*, Issue No. 4.

26. For one of the earlier expositions of this test, see *U.S.* v. *Carolene Products Co.*, 304 U.S. 144, 152-153, n. 4 (1938). For later applications, see *Baker* v. *Carr*, 369 U.S. 186 (1962); *Reynolds* v. *Sims*, 377 U.S. 533 (1964). For more recent references to this test, see *Regents of the University of California* v. *Bakke*, 438 U.S. 265.

economic and social characteristics.[27] With respect to such distinctions, a valid legislative purpose is presumed. Therefore, unless the one challenging the law can show that it has no rational relationship to a legitimate legislative purpose, the distinction stands.[28] In the case of section 15(1) of the Charter, such a test could be suggested for distinctions which are *not* listed in that provision.

In recent years the U.S. Supreme Court has evolved what has come to be known as intermediate scrutiny for distinctions made on the basis of sex and legitimacy. Under this test, the government must show an important governmental objective in order for a distinction to be held valid.[29] In Canada, under section 15(1), age and mental or physical disabilities are listed. Since bona fide qualifications and requirements are more readily evident with respect to these grounds, they might be considered subject to an intermediate scrutiny test rather than be considered inherently suspect.

Because of subsection (2) of section 15, there appears to be no question in Canada but that affirmative action programs do not contravene the equality clauses in subsection (1). Even though in the United States both the *Bakke*[30] and *Weber*[31] cases were decided on the basis of the Civil Rights Act of 1964, rather than the equal protection clause of the Fourteenth Amendment and the *Bakke* case invalidated only certain kinds of strict quotas, without affecting the plethora of measures which constitutes affirmative action, there was enough suspicion in Canada that the courts might find such programs to contravene equality clauses that the draftsmen decided to be absolutely certain.

Finally, one could suggest that section 15 will not be applied to private action, but rather will be restricted to government action. It is true that the equal protection clause of the American Fourteenth Amendment has arguably had limited application to private action; but this may be explained by the fact that when this interpretation was developed, i.e., after 1954 when racial segregation was held to contravene the equal protection clause,[32] there were no antidiscrimination

27. *McGowan* v. *Maryland*, 366 U.S. 420 (1961).
28. *Geduldig* v. *Aiello*, 417 U.S. 484 (1974); *New Orleans* v. *Dukes*, 427 U.S. 297 (1976); *Cleland* v. *National College of Business*, 435 U.S. 213 (1978). This test would appear to be similar to, although stricter than, the "valid federal [legislative] objective" test that the Supreme Court of Canada applied to the "equality before the law" clause of s. 1(b) of the *Canadian Bill of Rights*, see *The Queen* v. *Burnshine* [1975] 1 S.C.R. 693; *Prata* v. *Minister of Manpower and Immigration* [1976] 1 S.C.R. 376. It was refined by McIntyre, J., in *Mackay* v. *The Queen* [1980] 2 S.C.R. 370, 405-406, to a test of a "desirable social objective".
29. *Craig* v. *Boren*, 429 U.S. 190 (1976); *Califano* v. *Goldfarb*, 430 U.S. 199 (1977); *Califano* v. *Webster*, 430 U.S. 313 (1977).
30. *Regents of the University of California* v. *Bakke*, 438 U.S. 265 (1978).
31. *United Steelworkers of America* v. *Weber*, 444 U.S. 889 (1979).
32. *Brown* v. *Board of Education*, 347 U.S. 483 (1954).

(civil rights) acts in fifteen of the states and very little legislation in this area at the federal level. Even so, the U.S. Supreme Court extended state action to only a few areas, such as privately owned but municipally managed parks,[33] private restaurants in publicly owned facilities,[34] and restrictive covenants because of the state (court) action involved in their enforcement.[35] When the Civil Rights Act of 1964 was passed, it applied not only in the federal sphere but also in all the states. Thus, resort to the Fourteenth Amendment became less crucial.

In Canada's case, one might expect that section 15 will not apply to private action, for three reasons. First, section 32(1) states that the Charter applies ''to the Parliament and Government of Canada'' and to ''the legislature and government of each province... *in respect of all matters within the authority*'' of the respective legislative body. This wording was specifically changed from the version proposed as late as 24 April, 1981, which used the words ''and to'' in place of the words ''in respect of''. The intent to restrict application of the Charter to legislative and government action seems clear.[36]

Second, section 15 refers to equality under and before the *law*, and to equal protection and benefit of the *law*. The intent to refer only to inequality arising out of any application of the *law* appears clear. Third, every jurisdiction in Canada has an antidiscrimination (human rights) statute, and all of these apply to the Crown, i.e., to executive action. Therefore, section 15 will clearly apply when a discriminatory act is committed by legislative action, and the jurisdiction concerned does not have an overriding clause in its Human Rights Code, as do Alberta, Quebec, and Saskatchewan. With respect to executive or governmental action, section 15 and the various antidiscrimination statutes will overlap. With respect to private discrimination, it would appear that the Human Rights Codes will apply, although they cannot contravene section 15.

Section 27 purports to give constitutional rank to the principle of ''bilingualism within a multicultural'' context declared by the government of Canada in 1971. Because, by the nineteenth century, it had become evident that the French-speaking inhabitants of Canada could not be assimilated and because later immigrants (whose descendants now number about twenty-eight percent of the population) claimed equality of status with the two ''founding'' peoples (i.e., those descended from French and British immigrants), whose ''founding'' status was in

---

33. *Evans* v. *Newton*, 382 U.S. 296 (1966).
34. *Burton* v. *Wilmington Parking Authority*, 365 U.S. 715 (1961).
35. *Shelley* v. *Kraemer*, 334 U.S. 1 (1948).
36. For a discussion of s. 32, see K. Swinton, ''Application of the Canadian Charter of Rights and Freedoms'', in Tarnopolsky and Beaudoin, eds. *Canadian Charter of Rights and Fredoms: Commentary*, Toronto: Carswell, 1982, ch. 3.

any event later than that of the native peoples, the official government policy became one of protecting the ethnic pluralism of the country. It has been described as a cultural mosaic, in contrast to the American melting pot. Even though Canada's mosaic may be rather vertical, to the advantage of those of British stock, nevertheless section 27 of the new Charter now gives constitutional status to what was merely proclaimed government policy. Section 27 could play a role in interpretation of section 15, to the extent that ethnocultural groups can show disadvantage. Furthermore, it could form the basis of claims for the benefits coming from government funding of culturally related programs, if these benefits are not equal in a manner consistent with the preservation and enhancement of the multicultural heritage of Canadians.

It might be added that s. 27 was referred to by the Ontario Court of Appeal in *Reference re The Education Act and Minority Language Education Rights* (June, 1984, unreported) to support its conclusion that s. 23 of the *Charter* contemplates participation of the language minority in the management of minority language education facilities.

Language Rights

Sections 16 to 20 of the Canadian Charter provide that English and French shall be the "official languages" of Canada and of New Brunswick. Until the Constitution Act of 1982, the only constitutional language protection was afforded by section 133 of the Constitution Act, 1867 and section 23 of the Manitoba Act. Section 21 of the Charter preserves this situation with respect to Manitoba and Quebec. Section 133 of the Constitution Act of 1867 is extended to apply to New Brunswick. Sections 16 to 20 not only extend the official languages requirement to that province, but they are more extensive than section 133. They apply not only to courts and legislative bodies, but to the whole gamut of government services, and section 20 requires that communication be permitted in the official language chosen by "any member of the public". In essence, these provisions reflect the protection afforded by the *Official Languages Act*[37] at the federal level.[38]

Section 22 requires little elaboration beyond its terms. It does not require that any other language be given official status, but it certainly does not preclude it; and it could give rise to a political argument that official status should be extended, e.g., to the language of the aboriginal peoples, at least in the northern territories.

---

37. R.S.C. 1970, c. O-2.
38. A. Tremblay, "The Language Rights", in Tarnopolsky and Beaudoin, *supra*, n. 36, ch. 14.

The major change concerning language rights is to be found in section 23, which sets forth the requirement that "minority language educational rights" be provided.

It will be noted that section 23 rights are restricted to citizens who have themselves received instruction in English or French (subsection (1)) either in the province in which they still reside (para. (1)(a)) or in any other part of Canada (para. (1)(b)), or whose other children have received or are receiving such instruction (subsection (2)), to have their children receive primary and secondary school instruction in that language. This right, which, by subsection (3) applies "where numbers warrant", includes the right to public funding or "minority language instruction" (para. (3)(a)) as well as "minority language educational facilities" (para. (3)(b)).

It is impossible to forecast what kind of judicial supervision will be required to enforce section 23. Under what circumstances will bussing suffice? When will public authorities have to construct separate school buildings? Will merely separate classrooms suffice? What is the number necessary to meet the test of "where numbers warrant"? Certainly Canadian courts will have to consider the American court experience with supervision of busing for purposes of desegregation.

Two points have been determined by our courts under this section. One, by the Ontario Court of Appeal, I have mentioned earlier. In the other, the *Quebec Language Charter* case, the Supreme Court of Canada held that the provision in Quebec's Language Charter which would deny the rights in section 23 to parents who received their English language education *outside of Quebec*, is invalid. Unlike Chief Justice Deschênes, who held that the evidence before him was not sufficient to indicate that this restriction was a reasonable limit under section 1 of the Charter for the purpose of protecting the French language in Quebec, the Supreme Court seemed to base its decision on the historical fact that s. 23 was enacted for the purpose of overcoming such provisions as that impugned in the *Quebec Language Charter case*.

The Aboriginal Peoples

In Canada, as in the United States, Indians have a special status under federal jurisdiction. Unlike the United States, however, where this jurisdiction seems[39] to spring from several constitutional sources, including the treaty power, the rather vague reference in Article 1, section 8, of the U.S. Constitution to regulating "Commerce.. with the Indian Tribes", the power to dispose of United States territory and property, and even national defence, the Canadian provision, in section

---

39. F.S. Cohen, *Handbook of Federal Indian Law* (Washington: U.S. Government Printing Office, 1942, reprinted New York: AMS Press Inc., 1972) ch. 5.

91(24) of the Constitution Act of 1867, is explicit in giving the federal Parliament jurisdiction with respect to "Indians, and Land reserved for the Indians".

The Canadian provision has been interpreted to apply more widely than the text would indicate: the Judicial Committee of the Privy Council held that it included Eskimos.[40] The *Indian Act*,[41] enacted pursuant to section 91(24) of the Constitution Act of 1867, does not refer specifically to Eskimos or Inuit, and not even to all Indians, because the *Indian Act* is mostly inapplicable to Indians who leave the reserves,[42] to Indian women who marry non-Indians, and to their issue. Indian women are all excluded from the Act's coverage upon such marriage.[43] Although the distinction between Indian men who intermarry (and do not lose their status) and Indian women who intermarry (and do lose their status) was held not to constitute an infringement of the "equality before the law" clause in section 1(b) of the *Canadian Bill of Rights*,[44] there is now reason to believe that under the new equality rights provisions in section 15, combined with section 28, the Supreme Court may come to a different conclusion.

However that issue may be resolved under the new Charter, there is a specific provision that extends constitutional protection to all "aboriginal peoples", who are defined by section 35 of the *Constitution Act of 1982* as including "the Indian, Inuit and Metis [being of mixed Indian and non-Indian descent] peoples of Canada". The new constitutional protections are very limited and undetermined. Thus, although section 25 merely assures, as is explained in the marginal note thereto, that "aboriginal rights and freedoms [are] not affected by the Charter", these rights and freedoms are not specified, beyond declaring that they include (1) any recognized by the Royal Proclamation of 1763 and (2) any that may be acquired by way of land claims settlement.

Concerning the first source, i.e., the reference to the *Royal Proclamation of 1763*, Canada's first imperial constitution, its symbolic significance was described by Hall J., in the leading decision of the Supreme Court of Canada on Indian title, the *Calder* case,[45] as follows:

> This Proclamation was an Executive Order having the force and effect of an Act of Parliament and was described by Gwynne J. in *St. Catharines Milling* case[46] at p. 652 as the "Indian Bill of Rights": see also *Campbell*

---

40. *Reference re Eskimos* [1939] S.C.R. 104.
41. R.S.C. 1970, c. I-6.
42. Sections 4, 11, 12, and especially 109 to 113 inclusive.
43. Section 12(1)(b).
44. *Lavell* case, *supra*, no. 22.
45. *Calder* v. *A.-G. for B.C.* [1973] S.C.R. 313.
46. *St. Catharines Milling Co. Ltd.* v. *The Queen* (1888), 14 A.C. 46 (P.C.).

v. *Hall*. Its force as a statute is analogous to the status of Magna Carta which has always been considered to be the law throughout the Empire.[47]

Professor Lysyk summarized the actual requirements of the Royal Proclamation as follows:

> The Proclamation reserved certain lands to the Indians and provided that Indian land could not be purchased or otherwise alienated except by way of surrender to the Crown, and then only according to procedures prescribed in the Proclamation for obtaining agreement of the Indians occupying those lands.[48]

However, as suggested earlier, Professor Lysyk indicated that the significance to the Indian people of the *Royal Proclamation* is much greater:

> It has been suggested that in addition the Proclamation extends, by implication if not expressly, to a considerably broader range of rights. Several spokesmen for native organizations developed this theme before the Parliamentary Committee, drawing from the Proclamation such principles as the recognition of aboriginal peoples as nations, the implied necessity of mutual consent to alteration of their relationship with the Crown, the protection of aboriginal rights, and an implied right to self government in areas not ceded to the Crown.[49]

Whatever is the extent of these rights, they appear to be supplemented with a provision outside the Charter, section 35, which by itself constitutes Part II of the Constitution Act of 1982. As mentioned earlier, besides defining ''the aboriginal peoples of Canada'', this provision recognizes and affirms ''the existing aboriginal and treaty rights'' of these peoples (subsection (1)). It would be beyond the scope of this review to try to outline what these aboriginal rights[50] or treaty rights[51] are, except to note that even though they have never been very precisely defined by the courts, they now have constitutional status and therefore should override any inconsistent federal or provincial laws.[52]

For a more ample and precise definition of aboriginal and treaty rights, we must await subsequent constitutional developments. The first constitutional conference at which agreements were to be sought was required by section 37 of the Constitution Act of 1982 to be held within one year after the coming into force of the act. Subsection (2) of this section required that: (1) this conference include in its agenda an item respecting constitutional matters affecting aboriginal peoples and (2)

---

47. *Supra*, n. 45, 394-395.
48. K. M. Lysyk, ''The Rights and Freedoms of the Aboriginal Peoples of Canada'', in Tarnopolsky and Beaudoin, *supra*, n. 36, ch. 15, 473.
49. *Ibid.*, 475.
50. *Ibid.*, 476-484. D.E. Sanders, ''Aboriginal Peoples and the Constitution'' (1981), 19 *Alta. L. Rev.* 410.
51. Lysyk, *supra*, n. 48, 484-487.
52. *Ibid.*, 487.

the Prime Minister invite representatives of those people to participate in the discussions on that item.

The first such conference was held in Ottawa on 15 and 16 March 1983. Predictably, it did not complete the task of refining the definition of these rights, although certain technical amendments to the aboriginal rights provisions were agreed upon. Section 25 was amended to substitute a new paragraph [b] to make clear that what is protected are "any rights or freedoms that now exist by way of land claims agreements or may be so acquired", while section 35 has a similar clarification to provide that "treaty rights" include "rights that now exist by way of land claims agreements or may be so acquired".

In addition, amendments to sections 35 and 37 were agreed to. As a result sections 35.1 and 37.1 were added by the *Constitution Amendment Proclamation, 1983*. Section 35.1 provides that no amendment can be made to section 24 of the *Constitution Act, 1867* or to section 25 or Part II of the *Constitution Act, 1982*, without the prior holding of a constitutional conference to which representatives of the aboriginal peoples are invited and at which "an item relating to the proposed amendment" is included on the agenda. Section 37.1 extends the requirements of section 37 to two further conferences — one to be convened within three years after 17 April, 1982 and the second within five years after that date. With the adoption of section 37.1, section 37 was automatically repealed, on 18 April, 1983, by operation of section 54 of the *Constitution Act*.

Equality and Minorities

Daniel G. Hill*

As 1984 draws to a close, we have heard every conceivable Orwellian caveat and prophecy. Even those who have never read Mr. Orwell's novel have internalized a vision of rampant totalitarianism, which is often closer to fiction than fact. In our society justice, like a firm but loving parent, has tempered the potential for authoritarianism, so the latter remains an atrocity few Canadians can comprehend.

Big brother does exist, but he is certainly not the same creature depicted in Orwell's novel. The big brother we live with is often overbearing and occasionally clumsy but the constraints we feel under him are less the result of malice than simply the complexity of his size.

But in spite of his usually good intentions, those of us who come from minority populations often see our big brother as a bully - a progeny of entrenched power - who demands conformity at our expense. The sad reality is that these perceptions are frequently accurate - discrimination is readily institutionalized.

Ironically, the Ombudsman is both a creation of, and a check on, the power of big brother. Our desire for efficiency and order must never outpace our commitment to human rights and equity. There can be no definition of civilization that neglects equality - in the course of our advancement, human rights are not concrete entities, but rather the standards by which we define our human relationships and our collective morality.

As a human rights worker, I have personally witnessed the hearts of men and women at their best and at their worst. Yet throughout this diversity of experience I remain convinced that the human spirit is a force of positive good which should give us occasion for hope and optimism. My belief is based not on blind faith, but rather on the evolution of practical mechanisms designed to protect individual rights and dignity.

My commitment to human rights did not emerge in a vacuum, but was nurtured and developed in the context of our wider historical tra-

---

* Ombudsman of Ontario.

ditions. The past is evidence of both our shortcomings and triumphs where justice is concerned. Some events are truly shameful and others inspirational, but all serve as our yardstick for reform.

Canada has long been a sanctuary for those who sought the twin ideals of freedom and equality. As far back as 1793, seventy years before Abraham Lincoln's emancipation proclamation, the first parliament of Upper Canada, under lieutenant governor John Graves Simcoe, passed an Act prohibiting the further importing of slaves into Upper Canada.

There was no positive enforceable legislation to speak of for almost a full century thereafter, until the Ontario Government amended its *Insurance Act* in 1932 to prohibit racial and religious discrimination in the provision of coverage. Then, in 1934, Manitoba amended its *Libel Act* to cover racial and religious libel.

Aside from these two relatively minor adjustments, however, there was practically no legislation in support of human rights in Canada from 1833 to the mid-1940s. In fact, in the first half century after Confederation, Canadian Legislation affecting the rights of Blacks, Asians and Native Peoples was largely discriminatory. Asians, for example, were legislatively prohibited from voting, restricted in employment and barred from purchasing land in certain areas. Indians and Inuit were denied the right to vote and also excluded from certain jobs. And among the indignities visited upon Blacks in some parts of Canada were segregated schools to which their children were assigned by law.

In 1944, the *Racial Discrimination Act* was enacted in Ontario. This statute prohibited the publication or displaying of signs, symbols or other representations expressing racist or religious discrimination. An even more comprehensive statute was enacted by the Province of Saskatchewan in 1947 as the *Saskatchewan Bill of Rights Act*.

By the mid-1960s, every province, except Quebec, had adopted some form of human rights legislation.

Throughout the 1960s and '70s, new human rights issues were emerging in Canada. Discrimination based on sex and disability were two prominent areas of heightened concern. Much of the blatant and overt discrimination practised against individuals had been reduced due to past legislative efforts, but subtle and insidious forms of prejudice embedded in our social and institutional structures persisted.

As a result of this growing awareness, the new Ontario Human Rights Code was proclaimed on June 15, 1982, exactly 20 years to the day since the enactment of the first code.

The new code greatly extends both the grounds of discrimination and the consequent mandate of protection. For example, it is the first anti-discrimination legislation in Canada to explicitly prohibit harassment, sexual advances or solicitations.

Section 10 of the new code is directed towards the elimination of those supposedly neutral employment practices which have the effect of restricting the opportunities of certain groups, although they are not intentionally discriminatory or in bad faith.

Structural features in an organization that operate to exclude particular groups, can now be identified and replaced with fair and reasonable remedies. In addition, the new code empowers the Commission to recommend that special programs designed to reverse established patterns of discrimination be implemented.

The enactment of this new code is a major step forward in the ongoing struggle for equality - it recognizes the true nature of discrimination as pervasive rather than isolated or sporadic. Discrimination is inherent in the institutions of our society and can not be reduced to a series of single occurrences. In order to facilitate a climate of equal opportunity, Human Rights Commissions can now both support and initiate efforts to break down structural and organizational barriers that sustain discriminatory practices.

Human Rights Commissions are really in the business of changing and influencing public attitudes.

Much of our present need for Human Rights Commissions is in recognition of our past. As our history has shown, the majority society in Canada has been known to enslave, oppress and exterminate racial minorities. For example, they enslaved Blacks and Indians in Lower and Upper Canada. They oppressed and exploited the Chinese railroad workers. They interned, for no valid reason, Canadian Japanese during World War II, and white settlers exterminated the Beothuk Indians in Newfoundland.

Today the issues have changed but the memories are intact. Human Rights Commissions must not hesitate to enforce the law. Their emphasis must properly remain on the conciliation of individual disputes and broad programs of public education. Those who claim we can not legislate equality fail to appreciate the wider implications and benefits of the Commissions' work. Dean Rostow, formerly of the Yale University Law School, made this point when he said, "Men often say that one cannot legislate morality. I should say that we legislate hardly anything else. All movements of law reform seek to carry out certain social judgements as to what is fair and just in the conduct of society".

Recently Human Rights Commissions have been subject to a certain measure of public criticism. There are those who claim their work is insubstantial or lacks direction. Frankly, there is probably not a Commission in Canada that would win an unrestrained endorsement from minorities within its jurisdiction. In fact, even the most active and effective Commission would have to expect periodic volleys of brickbats. Being a creature of government, inevitably a Commission is suspect. Within the context of minority community politics, flaying a Commission is often considered a way for an aspiring leader to demonstrate militancy.

Existing legislation is not comprehensive enough and its administrative machinery must be tightened. Most Commissions have been active and effective in their case-by-case approach to complaints, but they have not pressed hard for long overdue extensions of their authority to combat institutionalized racism, nor have they tested their existing statutory powers rigorously.

I also urge the creation of independent bodies to review the activities of both Federal and Provincial Commissions. I am confident that such an assessment will restore the faith of critics and prevent the erosion of these vital organizations. In the event that weaknesses in the Commissions are identified, constructive remedies presented by an independent research and review body would be of positive benefit.

One effort I believe we must make is toward the establishment of contract compliance legislation. Presently, contract compliance exists in the United States under a Presidential executive order. The order prohibits federal government contractors and sub-contractors from job discrimination based on race, sex, colour, religion or national origin. Such regulations uphold affirmative action programs and insure that employees are placed, trained, upgraded, promoted and otherwise treated equally.

Although the present U.S. administration has sought to limit many of the existing restrictions, contract compliance is extensive. Companies bidding for government contracts are screened thoroughly while those currently under contract are audited regularly. In those cases where non-compliance with affirmative action programs is determined, remedial steps are ordered. If the contractor fails to implement acceptable remedies, or when voluntary remedies are inappropriate, contracts can be cancelled, sanctions imposed and the company in violation can virtually be debarred from further government contracts.

This no-nonsense approach to equality in the work-place has proven effective. In 1979 for example, the Uniroyal Company was barred from government contracts for three months until they agreed to a 5.2 million dollar settlement for women workers at their Indiana facility. Debarment for even the largest of industries can have a crippling effect when lucrative government contracts are at stake.

Such legislation is both appropriate and necessary in this country if we are to continue dealing effectively with equal opportunity concerns. Contract compliance demands fair and equitable hiring practices — those in accordance with our existing laws and our collective conscience.

One area that is greatly under-represented by visible minorities is the media, and in particular advertising. The lack of ethno-cultural diversity in television commercials dramatically influences our attitudes, especially those of our children.

Last year Salome Bey, a well known black Canadian performer, made these observations:

Our children go to schools where, culturally and racially, whites have been dominant. At school they study together, they play together and then they go home to their individual television sets. And since they spend more time assimilating via television than they do in classrooms or on playfields, when television says that visible minority children do not exist, that they are to be considered less than the "real" children who do appear on programs and in television advertisements, can you wonder at the results? Can you wonder that the "real" children hold the others in low esteem? Can you wonder that our children, rendered perpetually invisible by television, themselves suffer from low self-esteem?

Visible minority groups must not be judged on their racial characteristics. The same opportunities must be available for them as are available for others. If it takes legislation similar to contract compliance to achieve this goal, this is the path we must choose.

As Ombudsman for the province of Ontario, I am committed to fair and equitable hiring practices. Women and visible minorities are well represented in the Office of the Ombudsman, a presence, I hope that will be an example for the community.

I believe that it is up to the government of a democratic society to protect the human rights and fundamental freedoms of its people. However, these rights and freedoms, so essential to the dignity of man are only words and phrases without substance unless accompanied by effective governmental machinery which will implement them.

Paradoxically, with each step our government takes toward social equity, the bureaucracy becomes larger and more complicated.

Our popular conception of bureaucracy is that of an alternately benevolent and oppressive force, impenetrable by the average citizen. We live in an age when governments are regarded by their people as custodians of human welfare in almost all physical and social respects. Government has naturally responded with the creation of a vast structure encompassing health, education, housing, social security and community services.

In the workings of the bureaucracy thousands of administrative decisions are made each year, many by minor officials. Most of these decisions will be justified, but some will not. By reason of human error alone, mistakes and misjudgements must necessarily occur. The well-connected and the well-to-do can usually deal with these situations; they know their legal rights and can afford to pursue them. But for the ordinary humble citizen, and even more for the underprivileged and disadvantaged, there is often no simple way to gain justice.

While all citizens are universally affected by burgeoning government regulation, the underprivileged and disadvantaged are by necessity the most dependent and the most vulnerable to administrative abuse. Therefore, these are also the groups that most need the protection of the Ombudsman.

The Ombudsman concept is not simply an isolated safeguard for those with complaints; it is rather the natural and necessary outgrowth of an extensive scheme of human rights legislation. The thrust of our human rights legislation has sought to prevent arbitrary discrimination and to provide equal access to the opportunities, benefits and safeguards of our social and legal framework.

But for those who are considered the Pariahs of our society, the institutionalized authority of government is suspect. Visible and ethnic minorities, and particularly our native people, feel that government has often demonstrated an insensitivity to their cultural and spiritual heritage.

We cannot support and promote the concept of multiculturalism if we are not prepared to reflect and respect diversity and difference in our administrative policy. Equality in this context not only accommodates differences in individuals or groups, equality demands diversity. People have the right to be heard and understood in their own cultural and linguistic settings - anything less is unacceptable coercion by the majority.

As Gloria Montero has aptly put it in her article, "Facing up to Multiculturalism":

> Our whole attitude to multiculturalism is in grave danger of becoming folkloric unless we see it as the warp it is, running right through the fabric of our society, and use it positively to provide the essential humanity our impersonal industrial society has all but destroyed.

> Culture is not something we bring with us like so much extra baggage. Culture is a living thing, an innate part of what we are. It determines the way we look at life, the way we laugh, and cry, and love.

Our human rights legislation can not by itself achieve the goal of equality for all. It depends on the commitment of those who implement the provisions of our various codes and declarations. Our mechanisms for enforcement must be both effective and rigorously applied. The scourge of racism is still very much alive - in fact a Gallup poll conducted in 1982 found that a shocking 31% of Canadians would support an all white Canada.

Obviously, there is still much work to be done. One area where the Ombudsman will make a special effort is in the area of native rights.

I need not remind you that before any of us came to this country, the native people were here. Perhaps none of us would be in this country today if they had not taught the early settlers survival tactics in a difficult climate and terrain.

But today it is an insult to the collective conscience of this country to witness the appalling poverty and consequent despair that is the lot of many Native Canadians. The Native people of Northern Ontario have a disproportionately high suicide rate, a high infant mortality rate and a host of other acute medical and social problems. But it is not my intention to simply proclaim the familiar litany of injustices that these people have suffered. We can no longer just pay lip service to equality for our native population - we must initiate new and innovative approaches, to make their rights realities. Within my mandate, I intend to do this.

My staff in the far north has been expanded to include two native-speaking students from the Lac-Seul Indian Band, who have visited remote reserves and explained the Ombudsman concept to the residents in their own language and cultural context. This may seem like a very fundamental step in breaking down the barriers of mistrust that have developed between native people and government bureaucracy - but it is exactly this kind of sensitivity to language, culture and tradition that has been neglected in the past. Moreover, my office will reflect the ethnic and cultural diversity of those we serve, to avoid an entrenched "us and them" mentality. Programs and policies intended to alleviate the conditions of Native Canadians must be designed from a native perspective, with their input as the major determining factor.

As Ombudsman, I will regard the principle of native self-determination as the key to my dealings with reserves, and I will urge government bodies to do the same. I am encouraged by the recent initiative of the Ontario Ministry of Correctional Services to provide a grant to the Ne-Chee Friendship Centre in Kenora. This grant will be used for the establishment of a wilderness work camp for native persons convicted of liquor offences. It is hoped that the development of this kind of alternative will give greater hope of assistance to individuals affected with alcohol related problems. Work projects will include tree planting, forest fire fighting, building of facilities and other community services. In addition alcohol counselling, literacy training and native cultural and spiritual reinforcement will also be provided. Understanding native people in the context of their own environment and culture is not a benevolent gesture by government; it is rather, a human right dictated by our vision of equality and justice.

Our search for constructive alternatives is especially important in light of the double standard of equality which has often existed in the past. For example, when the interchange at the 401 and 427 highways was completed, a small graveyard containing 12 white bodies was conspicuously preserved. The same consideration was not given to our native people when the construction of a hydro dam at Ear Falls flooded the sacred burial ground of the Lac Seul Band. Although monetary compensation was obtained after the fact, the insensitivity of this act is telling.

Because I operate within the sphere of the provincial government, the majority of issues affecting the native population are outside my jurisdiction. Therefore, I urge the creation of a federal Ombudsman, an office that could make a tremendous impact in the protection of native rights. This issue is a burning one. We can only take pride in our strides toward a just society if we leave no one behind.

Justice demands that there be equality of access to government services and benefits. Policies or conventions which militate against the rights of particular individuals or groups must be eradicated - especially in the realm of government authority where institutionalized discrimination or unfairness must not be allowed to fester.

A broad spectrum of complaints ranging from parity of pensions for native police to adequate provisions of access for the disabled, are all positive rights with respect to government services. The Ombudsman's role is to defend the individual against abuses of executive power, and to facilitate the appropriate execution of rights.

The Ombudsman Act is one link in an evolving chain of human rights legislation going back from the *Magna Carta* to our most recent Charter of Rights and Freedoms.

A landmark event in this process was the *United Nations Universal Declaration of Human Rights.*

The Universal Declaration, composed of 30 articles, sets forth not only a list of traditional civil and political rights, but also rights in the social, economic and cultural fields. It includes such provisions as the right to work, protection against unemployment, the right to rest and leisure and the right to an adequate standard of living including food, clothing, housing and medical care.

Equality of access to the public service and the right to social security are also specifically guaranteed.

The Universal Declaration is based upon the proposition that all human rights are indivisible and interdependent. Beyond the recognition of the traditional civil and political rights, it demands that governments initiate positive action aimed at alleviating the plight of the underprivileged.

The following example drawn from our most recent Annual Report is illustrative of the Ombudsman's capacity to influence government policies - so they more clearly reflect the principles set out in this declaration.

This case concerned the mother of a paraplegic student, in her bid to have a mechanical lifting device installed in her son's school. The complainant's son was confined to a wheelchair and it was both difficult and hazardous for him to climb stairs.

The school that this boy wanted to attend had two levels with no elevator. Initially the school board refused to install an elevator in the school despite the availability of a substantial grant from the Ministry of Education.

Our office informed the Ministry that other types of less expensive but equally practical lifting devices were available and that the complainant would be satisfied with this alternative.

The Minister advised our office that the school board had decided to purchase the less costly device and that other school boards in the province were anxious to do the same.

Although the mandate of the Ombudsman is primarily concerned with individual grievances, reform on a wider scale is often the inevitable by-product of a single complaint.

Another integral part of the Ombudsman's job is to set standards aimed at enhancing the protection of the individual in his or her dealing with government authorities.

Thus it is consistent with his function to implement and support the developing international standards of human rights such as those of the United Nations Universal Declaration, of which Canada is a signatory.

In my first Annual Report the proposal of a Bill of Administrative Rights is made exactly in that spirit. It gives both the public and the public service an idea of what rights bind the relationship between the citizen and the government.

In my opinion, all persons are entitled to fair, just, and reasonable treatment from government authorities and every person in dealing with our provincial authorities is entitled to the following:

1. Respect for individual rights and personal dignity.
2. Prompt and clear responses to all requests for information or action.
3. Decisions that are arrived at without undue delay.
4. Decisions which are based only on relevant considerations, and on *all* relevant considerations.
5. Clear statements of the reasons for all decisions.
6. Clear and adequate notice of pending decisions.
7. A reasonable opportunity to be informed of relevant facts and law upon which decisions are based.
8. The opportunity to respond to any point in the decision-making process with additional revelant information.

9.   Clear information about rights of appeal against any decision affecting them and reasonable assistance in pursuing appeal procedures.

10. Clear information with respect to government policies and actions, presented in a manner understandable to all those affected.

If these considerations were adhered to in the relationship between the provincial authorities and the citizen, I would venture that few complaints would come to the Ombudsman's attention.

Canada has a human rights tradition that gives us great cause for hope. Along with our expanding population, we have always chosen progressive attitudes and actions rather than living in the past. This is not to say that we have not had our share of problems. But I believe that our accomplishments and our willingness to confront the issues will overcome our differences.

In conclusion, please allow me to resist the temptation to deal in rhetoric. I will say quite simply, that equality is the most important element in our civilization. If we must surrender small parts of our individual interest to build a society devoid of discrimination, it is well worth the price. Freedom enjoyed in the face of exploitation, disadvantage and despair is not really freedom at all.

Those of us gathered at a conference such as this are the privileged and the powerful. To some extent, as the custodians of justice, we have the ability to define equality for others. It is an awesome responsibility.

I believe we have both the will and the means to make human rights into living, purposeful realities. But the struggle is never static. Unless we positively move forward, we will inevitably move backward.

As long as I am Ombudsman, I hope to be able to say - as was said by an ancient roman leader Terence, the son of a Libyan slave - "I am a human being and nothing human is foreign to me".

Equality and Women

Chaviva Hosek*

What could equality between women and men look like? Perhaps I can start with what inequality looks like.

The United Nations in 1980 estimated that women do 70% of the world's work, that they grow most of the world's food, and that they own 1% of the world's property. In Canada the signs of inequality are somewhat different. Two-thirds of the women over 65 in Canada who live alone are living below the poverty line. Almost half of the women who are single parents live in poverty. The average wage of full-time women workers are about 60% of the average wages of full-time male workers. Women working in the paid labour force continue to do the vast majority of the household work and child rearing for their families. In effect, they carry a double shift.

In the paid workforce, women represent about 5% of the people in management. The pattern of occupational segregation is so profound, that we can be said to have two labour markets in Canada, one for men and one for women. With two-thirds of the women working in clerical, sales and service occupations at the lowest end of the wage scale, women have twice as much chance as men to be poor some time in their lives. In fact, poverty is increasingly a female phenomenon. One woman in ten is beaten by the man she lives with, and women as women are routinely devalued and trivialized in our jokes, in our pornographic magazines and in the unguarded talk of both men and women.

That is what inequality looks like. Inequality conditions not just our lives but our imaginations. We give lip service to the importance of child rearing but we concentrate that work only in the hands of one gender, and that is the group with the least money, the least power and least status in our society. The people in power in government and in the professions, the churches, in the labour unions, in the political parties, in big business, in the banks, in public institutions, in universities, in the media, are men. The decision-making in our society is done

* President, National Action Committee on the Status of Women 1984-6.

largely by men. The terms of the discussion with which we define reality are largely set by men.

In all these places we can point to some women, and more now than twenty-years ago. But those women are still exceptions who prove the rule. We all know their names because they are still exceptions. The gate-keepers to all those positions of power and influence continue to be men. We congratulate ourselves on the existence of these exceptional women and perhaps on their success as a sign of our progress in our society, and I do believe we have made that progress.

But I think that we sometimes think carefully before taking more steps because a society closer to true equality between the sexes would be very different from the one we live in now, and perhaps we are more than a little afraid to think about it or imagine it. In such a society you would not be able to guess from a person's sex what it is they might do for a living. You would not be able to assume from a person's sex that they spend a significant amount of their time cooking meals or doing laundry or raising children. Indeed all that work would be done but full responsibility for it would be assumed by men and women both. Women would not need to be somewhat legitimatized by their attachment to a man. The Prime Minister would sometimes be a woman. The Cabinet would sometimes have more women than men. The House of Commons might be female and the childcare workers might be male. The average wages of men and women would be close to identical and the people in decision-making positions would be women as likely as men. The nuclear physicists might be women as likely as a man. And the people serving the food at the local diner, the people cleaning the hospitals and the hotels, the people sewing buttons in factories, the nurses, the legal secretaries, the administrative assistants would just as likely be men as women. In fact, we would not notice any of them as exceptions because the rules would no longer be so rigid that the exceptions would stand out. And there would no longer be a billion dollar industry predicated on selling images of women being sexually abused, degraded or exploited. I believe even our sexuality and the way we express it would be very different, perhaps unimaginably different, in a world in which women and men were nearly equal.

The question for you after all this is, how do we get from that world to this one. And what does the formal justice system have to do with such a major transformation of Canadian society. I don't believe that the Charter of Rights in the Constitution alone will get us from that world to this but there are some connections. When the Canadian Constitution with its new Charter of Rights and Freedoms was passed into law in April of 1982, most of the women in Canada had high hopes and expectations about the potential impact of the Charter on the position of women in Canada. The hope was that this new Charter would be both a legal instrument to bring about equality, and that the law and administrative practices associated with the law and with government initiatives in concert with the Charter's equality provisions would be a beginning for creating and encouraging a spirit of equality in Canada.

The basic point to make about women's expectations from the Charter of Rights and Freedoms is that we want to see the spirit of equality in the law in Canada and not just the look of equality. We take a broad view of the Charter and see it in an international context. Canada is a signatory to the United Nations *Convention on the Elimination on all Forms of Discrimination Against Women*. The United Nations document obliges us not merely to state in our Constitution that we are a nation committed to the equality of the sexes in principle, but that we be active in our work to make equality a fact. We are obliged by the signing the U.N. Declaration to the international community to take all appropriate measures, and "to ensure the elimination of all forms of discrimination against women". We are obliged by it not merely to prohibit inequality but to ensure equality. We therefore look for de facto discrimination to be prohibited, not just de jure discrimination as Article 3 of the U.N. Convention enjoins us. These are the words of that Article": To take all appropriate measures including legislation to ensure the full development and advancement of women for the purpose of guaranteeing them the exercise and enjoyment of human rights and fundamental freedoms on the basis of equality with men". The Declaration therefore takes as given that women as a group have not achieved equality with men and that it requires the active advancement of women ensuring the full development of women, to bring us one day into a state of equality with men. Advancement and development of women are part of what we have agreed to in signing the Declaration and it is in that context that we see the Charter's provisions.

Titles VI and VII of the Civil Rights Act of the United States are one example of an attempt to ensure equality rather than merely prohibiting inequality. They provide for the effectuation of a broadly worded article prohibiting discrimination and education by very specific and concrete measures. Our own Charter in section 15(2) also explicitly states that it is not inappropriate to use positive action, affirmative action, to correct past discrimination. I would go so far as to say that not instituting special measures for accelerating de facto inequality is the equivalent of being prepared to let time do the work or not as time choses, and that this constitutes an acceptance of injustice which contradicts the spirit of equality with which we begin. We therefore expect to see at some point, if necessary, legislated affirmative action programmes in Canada as one aspect of an active search for equality.

But I don't want to fixate on mandatory affirmative action or any one particular remedy. The major point I want to make is that a search for equality between the sexes must involve women's advancement and development. It must involve positive action, not merely the removal of barriers. And it must involve a more sophisticated, indeed a developing understanding, of what the barriers to women's equality really are.

There are laws on the books which create systemic discrimination without being overtly discriminatory. The two following examples demonstrate the issue: domestic workers are rarely included in the provisions of the employment standards acts, and part-time workers are rarely allowed equal pay and pro-rated benefits along with full-time workers. Most domestic workers are women. Seventy-five percent of part-time workers are women. Therefore those laws which on their face are neutral have in fact an adverse impact on women. Other examples have to do with laws passed by the federal government like the *National Training Act* or job creation acts which are targetted specifically to the industrial sector and which turn out de facto to do very little for women, who do not work in that sector.

It is not necessarily just to treat women and men exactly the same if their situations are different. Mr. Fairweather has given the example that a building without a wheelchair ramp looks basically neutral but actually excludes people in wheelchairs from having access to the building. For women's employment needs, access to affordable childcare is parallel to the need for ramps for the disabled. In the current situation, women who are the parents of young children are unable to enter the labour market on an equal basis with men. Indeed, the burden of being a parent falls largely on women who pay the economic price of parenting. They pay it in a lesser attachment to the labour force, in being more likely to be working part-time, in having less developed career paths, lower wages, lower pensions or no pensions, and lesser opportunities for work if they divorce.

Government employment and training programmes which are organized in the absence of affordable childcare are basically not available to women with young children and thus discriminate against them. The same principle applies to barriers based on pregnancy and childbearing as well as child rearing. Without paid child-bearing leave, we as a society penalize women who choose to bear children and we make child-bearing an economic and social disability. The fact that only women bear children should not become a reason to penalize them for it. The principle to apply is where men and women are in radically different situations, like child-bearing, the same law would not be equitable for treating both of them. Identical treatment, in this case of a pregnant woman and non-pregnant people, constitutes a form of discrimination. The principle is that women should be treated differently when their situation is different, as in child-bearing, and where different treatment is necessary to achieve equality of opportunity in rights, privileges and benefits under the law.

I would like quickly to suggest a few ways in which the Charter of Rights can be an instrument for women's equality, particularly if it is interpreted in a liberal fashion. When women's groups appeared before the Joint Senate and House Committee on the Charter of Rights and Freedoms, most of them wanted the equality rights provisions under s. 15(1) to include the words or categories "marital status, sexual orientation and political belief". It is not clear whether the terms that are now there can be stretched to mean any of those categories, though we know that the enumerated categories are listed in particular and that therefore the list is meant to be exemplary rather than exhaustive. It is not yet clear whether those three categories can be extended out of the ones we currently have.

The "equal benefit of the law" provision in s. 15 could lead to sex equality through the distribution of benefits that come out of transfer payments between the federal government and the provinces. This is an area which I find particularly interesting. Since the definition of equality would require not merely facial equality but de facto equality as we see it, this could have some very interesting implications on current government expenditures. The federal government at the moment, through various financing programmes, transfers massive amounts of money to the provinces to help pay for medical services and post-secondary education. We have, so far, national standards of access to medical services but we don't have national standards of access to post-secondary education. If the standard applied to the distribution of funds through transfer payments could also make a difference to the people employed in the provision of those services in the medical sector or the post-secondary education sector, it could require that payments made by the federal government would have to be made on the basis of the laws the federal government uses for itself, and the standards it uses for itself applied to the provinces.

The mobility rights section of the Charter allows any Canadian citizen to pursue the gaining of a livelihood in any province. For women with young children for whom gaining a livelihood is impossible without accessible childcare, moving from Quebec to say New Brunswick might indeed infringe on their ability to pursue a livelihood if they cannot get support for childcare in New Brunswick on the same criteria as in Quebec. Therefore the whole question of mobility rights and the Charter with respect to access to services which allow one to pursue a livelihood could be a very interesting aspect of Charter questions in the future.

The list of areas that could be influenced by the Charter goes on and could include many others, including the pension system, Indian rights, and the protection of women's equality in relation to cultural practices in a multicultural society. However, I will end by saying that the Charter of Rights offers us a new location, a new legal space within which we can work to bring about a more equitable society.

The legal system as a whole reflects the values and ideals of the society in which we live. None of us have lived in a society in which women and men are equals. It will be new to all of us and unless we become a much richer society, a more equal society could imply a redistribution of the wealth and power that we now have along very different lines. All of us might wish for a richer society in which it would be easier to achieve this kind of redistribution. But women have been told for too long a time to wait for their turn until the mythical day when other problems seen as more crucial, will be solved. We cannot wait to work for justice until that mythical day. We work for it now in the knowledge that working for justice may be as close to true justice as we can ever get.

Equality and Native People

Roberta Jamieson*

Today it is an accepted fact that Indian communities are entitled to a special place, a special status as distinct peoples within Canada. Perhaps the most accomplished academic in the field of Indian rights, Professor Douglas Sanders, has called this acceptance the most significant post-war development in Canadian aboriginal policy.[1] It is an acceptance which has not come easily or quickly, and it is important, in order to understand the broader question of Canada's policy towards minorities and this minority in particular, to understand how and why it developed.

In essence, for a policy toward a minority to work, it has to take into account the characteristics of that minority. If Indian communities have unique status, it is because their characteristics as a minority are unique. I would like to bring to your attention at this point eight of the characteristics which make the communities of the First Nations peoples special.

First, Indian peoples are not a single minority, but groups of minorities separated by such major distinguishing factors as language. There are in fact eleven distinct language groups represented among the peoples of the First Nations of Canada.

Second, peoples of the First Nations are found in all geographic regions of Canada, thus making them perhaps the most dispersed minority in the country.

Third, the cultures of Indian peoples are as different from each other as the cultures of European nations, as different as, for example, the French are from the German. But whereas other cultures can look to a mother country overseas to support their existence in Canada, the cultures of the Indian peoples cannot. The fact that they are **indigenous** cultures means they are dependent on forces within Canada to survive.

---

* Indian Commissioner of Ontario.
1. Sanders, Douglas "The Renewal of Indian Special Status", unpublished manuscript, 1983, p. 1.

Fourth, each culture amongst First Nations has its own and distinct kinship pattern. Some are matrilinial, some are patrilinial, and some are a combination of the two.

Fifth, Indian peoples are found in small groups. The size of the average band is about 300. In the community where I live, the Six Nations Indian Reserve, we are 11,000. We are fortunate.

Sixth, no other minority is associated with a distinct land base. In Canada today there are a total of 2,200 Indian reserves.

Seventh, Indian peoples have always had some form of self-government. This feature of First Nation communities has continued unbroken, even during the less enlightened periods of Canadian policy, with links to original sovereignty still preserved.

Finally, the relationship which exists between First Nations and Canada is unique; it has a political and legal history stretching back to the earliest period of contact.

Clearly, no other group can claim to be as unique in terms of sharing such special characteristics. It is therefore only fitting that Canada's response be a special one. If we are trying to understand how the characteristics of a minority define the kinds of approaches which are appropriate, we might compare the situation of the First Nations with a typical example of other kinds of minority relationships to the government. If we are looking, say, at the fact that there are a number of Roman Catholics in British Columbia, we would find 1) that they are dispersed across the province, as opposed to living in communities whose common factor is the fact that all members are members of the minority, and 2) that they may have little in common aside from the fact that they are Roman Catholics. It is appropriate that the state respond to this group by making some form of accommodation. In this example, a response of a sectorial nature would be viewed as entirely satisfactory: special provisions in the education system, for example. Because the characteristics of the peoples of the First Nations are more diverse, and because they are unique, particularly with reference to the latter points I have mentioned, a similar response would not be acceptable.

Then what would constitute an acceptable response? I say to you that the **only** acceptable response would be one that had as its central core the accommodation of Indian communities as autonomous units, that is to say, as self-governing units.

The reasons for this assertion are three-fold. First, we have said, in describing the characteristics of First Nations, that they are indigenous peoples. They have original sovereignty, which includes clearly defined territories and full autonomy therein. This original autonomy, contrary to what history books and popular belief would have it, was marked by highly sophisticated systems of government in existence long before the first European contact. For example the Iroquois Confederacy, a governmental system which existed among my own people, is one which is bicameral in nature. Checks and balances were created to safeguard both individual and collective rights; even children were accorded a voice in decision making. It was a democratic system of government which was essentially egalitarian in nature. Everyone had a role to fulfill and no one was more important than the other. Certain of the women were selected to act as clan mothers, a significant role, the duties of which included the selection and appointment of chiefs as well as the right to discipline, withdraw or "dehorn" a chief for just cause.

There were systems of justice, of education, of health care. Diplomatic channels and notions of protocol were well established. The model worked so well that the Iroquois Confederacy is said to be the basis of the League of Nations and to have influenced the drafting of the Constitution of the United States of America.[2] And it is but one example of a system of government developed by a First Nation. There are many more, including the Potlatch which still exists on the west coast of British Columbia.

The fact that the First Nations had well-developed societies and defined political boundaries was acknowledged at the time of contact and in early treaty-making. The nature of the relations between the ancestors of the First Nations and Europeans at contact was determined even before the Royal Proclamation of 1763, which recognized and confirmed a relationship that first found expression in codified form in the Gus-Wen-Tah or Two-Row-Wampum belt. The Two-Row-Wampum records a formal agreement between the Dutch and the Iroquois in the middle of the sixteenth century.

> When the Haudenosaunee first came into contact with the European nations, treaties of peace and friendship were made. Each was symbolized by the Gus-Wen-Tah or Two-Row-Wampum. There is a bed of white wampum which symbolizes the purity of the agreement. There are two rows of purple, and those two rows have the spirit of your ancestors and mine. There are three beads of wampum separating the two rows and they symbolize peace, friendship and respect.

> These two rows will symbolize two paths or two vessels, travelling down the same river together. One, a birch bark canoe, will be for the Indian people, their laws, their customs and their ways. The other, a ship, will be for the white people and their laws, their customs and their ways. We shall each travel the river together, side by side, but in our own boat. Neither of us will try to steer the other's vessel.

---

2. *Report of the Special Committee on Indian Self-Government in Canada* (Parliamentary Task Force), Queen's Printer: Ottawa, 1983, p. 12.

The principles of the Two-Row-Wampum became the basis for all treaties and agreements that were made with the Europeans and later the Americans.[3]

Certainly the Royal Proclamation, which many refer to as Canada's first Imperial Constitution and which Mr. Justice Hall in the *Calder* case referred to as having the force of law analogous to the Magna Carta,[4] confirmed the recognition of Indian peoples as distinct political units. It referred to Indian peoples as the "several nations or tribes of Indians with whom we are connected." This same Proclamation, which is referred to in section 25 of the *Constitution Act 1982*, also formalized the treaty-making process. No attempts were made to deal with the internal sovereignty of the Indian nations, rather, a standard of conduct for relations with Indian nations was prescribed, one which accorded these nations political equality.

My second reason for suggesting that an accommodation to Indian peoples must include a provision for self-government is that the peoples of the First Nations have never given up their original internal sovereignty and it continues to exist as a right today.

I spoke, for example, of the definition of relations in the Royal Proclamation of 1763. As late as 1956 Canada negotiated a "treaty" with First Nations peoples using no other authority than that established by the Royal Proclamation[5].

And there is other support for the view that Indian peoples have a right to exercise their original internal sovereignty. If one examines the constitutional arrangements of 1867, it is clear that Indian peoples were exempted from the negotiations and agreements. While it is true that "Indians and lands reserved for Indians" is a heading which is listed under the federal jurisdiction, there is ample historical evidence to support the view that such a move was motivated by a sentiment of protection, one which recognized the need to safeguard the continued existence of political autonomy within Indian communities.

The *Indian Act* of 1876 also represented a recognition of a special set of collective rights and that especially at a time when provisions for collective rights was at odds with the values of individual equality and mobility, the cornerstones of nineteenth century liberal thinking. It defined who was entitled to be an Indian within the meaning of the Act, it set up the reserve system, and it spoke significantly of the rights to

---

3. Ibid., excerpts from presentations to the Special Committee by the Haudenosaunee Confederacy and from Wampum Belts by Tehanetorens, back cover of *Report*.
4. *Calder* v. *Attorney General for British Columbia*, [1973] S.C.R. 313.
5. Sanders, op. cit., p. 2, which refers readers to the Adhesion to Treaty 6 signed by members of the Saulteaux Indian Band in Saskatchewan, Treaty No. 6, Queen's Printer, Ottawa, 1964, p. 32.

reside on an Indian reserve[6]. Only minor modifications have changed the *Indian Act* from that day to the present.

Section 35 of the *Constitution Act 1982* has now affirmed and recognized the "existing aboriginal and treaty rights" of the aboriginal peoples of Canada. There has been, and there will continue to be, much debate as to the exact nature of the rights referred to in this section. It has been argued that the section represents a capsulization or a "full box" of all rights given to the First Nations by the Creator, including with the rights to hunt, fish, and gather, the right to self-government. It has also been argued that the rights referred to in this section represent something less than a full box of rights, and include only those collective rights of a quasi-property nature which are limited to the extent to which they were exercised by aboriginal ancestors and which have neither been the subject of treaty nor overridden by either federal or provincial legislation. Regardless of which view is taken as to the exact nature of these rights, it is clear that Canada has reaffirmed the collective rights of Indian peoples and has accorded them a special status. Section 25 of the same Act ensures that these rights will be protected by shielding them from any adverse effects of the *Charter of Rights and Freedoms*.

Again in the fall of 1982, the special status of Indian peoples was acknowledged when the House of Commons commissioned an all-party Special Parliamentary Task Force to study the issues related to Indian self-government in Canada. After extensive hearings throughout Canada involving more than five hundred submissions, the Task Force tabled its unanimous report in November, 1983. The Task Force concluded that the early relationship confirmed by the Royal Proclamation of 1763 had deteriorated. As a result of the deterioration in that relationship, Indian peoples had been largely ignored, and this neglect had led to a situation in which Indian communities were characterized by deplorable economic, political, and social conditions.

The Task Force in its first pages recommended that "the federal government establish a new relationship with Indian First Nations and that an essential element of this relationship be recognition of Indian self-government."[7] The Indian peoples must be able to move away from the deplorable social conditions which afflict their communities, there must be a fresh and a just opportunity for a secure role for the First Nations within Canada. Accommodation of Indian self-government is the answer; to achieve it means defining a distinct order of government in the Constitution, cooperating to develop intergovernmental agreements, and ensuring a sound and continuing fiscal and economic foundation.

---

6. Ibid., pp. 5, 52.
7. *Report of the Special Committee on Indian Self-Government*, op. cit., p. 41.

I have mentioned certain markers in the history of the relationship between Canada and the peoples of the First Nations because they illustrate the trends. Certainly there have been other policy initiatives which I might have discussed, such as the infamous "White Paper Policy" of 1969. Had it been implemented, it would have ended special status for Indian people, abolished Indian reserves, and as a result, assimilated Indian people into mainstream Canadian society. Fortunately, this policy was widely condemned and subsequently withdrawn. And there have been other fascinating political developments, the seating of Indian representatives at the First Ministers Constitutional Conference of March, 1983, for example.

So far I have made two points: I have said that the First Nations have certain rights, based on original sovereignty, and I have said that this sovereignty and the rights that flow from it have been confirmed time and time again. I would now like to turn to my third point, which is that there are international laws and international precedents which do and which should guide Canadian policy with regard to the First Nations.

To begin with, Canada has signed a number of international covenants which guarantee, in addition to the basic human rights of individuals, the fundamental collective rights of peoples to be self-governing. I draw your attention to the *United Nations Covenant on Economic, Social, and Cultural Rights,* the *Covenant on Civil and Political Rights,* and the *Helsinki Final Act* of 1975. During its deliberations, the above-mentioned Parliamentary Task Force took Canada's international obligations into consideration. In other words, the measures which were recommended were such as to satisfy the commitments which Canada has made to uphold international standards.

The concept of accommodation in the form of self-government is not unheard of. The fact that the cultural survival of indigenous populations was recognized as an important goal in the *United Nations Declaration of the International Code of Standards* in 1976 has led to the development of policy throughout the world which supports this goal. Part of the wording of this *Declaration* specifically refers to the "collective rights of a people to govern their own affairs".

Obviously arrangements that have been worked out in other countries are not necessarily the best model for Canada. A review of international developments will show, however, the variety of special arrangements that have been developed to accommodate indigenous or regional minorities. Spain and France are particularly interesting as the movements towards regional autonomy followed a long period of centralized power. In Spain, regional parliaments were established in 1979 in Catalonia and in the Basque region. France, in 1982, recognized the special status of Corsica by granting it a separate local parliament; two additional regional assemblies were to be elected in 1984. In Micronesia, and in other parts of the world, the concept of free association of independent states has been adopted.

In Canada, we have seen that one minority, the French Canadian population, has managed in one geographic area to gain a degree of self-government in areas of education, culture, and civil law. This has come about because the concentration of the population in large numbers in one province has resulted in a degree of political autonomy. This autonomy has in turn allowed them to work for the goal of cultural survival.

My point is simply this, that accommodations for regional and indigenous populations can and have been reached internationally, and within Canada as well. The only prerequisite is the political will to create such arrangements. With these arrangements, the First Nations will be able to play a meaningful role in Canada's future, and Canada will be able to fulfill its role as an international leader in indigenous relations.

The forum for the development of such accommodations is available; there is the Constitutional forum, and in Ontario, the Tripartite process. The climate is right. Canadians are aware as never before of the importance of safeguarding the cultures which define its make-up, of the strength which comes from diversity. What we need now is the will of the parties involved to address long-standing grievances, to get on with what is crucial, namely the accommodation of self-government for the First Nations, a right which has survived and a necessity for survival in the future.

Equality and Disabled Persons

M. David Lepofsky*

INTRODUCTION

For most, the problem of inequality confronting mentally and physically handicapped persons is quite unfamiliar. The very fact that disabled persons are subject to discrimination catches many by bewildered surprise. The two traditional legal sources for the correction of social injustices, namely statute and common law, have not comprehensively addressed this often unrecognized problem. The common law has never recognized a legal right to equality of opportunity for handicapped persons, while only in recent years have human rights statutes been amended to extend to disabled persons some protection against discrimination in employment, housing and the provision of goods, facilities and services.

In this context, it is hardly surprising that when the Charter of Rights was first introduced into Parliament in 1980, its new equality rights provision afforded no protection whatsoever against governmental discrimination because of handicap.[1] In the face of representations made by and on behalf of Canada's handicapped population, the framers of Canada's new Constitution later took the bold and powerful step of amending Charter section 15, so that it would include a right to equality before and under the law, and a guarantee of the equal protection and equal benefit of the law, without discrimination because of

---

* Counsel for the Ministry of the Attorney General for the Province of Ontario, Crown Law Office - Civil. This article is written in the author's personal capacity and does not purport to represent the views of Ontario's Attorney General.
1. The original version of section 15(1) as proposed in Fall 1980 provided as follows:
    15(1) Everyone has the right to equality before the law and to equal protection of the law without discrimination because of race, national or ethnic origin, colour, religion, age or sex.

mental or physical disability.[2] By its enactment of the handicap amendment, Parliament initiated a new era, in which Canadian judges, legislators and other public officials will be required to become more familiar with and responsive to the circumstances of disabled people, and their efforts towards achieving a status of equality. Not coincidentally, this new era was initiated in 1981, the International Year of the Disabled Person, whose theme was Equality and Full Participation.

This article provides an introduction to the new constitutional right of handicapped persons to equality at the hands of government. It surveys salient issues which will arise in handicap equality rights cases in an effort to plot out the new obligations imposed on legislatures, administrative officials, and courts.[3] It establishes the core principle that Charter section 15 compels governments to ensure that handicapped persons are afforded an equal opportunity to undertake and enjoy the rights, privileges or benefits extended to Canadians by the making or implementation of laws or other government initiatives. Pursuant to Charter section 15, the handicapped may neither be deliberately left out nor be omitted because of governmental oversight or inattentiveness towards the full participation of handicapped persons. As well, it proposes that governmental decisions affecting the rights, privileges and opportunities of handicapped persons may not be based upon inaccurate or stereotyped presumptions about disabilities. Decisions affecting the handicapped must be predicated upon a fair and accurate assessment of their true capabilities.

THE HANDICAPPED AS A DISADVANTAGED MINORITY

The Charter was not passed in a vacuum.[4] In enacting the Charter, Parliament recognized that hitherto, deficiencies had existed in Canada with regard to the protection of certain rights considered fundamental to the free and democratic society which the Constitution was intended to secure for Canadians. To discover the message which Charter section

---

2. Charter section 15(1) provides:
    15(1) Every individual is equal before and under the law and has the right to the equal protection and equal benefit of the law without discrimination and, in particular, without discrimination based on race, national or ethnic origin, colour, religion, sex, age or mental or physical disability.
3. For a more extensive development of the approach to Charter section 15's guarantee to disabled persons offered here, see M.D. Lepofsky and J.E. Bickenbach, ''Equality Rights and Physical Disability'', found in Bayefsky and Eberts, *Equality Rights and the Canadian Charter of Rights and Freedoms*, Carswell Company Ltd., Toronto publication late 1985.
4. *A.G. Quebec* v. *Quebec Association of Protestant School Boards et al.* 10 D.L.R. (4th) 321 at p. 331 (S.C.C.).

15 directs at governments, it is necessary to identify those pre-existing problems which this guarantee was intended to solve.[5] The inquiry into section 15's purposes or objectives should begin not with a technical parsing of the provision's literal words, but instead with an examination of the circumstances of inequality at the hands of government which have been confronted by handicapped Canadians.

Who are the physically and mentally handicapped?[6] This minority includes those persons with any identifiable physical characteristic or mental condition, however serious or minor, which can impair the ability to undertake a particular desired task. A Parliamentary Committee probing into the plight of handicapped Canadians found that more than two million Canadians are mentally or physically handicapped, a figure amounting to a staggering one tenth of the country's population.[7] Elsewhere it has been established that a substantial proportion of this population are unemployed and impoverished.[8]

What impact does a physical or mental disability have on an individual's life? In some circumstances, a physical or mental handicap can impede a person from undertaking a particular activity which would have been easily performed had the person been non-handicapped. A person who is permanently reliant upon a wheelchair due to paralysis from the neck down cannot jog. A totally blind person cannot safely drive a car.

The extent to which a specific handicap restricts a person from undertaking a task can vary, depending on a number of circumstances. Although a blind person cannot operate a motor vehicle, adequate training in the use of a white cane or guide dog can enable him or her to be quite mobile, travelling independently on foot and by means of public transit. The same handicapping condition can place very different restrictions on the abilities of different persons, depending on factors such as a person's intelligence, education, rehabilitation training, and attitude towards his or her disability.

The capabilities of handicapped persons have been radically increased in recent years by the revolution in technological aids for the handicapped. To offer one example, the advent of a computer equipped

---

5. *Hunter* v. *Southam et al.* 11 D.L.R. (4th) 641 (S.C.C.).
6. In this article, the terms ''disabled'' and ''handicapped'' are used interchangeably, and have the same meaning.
7. Canada, House of Commons, *Obstacles* Third Report of the Special Committee on the Disabled and the Handicapped (February 1981), at 131.
8. D. Baker, *Essential Duties, Reasonable Accommodation and Constructive Discrimination. The Evolution of Human Rights Protection for the Handicapped in Ontario*, p. 1. Law Society of Upper Canada Human Rights Program, Toronto, 1983.

with a synthesized voice which reads aloud the text displayed on its screen, as well as the invention of a computer which can generate output in Braille, have together provided visually handicapped persons with extensive access to computer-related fields hitherto inaccessible to them.

How are disabled persons perceived in society? The public is largely unaware of the fact that a combination of individual initiative, education, rehabilitation training and technical aids can provide an effective means for overcoming most obstacles to full participation in society. Accordingly, the public often harbours well-intentioned though misinformed and inaccurate preconceptions about hardships facing the handicapped in their day-to-day life. It is often assumed that a disability such as deafness, cerebral palsy, mental retardation or blindness poses an insurmountable barrier to the enjoyment of a normal life, one replete with challenges, joys, successes and failures. Life with a disability is perceived as tragic.

As a result of the underestimation of a handicapped person's abilities, coupled with an overestimation of the problems with which he must deal, the public often harbours attitudes of pity, patronization, and paternalism towards the disabled. These attitudes can at times be combined with a feeling of uneasiness or awkwardness when a handicap is accompanied by some physical disfigurement, lack of co-ordination or speech impairment.

Springing from these pervasive public attitudes comes a perception that handicapped persons are not ''normal'' people. This impression can also be traced to the fact that traditionally, physically and mentally handicapped individuals have often been channelled out of the normal mainstream of Canadian society. They were generally segregated into special schools, special workplaces or special residential facilities for the handicapped, with responsibility for their every need being delegated to charitable organizations for the disabled. Handicapped persons were ordinarily out of the sight of the public, and hence, were out of the minds of the public.

Accordingly, society has generally entertained no general expectation that handicapped persons would form part of the mainstream of Canadian life. A few peculiarly talented or gifted disabled individuals could be expected to become full participants in society. Yet these persons were viewed more as exceptional superstars than as normal individuals.

Because physically and mentally handicapped persons have traditionally not been seen as full participants in Canadian society, employers, providers of goods and services, property owners and developers, as well as governments and others often have gone about their business working on the assumption that the handicapped could not or would not involve themselves in many of the opportunities which they afford to society. Accordingly, the handicapped can be described as the "forgotten minority". It must be emphasized that this result, and the panoply of conventional attitudes which underlies it, are well-intentioned and not malicious in origin. These perceptions have been enhanced both by the traditional way in which the mass media portrayed disabled persons, and by the simple absence of a significant number of handicapped persons from Canada's public schools, workplaces and other social settings.

Indeed, far from being malicious in character, public attitudes of pity for handicapped persons are usually coupled with a genuine desire to help the handicapped by alleviating some of the perceived misery which is presumed to go along with living with a disability. In this respect, pervasive stereotypes about handicapped persons are generally different from the hateful stereotypes *vis-à-vis* some racial and religious minorities which persist in some quarters. The only exception to this generalization is the case of persons with a history of mental illness, actual or perceived, who can be subject to attitudes of distrust, fear and intolerance.

Despite this difference, there is a profound similarity between the treatment of handicapped persons and the stereotyping of racial or religious minorities. Each situation involves a tendency to generalize about "normal" people in society, and a failure to examine the true capabilities of individuals on the strength of their merits. Each involves an inaccurate prejudgment of a group of persons, for which individual members of that group must consequently suffer.

What inequalities confront handicapped persons? Three kinds of inequalities are linked to the conventional attitudes towards the disabled. First, fear, intolerance or discomfort about a disability lead some to avoid dealing with a handicapped person. Second, handicapped persons are often denied an opportunity to participate in an activity such as employment because of an inaccurate underestimation of their ability to undertake the activity and gain from it. Third, when a program is designed, a venture is undertaken or a building is built, due regard is often not paid to the ability of handicapped persons to participate in the program or venture, or to use the building. The program, venture or building is designed on the implicit and incorrect assumption that it would be of interest only to the non-handicapped, with the participation of disabled persons being disregarded or neglected.

When a mental or physical disability renders it impossible for an individual to participate in an opportunity, there is no denial of equality of opportunity where that opportunity is unavailable to him. However, when an opportunity is foreclosed to an otherwise qualified handicapped person either through a deliberate decision to exclude persons with his disability, or through a neglect to consider the participation of

qualified handicapped persons and to make reasonable provisions there-
for, an inequality of opportunity because of handicap has occurred.

While these attitudes and practices towards handicapped Canadians have lessened somewhat in recent years, they remain pervasive
nevertheless. They are not confined exclusively to legislators when they
make laws. They can play upon administrative officials when they
implement laws and formulate executive policies. They can influence
courts as they interpret statutes and fashion principles of common law.
When any of the three branches of government causes an inequality of
opportunity because of disability, Charter section 15 is triggered.

CORE CONTENT OF THE EQUALITY GUARANTEE

At its core, what does section 15 demand of governments and
promise to physically and mentally handicapped Canadians? Three root
principles can be derived from the seemingly complex wording of
Charter section 15(1), which are directed at all branches of government.[9]

First, a legislature, government agency or court may not single out
handicapped persons for disadvantageous treatment by denying or lim-
iting the participation of persons having a particular disability in a right,
privilege, benefit or other opportunity afforded to the non-handicapped
under a law or other government action. In this context, a governmental
decision to deny or limit the availability to a handicapped person of a
right, benefit or privilege is actionable under Charter section 15 where
the decision is expressly spelled out in black and white on the face of a
statute. An example of such a statute would be one which provides
expressly that no person with a physical handicap may be admitted to
the practice of law in a province. It is also actionable where the decision
was made by an administrative official in the exercise of discretionary
authority. An example of this occurs where a licensing official adopts
a policy never to grant a licence to operate a used car dealership to any
person who has ever been treated by a psychiatrist regardless of their
true qualifications.

The second message which section 15 directs at governments is a
command that governments not ignore, disregard, neglect or forget about
the handicapped when exercising legislative, administrative or judicial
authority to extend rights, benefits, privileges or opportunities to Cana-

---

9. It is accepted that the Charter's guarantees limit the authority of all three branches
    of government, including Parliament and the legislatures, the executive ministries,
    departments and agencies and the courts. See *Southam* v. *The Queen* (1983), 41
    O.R. (2d) 113; (1983), 146 D.L.R. (3d) 408; *R.* v. *Begley* (1982), 38 O.R. (2d)
    549. It is also accepted that the Charter places limits only on government action and
    does not purport to restrict private action. *Canadian Newspapers Co.* v. *The Queen*,
    [1984] 1 D.L.R. (4th) 183. See also Charter section 32(1).

dians. Governments should pay due attention to the needs, abilities and circumstances of qualified disabled persons in order to ensure that handicapped persons are afforded equality of opportunity with respect to participation in the governmental initiative. If under the law, program or other government activity, handicapped persons might be denied "equal benefit of the law", or the opportunity to fully participate to the extent of their individual capabilities, then government should show flexibility, by taking reasonable steps to ensure to the handicapped an opportunity to participate.

Where a law, program or other government initiative operates in a manner which denies or restricts the opportunity to participate in its fruits to qualified disabled persons, the denial of equal benefit is not justified simply because it is due to governmental neglect, ignorance or forgetfulness. Far from being mitigating circumstances, these factors tend to reflect the core of the problem of inequality confronting disabled Canadians and so demand redress.

The Charter's guarantee of equality to the handicapped does not operate on an assumption that handicapped persons are in all respects identical to non-handicapped persons. Neither does Charter section 15 incorporate a simplistic *per se* requirement that the handicapped must always be treated identically to the non-handicapped by government, and nothing more. Section 15 begins with the proclamation that all individuals are "equal". It does not purport to suggest the absurd proposition that all persons are identical regardless of disability. Identical treatment of a handicapped person and a non-handicapped person in instances where the disability places the two in different circumstances can at times itself amount to an obvious and gross example of discrimination.

The third obligation on governments, emerging from section 15, provides that in circumstances where governments have grounds for believing that a disability imposes an insurmountable barrier to full participation in a right, privilege, benefit or opportunity afforded under a law or other government initiative, it should afford to handicapped persons a reasonable opportunity to demonstrate that they *are* in fact capable of full participation, regardless of their disability. Legislators and other government officials should not too hastily jump to categorical conclusions about the capabilities of all persons having a particular disability. Neither legislation nor government policies should incorporate irrebuttable presumptions about the abilities of persons having a specified handicap through the adoption of flat rules about "all blind persons" or "all persons using a wheelchair", except in instances where there is sufficiently compelling evidence to support such an across-the-board determination about the entire group. It would be permissible, for example, for a legislature to enact an irrebuttable presumption in its Highway Traffic Act that totally blind persons are unqualified to drive through the adoption of a *per se* ban on the licensing of totally blind persons to drive.

This third obligation is traceable both to section 15 itself and to Charter section 7's directive that governments not deprive a person of life, liberty or security of the person except in accordance with the principles of fundamental justice. If the "right to liberty" guaranteed in section 7, includes *inter alia*, those rights and freedoms so fundamental to Canada's free and democratic society as to warrant express enumeration in the supreme law of the land (including section 15's right to freedom from governmental discrimination), then it would follow that any attempt by government to interfere with handicap equality rights must be preceded by compliance with the principles of fundamental justice. These principles would demand the employment of a fundamentally fair procedure for an accurate determination as to whether, in the particular circumstances, a person's disability incapacitates him from an effective undertaking of the right, benefit or privilege which he seeks. In this regard, both sections 7 and 15 share the common core purpose of ensuring that governments recognize and respect the individuality of citizens, and that governments not treat individuals in an arbitrary manner through a disregard of their individuality.

EXCEPTIONS TO THE REQUIREMENT OF EQUALITY

Exceptions to section 15's guarantee of equality are found in three Charter provisions, namely section 15(1), section 15(2) and section 1. As a general principle, the Charter's affirmative guarantees should be liberally construed,[10] while limitations on these guarantees should be interpreted narrowly.

The Impossibility or Incapacity Defence (Section 15(2))

Where a handicapped person has established that because of his disability he has been denied an opportunity to fully participate in or undertake a right, benefit or privilege afforded under a law or other government initiative, it is open to the Charter defendant to establish the defence of impossibility or incapacity.[11] The defendant must prove that the plaintiff's disability renders him wholly incapable of undertaking the essential burdens and responsibilities associated with the right, privilege, or benefit which has been denied or qualified. This factual matter must be established by clear and persuasive evidence and not by

---

10. *The Law Society of Upper Canada* v. *Skapinker* (1984), 53 N.R. 169, *per* Estey, J.
11. These terms are used interchangeably.

mere intuitive assumptions or impressionistic suppositions.[12] In circumstances where the same handicapping condition can have differing impacts on the functional capabilities of different persons, it will be necessary for the Charter defendant to present convincing evidence showing that the handicap irremediably incapacitates the particular plaintiff who is before the court.

In order to reach a fair and accurate assessment of the functional capacities of a handicapped individual, his abilities should be examined on the assumption that he has the use of reasonable accommodations (such as Braille material for a blind person, glasses for a person with low vision, or a hearing aid for a hearing-impaired individual). If a person's capacity to undertake a particular task were appraised without taking into account the availability of such adaptations, an inaccurate underestimation of his abilities would result, based on an unfounded and unfair disregard of the reality of adjustment to handicapping conditions afforded in a modern technological society. It would be absurd for example, to test a person's ability to function as a lawyer while demanding that he not wear eyeglasses during the test. Reasonable accommodations can include matters other than adaptive equipment. They can include reasonable alterations to the process by which a task is undertaken, or reasonable modifications of the activity setting.

The burden of proof in establishing the incapacity defence properly lies upon the defendant asserting it. This proposition derives from the traditional maxim that he who asserts must prove. It is also rooted in the fact that any other allocation of the burden of proof would be inconsistent with the core rationale of equality for handicapped persons. To place the burden of proof with respect to the impossibility defence on a handicapped individual would involve an *a priori* assumption that handicapped persons are incapable of undertaking government initiatives, absent contraindicating evidence. Such a presumption would amount to a constitutionalization of one of the very stereotypes about the handicapped which Charter section 15 is intended to eradicate, not perpetuate.

Why should the impossibility defence be situated in Charter section 15 and not in section 1? Certainly, the words of section 1 could theoretically allow for the assertion of an incapacity defence under that provision if such a defence were found to be unavailable under section 15. The principal reason for allocating the incapacity defence to section 15 and not to section 1 is that this approach allows the concept of

---

12. A comparable principle was established in a non-Charter context in *Ontario Human Rights Commission* v. *Etobicoke* [1982] 1 S.C.R. 202. See also, *Cameron* v. *Nel Gor Castle Nursing Home*, 5 C.H.R.R. D/2170.

equality to make more sense and allow its construction to be consistent with section 15's core purpose of furthering equality of opportunity.

At the heart of the concept of equality proposed in this article are twin propositions: first, handicapped persons should be treated like the non-handicapped by governments in circumstances where two groups are similarly situated; second, the handicapped should be treated differently than the non-handicapped by government in those circumstances where the handicapped are differently situated, and where such treatment is necessary to achieve equality of opportunity for the disabled with respect to rights, privileges and benefits afforded under law or other government initiatives. To implement this conception of equality, it is necessary in the context of section 15 analysis (instead of the section 1 context) to inquire into the functional capabilities of a handicapped Charter plaintiff, where such is in dispute, in order to ascertain when he is similarly situated to the non-handicapped, and when he is differently situated.

An example illustrates why Charter interpretation would take a more sensible course if the impossibility defence were located in section 15(1). Assume that a law, which provides that totally blind persons may not be given a driver's licence, was challenged as contravening section 15's ban on governmental discrimination against physically handicapped persons. If the impossibility defence were available under section 15, then this law would be upheld without resort to section 1, since it can easily be shown that at present, it is impossible for a totally blind person to drive a car. No *inequality* would be found in this law.

If, on the other hand, the incapacity defence were to be available under section 1, this law would be found to violate section 15 since it denies to blind persons a right or privilege available to all others. The law would subsequently be upheld under section 1 as a defensible limit on equality rights. However, it would be necessary for a court first, to reach the seemingly perverse finding that the fundamental right to equality for handicapped persons is contravened when a blind person is refused a driver's licence. Such an approach to the principle of equality is implicitly rooted in a supposition that section 15 simply requires governments to treat handicapped persons as if they were always identical to non-handicapped persons. Such a conception of equality is singularly inappropriate to the character of handicapped persons as a disadvantaged minority.

Affirmative Action Programs (Section 15(2))

The second exception to the equality guarantee arises from section 15(2)'s stipulation that equality rights are not infringed by any law or other governmental program or activity which has as its objective the amelioration of the conditions of physically or mentally handicapped

persons as a disadvantaged group in Canadian society.[13] This provision
was inserted in the Charter as a parallel to similar exemption provisions
found in statutory human rights codes in order to allow governments to
undertake programs and policies which extend added rights, privileges
or benefits to traditionally disadvantaged minorities such as handicapped persons, with the aim of helping them reach a position of equality in Canadian society.

The need for this exception to the equality rights guarantee can be
traced to the suggestion made by a badly divided U.S. Supreme Court
that some forms of affirmative action programs, designed to aid racial
minorities to attain equality of opportunity, contravene the racial majority's right to the equal protection of the laws, guaranteed by the 14th
Amendment to the U.S. Constitution.[14] The affirmative action exemption constitutes a narrow exception to the equality rights of majorities
tolerated in the short run, which is calculated to further section 15's
overall goal of securing for all equality of opportunity in the long run.
Section 15(1) and section 15(2) are thus both targetted at the same
objective.

If section 15(2) is construed in this principled and historically justified way, then it would follow that in order for a law or other government initiative to merit section 15(2) protection, it must be proven that
the impugned law or program has both an ameliorative purpose and an
ameliorative effect. It would not be sufficient for a Charter defendant
baldly to assert that the impugned law or program "was intended to
help the handicapped". If such a bald assertion of a benign governmental motive had been enough to save a law or program from constitutional attack, then virtually all laws or governmental programs could
readily be immunized from Charter challenge through either boiler plate
legislative provisions, or post hoc declarations of good governmental
intentions. The purposes which section 15(1) and section 15(2) were
jointly designed to achieve could be subverted thereby.

Laws or Programs Necessary to Achieve Compelling Governmental Objectives (Section 1)

Charter section 1, which authorizes the final exception to equality
rights, allows governments to impose reasonable limits on equality rights
if they are prescribed by law, and if they are demonstrably justified in

---

13. Section 15(2) provides:

    15(2) Subsection (1) does not preclude any law, program or activity that has as
    its object the amelioration of conditions of disadvantaged individuals or groups
    including those that are disadvantaged because of race, national or ethnic origin,
    colour, religion, sex, age or mental or physical disability.

14. See *University of California Regents* v. *Bakke*, 438 U.S. 265, 98 S.Ct. 2733
    (1978). See also, *Fullilove* v. *Klutznick*, 100 S.Ct. 2758 (1980).

a free and democratic society.[15] This exception is aimed at allowing governments to undertake activities which infringe constitutional rights enumerated in the Charter in those rare circumstances where the needs of society are so compelling and any other means for fulfilling those needs are so inadequate that the price of sacrificing fundamental rights is worth paying in a society which wishes to be free and democratic. A range of different approaches can be contemplated for the interpretation of section 1. One particular approach is offered in this article. Justification for its adoption in principle and precedent are examined elsewhere.[16]

By this approach one must first ascertain whether the Charter infringement is prescribed by law. If it is, one next determines whether the purpose for which it was undertaken is so important that its achievement would demonstrably justify a suppression of equality rights. Finally, one must consider whether the limit employs a reasonable means for achieving its compelling social objective.

To be "prescribed by law", a Charter contravention must be clearly and specifically authorized by a statute, regulation or common law rule[17] which is articulated with reasonable clarity, and which is not vague or totally discretionary.[18] For an impugned law or other government action to be "demonstrably justified in a free and democratic society", it must be targetted at the achievement of a specific policy objective whose attainment is so crucial to a free and democratic society that its achievement prevails over the protection of equality rights in such a society. To meet this burden, regard must be had to the comparative importance in a free and democratic society of the objectives of the impugned law

---

15. Section 1 provides:
   1. The Canadian Charter of Rights and Freedoms guarantees the rights and freedoms set out in it subject only to such reasonable limits prescribed by law as can be demonstrably justified in a free and democratic society.
16. See e.g. M.D. Lepofsky and J.E. Bickenbach, "Equality Rights and the Physical Disability", *supra* note 3. For a consideration of this article's approach to section 1 in the context of claims of freedom of expression, see M.D. Lepofsky, "Constitutional Right to Attend and Speak About Criminal Proceedings - An Emerging Liberty" (1983), 30 C.R. (3d) 87; M.D. Lepofsky, "Section 2(b) of the Charter and Media Coverage of Criminal Court Proceedings" (1983), 34 C.R. (3d) 63; M.D. Lepofsky, *Open Justice - The Constitutional Right to Attend and Speak About Criminal Proceedings*, Butterworths, Toronto, Canada, 1985, pp. 184-195.
17. *McCutcheon and Toronto* (1983), 147 D.L.R. (3d) 195; 41 O.R. (2d) 652; *R. v. Begley, supra*, note 9.
18. *Ontario Film and Video Appreciation Society* v. *Ontario Board of Censors* (1983), 147 D.L.R. (3d) 58 (S.C.O. Div. Ct.); affirmed sub nom. *Ontario Board of Censors* v. *Ontario Film and Video Appreciation Society* (1984), 5 D.L.R. (4th) 766 (Ont. C.A.).

or other government action, on the one hand, and the achievement of the goals of the equality guarantee on the other.

Assuming that the limit on equality rights is prescribed by law, and is aimed at a policy objective which is so compelling as to be demonstrably justified, it is then necessary to determine whether the means chosen by government to attain its ends are "reasonable". To be reasonable, the Charter contravention must be more than merely rational. The test for reasonableness is not whether the limit is subjectively acceptable to a reviewing court, nor whether it may be generally acceptable to a majority of Canadians, according to a reviewing court's perception of public opinion.

Rather, to be "reasonable", the limit on equality rights should meet two objective criteria: first, the limit must employ an effective means for securing its objectives; second, where there are more than one alternative means open to government to secure the compelling governmental objective, the means selected by government to attain its ends may incorporate a Charter violation only where it is the alternative which imposes the least restriction on constitutional rights necessary to the attainment of its goal. Where government has open to it two alternative sufficiently effective methods for securing a chosen objective, one which involves a restriction on equality rights and the other which does not, Charter section 1 obliges government to adopt the option which leaves Charter rights intact, since a Charter contravention can not be "reasonable" where it is wholly unnecessary.

SALIENT ISSUES IN HANDICAP EQUALITY CASES

Several issues will inevitably arise in handicap equality cases, and merit examination.

Does Section 15 Oblige Governments to Take Positive Measures vis-à-vis Handicapped Persons?

Does the Charter's equality guarantee require governments to undertake any actions which they did not hitherto undertake, or is it merely a restriction on proscribed governmental activities? It is an incorrect generalization to state that the Charter merely limits government powers, and that it does nothing more. It also places specific duties upon governments. By section 23, the Charter specifically obliges governments to provide educational opportunities to French and English linguistic minorities. Sections 16 to 20 oblige governments to make certain facilities accessible to the public in both official languages. Section 11(d) provides that a person charged with an offence must be provided with a fair trial before he can be convicted. Most important, the entirety of the Charter places an over-arching positive duty on governments not to violate the rights enumerated in it, while it provides specifically that an aggrieved individual can secure a remedy (which presumably can include an order requiring government to comply with the Charter) where this duty is breached.

In the equality rights context, the positive duty imposed on governments is a contingent one. It provides on one hand that in general, governments are not required to undertake any initiatives whatsoever. But that on the other hand, if a governmental initiative is undertaken, equality of opportunity for the handicapped with respect to participation in it must be afforded. For example, section 15 does not oblige governments to establish a general program of unemployment insurance payments. A government which determined that it would not provide anyone with social assistance as a result of their lack of success at finding a job does not thereby violate section 15. However, if that government does decide to establish an unemployment insurance scheme, Charter section 15 obliges the government to ensure that handicapped persons are afforded equality of opportunity with respect to participation in it.

The foregoing example further illustrates the point. If an unemployment insurance scheme were established and if handicapped persons were not afforded an equal opportunity to participate in it to the extent of their abilities, would a reviewing court be obliged to order the government to extend the benefits program to disabled persons in order to bring itself into compliance with section 15? In light of the fact that the duty imposed on governments by section 15 is a contingent one, it would follow that the more appropriate remedy would be for a court to offer the government the choice of either (a) bringing its conduct in line with section 15 by extending equality of opportunity to disabled persons *vis-à-vis* the unemployment insurance scheme, or (b) discontinuing the unemployment insurance scheme altogether. When confronted with this choice, a government may well prefer to choose the course of extending equality of opportunity to the handicapped rather than shutting down the program entirely as a practical matter. However, this choice is a legislative and not a judicial one.[19]

---

19. This discussion of positive duties on governments arising out of section 15 should not be confused with the question of the status of ''affirmative action programs'' under the Charter. An affirmative action program is a special genus of government activity aimed at improving the status of traditionally disadvantaged minorities. As discussed in section 4(b), the constitutionality of these programs is preserved

Does Section 1 Impose on Governments the Same Burden of Justification in Handicap Cases as in Cases of Discrimination Because of Race, Sex and Other Enumerated Grounds?

It might be suggested that a Charter defendant should shoulder a lesser burden of proof, or should be obliged to meet a lesser test to justify an interference with the equality rights of handicapped persons than it should when defending governmental discrimination because of race, religion or sex. In support of such a claim, it might be contended that discrimination based on handicap is less invidious than is racial, religious or sex discrimination, since a handicap can interfere with a person's ability, while one's sex, religion or race usually can not.

In support of such a view, attention might be focussed on the American experience under the equal protection clause of the 14th Amendment to the U.S. Constitution. American courts have deemed certain forms of discrimination, such as racial inequalities, as invidious, and have subjected them to strict scrutiny. Thus, it is very difficult for governments to justify racial discrimination. Most other kinds of discrimination, such as handicap-based inequalities, have often been characterized as non-invidious, and have been generally tolerated so long as they are minimally rational.[20] Recently, an intermediate level of judicial scrutiny has been afforded to sex discrimination in the U.S., revealing that in the opinion of U.S. courts, sex discrimination is not as bad as racial discrimination, but is worse than other kinds of inequality.[21]

Several principles demonstrate however why the Charter does not allow for handicap-based discrimination to be subject to any lesser measure of judicial scrutiny and vigilance than does inequality based on other grounds explicitly enumerated in Charter s. 15.[22] First, the plain words of sections 15 and 1 compel a uniform test with the same standard of justification to be demanded of governments with respect to all enumerated grounds of proscribed discrimination. In section 15, "mental or physical disability" occurs in the same sentence, and in the same context as do the other enumerated grounds. As well, section 1 states that "the rights and freedoms" set out in the Charter (which would include the equality rights of each of the classes enumerated in section 15) are subject only to those limitations which meet the threefold requirement of legal prescription, demonstrable justifiability and

---

by Charter section 15(2), although section 15(1) does not generally oblige governments to adopt them.

20. Gunther, *Constitutional Law*, (10th ed., 1979) 670.

21. *Craig* v. *Boren*, 429 U.S. 190, 97 S.Ct. 451 (1976).

22. The question whether a lesser standard of review under section 1 would apply in connection with discrimination based on grounds not specifically enumerated in section 15 is not considered here.

reasonableness. No separately worded limitation clause is set out for handicap cases.

Second, the Charter's legislative history reveals that the framers rejected the proposition that the equality right of handicapped persons be subject to a lesser standard of justification than would be required in the case of discrimination against certain other enumerated groups. During the proceedings prior to the Constitution's patriation of the Special Joint Committee of the Senate and the House of Commons on the Constitution of Canada, one group recommended that section 15 be amended so that in cases of discrimination on certain grounds such as handicap, a different and lesser standard of justification would apply than would be the case in instances of discrimination based on certain other grounds such as sex.[23] The Committee rejected this recommendation, retaining the uniform approach in section 15.

Fourth, the American experience does not afford much guidance in this connection. An adoption of the U.S. approach would require a complete disregard of the compelling difference between the wording of Charter section 15, which specifically enumerates the handicapped as one of the traditionally disadvantaged minorities who merit protection from discrimination "in particular", and the 14th Amendment's equal protection clause which does not. It also necessitates a disregard of the fact that the 14th Amendment was enacted a century ago in response to racial inequalities at the heart of the U.S. Civil War, and not in response to claims of handicapped persons to equality rights. In contrast, the Charter includes protection for the handicapped specifically because of Parliamentary recognition of the need for such protection.

Fifth, it would be wholly contrary to the core purpose of the Charter's equality guarantee to disabled persons for a court to disregard the uniform language of sections 15 and 1, and to superimpose upon the Charter the court's own views as to which kinds of discrimination are worse, those based on race, sex or disability. Section 15 was amended by Parliament prior to patriation to extend its protection to the handicapped precisely because it seemed unfair to afford to disabled persons any lesser measure of protection from governmental discrimination than was to be extended to the other disadvantaged minorities enumerated in the Charter. If a court were to rule that governments need meet a lesser standard of justification in handicap cases, it would thereby reverse in part this parliamentary decision.

Finally, it is of course true that one's handicapping condition is different from one's race or religion in that a handicap is more likely to impair one's abilities than is one's religion or race. However, this fact

---

23. Special Joint Committee on the Constitution of Canada (32nd Parliament, 1st Session) issue 10, pages 58-60 (9.12.80).

does not support the proposition that governments should be allowed to meet a lesser standard of justification under section 1 in handicap cases. It merely supports the proposition that an interpretive doctrine must be fashioned to accommodate this difference between the circumstances of race and religion cases on one hand, and handicap cases on the other. The impossibility or incapacity defence referred to in section 4(a) of this article will effectively sort out the differences between these grounds of discrimination. While this defence will be equally available to governments in all section 15 cases and not merely in handicap cases, as a practical matter, this defence will be successfully asserted by governments more frequently in disability cases than in cases involving race or sex.

Can the Cost of Providing Equality Rights to the Handicapped Form a Defence Under Section 1?

Whenever equality for handicapped persons is discussed, those required by law to provide equal opportunity often manifest great concern over the cost of accommodating the handicapped. At times, their concern over costs become exaggerated, reflecting a stereotyped attitude towards the handicapped, which involves a gross over-estimation of the help which they might need to function in society. It is revealing that in the case of equality of opportunity for other traditionally disadvantaged minorities, fears about the cost of providing equality are not as frequently emphasized, even though the provision of equality to these minorities may well have a hefty pricetag.

Practical experience with the accommodation of disabled persons reveals that once it has been positively decided to provide equality of opportunity, little or no costs need be incurred to accomplish this goal in most cases. Creativity and imagination often can go a long way. Thus, if a Charter defendant wished to rely upon cost as a section 1 defence to a handicap equality claim, it would have at a minimum to show with convincing evidence that very substantial cost consequences necessarily attend the honouring of handicap equality rights. A government could not merely hypothesize that the costs of equality are too high, absent proof that these costs are real, and absent proof that there is no way of extending equality of opportunity to the handicapped without incurring them. Proof of mere inconvenience for or administrative burden upon the government are not in themselves sufficient to excuse non-performance under section 1.

Assuming that a Charter defendant can show that the costs attending the provision of equality rights to handicapped persons with respect to a particular right, benefit or privilege afforded under law or other government action are necessarily very substantial, can a cost defence be asserted under section 1? Due regard for the legislative history of the handicap equality guarantee reveals that cost cannot form an absolute defence. When the Charter was proposed in the fall of 1980, its drafters deliberately excluded from it any protection for handicapped persons, in large part because the governments of the day felt that equality rights for the handicapped would cost too much. In response, advocates for the handicap amendment argued that the cost of equality was not great as was feared, that even if the cost were great, equality should not be denied simply because of its cost,[24] and that it was unfair to exclude equality rights for the handicapped by virtue of its pricetag, when other Charter rights were not being subjected to similar cost-based scrutiny.[25]

After considering the arguments advanced by the handicap amendment's proponents, the Federal Government reversed its stand, and the disabled were incorporated into section 15 by an all-party resolution. Construing section 15 in this context, a court ought not to allow a government to assert an absolute defence under section 1, since Parliament has already made a deliberate decision that the costs of providing equality at the hands of government to disabled Canadians is worth paying, and that an absolute cost defence to the extension of equality to the handicapped was unmeritorious. Moreover, concealed in an absolute cost defence is the arguably indefensible view that society is prepared to extend equality rights to the handicapped on paper, but that when it comes to putting these printed words into action, society would prefer to spend its money on other things.

Even though cost cannot form an absolute defence under section 1 to a denial of equal opportunity with respect to the participation in opportunities afforded under law or other government initiatives to qualified disabled persons, it may form a limited defence. If a government must expend a very substantial amount of money in order to bring itself into compliance with section 15, it is arguable that the expenditure can be spread over a reasonable number of years, where full compliance immediately would provably be fundamentally disruptive to the existing government program. In order to rely on this time-limited cost defence, a government defendant would have to present a reasonable and feasible plan for bringing itself into conformity within a reasonable time, a plan which does not involve either undue delay or a practical nullification of equalilty rights.

This approach would allow the costs to be spread out, and absorbed without undue disruption to government activities, and yet, it allows for the achievement of the goal of equality. It affords a reasonable balance between the achievement of the Charter's goals on one hand, and the reality that productive, meaningful change takes time. It is also

---

24. Special Joint Committee on the Constitution of Canada (32nd Parliament, 1st Session) issue 10, page 13, (21.11.80). Hon. Mr. Walter Dinsdale.
25. Special Joint Committee on the Constitution of Canada (32nd Parliament, 1st Session) issue 25, page 11 (12.12.80) Mr. David Lepofsky, CNIB.

faithful to Parliament's decision in adopting the handicap amendment that the costs of equality for the handicapped is worth paying.

How Does Section 15 Interact With Statutory Human Rights Codes?

Federal and provincial human rights statutes prohibit discrimination against certain groups in a specified range of economic activity such as employment, housing and the offering of goods, services or facilities to the public. This prohibition applies to the Crown as well as to the private sector. Certain human rights codes also provide that statutes and regulations, purporting to authorize conduct contrary to the ban on discrimination are inoperative to the extent of their conflict with the anti-discrimination law.[26] While every code bans discrimination on the grounds of physical disability, only some ban discrimination based on mental disability as well.[27]

Human rights codes interact with Charter section 15 in four ways. First, in the area of private discriminatory conduct with which government is not involved, human rights statutes provide a remedy while the Charter does not. A private employer, refusing to hire a fully qualified deaf person on the grounds of his deafness can be held liable under the applicable human rights code, while he has no obligations under the Charter.

Second, in those areas of government activity which are specifically regulated by human rights statutes, such as public employment and public housing, both the Charter and the Human Rights Codes may concurrently afford remedies to a victim of discrimination at the hands of government. If a qualified deaf person is refused a job by a government agency because of his deafness, he could obtain a remedy under both the Charter and the Human Rights Code. Here, the principle of judicial restraint in the constitutional area might favour the grant of a statutory remedy without resort to the Charter, if a sufficient remedy can be adequately and speedily secured in this manner.

Third, in those areas of governmental activities which are not addressed by human rights statutes the Charter will afford redress while human rights statutes will not. For example, assuming arguendo that a law authorizing the forced confinement of a mentally disordered person without the same procedural safeguards as attend the confinement of a non-handicapped person is challengeable under Charter section 15, redress against such a law would only be available under the Charter,

---

26. See e.g. *Ontario Human Rights Code*, S.O. 1981, c. 53 s. 46.
27. Compare the *Ontario Human Rights Code, supra*, note 26 which bans discrimination against both the physically and mentally handicapped with the *Saskatchewan Human Rights Code*, S.S. 1979, c. D-24 which bans only discrimination because of physical disability.

since statutory Human Rights Codes do not address discrimination in this area.

Fourth, some human rights statutes might conflict with the Charter's equality guarantee, and hence be unconstitutional to the extent of the inconsistency. A human rights statute which extends anti-discrimination protection to physically handicapped persons, but which does not extend the same protection to the mentally handicapped, might deny the handicapped the equal protection and equal benefit of the law. Such a statute denies to a mentally handicapped person legal redress against private parties who discriminate against him because of his disability, solely because his disability is mental and not physical.

CONCLUSION

The Charter's guarantee of equal rights and opportunities for handicapped persons with respect to government action stands in marked contrast to many other Charter guarantees. Constitutional rights to a fair criminal trial, reasonable bail and habeas corpus have a longstanding pre-Charter heritage in Canada, so that judges, legislators and other public officials have both familiarity and experience with the principles and practicalities underlying them. Yet, the Charter's command that handicapped persons are to be afforded equal opportunity to enjoy rights and participate in government programs to the extent of their individual abilities as a matter of constitutional right has no longstanding legal or political tradition or heritage in Canada.

In confronting the challenge of implementing this new constitutional right, Canadian courts, legislatures and administrative officials will be required to learn extensively about the status and circumstances of physically and mentally handicapped persons in Canadian society, and to make decisions affecting the rights and opportunities of this traditionally disadvantaged minority on the strength of this new familiarity.

To aid those responsible for implementing the Charter to learn about the present status of handicapped Canadians as a disadvantaged minority, and to work out the practical steps needed to bring government into conformity with the requirements of Charter section 15, judges and other public officials will have the benefit of two enormously helpful bodies of information. First, they can turn to the proceedings of the Special Joint Committee of the Senate and the House of Commons on the Constitution of Canada in 1980-81, which heard extensive evidence on the need for and implications of constitutional equality rights for the handicapped. Second, they can examine the comprehensive 1981 report of the Special Committee of the House of Commons on the Disabled and the Handicapped, entitled ''Obstacles''.[28] A product of public hear-

---

28. *Supra*, note 7.

ings held accross Canada in 1980, this all-party committee's report was before Parliament when the Charter was being debated, and its content played a significant role in the events leading up to the enactment of a Charter incorporating equality rights for handicapped persons. It may well be easier to implement the Charter's equality guarantee for the handicapped in a manner consonant with Parliament's intentions than it would be to implement some other rights found in the Charter, precisely because these sources of legislative history *vis-à-vis* the handicap guarantee are so readily available.

The task of implementing section 15's equality guarantee for disabled persons will be neither a simple nor a quick one. The Charter's framers were well-aware at the time of the handicap amendment's adoption that it would have a significant impact on the business of governments. By undertaking the challenge of the new era invoked by Charter section 15's handicap guarantee, attention should constantly be focussed on the purpose for guaranteeing equality rights to handicapped persons in a free and democratic society, namely, an achievement of equality of opportunity.

"Are you guilty?
— Of course I'm guilty. You
don't think (they) would
arrest an innocent man,
do you?"

"Êtes-vous coupable?
— Bien sûr, je suis
coupable! Vous ne
pensez pas (qu'ils)
arrêteraient un innocent,
n'est-ce pas?"

George Orwell, *1984*

THE RIGHT TO PROTECTION: FREEDOM FROM REHABILITATION

LE DROIT À LA PROTECTION: LE DROIT DE NE PAS SE SOUMETTRE À LA RÉHABILITATION

Rehabilitation: The Justice Model and the Victim

Edward L. Greenspan*

There seems to be a great fear in Canadians about crime. Whether this fear is as a result of an increase in crime reporting rates which creates the illusion of a rise in crime, massive publicity for certain spectacular crimes, or the manipulation of public opinion through the media by various interest groups, the fact remains that there appears to be a public clamour for increased protection and the most visible and effective way of providing protection is to increase the budget of law enforcement agents which has the effect of putting more officers on the street. These officers find more crime regardless of whether more crime actually occurs and we end up with a vicious circle that increases the fear in our people about crime. This fear has had a major impact on the concept of sentencing in criminal law.

Nearly all criminals and most people involved in the administration of justice used to believe that the solution to crime was to rehabilitate the offender and that humane and effective treatment would prove to be capable of changing the psychology and life of serious criminals. It was felt for the longest time that criminal behaviour was caused by factors beyond the control of the offender and by factors that could be remedied by treatment programs. This was the dominant theme of disparate treatment. As Judge Bazelon points out "This guiding faith of corrections has now been declared a false god."[1]

The popularity of the rehabilitation ideal has essentially collapsed. It has been condemned as an ineffective crime control strategy when evaluated in terms of recidivism. Additionally, it has been condemned as a policy that fostered unfairness. Under the guise of benevolence, rehabilitation supposedly encouraged disparate treatment of offenders and permitted an unjustifiable degree of state intervention into the lives of the offenders. But people now believe that rehabilitation must cease

---

* Lawyer, Toronto, Ontario.
1. David L. Bazelon, "Missed Opportunities in Sentencing Reform" 7 *Hofstra Law Review* 57 at 58.

to be the purpose of sentencing. Criminals are not to be sent to prison for "treatment". The alternative which has emerged is a very harsh, inflexible sentencing policy without compassion. Before I look briefly at the new, more popular sentencing policy, there are some comments I feel must be made about the rehabilitative model.

Even if rehabilitation has not succeeded as a goal of sentencing, there is nothing in my view to suggest that more uniform or even stiffer sentences will reduce crime, nor to conclude that the criminal mind is impervious to change so that there is nothing to do but punish criminals severely enough to modify the benefits of crime. Sending someone to a penitentiary where there is no rehabilitation mechanism is the first step in killing an offender's motivation to come to grips with himself and if you kill motivation you come close to killing the person.

Leaving apart a very small percentage that should never be restored to society and should never be released under any conditions, I have no doubt that it would make a difference if a prisoner felt he was being put in a system that would help him become a productive citizen, if he could be told that as he demonstrated his improvement he would be able to earn his way to freedom. Surely that would be better than having a prisoner wake up every day with total misery in his heart, because when you do that you will merely cycle and recycle inmates like dirty laundry. The prisoner will never be equipped to make it in the outside world. I would suggest that treatment has not really failed, it was never given a real chance due to woefully inadequate funding and has been abandoned as a matter of political and economic expediency.

The rehabilitative model has not failed us. We have failed it. Our collective respect for human dignity and worth should cause us to be very careful in our search for a different solution than the rehabilitative model. But, because it is the way of things, that some sentencing rationale must be dominant at a given time, the most popular justification for the criminal sanction now is incapacitation, retribution and deterrence.

This new emerging sentencing policy is designated by criminologists as the justice model. The features of the justice model are mandatory sentences for selected crimes, sentencing commissions and guidelines, reduction of parole and strict parole guidelines, and parole release decisions that are independent of participation in therapeutic programs.

But the real keystone of the justice model is retribution, just desserts, i.e., the idea that rational people deserve punishment if they violate the law. It is curious that in the abandonment of one model (rehabilitative model) of sentencing in favour of another model (justice model), that there has been a massive movement to expand the role of the victim in the formal criminal process with the aim of improving the position of the victim. The route taken, and in my view a misguided route, has been the elevation of the victim to the role of party in the criminal trial. Abraham Goldstein has become a proponent of this view: "I would bring the victim into the system by authorizing him to participate as a party... after conviction, on issues connected with restitution and sentencing, and before conviction, in hearings on dismissals, charge reductions, and guilty pleas."[2]

I can suggest a number of reasons for the emerging popularity of the victim:

(1)   Those "do gooders" in the system who have given up on the accused, when they came to the view the rehabilitative model had failed, had to transfer their sympathy to others and they discovered the victims. "Do gooders" need to be do gooders to someone - the new object of their affection - the victim.

(2)   Those former firm believers in the rehabilitative model who, seeing what they think is a failure of the rehabilitative model, are nevertheless horrified at the tough jail oriented justice model. Thus they have embraced the victim in an attempt to create an alternative for the judiciary to either avoid the apparently inevitable sentence of incarceration under the new, more popular justice model, or to minimize the period of incarceration by a victim oriented program.

(3)   Those who still believe in the rehabilitative model, but are pragmatic enough to make it appear that they are abandoning the model are emphasizing the role of victims in the short run in the hope that the rehabilitative model will re-emerge soon with less flaws than it presently has.

(4)   The perception of an increase in crime, particularly violent crime, coupled with a shift to a belief that the proper role of the state is of vindicating individual rights rather than intervening in the lives of individuals tends to lead to a focus on crime itself as a violation of individual rights rather than a collective failure to adequately deal with deviancy.

Whatever the reason for the rising popularity of the victim, the new suggested role for the victim is at odds with the tenets of democratic justice. The function of criminal law in theory and in fact is not the resolution of disputes between individuals. In the law of torts it is the individual suffering the delict who is conceived to be wronged. In criminal law, though the act may be and often is a recognizable tort, the important difference is the notion that it is the state or the collective community that has been injured.[3] The substantive criminal law is not

---

2. Abraham S. Goldstein, "Defining the Role of the Victim in Criminal Prosecution" (1982), 52 *Mississippi Law Journal* 515 at 557.

3. Henry Sumner Maine, *Ancient Law: Its Connection with the Early History of Society and its Relation to Modern Ideas*. London: John Murray 1884, Ch. X.

concerned with violations of the rights of individuals, but with violations of the collective interest in the security of the state, the safety of its citizens, or the shared morality of the community. A civil trial may be a fight between neighbours, each asserting his individual rights. In a criminal trial, the state, on behalf of the community, accuses an individual of violating some collective value in the society.

A democratic society is not however solely concerned with dealing with crime as an attack on the law-abiding majority. We also value freedom and dignity of the individual and this has implications for the way in which we treat the accused throughout the criminal process. It is the need to recognize these values which creates what may appear to be an imbalance, or as Ronald Dworkin thinks of it, an asymmetry. "The geometry of a criminal prosecution, which does not set opposing rights in a case against one another, differs from the standard civil case in which the rights thesis holds symmetrically."[4]

William H. Simon has written a thorough, brilliant and devastating attack on the "ideology of advocacy."[5] Yet, as he admits, his criticisms are weakest against advocacy in criminal law. I suggest that it is this peculiar configuration of the sides in criminal cases, the prosecution representing the collective values of our society set against the defence representing not only the individual defendant but the individualist values of our society, which gives him pause. And it is this which makes it critical that we never blur the distinction between civil and criminal law.

Both sets of values are of great importance and are seemingly irreconcilable in the criminal trial. When Goldstein observes that, "For centuries the criminal trial has been held out as the most distinctive embodiment of societal interest in the process of administering law,"[6] it is the societal interest in upholding the dignity of the individual to which he is referring and which is symbolized and seen to be aspired to (if not often given effect) in the rules of the criminal process. The ever increasing popularity of the victim and the new role for the victim obscures the role of the state, attempts to legitimate personal revenge as a justification for public punishment, and tends to overshadow the primary focus of the criminal trial - the legalized attempt by the state to deprive the individual of his liberty. There are other forums for redress of the violence done to victims. The legitimacy of the violence we do to an individual accused of a crime can only be determined in the crim-

---

4. Ronald Dworkin, *Taking Rights Seriously*. Cambridge, Mass. Harvard University Press, (1978), at p. 100.
5. William H. Simon, "The Ideology of Advocacy: Procedural Justice and Professional Ethics". (1978) *University of Wisconsin Law Review* 29.
6. Abraham S. Goldstein, "The State and the Accused: Balance of Advantage in Criminal Procedure", (1960) 69 *Yale Law Journal* 1149 at 1150.

inal trial. It is my view that changing the position of the victim in criminal justice through the formal criminal process does not alter the role of the state, but lends to the justice model the appearance of benignancy.

Exercising Discretion in Sentencing

William A. Craig*

The title of the topic is the "Right to Protection: Freedom from Rehabilitation". The title is a very imposing one, particularly the words "Freedom from Rehabilitation". When I saw this title I boggled somewhat, but after examining the matter I decided the concern of the people who were putting on the programme was to have a discussion on how the sentencing process could operate so as to develop a proper proportion between the interests of the public and the interests of the accused.

The fundamental principle of basic law has always been that society must impose sanctions for criminal conduct, not to exact vengeful retribution, but to maintain and protect the welfare of society. I am sure that everyone agrees that that ideal is as sound now as it was fifty years ago.

The courts generally have tried to accomplish that object in the sentencing process by looking at three main factors: punishment of the offender, deterrence not only to the offender but to others who might be inclined to commit a similar crime, and rehabilitation. In assessing these factors, the court has regard to many things: the nature of the crime, the circumstances, the degree of premeditation involved, the background of the offender, his or her age, the existence of criminal record, and other relevant considerations. My view is that notwithstanding the criticisms that are levelled at the sentencing process, a proper application of these factors is the most appropriate way to deal with sentencing and will produce the result which we seek to achieve, namely, a proper protection of the public's interest and at the same time a regard for the interests of the accused.

There are and have been and will continue to be many criticisms of the sentencing process. Some of it is well informed, other criticism is not. One of the criticisms is that when court talks about the punishment for an offender, court starts with the basic premise that punishment must involve a jail sentence. In other words, the court ignores or tends to ignore other forms of punishment. The thesis of these critics is

---

* Justice, British Columbia Court of Appeal.

that punishment in the form of a jail sentence should only be the last resort.

There is a very vocal group who maintain that it is nonsense to talk about deterrence. They say that if jail deters, why is our crime rate higher now than it has ever been? Like many people who have been involved with the criminal law, I have asked myself some of these questions and debated with myself on many occasions. But whenever I come to this proposition about deterrence, I always tell myself that I have represented many criminals in my time, but I have never met a man yet who ever wanted to go to jail. I am convinced in my own mind and have been for years that while a jail sentence does not act as a universal deterrent, it is a significant factor in controlling crime. I believe that if the courts did not make this clear there would be much more violence in our country than there is today. The courts generally, and I know it is certainly true in British Columbia, are taking a hard look at crimes involving violence and are stating that it must be severely dealt with to the extent that on the whole there should be a jail sentence even in the case of a first offender.

Another criticism is that it is nonsence to talk about jail acting as a rehabilitative factor. Again, I think a proper regard for the aspect of rehabilitation is an important factor in some sentences. How much weight in any particular case we assign to deterrence or such things as rehabilitation depends on many circumstances. In some cases our major if not only concern will be deterrence and punishment, and no concern can or should be given to rehabilitation. In other cases, deterrence or the principle of deterrence does not require a substantial jail sentence and the court may well consider that in the interest of rehabilitation a lesser jail sentence is appropriate. We know that with respect to many offenders, it is pointless to talk about rehabilitation but you cannot destroy hope in every case and that is an aspect which we must consider in rehabilitation considerations.

Another criticism is that there is too much disparity between sentences. These critics seem to think that there is some virtue in uniformity in all respects. There is not. We must look at each person as an individual. We can only give due regard to that aspect by considering carefully each case as it pertains to the individual before the court. Each case must be decided on its own facts, and this is particularly true in sentencing. These critics seem to think that a judge should not be involved in the sentencing process and that only a sentencing panel should be involved. Others who are concerned about the disparity in sentences suggest that there should be guidelines. Certain punishment should fit certain crimes.

Recently the United States has had a drastic overhaul of its federal criminal laws which I think Attorney General Smith referred to as ''the most far-reaching and substantial reform of the criminal justice system in our history''. This legislation abolishes parole. It also establishes a seven-person commission which includes three federal court judges who are to draft sentencing guidelines within eighteen months. In other words, for breaking and entering an offender might get four years and not less than two. It becomes very circumscribed. A judge who goes beyond those guidelines will be required to state in writing why he or she has strayed. I would not want to see us adopting such a scheme. It takes away that discretion which is so important to the due administration of justice.

The fundamental principle of criminal law will be best served by our continuing to follow the traditional methods we have employed heretofore in the sentencing process which involves a great deal of discretion for a trial judge. Obviously there is room for improvement. But the most important thing is that we follow or try to maintain this principle and that we try also to do it within the framework with which we are familiar.

Predicting Violence and Recidivism

Vivian M. Rakoff and Stephen J. Hucker*

Most practicing psychiatrists will do almost anything not to appear in court. There is a perception that they are entering into an arena where their best intentions will be perverted by the process, that they may become victims of narrowly-focused legal cross-examination, that they will appear foolish. These are, of course, risks that will confront any citizen in court, but for the psychiatrist, the discomfort and embarrassment exists not only at the individual level but also in a not always fully understood social role.

The two forms of rhetoric that we are concerned with here, namely medicine and the law, constantly overlap and occasionally come into conflict when a psychiatrist or other physician is called into the court.

To be brief, the legal system, in its purest essence, operates within the Kantian categorical imperative. Particular action and particular judgement should all, in the abstract, be generalizable in all circumstances. The function of the law, at its most extreme, is dispassionate. It relates to the public expression and legislation of a moral code. Law is tied to ethical conduct in society, and is concerned with the management of failure to behave in accordance with the ethical.

The principal categorical imperative of medicine is very different. It is concerned primarily with responsiveness to suffering in as general a way as possible, and specifically precludes concern with the ethical or moral components of behaviour. At its most extreme, the medical ethic demands from the physician that he treat the wounded soldiers of the enemy in exactly the same way as he would the wounded of his own side. Similarly, diseases, disabilities and conditions incurred through what society conventionally calls immoral or illegal behaviour, must also be treated by the physician in the most compassionate and effective way available at any given moment of history. Where the law operates

* Vivian M. Rakoff is Professor and Chairman, Department of Psychiatry, University of Toronto and Director and Psychiatrist-in-Chief, Clarke Institute of Psychiatry. Stephen J. Hucker is Associate Professor, Department of Psychiatry, University of Toronto and Chief of Forensic Service, Clarke Institute of Psychiatry.

on general principles, psychiatry is concerned with particular behaviour.

Where the law is judgemental, the psychiatrist is non-judgemental. Where the process of law is coercive and supported by the instruments of state, the psychiatrist is persuasive and can operate only with the support of empathic concern and the trust of relationship. Where the law is punitive, medicine is non-punitive. In law the examination of suffering is essentially public; in psychiatry the examination of suffering is essentially private.

Clearly, this almost diagramatic distinction and opposition between the two structures is infinitely modulated in practice. The legal system does not operate blindly and works within a social context of institutionalized mediation and altruism. It has long moved beyond primitive retribution to notions of rehabilitation and concern for individual rights. And medicine does not exist in pure essence, and the physician, in addition to his Hippocratic role within which he uses his Aesculapian authority, remains a citizen. He also is subject to the fashions, prejudices, judgements of his time that will colour the ideal mode he may believe he is subscribing to.

The concept of *mens rea* has long been a bridge between what we now call psychiatry and the law. The judgement of the clarity of mind, and therefore responsibility, moves between the forensic and the clinical and straddles the two structures. Similarly, the concern in our society with mitigation and charity presents the notion of mercy as central to the legal process. To be aphoristic, mercy is the essence of our dilemma. It is the central virtue of medicine but it is a modulating or secondary virtue in law. Ideally, the relationship between patient and doctor is one of absolute trust. The notion of confidentiality derives from and assures this trust. The behaviour of the patient and what he communicates to the doctor is encapsulated within the relationship of physician and patient in an almost discontinuous way from behaviour in the other arenas of society. Clinical communication is not expected to have consequences in the work-a-day world of the patient in terms of retribution, scandal, punishment, loss of status, or social role. The individual is, both metaphorically and actually, naked before medicine and the law. His vulnerability in medicine should never lead to pain, whereas his nakedness in law, where he is unprotected by status, connection, wealth, should not protect him from hurt if the law deems that he should be hurt.

I am, perhaps, labouring a distinction but it is so fundamental and potentially so bewildering that it cannot be stated too strongly. The contradictions or divergences that I have just referred to come most crucially into conflict when the psychiatrist is called upon to predict dangerousness, to ascribe rehabilitation, or has to inform society about difficult behaviour. Warning society is a fairly well established usage in Canada. Certain venereal diseases have to be reported; child abuse has to be reported. This kind of disruption of confidentiality relates to acts or conditions which exist. They are difficult enough for the physician to cope with, but the problems surrounding potential behaviour and future harm are much more complex.

Almost every psychiatrist has heard of the Tarasoff case.

The facts of the case were as follows: Prosenjit Poddar, a student at the University of California, became erotically obsessed with a young woman, Tatiana Tarasoff. He was being seen as an out-patient by a psychiatrist, Dr. Gold, who transferred his case to a clinical psychologist working in the out-patient department, Dr. Moore. Poddar described his erotic phantasies to Dr. Moore and articulated phantasies of harming or killing Tarasoff. A friend of Poddar's told the therapist that Poddar was planning to buy a gun. Dr. Moore consulted Dr. Gold and the two of them informed the university police about Poddar's dangerous phantasies. The campus police questioned Poddar about his plans at his apartment and Poddar denied any harmful intent towards Tarasoff. However, two months later, he stabbed her to death.

Poddar was charged with first-degree murder. Tarasoff's parents sued the campus police and the psychotherapists employed by the student health service. In essence, Tatiana's parents alleged that the police had been negligent in not detaining Poddar, and that the psychotherapists had been negligent in not warning Tatiana of Poddar's threats and in not confining Poddar. The university, in its defence, argued that there was no legal duty on the part of either the police or the psychotherapists to protect or to warn. The case was appealed to the California Supreme Court. This court ruled in 1974 that the psychotherapists had a duty to warn. Nevertheless, the court did not find the psychotherapists culpable for failing "to confine" Poddar.

Understandably, the court's ruling that potential victims had to be warned of their danger alarmed official psychiatric bodies. It was clearly a legal instruction to betray confidentiality. The consequences of this for the therapeutic relationship were of immediate concern, and some psychotherapists believed that patients would have to be warned about the duty to warn. The fundamental contract between patient and therapist that disclosure would not have consequence was violated. The American Psychiatric Association took the case to the California Supreme Court which changed the language from "the duty to warn" to "the duty to protect".

Other cases of a similar kind have been heard since then and, most recently, there was a great concern in Toronto when, on the occasion of the Pope's and Queen's visits, psychiatrists at Queen Street Mental Health Centre were invited to inform the police of patients who might have expressed dangerous thoughts directed at the Pope or the Royal

Family. The subsequent bomb explosion in Montreal's Central Station poignantly underlines the particular dilemma.

Instructions from various courts and cases have been, if not contradictory, at variance with one another making the task of the psychiatrist particularly difficult. For example, in the case of Thompson, the California Supreme Court ruled "that where the specific victim was not known and was therefore not foreseeable there was no duty to protect". However, in the case of Lepare a federal district court ruled that "there was a duty to protect even when the specific identities of the victims were unknown so long as the psychotherapists knew or reasonably should have known that the patient was dangerous".

Let me directly address the problem of dangerousness because it focuses our dilemmas today. It is now well established that psychiatrists are not particularly good at predicting dangerousness. In brief, a report by Professors Christopher Webster and Bernard Dickens of the Centre of Criminology of the University of Toronto stated: "An ad hoc interview study based on the opinions of some 40 Canadian forensic psychiatrists, forensic psychologists, and criminologists showed that these professionals themselves would claim little ability to predict the future violent behaviour of Dangerous Offenders of the kind dealt with under Part XXI of the Criminal Code of Canada... Predicting violence at the level of the individual prisoner is practically impossible without an almost inconceivable degree of control over key environmental, treatment, and biomedical variables.

It is imperative to recognize that the most any clinician or researcher can *ever* offer is a "probability estimate of future violent behaviour". And the pamphlet of the American Psychiatric Association on "Psychiatry in the Sentencing Process" specifically states that "... psychiatrists are severely limited in their capacity to predict violence or to describe mechanisms by which certain character disorders or psychotic syndromes influence moral judgments". If the court desires information on these it must be told as clearly as possible that the data here is either sparse or non-existent.

Psychiatrists have attempted to express their discomfort with being called upon to predict dangerous behaviour in the United States. Their modest disclaimers of expertise have not been accepted by all jurists and, in fact, the reluctance of the psychiatrists has been rejected by some on the basis that it would be "like trying to dis-invent the wheel". My colleagues, Drs. Christopher Webster and Stephen Hucker, Chief of Forensic Services at the Clarke Institute of Psychiatry, testified in a recent case in which "Dangerous Offenders" legislation was invoked. After they gave their opinions that psychiatrists' expertise, like everyone else's, on prediction of dangerousness is demonstrably weak, the judge, in giving his reasons for allowing the prosecution's application to go forward, stated that he acknowledged our abilities in this regard are limited but added "the law requires that we try" (to predict dangerousness).

The American Psychiatric Association pamphlet suggests that the most valid role for the psychiatrist in court is as "a friend of the court". In this way, a psychiatrist may give an opinion qualified and modified by the uncertainties of his knowledge without being forced into a position of pseudo-exactitude by either the defence or the prosecution. "In this role", states the American Psychiatric Association pamphlet, "the psychiatrist is employed by the court to conduct an evaluation... This mode of involvement is the mode traditionally favoured by most psychiatrists and does not place the psychiatrist in an adversary role... In such a position the psychiatrist must, of course, scrupulously seek to avoid bias simply because his or her report is unlikely to be challenged and may have an especially powerful influence."

Not only is the predictability of violence or dangerousness in doubt, but the casting of such prediction into a legal, as opposed to a clinical, expectation produces in the clinician what psychologists have called "cognitive dissonance" or discomfort. The contrary structures of the law and psychiatry, by their different labelling of particular acts, introduce an almost irresoluble dilemma. The law quite clearly wishes to prevent criminal recidivism and, for this purpose, will use either deterrents or rehabilitation. Repetition in general leads to closer scrutiny and surveillance of the patient and increased retribution and control.

In medicine, on the other hand, repetition of aberrant behaviour or clinically pathological behaviour is transformed into the notion of "the chronic sufferer". To perhaps dramatize the contrast, the long-term cardiac patient is recidivist. If schizophrenia were a crime (which it sometimes has been in history) the numerous relapses that are characteristic of the long-term schizophrenic "career" could be perceived as recidivist, and so on. The dilemma becomes clearer if one pursues the subject. If the behaviour of the accused is defined as a medical (psychiatrically) pathological entity, then the description of the behaviour has to be in terms of chronicity and relapse rather than recidivism. The physician, unlike the law, has no right to diminish charity because of repetition. The law behaves with diminution of charity in the face of repetition.

In addition, the psychiatrist must avoid applying psychological or pathological symptom labels to behaviour that is aberrant or violent in the absence of clinical data. The American Psychiatric Association's report addresses itself particularly to the confusion surrounding the now out-moded label of sociopathy. It states, "The psychiatrist who is not careful can mislead the judge or jury into believing that a person has a major mental disease simply on the basis of a description of prior criminal behaviour".

There is, unfortunately, only slight evidence that psychiatric treatment averts recidivism and increases rehabilitation except in sporadic and anecdotal reported cases. Imposing psychiatric treatment in the hope of diminishing recidivism extends the legal disruption of patient/physician relationship. The hope and the expectation that therapeutic intervention will avert antisocial behaviour is one of the best hopes of our society. Nevertheless, the coercion of a therapeutic relationship is extremely problematic. While it may sometimes succeed, in principle and in most instances, the relationship is fundamentally undermined by having been legislated rather than having been entered into on a voluntary basis. In the most formal terms, the medical relationship in an institutionally ordered setting represents a corruption and a contradiction of society's expectation of the patient/physician contract. Not only is the manifestly coerced relationship problematic, but in settings of prisons and institutions even those relationships that appear to be voluntary may suffer as one remove from the source the negative influences of coercion.

Yet, having said this, it would be an exercise in purest luxury, and denial of common sense and simple humanity, for psychiatrists to assume that they can totally deny participation in the legal process. The intellectual difficulties remain; the citizen must go to court and the citizen must speak the truth. The psychiatrist, when he is a psychiatrist, is not an ordinary citizen but the representative of an ancient and highly conventionalized social role that demands of him resistance to "speaking the truth" when speaking that truth may damage his patient. The Hippocratic injunction: *"Primum non nocere"* remains a fundamental medical premise. Yet the citizen and physician are blended in one body and the law frequently fails to respect the distinction between the two entities when the psychiatrist stands before a cross-examining counsel.

Yet, as the American Psychiatric Association report states, "It is ultimately for the courts to determine the utility of psychiatric participation... It would be arrogant of psychiatrists and neglectful of their social responsibilities for them to summarily reject what the courts view as a legitimate demand for service". But having said that, the report reminds us "to ask psychiatrists blindly to accept the mandate of the courts in all circumstances is to ask them to ignore their duty to exercise independent moral judgement concerning the legitimate use of their skill". I am certain that delegates to this meeting are more aware of the details of Bill S-33 now before the Senate than I am. In brief, the Bill protects the information gained by psychiatrists in particular cases unless the insanity defence is invoked. We welcome this Bill since it will legislate what is essentially an implicit rather than explicit social contract between patient and therapist.

The fact remains that the courts will continue to ask psychiatrists for their opinion, and psychiatrists, however much they may be distressed or wriggle, will have to appear in court and give of their best. To be blunt, I believe that the fundamental issues cannot be fully resolved. The two structures of medical charity and the law are in a constant and necessary conflict. The protection of these separate structures is part of the continuing work of a civilized society. The resolution cannot lie in exact and exquisite intellectual parcelling out of the territories since they will always overlap. The inter-penetration of the two social structures does not depend upon their fine articulation but upon the social climate.

Both psychiatry and the law will reflect the values current in the society at a given time. The interpretation of law is, after all, your business as judges and jurists. The fact that these interpretations vary from court to court, from time to time, reflect the human issues of value and social altruism that are involved. In the same way, psychiatrists who emanate from an ancient medical tradition must not deceive themselves that there is some pure form of practice and response which keeps them encapsulated from the social process.

Both medicine and the law are affected by emphasis on civil liberties. Common sense is not always a good guide to the erosion of civil liberties and yet the demand for a civil libertarian position in all instances may be contrary to important and over-arching concerns of altruism which need to be explicitly expressed. I am trying to state in, perhaps, a somewhat round-about fashion that both law and psychiatry derive from central ethical concerns of the society. The clinical traditions of the one or the verbal expressions of the other cannot escape the fundamental premise of our kind of socio-political organization that we should be concerned with the welfare of the individual. The notions of charity and mercy to which I referred earlier are the bond between our institutions. They are only in conflict if they are seen outside the context of an essentially (although often very fallible) humanely-directed social contract.

*"The aim… was… to
prevent men and women
from forming loyalties."*

*"Le but… était…
d'empêcher les hommes
et les femmes de se vouer
une fidélité."*

George Orwell, *1984*

THE RIGHTS OF FAMILIES:
FREEDOM FROM ASSOCIATION

LES DROITS DE LA FAMILLE:
LE DROIT DE NE PAS S'ASSOCIER

State Intervention in the Family

Bertha Wilson*

It is something of a truism, bordering on triteness, to say that the family is one of the fundamental institutions of our society. It is nowadays becoming equally truistic, however, to observe that as a social institution the family is rather less fundamental than it used to be. This certainly seems to be the case if we are to judge by what has happened to the divorce rate in this country in recent years. It increased nearly 5-fold between 1966 and 1978 and has continued to escalate since - until last year when it showed a modest decline. It is against that factual background that we must approach the subject of today's session which is the "balancing [of] the rights of children, spouses and the state, in issues of custody, divorce and economic distribution". Given the general theme of the conference, I take it that our concern is the character and extent of state intervention in the family and the possible justifications for such intervention in these areas of family law.

Before attempting to come to grips with this rather daunting topic, I should like to make the preliminary observation that I prefer to speak of the "interests" rather than the "rights" of the state. The recognition of rights grows, it seems to me, out of the respect and dignity which is properly to be accorded to individual human beings, whether by other human beings or by the state. It follows that while the state can have interests, in the sense that it can pursue collective goals which will have the effect of promoting the general well-being of society at large, and while it can take upon itself the role of protecting the rights of others, it cannot itself assert rights against individuals. I think it will help to clarify what follows if we bear this point in mind.

Returning then to our main theme, I should like to consider with you a number of different ways in which state intervention in the family can be characterized, and to discuss those possible characterizations with reference to current trends in Canadian family law. One obvious way of viewing state intervention in the family, but not one which I propose to consider at any length, is in terms of a contravention of

---

* Justice, Supreme Court of Canada.

whatever constitutional rights accrue to individuals by reason of their status as actual or potential members of a family. This is a well-developed area of constitutional law in the United States where the Supreme Court has recognized, mainly as an incident of substantive due process, a number of different family-related rights. These include the right to marry, the right to have children and the right to decide how those children will be raised and educated. More generally, the United States Supreme Court has recognized a constitutionally protected "private realm of family life which the state cannot enter" [*Moore* v. *City of East Cleveland* (1979), 431 U.S. 494 at 499 *per* Powell J., delivering a plurality opinion].

I do not intend to canvass the question whether state intervention in the family possesses a constitutional dimension in Canada, however, and this for two reasons. First, any constraints which the Canadian Constitution might place on such intervention are most likely to derive from the *Charter of Rights and Freedoms*. The Charter is a recent development in the political and legal life of our country and one whose implications for the development of the law have yet to be definitively mapped out. For reasons that I think are obvious, it would therefore be inappropriate for me to comment on — or speculate about — its implications for the development of family law.

There is another reason, however, for not entering on a discussion of the constitutional aspects of state intervention in the family and that is that the conference programme directs us towards a consideration of the rights of family members in the context of marriage breakdown when divorce, custody matters, and questions of economic distribution are at issue. These questions generally involve the rights of individuals as against one another rather than directly as against the state and for that reason their constitutional aspects are likely to be more attenuated than when the state intervenes in a family that is still intact or where it acts so as to prevent two persons from forming a family. Even in the United States, the constitutional ramifications of divorce, custody and economic distribution following marriage breakdown remain largely unexplored.

Having put aside the constitutional aspects of state intervention in the family, then, it might seem that there is not a great deal left to speak about. Divorce proceedings and the related issues of custody, maintenance and distribution of matrimonial property are, it might be said, essentially civil disputes between two private parties. Once it is granted that the state has no choice but to lay down ground-rules for the resolution of such disputes, and to provide a judiciary to preside over their adjudication, it might appear that the concept of state intervention has no greater application here than it would in any other area of civil law; that where there exist irreconcilable differences between private persons then the state has no choice but to take a hand in the matter and that the extent to which this is so is no greater in family law than it is in property, tort or contract.

Such a view would, I think, be overly simplistic. It ignores the fact that in setting the ground-rules for divorce the state has, traditionally, overridden even *consensual* agreements to end a marriage. Unlike other kinds of contract a marriage cannot be terminated by simple agreement between the parties. Until relatively recently a husband and wife had to go to court and one of the two had to prove that the other was at fault in some way, for example, through the infliction of cruelty or the commission of adultery. Since 1968 the grounds for the dissolution of marriage in this country have been expanded beyond those based solely on fault but it is still not possible to obtain a divorce without first going to court and being granted a judicial decree. This kind of regulation of the dissolution of marriage is clearly a form of state intervention in the family. While it might seem an odd way of putting the point, such regulation is, in effect, a restriction on freedom of contract and freedom of contract has traditionally been regarded as one of the characteristic features of a non-interventionist political philosophy.

The possible reasons why the state has not yet abandoned the regulation of the dissolution of marriage, even where both parties desire that the marriage should be brought to an end, are, in my opinion, twofold. First, there is the interest the state has in preserving the strength and autonomy of the family as one of the fundamental social institutions of the community. One important aspect of this interest is that the nuclear family has traditionally been the focus in our society for the raising and educating of children. Another important aspect is the fact that spouses, especially wives, often make personal and economic sacrifices in order to create a family. Before I come to discuss these features of family life, however, and the possibility that they might best be protected by means other than the strict regulation of divorce, I would like to spend a few moments speaking about the second interest that the state could have as a justification for placing legal restrictions on the dissolution of marriage. That interest is the protection and preservation of the central role that marriage and the family play, or at least have traditionally played, in the moral life of the community. The interest can best be characterized as the *moral* dimension of state intervention in the family.

In his well-known Maccabaean Lecture in Jurisprudence of 1959, "The Enforcement of Morals", Lord Devlin maintained that the preservation by the state of a society's social morality was necessary in order to protect the society itself from disintegration [now published as ch. 1 of *The Enforcement of Morals*, hereafter EM]. Any breach of a generally-accepted social morality was capable, he argued, of affecting society injuriously. It followed that just as a society was entitled to protect itself from any activity that was subversive or treasonous, so there was no theoretical limitation on a society's power to enforce its underlying social morality through legislation. This was said to be so even where the immoral activity did not directly injure any persons other than, perhaps, those who indulged in it.

Although in his original Maccabaean Lecture Lord Devlin limited his discussion to the enforcement of morals by means of the criminal law, he subsequently made clear that the implications of the thesis he was propounding extended much further. In a lecture delivered in 1963 he made explicit its application to laws regulating marriage and divorce, saying that "because the institution of marriage is fundamental to society the moral law regulates it very closely — much more closely than in most other subjects in which the moral and secular law both operate" [EM, ch. 4, p. 61]. While he acknowledged the religious origins and incidents of marriage, Lord Devlin insisted that the state's justification for its regulation derived, rather, from the general moral acceptance of the institution within the community. "Wherever the ideas come from", he said, "they now form the community's notion of good and evil... The law must be taken from present and not past morality and cannot be justified simply on the basis that it accords with Christian doctrine" [EM, p. 62].

It is thus evident that the morality with which Lord Devlin was concerned is *conventional* morality forged by social consensus; it is, in his words, "a fundamental *agreement* about good and evil" [EM, p. 10], consisting of principles "which every right-minded person would accept as valid" [EM, p. 15]. In his equally well-known reply to Lord Devlin, Professor H.L.A. Hart made the point that conventional moralities do change over time and often without any perceptible harm to the societies in which they are found. Lord Devlin in fact accepted that proposition as true although it is not immediately clear how he could reconcile it with other aspects of his theory. That is an interesting question, but not one which can be pursued here. The point which I wish to emphasize for our present purpose is simply this: even if one were to accept Lord Devlin's thesis that the state is entitled to enforce moral standards in areas that are generally regarded as being of only private concern, the fact remains that this requires those standards to be backed up by a presently-existing social consensus. If that consensus changes or disappears, then the state's justification for intervention disappears as well.

The relevance of this philosophical discussion to our present topic is, I hope, fairly clear. The fact of the matter is that in recent times there have been radical shifts in social attitudes towards marriage and divorce, especially over the past two decades. To some extent this is indicated by the drastic increase in the divorce rate to which I alluded earlier. Even apart from the statistics, however, it seems to me that there has been a perceptible shift in how marriage is viewed within our society. No longer is it generally regarded as a permanent partnership that can be expected to last for life. Nor is there nowadays much, if any, social stigma attached to being separated or divorced. In other words, the consensus of traditional social morality, that a marriage cannot be brought to an end except on the basis of a limited number of serious grounds, can no longer be plausibly said to exist.

The implications of this fact for the moral dimension of the state's regulation of divorce are, I think, evident. Even on the rather conservative view of the relationship between law and morality that is taken by Lord Devlin the state's justification for intervention on moral grounds has been very much diminished. Lord Devlin in fact recognized as much in his 1963 lecture although the social change of which we are speaking had not then progressed as far as it has today. He nonetheless acknowledged that marriage had become more of a secular than a religious institution and that it could no longer be regarded as an indissoluble partnership for life.

I should emphasize that I do not mean to imply that marriage has become an unimportant institution in our society, which is clearly far from the case, or that any justification which the state could have for regulating the dissolution of marriage has disappeared. I am saying only that social attitudes to the indissolubility of marriage have changed and that in consequence the strictly *moral* dimension of state regulation has been very much reduced in importance.

I have already alluded briefly to an alternative ground which could be put forward by the state to justify restrictions on at least some divorces and that is the preservation of the family as the traditional means by which children are raised. Once you have had children, it might be argued, the state's interest in their welfare is strong enough to justify the state's refusing to let you divorce. In fact, no such distinction is drawn for purposes of divorce between couples with children and those without, although the need to protect the interests of children is undoubtedly one of the factors underlying the general lack of support for completely unrestricted divorce. Apart from that, however, there seems to have been a pragmatic recognition that a refusal by the state to grant a decree of divorce cannot, in and of itself, preserve a child's home from breaking up since such a refusal cannot prevent the parents from going ahead and separating anyway.

The law must still make some provision for the children of a broken marriage, of course, and that is a matter to which I shall return. But as far as the dissolution of the marriage is concerned, changes in the law have, in this country and elsewhere in North America and Europe, reflected the changes in social attitudes which I have been discussing. In Canada, as I have already mentioned, the 1968 *Divorce Act* introduced certain no-fault grounds for divorce alongside the traditional fault grounds. The most important of these was a permanent marriage breakdown due to the spouses having lived separate and apart for three years, although in the case of someone who had deserted his or her spouse the period was extended to five years. Bill C-10, which was before the last Parliament, would have gone much further and abolished the fault grounds for divorce altogether. It would have introduced a single criterion for divorce - marriage breakdown - which could be established either by the husband or wife asserting that the marriage had broken down or by their living separate and apart for a minimum of one year. If this latter condition had not been fulfilled, however, no decree could be granted until at least a year had passed after the petition for divorce had been filed.

This trend in divorce legislation clearly represents a decrease in state intervention in the dissolution of marriage. It represents, that is, a legislative recognition, in line with prevailing social attitudes, that there should be greater individual autonomy in the decision to end a marriage. It might seem that individual autonomy is not in fact being fully respected in those cases where only *one* partner of the marriage desires a divorce, but it should be borne in mind that the state cannot force an unwilling husband or wife to live with his or her spouse. If social pressures can no longer keep couples from separating, then it is not for the state to take that role upon itself by requiring people to live together against their will. In fact, that being so, the easing of legal restrictions on divorce can be regarded as just a matter of form following substance. It is, essentially, a recognition by the state of what great numbers of people are doing in any event.

Nothing in this discussion is meant to suggest that the state is no longer entitled to act upon the *first* of the two possible reasons for state intervention in the family that I identified earlier. That reason, which was the state's interest in protecting the strength and autonomy of the family as one of the fundamental institutions of the community, may well explain why under Bill C-10 it still was not possible to end a marriage at will. More important, though, is the possibility that respect for the institution of the family and the obligations it entails can be fostered by means other than by making it difficult to obtain a divorce. This possibility is exemplified by the legislation that has now been enacted in every province requiring, under certain circumstances, an adjustment of property rights between separating spouses. The effect of this sort of legislation is that, at the same time as it is becoming easier to dissolve a broken-down marriage, spouses are being required to acknowledge the nature of the relationship they are dissolving by means of a redistribution of their respective property holdings.

The purpose of protecting the importance of the family as a social institution is often explicitly acknowledged in matrimonial property legislation. In the preamble to the Ontario *Family Law Reform Act* we read, for example, that "... it is desirable to encourage and strengthen the role of the family in society; and ... for that purpose it is necessary to recognize the equal position of spouses as individuals within the marriage and to recognize marriage as a form of partnership''. The preamble then goes on to say that ''... in support of such recognition it is necessary to provide in law for the orderly and equitable settlement of the affairs of the spouses upon the breakdown of the partnership...'' The various provincial statutes differ quite widely in detail, but the typical scheme involves the classification of a married couple's property into matrimonial and non-matrimonial assets with the former then being subject to a *prima facie* equal division between the spouses upon the occurrence of marriage breakdown. The purpose of this kind of regime is, clearly, to recognize that contributions by a spouse to a family's well-being, including its economic well-being, may not necessarily be reflected by the couple's separate property holdings. This is especially true where only one spouse works and contributes financially while the other's contributions take the form of home-making or the raising of children.

The judicial development of the constructive trust in such cases as *Rathwell* v. *Rathwell* and *Pettkus* v. *Becker* manifests a similar, albeit more limited, recognition of the fact that, where the financial contribution or labour of one spouse has enabled the other to acquire a particular asset, the court should assess the contributions of each and ''make a fair, equitable distribution having regard to [their] respective contributions'' [Dickson J. in *Rathwell*].

These legislative and judicial developments seem to me to protect two quite separate types of interests. The first, which is made explicit in the preamble to the Ontario *Family Law Reform Act* that I quoted a moment ago, is the direct interest of the state in ''encourag[ing] and strengthen[ing] the role of the family in society''. The second interest is that of those spouses, mostly wives, whose legal position would otherwise not have been as strong as that of the other spouse. This second interest is protected through the recognition of marriage as a partnership in which the partners, despite the fact that their respective contributions may be quite different in form, nonetheless have equal rights and obligations.

These two types of interest which I have identified, although distinct, are clearly related: the interest of the state in strengthening the role of the family in society is served by the recognition that spouses have equal rights whose protection may require the redistribution of property. Given that the state's interest is therefore only served indirectly, through an equitable readjustment of private rights, to what extent can we speak of matrimonial property schemes as constituting state intervention in the family? While there is no intervention here of the strong kind that I discussed in connection with divorce law, where even consensual arrangements may theoretically be overridden by the state, I think it is legitimate to speak of state intervention in the weaker sense of a deviation from general legal standards which would otherwise be applicable. The standards being departed from in matrimonial property regimes are, of course, the usual rules and principles of property law.

There are two points I should like to make with respect to this form of state intervention into matters concerning the family. The first is that it is by no means new. At common law a wife was regarded as nothing more than an extension of her husband's legal personality, which meant that any property which she held at the time of her marriage vested absolutely in her husband. When a woman married she became legally incapable of owning property in her own right, and that, I think you will agree, is a fairly radical departure from the usual principles of property law. While the married women's property Acts rectified this situation to the extent of making it possible for wives to hold separate property, it is only if we do not look beyond that relatively recent development in the law that it is possible to regard the new matrimonial property regimes as an unprecedented form of state interference with the private property rights of spouses.

The second point I want to make is that the extent of this intervention is in any event minimal. Generally speaking, the provincial matrimonial property regimes are not imposed automatically but only after one of the parties has obtained a court order. More important, however, is the fact that it is generally possible to opt out of these regimes by means of an agreement between the spouses [see e.g. McClean, "Matrimonial Property, Canadian Style" (1981), 31 *U.T.L.J.* 363 at pp. 368-71]. A number of provinces give the courts a discretion to override such an agreement in certain very limited circumstances, but for the most part spouses have the power to regulate by means of a previous consensual arrangement the disposition of their property in the event their marriage breaks down. The impact of the new matrimonial property schemes on individual autonomy is therefore limited and it is in that sense that the extent of state intervention which they represent can properly be characterized as minimal.

I should now like to turn to the third area of substantive family law with which we are concerned today, namely child custody. The basis for resolving custody disputes between two parents is the test of the best interests of the child, which has now been accorded legislative recognition in almost every province. Bill C-10 would, if it had been enacted, have incorporated the test into federal divorce law as well, although the courts have in fact been applying it for some time in divorce actions where custody is being sought as ancillary relief. The "best interests" doctrine represents another possible form of state intervention in the family. It is, again, not a new form of intervention since the doctrine has its roots in the centuries-old *parens patriae* jurisdiction of the courts of equity to protect the rights of anyone who is under a legal disability. It is true, however, that that jurisdiction was only rarely exercised against the near-absolute right of a father to custody of his child at common law until well into the nineteenth century when the interests of the child had already begun to receive statutory protection.

We are not here concerned with custody disputes between parents and non-parents where the interventionist aspect of the best interests doctrine is at its strongest. I might note in passing that in the United States there are constitutional limits on the ability of the state to remove the child from its parents. The focus of our present discussion is the determination of custody as between two natural parents, but even in those cases there is a definite interventionist flavour to the best interests test. In applying the test a court is free to make whatever order it sees fit, regardless of whether either party has requested that order, and in fact the court can, at least in theory, ignore even consensual custody arrangements that the parties might have settled upon themselves.

I think it would be a mistake, however, to regard this form of state intervention as analogous to that which is involved in state regulation of divorce, that is, as a power to interfere with even the consensual resolution of bilateral civil disputes and nothing more. While custody actions may appear *formally* similar to other forms of civil litigation, they are not truly bilateral in nature. This is because the interests and well-being of a *third* person, not technically a party to the action, lie at the heart of the case. That person is, of course, the child whose custody is at issue. The form of state intervention that is represented by the best interests doctrine can therefore best be characterized, it seems to me, as the protection of the interests of an individual who is not yet capable of looking after his or her own interests. That is, I think, a much more easily justified form of intervention than interference with the resolution of private disputes between legally competent persons.

Furthermore, while the potential for state intervention in family matters on the basis of the best interests may, in theory, be very great, in practice it is likely to be quite limited. It is only very rarely that a court will ignore a consensual custody arrangement that the parties have agreed upon themselves. Indeed, there seems to be a strong trend towards de-emphasizing the adversarial nature of family litigation through the encouragement of the consensual settlement of marital disputes, especially where the custody of children is involved. This trend is evidenced, for instance, by the introduction in a number of provinces of court-connected conciliation services which have proved to be both popular and successful. The trend is also related to the growing recognition among behavioural scientists that it is almost always in a child's best interests to maintain meaningful contact with *both* parents after separation or divorce, something which becomes most feasible when custody matters are determined on a consensual basis. A related aspect of this general trend is the growing popularity of joint custody, an arrangement which maintains the same family relationships that a child has always known although in an altered form.

This trend towards settling custody issues by consensus enhances the autonomy of the family and of its members by reducing the need for state intervention to a minimum. This is in marked contrast to the famous — or infamous — proposal of Goldstein, Freud and Solnit in their book *Beyond the Best Interests of the Child* that custody should generally be granted to one parent only together with the authority to determine whether the other parent should or should not have access. Far from reducing the role of the state in custody matters, as the authors suggest would be the case, I tend to think that the drastic nature of this solution would, if implemented, increase by a significant degree the number of cases that have to be decided by the state through litigation.

What can we say of the rights of the child itself in custody cases? Younger children, at least, clearly do not have a right to live with the parent of their choice, but if the custody issue reaches court they do have a right to have their wishes heard and taken into account. The courts have, in effect, been giving consideration to children's wishes in these matters for some time and a number of provinces have recently given legislative recognition to that principle. There has also been a related trend, manifested in both legislative and judicial developments, towards appointing independent counsel for a child where the protection of his or her interests requires it. It is thus fair to say, I think, that while the *substantive* rights of children in custody matters are relatively limited, they do have certain *procedural* rights which are gaining increased recognition and respect.

In summarizing the rather extensive ground I have covered in this survey of family rights and the interest of the state in family matters, I should note first the trend towards the recognition of equal rights between spouses and also the increasing protection that is being accorded to children's procedural rights in custody matters. As to whether state intervention in the family is increasing or decreasing in the areas of family law I have been discussing, that is a difficult question to answer. State intervention can, as we have seen, take a number of different forms, not all of which are susceptible to easy comparison. I think it is nonetheless safe to say that state intervention is decreasing at least in the sense that the overall trend seems to be towards a greater recognition of individual autonomy in family matters. This can be seen in the introduction of less restrictive grounds of divorce as well as in the trend towards the consensual settlement of custody issues. It can also be seen in the relatively minimal inroads into private property rights that have been made by the recent developments in matrimonial property law.

At the same time, however, the state has not abandoned its interest in protecting and fostering respect for the family as one of the fundamental social institutions of the community although its means of doing so have moved away from forcing couples to remain married. Instead, it now encourages them to end their marriage in a way that is consonant with the responsibilities and obligations that forming a family entails. This is clearly the thrust of the new matrimonial property regimes, for example, and we see it as well in the trend favouring the raising of children by both their parents even after the parents have separated or divorced.

This balance between respect for individual autonomy on the one hand and protecting the institution of the family on the other is a difficult one to find and maintain. This is especially so when social attitudes to marriage and the family continue to be in a state of flux. We almost certainly have yet to strike the proper balance. The most we can say at present, I think, is that at least we are taking a fresh look at the issues and asking the right questions.

Children's and Family Rights and the Role of the State in Custody and Child Protection Matters

Kate A. Hughes and H.T.G. Andrews*

The field of children's family and state rights in the context of custody and child protection law has offered shelter to many misconceptions that, for a variety of reasons, have been perpetuated even in the legal literature. Some, such as the myth that children have, until recently, had no rights under the law, seem to be rhetorical fabrications intended to elicit sympathy and to motivate legislators to effect some desired reform. Others, such as the often repeated assurance that the family as a unit is supposed to enjoy certain basic rights under the law, tend to be romantic and cherished inventions perhaps born out of a desire to believe that society's most basic institutions are firmly entrenched in the law of the land. Any examination of the rights of the child, the family and the state would profit by a prudent weeding out of these fictions and it is one of the objectives of this paper to attempt to present a more balanced view.

MYTHS AND RIGHTS

A discussion of rights in family law is particularly problematic not only because of the misconceptions that abound, but also because of the large role that the state plays in family law. Disputes such as custody or child protection cannot be solved simply at the level of parent's or children's rights, for the state has a duty to protect the best interests of children and of society as a whole. The crucial question is how active a role the state should take in family matters. The ancient Greek philosopher Plato advocated that the state apprehend children at birth and

---

* Kate A. Hughes, Lawyer, Toronto, Ontario. H.T.G. Andrews, Chief Judge of the Provincial Court (Family Division) of Ontario.

raise them collectively without any contact with their parents.[1] Such a suggestion seems abhorrent in contemporary western society, yet equally appalling is the prospect of the state's never intervening, particularly in the case of child abuse.

Children's Rights

There are many voices calling for more rights for children. The United Nations proclaimed in its *Declaration of the Rights of Children* that all children are entitled to a "happy childhood".[2] The British Columbia Royal Commission on Family and Children's Law[3] proposed that an extensive bill of children's rights be introduced into legislation and similar legislation for Ontario has recently been advanced in a private members bill.[4] Legal commentators, as well, have advocated introducing rights for children into law, including the "legal right... [t]o receive parental love and affection".[5] Occasionally even judges lapse into this zeal. In his reasons for judgment, one Ontario county court judge wrote:[6]

> Every child should have certain basic rights such as: the right to be wanted, the right to be healthy, the right to live in a healthy environment... and the right to continuous loving care.

Noble and well meaning as these sentiments are, they would hardly constitute meaningful legal rights even if enshrined in legislation. No one would dispute that ideally children should be "happy" and "loved" and that socially children should have such "basic rights". These interests, however, would at best constitute symbolic legal rights, if only because there is no mechanism to enforce them in law. In order to have a non-trivial right, one must have a means to vindicate it.[7] Children, or their legal representatives, cannot compel their parents or anyone else to love or to want them, nor is there any recognized action to sue for

---

1. *The Republic of Plato*, trans. by Francis Cornford, Oxford, Oxford University Press, 1977.
2. Preamble to G.A. Res. 1386, 14 U.N. GAOR Supp. (No. 16) at 19, U.N. Doc. A/4249 (1959).
3. British Columbia Royal Commission on Family and Children's Law, *Fifth Report — Part III: Children's Rights*, Victoria, Queen's Printer, 1975.
4. Bill 86 (*Children's Rights Act, 1984*) of the 4th Session of the 32nd Legislative Assembly of Ontario, First Reading on May 29, 1984.
5. Henry H. Foster, Jr. and Doris J. Freed, "A Bill of Rights for Children" (1972), 6 *Fam. L.Q.* 343 at 347.
6. *Re Brown* (1975), 9 O.R. (2d) 185 at 192, 21 R.F.L. 315 at 323 (Ont. Co. Ct.), *per* Stortini, Co. Ct. J.
7. *Ashby* v. *White* (1703), 2 Ld. Raym 938 at 953, Holt K.B. 524, 6 Mod. Rep. 45, 1 Salk 19, 3 Salk 17, 92 E.R. 126, quoted with approval by Mr. Justice Rand of the Supreme Court of Canada in *Orchard* v. *Tunney*, [1957] S.C.R. 436 at 447, 8 D.L.R. (2d) 273 at 283.

damages.[8] Apart from symbolic value, there is no point in introducing unenforceable rights.

Often, the motivation in this call for "basic rights" for children has been the belief that children have little or no rights and that they have the status of chattels or, at best, "quasi-persons" at law.[9] It is not clear what basic rights reformers perceive children as lacking that adults enjoy. At common law, a child has always had the same rights as an adult. Unlike a married woman whose identity at law was taken over by that of her husband, children have always possessed a separate legal status from their parents.[10] Although the parents are natural custodians of the child and exercise certain powers, such as that of reasonable disciple, the child has remained a separate legal person, entitled to the benefits of property and to the enforcement of his or her choses in action, and was liable in turn as an individual for his or her own crimes and torts.[11] In order to sue or to be sued or to be subject to criminal prosecution, one must be a "person" rather than a chattel. By this measure, clearly, children are persons, not property nor even "quasi-persons".

Although children have independent rights, they have rarely been independent agents. Despite their theoretical legal equality with adults, the disability of infancy means that the child must almost always act through a guardian to enforce his or her rights. The practical problem has been how to get the guardian (parents being natural guardians) to act on behalf of the child. This is particularly troublesome when the guardian's personal or property interests do not coincide with those of the child. In property matters, the English Court of Chancery developed very rigid rules of equity to avoid such conflicts; for example, the guardian could not purchase the property of his infant ward, nor could he sell his property to the ward. Unfortunately the Court of Chancery did not traditionally concern itself in the non-proprietary matters of the

---

8. *Schrenk* v. *Schrenk* (1981), 32 O.R. (2d) 122 (Ont. H.C.).

9. In "The Child's Right to "Life, Liberty and the Pursuit of Happiness"" (1981), 34 *Rutgers L. Rev.* 154, author Maureen S. Binetti argued that children are in effect "quasi-persons" who are treated as the private property of their parents.

10. William L. Prosser, *The Handbook of the Law of Torts*, 3d ed., St. Paul, Minn., West Publishing, 1964, at 885.

11. *Id.* See also *Deziel* v. *Deziel*, [1953] 1 D.L.R. 651 (Ont. H.C.); *Fidelity Casualty Co.* v. *Marchand*, [1924] S.C.R. 86, [1924] 4 D.L.R. 157, reversing 35 B.R. 5, 29 Rev. Leg. N.S. 5, [1923] 4 D.L.R. 913. Section 66 of Ontario's *Family Law Reform Act*, R.S.O. 1980, c. 152, states in fact:
    No person shall be disentitled from bringing an action or other proceeding against another for the reason only that they stand in the relationship of parent and child.
    This provision apparently codifies the rule at common law for Ontario. See James C. Macdonald, Karen M. Weiler, Ruth E. Mesbur and Craig Perkins, *Law and Practice under the Family Law Reform Act*, Toronto, Carswell, 1980, vol. 1.

child.[12] Only in the twentieth century have the courts of equity expanded the state's *parens patriae* role beyond property matters, with Canada leading the United Kingdom in this advance.[13] In the meantime, the legislative arm of the state worked to fill this void by enacting new laws that created new institutions, new programmes, and new causes of action, such as child support laws, child protection statutes and adoption legislation.

Such intervention by the state is occasioned not because children lack the status of persons with full rights but because it is a means to ensure that children are able to put into practice the theoretical equality that they have with adults. These actions are analogous to interventions by the state on behalf of other politically weak minorities, such as affirmative action programmes or protective measures. These measures are not a means of raising minorities to the status of persons but are an attempt to overcome their political and social inequality. In the same way, child protection legislation is not enacted because children lack rights but because the state realizes that without intervention, children are unlikely to assert their rights on their own behalf. It is for this reason that procedural rights, such as the right to legal counselling and representation, are so important and "bills of rights" for children that emphasize these procedural rights are not subject to the earlier criticism of being unenforceable.[14]

"Family" Rights

Contrary to much rhetoric, there is no such thing in Canada as "family rights". The family is not a unit that has any standing in law as do other associations of human beings (such as corporations, labour unions and partnerships). The family is merely a collection of individuals but it is the individuals who possess rights in contemporary western society. If there is some perceived wrong inflicted, the family cannot sue in the courts, although its members may join as co-plaintiffs to launch an action. But just as a family cannot sue, so it cannot be sued or prosecuted, although again, its individual members may be singled out as defendants.

In more ancient societies, man was legally perceived not as an individual but as a member of a group — his *gens*, house, clan or

---

12. *Wellesley* v. *Duke of Beaufort* (1827), 2 Russ. 1 at 21, 5 L.J.O.S. 85 at 93, 38 E.R. 236 at 243 (Ch.), *per* Lord Chancellor Eldon.
13. Olive M. Stone, "Jurisdictions over the Custody and Upbringing of Children in Canada and Their Judicial Exercise" (1979), 2 *Can. J. Fam. L.* 365 at 386.
14. For example, the proposed *Children's Act, 1976*, drafted by the British Columbia Royal Commission on Family and Children's Law, *supra*, fn. 3, stressed procedural rights and included a provision warning that failure to respect these procedural rights would render any judicial or administrative act or decision voidable. For further discussion, see Jeffrey S. Leon, "Canadian Children: Prospects for Legal Rights and Representation" (1979), 2 *Fam. L. Rev.* 16 at 23.

family.[15] It was this unit that was held accountable for any wrong committed by one of its members and conversely it would seek amends for any wrong committed against one of its members. Roman civil law revolutionised much of this traditional thinking, for although the *familia* was still a powerful institution in Roman society, the concepts of rights and responsibilities became attached to separate individuals rather than to the *familia*. Personal accountability permeated the law of Rome and of those societies that have adopted its culture. Indeed, from one point of view, the history of contemporary western society is a movement shaped by the gradual dissolution of familial and feudal dependencies and the growth of individual obligation in its place.[16] For better or for worse, the family has now ceased totally to be the pursuer of legal rights or the target of legal responsibilities in society and the individual generally remains as the entity who is accountable at law for his or her own acts.

The law does, however, do much to encourage the formation and maintenance of families. Tax laws, for example, offer incentives or preferential treatment in the case of families, but the benefits accrue to and can be claimed only by the *individual taxpayer* and not the family unit. For economic and social reasons, the family is a highly valued institution and there is accordingly much legal support and regulation of its existence. Occasionally, however, courts will refer to "family privacy", "family autonomy" and "family integrity" and some legal commentators have argued that these are constitutionally protected values.[17] In a recent highly publicized Ontario case concerning abortion, a High Court Justice suggested that at least some elements of family life are "rights":[18]

> The decision to marry and to have children might be granted constitutional protection because they are considered deeply rooted in our traditions, and fundamental to our way of life.

Nevertheless, if such rights are acknowledged even to exist, they will be recognized as *individual* rights to family relations rather than as family rights. For instance, the right of an individual to belong to a family, as in the right to participate in any group, is basically an exer-

---

15. Henry Sumner Maine, *Ancient Law - Its Connection with the Early History of Society and Its Relation to Modern Ideas*, London, John Murray, 1861, at 183.

16. *Ibid.*

17. For a discussion of the "three distinct, yet interrelated constitutional principles" of parental authority, family privacy and family institutional integrity, see Robert Keiter, "Privacy, Children and Their Parents - Reflections on and beyond the Supreme Court's Approach" (1982), 66 *Mich. L. Rev.* 459.

18. *The Queen* v. *Morgentaler, Smoling and Scott* (1984), 47 O.R. (2d) 353 at 407, 12 D.L.R. (4th) 502 at 556, 11 C.R.R. 116 at 172, 14 C.C.C. (2d) 258 at 312, 41 C.R. (3d) 193 at 253 (Ont. H.C.); appeal quashed at (1984), 48 O.R. (2d) 519, 6 O.A.C. 53, 16 C.C.C. (2d) 1, 41 C.R. (3d) 262 (Ont. C.A.).

cise of a person's freedom of association. Only an individual, not the whole group, can enforce this right. Even family integrity, as described by one of proponents for the recognition of such a right, is an individual right not a group right. Joseph Goldstein, American law professor, psychoanalyst and co-author of the controversial book *Beyond the Best Interests of the Child*, defined family integrity as a bundle of rights held by individual family members:[19]

> The child's need for safety within the confines of the family must be met by the law through its recognition of family privacy as the barrier to state intrusion upon parental autonomy in child rearing. These rights — parental autonomy, a child entitlement to autonomous parents, and privacy — are essential ingredients in "family integrity".

Although the family was mentioned in the preamble of the *Canadian Bill of Rights*,[20] there is no reference to the family in the *Canadian Charter of Rights and Freedoms*.[21] This is not surprising given that the *Charter*, like the common law, purports to protect the rights of individuals. The most likely charter section applicable to individual rights within the family would be section 7 which guarantees the:

> ... right to life, liberty and security of the person and the right not to be deprived thereof except in accordance with the principles of fundamental justice.

Section 7 would apply to family law if given a broader interpretation than merely freedom from physical constraint. Canadian authorities appear to be divided on the issue, with some advocating that "liberty" includes the right to privacy,[22] others arguing it should be given a narrow interpretation to cover only physical freedom.[23]

In the United States, it is settled that "liberty" is to be given a broad meaning. The United States Supreme Court has repeatedly recognized as fundamental the right of individual autonomy in activities relating to marriage, procreation, contraception, abortion, family relationships and the rearing and educating of children.[24] That court has also rejected the argument that the absence of explicit protection for the family leads to the conclusion that liberty does not encompass freedom

---

19. Joseph Goldstein, "In Whose Best Interest?", in *Family Law - Dimensions of Justice*, ed. by Rosalie S. Abella and Claire L'Heureux-Dubé, Toronto, Butterworths, 1983, at 122.
20. R.S.C. 1970, App. III.
21. Part I of Schedule B to the *Canada Act, 1982*, c. 11 (Imp.).
22. See, for instance, Morris Manning, *Rights, Freedoms and the Courts - A Practical Analysis of the Constitution Act, 1982*, Toronto, Emond-Montgomery, 1983, at 243.
23. Patrice Garant, "Fundamental Freedoms and Natural Justice", in *The Canadian Charter of Rights and Freedoms*, ed. by Walter S. Tarnopolsky and Gerald A. Beaudoin, Toronto, Carswell, 1982, at 270.
24. For a full discussion of the American case law, see the unauthored "The Constitution and the Family" (1980), 93 *Harv. L. Rev.* 1156.

in the area of family life.[25] Protection has been specifically given to rights relating to child custody[26] and child protection.[27] After surveying a long line of cases, one Supreme Court justice concluded that the jurisprudence had created "a private realm of family life which the state cannot enter".[28]

In Canada, section 7 of the Charter has been invoked in a number of non-criminal cases[29] and, although it may be premature to make any sweeping pronouncements, it appears to date that the words "life, liberty and security of the person" enjoy a broad interpretation. This section is particularly relevant to child protection hearings where the potential infringement of liberty can be acute. At the time of this writing, however, only two judgments have come to the authors' attention that have discussed section 7 in a child protection context. The section was held to apply in a recent Manitoba judgment where a thirteen-year-old boy successfully argued that he was entitled to be present and have counsel at a protection hearing because his liberty and security would be affected.[30] In a Saskatchewan case, a mother tried to convince the court that the province's child protection laws violated section 7 of the Charter on the grounds that they allowed waiver of notice of hearing and delays between apprehension and trial and denied the children the right to be heard[31]. Although she was unsuccessful, one commentator concluded that "implicit" in the reasons for judgment is an acceptance of the applicability of section 7 to protection proceedings.[32]

Of themselves, these two cases are scarcely grounds for optimism, but there is a body of pre-charter case law in which Canadian courts have been very receptive to arguments favouring the "rights" that members enjoy in the integrity and privacy of their family unit.[33] It

---

25. *Roe* v. *Wade* (1973), 410 U.S. 113, 93 S. Ct. 705, 35 L. Ed. 2d 147.

26. *Stanley* v. *State of Illinois* (1972), 405 U.S. 645, 92 S. Ct. 1208, 31 L. Ed. 2d 551.

27. *Santosky* v. *Kramer* (1982), 455 U.S. 745, 102 S. Ct. 1388, 71 L. Ed. 2d 599.

28. *Moore* v. *City of East Cleveland* (1977), 431 U.S. 494, 97 S. Ct. 1932, 52 L. Ed. 2d 531.

29. For instance, see *Re Poirier and Simmonds*, unreported decision of Mahoney, J., July 6, 1983, Fed. Ct. Tr. Div., digested at 21 A.C.W.S. (2d) 230. But see also *Operation Dismantle* v. *Government of Canada et al.*, [1983] 1 F.C. 745, 49 N.R. 363, 3 D.L.R. (4th) 193 (Fed. App. Div.), where Pratte J., interpreted the provision as protecting against arbitrary arrest and detention.

30. *Re Martin, Children's Aid Society of Winnipeg* v. *Martin et al.* (1983), 25 Man. R. (2d) 143, [1984] 2 W.W.R. 742, 37 R.F.L. (2d) 113, 7 C.R.R. 246 (Man. C.A.), reversed on another ground at 26 Man. R. (2d) 312, [1984] 4 W.W.R. 478, 39 R.F.L. (2d) 239 (Man. C.A.).

31. *Shingoose* v. *Minister of Social Services* (1983), 26 Sask. R. 235, 149 D.L.R. (3d) 400 (Sask. Q.B.).

32. Nicholas Bala, "Family Law and the Charter of Rights", an unpublished paper delivered at the annual conference of the Ontario Family Court Judges' Association at Brampton on May 23, 1984, at 8 (manuscript).

33. *Id.*, at 7-8 (manuscript).

seems unlikely that an entrenched charter of rights should interfere with this tradition.

Parental Rights

Pre-charter case law is particularly protective of parental rights. The law has for some time allowed a number of rights to parents including the right to custody and access, the right to determine religion and education, the right to consent to medical treatment and to marriage as well as the right to discipline and the right to the child's services.[34] Despite legislation that clearly limits these rights, Canadian courts have continued to protect the rights of parents, notably natural parents, who are threatened with the loss of custody of their children to third parties. In a frequently cited case, the Supreme Court of Canada held that is was:[35]

> ... settled law that the natural parents of an infant have a right to its custody which apart from statute, they can lose only by abandoning the child or so misconducting themselves that in the opinion of the Court, it would be improper that the child should be allowed to remain with them, and that effect must be given to their wishes unless "very serious and important reasons" require that, having regard to the child's welfare, they must be disregarded.

The principle seems almost to suggest that parental rights can override the best interests of the child and it is for this reason that courts in Ontario and Nova Scotia at least have chosen to modify it (or to deviate from it) by focusing only on the welfare of the child.[36] To date, how-

---

34. For a full discussion of parental rights, see John M. Eekelaar, "What Are Parental Rights?" (1973), 89 *L.Q. Rev.* 210.

35. *Hepton* v. *Maat*, [1957] S.C.R. 606, 10 D.L.R. (2d) 1.

36. *Re Moores and Feldstein*, [1973] 3 O.R. 921, 38 D.L.R. (3d) 54, 12 R.F.L. 273 (Ont. C.A.); *C.A.C.* v. *F.D.R. and S.J.R.* (1977), 21 N.S.R. (2d) 631, 28 A.P.R. 631 (N.S. App. Div.). For an examination of Ontario's and Nova Scotia's attempts to "re-interpret" the principle in *Hepton* v. *Matt*, see *Funk et al.* v. *Funk et al.*, [1978] 6 W.W.R. 136 at 148-151, 6 R.F.L. (2d) 151 at 165-168, 2 *Fam. L. Rev.* 121 at 126-127 (Man. Prov. J. Ct., Fam. Div.), *per* Carr, Prov. J. Paradoxically, in dispensing with a parent's consent to an adoption, the Ontario courts have, at the very highest level, adhered to the more conservative test of parental rights, namely that those rights are not to be removed unless, by a course of serious misconduct or by abandonment of the child, the parent has disentitled himself or herself from having further relations with the child. See *Re Desmarais; Desmarais* v. *Casper*, [1969] 1 O.R. 700, 3 D.L.R. (3d) 617 (Ont. C.A.); *Re Liffiton and Campbell*, [1972] 2 O.R. 592, 26 D.L.R. (3d) 360, 7 R.F.L. 353 (Ont. C.A.); *Children's Aid Society of Metropolitan Toronto* v. *Lyttle*, [1973] S.C.R. 568, 34 D.L.R. (3d) 127, 10 R.F.L. 133; *Smith* v. *Harvey* (1974), 19 R.F.L. 373 (Ont. C.A.); *Re Gardiner* (1977), 4 R.F.L. (2d) 394 (Ont. C.A.); *Vincent and Vincent* v. *Wall* (1980), 19 R.F.L. (2d) 342 (Ont. Prov. Ct., Fam. Div.); *S.K. and T.K.* v. *M.S.D.* (1980), 21 R.F.L. (2d) 271 at 281 (Ont. U.F.C.). See *contra*, *W.A.* v. *W.B.* (1981), 34 O.R. (2d) 716, 23 R.F.L. (2d) 371 (Ont. Prov. Ct., Fam. Div.); and *W. and W.* v. *C.* (1981), 35 O.R. (2d) 730 (Ont. Prov. Ct., Fam. Div.), where the "best interests" test was held to prevail.

ever, the Supreme Court of Canada has consistently upheld the parental rights doctrine.[37]

To speak of parental "rights" is actually misleading for, as one jurist commented, the expression is actually a "loose way of describing the conglomeration of rights, powers, liberties and (perhaps) duties that a parent has with respect to his children".[38] For instance, the parental "right" to discipline is more accurately described as a privilege or a limited form of civil and criminal immunity in that the law will not interfere where parents inflict reasonable punishment but that it will if the discipline amounts to abuse or where the child is found to be in need of protection. If discipline was truly a right, the state and all others would be under a duty to permit the act or to forbear from preventing it.[39] Moreover, as the English Court of Appeal observed, a parental right is:[40]

> ... a dwindling right which the courts will hesitate to enforce against the wishes of the child the older he is. It starts with a right of control and ends with little more than [a right of] advice.

Modern legislation tends to emphasize parental duties to the child and downplays parental rights.[41] For instance, child labour legislation and compulsory school laws have taken considerable control of children out of the hands of parents on matters covered by these statutes, while at the same time legislation has refined a duty not recognized at common law, namely the financial support of infant children by their parents[42] and the support of destitute parents by their adult children. There is speculation that further "moral" duties of parents will ripen into legal duties, such as the duty to support children beyond the age of majority or the duty to provide surgery, dental work or recreational facilities for children.[43] Parental rights have also been limited in case law recently by courts' transforming traditional parental rights into children's rights. Increasingly, for instance, courts are interpreting access

---

37. *Hepton* v. *Maat, supra,* fn. 35; *Re Duffell; Martin* v. *Duffell,* [1950] S.C.R. 737, [1950] 4 D.L.R. 1, affirming [1950] O.R. 35, [1950] 1 D.L.R. 694 (Ont. C.A.); *McNeilly* v. *Agar,* [1958] S.C.R. 52, 11 D.L.R. (2d) 721, affirming [1957] O.R. 359, 8 D.L.R. (2d) 353 (Ont. C.A.); *Children's Aid Society of Ottawa* v. *Mugford,* [1970] S.C.R. 261, [1970] 1 O.R. at 610n, 9 D.L.R. (3d) at 123n, affirming [1970] 1 O.R. 601, 9 D.L.R. (3d) 113 (Ont. C.A.).
38. Eekelaar, *supra,* fn. 34, at 212.
39. Wesley N. Hohfeld, "Some Fundamental Legal Conceptions as Applied in Judicial Reasoning" (1977), 26 *Yale L.J.* 710. For an application of Hohfeld's concepts to family law, see Eekelaar, *supra* fn. 34, and Bernard M. Dickens, "The Modern Function and Limits of Parental Rights" (1981), 97 *L.Q. Rev.* 462.
40. *Hewer* v. *Bryant,* [1970] 1 Q.B. 357 at 369, [1969] 3 All E.R. 578 at 582, [1969] 3 W.L.R. 425 at 430, *per* Denning, M.R.
41. Dickens, *supra,* fn. 39, at 463.
42. Walder G.W. White, "A Comparison of Some Parental and Guardian Rights" (1980), 3 *Can. J. Fam. L.* 219 at 231-232.
43. *Id.,* at 248.

as the right of the child, rather than of the parent.[44] While there is no deliberate or concerted attack on parents by some imagined alliance between the state and advocates of children's rights, it is clear that traditional parental rights are nevertheless under scrutiny and in some cases are either being regulated or severely eroded.

THE ROLE OF THE STATE IN THE FAMILY

The family has been romanticized as the private world separate from the public sphere of politics and state intervention. In particular, because of the rapid growth of industrialization, nineteenth-century western society glorified the family as a "haven in the heartless world"[45] and as the "repository for values being destroyed in the market-place".[46] It is, however, a myth that the family is self-regulating for the state is and has always been intimately connected with the family. There is no *a priori* concept of the family that would allow it to exist separate from its culture. The very structure that the family takes is influenced greatly by the state. A blatent example in western society is the criminalization of bigamy and incest, which has a profound effect on the composition of the family. A more subtle example is the financial and tax incentives or disincentives on marriage, children and divorce as well as the effect of private and government pensions in the decay of the extended family and the promotion of the nuclear family. The state also regulates the break-up of the family and can have a major impact by favouring a certain configuration among the survivors of the defunct family by, for instance, the way in which it encourages its courts to issue and enforce custody orders in respect of separated parents.

The motives most frequently ascribed for state regulation of the family are its interest in strengthening the institution of the family, its "police power" in regulating morals, and its responsibility as *parens patriae* to protect the interests of the child.[47] This creates a precarious role for the state as there are no absolutes regarding the best interests of the child, no social consensus on morals and, as briefly mentioned, the institution of the family is constantly in flux. While the state cannot but have an influence on the family, it can play a greater or lesser role in regulating it.

---

44. See, for example, *M.* v. *M. (Child: Access)*, [1973] 2 All E.R. 81 at 85 (Fam. Div.), *per* Wrangham, J.; *Currie* v. *Currie* (1975), 18 R.F.L. 47 at 51-52 (Alta. Tr. Div.), *per* D.C. McDonald, J.; *Knudslien* v. *Rivard* (1978), 5 R.F.L. (2d) 264 at 269 (Alta. Fam. Ct.), *per* White, Asst. Ch. Prov. J.
45. For a full discussion, see Christopher Lasch, *Haven in a Heartless World - The Family Besieged*, New York, Basic Book, 1977.
46. Frances E. Olsen, "The Family and the Market - A Study of Ideology and Legal Reform" (1983), 96 *Harv. L. Rev.* 1497 at 1504.
47. "The Constitution and the Family", *supra* fn. 24 at 1160.

Spokesmen from many quarters, including the Ontario Ministry of Community and Social Services, have recommended a policy of minimum state interference in the family.[48] Bertrand Russell, the English philosopher and social reformer, pointed out at the beginning of this century that the state had a vested interest in minimizing intervention in the family. A later writer condensed Russell's views as follows:[49]

> The state's desire to maintain family autonomy is not only a matter of tradition, but also reflects a recognition of the family's effectiveness as a social institution; no one has devised a better system for overseeing the rearing of most children. Autonomous families not only provide the conditions needed for the physical and emotional development of individual children, but also make possible a religious and cultural diversity that might disappear if the state extensively regulated or controlled child rearing.

Many legal commentators continue to agree that the state cannot replace the "flesh and blood" role of the family,[50] nor can it enforce emotional support or human loving.[51] American courts have expressed a desire to encourage a pluralistic society through minimum state interference in the family and have upheld the rights of parents to raise their children according to the traditions of different cultures.[52]

While there are good reasons for keeping state involvement in the family to a minimum, a policy of total non-intervention would prove wholly unacceptable. State intervention in the form of compulsory school attendance and the abolition of industrial child labour has done much to advance society, although it significantly infringes on parental "rights". Furthermore, the state has an obligation to set standards to protect the lives of its individual members. Even the staunchest advocate of family autonomy and of parental rights would surely accept as a sound reason for state involvement in the family the justification advanced by John Stuart Mill for infringement of individual freedom. In his essay, "On Liberty", the British philosopher and publicist John Stuart Mill stated:[53]

> The only purpose for which power can be rightfully exercised over any member of a civilised community, against his will, is to prevent harm to others.

---

48. Ontario, Ministry of Community and Social Services, *The Children's Act - A Consultation Paper*, Toronto, Queen's Printer, 1982.
49. Judith Areen, "Intervention between Parent and Child - A Reappraisal of the State's Role in Child Neglect and Abuse Cases" (1975), 63 *Georgetown L.J.* 887 at 893.
50. Goldstein, *supra*, fn. 19, at 123.
51. White, *supra*, fn. 42 at 243.
52. See, for example, *State of Wisconsin* v. *Yoder* (1972), 406 U.S. 205, 92 S. Ct. 1526, 32 L. Ed. 2d 15. See also *In re J.P.* (1982), 648 P. 2d 1364 (Utah S.C.).
53. John Stuart Mill, *On Liberty*, Markham, Penguin, 1974, at 68.

On this basis, at the least, the state is warranted to step into the "private" realm of the household whenever there are grounds to suspect domestic violence and more particularly child neglect and abuse.

The State's Role in Child Protection

Child protection law is the most blatant example of state intervention in the family. All provinces and territories have legislation permitting the state, either through a government department or through a private child protection society, to apprehend a child apparently "in need of protection". Such legislation is relatively recent and in fact, legislation protecting animals preceded child protection laws in many jurisdictions. So powerless was the state in the face of parental autonomy that, in 1874, for example, the New York Society for the Prevention of Cruelty to Animals had to resort to arguing that an eight-year-old girl was a member of the animal kingdom in order to protect her from abusive step-parents.[54] Immediately following this case, the Society for the Prevention of Cruelty to Children was created in New York and the next year the Toronto Children's Aid Society was formed.[55] Legislation in Canada in a form that would be recognized as a modern child protection law was first enacted in Ontario in 1893,[56] although the roots of such statutes can be traced to the much earlier English Poor Laws.[57]

The potential for state interference through the use of child protection legislation is enormous. If a court concludes that a child is indeed in need of protection, parental rights are not only infringed upon, but may even be terminated. Although the criteria for the apprehension of children suspected to be in need of protection have been limited in recent years,[58] the statutory definition of a child "in need of protec-

---

54. Bernard M. Dickens, "Representing the Child in the Courts", in *The Child and the Courts*, ed. by Ian F.G. Baxter and Mary A. Eberts, Toronto, Carswell, 1978, at 295, footnote 7. See also Areen, *supra*, fn. 49, at 903.

55. For a more detailed history of children's aid societies in Ontario, see Richard B. Splane, *Social Welfare in Ontario, 1791-1893*, Toronto, University of Toronto Press, 1965; and Andrew Jones and Leonard Rutman, *In the Children's Aid - J.J. Kelso and Child Welfare in Ontario*, Toronto, University of Toronto Press, 1981.

56. *An Act for the Prevention of Cruelty to, and better Protection of Children*, S.O. 1893, c. 45.

57. White, *supra*, fn. 42, at 229.

58. For instance, since 1977, it is no longer a ground for state intervention that a child is found loitering, selling newspapers, found in a disorderly house, engaged in street trades, conducting himself immorally or in possession of obscene materials. Amendments to the various provincial child protection laws have eliminated these criteria.

tion'' still remains broad and open-ended in all provinces and territories.[59]

The legislation is frequently biased in favour of the state in other ways, such as the right to appeal or to seek modification (''review'') of an existing court order. In Prince Edward Island, for example, there was until 1977 no right to appeal any decision of a child protection court.[60] Even at the present time, parents on the island province apparently lack any right to ask a court to review its order, although the Director of Child Welfare may request a review at any time.[61] In Quebec, by contrast, any child fourteen years of age or more, the parents of the child, the *comité de la protection de la jeunesse* or a director of youth protection may apply to the court for a review of a decision or order whenever new facts arise.[62]

Provisions allowing for delays in child protection proceedings also severely threaten the rights of children and parents. In Alberta, for

---

59. All provinces and territories have a slightly different definition of ''child in need of protection'', but all include such vague provisions as ''a child [who] is not being properly cared for'', a child who is subjected to emotional or mental neglect, lack of affection and the like, or a child who is ''beyond the control of his parents''. The various definitions can be found in:

Alberta: clause 6(*e*) of the *Child Welfare Act*, R.S.A. 1980, c. C-8; to be superseded by subsections 1(2) and 1(3) of the *Child Welfare Act*, 1984, c. C-8.1 [not yet in force];

British Columbia: section 1 of the *Family and Child Service Act*, 1980, c. 11;

Manitoba: section 16 of *The Child Welfare Act*, 1974, c. 30, as amended by 1979, c. 22; 1980, c. 41; 1982, c. 45; 1983, c. 55;

New Brunswick: subsection 31(1) of the *Child and Family Services and Family Relations Act*, 1980, c. C-2.1;

Newfoundland: paragraph 2(*a*.1) of *The Child Welfare Act, 1972*, No. 37, as amended by 1977, c. 69; 1981, c. 54; 1984, c. 2;

Northwest Territories: subsection 14(1) of the *Child Welfare Ordinance*, R.O.N.W.T. 1974, c. C-3;

Nova Scotia: clause 2(*m*) of the *Children's Services Act*, 1976, c. 8;

Ontario: clause 19(1)(b) of the *Child Welfare Act*, R.S.O. 1980, c. 66; to be superseded by subsection 37(2) of the *Child and Family Services Act*, 1984, c. 55 [not yet in force];

Prince Edward Island: subsection 1(2) of the *Family and Child Services Act*, 1981, c. 12, as amended by 1983, c. 14;

Quebec: sections 38 and 38.1 of the *Youth Protection Act*, R.S.Q. 1977, c. P-34.1, as amended by 1981, c. 2 and 1984, c. 4;

Saskatchewan: section 15 of *Family Services Act*, R.S.S. 1978, c. F-7;

Yukon Territory: section 118 of the *Children's Act*, 1984, c. 2.

60. See section 15.1 of the *Children's Protection Act*, R.S.P.E.I. 1974, c. C-7, as added by 1977, c. 4; now repealed and superseded by the *Family and Child Services Act, supra*, fn. 59.

61. Under section 35 of the *Family and Child Services Act* of Prince Edward Island, *supra*, fn. 59, the Director of Child Welfare can review a supervision order; under section 36, he can review a temporary wardship order; and under section 37, a permanent wardship order.

62. See section 95 of Quebec's *Youth Protection Act, supra*, fn. 59.

instance, a hearing does not have to be held until twenty days after the child is apprehended and at that time, the judge can adjourn the hearing for as long as he or she wishes.[63] Understandably, the child protection authorities need time to marshall their evidence against the parents or guardians of the child, but such infringements on liberty would hardly be allowed under the criminal law and it may become increasingly more difficult to defend such delays in child protection law, especially when it is recalled that minimizing delays in any litigation involving a child actually advances the child's best interests. Should the case be withdrawn during this interval and the child be returned to the parents, the legislation offers no mechanism for holding the child protection authorities accountable or for any sort of hearing into this abortive invasion into the life of the family that might have lasted for many weeks.[64]

Child protection laws were frequently accused of having a disparate impact on certain classes and cultures.[65] Even in the late eighteenth century, the English jurist Sir William Blackstone recognized that the introduction of the Poor Laws established a dual standard for state scrutiny of the family. They allowed the children of the poor to be "taken out of the hands of their parents" while the rich were "left at their own option, whether they will breed up their children to be ornaments or disgraces to their families".[66] Canadian legal commentators have also noted that it is the poor household in Canada, the "welfare" family that often becomes the subject of public inspection and public discipline.[67] Canadian judges are now sensitive to this issue and have stressed that a court must never assess the child care of a poor family by the unrealistic standards of the middle class[68] or of another culture.[69]

To its credit, the state has assumed a supplementary role in the field of child protection that goes beyond its *parens patriae* functions.

---

63. Subsection 10(1) of Alberta's *Child Welfare Act, supra*, fn. 59. Subsection 19(2) of the 1984 superseding Act would reduce the interval between apprehension and the first hearing to ten days, while subsection 24(1) would limit an adjournment to no more than forty days or for such longer period as to which the parties agree.
64. David A. Cruikshank, "Court Avoidance in Child Neglect Cases", in *The Child and the Courts, supra*, fn. 54, at 207.
65. Areen, *supra*, fn. 49, at 888-889, remarked that:
    Perhaps the most prevalent characteristic of families charged with neglect is poverty; this raises the troubling possibility that class or cultural bias plays a significant role in decisions to label children neglected or abused.
    Canadian professor of law, medicine and criminology, Bernard M. Dickens, noted Areen's comments with approval in his paper, "Legal Responses to Child Abuse in Canada" (1978), 1 *Can. J. Fam. L.* 87 at 93.
66. William Blackstone, *Commentaries on the Laws of England in Four Books*, Oxford, Clarendon Press, 1765-1769, vol. 1, at 451.
67. Dickens, *supra*, fn. 39, at 466.
68. *Re Warren* (1973), 13 R.F.L. 51 (Ont. Co. Ct.).
69. *Mooswa* v. *Minister of Social Services for Saskatchewan* (1976), 30 R.F.L. 101 (Sask. Q.B.).

It provides counselling and guidance service to families through its child protection offices before, during and after (and even in lieu of) court proceedings. It operates group homes and other service facilities that, with varying degrees of success or failure, attempt to simulate a family setting for children. And it facilitates adoption and offers home-maker services. This "helping" aspect of the state's involvement in the family is costly, however, and for that reason, suspicions are generated about the possible conflict between this aspect and that of *parens patriae*, where the prospect of terminating parental rights becomes economically attractive. One American court warned that termination of parental rights in child protection cases can be made to promote the financial interests of the state rather than the best interests of any particular child, simply because:[70]

> ... terminations aid the state in meeting the demand for "adoptable" children while also relieving it from the financial cost of long-term foster care, homemaker, services, and other welfare or public services.

The State's Role in Child Custody

As in the case of child protection, a state policy of non-intervention in custody disputes is neither possible nor desirable. Nineteenth-century feminists pointed out that state neutrality with respect to the family meant that the openly hierarchical social roles within the family at the time were only being supported and reinforced.[71] At common law, for example, the father had full custodial rights over his children and the mother had none, not even a right to access.[72] State neutrality to such a domestic regime clearly amounted to acquiescence. Paradoxically, to enforce his rights, the father could invoke the assistance of the state's court system that would furnish him with a writ of *habeas corpus* for the physical possession of the children. The logic here was that refusal by the state to lend enforcement to the father's rights would have been considered state interference into the internal government and sanctity of the home.[73] It was not until the twentieth century that the state began to interfere by enacting legislation granting equal entitlement of custody to both parents. British Columbia led both the rest

---

70. *State of Oregon, ex rel. Juvenile Department of Multnomah County* v. *Wade* (1974), 19 Or. App. 314, 527 P. 2d 753 (Ore. C.A.).

71. See the "Seneca Falls Declaration of 1848", discussed by Olsen, *supra*, fn. 46, at 1511.

72. *In re Allen* (1869), 5 P.R. 443 at 453 (Upp. Can. Q.B.), *per* Morrison, J., reversed at (1871), 31 U.C.Q.B. 458 (*in banco*). See also Constance B. Backhouse, "Shifting Patterns in Nineteenth-Century Canadian Custody Law", in *Essays in History of Canadian Law*, ed. by David H. Flaherty, Toronto, Osgoode Society, 1981, vol. 1, at 212.

73. Olsen, *supra*, fn. 46, at 1505.

of Canada and England by being the first to pass legislation in 1917.[74] Newfoundland still has no equal guardianship legislation and presumably follows the common law rule giving full rights to the father.[75]

Equal guardianship legislation was an active step toward the decomposition of the traditional patriarchal structure of the family. In the same way, custody legislation can and has had a large impact on the new configuration that the remnants of a family take after its breakdown.[76] For example, legislation creating a presumption for separated or divorced parents in favour of "joint custody" of their children, as was recently enacted in California,[77] could have an equally profound effect on the power distribution among family members.

---

74. In chronological order of promulgation:

British Columbia: *Equal Guardianship of Infants Act*, 1917, c. 27; now section 27 of the *Family Relations Act*, R.S.B.C. 1979, c. 121;

Alberta: *An Act to amend An Act respecting Infants and to Provide for Equal Parental Rights*, 1920, c. 10; now section 47 of the *Domestic Relations Act*, R.S.A. 1980, c. D-37;

Manitoba: section 135 of *An Act respecting the Welfare of Children*, 1922, c. 2; now section 14.1 of *The Family Maintenance Act*, 1978, c. 25, as added by 1983, c. 54;

Ontario: section 3 of *The Infants Amendment Act*, 1923, c. 33; now section 20 of the *Children's Law Reform Act*, R.S.O. 1980, c. 68, as added by 1982, c. 20;

Saskatchewan: section 3 of *An Act to Amend the Infants Act*, 1925-26, c. 42; now section 22 of *The Infants Act*, R.S.S. 1978, c. I-9;

Prince Edward Island: *An Act to Amend the Children's Act*, 1968, c. 5; now section 80 of the *Children's Act*, R.S.P.E.I. 1974, c. C-6;

Northwest Territories: section 28 of the *Domestic Relations Ordinance*, (1969) 2d Sess.), c. 10; now section 28 of the *Domestic Relations Ordinance*, R.O.N.W.T. 1974, c. D-9;

Quebec: section 5 of *An Act to Amend the Civil Code [of Lower Canada]*, 1977, c. 72; now article 648 of the *Civil Code of Quebec*;

New Brunswick: section 1 of *An Act to Amend the Deserted Wives and Children Maintenance Act*, 1977, c. 17; now section 129 of the *Child and Family Services and Family Relations Act*, 1980, c. C-2.1; also subsection 13(1) of the *Habeas Corpus Act*, R.S.N.B. 1973, c. H-1, as amended by 1977, c. 25;

Nova Scotia: subsection 18(4) of the *Family Maintenance Act*, 1980, c. 6;

Yukon Territory: subsection 32(1) of the *Children's Act*, 1984, c. 2.

The United Kingdom adopted equal guardianship in *An Act to Amend the Law with Respect to the Guardianship, Custody and Marriage of Infants*, 15 & 16 Geo. V (1925), c. 45.

75. In the case of Newfoundland, its Court of Appeal made a highly questionable pronouncement that equal guardianship by both parents is a rule of common law. See *Re Hutchings* (1977), 9 N. & P.E.I.R. 438 at 442, 12 A.P.R. 438 at 442, 71 D.L.R. (3d) 356 at 358, 24 R.F.L. 328 at 330, *per* Furlong, C.J.N.

76. Julia Brody, "Parental Rights and Children's Welfare - Some Problems of Feminists' Strategy in the 1920s" (1982), 10 *Int. J. Soc. L.* 146, where the author pointed out that custody has considerable influence on power relations between husbands and wives. She argued that joint custody has the potential to have regressive implications for women.

77. See Nancy K. Lemon, "Joint Custody as a Statutory Presumption - California's New Civil Code Section 4600 and 4600.5" (1981), 11 *Golden Gate Univ. L. Rev.*

Unlike child protection laws, however, custody legislation tends not to require the participation of the state as an active litigant. There are exceptions, to be sure, and the offices of the Official Guardian, Official Trustee, Family Advocate or whatever other name by which he or she may go, are occasionally met with requests to step into a custody dispute, but even here, the intervention is not on account of some positive rule, but rather at the request of a litigant or even of the court. Even fairly "activist" legislation such as that ratifying and implementing the Hague *Convention on the Civil Aspects of International Child Abduction*[78] in which the participating state offers its facilities for tracking down and locating the abducted-child and the abducting parent, and by which it is bound to use its administrative and judicial facilities to enforce a foreign custody order even to the point of returning the child, offers a remedy that is activated by a litigant and not by the state of its own initiative.

The high cost of the justice system generally and in the area of custody litigation in particular has motivated many jurisdictions to create, either by means of legislation, by rules of court practice or by administrative action, avenues of dispute resolution that either parallel the court system or are part of it.[79] There is a vast range of services

---

485. Lemon shared many concerns with Brody, *supra*, fn. 76, regarding the impact of joint custody on women and the motives of those who are promoting joint custody.

78. Nine jurisdictions in Canada have adopted the Convention into legislation:
British Columbia: section 42.1 of the *Family Relations Act*, R.S.B.C. 1979, c. 121, as added by 1982, c. 8;
Manitoba: section 17 of *The Child Custody Enforcement Act*, 1982, c. 27;
New Brunswick: *International Child Abduction Act*, 1982, c. I-12.1;
Newfoundland: *The International Child Abduction Act*, 1983, c. 29;
Nova Scotia: *Child Abduction Act*, 1982, c. 4;
Ontario: section 47 of the *Children's Law Reform Act*, R.S.O. 1980, c. 68, as added by 1982, c. 20;
Prince Edward Island: section 28 of the *Custody Jurisdiction and Enforcement Act*, 1984, c. 17;
Quebec: *An Act respecting the Civil Aspects of International and Interprovincial Child Abduction*, 1984, c. 12;
Yukon Territory: sections 56 to 61 of the *Children's Act*, 1984, c. 2.

79. In the case of pre-trials, for example, see:
Alberta: rule 219 of the *Supreme Court Rules*, Alta Reg. 390/68, as amended by Alta Reg. 124/73;
British Columbia: rule 25 of the *Rules of Court*, B.C. Reg. 634/76; and rule 13 of the *Family Relations Rules and Regulations*, B.C. Reg. 141/79;
New Brunswick: rule 50 and subrule 73.12 of the *Rules of Court*, N.B. Reg. 82-73;
Newfoundland: rules 31, 32 and 33 of the *Rules of the Unified Family Court, 1979*, Nfld. Reg. 99/79;
Northwest Territories: rule 231 of *The Supreme Court Rules*, S.O.R./79-768;
Nova Scotia: rules 25, 26 and 27 of the *Civil Procedure Rules, 1971*;
Ontario: rule 50 of the *Rules of Civil Procedure*, O. Reg. 560/84; rules 19, 20 and 21 of the *Rules of Practice and Procedure of the Unified Family Court*, R.R.O.

such as pre-trials, mediation, conciliation and marriage counselling that litigants are either encouraged or compelled to seek out before they can enter upon a formal trial in a court of law. But even here, the state has no interest in the outcome of the dispute (other than to be satisfied that the child is not in danger) and maintains an ''arm's length'' impartiality with the parties.

In the field of custody, therefore, unlike that of child protection, the state is still very much inclined to respect the ''private realm'' and to avoid any overt intervention.

CONCLUSION

Assessed in a reflective manner, free of the myths that haunt the field of family law, state intervention into the sanctity of the ''private realm'' no longer seems as ominous as is often portrayed. True, the state is now so intimately implicated in family life that it is often impossible to separate the different functions of parents and of the state or indeed even to identify them as parental functions or as state functions. Yet there is no indication in western societies that the state is committed to replacing the ''flesh and blood'' role of the family with its own creations. On the contrary, much of the state's efforts are directed to supporting and reinforcing the family unit.

The biggest fear today is not that the state will invent new and more disturbing interventions into the privacy of the home — a distinct prospect for which the technology already exists — but rather that economic pressures will compel the state to lessen its support for the family and to withdraw important and even vital resources. The austere economic policy has already manifested itself in the field of child protection, where the trend in several provinces is noticeably towards minimising state involvement in the family. With more limited resources, the remaining servants of the state will find it difficult to provide the services to which they are already committed, such as foster care, counselling, mediation and family court clinics, to name a few. The full impact of a major retrenchment can be tragic, not least because the economies that it is intended to make may simply never materialize and may be more than swallowed up by the ultimate cost to the taxpayers of years of neglect to the social obligations reasonably expected of a modern industrial state.

1980, Reg. 939; rules 21, 22 and 23 of the *Rules of Practice and Procedure of the Provincial Court (Family Division)*, R.R.O. 1980, Reg. 810;
Prince Edward Island: rules 25, 26 and 27 of the *Civil Procedure Rules, 1977*;
Quebec: article 279 of the *Code of Civil Procedure*, R.S.Q. 1977, c. C-25;
Saskatchewan: rule 196A of *The Queen's Bench Rules*, 1961, as amended; rules 26 and 27 of the *Rules of the Unified Family Court*, (1978) 74 Sask. Gaz. 1364.

Trends can change, however, and recent media attention to disturbing statistics concerning the high incidence of sexual abuse of children in their own homes may give policy makers and legislators second thought to budget cuts in certain fields. All is not gloom yet, but for the forseeable future, the problem will be not so much how to keep the state out of the family but where to keep it in.

Family Policy in Canada: From Where to Where?

Margrit Eichler*

INTRODUCTION

Families in Canada have always displayed some variability. In societies in which we find important social changes, these changes inevitably have some effect on families, for the simple reason that people are affected by such changes and that these same people are likely to live in families. Families in Canada have, therefore, never been static structures, and they have never been all of the same kind.[1] The nuclear family in which father, mother, their own biological children and nobody else lived happily together has always largely been a myth: families were not necessarily happy just because they lived under the same roof; and there have always been family disruptions for reasons of death and desertion, as well as migration because of economic necessity.[2]

Nevertheless, there are times in which changes are particularly marked, and in which one pattern is being visibly replaced by another pattern. I will argue in this paper that we are currently living in such a period where one type of family pattern is being replaced by another one, without the process having been completed. In the following, I will briefly describe some of the prominent features of contemporary Canadian families. I will then construct a model of what I call the "old" family which represents a simplified theoretical construction of what

---

* Professor of Sociology, Ontario Institute for Studies in Education.
1. *Cf.* Emily Nett, "Canadian Families in Social-Historical Perspective", (1981) 6 *Canadian Journal of Sociology* 239-260.
2. For American data, see Mary Jo Bane, "Marital Disruption and the Lives of Children", in George Levinger and Oliver C. Moles (eds.), *Divorce and Separation: Context, Causes, and Consequences*, New York, Basic Books, 1979, p. 276-286; for a historical Canadian example see Tamara K. Hareven, "The Dynamics of Kin in an Industrial Community", in (1978) 84 *The American Journal of Sociology*, 5151-5182. See also R. Pike, "Legal Access and the Incidence of Divorce in Canada: A socio-historical Analysis", (1975) 12 *Canadian Review of Sociology and Anthropology* 115-133.

was. Following this, I will construct a model of the "new" family which is a simplified hypothetical construction of where I see us, as a society, moving, and I shall locate our contemporary families somewhere between these two end points.

Following this, I shall look at social policies which are appropriate for the "old" model of the family, and thereafter at those which are appropriate for the "new" model of the family, and I shall note the fit (or lack of fit) between the micro and macro-levels. Lastly, I will briefly discuss some of the implications of these considerations for law.

DESCRIPTIONS OF CONTEMPORARY FAMILIES IN CANADA

Recently, there have been some major changes in Canadian households and families, which can be addressed under the headings of (a) demographic changes, (b) changes in the nature of economic co-operation, (c) changes in the awareness with respect to family violence, and (d), consequences of (a) and (b).

Demographic changes

One of the most striking changes we can observe is the decrease in fertility. Canadian women have fewer children than ever before. While in 1960 the average number of children per woman was about 3.9, in 1982 it had sunk to about 1.7.[3] That is, fertility has decreased by more than half in approximately two decades.

Life expectancy, by contrast, has risen constantly. For a male born in Canada in 1931, the life expectancy at birth was 60 years, and for a female born in that year, it was 62.1 years. For a male born in Canada in 1976, the life expectancy is 69.6 years, and for a female born in that year it is 76.9 years.[4] Barring unforeseen disasters of a national scope, one would expect the life expectancy to continue to rise in the future. This means that there will be more older people around who will eventually need to be taken care of, and fewer younger people to provide this care. In terms of family relationships this means that there are likely to be more grandparents alive during the youth and young adulthood of their grandchildren, and fewer grandchildren per grandparent.

The divorce rate has increased steadily and consistently over the past decades, rising from a rate of 39.1 in 1960, which represents 6,980 divorces in that year in Canada, to a rate of 275.5 in 1982 which rep-

---

3. For trend data and 1960 data see Margrit Eichler, *Families in Canada Today. Recent Changes and their Policy Consequences*, Toronto, Gage, 1983, p. 37, t. 2.2; for 1982 data, see Canada, Statistics Canada, *Vital Statistics, Vol. I, Births and Deaths 1982*, Catalogue 84-204, Ottawa, Minister of Supply and Services, 1984.
4. Canada, Statistics Canada, *Population Projections for Canada and the Provinces, 1976-2001*, Ottawa, Statistics Canada, 1979.

resents 70,436 divorces. In 1983, for the first time in a long period, there was a small decline both in the rate as well as in the number of divorces. The divorce rate declined by 3.6% to 275.5, while the number of divorces granted in that year declined by 2.7% to 68,567.[5] It is too early to state whether this slight decline marks the beginning of the end of the previous trend - a beginning reversal, a slowing - or constitutes merely a temporary anomaly. My guess would be that it is an anomaly, possibly generated by speculation in 1983 that there would be an incipient change in the divorce law (which did not materialize) rather than a radical shift in the overall trend. Only time will tell, however, whether this guess is accurate.

Due to the great increase in divorce, there has been a great increase in remarriages. In 1982, 28% of all marriages contracted in that year involved at least one previously married partner, compared to 12.3% of all marriages in 1967.[6] The great bulk of that increase is due to divorced rather than widowed persons remarrying; indeed, the proportion of widowed people remarrying has consistently declined, no doubt due to the increased life expectancy. One would expect this trend to continue for as long as the divorce rate remains high or increases.

Further, there has been a large (although inconsistent) increase in the percentage of births to unmarried mothers. While in 1960 only 4.3% of all children were born to unmarried women, representing 20,413 children, the percentage had risen to 15.3% in 1982, representing 55,625 children.[7]

One consequence of the increase in divorce and in the births to unmarried women is that the proportion of children living in one-parent households has increased. Approximately 17% of all families with children consisted of one-parent households in 1981,[8] mostly headed by women, and three out of seven of them were below the poverty line in 1981.[9] The two factors, having a female head and poverty, are closely connected.[10]

5. For 1960 and trend data, see Eichler, 1983, *op. cit.*, p. 48, t. 2.6; for 1982, see Canada, Statistics Canada, *Vital Statistics, Vol. II - Marriages and Divorces*, Catalogue 84-205, p. 16, t. 10. Information for 1983 was obtained via telephone from the Toronto regional office of Statistics Canada.

6. For 1967 and trend data, see Eichler, 1983, *op. cit.*, p. 232-233, t. 7.7, for 1982, see Canada, Statistics Canada, *Vital Statistics, Vol. II - Marriages and Divorces*, Catalogue 84-205, p. 8, t. 5.

7. For 1960 and trend data, see Eichler, 1983, *op. cit.*, p. 206, t. 7.2. Figures for 1982 were calculated for Canada, Statistics Canada, *Vital Statistics, Vol. I, Births and Deaths*, Catalogue 84-204, p. 11, t. 7.

8. Economic Council of Canada, *On the Mend, Twentieth Annual Review 1983*, Ottawa, Minister of Supply and Services, 1983, p. 90.

9. *Ibid.*

10. *Cf.* National Council of Welfare, *One in a World of Two's* (A Report by the National Council of Welfare on One-parent Families in Canada), Ottawa, National

Changes in economic co-operation

It used to be the case that women dropped out of the labour force when they married. In the sixties, the prevalent pattern was that they remained in the labour force after marriage until the birth of the first child, at which time they dropped out of the labour force, sometimes to return after the last child had entered school.[11]

The labour force participation of married women has increased consistently,[12] and today the majority of Canadian wives are in the paid labour force. We have thus crossed a threshold (at around 1980) which changes the majority pattern for husband-wife families from a bread-winner family to a two-earner family.

A corollary of this change is that the majority of Canadian children now have a mother who is in the paid labour force,[13] although wives and mothers are, of course, not an identical group.

Changes in the awareness of family violence

Until quite recently, violence within families was effectively hidden. It is only since the mid-seventies that some consistent scholarly and public attention has been focussed on this problem. As a consequence, we have no reliable information about the incidence of any form of family violence in the past, and very little information about the incidence and its nature in the present. This makes any statements about changes in any type of familial violence impossible, since there is no basis against which to assess contemporary information (to the degree that it exists).

The editors of one of the most recent comprehensive American books on family violence conclude:

> ... the family is the predominant setting for every form of physical violence from slaps to torture and murder. In fact, some form of physical violence in the life cycle of family members is so likely that it can be said to be almost universal. ... If this is indeed the case, then violence is as typical of family relationships as is love.[14]

Council of Welfare, 1976, for the argument; see Canada, Statistics Canada, *Canada's Lone-Parent Families*, Catalogue 99-933, Ottawa, Minister of Supply and Services, 1984, for the most recent figures.

11. *Cf.* Sylvia Ostry, *The Female Worker in Canada* (One of a series of labour force studies in the 1961 Census Monograph Programme), Ottawa, Dominion Bureau of Statistics, 1968.

12. See Eichler, 1983, *op. cit.*, p. 170, t. 6.1.

13. See Eichler, 1983, *op. cit.*, p. 248, t. 8.2

14. Gerald T. Hotaling and Murray A. Straus, "Culture, Social Organization, and Irony in the Study of Family Violence", in Murray A. Straus and Gerald T. Hotaling (eds.), *The Social Causes of Husband-Wife Violence*, Minneapolis, University of Minnesota Press, 1980, p. 4.

There is no reason to suspect that Canada would fare any better if we had a representative study of violence within families in Canada. One usual estimate that is often cited is that 10% of all Canadian wives are being battered by their husbands (common law a well as legal).[15]

As for sexual abuse of children, the Committee on Sexual Offenses Against Children and Youths found in a National Population Survey that 30.4% of all males and 53.9% of all females reported that they had been victims of sexual offenses, ranging from unwanted exposure to a sexual attack.[16]

Looking only at the most serious form of assault, namely whether anyone had ever tried to have sex with them or had forcibly sexually assaulted them, the committee found that 22.1% of the women and 10.6% of the men had experienced this form of assault.[17]

The committee concluded in terms of changes in incidence that

> The best evidence available ... suggests that the volume of these crimes in relation to population growth has remained at a relatively constant level for some time. In this respect, the major change that appears to have occurred is not so much an alteration in the incidence of these offences, but the fact that Canadians as a whole are becoming more aware of a deeply rooted problem whose dimensions have not significantly shifted in recent decades.[18]

Finally, the committee found that well over half of all sexual assaults occurred in the homes of victims or suspects,[19] and that the majority of the assailants were already known to and possibly trusted by the assaulted victims thus placing it well into the circle of the family.[20]

Consequences of demographic changes and changes in economic co-operation

Due to the noted increases in divorce, unmarried motherhood, and remarriage, we find an increasing separation between marital and spousal roles. This shows itself in a high proportion of households in which dependent children live together with only one of their biological parents, while the other biological parent is still alive but living in another household, moreover either one or both biological parents may have

---

15. *Cf.* Linda MacLeod, *Wife Battering in Canada: The Vicious Circle*, Advisory Council for the Status of Women, Ottawa, Minister of Supply and Services, 1980.
16. Canada. Minister of Justice and Attorney General of Canada, Minister of National Health and Welfare, *Sexual Offences Against Children*, Vol. I (Report of the Committee on Sexual Offences Against Children and Youths), 1984, p. 185.
17. *Ibid.*, p. 181.
18. *Ibid.*, p. 186.
19. *Ibid.*, p. 201.
20. *Ibid.*, p. 218.

remarried a spouse who thus becomes a wife or husband but not a biological mother or father to the children involved. Whether or not such a "stepparent" actually is experienced as a social parent by the children concerned seems to vary greatly.[21] It is not the fact of stepparenting which is startlingly new, but the scope of the phenomenon as well as the continuing existence (and often involvement) of the non-coresidential parent in the parenting process.

Another consequence of these same factors, simply stating the same facts differently, is a large (and increasing) incongruity between household and family membership. In other words, the members of one household do not necessarily have the same family members. Imagine the case of a family with two children, in which the husband and wife (who are father and mother to the children) divorce, and the father maintains contact, through visiting arrangements with his children, while the mother has custody and the children reside with her. In that case, the mother and the children form one household, and for the mother, they form her family, while the children have family members in two households, namely their own and their father's.

Now let us assume that the father marries another woman who also brings a child from a previous union into this marriage, and that eventually the father and his new wife have another child together. The children of the first family now have a halfsibling and a stepsibling, as well as potentially a stepmother in their father's household; however, the child whom the father's second wife brought into her marriage also maintains contact with his father. This example can be continued by assuming that the first wife also remarries, a man with or without children, that the previous partner of the second wife of the original children's father has remarried, and so on. It is, however, sufficient to illustrate the point that household and family membership is no longer necessarily congruent, and that as a consequence members of one household may have different family members.

This opens up new sets of relationships which did not previously exist to the same degree as well as creating problems in relationships which also did not previously exist to the same degree. Parents of adult children who marry a partner who brings a child into this marriage may find themselves in a quasi - or step - grandparental relationship to this child, and children who are not biologically related may nevertheless be stepsiblings and share halfsiblings. On the other hand, parents of adult children who have lost custody of their own children may have difficulty maintaining contact with their grandchildren, if the custodial parent does not wish for such contact.

---

21. Penny Gross, *Kinship Among Remarriage Families*, Ph. D. dissertation, University of Toronto, Dept. of Sociology, in progress.

As a consequence of the changed pattern of economic co-operation, we can note that a shift has occurred from the breadwinner couple to the two-earner couple as the norm, and that at the same time the full-time mother has become a minority phenomenon and that the majority of Canadian children experience some form of shared childcare.

Finally, because of a number of factors, we note that an increasing proportion of women and children are living in poverty. This is due to the increase in one-parent households, noted above, and the fact that many of these households are living in or near poverty, especially if the head is female, as is the case in the vast majority of one-parent households. The fact that women generally have lower paying jobs than men and that maintenance payments are generally exceedingly low, not reflecting real costs of providing for a child let alone childcare,[22] are major causes for this situation. The situation is exacerbated by the fact that our child-related benefits are low by comparative international standards,[23] and that our social welfare legislation actively discourages the change-over from a poor female-headed household on social assistance to a husband-wife family with somewhat higher resources.[24]

To sum up, Canadian families today are characterized by a wide degree of differences in terms of composition, structure, type of economic co-operation (or lack thereof), with quite divergent consequences for different families. There are one parent and two parent households, husband-wife households who are not joint parents to all or some children involved, there is an increasing separation between marital and spousal roles, and increasing incongruity between family and household memberships, a majority of wives are in the labour force, making the husband-wife breadwinner family a minority, while we do find an increase in the proportion of one-parent breadwinner household. The majority pattern for Canadian children today is not to have a full-time mother at home and therefore to experience some form of shared childcare. It should be added here that only a small minority of these children find places in a licensed, supervised day care setting. The majority of them are cared for in unlicensed, unsupervised settings,

22. See Louise Dulude, *Love, Marriage and Money ... An Analysis of Financial Relations Between the Spouses*, Ottawa, Canadian Advisory Council on the Status of Women, 1984.

23. See Sheila B. Kamerman and Alfred J. Kahn, *Child Care, Family Benefits, and Working Parents. A Study in Comparative Policy*, New York, Columbia University Press, 1981; also Sheila B. Kamerman and Alfred J. Kahn (eds.), *Family Policy. Government and Families in Fourteen Countries*, New York, Columbia University Press, 1978.

24. *Cf.* Margrit Eichler, "The Familism-Individualism Flip-Flop and its Implications for Economic and Social Welfare Policies", *Social Change and Family Policies*, XXth International CFR Seminar, Key Papers, part 2, p. 431-472, Melbourne, Australian Institute of Family Studies and ISA International Sociological Association (CFR Committee on Family Research), 1984.

where the care ranges from excellent to appalling.[25] Finally, a growing number of women and children find themselves in or near poverty.

It should be noted that Canada is not alone in experiencing these trends. At least some of them seem to be causally connected with the process of industrialization, since we find similarities in familial structures among all highly industrialized countries. The demographic changes noted in Canada can also be observed in other highly industrialized countries, as well as a trend for women to participate in the paid labour force (and therefore presumably for wives and mothers to participate in the paid labour force) in large numbers. Overall, we can also note a large discrepancy between household and family membership, as suggested by internationally high divorce rates and/or illegitimacy rates.[26] It is interesting to note that these trends are observable in all highly industrialized countries, irrespective of political regime, i.e., they are equally found in Eastern Europe as well as in Western Europe, North America, Japan, New Zealand and Australia.[27] It was for this reason that I speculated above that the current small change in the Canadian divorce rate is a temporary abnormality rather than signalling an overall shift in trends.

Clearly, then, we are in a period of considerable social change as far as familial structures are concerned. It now becomes important to attempt to identify the direction of the ongoing changes, especially if we wish to assess the adequacy of policies affecting families, now and in the future.

THE "OLD" AND "NEW" MODEL OF THE FAMILY

Mary Ann Glendon has argued that we are currently in a period of "unsettled assumptions" about marriage. She suggests that we are moving towards a "new marriage" which is complemented by a "new property" both of which are the result of a complex shift in the relative importance of family, work, and government as status determinants and sources of support.[28] She characterizes the "new marriage, American Style", as having

---

25. For an overview of the literature, see Eichler, 1983, *op. cit.*, p. 249-2622.
26. For comparative data on illegitimacy rates, divorce rates, and labour force participation rates of women, see Eichler, 1984, *op. cit.* For comparative rates of fertility and other factors, see Alex Inkeles, "Modernization and Family Patterns: A Test of Convergence Theory", in Dwight W. Hoover and John T.A. Koumoulides (eds.), *Conspectus of History*, Vol. I, No. 6, 1980, Family History, Muncie, Ind., Dept. of History, Ball State University, 1981.
27. *Ibid.*
28. Mary Ann Glenden, "The New Marriage and the New Property", in John M. Eekelaar and Sanford N. Katz (eds.), *Marriage and Cohabitation in Contemporary Societies. Areas of Legal, Social and Ethical Change. An International and Interdisciplinary Study*, Toronto, Butterworths, 1980, p. 59-70.

two earners, mutually dependent on their combined sources of income, the wife earning less than the husband. The wife's earning, though low, seem, together with her earning potential, to be a major factor that makes it easier for husbands as well as wives to depart from a marriage. ... Since three out of four divorced persons remarry, the new marriage is often a subsequent marriage. ... Thus, one can fairly say that in the United States, there is now a fundamental right to marry, and marry, and marry.[29]

Building on this analysis, I shall attempt to develop a model of the "old family" and of the "new family" (rather than the "new marriage") since, as far as social policies are concerned, it is the entire family (including the children) which should be considered as of central importance. If the above summary of trends is correct, and there is indeed a growing dissociation between marital and parental roles, then obviously this aspect must be systematically integrated into any consideration of the adequacies of social policies.

After having presented models of the "old" and "new" family, I shall develop models of social policies which correspond to the "old" and the "new" family at the macro-level, if we assume that there was congruity between behaviours at the micro-level and assumptions about such behaviours as displayed in policies at the macro-level. This will then allow us to place current familial styles of behaviour somewhere on a continuum between "old" and "new" families, and to assess the degree of congruence (or lack thereof) of current social policies in view of the placement of contemporary Canadian families on the old-new continuum.

The model of the "old family"

I shall structure the discussion in terms of four dimensions: ideology, economy (in terms of responsibility and dependency) household composition and management, and personal care.

As far as the ideological dimension is concerned, the old family is characterized by a very strong sex-role differentiation which affects all other dimensions. The roles of wives and husbands, fathers and mothers, are clearly distinguished and largely non-overlapping. This is manifested in the assignment of economic responsibility and household management as well as in the responsibility for personal care. The father/husband is seen as responsible for the economic well-being of the entire family, while the mother/wife is seen as responsible for the physical, emotional and overall well-being of family members. This includes providing care to family members in need of care, including sometimes aged parents. By corollary, the father/husband is *not* seen as responsible for the physical, emotional and overall well-being of family members,

---

29. *Ibid.*, p. 62/3.

except in economic terms, and for providing care to family members in need of care, while the mother/wife is not seen as responsible for the economic well-being of the family.

Wife and children are thus conceptualized as economic dependents of the husband/father, and the work that wives perform within the household as full-time or part-time homemakers is for that reason necessarily invisible with respect to its economic value.[30] If wives or mothers are in the labour force, their work is in addition to their homemaking functions and earnings are seen as of secondary importance.

As far as household composition is concerned, the nuclear family, consisting of a husband, wife, and their own biological children (and nobody else) is seen as normative. As a consequence, household and family memberships are treated as congruent. Further, there is an unclear division between spousal and parental obligations, and as a consequence, wives are equated with mothers, and husbands are equated with fathers, while parents who are non-coresidential with their children are treated as non-parents.

The old model of the family can be summarized as follows:

THE "OLD" FAMILY MODEL

Ideology	Sex-role differentiation
Economic Responsibility	Husbands/fathers as breadwinners, wives secondary earners or non-earners
Economic Dependency	Wives/children as dependents of husbands/fathers
Household Composition	Assumption of congruence between household and family membership
	The nuclear family seen as normative
	Wives equated with mothers, husbands equated with fathers
Household Management	Wives/mothers as full-time or part-time homemakers with sole responsibility for household management
	Husbands/fathers not responsible for household management

---

30. *Cf.* Margrit Eichler, *The Connection Between Paid and Unpaid Labour and its Implication for Creating Equality for Women in Employment*, in Rosalie S. Abella (ed.), *Research Studies of the Commission of Equality in Employment*, Ottawa, Ministry of Supply and Services, 1985, pp. 537-546.

	Unclear distinction between spousal and parental obligations
Personal Care	Mothers/wives/adult daughters/(-in-law) responsible for provision of care for children and adults
	Fathers/husbands/sons/(-in-law) not responsible for provision of care for children and adults

The model of the "new family"

By contrast with the "old family", the "new family" is premissed on the notion of sex equality rather than sex-role differentiation. This applies to all dimensions of interaction. Consequently, the roles of husbands and wives, mothers and fathers are not differentiated on the basis of sex but on the basis of individualistic factors and they overlap to a high degree. Household management as well as economic responsibilities are shared by husband and wife. Both father and mother are seen as responsible for the economic, physical, emotional and overall well-being of the various family members.

Children are seen as the economic dependents of both mother and father, and both wife and husband are full-time participants in the labour force and are in addition responsible for the housework.

Male relatives are co-responsible with female relatives for the care of family members in need of care.

As far as household composition is concerned, variable structures are recognized as constituting different types of families. A potential incongruity between spousal and parental roles due to unmarried motherhood, divorce, remarriage and other factors is acknowledged and accepted. Consequently, there is a clear distinction between spousal and parental obligations, since husbands are not necessarily equated with fathers, wives are not necessarily equated with mothers, and noncoresidential parents are recognized as such.

The model of the "new family" can be summarized as follows:

THE "NEW" FAMILY MODEL

Ideology	Sex equality
Economic Responsibility	Husbands and wives (fathers and mothers) are both earners, equally responsible for their own support and that of the children

Economic Dependency	Children are dependents of their mothers and fathers
Household Composition	Assumption of congruence between household and family members
	A variety of family types acknowledged and accepted
	Wives not unquestioningly equated with mothers, nor husbands with fathers
Household Management	Shared responsibility between husband and wife
	Clear distinction between spousal and parental obligations
Personal Care	Mothers/fathers, wives/husbands, daughters/sons, daughters-in-law/sons-in-law equally responsible for provision of care for family members in need of care to the degree that this can be combined with full-time paid work

SOCIAL POLICIES APPROPRIATE FOR THE NEW AND OLD FAMILIES

In this section, we will consider each of the items of the "new" and the "old" family and consider what type of social (including economic) policy would be appropriate to each of the models of the family. In order to be able to do so, we need to shift our attention from the micro level to the macro level and consequently translate some of the dimensions employed at the micro level to those appropriate for the macro-level.

The ideological dimension remains such, but the economic dimension, which was split into responsibility and dependency for the micro-level, needs to be split into labour market policies, the tax structure, and other government transfers to consider some of the implications of the old and new model of the family. Household composition remains as a dimension, and personal care translates into social services. Household management, i.e. unpaid housework, is integrated as a tacit assumption into labour market policies, the tax structure, other government transfer programmes, and social services.

In the following section, I shall consider which policies are logically congruent with both the "old" and the "new" model of the family.

Policies congruent with the "old family"

As far as the ideological dimension is concerned, policies must obviously be based on the notion of sex role differentiation in order to match the "old" model of the family. This means that for the purpose of labour market policies, men are treated as the primary earners, and women as the secondary earners or non-earners. Since women are seen as solely responsible for household management, it follows that men, whether they do or do not have a family, are seen as completely unencumbered by family responsibilities, while conversely all women with families are seen as encumbered by their familial responsibilities, or, if without family, seen as potentially encumbered depending on age and other characteristics (such as the assessed likelihood to get married, or to have a child). Only if, in the eyes of an employer, a woman is highly unlikely to ever acquire a family of her own, could she possibly be considered as a worker of equal value to a male worker, but since she, by definition, does not have dependents, therefore she requires a lower wage than a comparable male worker.

The tax structure will, logically, provide some tax relief to the man who has dependents (such as a wife and children), for example via a spousal exemption.

Other government programmes will provide replacement income in case of the incapacity or absence of a male breadwinner. Social assistance programmes, for example, will provide financial assistance to mothers with dependent children but without a male to depend on, but will withdraw such assistance when a man who is theoretically capable of earning an income assumes some aspects of a husband role. Since husbands are equated with fathers, this is a logical policy to pursue. By contrast, if a wife's earnings cease, this loss of income will not entitle the family to a replacement income.

Conversely, when a wife/mother is incapable of providing care to family members for reasons of incapacity or absence, the state will provide replacement service. By way of example, when a wife or mother is unable to do housework due to a serious and prolonged illness, the provincial hospital insurance plan may provide a substitute homemaker, but will fail to do so when a man is incapacitated or absent and therefore cannot do housework, irrespective of whether he has or had not done so before he became incapacitated.

As far as household composition is concerned, the assumption underlying policies is that membership in a household is identical with family membership, and conversely, that there are no nuclear family relationships of importance between households. There will be little concern, then, with enforcing the economic responsibility of parents (predominantly fathers) towards their dependent children if they no longer (or never did) reside together with them, for whatever reason.

With respect to social services, women are assumed to be available for the care of family members in need of care, whether these women do or do not have paid employment (which is always of secondary importance compared to their family responsibilities while the reverse is true for men). Accordingly, there is no societal reason for providing childcare for husband-wife families, since the wife is (and if she is not, she should be) available for looking after the children, nor is there much concern with providing care for people who need care but who have mothers, wives, adult daughters or daughters-in-law nearby.

We can summarize policies appropriate for the old model of the family as follows:

POLICIES CONGRUENT WITH THE OLD FAMILY MODEL

Ideology	Sex-role differentiation
Economy:	
Labor Market Policy	Men seen as primary earners, women as secondary earners or non-earners
	Preference is therefore given to men over women in all employment programmes, women are treated as labour force reserve
	A large wage-differential by sex
	Employers and labour law regulations treat male workers as unencumbered by family responsibilities, and female workers as encumbered or potentially encumbered
Tax Structure	Provides relief to male earners with dependents (i.e., wife and/or children)
Other Government Transfers	Provide replacement income in case of absence of male breadwinner or presence but incapacity to earn income
	Provide replacement care in case of incapacity or absence of wife/mother
Household Composition	For purposes of eligibility to benefits, household membership is equated with family membership, and eligibility is determined on basis of family need rather than individual entitlement
	Rights and obligations of non-coresidential parents are not enforced

| Social services | No universal day care, no universal relief for care for adult family members in need of care, no institutionalized right to care for temporarily sick family members on the part of workers |

Policies congruent with the "new family"

If policies appropriate for the old family - "old policies", so to speak - are premised on the notion of sex differentiation in the ideological dimension, policies appropriate for the new family - "new policies" - must be premised on the notion of sex equality. From this, a large number of consequences flow for all other social policies.

With respect to the economy, and for purposes of labour market policy, women and men are treated equally as primary earners, all employment programmes are equally targetted towards women and men, there is no wage differential on the basis of sex and employers as well as labour law recognize that the vast majority of workers - male as well as female - do have some familial relationships and therefore do have some responsibility towards their family members. There is no difference on the basis of sex in the manner in which these familial responsibilities are recognized and accepted.

The tax structure provides relief to parents with respect to the costs attached to rearing children, but adults are not conceptualized as dependents of other adults.

Other government transfers provide replacement income and replacement care in case of incapacity or absence of one parent (either mother or father).

For the purposes of government programmes, variability in family structures is recognized and accepted. In other words, household membership is not automatically equated with family membership, and ongoing parental responsibilities of non-coresidential parents are continuously enforced.

As far as social services are concerned, it is recognized that it is in principle impossible for any person to be responsible for his or her own economic welfare and therefore to have a full-time paid job while at the same time being responsible for a person in need of care on a full-time basis, such as a dependent child or an adult in need of care. Therefore, there is a system of social services which through a network of services provide care for children as well as for adults in need of care. Alternatively, there is a wage replacement system in place which reimburses adults who care for other people, including their own family members, for their losses in income. Labour law recognizes the right of paid workers to some paid time off for family responsibility, just as we now recognize the right to paid statutory holidays and vacation and sick leave.

We can summarize policies appropriate for the new model of the family as follows:

POLICIES CONGRUENT WITH THE NEW FAMILY MODEL

Ideology	Sex equality
Economy	
Labour Market Policy	Women and men seen as primary wage earners
	All employment programmes equally targetted to female and male workers
	No wage differential by sex
	Family responsibilities of male and female workers equally recognized and accepted
Tax Structure	Provides relief to parents
Other Government Transfers	Provide replacement income and replacement care in case of absence or inability of one parent
Household Composition	Eligibility to benefits is based on individual entitlement rather than family status. Household and family memberships are not equated, unless, in fact, congruent
	Rights and obligations of non-coresidential parents are enforced
Social Services	Wide network of social services for childcare and adults in need of care and/ or wage replacement system for people caring full-time for family members

Placement of contemporary families and policies on the old-new continuum

Looking at families in Canada today, it becomes obvious that at the micro-level we have moved a fair distance towards the "new family". Sex equality as an ideology is more often accepted than not, more wives are earning money than are completely economically dependent on their husbands, family laws have been amended to make both parents responsible for the economic well-being of their children as well as for their care and other housework, a variety of family types co-exist although they are not always acknowledged or socially accepted, the increase in remarriages has generated some awareness that not all wives are mothers nor all husbands fathers, which has led to some awareness that spousal and parental obligations must be distinguished, especially when dealing with the aftermath of divorce. We do not really know to what degree male relatives are involved in the care of their family members in need of care.

Nevertheless, it would be quite incorrect to say that as a society we have generally adopted the new family as the model of the family. We are, at present, clearly in a transitional stage, which expresses itself in two different ways. For one, a substantial proportion of the population, in particular its middle-aged and older segments, were brought up while the old model was the accepted model of the family. These people presently must cope with circumstances which have changed. Even if they themselves eventually adopt a new style of life, part of their history will remain tied up with the old model of the family. For instance, if a wife takes on full-time paid employment after she has been a homemaker for twenty years, she will never make up the loss in seniority and pay which is due to the time she worked as an unpaid homemaker.

Secondly, some people still choose to follow a modified version of the old model of the family in their own behaviour. Although the majority of mothers work for pay, there are still substantial numbers of mothers who drop out of the labour force when their first child is born. Presumably, these people will eventually find themselves in a situation similar to that presently encountered by those of middle or older ages who have conformed to the old model of the family.

Due to this second group of relatively young people we will remain in a transitional stage for at least another thirty years, because even when these women go into the labour force later on, most of them will not be able to make up for the years they worked without pay in their homes in areas such as career progress, acquisition of seniority, or income potential.

To the degree that women are less likely to be full-time members of the paid labour force, it makes sense for them to do more of the caring for family members, thereby continuing sex role differentiation in the personal care dimension.

Nevertheless, we seem to be well on our way towards the new model of the family.

When we turn to policies, a totally different picture emerges. Our present policies are in general better described as policies congruent with the old model of the family than with the new model of the family.

Inspite of the fact that more women than ever before are currently in the paid labour force, sex segregation of occupations has not decreased in the recent past but may even have increased.[31] The wage differential between the sexes continues to be large, and while there is a very limited (by international standards) acceptance of female family responsibilities, there is hardly any recognition of male family responsibilities, although paternity leaves can be obtained in some professions by male employees. Parental leaves are, of course, only one component of recognizing family responsibilities of workers. A statutory right to time off in case of illness of family members would be another crucial aspect which is generally not available to either male or female employees at the present time in Canada, although such provisions do exist in other countries.

The tax structure provides some relief to parents, but also to breadwinners with dependents (the spousal exemption). Our social assistance programmes tend to be completely premised on the notion of the old family.[32] Eligibility to benefits is partially premissed on family membership and partially on individual entitlement,[33] and in general it is fair to say that the rights and obligations of non-coresidential parents (usually parents without custody) are not enforced.[34]

As far as social services are concerned, there is no wide public network for childcare and adults in need of care available. For instance, only a small minority of our children are cared for in public day care settings, and the majority are in ad hoc private care situations.

This presents a serious problem. Our family structure has been changing quite rapidly, and as a consequence, our social policies are "out of whack" since they have not changed at the same speed.

One of the many consequences of the mismatch between the "new family" and "old policies" is the increasing incidence of poverty among women and children which has been noted in the first section of this paper. Much of present day efforts to further reform the family law can, in fact, be understood as an attempt to remedy this situation by sharing assets between ex-spouses more equally. In the last section of this paper, then, I shall in a rather cursory manner consider some of the implications of the above discussion for law.

IMPLICATIONS OF THE MOVE TOWARDS THE NEW FAMILY FOR LAW

Prior to the latest spates of revisions of the various family laws which started with the enactment of the Ontario Family Law Reform

---

31. Economic Council of Canada, *op. cit.*, p. 87.
32. *Cf.* Eichler, 1984a, *op. cit.*
33. See Eichler, 1983, *op. cit.*, chapter 10.
34. Dulude, *op. cit.*

Act in 1978, family law tended to be firmly based on the model of the old family. Laws were, as a rule, premised on the assumption of sex role differentiation, the breadwinning role of the father, the homemaking role of the mother, female responsibility for the provision of care, and congruence between household and family membership which is perhaps most clearly exemplified in the notion of illegitimacy.

With the new legislation which has been enacted, the law has moved quite decisively in the direction of adopting the premises of the new family model. In practice, however, we are faced with some significant problems, because we are at present in a transitional period. Ex-wives and their children tend to fall into poverty upon divorce, while ex-husbands tend to be better off economically after divorce.[35]

While there are many other issues which are problematic and which can be traced back to this very basic disjunction between how people actually live together and how economic and social policies assume they live together, the desperate economic situation of many ex-wives and their children seems to be one of the issues around which a considerable amount of concern is focussed. One of the major attempts to improve their situation can be found in a push for complete sharing of all assets (including business assets) between ex-spouses.

I see several problems with a full community of property regime which would apply to everybody. If the foregoing analysis is correct, the major problem is located at the level of economic and social policies, and not primarily at the level of family law. Legal reformers might therefore profitably shift their attention to developing and implementing legal measures to improve the economic position of all women. Further, we must devise legal obligations and entitlements for men to discharge their part of familial responsibilities, so that the burden (and joy) of caring for others can, in fact, be shared between women and men. While this seems to me clearly the long range direction to go into, it must be acknowledged that there are many casualties due to the fact that we are finding ourselves in a transition period which will go on for a long time yet. In cases in which women entered a marriage under the old terms assuming that they would be economically provided for, a community of property regime would certainly be appropriate.

However, a compulsory community of property regime for everybody would in principle reward women on the basis of their husband's economic contributions, not on the basis of their own work. This means, that under the euphemism of ''partnership'' women would continue to be treated as their husbands' dependents. By contrast, I would argue that some women should get all the property, for instance, if they have raised children, and also had a paying job, while other women, who

---

35. *Ibid.*

have not raised children or cared for adults who are unable to care for themselves and who have not had a paying job maybe do not deserve half of all the property accumulated by the husband. And what do we do with wives who have supported husbands and done all or most of the housework as well as the care of others? Will they have to split their property with a man who has not contributed his share?

It seems somewhat ironic to me to argue for any one property regime for all families at the exact time when we are faced with a wide diversity of family types which will inevitably be with us for a long time to come. It seems also ironic to me to argue for ex-wives primarily on the basis of their spousal role, rather than on their spousal as well as their parental role, given that we are faced with an increasing dissociation between spousal and parental roles. In other words, the contributions of women as wives and as mothers should be separately assessed, just as the contributions (or lack thereof) of men as husbands and as fathers should be separately assessed. If a woman has been carrying the parenting role for the father as well as for herself, this should be acknowledged in property settlements.

Nevertheless, economic equality for women will not come about by reforming the family law, it will come about by reforming labour law, revising our tax structure, and reshaping our economy. That is not to say that further reform of family law is unimportant, but merely to point out that it must not be seen as solving some problems which are beyond its purview. People who do socially useful work in their homes must be rewarded for this work socially, not privately, raising children must be seen as a social contribution, not only as a private contribution, and men and women must equally share family responsibilities in spite of their paid work just as women must have the same access to jobs and the benefits attached to them as men have.[36] Once we achieve these goals, ex-wives will not be so poor and children will not sink into poverty merely because their parents divorce or were never married in the first place.

---

36. See Margrit Eichler, *Applying Equality to Employment*, p. 205-214.

Canadian Family Law: Mixed Messages and Conflicting Signals

F. Murray Fraser*

INTRODUCTION

My original mandate was to use the specific provisions of Bill C-10 - an *Act to Amend the Divorce Act*[1] - as a point of departure for a discussion of the ways in which divorce reform would affect family law in Canada. I was to draw a narrower focus upon some of the issues raised by Madam Justice Wilson in her opening statement.[2]

With the demise of Bill C-10 and, indeed, the government that sponsored it, I concluded that a more appropriate course of action would be to comment on a number of examples drawn from family law in which rights and interests are or should be identified and accommodated in a modern system of justice. In that context one may undertake a modest review of some of the major recent developments in Canadian family law at both the substantive and procedural levels. Therefore, I shall discuss a series of concepts - existing and proposed - in family relations in which rights of individuals and the interest of the state are under consideration.

By way of introductory remarks, however, I wish to comment briefly on certain aspects of the paper presented by Madam Justice Wilson. For the purposes of this discussion I accept the categorization of "interests" of the state and "rights" of individuals. Justice Wilson presents two major reasons for the state's continuing regulation of the dissolution of marriage and, by implication, the continuing involvement of the state in other aspects of family relations:

1.   The state has an interest in preserving the strength and autonomy of the family as a fundamental social institution;

---

* Vice-Président Academic and Professor of Law, University of Victoria, Victoria, B.C. Professor Fraser wishes to acknowledge the assistance of Peter Behie (LL.B., University of Victoria) in the preparation of this paper.

1. Bill C-10, First Reading January 19, 1984, Second Session, Thirty-second Parliament, 1983-84.
2. B. Wilson, "State Intervention in the Family", paper delivered at *C.I.A.J.*, 10th Annual Conference, Ottawa, October 21, 1984.

2.   The "moral dimension" of the state's intervention in family rela-
      tions - the protection and preservation of the role of marriage and
      the family in the moral life of the country.

Madam Justice Wilson concludes that with the dramatic changes
in social attitudes toward the indissolubility of marriage, the moral
dimension of state regulation has been very much reduced in importance. She implies that the state's interest in protecting the family as a
fundamental institution is vigorously assisted in legislative and judicial
pronouncements. It is here that we may have a point of disagreement.

My point is that Canadian family law lacks a coherent policy basis.
Legislation on family relations is piecemeal at best and judicial decisions often add to the confusion. The result is that conflicting signals
and mixed messages are sent to the community at large with respect to
the rationale for the involvement of the state in family matters.

Let me illustrate as follows. There is no agreement in law as to
what constitutes "the family". The definitional factor is missing. Dr.
Eichler illustrates the difficulty of providing a definition to apply to
family situations today,

> A family is a social group which may or may not include adults of both
> sexes (e.g. lone-parent families) may or may not include one or more
> children, (e.g. childless couples), who may or may not have been in their
> wedlock, (e.g. adopted children, or children by one adult partner of a
> previous union). The relationship of the adults may or may not have its
> origin in marriage (e.g., common law couples), they may or may not
> share a common residence (e.g., commuting couples). The adults may
> or may not cohabit sexually, and the relationship may or may not involve
> such socially patterned feelings as love, attraction, piety, and awe.[3]

Dr. Eichler points out that an examination of laws and policies will
provide specific definitions of family for particular purposes such as
marriage, property division, support, tax purposes and social welfare
purposes. This results in what she describes as "a multiplicity of family
definitions".[4]

Legislative provisions reflect this picture. Marriage laws exist,
one might argue, to enforce or support a societal view of a family or
marriage partnership - one must obey the rules and follow the procedures in order to acquire the status from which rights and obligations
flow. Not only are the sanctions for breach of these requirements relatively light, but a parallel system exists within the law whereby those

---

3. M. Eichler, *Families in Canada Today: Recent Changes and Their Policy Consequences*, Toronto, Gage, 1983, p. 3-4.

4. *Ibid.*, p. 5.

who choose to live together outside marriage acquire similar and in some cases identical rights and obligations.[5]

Similar arguments may be made with respect to the law relating to children which, for centuries, discriminated between legitimate and illegitimate children, vesting in the former significant advantages with respect to the rights of support, entitlement to property, use of name, inheritance and so on, whilst restricting at a minimal level the rights of the latter. In recent years the focus upon the "rights" of children has resulted in a blurring of the distinction and in some provinces the complete elimination of discriminatory provisions.[6]

Examples from reported cases are many but two will suffice as being illustrative of the difficulty of definition. In *R. v. R.*,[7] Mr. Justice Kerans stated,

> The fact is that there have been substantial changes over the past century in the attitude of our society about the ideal family situation. Once it was accepted that the husband and father was the decision-maker for the family, even about child-rearing questions and even after a marriage breakdown... the new "modern" marriage model involves not only the idea of the nuclear family, but also of the marital partnership where all major decision-making is shared. The partnership model has only just recently been accepted fully into the law by the enactment of the matrimonial property Act... the modern marriage model does not concede any special status to the father and therefore requires a new standard to decide custody cases...

> Some divergence in the roles of male and female was accepted in the newer model. The husband could continue to be the bread-winner and the wife could have a special responsibility as a professional homemaker. This does not say that she alone must carry the burden of child-rearing. But there were and are, in this model, a measure of acceptably different parental roles based upon gender...

> In what may be called the supra-modern marriage, strenuous efforts are made to avoid any role distinction based upon sex. The many tasks of homemaking and child-rearing - indeed, child bearing - are shared as completely as possible, and not on any gender basis. It follows, of course, that both fathers and mothers must, if this model is to work, acquire the skills and make the commitment which is required for effective parenting.[8]

---

5. For a detailed discussion see, W. Holland, *Unmarried Couples: Legal Aspects of Cohabitation*, Toronto, Carswell, 1982.

6. Some examples are, British Columbia, *Legitimacy Act*, R.S.B.C. 1979, c. 232; Ontario, *Legitimacy Act*, R.S.O. 1980, c. 68; New Brunswick *Legitimation Act*, R.S.N.B. 1973, c. L-4; see Holland, *supra*, note 5, p. 152 ff. for further discussion.

7. (1983), 34 R.F.L. (2d) 277 (Alta. C.A.).

8. *Ibid..*, p. 286-287.

Another example is the decision of the Supreme Court of Canada per Dickson, J., as he then was, in *Pettkus* v. *Becker*.[9] The case held, *inter alia*, that there was no basis for any distinction in dividing property and assets on equitable grounds between marital relationships and informal relationships which had lasted for a lengthy period of time. In a comment[10] Professor McLeod states,

> Historically, people who live together outside of marriage have been in large part ignored. Current society has generated so many such unions that the law has been forced to face the issue. By legislation children born of such unions are given greater rights than before, "spouses" are given support rights and the Supreme Court of Canada has extended modified property rights. The family is a building block of society. The same social and economic effect of breakdown is felt by members of extra-legal families as by those of legal families. Although extra security may justifiably be given to legal family members because of social pressure, to ignore extra-legal families is unrealistic...
>
> Not all couples living together should fall within the scope of the decision, but only those whose long-standing in relationship has generated the trust and lack of formality which surrounds married couples. The search for this boundary may prove to be the most difficult legacy of the decision. The relaxation in matrimonial cases of the principles utilised in "stranger" property cases justifies the relaxation of such principles in cases of unmarried couples falling within the boundary. What lies unexpressed in the reasons for the judgment of Dickson, J. is that current morality will accept "special treatment" of unmarried couples.

It is arguable that these jurisprudential developments simply mirror the confusion and reflect the ambivalence of society with respect to the variety of family and marital arrangements which presently exist. In essence, they reduce the "interests" of the state to an economic role vis-a-vis spouses and a protective and economic role in the case of children.

Family law can be said, therefore, to be reactive to societal situations rather than enforcing a perceived moral or institutional stance. Family law may well be all things to all men, women and children.

THE DISSOLUTION OF MARRIAGE AND ITS ECONOMIC CONSEQUENCES

Madam Justice Wilson has referred to the evolution of divorce law in Canada. In 1968 we moved from a restrictive offence-based law to a system in which matrimonial offence and marriage breakdown coexist - a politically and socially acceptable half-way house between fault and no-fault.

---

9. [1980] 2 S.C.R. 834, 19 R.F.L. (2d) 165, 8 E.T.R. 143, 177 D.L.R. (3d) 257.
10. (1980) 19 R.F.L. (2d) 165.

Reforms of 1968 did not complete the process. The Law Reform Commission of Canada undertook as one of its major priorities a project on family law. The Commission recommended the elimination of the fault concept as a basis for the dissolution of marriage. In its place there would be recognition of the right to divorce upon evidence by either spouse that there had been an irretrievable breakdown of the marriage.[11] The Commission recommended strongly that the process of dissolution should be placed, as far as possible, in a non-adversarial setting.

Bill C-10[12] was introduced in the House of Commons in January, 1984. It purported to eliminate ''fault'' as a basis for divorce and as a factor in decisions concerning spousal maintenance. It strengthened the rights of children by recognizing the need for legal representation in certain cases and by placing a greater emphasis upon the best interests of the child. But the dissolution process was to remain rooted in the adversarial mold subject only to a clause permitting the provinces to introduce new rules of court.

It is likely that the elimination of fault would have received general approval indicating a further lessening of the role of the state in bolstering the family unit.[13]

The major focus of the ''interest'' of the state in the regulation of the dissolution of marriage is of an economic nature. The economic rights of spouses upon dissolution are seen as requiring state intervention, and, for the most part, are not to be left to private ordering.

There have been fundamental legislative changes concerning support obligation and property rights in Canada. Time permits only brief reference in general terms.

The ''offence'' or ''fault'' of a spouse has been eliminated in most provinces as a consideration in the determination of support obligations. Section 10 of Bill C-10 would have accomplished this objective in divorce legislation. The law recognizes *mutual* support obligations of spouses rather than the traditional responsibility of the husband. The emphasis in legislation and in judicial decisions has moved from the objective of ''financial support for a lifetime'' to a consideration of needs and capacity to pay together with the expressed legislative objective of the attainment of financial self-sufficiency within a period of time.

In spite of extensive reforms in substantive and to some degree in procedural law, serious problems remain. An emphasis upon the attainment of self-sufficiency creates considerable difficulty, particularly for

---

11. Law Reform Commission of Canada, *Divorce*, Working Paper No. 13, 1975, p. 33-34.
12. *Supra*, note 1.
13. Wilson, *supra*, note 2, p. 14.

homemakers. Judicial discretion abounds in the assessment of support obligations and has resulted in conflicting and irreconcilable results. The failure of the enforcement system for support obligations is a dramatic illustration of the limitations of reality. And the formation of new family units by former spouses has resulted in wide variations in cases where judges, without the benefit of specific legislative direction, must deal with competing demands for support from various parties.

The result of legislative recognition of support obligations of spouses in today's society has demonstrated the need for comprehensive policies in which private law and public or social policy objectives are interlocked.

FAMILY PROPERTY

Comprehensive reforms have occurred in the law of family property. A responsive and expectant social climate, the politicization of the issues, the comprehensive work of Law Reform Commissions and the leadership of the courts in certain instances[14] laid the groundwork for legislative changes directed to achieve an equitable sharing of assets upon the dissolution of a marriage. In addition to this objective, many reformers and observers had hoped that legislative action would bring about major changes in the way in which marital disputes were dealt with. In particular, there was anticipation that procedures could be devised to reduce the adversarial nature of proceedings, to reduce the bitterness of the parties who were engaged in the dissolution of their marriage, to encourage dispute resolution by processes short of the judicial proceedings, and to lessen the financial costs and time involved in the processing of divorce and related proceedings. Mediation, arbitration and conciliation were seen as attractive alternative dispute resolution techniques.

In many provinces these objectives have not been achieved and, in fact, there has been a dramatic increase in family litigation concurrent with an increased emphasis upon the adversarial nature of the proceedings and a significant increase in costs.

This matter was touched upon recently by the Honourable Allan McEachern, Chief Justice of the Supreme Court of British Columbia.[15]

Chief Justice McEachern stated,

Family law has been completely captured by the experts, particularly actuaries, appraisers, pension consultants and business valuators, mainly,

---

14. Laskin, J. in *Murdoch* v. *Murdoch* (1975), 13 R.F.L. 185; *Rathwell* v. *Rathwell*, [1974] R.F.L. 297; *Pettkus* v. *Becker* (1980), 19 R.F.L. (2d) 165.
15. A. McEachern, *The Suffocation of the Court System*, paper delivered at the International Symposium on the Role of the Legal Profession in the Twenty-First Century, in Vancouver, August, 1984.

I am told, because counsel think they will be found guilty of negligence if they do not match the other side, expert for expert, even though no lawyer has ever been found guilty of negligence for failing to call experts.[16]

Describing the unsatisfactory state of family law, he went on to say,

Many judges think family law is not as it should be in that it has become too expensive for most disputants. Never before in the history of human legal conflict have so many spouses paid so much to have their assets apportioned between themselves and their advisors. Never before have we had a situation where opposing lawyers in litigation each have an assurance that they will be well-paid regardless of how well or how poorly they perform as long as there is equity in the family home. And never before has legislation made so much litigation possible.

I wonder if our legislators understood when the *Family Relations Act* was enacted, that angry spouses, with or without cause, can now arbitrarily insist upon division of assets which often makes it necessary for homes, farms and businesses to be sold without regard to good economic practices. The result is often that a healthy economic unit becomes two units that are not healthy and that, because of legal and expert fees, taxes and market losses, the sum of the two parts is nowhere close to what the parties started with.[17]

This state of affairs was foreseen in some jurisdictions. Rosemary Brown, M.L.A., speaking in the B.C. Legislature on the proposed family relations legislation said,

We recognize that it's really a lawyer's bill, and that the lawyers are going to have a field day with it - creating new precedents, interpreting words, interpreting meanings, and dealing with new principles which they've never had to deal with before such as the whole concept of equality in marriage. And we recognize for the next three or four or may be even ten years there's going to be utter chaos in the province in terms of really working out this piece of legislation.[18]

In a perceptive and comprehensive analysis of the new legislation[19] and its interpretation after a few years before the courts, Professor Keith Farquhar wrote,

For what it is worth, the gloomy prediction is offered that, while the legislation remains in its present form, there is very little hope for certainty in either the short or long term. The point has been made several times, and is made once again with respect, that the present state of the law has little to do with the courts. They have done the best they could with legislation which is difficult and confusing, but at the last they have been defeated by the paradoxes of the legislation itself. The antithetical principles of "equal division" and "unfairness" and the marked delim-

---

16. *Ibid.*, p. 24.
17. *Ibid.*, p. 35-36.
18. *Debates of the B.C. Legislature*, 3rd Session, 31st Parliament, 2nd Reading, Bill 22, p. 2677.
19. *Family Relations Act*, R.S.B.C. 1979, c. 121.

itation of the principles of property entitlement on the one side and the principles of maintenance on the other, are not calculated to bring about a subtle line of authority.[20]

It may well be fortuitous that Bill C-10 died on the order paper. With federal-provincial cooperation, opportunities abound for the development of rational policies with respect to the dissolution of marriage and its economic consequences. In addition, action must be taken to develop a coherence between the rights and obligations under private family law and the complementary role of the state in providing support through social legislation.

Professor Payne has stated the challenge as follows,

> In summation, the economic crises provoked by the breakdown of marriage are unlikely to be resolved by the private family law system or the public law system. The concept that marriage constitutes a basis for economic security for a dependent spouse is no longer tenable but the answer does not lie in the legal system but in the development of coordinated policies that will facilitate economic viability through job security and equal opportunities for career advancement for all Canadians, whether male or female.[21]

RIGHTS OF CHILDREN

In spite of the considerable activity of Law Reform Commissions, scholars, government, policy advisors and advocacy groups, children in Canada have limited legal rights. Some progress has been made in the past ten years and to illustrate developments I want to touch upon three separate issues: the rights of parties in adoption proceedings, the attempts to recognize the rights of children in the law of custody, and the procedural recognition of the right to independent legal representation of children.

ADOPTION

It is in the area of adoption law and policy that one can predict with some certainty considerable public debate and possible legislative action within the next few years.

An examination of the rights of individuals and the interest of the state in adoption matters yields a host of conflicting administrative policies, legislative provisions and judicial pronouncements.[22]

---

20. K. Farquhar, ''The New Matrimonial Property Legislation in British Columbia: The First Year'' (1981), 15 *U.B.C.L. Rev.* 1-86, p. 81.
21. Julien Payne, *The Impact of Family Law on the Economic and Social Well Being of Families in Canada*, unpublished report, prepared for the Royal Commission on the Economic Union on the Development Prospects for Canada, 1984.
22. Compare the views of each of the following authors, R. Abella, ''Procedural Aspects for Children Upon Divorce in Canada'' (1983), 61 *Can. Bar. Rev.* 443; S. Borins,

Viewed in an historical context, adoption in Canada served a limited number of objectives. It provided homes and traditional "two-parent families" for infants, the great majority of whom were born out of wedlock. It provided "families" for those who were unable to bear children. It served the economic interests of the state by transferring to the adoptive family the economic responsibility for longterm child care in the situations which otherwise might result in financial expenditure by the state to support foster parents. Occasionally, it provided welfare for a single mother who might attempt to support her illegitimate child.

To support these objectives, the law developed over the years to a point where the adopted child became, in legal terms, equivalent to a natural child of the family, thereby obtaining inheritance, maintenance and other rights from its adoptive parents. At the same time the adopted child was amputated in law from its natural parents. The "right" of an infant to a "normal" family upbringing, the interest of family members in "acquiring" children, and the interest of the state - all were said to be met by these arrangements.

With the passage of the *Divorce Act* of 1968 came the phenomenon of step-parent adoptions. Divorced persons created new family units through marriage with new partners who were anxious to solidify the "family" by appropriate legal means - in many cases by the adoption of the child or children of the new partner. In most provinces step-parent adoptions are now in the majority and, in many cases, provincial authorities are not required to carry out home studies or make recommendations on the appropriateness of the proposed adoption.

Step-parent adoptions were not contemplated by legislation passed decades ago, yet they produce results in law that are identical to those which are achieved in other adoptions. But different questions arise.

In step-parent adoptions, generally speaking, older children are adopted. They know their natural parents, or their grandparents. They have grown up with their family name. They are already part of a traditional family unit. They are legitimate children whose status will not be improved by adoption. In fact, some provinces have abolished the distinction in law between illegitimate and legitimate children, thereby removing an argument in favour of the legal results of the traditional adoption.[23] Legislation in some provinces provides for the proposed adoptee to signify his or her consent but this is of little use to many children in the process.

"Family Assessments in Custody And Access Disputes Under the Children's Law Reform Act, 1977" (1982), 24 *R.F.L.* (2d) 90-98; B. Chisholm, "Obtaining and Weighing the Children's Wishes - Private Interviews with a Judge or Assessment by an Expert Report" (1976), 23 *R.F.L.* 1-12.

23. See Holland, *supra*, note 5.

It is debatable whether the rights of the parties are secured by the application of existing adoption legislation and policy to these situations, particularly in light of data which indicate the failure of second marriages on a rather large scale and an increasing number of failed adoptions.

A related but separate issue is the "right" to access to information concerning birth parents or natural children. This issue continues to surface in Canada where a variety of devices - active registries, passive registries, ministerial discretion, judicial discretion and self-help remedies - exist to deal with the situation.[24]

One concludes with a series of questions. Are the rights of the individual adequately recognized in the present circumstances? Should modifications be made to grant a child, upon the attainment of the age of majority, a right to receive information concerning its natural parents? Should such a right be unfettered or should it be limited to purposes related to health? These and other issues relating to rights of the parties to adoption proceedings require careful attention.

CUSTODY

Decisions concerning the custody of an infant are among the most perplexing questions for the law. The evolution of the law of custody reflects changing attitudes in society. It develops from the "parental right" or "chattel theory" dominated early on by the recognition of the father's role as head of the household but tempered by the device of awarding care and control to the mother, to the gradual recognition of the "right of the child" to have his/her "best interests" recognized as the major, and recently, the sole determinant of the issue. There was general adherence to the "best interests of the child" principle which was determined in each case by the judicial selection and application of "rules of thumb" such as the tender years doctrine. On occasion a third party - a grandparent, an aunt or uncle, or even a non-relative - would receive recognition by the courts as a person to whom custody might be granted but, generally speaking, the mother received custody in the great majority of cases, and the father in the remainder.

In recent years there has been increasing recognition by the judiciary of the importance of expert evidence in custody cases. This factor and more vigorous representation of children's interest by legal counsel have resulted in a greater variety of and more flexibility in arrangements to meet the best interests of children in custody matters.

---

24. F.M. Fraser and H.D. Kirk, "Cui Bono? Some Questions Concerning the Best Interests of the Child Principle in Canadian Adoption Laws and Practices", in K. Connell-Thouez and B. Knoppers, eds., *Contemporary Trends in Family Law: A National Perspective*, Toronto, Carswell, 1984, p. 105-119.

The most comprehensive attempts by way of legislation are found in recent amendments, for example, in British Columbia, where the family relations act[25] provides as follows,

> 24. Best interests of child are paramount. —
> (1) Where making, varying or rescinding an order under this part, a court shall give paramount consideration to the best interests of the child and, in assessing these interests, shall consider these factors:
>
> (a) the health and emotional well being of the child including any special needs for care and treatment;
> (b) where appropriate, the views of the child;
> (c) the love, affection, and similar ties that exist between the child and other person;
> (d) education and training for the child; and
> (e) the capacity of each person to whom guardianship, custody or access rights and duties may be granted to exercise these rights and duties adequately; and give emphasis to each factor according to the child's needs and circumstances.
>
> (2) Where the guardianship of the estate of a child is at issue, a court shall consider as an additional factor the material well being of the child.
>
> (3) Where the conduct of a person does not substantially effect a factor set out in sub-section (1) or (2), the court shall not consider that conduct in a proceeding respecting an order under this part.
>
> (4) Where under subsection (3) the conduct of a person may be considered by a court, the court shall consider the conduct only to the extent that the conduct affects a factor set out in subsection (1) or (2).

Progress has also occurred, at least insofar as legislative action is concerned, in attempts to determine and enforce the best interests of the child. For example, in Ontario, recent amendments to the *Children's Law Reform Act*[26] illustrate the interventionist role of the state by providing for assessments, mediation, investigation and the supervision of orders. It is too early to evaluate these provisions but they emphasize the increasing role of the state on behalf of children.[27]

LEGAL REPRESENTATION OF CHILDREN

In the past ten to fifteen years significant changes have occurred in providing mechanisms to ensure that those interests are identified and canvassed thoroughly before the courts. I have referred earlier to

---

25. R.S.B.C. 1979, c. 121.
26. *Children's Law Reform Act*, R.S.O. 1980, c. 68, as am. by Stats. Ont. 1982, c. 20.
27. Views of experts are by no means unanimous. See *supra*, note 20.

changes in the substantive law of custody. At the procedural level there is now general acceptance of the right of the child to independent legal counsel.

As Judge Abella points out,

> But if one perceives the essence of custody actions to be not the right of a parent to custody of a child, but rather the right of the child to have his or her needs met by the person best able to meet those needs, then the focus must be on the child. To ensure that this continues to be the focus, an advocate for the child is often helpful, and frequently indispensable. The existence of a child advocate allows full participation in decisions that affect the child, and enhance the child's perception of the process as a fair one.[28]

In many jurisdictions specific legislative amendments have been introduced.[29] It must be noted, however, that in some jurisdictions the decision to appoint a legal representative or family advocate remains with a party outside the proceedings and, for economic and other reasons, the discretion may not be exercised to the benefit of the child.[30]

A further problem is that the legislation establishing the right of a child to independent legal counsel has failed to define the role and responsibilities of such counsel and has resulted in confusion and ambiguity with respect to this concept.[31]

Dr. Eichler comments,

> One last consideration in this context concerns procedural rather than substantive law. If the emphasis in custody decisions is on serving the best interests of the child rather than the rights of the parents, then this involves a change from assessing past behaviours of parents (''which parent has behaved best'') to an assessment of the future, ''a process more ethereal than a review of historical occurrences'' (Bayda 1980:66) given that such a dramatic shift in substantive law has occurred, Bayda argues that it must be accompanied by an equally dramatic shift in adjective law. It has been found over the years that the technique most suited to coping with the future, with a formulation of plans and the like, is not the adversarial approach but the investigative or scientific method. (Bayda, 1980:66). He therefore suggests that only two rules should apply in the future in any enquiry:
> > (1) Anything reasonable that will assist in this search should be brought forward and examined, and

---

28. R. Abella, ''Procedural Aspects of Arrangements for Children Upon Divorce in Canada'' (1983), 61 *Can. Bar. Rev.* 443, 446.

29. *Children's Law Reform Act*, R.S.O. 1980, c. 68, as am. by Stats. Ont. 1982, c. 20, s. 1(60).

30. See, for example, the B.C. legislation, *Family Relations Act*, R.S.B.C. 1979, c. 121, s. 2, which provides for the appointment of a Family Advocate at the discretion of the Attorney General.

31. See M.J.J. McHale, ''The Proper Role of the Lawyer as Legal Representative of the Child'' (1980), 18 Alta. L. Rev. 216.

(2) The setting should be one of informality, but a *predictable* informality.[32]

There has been legislative acceptance of the principle of legal representation but a failure to define the role and responsibilities of the office.

FAMILY COURTS

In 1974, the Law Reform Commission of Canada[33] recommended the implementation of a system of unified family courts as a "logical first step to meet a pressing need". The need might be identified as the right of participants in disputes arising from family relationships to a system of justice which ensures, as far as is possible, the resolution of these disputes in a dignified, supportive and inexpensive manner. The essential elements include a court with exclusive and comprehensive jurisdiction in family matters and the existence of auxiliary services for the parties. Mediation, arbitration and conciliation are more appropriate than adversarial procedures in the resolution of family disputes.

The commission commented upon the confusion, despair and frustration of the parties in family disputes as being caused by the fragmented jurisdiction of the courts, adversarial procedures, inadequate or non-existent support services, conflicting philosophies and heavy costs of litigation, all of which led to a lack of respect for the courts and the legal system.[34]

In some jurisdictions unified family courts have been established. For the most part, however, the family court suffers the disabilities which were identified more than a decade ago.

THE LEGAL PROFESSION

A study of the evolution of family law in Canada would be incomplete without a detailed understanding of the actions and attitudes of the members of the legal profession and their representative institutions.

It is fair to state that the profession paid little attention to family law until the early 1960's. Prior to that time the only area of interest was divorce and, with some exceptions, divorce practitioners were not highly regarded by their colleagues. They seemed to operate, for the most part, in the shadow of the process. In spite of the obvious inade-

---

32. Eichler, *supra*, note 3, at pp. 295 to 296.
33. Law Reform Commission of Canada, *The Family Court*, Working Paper #1, 1974.
34. The Law Reform Commission of Canada endorsed those recommendations in a Report entitled *Family Law*, 1976.

quacies and hardships of existing law and practice of divorce, lawyers showed little interest in reform.

About twenty years ago a number of factors combined to heighten the profession's interest in family law. The introduction of legal aid schemes greatly expanded access to legal advice and the courts, particularly for women. Family law became respectable and, in many cases, profitable. Law Reform Commissions devoted considerable resources to the study and proposed reform of family law. At the same time, the issues took on an increasingly public dimension. For the first time the faculties of law established comprehensive courses in family law resulting in a more knowledgeable and critical legal profession.

In sum, there was a realisation, publicly and professionally, that reform was required and would likely be acceptable in the political sense. There was a commitment of resources to the search for the solution to the major legal problems in family relations.

Reforms did indeed occur and opened up new areas of practice for the legal profession. With these opportunities came a marked increase in the numbers of lawyers who practiced family law; not surprisingly, success and volume also brought about additional problems with respect to competence and related matters. Let me give one illustration. Governance of the legal profession rests with the law societies in each province. An underlying premise of professional self-government is that the profession will govern in the public interest. I want to examine this premise in the context of the issue of specialisation. The time has come for the legal profession to designate procedures by which, upon the completion of appropriate educational instruction and examination, practitioners may be certified as specialists and would remain so upon regular recertification. I am aware, of course, of the considerable efforts of certain segments of the bar to introduce specialisation as an acceptable concept. But the goal has not yet been achieved. It is in the public interest that there be a system of specialisation in family law rather than the continued acceptance of back-door specialisation through the holding out of family law as a preferred area or by the restriction of one's practice to family law. This amounts to misleading advertising by the legal profession. Members of the general public do not understand the fine distinction, if one exists, between these designations and that of a full-fledged, properly qualified specialist.

There is without a doubt a specialised body of law and procedure in family law which commands the attention of specially qualified practitioners. The profession should resolve the matter now.

An optimist may see a breakthrough in recent developments concerning mediation by lawyers in British Columbia. In that province the benchers have received the report of a sub-committee which has resulted in the adoption of the following ruling by the law society of British Columbia,

3. A member may act as a family law mediator only if he or she

(a) (i) has been engaged in the full-time practice of law for at least three years or the equivalent in part-time practice,

or (ii) has been approved by the professional standards committee because of special qualifications or experience: and

(b) has completed a course of study in family law and mediation approved by the professional standards committee.

Recognition that continuing education and/or special qualifications are required in mediation opens the door to similar developments in the general area of family law.

CONCLUSIONS

The justification for the intervention of the state in the regulation of family relations rests upon an interest in the economic relations of the parties and the protection of the rights of children.

Private family law does not reflect a coherent policy with regard to rights and obligations of the individuals involved in family relations. There is a need for the development of policies which interlock the objectives of private family law and those of public social legislation.

The rights of individuals within "the family", broadly defined, will receive increasing attention in the legislatures and the courts.

PART II

THE ENFORCEMENT OF RIGHTS

L'EXÉCUTION DES DROITS

"The choice for mankind lay between freedom and happiness..., for the great bulk... happiness was better."

"... l'espèce humaine avait le choix entre la liberté et le bonheur, ... et le bonheur valait mieux."

George Orwell, *1984*

ACCESS TO LAW

L'ACCÈS À LA LOI

The Role of Legal Aid and Legal Clinics

Archie Campbell*

My particular topic focuses on access to the law with specific reference to the delivery of legal aid and most particularly the growth of community legal aid clinics as one of the methods of making the law much more widely accessible to those people who are most in need of the protection of the law.

Those of us in this room who spend most or all of our working life interpreting laws, applying laws, working with laws, making laws, are very keenly aware of the importance of the rule of law. I think that is a very special awareness which we have which is not shared generally by the public at large to any great extent. You don't hear people on the streetcar muttering about the rule of law; you don't see people walking up and down the street with signs picketing to support the rule of law.

The difficulty with the rule of law in Canada today is very largely that the laws are so complex, there are so many of them, they are such a bewildering quandry to people who find themselves caught up in the web of the law, that ordinary people find it very difficult to understand that whole system. Perhaps if we had fewer laws or if the laws were more clear, that situation would be a little bit better. But generally speaking, no matter how clear we try to make our laws, you always need someone who is skilled - an articulate legal adviser, perhaps a lawyer, perhaps a community legal worker - somebody who is familiar with the system and who can bring it home to the ordinary person who needs the law or who needs the protection of the law.

The Attorney General for Ontario recently said to the Standing Committee of the Administration of Justice in a debate about the need for the legal aid and the need for public support for the legal aid system, that those of us who spend our lives working with laws often forget what a bewildering and often intimidating patch-work legal rules form. Moreover, we may also forget that achieving the passage of a law is

---

* Deputy Attorney General for Ontario. Formerly Director of Parkdale Community Legal Services, Toronto.

quite a different thing from ensuring its effect and equal application. Laws govern vital aspects of the lives of every resident of this province. To deny any citizen access to legal services is to reduce citizens to subjects and to entrench inequality in its most fundamental and unjust sense. To the extent that any person is excluded from the rule of law, the rule of law is weakened; and to the extent that it can be said realistically that there is one rule of law for the rich and another law for the poor, then to that extent the rule of law is not what it's made out to be. If people don't have access to legal advice or to legal services, all of the work we do and all of the work that is done in the legislatures is really of no force and effect.

The legal profession for centuries has had a fine tradition of public service, pro-bono work before the widespread introduction of legal aid plans in Canada. To some extent still today, a great number of lawyers would give their services free of charge or with very little charge to people who could not afford legal representation. That kind of a system worked relatively well until the 1950's and 1960's when it became rapidly apparent that the occasional charity of the public-spirited lawyer was no systematic machinery for making legal services available to those who couldn't afford them. In most of the provinces in the 1960's or 1970's full-scale legal aid plans were launched.

Legal Aid is generally described as a partnership between the government and the private Bar. Of course it works differently from province to province. Because the legal advice has to be absolutely independent of government, you get some very interesting and healthy tensions between the kind of independence you have to have in the delivery of legal advice, and the kind of accountability that is always required when you are working with the taxpayers money.

One of the most interesting developments I think in legal aid in the last fifteen years or so, has been the steady growth of the community legal aid clinics. People have come to realize generally that the kinds of problems that poor people have are not readily susceptible of service in a traditional law office. Stephen Waxler, the Harvard professor who is such a pioneer of the community legal aid clinic model in the United States, persistently pointed out that poor people are not like rich people without money. They have very special categories of legal problems of their own. He said poor people are always bumping into sharp legal things. It is to bridge that gap between the traditional methods of delivering legal services and the tremendous unmet need that existed in the public, that the community clinic movement started to develop. There were a couple of university-based clinics and then in Ontario, around 1975, the system was regularized and put on a much more formal footing.

In a province like Ontario where growth and public funding has not been dramatic in many areas and where there has been a great deal of constraint in many years, the community legal aid clinic budget has probably grown faster than any other area of public funding in Ontario during that period of time. It started with eight clinics and a budget of two or three hundred thousand dollars. Now we have about forty-four clinics and there are four more on the way within the next six months. The budget now is about 10 million dollars. That has not been the result of unbridled growth, it has been largely planned.

One of the most exciting ways that the legal aid community clinic movement has developed in Ontario is how it developed in response to individual communities and individual kinds of needs. There is a wide diversity from one part of the province to the other in the kind of clinics they are, the kinds of local boards they have, and the kind of work they do.

Just to take two examples out of the forty-four clinics, the Canadian Environmental Law Association does a full case service for individuals and other public bodies and hearings, official plan references, pit inquiry applications, waste disposal, land site applications, nuisance and negligence actions, and a whole range of environmental concerns. There is another clinic called the Central Toronto Community Legal Clinic on Bathurst Street dealing with most areas of low income law, administrative tribunals, Immigration Appeal Board, Workmen's Compensation Board, Social Assistance Review Board, rent review, employment standard branches, and small claims courts. Until you actually sit down and take a look at a set of welfare regulations one cannot appreciate how complicated things can be, and that is just one example of the kind of thing that an ordinary law office is simply not equipped to deliver to an ordinary client. But with legal aid clinics with economies of scale and the specialization of community-based legal aid workers who are not lawyers but who are supervised by lawyers, you can get that service much more readily understood by the client and yet have it much more effectively delivered.

The Report of the Clinic Funding Commission under the Honourable Mr. Justice Grange in 1968, reviewed the gaps in the Legal Aid Plan and pointed out that the private Bar and its clients know that it is sometimes not sufficient merely to resolve an immediate problem. Often the client's welfare dictates more. He or she must know the dangers in order to avoid them in the future, and if they cannot be avoided the client may have to combine with others to attack the root of the problem. If the aims of legal aid as often stated are extending to the poor the same legal benefits as those available to their fortunate brothers, some method must be needed to provide for them.

I think that the growth of the clinics in Ontario has been one of the most dramatic improvements to the administration of justice that we have had in the last decade. I know the theme of the conference is

"Beyond 1984" and one of the liveliest issues with community legal aid clinics in the next few years could well turn out to be the precise boundary line between what is a legal service and what is something else. It is obvious that test case litigation is a legal service, and so is advising a community group on how to secure a legislative change, or a change in a by-law. The difficulty comes where you find large numbers of people with the same problem. It then becomes very obvious that it is only if they organize and get together that they are going to be able to change the general nature of the problem. You then enter into that never never land, the borderline between what is really political activity by a clinic and what is the delivery of the legal service. So far in Ontario, we have been very fortunate and I think the other provinces have been fortunate as well in that it has not been necessary to confront that delicate line. Hopefully, the continued development in Ontario and other provinces of the clinical movement will keep those lines clear and ensure that the development of the clinical movement will not be unduiy politicized.

The Media and the Legal System

Peter Herrndorf*

I should warn you right from the start that I'm here juggling two hats... somewhat precariously:

One, as a former television journalist and network executive, who still feels a strong sense of pride in the work of broadcast journalism in this country;

And two, as a law graduate who's just completed a refresher course by osmosis during my wife's three year stint as a producer on the CBC's series *"The Lawyers"*.

And so, with a foot tenuously in each camp, I have either the best or the worst perspective from which to deal with our topic today.

Although I'd like to keep my remarks quite short, I do want to deal briefly with three subjects:
* the impact of television as a medium and as a journalistic force;
* a somewhat revisionist view of the uneasy relationship between the media and the justice system; and
* some thoughts about how to improve that relationship for the benefit of the Canadian public.

As I've indicated, I'll be concentrating most of my remarks on television and television journalism, but many of the observations will relate equally to radio and print journalism.

Let me begin by giving you some facts about the Canadian television industry, and the broadcasting environment within which it operates.

Canadian television networks and stations face an extraordinary range of competition. In addition to the four American networks which are seen in most parts of the country, Canadian viewers have access to two publicly owned Canadian networks (CBC and Radio Canada); three private Canadian networks (CTV, Global & TVA); four educational

---

* Publisher, Toronto Life Magazine.

networks, seen in different parts of the country; eight pay television services; and a number of independent stations on both sides of the border. As a result, many viewers in cities such as Toronto, Montreal and Vancouver can now choose from more than twenty American and Canadian channels.

CBC radio and television operates the largest journalistic organization in the country and provides a continuous diet of news and current affairs programming on a local, regional and network level almost every hour of every day of the year;

The impact of television continues to be profound in Canada. I'd like to give you a few examples:

- One episode of a popular Canadian drama series (like "*Empire*") has a larger audience in a single night than all of Canadian theatre in an entire year; the audience for last night's edition of "*The National*" and "*The Journal*" will have been considerably larger than the combined daily circulation of the Globe, the Toronto Star, the Montreal Gazette and Le Devoir;
- Canadians now spend about half of their leisure time watching T.V., an average of about 23 hours per Canadian per week or 3 hours per day for every man, woman and child in Canada;
- All the time that Canadians spend reading books, newspapers and magazines, going to the movies, theatre, ballet, or the symphony, cheering on Wayne Gretzky or Guy Lafleur, or thinking about raking the leaves, is only a tiny fraction of the time they spend watching television;
- Most research surveys now suggest that Canadians get the great bulk of their information from T.V., far more than from newspapers or magazines;
- By the time our children reach the age of twelve, they will have seen *12,000* hours of television, something like twice as much time as they've spent in school;
- And, at the almost bizarre level, it's now projected that the average Canadian will spend nine years of his or her life in front of a television set. Think about that when you're watching Knowlton reading "*The National*".

Given that amount of television viewing, particularly by children, and the persuasive and impressionistic nature of the medium, it's safe to assume that television is awesome as a cultural conditioner. It conditions, in a subtle and often insidious way, our values and assumptions, creates many of our heroes, myths, role models, and our expectations about life. It accelerates social trends and often determines our views about what's good and what's second rate and, most significantly, it conditions our attitudes to our history, traditions, institutions and our sense of self esteem as a people.

In these circumstances, Canadians have every right to expect that television should provide them with a range of first class news and current affairs programming keeping them fully informed, helping them to understand the major issues of the times, and helping them to make the endless choices (large and small) that all of us are required to make on a daily basis.

By and large, I think that Canadian television lives up to *that standard*, and I could argue that it does so more effectively than is the case in either the United States or Britain.

But before I come across as some latter day "Candide", I should quickly point out that T.V. news and current affairs in Canada still has a lot of shortcomings and can often be quite maddening in its limitations.

Let me, for the moment, confine my remarks to the CBC, and give you my assessment of the strengths and weaknesses of its network service:

a) The plus side of the ledger has to begin with a simple assertion: CBC News and current affairs is doing a better job of informing its audiences than ever before. It provides more information, more rapidly, more accurately, and from more parts of the country and the world than anyone would have thought possible even a decade ago.

b) CBC Television provides more news and current affairs programming in its prime time schedule than the BBC, the three American commercial networks, CTV or Global, and it's part of a conscious effort to make the CBC *the* information network in Canada.

c) The introduction of the news at 10:00 and *"The Journal"* has improved the CBC's journalistic service significantly. It's provided a national forum for the major stories, issues and personalities in Canada and given a uniquely Canadian perspective on an increasingly volatile international scene.

d) *"The Fifth Estate"* performs a different function for the CBC. It provides Canadians with some of the best original reporting in journalism. Programs such as Eric Malling's *"Canadair Special"*, John Zaritsky's *"Just Another Missing Kind"*, and Hana Gartner's portrait of *The Ocean Ranger Disaster* represent an invaluable journalistic service.

e) Simultaneously, CBC documentary series continue to be among the finest in the world. I find it difficult to imagine that documentary mini-series like the *"Canadian Establishment"*, *"Connections"*, *"War"*, *"The Music of Man"* and the upcoming series on *The Canadian Legal Profession* would be produced by any other North American network.

f)   The CBC's commitment to news and current affairs over the past
      fifteen years has also led to the development of a large number of
      highly talented reporters, editors, hosts, and producers. They're
      more experienced, better educated, and have more specialized
      skills than ever before.

g)   The CBC also has a strong tradition of journalistic independence,
      and despite periodic efforts to pressure or cajole CBC journalists,
      that "Arm's length tradition" has made it possible for the CBC
      to be quite rigorous in its coverage of business and political insti-
      tutions in this country.

But there's also a downside to the CBC news and current affairs
coverage, much of it endemic to North American television journalism.
And it's these journalistic limitations that have fuelled a good deal of
the criticism and mistrust of the media that I've heard expressed within
the legal community.

It may be worthwhile running through the litany of complaints that
particularly rankle the legal profession these days. As you'll notice,
very few of these criticisms are couched in the muted and cerebral tones
for which lawyers are so renowned. They include the following:

i)   The media is simply ill informed about legal issues, and the
      reporting and editing are largely simplistic and shallow and fre-
      quently inaccurate;

ii)   In its haste to get a story on air (or into a newspaper), the media
      often trivializes important decisions by concentrating on the most
      contentious aspects of a case without contributing to a deeper
      understanding of the complex issues involved;

iii) Network newscasts are unwilling to devote more than ninety sec-
      onds of airtime to complicated legal stories or decisions and con-
      sistently fail to provide the necessary texture or subtlety to their
      coverage;

iv)   The media often ignores the legal system and is unwilling to give
      it the kind of space more regularly devoted to politics, wars, plane
      crashes, fires, and strikes. The media pursues this editorial line
      because of a reluctance to tackle difficult and abstract stories,
      stories that don't have the "visuals" that producers are looking
      for;

v)   When the media does cover the legal system in a major way,
      competitive considerations dictate the coverage of the most noto-
      rious cases (like Colin Thatcher and Susan Nelles) rather than the
      cases that break new legal ground. The media would far rather
      pursue colourful legal personalities and human interest features
      than have to deal with the balancing of complex legal interests.

As you might imagine, I don't accept all of these criticisms; but if
you disregard some of the rhetoric, there's an element of truth in each
of the allegations.

I happen to believe that the quality of the specialist reporters covering our courts has improved dramatically in recent years. But I have to admit that we had a long way to go. I'll also acknowledge that my profession sometimes trivializes major stories, that it's hampered by time constraints (both deadlines and space), and that television is often more preoccupied with ''great pictures'' than it needs to be.

But I also want to stress that the relationship between the media and the legal profession is very much a two-way street. Most of the reporters and editors in this field are highly skilled and take their responsibility very seriously, not only because the public relies on their work, but because they're professionals who take a great deal of pride in their craft.To a great degree, they feel that the Canadian justice system is often its own worst enemy when it comes to dealing with the press. They feel strongly that the courts and the legal profession have a significant role to play in improving the quality of journalistic coverage.

Over the past few weeks in preparing these remarks, I canvassed half of a dozen senior journalists who've specialized in this field in recent years. I think it might be instructive to hear their side of the story - what it's like covering the Canadian justice system.

I should begin by saying that all of these journalists are determined to protect the dignity and integrity of the judicial system, and all of them speak with respect for the values and traditions of our legal system.

But they're also unanimous on one other point - all of them feel that ''the legal affairs beat'' is a particularly difficult and frustrating one for them. They sense a tremendous ambivalence about the press on the part of the courts and the legal profession:

- on the one hand, the courts and the legal profession want more accurate and thorough coverage and look to the media to explain and publicize the way the legal process works;

- but on the other hand, most of the courts aren't organized to assist the press in either function. The courts and the law societies frequently hinder and restrict a reasonably free flow of information. The press is often treated as a nuisance (at best) and as a potential impediment to the administration of justice.

This ambivalence, the reporters argue, does real damage to the public's understanding of one of our great democratic cornerstones and it makes it far more difficult to bring the law within the reach of those whom it is intended to serve. More specifically they argue that:

1) The courts are poorly equipped to deal with the basic day to day requirements of the working press. Reporters sometimes have difficulty finding out when cases are coming up and where they'll be heard, the probable length of the trial or when the judgments are being handed down (unless they've really cultivated the judge's secretary). They have difficulty getting enough copies of a decision and it's sometimes difficult to order them in advance. Courtrooms are often booked without any thought given to accommodating all of the reporters covering the court. These aren't exactly cosmic issues, but they make it more difficult for journalists, working under deadline pressures, to function effectively;

2) The reporters also argue that most courts have outdated restrictions on access to the judicial system. They're particularly critical about the prohibition on the use of small, portable tape recorders in the courtroom, contending that the tape recorder is the electronic equivalent of a print reporter's note pad and pencil. The tape recorders are unobtrusive and soundless and allow reporters to retain complex parts of the proceedings in a much more precise and accurate way than by shorthand;

3) Although there's a good deal of debate within the journalistic community about giving courtroom access to television cameras, the electronic press makes the case forcefully:

   i) Since radio and television journalism need sound and pictures to convey an accurate reflection of a story, why should the electronic press have to live with court rules designed many years ago for the print press.

   The complete denial of electronic access, a blackout, if you will, severely restricts radio and television reporters in portraying a real picture of our courts proceedings.

   ii) Television cameras have become much smaller, can be operated without lights, and can function in a fixed and unobtrusive position in the court;

   iii) The CRTC and the Grange Commission have both given extended access to cameras, without it interfering in the process, changing the behaviour of the participants, or inviting "dramatics and confrontation". In each case, the continuous coverage on cable and the excerpts used on nightly newscasts represented an important educational service to the public. And, it's worth noting that the print coverage of the Grange Commission was a good deal more flamboyant than the televised coverage;

   iv) The Supreme Court of Canada conducted a closed circuit experiment last year using CBC cameras and satellite feeds to hear arguments from lawyers in British Columbia. The electronic equipment did not become obtrusive, and the Chief

Justice recently described the initiative as a "complete success";

v) More than forty American states are now experimenting with the use of television cameras, most of them operating under guidelines established by the courts. Where those guidelines have been rigorously developed and rigorously observed, it seems to be working reasonably well.

4) The reporters are also frustrated by the lack of access in another area of the legal system, namely, the ongoing opposition of the courts and the law societies to a more open relationship between the legal profession and the media. Earlier this year, as you all know, the Law Society of Upper Canada reminded its members in a communiqué about excessive contact with the media. The communiqué expressed concern that such contact might "invite the inference that it was given to publicize the lawyer, and carries the danger of being in contempt of court."

The communiqué had an immediate consequence for the media. It made it even more difficult for journalists to get the necessary background briefings and interviews about complex legal proceedings and inhibited even those lawyers who tended to cooperate with the press. As a result, when journalists ask the legal profession "can you help me get this story right?" they often face a wall of silence from both lawyers and judges.

5) And finally, a number of the reporters I talked to expressed their frustration with the "catch 22" aspects of covering the most important and far-reaching Supreme Court decisions. Reporters always find themselves trying to reconcile two fundamental journalistic imperatives: they have to make sure that they're competitive in filing stories and reports on major court decisions... and that usually means that they have to file as quickly as possible; but they also want the extra time to study the lengthy judgments in detail and to give the decisions the care, the texture, and the significance they deserve.

A number of the reporters feel that the courts could help to solve this classic dilemma by initiating "lock-ups" (similar to the federal budget) for major decisions on issues such as the Charter of Rights. The reporters would all be kept in the lock-up for five or six hours prior to the decision to allow them to do a thorough analysis of the judgment without the buffeting of deadlines or competitive considerations. Most of the reporters feel that this would result in a marked improvement in the quality of reporting in these "milestone" cases.

Let me conclude with some brief thoughts about making the "uneasy relationship" between the legal system and the media a little easier.

a)   I would recommend that the legal community take the Chief Justice's comments in Winnipeg in August to heart. In his speech to the Canadian Bar Association, Chief Justice Dickson urged reasonable cooperation with the media for judges, lawyers, and academics. "We can give comprehensive answers in response to genuine requests for information", the Chief Justice said, "and take the time to explain the background that will make sense of a legal issue of current interest."

b)   I also think the report of the "subcommittee on lawyers and the media" of the Law Society of Upper Canada, which was circulated on September 24th is a step in the right direction.

The report suggests that "where the lawyer, by reason of his professional involvement or otherwise, has knowledge to assist the media in conveying accurate information to the public, it is proper that the lawyer do so, so long as there is no infringement of his obligations to his client, the profession, the courts and the administration of justice."

Both of these suggestions would be of great help to the journalists handling legal affairs beats.

c)   I would urge many of the courts across the country to look at some of the recent initiatives taken by the Supreme Court of Canada in assisting working journalists in a day to day sense. These changes are administrative and logistical in nature, but they make journalists covering the courts a great deal more effective.

d)   I would recommend that the Supreme Court of Canada initiate an experiment with the "lock-up" procedure in a major case in the near future to test the benefits and implications for the public, the journalists, and the legal profession.

e)   And finally, I would also recommend that the courts continue to experiment with access to television cameras and that the Supreme Court take the lead in this regard.

As Chief Justice Dickson said in Winnipeg: "our courts, by reason of the *Charter*, have begun to assume the role of referee between the individual and the state".

Given this new role and the importance of many of the cases the Supreme Court will be hearing in the next few years, almost every Canadian has an interest in the results. They're entitled to see and hear the arguments presented, as eloquently and as effectively as they are made. And they're entitled to see and hear the decisions rendered by those judges who are responsible for making them. I can't think of any better way of educating and informing Canadians about the legal system, how it works, and what the court's decisions mean to them.

*"In the end (they) would
announce that two and
two made five, and you
would have to believe it."*

*"… (Ils) finiraient par annoncer
que deux et deux font cinq et
il faudrait le croire."*

George Orwell, *1984*

ACCESS TO JUSTICE

L'ACCÈS À LA JUSTICE

The Processes of Dispute Resolution

Edward D. Bayda*

My remit is as follows:

> ... to discuss the decision-making process as it currently operates in the courts... [to express] views on specialized courts, institutional changes which should be made to facilitate the decision making process, and [to make] any other comments... on the structure and institutions of decision making in the court system.

The remit raises a plethora of associated questions. What are the tasks of the decision-making process? Put another way, what does society expect the decision making process to accomplish? What are the underlying assumptions that society has about the process? What is it about the process that makes it acceptable to society? How is the process perceived to operate? How does it really operate? How much disturbance and injection of change can the process withstand before it begins to suffer and before society will find it unacceptable? The list is hardly exhaustive. This paper attempts to answer some of those questions.

THE TASKS IN GENERAL

The most obvious and universally recognized task of the decision-making process — the court process — is to resolve conflicts between disputants. But it is not the only task. The other tasks — perhaps not as readily apparent or recognized — are social control, lawmaking and government (legislative and executive) control. An understanding of the decision-making process as a whole necessitates breaking it down into these four tasks and viewing the process from the standpoint of each.

THE PROCESS AS CONFLICT RESOLVER

The average member of society thinks of the court as performing but one task, that of resolving disputes. His perception of the decision-making process — the court — encompasses a knowledgeable inde-

---

* Chief Justice of Saskatchewan.

pendent decision-maker (i.e. a fair judge who is not the pocket of either party), the existence of laws to govern the situation (i.e. judges do not make up laws as they go along), the adversary nature of the proceedings (i.e. a legal battle for which each party is advised to retain a lawyer) and a winner-take-all result (i.e. one side wins, the other loses). A compendious description would probably go something like this: The process consists of (1) an independent judge applying (2) pre-existing legal norms after (3) adversary proceedings in order to achieve (4) a dichotomous decision in which one party is found legally right and the other legally wrong.[1]

It is fair, I think, to say that the average member of society finds the process, as he or she perceives it, acceptable. Why is it acceptable? The answer is not uncomplicated but in the end may be reduced to one word: consent. Man has been resolving disputes from the beginning of time. Often the two disputants will resolve the conflict between themselves. Their consent is inherent in the resolution. But when they are unable to resolve it between them, they may seek assistance. The resolution will then involve three persons: the two disputants and the conflict resolver. In its rudimentary form the process calls for the two disputants to choose (i.e. consent to) the conflict resolver. Thus, at the point of choosing, neither can have any objection to the conflict resolver exercising his role. The acceptability of the process by both may change, however, after the resolver has made his or her decision. The loser may then perceive the one-against-one-and-a-neutral structure as deteriorating into two against one. To the loser, that is unacceptable. The answer is to create a situation where the element of consent by the disputants will percolate through the whole process and survive the making of the decision. In short, the answer resides in maintaining the one-against-one-and-a-neutral structure.

The realization of the answer in large measure centers around the approach the conflict resolver is expected to use to perform his or her function and around the quality of the decision he or she is expected to produce. Professor Shapiro suggests four classes of resolvers, each with a different approach: the go-between, the mediator, the arbitrator, and the judge. These should be imagined on a continuum in that order. The placement of each on the continuum is determined by the degree of consent by the disputants in the selection of the resolver and on the extent of the non-dichotomous or mediate quality expected in the decision by the resolver.

The go-between is a person who offers his good offices to negotiate a settlement. He operates in a pure consent, pure mediated solu-

---

1. See: Martin Shapiro, *COURTS: A Comparative and Political Analysis* (1981) — a work, I add, which both spawned many of the ideas elucidated in this paper, and confirmed, for me, the soundness of many ideas I already entertained. I am much indebted to Professor Shapiro.

tion, situation. Whatever resolution results from his efforts is purely one by the parties themselves. A real estate broker shuttling between seller and prospective buyer (who are having a difference concerning the price) is a good example of a go-between. Whatever influence he has lies in the manner in which he expresses the message he is carrying.

The distinction between a go-between and a mediator is that the latter is allowed some latitude in moulding the decision. The mediator, like the go-between, can operate only with the consent of both parties. He may not impose solutions. The parties prescribe the norms and they themselves produce the solution. The mediator may suggest or help mould the solution. By shuttling back and forth with proposals and counter proposals, he may actively assist in producing the solution but it must be said that the solution is the parties' own.

An arbitrator is in a somewhat different position. Usually the two parties have to agree upon an arbitrator. Often the parties agree in advance what should happen if they cannot agree. Hence, an arbitrator cannot function without the consent of both parties. The main distinction between an arbitrator and a mediator is that an arbitrator is expected to mould his own solution to the conflict. He does not simply assist the parties in arriving at their own solution. In those cases where the arbitration is binding, the arbitrator has the right to actually impose his solution on both parties. The norms within which the arbitration is expected to function are sometimes chosen by the parties but not always. An example from labour law is appropriate. In a "rights" arbitration the parties expect a resolution according to who is right and who is wrong. In an "interest" arbitration, they expect something more akin to a mediated solution.

The lines between the different positions on the continuum are sometimes blurred. For example, when arbitration is in no sense binding, it merges with mediation. When arbitration is binding, both in the sense that the two parties must go to arbitration on the demand of either or upon the fiat of the legislature and must then abide by the arbitrator's decision, it tends to merge into judicial judgment. This is particularly true in those cases where the arbitrator is expected to reach a legally correct as opposed to a mediated solution (e.g. a "rights" arbitration in labour matters). An arbitrator in these cases really sits as a private judge.

The conflict resolver occupying the last position on the continuum is the judge. The judge acts as conflict resolver not because the parties have chosen him but because he occupies an office. He applies not norms of the parties' choosing but pre-existing law. The decision expected of him is not a mediated one but a dichotomous one which he imposes upon the parties. The emergence of the shift from direct consent (in the case of the go-between, mediator and arbitrator) to what appears on the face as no consent (in the case of a judge) is explained by the developing complexities of society and the need for certainty.

But if the parties do not consent, why then is the judge accepted as a conflict resolver? Part of the answer is that the parties indirectly consent to the judge assuming his role. After all, he is appointed to his office by representatives elected by an electoral process in which the parties are entitled to participate. But mostly the answer lies in the acceptance by the parties of the judge as the neutral in the one-against-one-and-a-neutral structure. The judge is perceived as truly independent and impartial and not in any way as acting for the opponent (so as to produce a two-against-one structure). Similarly, where the law applied by the judge is perceived as neutral and not favouring the opponent, the loser will accept the judge's dichotomous decision finding him legally wrong. The one-against-one-and-a-neutral structure persists and survives the decision.

But all this is apt to change where the judge is perceived as a governmental officer who injects into the process a third set of interests (the government's) quite independent of those of the two disputants or where the law is perceived as favouring a particular class in society (e.g. the property owner or the employer), as indeed many laws do. These perceptions tend naturally to produce the undesirable two-against-one structure.

How then can the decision-making process — the court process — in performing its first task of conflict resolution, assist in avoiding the undesirable two-against-one structure? It is helpful here to recall the average person's 4-point model of the decision-making process described above. The first point relates to independence and impartiality. It is axiomatic that the judge must always be and appear to be, inside the courtroom and out, independent of the opposing party and of any third party who may have an interest (e.g. government). He or she must in his dealings present a total picture of fairness and impartiality. The judge must have the ability to make up his mind when the case is complete, but equally important he must have the ability not to make it up until everyone has had his legitimate say.

Allow me to defer until later a consideration of the second point. I move to the third and fourth points: the adversary nature of the proceedings and the dichotomous decision. Should the decision-making process rely as heavily, as it now appears to, on the adversary nature of the proceeding? If before reaching the courtroom the emphasis in the proceeding were on mediation rather than adversarial posturing, are the chances not smaller for the undesirable two-against-one structure materializing? Indeed, if in the courtroom there were more heed paid by the judge and counsel to a mediated solution rather than a dichotomous one, would not the results be similar? Does strict adherence to the adversary procedures really produce the best results? If, as often happens, the truth in a case simply cannot be discovered (e.g. a motor vehicle collision where all parties are killed), should the adversary winner-take-all rule prevail? Should the judge be entitled to pretend he knows with certainty what the factual situation is when in reality no one knows? Or is there room in that situation for a mediated rather than a dichotomous decision and should not the court proceeding reflect more of a mediation *cum* adversary approach rather than a strict adversary approach?

Shapiro suggests that "mediating is not to be seen as an antithesis to judging but rather as a component in judging." He contends that most judicial systems retain strong elements of mediation. The common law system, for example, consistently converts indivisible disputes, that is, disputes over injury to person and property and disputes over fulfillment or nonfulfillment of obligations into disputes over sums of money. Mediate solutions are always possible in disputes over money.

Some areas of the law lend themselves more readily to mediation than others. In the commercial world, litigants often will have reduced to writing the detailed rule of decision for themselves in case of dispute. They are anxious to maintain their cordial business relations despite the dispute. There is much fertile ground here for mediation. The field of family law is a particularly good example, especially where children are involved, where the resolution to a dispute should be a mediated one and not a dichotomous one.

Undoubtedly the most bountiful and rewarding area for mediation lies in the pre-trial stage of the proceedings. There should, of course, have been much negotiation and mediation before the action is commenced, but there is no reason to let up after the action is commenced. At the present time the injection of an official mediator does not occur usually until a pre-trial conference is held (and then — at best — only very little mediation is done). A judge then acts as the mediator. Perhaps the official mediator should be injected at an earlier stage. Should the mediator be a judge? Should consideration be given to creating a new office — the office of mediator? Perhaps he or she should be no less a professional than a judge and should enjoy the prestige, privileges and independence of a judge. These official mediators could specialize in certain areas of conflict (e.g. family law, commercial law, tort law, etc.). It would be preferable, I think, to have specialized mediation services rather than specialized courts.

It would seem advantageous to inject the mediator into the proceedings not only early in the proceedings but at more than one stage, perhaps three or four. He should concern himself not only with producing a mediated resolution of the conflict but with assessing, refining and distilling the issues so as to ensure that only disputes truly deserving of a judicial adjudication end up in court. A judge should not be called upon to render a dichotomous decision where fairness and the nature of the case require a mediated solution. Nor should the court be required to deal with an action in a raw or semi-refined state.

The foregoing proposals are not inconsistent with the public's right of ready access to the courts. The public does indeed have that right. There is a concomitant duty on the courts to make themselves accessible. But there exists a corresponding duty on the members of the public and their counsel not to abuse the right of access.

It is not hyperbolic to say that 50% to 60% of the civil actions tried in most Canadian courts today should not have ended up there. In many of those cases the true answer mysteriously eluded the losing litigant and his counsel until the judge's decision was rendered. In many others, the proper solution was a mediated decision, not a dichotomous decision by a judge. In many cases, professional pre-trial mediation would have had the desired results.

A vast number of cases that do come to court are not ready for presentation to a judge. Whether the reason is lack of diligence or ability on the part of counsel, the pressures of too much work, or simply an unwholesome lackadaisical attitude to the process, is immaterial. Professional mediation could improve the quality of presentation in court. A proceeding in court should be regarded as something of an event, not some humdrum occurrence during an ordinary day.

Mediation, as an integral part of the judicial structure, works in other places and systems. Consider, for example, Japan. There are only 10,000 lawyers practising in the whole country of Japan, whose population is 100 million. In the United States there are 622,000 lawyers for a population of 250 million (one lawyer for each 400 persons). Today, two-thirds of the lawyers in the world live in the United States which has six percent of the world's population. Los Angeles County has more judges than all of France. The figures for Canada are not quite as startling but nevertheless are revealing. There are 44,000 lawyers for a population of 24,634,000 (one lawyer for each 559 persons). One reason for Japan's small number of lawyers is the tendency towards mediation in many areas of the law despite its having imported a highly adversary and dichotomous judicial style along with the German Civil Code.

There is good reason to believe that in Canada professional mediation operating as an integral and important part of the judicial system, after a while, would reduce the amount of time required to hear a case (mediation would properly prepare cases for a hearing), would substantially diminish the number of cases ending up in court (mediation would screen out the cases better suited for a mediated solution), would improve the quality of court decisions (judges would have more time to devote to fewer judgments), would increase certainty in the law (fewer judgments would restore judges' respect for precedent, not to mention that mediators would not be writing "definitive" judgments on every novel legal point as so many judges are now prone to do) and the number of satisfied litigants would increase noticeably (it is human to prefer to consent to a result affecting one rather than have it imposed and human also to prefer less anxiety and less expense). In the end, society's members, collectively and individually, would be the greatest beneficiaries.

The foregoing has particular application to civil disputes in the area of private law at the trial level. That is not to say that mediation in the area of public law, and particularly criminal law, is unworkable or unacceptable. Plea bargaining is, of course, a form of mediation. It works reasonably well and in some jurisdictions is not only workable but virtually indispensable to the survival of the criminal law system. It is proposed to deal more extensively with this aspect under the "social order" heading.

THE PROCESS AS SOCIAL CONTROLLER

There are many times when the decision-making process is concerned not only with resolving the dispute at hand but with much more. The judge will keep one eye on the disputants and their dispute and another eye on the general well-being of the community. The area of criminal law is the most obvious example where this occurs. It is interesting to note that this was not always the case in English criminal law. Not until the seventeenth century was criminal law clearly separated from tort. The area of tort — where conflict resolution is mostly an interpersonal process — offers another example. The notion of the "reasonable man" connotes social standards which direct how men should act.

The tool the process uses to effect social control is the application of pre-existing law. The judge is expected to apply not the norms chosen by the disputants to resolve their dispute or pre-existing rules shaped by them, but pre-existing law shaped and chosen by the system. Thus, when a battered wife reports the assault to the police, who then lay a charge against the husband, the judge before whom the issues are placed is expected to apply the criminal law as he or she finds it and not the rules that the disputants may choose to resolve their conflict. One of the consequences of that approach is the refusal by the Crown to stay the proceedings where the wife and husband have chosen to reconcile. What happens, of course, is that the process underscores social control to the point of virtually ignoring the resolution of the interpersonal dispute. Put another way, at that point the process — the judge — is importing a third set of interests, the interests of society as embodied in the criminal law, to be adjudicated along with the interests of the two disputants (the victim of the offence — or his family — is an aggrieved party and in that sense is a disputant). To the extent that the judge applies pre-existing law, he acts not independently but as a servant of the regime. He finds himself in the courtroom to impose Parliament's wishes and not to do justice as he sees it through his "common law" eyes.

A brief diversion into the historical background of judicial power is apposite. Originally, judges were advisors to the Crown and often its administrators, and as well, the dispensers of its justice. They took the King's justice to the people and generally assisted in holding the countryside. When Parliament wrested sovereignty from the Crown, the judges transferred their allegiance from King to Parliament. They succeeded, however, (in the 17th and 18th centuries) in building substantial autonomy based on the institutional incapacities of Parliament and (in Shapiro's words) ''the marvelously impenetrable lump of lore-ridden common law, common lawyers and common law courts.'' Then, in the 19th century Parliament asserted itself and through its legislative acts became the principal lawmaker. This resulted in a return by the judges to a species of dutiful subordination.

One of the goals of social control is to standardize the law and have it applied uniformly. The function of social control is exercised by courts at all levels. However, as one leaves the trial level and climbs the hierarchical ladder, it seems that the higher the appellate court the greater the degree of social control. Indeed, the highest courts are barely courts at all. It is true that they operate in the context of resolving a dispute between two litigants. Their principal role, however, is to provide uniform rules of law. As Shapiro points out: ''naturally such rules must be based on consideration far broader than the concerns of the two litigants, essentially on consideration of public policy that may have little to do with particular litigation. At worst the litigants are irrelevant [as Mr. Miranda may be prepared to attest]; at best they are examples or samples of general problems to be solved; [Mrs. Rathwell may agree]''.

In performing its task of social controller, is the decision-making process, as it is functioning today, acceptable to society? The general members of society who benefit from the control (they are the people for whom the third party's interests exist) tend not to complain. The members of society who are the immediate disputants may be in a different position. Consider, for example, the position of an accused person. He or she is faced with what he may originally perceive as a two-against-one-and-a-neutral structure (he sees not only the complainant/ victim as against him but the regime with its third party interest). The moment he perceives the judge — the neutral — as the servant of the regime imposing its interests (the pre-existing laws designed for social control) on the disputants, he is apt to perceive a three-against-one structure. There is thus inherent in the process a constant tension between the judge's need to assert his independence and his mandate to perform his task of social control.

The tension, I suggest, may be attenuated in certain cases by invoking the new Charter of Rights which provides for relief in some instances of harsh law. A successful invocation will tend to prevent the accused from perceiving a deterioration of the two-against-one-and-a-neutral structure into a three-against-one structure.

Is mediation consistent with an attempt by the court to perform its social control function? In certain areas I think it is. For example, social control encompasses the reformation and rehabilitation of the offender. It seems sensible, from the standpoint of reformation, that mediation or voluntary arbitration should be explored in cases of crimes committed within continuing relationships (e.g. assault by a husband upon a wife). It seems sensible, too, to explore diversion in cases of crime without direct victims such as drug cases. Only in serious crimes where reconciliation is out of the question, in crimes where one stranger victimizes another, and in crimes where there is a dispute as to material issues such as identity, should the adjudication course be adopted outright. It is noteworthy that a few recent proposed amendments to the Criminal Code incorporate thinking along these lines.

THE PROCESS AS LAWMAKER

The once raging question, "Do judges make law?" has now been settled. Of course they do. In order for judges to have only to "discover" law but never "make" it, they would need to have available to them a complete body of pre-set rules designed to govern every conceivable human act and every conceivable combination of human acts. No human society has compiled such a body of law. It is doubtful society is competent to do so. The question is not so much whether judges make law, but in what situations do they make it?

When the common law reigned supreme, judges made an extensive amount of law. Today they continue to make law despite the monumental proliferation of legislative and executive law. Indeed, it is that massive bulk of primary and secondary legislation that provides the relentless flow of opportunities for judicial lawmaking. Lord Hailsham guesses that over nine out of ten cases heard on appeal before either the Court of Appeal or the House of Lords either turn upon, or involve, the meaning of words contained in enactments of primary or secondary legislation. Generally, the appellate courts in Canada are experiencing a parallel phenomenon. I suggest five reasons for this: First, it is virtually impossible for even the most skillful legislative draftsman to put into an enactment all of the necessary details to cover the many situations intended to be governed by the enactment. The court must then engage in supplementary or interstitial lawmaking to fill in those details if it is to resolve the dispute before it.

Secondly, not all legislative draftsmen are skillful. Many are required to work under monstrous pressures of time. The consequence, often, is a vague, ambiguous, contradictory or non-sensical enactment. The inadvertent wording will require the court to engage in lawmaking to set it all right.

Thirdly, there are instances where the legislature advertently promulgates a vague enactment. In those cases, the legislature intends to, and does, pass the buck to the courts. When faced with such an enactment, it is futile for the court to look for legislative intent. There is not any. The court must legislate if it is to resolve a dispute based on such an enactment. Politically sensitive or politically cumbersome issues are susceptible to this sort of treatment. A recent example in our Saskatchewan courts pertains to a badly worded statute requiring teachers (or not requiring them) to supervise students during the noon hours. The legislature appears to have decided that the courts should resolve this politically cumbersome issue.

Fourthly, there are other instances where the legislature passes a general enactment and impliedly invites the court to make laws particularizing the generalities. The most striking example of this is our new Charter of Rights. In the case of a constitutional statute, the legislature often deliberately gives the court much scope for interpreting the statute because — to use Chief Justice Dickson words in *Hunter* v. *Southam*: ''Once enacted, its provisions cannot easily be repealed or amended. It must, therefore, be capable of growth and development over time to meet new social, political and historical realities often unimagined by its framers.'' He then observes: ''The judiciary is the guardian of the constitution and must, in interpreting its provisions, bear these considerations in mind.'' If the court is to discharge its mandate ''to meet [these] new social, political and historical realities'', then, by the very reason of the newness of the realities, the court will need to make law. It has no other means at its disposal.

Fifthly, often in matters of social policy, there exists a gap between what society wants and what the legislation extant provides. The gap can be filled by legislation but legislatures are slow to respond at times. The members of the public will sometimes appeal to the courts to fill that gap. In those situations the court makes law to fill the gap. A good example in relatively recent times is found in the decisions relating to the distribution of matrimonial property. Before *Murdoch* v. *Murdoch*, there clearly existed a gap between what society wanted and what the legislature provided. An appeal was made to courts to fill the gap. It did not work the first time. It did the second time in *Rathwell* v. *Rathwell*. Then, of course, the politicians decided to respond and began to make their own laws to fill the gap. In the United States the lawmaking powers of the courts have reached enormous proportions. Today their federal and state courts are drawing school district lines, administering prisons, supervising railroads, prescribing personal procedures for police departments, altering the time schedules and design features of vast construction projects, determining patterns of urban development, and preserving seacoasts.

If judges are inevitably lawmakers, what does that do to the 4-point model of independence, pre-existing legal rules, adversary proceedings and dichotomous solutions? It has a somewhat shattering effect. Take the first point: independence. Independence of the judiciary is incompatible with the task of lawmaking. Society will not countenance a group of persons making laws who are not responsible representatives of the people. Shapiro observes:

> To the extent that courts make law, judges will be incorporated into the governing coalition, the ruling elite, the responsible representatives of the people, or however else the political regime may be expressed. In most societies this presents no problem at all because judging is only one of the many tasks of the governing cadre. In societies that seek to create independent judiciaries, however, this reintegration will nonetheless occur, even at substantial costs to the proclaimed goal of judicial independence.

An example of reintegration in the United States is reflected in the continual debate over whether judges should be elected or appointed. In Canada, recently, concern has been expressed in some quarters about the appointment of judges. The Canadian Bar Association has established a committee to study the matter. One Attorney-General has complained that he is not being consulted by the federal Minister of Justice before an appointment to a superior court is made. Some Attorneys-Generals and some officials in the federal bureaucracy would like very much to see the proposed amendments to s. 96 of the British North America Act passed. They seem oblivious — perhaps some seek the result — to the fundamental change such a step would bring in our democratic structure. An emasculation of the courts' powers to the extent envisioned by those amendments and a subordination of the courts to the legislative arm, and particularly the executive arm of government, would inevitably result in that change — a change not only injudicious but inimical to society generally. This restlessness on the part of some politicians and some bureaucrats may be attributed in some measure to the realization by them of the power to legislate recently vested in the judges by the Charter of Rights and in some measure to their continual attempts to deal with the perpetual conflict between, on the one hand, the need for the judiciary to always be independent (so that in performing the task of conflict resolution, the structure never deteriorates to the undesirable two-against-one or three-against-one), and on the other hand, the need for the judiciary to make laws (if it is going to properly discharge the tasks assigned to it by litigants and by Parliament).

The second point in the 4-point model relates to an application of pre-existing rules. Clearly, case-by-case law-making negates the model's requisite for pre-existing rules. The common law system of "developing" the law as each case is heard presupposes that as the resolution of the conflict proceeds the rules will be "discovered" in the very process of resolving the conflict. The disputant does not know what rules govern his act until after he has acted. The rationalization for the system is, first, that these rules made by judges are nothing more than common sense with which everyone is or should be endowed; and second, that every new rule is but a small logical extension of a well-known and accepted legal principle. Everyone who acts in an area where an extension of the well-recognized principle may be required takes his chances. But in reality, however, the new rule often could not easily have been anticipated. The promulgation of such a new rule by a judge may take many pages in judgment. Often the rule is made because the judge desires to discourage future like conduct, but to do so he must penalize the conduct which gives rise to the conflict as if the rule existed before the conduct occurred.

The third point of the model, the adversary nature of the process, fares no better. Where judicial lawmaking occurs adversarial jousting must, of necessity, take a back seat. If a judge is engaged in making a rule for future application, he must be concerned with a much broader range of interests than those disclosed by the immediate dispute before him. Adversarial techniques are very helpful to discover some concrete thing that occurred in the past but lose considerable usefulness when they are applied to mould and formulate future policy.

In summary, then, where judges are entrusted with lawmaking powers, and in our society they often are, and are then asked to resolve a conflict applying pre-existing rules or rules mutually consented to by both parties, as well as rules they, the judges, may make, the loser of the case may well perceive himself to have been legislated against rather than impartially dealt with. This deviation, however, from the 4-point model is unavoidable.

THE PROCESS AS GOVERNMENT CONTROLLER

John G. Kester, a former law clerk to the late Associate Justice Hugo L. Black of the United States Supreme Court, said: ''The legal system is precious because it does more than settle disputes: It protects our freedom.''

Chief Justice Dickson's comment that the judiciary is the guardian of the Constitution conveys much the same notion.

Anthony Lewis, writing in the *International Harold Tribune* (July 10, 1984) said:

> The power of the modern state strains the central premise of American democracy, which is the belief that freedom requires limits on government. For the levers of power available to government today — economic, technological, physical — would amaze not only Jefferson but Franklin Roosevelt.

For the last 30 years America has relied overwhelmingly on a single institution to set the limits on state power. That institution is the Supreme Court. I think we did not altogether realize the extent of our reliance on it until the moment when the court made clear that it was no longer prepared to perform the function.

When the justices finished their term last week, there was a stunned reaction among the public as well as legal specialists. It was not this or that decision that produced the reaction. It was the sense that our fundamental assumptions about the Supreme Court must change.

I rue the day similar words are written suggesting a change in the assumptions about our Canadian courts. Before we are overtaken, however, by that peripatetic Canadian smugness, let us examine what is happening in our Canadian system.

Canada, like England, has in the 20th century become an executive state, an administrative state, a welfare state, with the attendant proliferation of administration boards and tribunals. In such a state, the centre of politics and law is the machinery of the central government. Parliament has transferred all of its authority over day-to-day policymaking and much of its ultimate authority, as well, to the cabinet and ministries. It is no secret that some departments of governments, some civil servants, some administrative tribunals, and some executive bodies, are very powerful forces in government.

Actions between individuals and an agency of government, between agencies of government, and between governments themselves, abound. Those actions are but one indication of the enormity of the activities carried out by this governmental monolith. What control mechanisms for checking the abuse of power of the agents of this colossus has the system put in place? One such mechanism is reflected in the power of the judiciary when exercising its administrative law function. That power, as any neophyte student of administrative law will know, is highly circumscribed. It is essentially the power to declare ultra vires any decision or act that strays outside the jurisdictional bounds set by Parliament. Within those bounds, and apart from the dictates of natural justice, the agents of the monolith can do virtually as they please. The role of the judge discharging his administrative law function is really not one of exercising his judicial independence but one of carrying out the will of Parliament. What does this come to? Shapiro's summation commends itself to me:

> This judicial surrender is all the more complete when it is acknowledged, as it must be, that the parliamentary power to which the courts pretend to be subordinating themselves has long since disappeared. In the last analysis *ultra vires* is a circular doctrine of surrender to administrative government. It proclaims that the courts will insure that the executive obeys Parliament. Parliament, however, has long since transferred all of its authority over day-to-day policymaking, and most of its ultimate

authority as well, to the cabinet and the ministries. Ultimately *ultra vires* means only that the executive must obey itself. As to natural justice, it means no more than that the ministries must grant hearings before deciding whatever they please. The process of both parliamentary and judicial abdication has gone so far that there are serious doubts about whether the rule of law survives in England at all. And if it does, it must do so in the ideological commitments of the executive elite itself rather than in the constraining powers of the courts.

Nothing could be more touching than the way in which, in the face of this overwhelming political reality, English authorities on administrative law continue to cite and re-cite a handful of cases that preserve the doctrines of judicial review. For those cases are not only very few but almost invariably result in the chastisement of some local authority for firing a policeman or harassing the owner of a mobile home site. To the extent that judicial review remains an active force at all, it serves largely as a handmaiden of central administration in its attempts to rationalize and control the mass of local authorities and subordinate tribunals ultimately responsible to the central ministries.

The infusion into the system of the Charter of Rights was not coincidental. The Charter's appearance on the scene was, in a sense, ordained. Had the Charter not come into being, the stresses created by the absence of mechanisms to check the monolith would have had serious repercussions for our democratic state. The Charter has put into the hands of the judiciary tools that go a long way in providing some of the necessary checks heretofore unavailable. But the Charter is only as potent as the judiciary. To render the judiciary a eunuch is to render the Charter a eunuch. It is thus distressing to see consideration being given to such "eunuchizing" legislation as the proposed amendments to s. 96 of the British North America Act. Chief Justice Nemetz put it well when he summed up the serious enervating effect the amendments to s. 96 would have:

> It is imperative that our heritage of a citizen's access to an independent judiciary should not be limited by impulsive action and the vagaries of changing governments. What we have in Canada is a functioning system. Federally-appointed superior courts without jurisdiction juxtaposed with provincially-appointed tribunals without independence would make a mockery of our system of justice.

I refer one last time to the 4-point model I sketched at the beginning of this paper. In particular, I refer to the first point — independence of the judge — in the context of government control. If in a conflict the court is required to exercise its task of government control and one of the disputants perceives the judge not as independent but as a servant of the regime, and in the result the conflict is reduced to a two-against-one structure, the phrase "... nothing was illegal since there were no longer any laws" will be more than just Orwellian rhetoric.

CONCLUSION

Respecting the court's task of conflict resolution, there is some room for change in attitude and approach by all concerned in the decision-making process. The same is true of the court's task of social control but perhaps not to the same degree. There seems little that can be done about the court's tasks of lawmaking and government control excepting that legislative steps are warranted to strengthen the court's independence. This would ensure the court's being better able to perform these tasks, both of which are becoming increasingly more important and necessary.

Administrative Tribunals: Is Justice Done?

Roy L. Heenan*

Mr. Justice Frankfurter wrote that "the history of Liberty has largely been the history of procedural safeguards".

It is with this in mind that I share the reluctance of many lawyers to see the historic function of the courts removed and given to administrative or quasi judicial Boards. The independence of the Courts and the procedural safeguards either inherent in or built into the court system remain, in my opinion, the best guarantees of justice for the citizen.

Nonetheless it is perhaps inevitable with the complexity of our societies and the sheer volume of matters to be adjudicated upon that alternate avenues to justice are sought which, we are told, will be less formal, more expeditious and more accessible to the average citizen. It is also suggested at times that these alternate forums will be more equitable.

THE ASSUMPTIONS BEHIND THE CREATION OF BOARDS

We have all had occasion now to experience these alternatives and I feel we are entitled to question the assumptions which underlie the creation of these Boards.

In the first place is this question of speedy decision making. There can be no question that one of the problems with the court system is the delays which have been experienced before a matter is disposed of. Because of the very procedural safeguards to be found in the court system perhaps delays are unavoidable. On the other hand, to this there are two answers:

(1) In the case of most administrative Boards, it is far from certain that speed is assured. Indeed in many cases the delays experienced before an administrative Board can be compared to the delays in the court system;

(2) Next, even if speed were assured, it must be ensured that it does not become an end in itself. Expedited proceedings must not lead to abbreviated justice. The removing of formality may speed things

---

* Lawyer, Montreal, Quebec.

up. It must not however be allowed to create arbitrary decision making.

Secondly, it is suggested that the administrative Boards have merit because of the expertise to be found on the Boards which may not be found in the Courts. With all respect to the Boards, the issue of expertise is a carefully cultivated myth.[1] There can be some expertise in the Boards, just as the same expertise can usually be found in the Courts. But that expertise can also become dated fairly rapidly.

Thirdly, the assumption that the administrative or quasi judicial Board will be more equitable is certainly open to question. These Boards are often given more powers and much more latitude than the courts. It is far from certain that they exercise that power more equitably. Some might, others might not; and abuse by an unrestrained Board is, I suggest, one of the most serious threats to justice in our present society. It is disturbing to me to see Courts of Appeal accepting and justifying standards of conduct and errors in decision making, including the creation of new law, from Boards that they would never tolerate in any form from judges in the first instance. Does our society become any more just because of it? I do not believe so.

As far as being more equitable, I have much sympathy with the reaction of Mr. Justice Dickson, as he then was, in the case of *In re Residential Tenancies Act*[1a] when he wrote:

> Implicit throughout the argument advanced on behalf of the Attorney General of Ontario is the assumption that the court system is too formal, too cumbersome, too expensive and therefore unable to respond properly to the social needs which *The Residential Tenancies Act* is intended to meet. All statutes respond to social needs. The courts are not unfamiliar with equity and the concepts of fairness, justice, convenience, reasonableness. Since the enactment in 1976 of the legislation assuring "security of tenure" the County Court judges of Ontario have been dealing with matters arising out of that legislation, apparently with reasonable despatch, as both landlords and tenants in the present proceedings have spoken clearly against transfer of jurisdiction in respect of eviction and compliance orders from the courts to a special commission. It is perhaps also of interest that there is no suggestion in the material filed with us that the Law Reform Commission favoured removal from the courts of the historic functions performed for over one hundred years by the courts.

---

1. See on this subject, with regard to labour relations boards, the series of articles by Julius Getman and Stephen Goldberg: "The Myth of Labor Board Expertise" (1972), 39 Univ. Chic. L.R. 681; "NLRB Regulation of Campaign Tactics" (1975), 27 Stanf. L.R. 1465; "The Behavioral Assumptions Underlying NLRB Regulation of Campaign Misrepresentations" (1976), 28 Stanf. L.R. 263.

1a. [1981] S.C.R. 714, 749.

DIFFERENT FORMS OF BOARDS

With the reservations, then, that come from questioning the assumptions leading to the establishment of the Boards, let us consider some of the alternate avenues. Since my own experience has largely been in the industrial relations and human rights field, it is from these Boards, commissions or institutions that I will take my examples, in the hope that the lesson learned may have wider application.

In terms of preference, the best alternative to the courts is a system in which the parties to a dispute choose their own adjudicator. In labour matters, the arbitration system is widely used and accepted. In the more informal approach, many of the procedural safeguards of the courts are bypassed. For instance, there are generally no prehearing procedures.[2] But the protection of fairness is built in with the concept of natural justice, enforced, when needed, by judicial review. More importantly, since the adjudicator is to be chosen by the parties, the impartiality is taken for granted and the adjudicators will generally assure the rights of both parties. Lastly the system is self-regulating in that a bad or unfair adjudicator will not be rechosen by the parties, and, since word travels fast, will not likely last in the system.

In labour matters, arbitration has existed for many years either by tripartite boards or single arbitrators. It has served the parties well. It has served the parties best however, when the arbitrator remembers that he or she is deciding in the interest of the immediate parties and avoids the danger of legal pontification. While it is desirable, and indeed essential, that the reasons for a decision be cogently written, it is quite a different matter for the arbitrator to approach each case as a great new legal principle waiting to be discovered.

Unfortunately, recently, a few arbitrators have envisioned their role as one of advancing the state of the law. The arbitration is viewed as an opportunity to unleash a new truth on an unsuspecting world. The decisions tend to be long, wordy, and very legalistic. More particularly they do not appear to be written with the immediate parties primarily in mind.

This brings to mind the noted American humorist who during his college days at Harvard was asked to write a thesis on the Newfoundland Fisheries case. His interpretation, though scholarly and well reasoned, was written entirely from the point of view of one of the fish! Although the intellectual exercise may be valid, it is preferable that arbitrators, at least, remember the immediate parties to the dispute.

Examples of this tendency to pontificate can be found in the growth of "legal doctrines" in arbitration. Thus the development in labour

---

2. *In re C.B.C. & Cupe* (1978), 18 L.A.C. (2d) 357, 361-2 (Adams); *In re Fabricated Steel Products (Windsor) Ltd.* (1977), 16 L.A.C. (2d) 148, 160-2 (O' Shea).

arbitration recently of the "doctrine of equitable estoppel" and of the "doctrine of fairness".

One of our best arbitrators, Ted Weatherhill, wrote recently[3]

> I don't suggest that these so-called "doctrines" are bad or out of place in arbitration: what is out of place, I think, is dressing up these fairly understandable ideas in this incomprehensible garb, and then drawing farreaching conclusions from the expansive, impressive but vague language used.

After noting that the word "doctrine" gives a cloak of "academic razzle dazzle", he went on to comment on the "doctrine of fairness". "A requirement of "fairness" while it sounds nice would appear to me to be a vehicle for imposing on the parties the view of the arbitrator - for going far beyond the carefully elaborated doctrine of estoppel and certainly for relegating to the background the collective agreement the parties have made".[4]

In the case of *York University and York University Faculty Association* the "doctrine of fairness" is elevated to a "duty (of an employer) to act fairly" and a majority of the arbitration Board wrote:

> In fact it seems to us that the duty to act fairly would logically be extended beyond a simple prohibition against discriminatory treatment without seriously blurring its meaning. In our view, the premises that support a prohibition of discriminatory decisions making would also logically imply a duty to execute the terms of an agreement arbitrarily or unreasonably.[5]

The Courts intervened and restored the state of the law to what it had been. Three decisions of the Ontario Court of Appeal reminded the arbitrators in gentle terms that the parties to a collective agreement make their own law and it is not incumbent on arbitrators to modify it.[6]

The decisions bring to mind the famous dicta of the United States Supreme Court in *United Steelworkers and Enterprise Wheel & Car Corp.*[7]

> An arbitrator is confined to interpretation and application of the collective bargaining agreement; he does not sit to dispense his own brand of industrial justice... When the arbitrator's words manifest an infidelity to this obligation, courts have no choice but to refuse enforcement of the award.

---

3. J.T.W. Weatherhill, in a paper so far unreported, given to the Canada Labour Conference, Toronto, March 10, 1983.
4. J.T.W. Weatherhill, in a paper so far unreported, given to the Canada Labour Conference, Toronto, March 10, 1983.
5. [1980] 2 L.A.C. 17, 19.
6. *Metropolitan Toronto Board of Commissioners of Police* v. *Metropolitan Toronto Police Association* (1981), 124 D.L.R. (3d) 684, 687 (Leave to appeal to the Supreme Court refused); *United Glass & Ceramic Workers & Libby St. Clair Inc. et al.* (1981), 125 D.L.R. (3d) 702; *In re Falconbridge Nickel Mines Ltd. & Brummer* (1981), 129 D.L.R. (3d) 561.
7. (1960) 363 U.S. 597.

"Equitable Estoppel" is a recent and impressive sounding addition to the arbitrator's stock of doctrines. Almost one third of recent labour arbitration case reports deal with cases in which the doctrine is applied or at least appealed to. No party's preparation for an arbitration can be complete until it is ready to discuss the intricacies of Lord Denning's judgments in the cases of *High Trees House* and *Coombe* v. *Coombe*.[8]

The progress of doctrine here has been remarkable. Indeed, Lord Denning's caution against the use of estoppel as a "sword" rather than as a "shield" is seen as outmoded by some arbitrators and positive rights not bargained for are bestowed almost with abandon. The concept that the arbitrator's role is to apply a collective agreement, which by statutory definition must be an agreement in writing, seems to have been ignored.

Yet it is one of the benefits of the arbitral system that doctrinal innovation will not receive universal approbation. Equitable estoppel has been treated as being less than a panacea by such other respected arbitrators as M. Teplitsky, Q.C. and J.D. O'Shea, Q.C.[9] who have refused to apply it to supplement the agreement of the parties.

Eventually, the Courts will be forced to intervene, I am convinced, to put this "doctrine" in perspective. Hopefully, we will then return to more normal arbitration.

If arbitration in labour matters may be considered to be basically successful, can the process have a role in general civil matters? I see no reason why not. In certain of the United States a form of pretrial voluntary arbitration has been tried, with the parties presenting their case to an arbitrator. The arbitrator's decision is not binding on the parties and cannot be used if the matter goes to trial. I am informed that the experience there is that between 75 and 90% of the matters so sent to arbitration are settled or dropped before coming to trial.

Chief Justice Alan B. Gold of the Quebec Superior Court is experimenting at the present time with a form of prehearing with senior counsel at the Bar presiding. He informs me that this has been relatively successful and the backlog of cases in the Superior Court is diminishing. He has also informed the Quebec Bar that if the present measures do not significantly reduce the backlog, he will recommend the implementation of a compulsory system of non-binding arbitration in cases up to a certain dollar value. He points out, however, half facetiously, that if this doesn't work he will resort to trial by fire: that is to say, he will burn the files of all the cases in arrears, knowing full well that the

---

8. *Central London Property Trust* v. *High Trees House* [1947], 1 K.B. 130; *Coombe & Coombe*, [1951] All E.R. 767.
9. *Domglas Ltd.* (1984), 8 L.A.C. (3d) 365; *Re Municipality of Metropolitan Toronto* (1984), 7 L.A.C. 74.

mere prospect of having to reconstitute some of those files would give the lawyers involved the strongest incentive to settlement!

If a system of arbitration with the parties choosing their own judges is a preferred alternative, this is not always possible because of the ad hoc nature inherent in it. If a board or commission is necessary, what should be its nature? Again drawing on a labour law background, I am convinced that every effort must be made to ensure that the Board does not lose touch with its essential constituency. If a Board and its decisions are to be acceptable, it must be known to be fair. The best way for this to be achieved is if the parties can themselves be represented on the Board.

Labour Boards in Canada have traditionally been composed of representatives of labour, management and the public.

Paul Weiler[10] has often attributed the success of the B.C. Labour Board when he was there to the tripartite nature of the Board. In his book *Reconcilable Differences*[11] he wrote:

> The B.C. Labour Board followed the tripartite pattern originally set by Ontario. Of these twenty-one members, seven were designated as representatives of employers, seven as representatives of employees and their unions, and seven were labeled neutral. The thrust of that institution was that the tribunal administering the law of industrial relations should be composed of people drawn from the labour-management community itself...

> I do not mean to suggest that these people were supposed to act as advocates for their constituency inside the Board. Significant cases before the Board were typically heard by a panel composed of a vice-chairman and a union and management ''winger''...

> Of course, the positive point is that the tribunal making those decisions consisted primarily of people who were still living and working in the environment which the Labour Board was trying to shape and contain. That kind of community participation is the ideal means of ensuring that the practical flavour of an industrial relations setting is apparent to the Board as it is reaching the judgments that it must make. It is also the best channel of communication to ensure that the thrust of the Board's policy is understood by those who must live under it, and for carrying back the reactions and difficulties that the policy may have evoked.

George Adams, the immediate past Chairman of the Ontario Labour Relations Board, has expressed similar sentiments.

---

10. Professor of Labour, Law Harvard Law School, formerly Chairman of the British Columbia Labour Board.
11. *Reconcilable Differences, New Directions in Canadian Labour Law*, The Carswell Company Limited, Toronto (1980) at page 294.

Although I did not realize it at the time, one of the most significant changes recommended by the Woods Report[12] was the elimination of the tripartite Canada Labour Relations Board. I would argue that it has not been a felicitous change. The neutrality and fairness of the Board has frequently been called into question. I would argue that it has succeeded in alienating itself from the parties. Yet the very reasons why a Labour Board should be tripartite were eloquently expressed in the Woods Report. Four reasons were given:

(1)   The presence of a person drawn from the ranks of a party is a source of assurance to that party that his case will be understood and carefully reviewed.

(2)   That same assurance usually makes the tribunal and its decisions more acceptable to the parties.

(3)   Since the Boards are often given wide discretion, a representative type tribunal offers a basis for assurance that discretion will be exercised on the basis of industrial relations experience.

(4)   Power of discretion involves a measure of compromise, and when a claim is to be settled on the basis of what the tribunal considers a fair reconciliation of conflicting interests and claims it is of some comfort for the tribunal to be representative.

It is significant that the study paper done for the Law Reform Commission of Canada by Stephen Kelleher on the Canada Labour Relations Board[13] has as its first recommendation that the Canada Labour Board be changed back to a tripartite Board[14] - for many of the reasons outlined above.

The last alternative presents, in my opinion, the greatest danger to justice. It is, unfortunately, a mode that has been increasingly popular in recent times. It consists of creating a Board or a commission on a permanent and non-representational basis and then bestowing on the body vast discretion both as to the subject matter and to the remedy. Is justice really served in our society by enacting a vague law and then giving to a board an enormous discretion to determine both what the law is and how a transgressor should be punished?

We must be doubly concerned when the full right to judicial review is curtailed. Professor H.W.R. Wade of Cambridge in his Hamlyn Lectures on *Constitutional Fundamentals*[15] summed up the problem in the following passage.

---

12. *Canadian Industrial Relations*, The Report of Task Force on Labour Relations, H.D. Woods, Chairman, December 1968 at page 207.
13. Law Reform Commission of Canada, Ottawa, 1980.
14. *Ibid.*, p. 24 and 83.
15. H.W.R. Wade, *Constitutional Fundamentals*, Hamlyn Lectures 32, Stevens & Sons, London, 1980, p. 66.

But, as I have just observed, to exempt a public authority from the jurisdiction of the courts of law is, to that extent, to grant dictatorial power. It is no exaggeration, therefore, to describe this as an abuse of the power of Parliament, speaking constitutionally. This is the justification, as I see it, for the strong, it might even be said rebellious, stand which the courts have made against allowing Acts of Parliament to create pockets of uncontrollable power in violation of the rule of law. Parliament is unduly addicted to this practice, giving too much weight to temporary convenience and too little to constitutional principle. The law's delay, together with its uncertainty and expense, tempts governments to take short cuts by elimination of the courts. But if the courts are prevented from enforcing the law, the remedy becomes worse than the disease.

JUDICIAL REVIEW

''For Judicial control, particularly over discretionary power, is a constitutional fundamental'' writes Wade.[16]

If the alternate forms of access to justice may be acceptable in certain circumstances, the practice of attempting to prevent any judicial review of their decisions is questionable, not only on the constitutional grounds raised by Professor Wade. If we are really concerned with justice as distinct from the mere speed of the decision, surely a discretionary tribunal must be made subject to court review on the grounds both of fairness as well as misuse of power.

Indeed the safety valve for the experiments with alternate forums is that when they misuse their powers, they can be called to order by the Courts. Misuse of power by a discretionary Board is the very antithesis of Justice. Is there to be no remedy under these circumstances?

Our courts have on occasions been remarkably timid about intervening in these decisions, and lengthy dissertations on the distinctions between errors of law within jurisdiction as against errors of law that exceed jurisdiction, have done as much to confuse as to enlighten.

In the recent House of Lords decision in England in *Reilley* v. *Mackman*[17] Lord Diplock wrote:

> It was this provision that provided the occasion for the landmark decision of this House in *Anisminic Ltd.* v. *Foreign Compensation Commission*, [1969] 2 A.C. 147, and particularly the leading speech of Lord Reid, which has liberated English public law from the fetters that the courts had theretofore imposed upon themselves so far as determinations of inferior courts and statutory tribunals were concerned, by drawing esoteric distinctions between errors of law committed by such tribunals that went to their jurisdiction, and errors of law committed by them within their jurisdiction. The breakthrough that the Anisminic case made was

---

16. Wade, *op. cit.*, p. 68.
17. [1983] 2 A.C. 237, 278.

the recognition by the majority of this House that if a tribunal whose jurisdiction was limited by statute or subordinate legislation mistook the law applicable to the facts as it had found them, it must have asked itself the wrong question, i.e., one into which it was not empowered to inquire and so had no jurisdiction to determine. Its purported "determination", not being a "determination" within the meaning of the empowering legislation, was accordingly a nullity.

Our recent jurisprudence, however, illustrates the ambivalence of Canadian Courts in this area. Again, drawing on the Labour Law experience, in the recent Supreme Court decision of *National Bank of Canada* v. *Retail Clerks and C.L.R.B.*[18] Mr. Justice Beetz in allowing an appeal against a decision of the C.L.R.B., could remark (with the concurrence of four other Judges)

> Remedies Nos. 5 and 6 thus force the Bank and its president to do something, and to write a letter, which may be misleading or untrue.
>
> This type of penalty is totalitarian and as such alien to the tradition of free nations like Canada, even for the repression of the most serious crimes. I cannot be persuaded that the Parliament of Canada intended to confer on the Canada Labour Relations Board the power to impose such extreme measures, even assuming that it could confer such a power bearing in mind the Canadian Charter of Rights and Freedoms, which guarantees freedom of thought, belief, opinion and expression. These freedoms guarantee to every person the right to express the opinions he may have: *a fortiori* they must prohibit compelling anyone to utter opinions that are not his own.

The strength of these comments is remarkable. What is even more remarkable, however, is that, in the Federal Court of Appeal, what Mr. Justice Beetz described as "totalitarian and as such alien to the tradition of free nations like Canada" was accepted as being within the Board's jurisdiction without even calling on the Respondents to justify the decision.

The need for Courts to intervene to restore procedural safeguards in the interest of justice is illustrated by the following two examples.

In the case of *McBain* v. *The Canadian Human Rights Commission*[19] the Honourable Mr. Justice Collier comments:

> Keeping in mind the test propounded in the *Marshall Crowe* case, opinions may well differ, in this case, as to whether, on all the facts here, a reasonable apprehension of bias on the part of the Human Rights Tribunal is well-founded...
>
> In my view, the reaction of a reasonable and rightminded person, viewing the whole procedure as set out in the statute and as adopted in respect of this particular complaint, would be to say: there is something wrong here;

18. [1984] 1 S.C.R. 269.
19. 84 C.L.L.C. 16104 at 16108-9.

the complaint against me has been ruled proved; now that complaint is going to be heard by a tribunal appointed by the body who said the complaint has been proved; that same body is going to appear against me in that hearing and urge the complaint to be found to be proved.

Again in the recent case of *Eastern Provincial Airlines* v. *The Canada Labour Relations Board et al.*[20] the Board's decision was quashed when it was shown that the Board refused to allow any recording whatsoever of its proceedings, cut off the defence after hearing only one witness, knowing there were several others waiting to be called, rendered a decision on the merits condemning the defendant, and prepared a "record" of the proceedings which did not reflect what happened. The Board had been unfair.

However when the matter was referred back to the C.L.R.B., a subsequent decision rendered was found by the Federal Court to be valid though in error. One of the Judges refers to the key conclusion as being "perverse" and "a tautology of exceptional transparency". However while the Judges were of the opinion that the Board erred in law, they decided that the error was "not a jurisdictional error".[21]

The reasons sometimes given for what I would submit is excessive deference to the decision of the Boards is because this was the legislators' intent. Much has been made, for instance, of the fact that the Canada Board is not subject to the review under section 28(1)(b) and (c) of the *Federal Court Act*. Forgetting for a moment that section 28(1)(a) was supposed to contain the full review available under the prerogative writs of prohibition and certiorari, it should be noted that the amendment which removed the review under part (b) and (c) was passed in approximately thirty seconds after being introduced between second and third reading of a Bill amending the Canada Labour Code. The total explanation for this change was given by the Honourable John Munro then Minister of Labour as follows:

> That is the amendment. I am sure honourable members are aware that this is designed to overcome frivolous delays by applications to the Federal Court *during* proceedings before the Board which delay the decision to the frustration of both parties involved. It is similar to proposals in other provincial legislation.[22]

There was no other debate or comment on the amendment in the Commons. Either the Minister was ill-informed, or the Courts have read far too much into the said amendment.[23] Again Professor Wade's writing comes to mind

---

20. [1984] 1 F.C. 732.
21. Federal Court of Appeal, No. A 1893-83.
22. Hansard Commons Debate, April 17th, 1978 p. 4261.
23. *La Banque provinciale du Canada* v. *Syndicat National des employés de Commerce et de Bureau du Comité Lapointe (C.S.N.)*, [1979] 2 F.C. 439 at 441-442; *Teamsters Union Local 938* v. *Massicotte*, [1982] 1 S.C.R. 710 at 712-713.

Here again is a remarkable instance of judicial policy on the constitutional level. The judges appreciate, much more than does Parliament, that to exempt any public authority from judicial control is to give it dictatorial power and that this is so fundamentally objectionable that Parliament cannot really intend it.[24]

This should, I submit, be kept in mind.

Many further illustrations could be drawn to underline the potential dangers of either unfairness or misuse of power by tribunals with discretionary power. If *access* to justice requires that Boards or Commissions be entrusted in some areas with the roles formerly played by the courts, *justice* itself requires that these bodies be subject to Judicial review.

Lord Atkin perhaps put it best:

Finality is a good thing, but justice is a better.[25]

---

24. *Op. cit.*, p. 65.
25. *Ras Behari Lal* v. *King-Emperor* (1933), 60 I.A. 354, 361.

Decision-Making

Garry Watson*

I would like to discuss two phenomena that have emerged in civil litigation and in the literature in the 70's and 80's. The first is alternative dispute resolution, and the other is the emergence of what have been called managerial judges. The alternative dispute resolution movement is primarily concerned with the exploitation and exploration of alternative methods to adjudication as a means of resolving disputes. The movement originated in the United States but has quickly become an international phenomenon. For reasons which are not altogether clear, it appears to perhaps have had less impact overtly in Canada than in some other places. I shall come back to this in a moment.

Managerial judges. The phrase itself is the title of a recent Harvard Law Review article by Professor Judith Resnick in which she describes the shift of judges from the role of totally disinterested adjudicators to a more managerial stance. For instance, managerial judges meet with counsel in chambers in an attempt to encourage settlement. They may supervise case preparation through the handling of all interlocutory motions in a case and they are concerned with calendar control. They have developed schemes for speeding up the disposition of cases and for persuading litigants to settle rather than to try cases, and they are concerned overall with the more efficient use of judges and of courtrooms. Are the two phenomena related? I believe so, at least in part. Both represent a reaction to court congestion and delay and to dissatisfaction with adjudication as a method of resolving disputes, at least with the cost and delay that is presently involved in adjudication. In addition both represent attempts to do a better job at resolving disputes.

Turning back to the alternative dispute resolution movement. It has as its major focus an attempt to increase the use of alternative methods to court-centered adjudication in resolving disputes. For example, mediation, conciliation, negotiation and arbitration. This however has not been the movement's only concern. It has a very strong academic component with a distinct interdisciplinary flavour. In universities and

* Professor, Osgoode Hall Law School.

research institutes not only lawyers but political scientists, socioligsts, anthropologists and historians are working actively in this field. Indeed, to date the most impressive achievements of the movement have been in the area of research directed to increasing our knowledge about what is often referred to as (and I think the phrase is an ugly one) "disputing". For example, some very large empirical research projects have demonstrated that what we see in the courts is merely the tiny tip of the dispute-processing iceberg. Just as the court's own caseload is "pyramidal" in the sense that only 3 to 6 percent of all law suits ever reach the point of being adjudicated, only a small percentage of all disputes or potential disputes in our society ever lead to the filing of a law suit. Most disputes are not resolved in the courts. They are resolved in the workplace, at school, in boardrooms, offices, homes and a myriad of other places by a variety of means that include, principally, negotiation or mediation. Moreover a large number of disputes or potential disputes are never resolved because people "lump it" (i.e. they decide to do nothing about it) or are never even perceived by the parties as giving rise to a claim. The research confirms, as might have been suspected, that the disputing process has a distinct socio-economic bias. Being educated and having money make people much more likely to pursue disputes. The short term practical achievements of this movement have, I believe, been less noticeable or impressive. Let me took briefly at some of the examples.

First of all, the movement towards justice centres. These are local, sometimes community based centres, their primary purpose being to attempt to resolve disputes without going to court. They are largely but not exclusively a U.S. phenomenon where considerable government and foundation funding was initially available. Their impact and success is unclear at the moment but it appears not to be having a major impact. Secondly, mediation. Mediation has clearly emerged as a useful alternative form a third party intervention or assistance in the resolution of disputes. Although it has been marketed in a variety of ways, for example, public and private mediation services have been established to deal with everything from consumer complaints to big business disputes, it has proved difficult to sell on a voluntary basis outside the court setting. However some limited success has been achieved in the matrimonial law area. The possible role of the legal profession as a deterrent to non-court based use of mediation has been suggested but remains unclear. But suspicions abound. Certainly mediation in the form of the pre-trial conference has become part of the weaponry of the managerial judge, but more of that in a moment.

One difficulty in measuring the impact of mediation as Professor Rick Abel and others have observed, is that most mediated cases would probably have been resolved by negotiation had they been left alone.

With regard to arbitration in the form that we most often encounter it today, it is unclear that it differs very significantly from adjudication as a dispute resolution technique. It looks very much like adjudication but with a non judge playing the adjudicative role. As with mediation, marketing to date has not been particularly successful. Obtaining wide-scale pre-or post dispute consent to arbitration has proven difficult and again there is a suspicion that lawyers have not helped in this role.

As for negotiation, the alternative dispute resolution movement has rediscovered negotiation and affirmed that it, and not motherhood or prostitution, is the oldest profession. Research, both theoretical and empirical, has elevated negotiation to the position of being clearly the major method of dispute resolution in our society and in most other societies, not only today but from time immemorial. Bargaining in the shadow of the law, to use Mnookin and Kornhauser's evocative phrase, is the method by which most disputes are resolved whether or not they ever become law suits.

While many proponents had hoped for more immediate gains I think it will take time for the full effect of the movement to show. Law students for the first time are seriously studying alternative methods of dispute resolution and receiving training in mediation and negotiation, and those methods are now being portrayed as vitally important and legitimate means of resolving conflict without adjudication.

Well where does this all leave us? What have alternative dispute resolution and managerial judges got to do with access to justice, the subject of this panel and with the theme of this conference? Let me briefly draw three points of contemporary concern that I have with the directions we are taking. First, managerial judging's embracing of the alternative dispute resolution technique of mediation and role conflict. I believe the emergence of managerial judges, if that is really the right term, has been both inevitable given the contemporary circumstances, and desirable. By managerial judges I mean judges who are concerned not with just providing impartial adjudication when called upon to do so, but also with exploring within the court context other methods of resolving litigants' disputes and with managing the caseload calendar which, until their intervention, was largely unmanaged by anyone.

In her Harvard Law Review article Judith Resnick raised some due process and what might be called "Big Brother" problems whith man-agerial juges. I think we have in many respects handled this develop-ment better than our American counterparts. For example, we have been more sensitive than they have in recognizing the risk of injustice that may result when a person whose primary role is adjudication indulges in mediation. A good example is a provision in the Ontario Rules of Civil Procedure that expressly prohibits a judge who conducts a pre-trial conference from presiding at the trial, and a provision prohibiting a judge who has been assigned to hear all pre-trial motions in a complicated case from presiding at the trial. But have we gone far enough in this direction?

Have we been sensitive enough to the risk of role conflict? I don't believe that we have. Judges are unique in that they alone have the compulsory power enforced by the state to adjudicate on people's claims. An adjudication must be impartial and must be seen to be impartial. Adjudication is frequently not seen as impartial when a judge, in mid-trial, resorts to the role of mediation that was appropriate at the pre-trial conference. That is, I suggest quite inappropriate in mid-trial without the express consent of counsel. I believe the late Walter Williston was correct when he recommended the passage of a rule in Ontario that would have expressly provided that a judge before whom a proceeding has been called for trial, could hold a conference either before or during the trial without disqualifying himself from presiding at the trial, provided however, that unless expressly consented to by all parties there shall be no discussion as to discharging the jury, the settlement of liability or the settlement of the quantum of damages.

There is a tendency I believe on the part of many judges to pass over or avoid the implications of such practices and to view such mid-trial intervention helpful to the parties, necessary and not improper. I disagree. I suggest that it is the soft underbelly of managerial judging. Many counsel complain today that with a few judges, by no means all, it is just not possible to get a fair impartial adjudication. Better to keep separate and distinct the roles of mediation and adjudication that lead to injustice in the name of managerial expediency. In the most recent volume of the Yale Law Journal, Professor Owen Fisk has written a provocative article entitled ''Against Settlement'' in which he attacks one of the basic assumptions of the alternative dispute resolution movement - that is, that settlement is preferable to adjudication in achieving justice. Few will agree with all of Fisk's arguments but he makes the important point that settlements resulting from economic coercion are unlikely to be just and those that result from judicial coercion are totally unacceptable.

The second matter I would like to refer to is the delegation of decision-making as an aspect of managerial judging. The delegation of certain aspects of adjudication by judges to subordinate judges or court officers through the power to direct a reference, to masters, commissioners, referees or registrars, has long been a feature, albeit a limited one, of our civil procedure. With the rise of managerial judging there is evidence of more aggressive use of this power, particularly by superior court judges in the area of family law. No longer are mere matters of accounting being referred, but also the determination of basic rights, for example, the right to maintenance, to the division of property, and custody. I believe this development is to be seriously questioned. The work involved can be time consuming, repetitive and less interesting than the trial of major commercial or product liability cases, but it is extremely important to the parties. The citizenry is entitled to a fair and impartial trial and, on the basic issues of entitlement, to a hearing before a judge, not before some surbordinate to whom the matter is being referred and effectively delegated. I suspect that in the near future that we may see the Supreme Court turn its attention to the constitutional permissibility of such broad exercise of the reference power. If so, I feel that the court may well point out that the newly rediscovered central role for the s. 96 judiciary carries with it not only powers but also responsibilities which may not be broadly delegated to non-section 96 judges.

My final point I will touch on only briefly. Under the influence of the alternative dispute resolution movement, the procedural device geared most directly to settlement, that is, payment into court, has been reshaped in many jurisdictions into a broader, "written offer to settle" procedure. This, in effect, allows both plaintiff and defendant alike to use the pressure of costs sanctions to force the opponent to carefully consider proposed offers to settle rather than proceeding to trial. There is much to be said for this development in that it makes available to the plaintiff a weapon formerly available only to the defendant. These written offers to settle procedures, with the possibility of the shifting of costs from one party to the other, are now even being seriously proposed in the United States where, as you probably know our costs indemnity system is generally unknown. These proposals have given rise to a flurry of writing in the United States on "attorney feeshifting", including some sophisticated economic analysis. This writing strongly reaffirms what we have tended to ignore - that cost-shifting, fair and equitable as it may appear on the surface, operates quite differentially on litigants depending on whether they are risk neutral or risk adverse.

Put bluntly, the fear or risk of having to pay the other side's costs is much more of a deterrent to the average individual litigant than it is to an insurance company which, after all, is in the risk business, or to a large corporation. Our cost rules undoubtedly deter litigation, but they deter some groups of litigants much more than they do others. The represent a restriction on access to justice which is a differential restriction and one biased against individuals of modest means. I believe that it is something we will likely closely re-examine in the next decade.

Let me close with an observation that has been made by the historian Jerry Auerbach in his recent book. "Justice without Law". Auerbach speculates that in the 25th century people will look back at the role played by lawyers and judges in the 20th century with the disbelief and lack of comprehension that we now display towards medieval religious zeal and piety in the 14th and 15th century.

*"Who wields power is not
important, provided that
the hierarchical structure
remains always the same."*

*"Il n'est pas important de
savoir qui détient le pouvoir,
pourvu que la structure
hiérarchique demeure
toujours la même."*

George Orwell, *1984*

THE PROFESSIONALS IN JUSTICE

LES PROFESSIONNELS DE LA JUSTICE

The Role of the Lawyer

L. Yves Fortier*

Notre société, ainsi que notre constitution, s'appuient sur la primauté du droit, sur le "rule of law", héritage précieux, s'il en est, du régime politique britannique. La primauté du droit, ça signifie, en peu de mots, que nous vivons dans le respect de valeurs morales et sociales mûries au cours des siècles, dans le respect de normes établies par nos parlements élus et dans le respect des décisions rendues par nos tribunaux.

One cannot speak of "rule of law" without speaking of the roles played in our society by our eleven parliaments, our eleven cabinets (for, as we know all too well, regulations as well as statutes form "the law"), our judges and our lawyers. One must also speak of the Canadian Charter of Rights and Freedoms which two and a half years ago, was draped like a blanket over our entire judicial system.

Simple avocat, je veux profiter de l'occasion qui m'est offerte aujourd'hui sur cette tribune avec un juge, un professeur de droit et un législateur, tous fort éminents dans leurs sphères respectives, pour poser quelques questions, formuler quelques critiques et susciter, je l'espère, une discussion constructive sur le rôle d'un chacun dans l'administration de la justice au Canada en 1984.

LE RÔLE DU LÉGISLATEUR

Let me begin with the role of lawmakers in our society. Members of Parliament in Ottawa, members of provincial legislatures, do not have as their sole responsibility the adoption of laws. Lawmakers must insure that good laws are adopted as well as laws properly drafted. Federal and provincial lawmakers have a duty to inform the citizens of their rights and obligations and they will only be able to discharge that duty conscientiously if the statutes which they have passed are readable and understandable.

Nous sommes ensevelis sous une masse de lois et de règlements qui, souvent à notre insu, régissent jusqu'aux plus menus détails de nos

* Ancien président, Association du Barreau canadien.

activités quotidiennes et qui brillent souvent davantage par leur quantité que par leur qualité. Il arrive malheureusement de plus en plus que nos députés ne savent pas ce qu'ils font, ce qui ne signifie pas qu'on doive leur pardonner pour autant. Il arrive de plus en plus que nos députés ne réalisent pas les conséquences des gestes législatifs qu'ils posent, mais ceci est loin de constituer pour eux une excuse valable.

In my opinion, we cannot condemn strongly enough this growing tendency on the part of our governments to legislate rashly, either out of panic or out of laziness. Omnibus bills, legislation by decree, voluminous regulations often published after their effective date — have become the rule rather than the exception. In effect, legislation has been taken away from Parliament and the legislatures where it belongs and entrusted to cabinet ministers or, worse, to civil servants who are elected by no one and whose roles should be to implement rather than to direct the electorate's will. It is not up to the lawyers alone to react to this erosion of legislative power and mushrooming of executive power — it is the responsibility of all citizens. But it is perhaps up to lawyers to draw to the attention of others that this is happening and that its consequences are extremely serious: everyone must be made to see this appalling situation and to react.

This problem is made even worse by an increasing difficulty in finding out what the laws and regulations are which apply to a particular question. Lawmakers, lawyers and judges experience this frustration today. Imagine how the individual untrained in the law will react. It is ironic to have to say this when we have finally succeeded in obtaining a Freedom of Information Act, both in Ottawa and in many provinces, but it is true. Not only the individual and not only corporations but also the lawyers whom they pay can be less and less sure of the real state of the law! We all have heard the adage: "Ignorance of the law is no excuse!" This perhaps had understandable good sense in the past but our law making today has made it ludicrously unfair.

Nous professionnels de la justice devons prendre conscience des lacunes du système législatif actuel. Si l'état, si la bureaucratie, veulent nous envahir, ce qui, en soi, est déjà inquiétant, au moins devraient-ils avoir la délicatesse de nous dire franchement avec quoi ils nous envahissent et de nous envahir avec des produits de qualité supérieure. La population n'a-t-elle pas le droit de connaître tous les règlements qui se cachent sous le cheval de Troie que sont devenues nos lois, et de savoir exactement quels droits et quelles obligations sont modifiés par chaque loi nouvelle et par chaque nouveau règlement?

LES AVOCATS

Après avoir lancé un caillou au législateur et avant de traiter des juges, je me permets quelques commentaires sur le Barreau et ses membres.

Sondages après sondages, révèlent que le public a une perception négative de l'avocat. Pourtant, ces mêmes sondages révèlent que cette image est négative surtout chez ceux-là qui n'ont jamais consulté d'avocat. Notre profession est donc, en quelque sorte, jugée, non pas sur ses actes, mais sur des impressions.

Je comprends, dans une certaine mesure, ces préjugés. Notre système judiciaire, comme notre société, est fondé sur la confrontation. La démocratie prospère, là où des parties s'affrontent. La justice est rendue, après que des parties se soient affrontées. Dans tout procès, il y a un gagnant, il y a un perdant, et, transposé dans les yeux d'un public mal éclairé, cela signifie souvent qu'un avocat sur deux s'oppose à ce que justice soit rendue.

But it would be simplistic to stop here and not to look clearly at the other factors which contribute to the lawyers' less than perfect image. Why do some laymen equate the morals of criminal lawyers with those of their guilty clients? Why do others blame lawyers for the cost of litigation? Why are lawyers seen as the cause of delays in getting to trial? Why do they have a reputation of inventing triable issues in what is seen as crystal-clear facts and crystal-clear law? Why is the isolated rotten apple of a fraudulent lawyer so easily extrapolated to the whole barrel of good ones? We have to answer these questions, we cannot duck them.

I recognize that lawyers deserve, to a large extent, the bad image which they have. We have not always played the role which has been assigned to us. Some of the criticism directed our way is justified. Les avocats se sont toujours, comme d'instinct, tenus trop près d'un pouvoir qu'ils n'osaient par conséquent dénoncer ou critiquer. Ils se sont opposés, pas toujours pour les bonnes raisons, à des mesures progressistes qui leur coupaient l'herbe sous le pied. Ils ont fait preuve, parfois, entre confrères, de trop de tolérance.

Nous n'impliquons pas assez le client dans les démarches complexes que nous devons effectuer, et nous sommes ensuite en peine de justifier des honoraires que de toutes façons nous n'expliquons pas assez. Il en est qui se livrent, dans l'intérêt de leur client, certes, mais au détriment de la justice, à des manoeuvres de diversion ou des tactiques dilatoires d'un goût douteux. Bref, il nous arrive parfois d'oublier que nous sommes, d'abord et avant tout, des officiers de la justice, et que notre maître est le droit avant que d'être le client.

Ces *mea culpa* complétés, je suis heureux de constater que les temps changent, et rapidement, et pour le mieux. Les Barreaux et leurs membres s'impliquent plus que jamais dans le processus législatif. Ils ne se gênent plus pour critiquer des lois et ceux qui les adoptent et la manière avec laquelle on les adopte. Ils se présentent en commission parlementaire. Ce sont eux, ne l'oublions pas, qui ont amené l'aide juridique. Ils se montrent plus sévères envers leurs membres et plus critiques à l'égard de la magistrature. Ils ont créé un fonds qui n'a pas son pareil, pour indemniser les clients victimes de fraude. Ils consacrent beaucoup d'énergie à l'amélioration de la qualité des lois et à l'information du grand public, notamment par le biais d'émissions de radio et de télévision.

Whether because they are more clever now than before or because their clients are learning to use lawyers more efficiently, lawyers are more and more involved in preventing trouble rather than getting their clients out of it. Je rêve, personnellement — le droit de rêver, s'il n'est pas enchâssé dans la constitution, n'en existe pas moins — au jour où les clients, comme font les patients des médecins et des dentistes, prendront rendez-vous d'avance, tous les six mois, pour faire évaluer leur état de santé juridique et aller au-devant de coûts inutiles. Du droit préventif, pourquoi pas? Furthermore, lawyers are more prone now, once a dispute has arisen, to seek ways of avoiding bringing it all the way to court: arbitration or earnest attempts at settlement are more common everywhere in Canada. Though it is hardly, at first glance, in the economic interest of their members, the various law societies and barreaux have set up arbitration mechanisms and they have been in the forefront of the battle to take the confrontation out of divorce. These developments are positive ones.

I am also pleased that the questions of lawyers' specialization and lawyers' advertising are now so widely and publicly debated. I am hopeful, indeed confident, that clients will before long be able to choose their lawyers knowing beforehand in what areas those lawyers are proficient and, generally, what kind of fees to expect. This will mean better service for the client.

J'affirme donc, sans hésitation, que l'avocat prend de plus en plus conscience de son rôle social, de son rôle d'officier de la cour, de son rôle, en quelque sorte, de protecteur du citoyen. Nous avons encore du chemin à faire mais nous sommes engagés, dans le plein sens du mot, dans la bonne voie.

LES JUGES

Parlons maintenant du rôle des juges dans cette équation. Une des pierres d'assise de notre société est l'indépendance et le respect du pouvoir judiciaire. Le juge est le gardien, en dernier ressort, de la paix sociale. Et même quand on est convaincu qu'il a eu tort, dans un cas donné, on se doit, tous, de distinguer entre une critique saine et constructive du jugement rendu, et une critique de l'institution judiciaire en tant que telle.

Les juges sont des proies faciles. Ils font, quoi qu'ils décident, des mécontents. Ils sont exposés à des critiques de nature professionnelle ou personnelle, et ne peuvent se défendre. Ils sont de plus en plus, et bien malgré eux, impliqués dans des débats politiques qui ne peuvent, à long terme, que saper leur crédibilité, donc mettre en péril l'ordre social.

We must all oppose most strenuously the politicization of our courts. I am not referring here to the judicial appointment process. I refer rather to the growing tendency of our legislators to abdicate their responsibilities by permitting some issues to be decided by our courts which should be decided by the lawmakers. It is unfair to the judges that they should be forced to decide constitutional questions which arise only because our governments have failed to agree with each other: medical and social problems which arise only because our legislators have not had the courage to deal with them directly: labour problems which come to court only because lawmakers have sought a hasty way out of them.

Je m'inquiète, en particulier, de ces déclarations à l'emporte pièce de politiciens qui discréditent à l'avance ou par après les jugements des tribunaux. Qu'on me comprenne bien. Je ne vise aucun gouvernement, aucun parti, aucun ministre en particulier: il y a des exemples à tous les niveaux. Mais je dis qu'il est inacceptable, dans une société fondée sur la règle du droit, que des politiciens qui n'ont pas su régler leurs différends, blâment de quelque manière que ce soit le tribunal qui l'a fait à leur place, au détriment, nécessairement, de certains d'entre eux.

Cela est vrai, aussi, de l'avocat perdant, qui ne doit pas se défouler d'une frustration peut-être légitime sur le dos du juge ou de la cour qui lui a donné tort. Toute forme de discrédit jetée sur le pouvoir judiciaire, autrement, je le répète, que par le biais d'une critique constructive, ne peut que desservir et la société et le système juridique.

To be fair, judges must share a part of the blame as they have on occasion yielded to the temptation offered by their privileged position and have willingly dipped some of their judgments into the juice of politics. But we can hardly call them back to the straight and narrow when our repatriated constitution calls on them to decide when collective rights must override individual rights and what are the frontiers of a "free and democratic society". These are political decisions. Judges now required to declare the invalidity of unacceptable laws must ask themselves "unacceptable to whom"?

In the first few years of breaking in the new Charter, we should be aware of the new pressures on our judges. They did not legislate the Charter. They did not ask for this extension of their judicial duties. However, in thirty short months, they have demonstrated that their traditional skills would serve them well in their new responsibilities. Judges in Canada have not shied away from interpreting the Charter, and lawmakers, lawyers and law professors should commend them for their bold efforts.

Je conclus en exprimant le souhait que nous tous, professionnels de la justice, prenions conscience de la dimension sociale de notre profession. Lorsque nous nous interrogeons, à l'occasion de colloques tel celui-ci, sur les sujets qui nous sont chers, l'indépendance de la magistrature et du barreau, la spécialisation, l'administration de la justice quoi, n'oublions jamais que nous n'opérons pas en vase clos.

The law is not made for judges, lawyers, legislators and law professors alone. We are all the servants of the people and of the law. The law belongs to all people and we must all protect it.

The Role of the Judge

Constance R. Glube*

INDEPENDENCE OF THE JUDICIARY AND THE ADMINISTRATION OF JUSTICE

I have decided to discuss these two topics together as they overlap in their result.

Judges cherish their independence and guard it jealously. They have to, even to extremes, otherwise their independence would be continuously eroded. So few people truly understand the position of judges. They do not understand that we are neither part of nor subservient to the executive branch of government. Bora Laskin, the former Chief Justice of Canada, in a speech entitled *The Institutional Character of The Judge,* April 11, 1972, discussed the principle of judicial independence and stated:

> The paradox of this principle is that in securing the individual responsibility of each judge of a court, once he is appointed, as against subservience to any fellow judge and as against external interference by others, it at the same time gives cohesion to the court as an institution distinct from other units of government.

He considered courts as a unit of government but distinct from other units.

Our courts are subjected to a number of administrative difficulties, in part due to budget constraints at the provincial level and in part due to a lack of understanding of the place of the judiciary in government. We are obliged to go cap in hand to government to request the simplest tools which must be available to properly perform our responsibilities. Administratively, the future must allow the judiciary greater control over its own destiny. There must be a recognition that governmental and judicial requirements do not always coincide. I have heard many judges say that administration is not our function. With respect, I disagree.

---

* Chief Justice of the Supreme Court of Nova Scotia, Trial Division.

There must be a way for the judiciary to administer itself. (See Masters In Their Own House by Mr. Justice Jules Deschenes). One way is for government to provide block funding to be totally administered by the courts. This would oblige the judges to examine their priorities with great care to ensure that funds are spent wisely and effectively, that is, where the need is greatest. To maintain our independence we must have the responsibility and control over the product. We must be able to manage in an effort to put our own house in order and improve what we know is wrong but have no means at present to correct. I believe this can be done without interfering with elected government. No judge should, by actual fact or by inference, be perceived as interfering with governments elected by the people. However, the judiciary must attempt to retain and protect their independence for those same people.

The judiciary must be in a position to respond to the rapidly changing world in which we live. How can we do that without computerization of our administration and without the ready availability of computers providing case retrieval. The world outside the courts has gone that route and we should not always be the last to receive up-to-date time-saving facilities.

There is a large area of independence of the judiciary which time does not permit me to develop, namely, the desire of Provincial Governments to amend the Constitution to allow them to set up tribunals to deal with many areas of civil litigation presently dealt with by federally-appointed judges. I see this as not only a threat to judicial independence but also as a threat to providing justice for the people. Others have, and will in the future, deal with this topic more fully, but it cannot be ignored as a way in which dispensing justice may evolve. I add my own fervent hope that it will not go that route.

Much more could be said of the independence of the judiciary but other topics need to be covered.

EDUCATING THE PROFESSION

Judges must recognize the need for judicial education and pursue it with diligence. We are in an age where technological change is occurring rapidly. The law is not static and if the law is to respond to those rapid changes the judiciary must learn and change so that we may keep up-to-date and continuously develop our understanding.

Computers are much more than glorified filing systems. A recent article in Business Week magazine dated July 9, 1984, is entitled "Artificial Intelligence Is Here". The article relates that computers which mimic human reasoning exist. Limitations are recognized but the computer engineers are working towards designing machines capable of doing multiple tasks simultaneously. The next step is to produce machines which are capable of commonsense reasoning. Perhaps by the year 2001, Judges will be obsolete! In the meantime let us use the available technology to assist us in our daily research requirements.

Today, the majority of judicial appointments are made from men and women in their forties and fifties who will occupy their positions for fifteen or twenty years. To believe that judges cannot or need not learn and keep up-to-date will result in a disservice to ourselves and to the public we serve. To remain current we must be both student and teacher. In every region of this country, we are so involved with our own duties that we tend to miss out on what is happening around us. Our exposure outside the courtroom will remain limited unless we deliberately plan otherwise.

We need communication with academics, lawyers and judges. We are partly technicians where nuts and bolts training is important but in addition, we are expected to make policy judgments. As a group we show a great reluctance to do more than apply the law. We need to understand the content and the back-ground of the law we apply, for without that understanding, we must question our ability to apply the law.

The performance of a judge may be adequate but none of us accepted our appointments with a view to accepting mediocrity as our standard. Our sights are high but most of us need help which education and training can provide. We may not be capable of writing great works of art but that is not our function. Our function is to understand the basis of the principles of law, to understand the approach to law which is affected by many different disciplines, and then to apply the law with greater understanding and meaning.

Powers of deduction and understanding must be constantly honed. This cannot occur solely in the courtroom setting. Too many of us rely upon what we learned ten, twenty or forty years ago, without ever opening our minds to new ideas. Education, meaningfully presented, essential to maintain, and above all improve, judicial pronouncements.

How can this be done? Judges must participate regularly in the many courses and conferences currently offered. In addition, there is the question of sabbaticals. They have been talked about, but as yet, they have not been implemented. The realization of sabbaticals for judges where judges would have the time to study and write could be one of the most productive proposals upon which we could embark. We all know of sabbaticals in the academic world, and in some commercial operations as well where they are seen as an important part of a person's working life. Why not for the judiciary?

SPECIALIZATION

Amongst the judiciary, specialization already exists, particularly at the provincial level in the field of criminal and juvenile law and at the provincial, and in some provinces at the federal level as well, in the field of family law. A few superior courts have judges who specialize in additional fields.

Is specialization a good thing? Is it necessary? And what of appellate courts?

I believe specialization of lawyers will happen more and more. In many places the idea of one lawyer handling all the requirements of an individual may soon disappear. No doubt there will always be the general practice of law just as we see in medicine today. However, I would suggest, in large centres, the generalist lawyer will soon become the minority rather than the majority.

It is difficult for me to say at this time whether I believe specialization is right or wrong. What I can say is that I believe specialization is beginning now in the legal profession.

Where does that leave the judges? If the numbers on the bench are sufficient it seems wrong to force a judge of a particular court, for example, to try matrimonial cases or criminal cases where the judge has no background in those areas of the law and perhaps actually dislikes dealing with those aspects of the law. If there are sufficient numbers, I can see judges specializing. Sufficient numbers are necessary so that the public will not be faced with only one person each time a particular type of case arises. Out of necessity, small courts will deal with all types of cases which could eventually prove difficult. That is the way most courts handle their current caseload and it is my belief that, for the most part, judges can and do dispense justice evenhandedly. For the human element exists — pride in what judges do. So much will depend upon counsel's ability to present their case if specialization comes into areas where the judiciary are few in number.

Even if a number of courts see judicial specialization as the way to go, it would not meet the needs of the public, nor would it be economically viable to carry specialization through to the appeal court level either provincially or at the Supreme Court of Canada. If specialization occurred at the appeal court you could end up with one man decisions from the initiation of the case to the final appeal. In my view, this could be contra-productive and lead to a break-down of justice.

MEETING THE PUBLIC'S EXPECTATIONS AND NEEDS — ASCERTAINING AND IMPLEMENTING PUBLIC POLICY

The role of the judge in ascertaining and implementing public policy and meeting the public's expectations and needs is an area which requires constant vigilance by all — politicians, law professors, lawyers and judges. Judges have been told to isolate themselves from many things. In so doing, we may be totally unswayed by the many controversies in society and end up totally unsuited to deal with the needs of a changing society. We must be aware and keep up-to-date — we must keep an open mind and constantly pursue our own edification and understanding of what is really happening in the world. We must place ourselves *in* the world — not on the doorstep. The day of the cloistered judge cannot, realistically, continue to exist. Judges need to broaden their horizons beyond the law. Within bounds, we must participate in society. Politically of course, we must maintain a "hands off" policy and any active participation in any controversial cause, political or otherwise, must be avoided as we never know when that cause may enter the courts.

However, knowledge of what is going on in society is important to avoid the perception that a judge is someone covered in mothballs who is dusted off to go into court and then returns to the attic. We tread a fine and difficult line at times. As we represent the court we must maintain constant vigilance to preserve the dignity and impartiality of the office.

Unfortunately, the public perception of a judge and the actuality may not coincide. Our roles are not to isolate ourselves and consider our judgments in a controlled atmosphere. We must understand what the world is up to, how other cultures live, and about the many different kinds of people who come before the courts. For who are we meant to serve? Ourselves or the public? Clearly it is the public, and so we had better know something about the public's needs, otherwise we shall not only fail to meet the public's expectations and needs but also our own expectations.

A current area of change which is the most important vis-a-vis the judge, lawyer, legal academic, parliamentarian and the public, is the *Charter*. This has turned judges on to a new path. We cannot continue to bury our heads in *stare decisis*. Like it or not we must try to meet the challenge of the *Charter* which, at the moment, has placed the judiciary in the forefront of assessing and effecting public policy. Many charter decisions are doing just that, and unless we are aware of the world outside the courthouse walls we shall not be able to pick up the torch of freedom and equality.

In the past, courts have been quite slow to make changes including overturning previous decisions which have been shown to be unjust in today's society. The *Charter* has said we have to make changes. Interpretations of the law based upon precedent which was "valid" one day was not valid the day after the proclamation of the *Charter*. This will be seen once again in 1985 when s. 15 comes into force.

Lawyers and academics can help the judiciary along this path with their legal arguments and writings, but in the end the judges have to make the decisions. They must be enlightened decisions, aware of the social fabric of our time, with our finger on the pulse of humanity.

THE FUTURE ROLE OF THE PROFESSION

Our future role is a challenge.

Maintaining and advancing our independence — will government recognize the validity of our positions? Without an independent judiciary one of the foundations for a free society would disappear, crumbling the underpinnings of democracy.

Facing responsibilities placed upon judges by the *Charter* — will we do the job satisfactorily, or will the public say it has not been done, forcing the government to define and refine?

Will we be forward in our thinking and providing justice or will we be cautious and, as a result, ineffective in our pronouncements?

It is up to us to meet the challenges which face us and move forward beyond 1984.

The Role of the Legal Academic

Ed Ratushny*

BACKGROUND

Although the program indicates that I will be talking about the role of the "legal academic", I prefer the term law professor. The reality is that the word "academic" has come to have a rather pejorative connotation, as in the comment: "There is no need to pursue that line of argument as we view it as being strictly academic". The implication is that an academic argument is one which is irrelevant to the business at hand.

Perhaps one should not be so sensitive about such a suggestion since, after all, the whole object of a university is to permit the unencumbered pursuit of knowledge and wisdom quite apart from any practical compulsion. However, in my view, the most important quality which a lawyer must have is a sense of *relevance*. Moreover, that quality is particularly important for a lawyer who also happens to be a law professor, when confronted with a tremendous volume of material, concepts and ideas which must be organized and presented as a logical and systematic subject within the constraints of a limited number of precious teaching hours.

At the same time, law professors must be careful not to be "spooked" by the practitioner who complains that his articling student spent three years at law school and never learned to search a title. That can be learned easily enough during the first week of articles. What law school offers is a unique opportunity to study laws, legal institutions and legal systems in a comprehensive, inter-related and theoretical as well as practical manner. The opportunity is unique since unless the student becomes a law professor or, perhaps, a professional law reformer, that student will spend his or her remaining career dealing with specific issues based upon specific factual situations. In other words, law school is not meant to provide the graduating lawyer with the training to dazzle the staff at the Registry Office. Rather it is to provide a conceptual framework, a knowledge of basic principles and, above all, a sense of relevance in dealing with legal issues for a lifetime.

* Faculty of Law, University of Ottawa.

The law professor has three basic responsibilities. The first and foremost is to teach. This includes not only the organization and presentation of courses, but also the preparation of materials and the counselling and guidance of law students. The second responsibility is to participate in the administration of the law school and the university in a manner which is somewhat analogous to that of a self-regulated profession. The third responsibility is to be productive in what might be described as "research and other professional activities".

In my view, the responsibility to teach and to be dedicated to teaching is the *sine qua non* of all other activities undertaken by law professors. The equitable sharing of administrative responsibilities is closely related. However, it is the third area that I wish to explore briefly today since it is an increasingly important dimension of the law professor's role. Finally, I should add by way of background that my own areas of teaching and specialization are in the Public Law area — Administrative Law, Criminal Procedure and Evidence, the Charter, Human Rights and aspects of Constitutional Law. My comments will, therefore, tend to draw upon examples from the Public Law field.

FUNDAMENTAL RESEARCH

The Arthurs Report on Research and Education in Law, observed that:

> ...there is not much fundamental scholarship undertaken in Canada by legal academics... to the extent that fundamental research is being carried out, we are indebted to a very small minority of legal scholars

The Report suggests that one reason for this state of affairs is that those who are committed to more "scholarly values" may be denied recognition and rewards when their work is perceived not to have "professional relevance":

> As a result, they may shift away from these areas to others that are more congruent with the interests of colleagues, students and the 'legal' world.

Another factor discouraging research was seen to be the enhanced status and recognition of law professors resulting in increased demands upon their time:

> Since the 1960s law professors have been more frequently appointed to the bench, to boards, commissions and inquiries and to senior university and public administrative posts. They have been asked to serve on committees of the bar, as counsel or researchers by law firms, governments and professional and community groups, and as arbitrators, mediators and trouble shooters.

The suggestion in the Report is that this development has had the negative consequences of discouraging fundamental research.

Perhaps it has. However, in some ways, the Arthurs Report adopts a very conservative view of this third dimension of the role of the law professor. It seems to insist upon placing the law professor in the traditional academic mainstream. A premium is placed upon doctrinal research, particularly where that proceeds from an inter-disciplinary foundation. Of course, that is a wonderful thing and it certainly justifies the study of law and the funding of research within the traditional university hierarchy. Moreover, the terms of reference of the Arthurs "Consultative Group" were restricted to "legal research and education". It may have been beyond the terms of reference of the Report to assess the significance of this recent phenomenon of the extraordinary demand for the services of law professors apart from its impact upon traditional academic research.

Nevertheless, the phenomenon is a reality and there are some very positive aspects to it. It has provided a direct nexus between the law school and the society which laws and legal institutions are created to serve.

That is not to say that doctrinal research should be neglected. Every self-respecting law professor wants to make a contribution and establish credibility in this respect. Frequently this contribution will arise out of thesis work during graduate studies and subsequent refinement and exposition of that work. However, is it reasonable or desirable or even possible to confine the law professor to doctrinal research for an entire career?

OTHER PROFESSIONAL ACTIVITIES

It may be useful to begin with a few concrete examples to illustrate what I mean when speaking of a direct nexus between the law school and the society which our laws and legal institutions are created to serve.

To start with my own law school, we have my Colleague Gérald Beaudoin, who recently served as a member of the Pépin-Robarts Commission. During the process of patriation of the Constitution he served as an advisor to the Government of Canada. On subsequent litigation in relation to language rights, he served as an advisor to the Québec Government. In the language rights litigation of recent years, another Colleague, Professor Joseph Magnet has been a frequent and forceful advocate. Professor Vern Krishna's work as an advisor to the Federal Finance Department led to his appointment as Chief of Tax Policy before his return to the role of law professor. Professor Rowland Harrison, an expert in Oil and Gas Law, served a similar stint with the Department of Energy, Mines and Resources. Professor Tarnopolsky was active in establishing human rights commissions in various parts of Canada and expended considerable time and energy on civil liberties causes before accepting a judicial appointment. Another Colleague, Professor Maxwell Cohen has had a distinguished career of public service in addition to his professional responsibilities and, most recently, sat on the International Court of Justice.

What of the role of Professor Lysyk in advising the Federal Government and then the Government of Saskatchewan in relation to Constitutional amendment? Or Professor Strayer who took the opposite route by starting with the Saskatchewan Government, and then joining the Federal Government? Consider the work of Professor Paul Weiler in relation to the British Columbia Labour Relations Board and the Ontario Workers Compensation Board, Professor Terry Ison in relation to the British Columbia Workers Compensation Board and the role of Professor Innes Christie as Chairman of the Nova Scotia Labour Relations Board and as a Member of the Anti-Inflation Appeal Tribunal. Indeed, Professor Harry Arthurs has had more than a passing impact upon the field of labour relations. Professor Giselle Côté-Harper sat on the United Nations Committee on Human Rights. Professor Irwin Cotler has been a highly visible advocate in the field of International Human Rights.

In the area of domestic Human Rights, an entire field of jurisprudence in relation to anti-discrimination law and procedure has been developed by law professors such as Peter Cumming, Dale Gibson, Bill Black, Ken Norman, and others. Professor Ian Hunter served as Counsel to the Ontario Human Rights Commission for many years and is now an outspoken critic of some recent developments in this area.

This random, spontaneous recitation is presented for only one purpose. That is to illustrate that law professors have been called upon to deal in a practical way with some of the most difficult and important legal issues facing Canadian society in recent years.

There are many reasons for this phenomenon. Perhaps the most significant is that law professors have the luxury of dealing with law from a "macro" perspective. In preparing and keeping current in a subject area, there is an opportunity to keep in constant focus the entire elephant while practising lawyers, judges and government officials are so often pre-occupied with remedying a leg, an eye or a trunk. Such a broad perspective is particularly important when dealing with new developments and new subject areas such as the recent examples of developments in the field of Human Rights and the coming into force of the Charter. It also requires some sensitivity to the governmental machinery and political process through which public laws are made and administered.

A second luxury is the special kind of independence offered by academic freedom and security. It permits research, advocacy and social criticism beyond what a client's needs or the firm's overhead would permit. Of course, the judicial role bears its own constraints in relation to public policy debate as we have seen in recent years and the lawyer in government faces similar constraints.

A third feature of the role of the law professor which contributes to this phenomenon is the tremendous career flexibility which exists. The teaching must be done well, administrative dues must be paid and research and publication must be visible. However, there is no weekly or monthly accounting. Intensive and productive work can build up "capital" which releases time for the kinds of activities described earlier. Moreover, there are sabbaticals and, it is relatively easy to arrange for an unpaid leave of absence for a year or more.

There are few difficulties in moving from full time law teaching to another role and back again. Unlike law practice, there does not exist the continuing responsibility for the affairs of special clients or the greater inter-dependence amongst partners. Apart from serving on commissions of inquiry, it is very difficult for most judges to leave the Bench for periods of time to pursue other interests or opportunities for periods of time notwithstanding the Rosie Abellas and Allen Lindens of this world.

IMPLICATIONS

In assessing the implications of this phenomenon, it is obvious that law professors have made a special contribution to many significant, recent developments in Canadian society. That is not likely to diminish. The ever-increasing influence of decision-making by governments and by non-judicial tribunals as well as the force of the Charter will increase the demands upon law professors. Increased service on task forces, in special studies and through assistance in implementing government policies and programs is, then, inevitable. In my view, this is an important and legitimate role for the law professor.

There is also an important benefit for the law school and law students. Such outside activity on the part of law professors can bring to the classroom acutely significant insights into the nature of law-making and administrative processes. This kind of experience can be extremely valuable in developing the public law professor's sense of relevance and sense of the broader context within which the law functions.

Of course, such knowledge and experience can also be transmitted to the legal profession through continuing education programs. By and large, I like to see such programs developed and taught by practitioners with law professors being called upon only to deal with broader issues or recent developments. An example is the initial series of seminars which the Human Rights Centre of the University of Ottawa organized to acquaint the Canadian judiciary with the Canadian Charter of Rights and Freedoms.

Of course, there is an obvious "down side" to all of this. That is the danger that law professors will become so pre-occupied with these "other activities" that they will neglect their teaching, their administrative responsibilities or their obligation to do "pure" research. The stimulation and rewards are very real. To be at the forefront of historical constitutional changes, working with the leading politicians and public servants, planning strategy and preparing for landmark court cases is pretty heady stuff. There is personal recognition and there are also financial rewards. It is obvious that publishing an article in a law journal which only a few other law professors are likely to read may pale by comparison.

In my view, the answer to this potential problem is simple. Teaching, administrative responsibilities and a reasonable publication record must come first. Unless these responsibilities are met, outside work should not be undertaken. (It is interesting to note that almost all of the professors mentioned earlier have distinguished themselves as teachers, administrators and legal authors in addition to the special professional contributions which they have made). Moreover, outside work should only be accepted where it can be clearly demonstrated to be directly related to the law professor's area of specialization. It should also be demonstrable that such work may contribute to society and to the professor's own professional development.

Law professors should not be attempting to carry on law practices. In my view, the attempt to churn out divorces or land deals does not fall within the range of acceptable outside activity. Moreover, it is unfair to the practitioner, particularly the sole practitioner who must rely on this kind of work to pay the over-head. At the same time, where the conditions suggested earlier have been met, the law professor should have no reservation about accepting any financial rewards which may exist for the work in question. Often it will be done at considerable personal sacrifice as a result of being added to the other responsibilities. As a professional, the law professor should be equally entitled to compensation for his or her time and skills.

However, the most serious implication of outside work for law professors is that so many of them are eventually lost to the teaching profession forever. Recognition by the legal profession and governments of a Borins, Le Dain, Linden, Lysyk, Strayer or Tarnopolsky does not arise completely out of teaching excellence or law journal publications. A number of Canadian university presidents are former law professors and a whole myriad have moved into careers in government tribunals and departments.

No one is likely to be offended if I relate a comment which was made to me approximately ten years ago by Professor Frank Scott at the time when the position of Chief Justice of Canada was due to become vacant. At the time, Bora Laskin was a puisne judge of the Supreme Court. Professor Scott told me that he had never forgiven "Bora" for accepting his appointment to the Ontario Court of Appeal because the law schools *needed* outstanding professors. Of course, one might debate

whether outstanding Chief Justices of Canada are at least equally important.

CONCLUSION

No doubt you have your own views about the role which law professors should assume beyond 1984. In the Public Law field, at least,
the demand for increased involvement outside of the law school is bound
to increase. I would echo Professor Scott's view of the need for brilliant
and dedicated law professors who do not view teaching as a ''stepping-
stone'' to other positions, but who view their profession as a unique
and privileged opportunity to influence the shape of our future laws, to
shape the influence of our future lawyers and to make a direct and
important contribution towards dealing with some of the most significant issues which our great country will face in the years to come.

*"Who controls the past
controls the future: who
controls the present
controls the past."*

*"Celui qui a le contrôle
du passé a le contrôle
du futur. Celui qui a le
contrôle du présent a le
contrôle du passé."*

George Orwell, *1984*

THE PROSPECTS FOR JUSTICE

LES PERSPECTIVES D'AVENIR DE LA JUSTICE

The Prospects for Justice

John J. Robinette*

The task which confronts me this morning is not only difficult but approaches the impossible. In the Gospel by St. Matthew it is said:

> Beware of false prophets which come to you in sheep's clothing but inwardly they are ravening wolves.

That does not help to restore my self-confidence.

In order to divine the future it is sometimes helpful to look at the past. Let us examine for a moment the last fifty years in the development of the common law. When Lord Devlin was a Law Lord he delivered a series of lectures and in one of them he said:

> The common law has grown by the formation of precedents and the division and multiplication of precedents until a complete organism is formed... But precedent could not make a rule if any Judge could alter it. So precedent, when finally established, becomes as rigid as the branch of a tree... The common law cannot abrogate an existing principle of law and I doubt whether it is now ever likely to invent a complete new one.

Consider fifty years ago in Canada. Our law schools had no courses on family relations, taxation, labour law or land use control. Some of these today are the busiest aspects of many practitioners' practices.

Think of the sweeping legislative changes in pure matters of law effected in the last fifty years, such as The Family Law Reform Act, The Landlord and Tenant Act and the drastic amendments to the Criminal Code.

Consider also the leading inventive decisions of the Courts in the last fifty years which completely contradict Lord Devlin's statements. They are impressive and I remind you of the following:

1. *Donahue vs Stephenson*, dealing with the liability of manufacturers to ultimate consumers;
2. The *Hedley Byrne* decision in 1963 recognizing liability for negligent use of words;
3. The doctrine of promissory estoppel as a shield and not a sword from the *High Trees* judgment of Lord Denning.

* Lawyer, Toronto, Ontario.

4. The concept that an administrative body even though it is not compelled to act judicially and is not bound by all the rules of natural justice must nevertheless act fairly when it is deciding a person's rights or privileges;

5. The developing suggestions in contract cases of the so-called unequal bargaining position theory and the change in the attitudes of the Courts to clauses which purport to exonerate a person entirely from liability.

6. Mareva injunction.

7. Anton-Piller order in copyright cases.

The developments in the common law in the last fifty years were brought about by the force of significant social, economic and technological changes in the community and the same fundamental forces will operate in the next fifty years, with what results no one can foretell.

All one can say is what Mr. Justice Felix Frankfurter said:

> Future lawyers should be more aware that law is not a system of abstract logic but the web of arrangements rooted in history but also *in hopes,* for promoting to a maximum the full use of a nation's resources and talent.

The major dilemma of the law will continue to be the solution of the inherent conflict between freedom of the individual and necessary state-imposed disciplines. We are living in a violent society in North America and, of course, state-imposed discipline is essential. The problem is to balance that with the essential right of freedom of individual men and women.

We should also recognize the limitations of the law to deal with current vulgarity, bad taste and obscenity. These are largely a matter of manners, education and ethics, and the power of the law to deal with them effectively will remain limited.

On the other hand, I do think that one can safely make some predictions with reference to the doctrine of *stare decisis.* Both the Supreme Court of Canada and the House of Lords have indicated and have held that they can overrule prior decisions. Even before the Supreme Court of Canada announced its intention not to be bound by decisions which the Court considered to be wrong, we did find our Supreme Court by judicial decision modifying the law of evidence in an important aspect. In 1965 the House of Lords had been confronted with a question of whether it should modify the hearsay rule in a situation where an accused had been charged with conspiracy to receive stolen automobiles. In order to establish that certain cars admittedly sold by the accused were in fact stolen, the prosecutor called as witnesses employees of the manufacturer of the cars to prove records compiled by various workmen as the cars were made, purporting to show the engine, chassis and cylinder block numbers which had been recorded on the car by employees of the manufacturer. The cylinder block number alone was marked in a secret part of the block and could not be obliterated or removed. Witnesses from the manufacturer were persons whose jobs were to keep the records and not compile them.

The House of Lords by three to two held that the evidence was inadmissible because it was hearsay. Lord Pearce, with whom another Law Lord agreed, dissented and said in his opinion that the evidence was fair, clear, reliable and sensible. He justified his decision by saying:

> This process of improvement and evolution was carried out by the inherent power of the Courts to conduct its process so as to prevent abuse and secure justice.

In 1970 the Supreme Court of Canada in *Ares v. Venner* [1970] S.C.R. 608, on an appeal from Alberta, had to deal with a similar problem involving nurses' notes on the hospital record of a patient. The Supreme Court speaking through Mr. Justice Hall adopted the views of Lord Pearce in the *Myers* case and rejected the contention that although the law needs to be restated to meet modern conditions the Court must leave it to Parliament and the ten Legislatures to do the job.

Goodness knows what social and economic changes will take place or what crises will present themselves to the Canadian people in the next few decades but I predict that the Courts will apply the so-called doctrine of *stare decisis* even more leniently than they have in the past and the Courts will have to recognize that changing and powerful public pressures may compel them to alter their provisionally expressed views on a subject matter. This is not applicable to such subjects as land law or trusts or wills or most commercial matters, but may turn out to be peculiarly and particularly true with reference to the Court's decisions on the Charter of Rights and Freedoms. As you are aware, section 1 of the Charter guarantees rights and freedoms set out in it, subject only to such reasonable limits prescribed by law as can be demonstrably justified in a free and democratic society. Free and democratic societies change, often very fundamentally, and in the decades ahead the Courts will likely recognize that the Charter of Rights and Freedoms has to be interpreted in the interests of Canadian society as a whole. With changing conditions they may well be compelled to review prior decisions on the Charter of Rights and Freedoms. I predict a much greater flexibility in the application of *stare decisis* to Charter cases depending entirely on the possible changes in the whole Canadian scene.

As to the future I think I can be much more definite about what we should be doing or will have to do with reference to the institutions which make, interpret and deal with the subject matter of law.

1. Legislatures must deal more expeditiously with necessary reforms in what I may call purely legal matters. Our Legislatures seem to be

more interested in other matters, forgetting that it is legal questions which affect the vast majority of the population.

2. The Judiciary

The independence of the judiciary free from the pressures or influence of either Parliament or the Executive must be maintained.

In a recent White Paper published by a Department of the Federal Government with reference to proposals for a review of the law of copyright it is stated:

> There presently exists in Canada a Crown prerogative right to authorize printing and publishing of works such as Act of Parliament and *judicial decisions*.

The White paper recommends that this Crown prerogative right remain.

This view as far as judicial decisions are concerned seems to be based on the theory that Judges are servants of the Crown and that, therefore, the Crown has the right to copyright any reasons for judgment and can permit or refuse to permit copying or give licenses to copy judgments of the Courts.

I submit that this is nonsense and fundamentally wrong, both historically and realistically. What it would mean is that the Federal Crown could make the decision as to whether any Court's judgment could be published at all or by whom it could be published.

That view ignores completely the constitutional history of England and Canada.

It may have been true under the Stuart Kings that the Judges were servants of the Crown but to suggest today that the Judges are servants of the Crown or that the Crown has some prerogative right of copyright entirely ignores the historical significance of the Whig or constitutional revolution in England culminating in the Bill of Rights and Act of Settlement in 1701.

The proper position is discussed by Sir William Holdsworth in his great history of the English law where he says:

> The separation of powers in the British constitution has never been complete but some of the powers in the constitution were and are so separated that their holders have autonomous powers, that is, powers which they can exercise independently subject only to the *law* enacted or unenacted. The Judges have powers of this nature because having been entrusted with the maintenance of the supremacy of the law they are and always have been regarded as a separate independent part of the constitution. It is true that this view of the law was contested by the Stuart Kings but the result of the great rebellion and the revolution was to affirm it.

Holdsworth correctly states the independent position of Judges both in Canada and England and any attempt to erode the independence of the Judges must be vigorously resisted.

3. Whatever else, our Judges should be free from financial anxiety with respect to themselves and their families, and since we are talking about the future at the moment, Parliament should, therefore, in the immediate future, accept and adopt in amendments to the Judges Act the fifteen recommendations in the Report of the First Triennial Commission on Judges' Salaries and Benefits. The Provinces likewise within their constitutional field have an obligation to the Judges and to the administration of justice to supply our Judges with competent staffs, proper offices, technical equipment and libraries so that they can work to maximum efficiency.

We may have to borrow from England two aspects of their practical administration of justice, one of which is some degree of specialization of Judges for particular types of cases. In England, the Justices of the Queen's Bench and the circuit Judges do the criminal work and those justices of the Queen's Bench who go on assizes have had vast experience in criminal matters both as counsel and in the Court. A Judge who is skilled in trusts and wills finds his way to the Chancery Division where he is exercising his specialized skills and experience and no one would ever think in England of having that Judge preside in a criminal trial.

I only mention this as an approach which may be desirable and probably could be worked out in the context of individual Courts.

Another approach which can be borrowed from England is that the Judges be reserved as far as possible in commercial cases for decisions of law and not for the tiresome burden of factfinding. In England today all construction contract cases are referred to experienced Official Referees who have the status of County Court Judges. They find the facts and they apply the law as they see it so that a burden is removed from the High Court Justices who in construction contract cases virtually only decide points of law on appeal to them.

Similarly the great English commercial Court to-day separates, in effect, law and factfinding. In London there are arbitrators who are experts in charter parties and other commercial issues; some of them are persons who have experience in a particular field and the arbitrators make the decision on the facts again applying the law as they understand it. There is an appeal to the commercial Court Judges in the Queen's Bench Division on questions of law but there is not even a right of appeal in cases involving possibly millions of pounds to the Court of Appeal without further leave. Some method may have to be devised to leave the factfinding tasks for others and leave the Superior Court Judges to decide the purely legal questions which arise out of those facts.

Finally, a word as to the appointment or selection of Judges. I am not going to elaborate on this but I am merely going to tell you a story about Abraham Lincoln.

> *"The best books are those
> that tell you what you
> know already."*

> *"Les meilleurs livres... sont
> ceux qui racontent ce que
> l'on sait déjà."*

George Orwell, *1984*

JUSTICE IN THE LITERARY TRADITION

LA JUSTICE DANS LA TRADITION LITTÉRAIRE

Justice in the Literary Tradition

Margaret Atwood*

PROLOGUE

I had a bet on that whoever introduced me would say, "My wife just loves your books." I lost.

Before I begin in earnest, I have to tell you that I've actually been in court three times. The first, as a witness in a case against a peeping Tom that we unfortunately caught on the third floor windowsill of our graduate women's residence in Boston, in 1961. Every night there you could hear the patter of little feet on the roof, but this one we trapped. He said he'd got arrested on purpose because he was having trouble with both his wife and his girlfriend and he figured it would be more peaceful in jail.

The second time was as a character witness for a friend of mine, a picket-line addict. I said I had never seen him spitting on policemen, which was true. The third time I was the plaintiff. I wanted restitution for three cows which had once belonged to me, and which had been kidnapped, and, I suspect, foully eaten. I won, and the judge said, "My wife just loves your books."

Now, on none of these occasions was I the accused, but on each of them I was paralyzed with terror throughout the proceedings - and I am not an easily terrorized person. I am not afraid (for instance) of snakes. I don't know what it is about judges and lawyers - maybe it's the suits. So you can imagine how I must be feeling.

When I told my accountant that I was going to do this thing, he said, "I can see the headlines: *Well-known Writer Makes Fool of Self.*"

On the other hand, when I told my lawyer - a certain Mr. Clean, from King and Bay, whom I employ on the well-known Mafia principle that the kinkier one's profession, the more pin-striped and well-vested should be one's advocate - he merely said, "Oh, no...", Seeing, no doubt, his years of careful coaching in respectable legal deportment sliding down the drain.

---

* Poet and novelist.

Such qualms aside, I have to say I've been having a wonderful time - I knew you guys had some big words in your vocabularies, but not *those* big words. Judges and lawyers, talking about the human condition? Things are looking up. I'm impressed as well as terrified - and for those of you who asked, no, I'm not collecting material. Lawyers, as I'm about to indicate, have been done.

Alors, l'adresse - en français de l'école secondaire de Leaside, Ontario.

Mesdames et messieurs, Vos Honneurs et Vos Honneureuses, Juges et Jugettes, Avocats et Avocatesses:

C'est une grande honneur et aussi une grande plaisir d'etre ici avec vous ce soir - dans une compagnie si distinguée, si intelligente, si pleine de sagesse et de charme, de savoir faire et aussi, et beaucoup plus important, de savoir vivre.

Le français, comme nous savons, est la langue de clarté, de précision, et aussi de nuance et des sentiments les plus délicats et raffinés que possible - mais ici ce soir, c'est une question des avocats, alors on n'a pas besoin de tout ça, et c'est malheureusement nécessaire de continuer en anglais.

Living in a double-language culture can sometimes help us gain insight into topics such as the one on our plates tonight. While I was reading a menu recently, it came to me in a flash of light that, in French, the word for *lawyer* is exactly the same as the word for *avocado*. As a writer, I'm in the habit of pondering over such things. Surely such a resemblance could not be mere coincidence. An avocado has a thick tough skin, a hard centre, and a texture like soft soap; you can get them stuffed or without dressing, and they're at their best when slightly rotten. Lawyers, however, are nothing at all like that; proving yet once again the slipperiness of semantic analysis.

Having bombed out with that one, I began to sweat. What ought a poor miserable scribbler say to a roomful of lawyers and judges? As I am metaphorically minded, I was already having visions of being lowered into a tankful of sharks, armed only with a teaspoon. All of a tremble, I called my friend, Judge Rosalie S. Abella, who by some judicious (that's a pun) armtwisting got me into this in the first place.

"What am I going to say to them?" I asked, clammy-handedly.

"You'll just tell a few judge and lawyer jokes," she replied. "And Atwood, you'll do me a favour. I know you're famous, but you're kind of short. You mind wearing just a little heel? So they can see your head".

"I don't know any judge and lawyer jokes", I said snotnosily. "Apart from Dorothy Parker's quip about having spent a lovely week-end in Boston sliding up and down the barristers - but that wouldn't apply in Canada, of course. Anyway, judges and lawyers aren't funny".

"Not *funny?*" she bridled. "Some of them make very funny jokes!"

"What about?" I asked, open-mindedly.

"Torts," she replied.

Judge Abella having been no use at all, I called my other friend, whom I shall call X.

"X", I said. "Help".

"Not to worry", said X. "They won't listen to a word you say anyway."

"Why, because I'm a woman?" I asked, knee-jerkingly.

"No, don't be silly. Those days are over. *I'm* a woman."

"Because I'm a writer?"

"No", she said. "Because you come on after the banquet".

Now, it hadn't escaped my attention that I came on after the banquet: in Cecil B. de Mille epic films about Rome or the Bible, *after the banquet* is the slot usually reserved for court jesters, dancing girls and orgies; in other words, cheap frills. And it is this fact - this *coming on after the banquet* - which takes us, finally, into the heart of our subject for this evening.

For the fact remains that the members of the legal profession - lawyers in particular - have, on the whole and historically speaking, had a bad press from writers. ("All of it deserved", muttered one lawyer I met at a party). There are several reasons for this. The first is, obviously, that judges and lawyers on the one hand, and writers on the other, both deal in language.

But let us pause here. "Judges and lawyers" is an awkward phrasing. I shall take a leaf from Lewis Carroll and from those who wish to substitute one sex-inclusive word for "he and she", and combine these two words into the single word "jawyers". You may find that slightly irreverent, but I *have* considered the alternative, which is "ludges". "Ludges", you must concede, is all too suggestive of some kind of bottom-sucking fish you might find in the depths of Lake Ontario, and we wouldn't want that, would we?

Jawyers and writers, then, both deal in language; but, as you can see, in entirely different ways. A jawyer wishes each word to mean one thing and one thing only. He is the foe of ambiguity, which he calls "vagueness", and will fight to the very last comma and semicolon to bend the language to his will, stuff it into his imprisoning clauses and subclauses, manacle it with heretofores, aforesaids and notwithstandings, and deliver it into his filing cabinet, sealed, signed, stamped, stapled and mutilated.

Writers, on the other hand, wish the language to expand into all available space: to resonate, to proliferate, to exfoliate; to play, sing, dance, and above all to suggest. Writers are sometimes accused of using suggestive language; but for a writer all language is suggestive. The writer wants language to be a top hat miraculously full of rabbits - magic, that which unites. The jawyer wants it to be a scalpel, a knife - logic, that which divides. The result is that writers don't believe jawyers communicate in any real language at all, but only in a kind of jawyerese, which is deficient in any of the qualities that make human intercourse worth while. In a word, for writers, jawyerese is not sexy.

That is of course an unfair assessment; but consider, on the other hand, what jawyers think of writers. Writers use language to tell stories, or, as we say, to fictionalize; but do that in court and you get hit for perjury. *My* lips move when I read contracts, it's true - I try to read them in the bath to counteract creeping rigidity - but some jawyer's lips move when they read anything else. The jawyer strikes the writer as incomprehensible, but the writer strikes the jawyer as crazy. Or, at the very best, dangerously unstable. As my own lawyer said to me once, "Harumph. Well, Margaret, you must admit that there are many more alcoholics among the members of your profession than there are among mine."

"In a pig's eye," I replied. "It's just that the members of your profession take better care to conceal it; and with good reason. If *I* get drunk and put my fist through a plate-glass window, that's a literary anecdote. I might even come out looking warm, human and accessible. It's not such bad p.r. But if *you* do it, you don't come out looking warm, human and accessible, you come out looking incompetent."

"But I *am* warm, human and accessible", he said, rather hurt.

"Don't let me catch you at it," said I. "This is the age of specialization. Leave that stuff to us writers. That's *our* job. You do the contracts." As for labouring under the impression that you're a tree or a skylark or - in the twentieth century - a fungus, or that there are angelic voices coming out of the bathroom sink, that's stock in trade for poets, but who would want it in their lawyer?

However, jawyers are merely sharing the views of their society when they think of writers either as a species of verbal tap-dancer or as a band of licensed zanies. And there's even some truth concealed behind this prejudice. One of the functions of the court jester was to hit the king over the head with a bladder filled with air and dried peas, to remind him that pomposity has its limits, and that, from one point of view, human life is a comedy and even the ruler is a part of it. If everyone went around saying that the emperor has no clothes on, we'd have anarchy. But if nobody were allowed to say it, we'd have tyranny. One of the first things to get chopped or forced underground in any totalitarian society is the sense of humour. The legal profession is society in its formal dress; hence the symbolic importance, in legal and professional circles, of the vest; from which we get the expression, "vested interests". The vest, apart from giving its wearer the sensation of keeping things close to his chest, is there to indicate that the wearer is well-buttoned in, and is not likely to break out into indecorous flights of comedy, romance, satire or tragedy, at least in public. I personally class lawyers by the number of visible buttons: thus, a ten-button lawyer, a twelve-button lawyer, and so on. Even female lawyers are prone to suits. However, the writer insists that under the narrow pin-stripes there exists a human being not much unlike others, and subject like them to the seven deadly sins as well as a few minor ridiculousnesses; a reminder which is not always entirely welcome.

Keeping this in mind, and keeping in mind also my belief that one of the things writing, especially the writing of prose fiction, actually *does* in society is to force a constant re-examination of the values we think we're living by, I'd like to consider three points on the interface - or, to purge a phrase and to replace a geometrical metaphor with a more organic one - three areas on the permeable membrane that connects the legal mind with the writerly one. These areas I will call the mimetic, the architectonic and the metaphysical.

By the mimetic area I mean that area of fiction (fiction taken to comprise not a certain form but any literary invention) in which life is held to be imitated by art. When a writer is thinking in this way, she will claim that the kinds of people that appear in her fictions are there because they are also there in real life; that she is, as it were, merely copying things down. This is never altogether true but it often has something to it. Looking at the figures of judges and lawyers that appear as characters in books over the centuries in - for instance - English-language literature (since that's the only one I know much about), we can see that lawyers in particular have definitely come up in the world, in literature as in life.

Going back as far as Chaucer, we find the law already flourishing, in a way, and already in disrepute with writers. The legal figure in *The Canterbury Tales* is the Sergeant of Law, sometimes called The Man of Law. He's fairly high up in the profession, an Assizes judge as well as a King's Counsel, but he is not much admired by Chaucer. He's depicted as somewhat obsequious, verbally adroit, good at collecting his fees, ostentatious about his own diligence, a social climber and a conservative dresser. Chaucer has him introducing his tale with a condemnation of the state of poverty and a truly greasy song of praise to riches and rich people, which shows where his interests lie.

The image of the lawyer as a grasping and tricky parvenue persists throughout the eighteenth century, though the figure of the judge splits off, sometimes appearing as a jolly hunting-and-drinking local squire. Both however tend towards Daumier caricature. Even when the judge-as-squire is an honest fellow, he's not overly bright, and the lawyers are definitely devoid of nobility. Neither are what you'd call heroes, and the idea of either one, but especially a lawyer, being the chief ruler of a country - as in "Prime Minister" - would have been mocked and flouted. Lawyering was something you did if you didn't have anything better to do, such as being a Lord.

Hero status tended to be reserved for those who broke the law, such as highwaymen - witness Jack Sheppard, which is not surprising in view of the harshness of the laws themselves. Fielding's *Amelia* shows the citizen as victim of the system, his *Jonathan Wilde* the system as manipulated by evil.

Up-against-the-justice-system novels, such as Scott's *Heart of Midlothian* and - perhaps the best 19th century European example - Hugo's *Les Miserables*, remind us that one function of the writer, in our tradition, from the Bible on, has been to speak for the powerless, to give a voice to the voiceless. The dominant English writer here is Charles Dickens.

In *Bleak House*, Dickens turns the Court of Chancery into a powerful metaphor - a sprawling uncontrollable monster made of paper, which can nevertheless eat people. It's like Dante's Hell, in that, once in, you can forget about getting out. The lawyer that goes with this vision is the foreboding Mr. Tulkinghorn, dry as dust, furtive and secretive, who knows as much as he can but keeps his knowledge to himself for his own purposes. Tulkinghorn is part shadow, part animated mummy, part spy, part vampire; his fearsomeness indicates that the law has grown in influence, pervasiveness and malignancy, at least in the popular imagination.

Dickens had ample opportunity to observe the law at work, as one of his first jobs was as a go-fer for a Gray's Inn solicitor, and he was, early on, a court reporter. He was not against the rule of law *per se*, but against its misuse, as he makes clear in *A Tale of Two Cities*. The French Revolution would never have happened, he says, had not the law been so corrupted and perverted. The real hero of this novel is, not incidentally, a lawyer. Sidney Carton isn't the hero in the sense of male ingenue. He is instead a Byronic anti-hero, who behaves more like the popular version of a poet than like the solicitor he is; that is, he drinks too much, he's a wastrel, he's cool and ironic, he dresses sloppily, and he's indifferent to his job. "I am a disappointed drudge", he says, prefiguring the Monday morning state of gloom at King and Bay. But he's also sentimental and chivalrous with women, and it's he who sacrifices himself to the guillotine so that the husband of the woman he loves may live. "It is a far far better thing I do than I have ever done", he thinks as he mounts the scaffold, thus putting the practice of law into its proper perspective. For Dickens, it's okay for a lawyer to be a hero, but only if he's a poor lawyer; poor in both senses of the word.

It was left to the twentieth century to invent that now-prevalent literary sub-genre, the courtroom drama, and to turn the erstwhile pettifogging and mistrusted lawyer into the stalwart hero. The lawyer-as-hero must surely have been consolidated, if not invented, by the very prolific Erle Stanley Gardner. Perry Mason, apart from the pedestrian literary style in which he's embedded, retains vestiges of previous lawyers - he's tricky and not above stretching an ethic - but really he's the man in the white hat, saving damsels in distress, his weapon not a smoking revolver but a shelf-full of well-thumbed casebooks. It was a long haul from Chaucer to Gardner, but we can see that, in the mimetic area -art as an imitation of life - the lawyer has definitely been upgraded. In literature, however, there's still a preference for the St. George or Robin Hood model. Lawyers who save the weak and innocent are preferred; those who help the rich get richer, though they may be amply rewarded in real life, still don't get many gold stars from writers.

I shall now turn to what I've called the architectonic area. This is the category to which this convention's mascot-book belongs, and it's of especial interest not only to me but to that brain-in-a-jar metaphor, the legal mind. Such books concern themselves with designing societies, which means designing their legal systems as well. Sometimes the societies they design are supposed to be models of the good, in which case we call them "Utopias", a word that does not signify "good" but "nowhere". Sometimes, on the other hand, they design societies that are supposed to be models of the bad, for which the literary powers that be have formulated the word "Dystopia". The bad design is really the good design in reverse: that is, we the readers are to deduce what a good society is by seeing in detail what it isn't, and thus by indirection find direction out.

The Utopia-Dystopia as a form tends to be produced only by cultures based on monotheism - or, like Plato's system, on a singular idea of the Good - which postulate also a linear goal-oriented time. Cultures based on polytheism and the circularity or simultaneity of time don't seem to produce them. Why bother to try to improve society when you know it's all just going to go round again, like clothes in the wash? But Judaeo-Christianity, being a linear monotheism, has given rise to several such cultures, our own and various orthodox Marxisms among them. In Marxism, history replaces God and the classless society replaces the New Jerusalem, but change-through-time, a change for the better, is similarly postulated. Thus in the background of every modern Utopia lurk Plato's Republic and the Book of Revelations, and modern Dystopias have not been uninfluenced by literary versions of Hell, especially those of Dante and Milton.

Sir Thomas More's *Utopia* gave its name to the genre, and it's noteworthy that the straw man More sets up to advocate positions he himself is against, such as the death penalty for stealing, is a lawyer. The Utopians themselves have no lawyers. They believe written laws should be few and understandable, and that every man should therefore be able to plead his own case, rather than having a lawyer to "instruct him in deceit".

The original *Utopia* has a long list of descendants, which includes Swift's *Gulliver's Travels*, and, in the nineteenth century, William Morris's *New From Nowhere*, in which the ideal society is a kind of artists' colony; H.G. Wells's *Time Machine*, in which the lower classes actually eat the upper; Butler's *Erewhon*, in which crime is a sickness and sickness is a crime; and W.H. Hudson's *A Crystal Age*, in which there is not much sex. In our own century, the classics are Huxley's *Brave New World*, Bellamy's *Loading Backwards*, and, of course, *1984*, to mention a few. Utopias by women are also of note, though not as numerous. There are, for instance, *Herstory* by Charlotte Perkins Gillman and *Woman on the Edge of Time* by Marge Piercey.

Utopias are often satirical, the satire being directed at whatever society the writer is currently living in: that is, the superior arrangements of the Utopians reflect badly on *us*. Dystopias are often more like dire warnings than satires, dark shadows cast by the present into the future. They are what will happen to us if we don't pull up our socks. Both, however, show the architectonic imagination at work, as it busily rearranges our all-too-imperfect human life on earth.

What aspects of this life interest such writers? To no one's surprise, their concerns turn out to be much the same as those of this conference. There are, of course, the superficial matters of clothing and cuisine, partial nudity and vegetarianism making regular appearances. But the main problems are the distribution of wealth, labour relations, power structures, the protection of the powerless, if any, relations between the sexes, population control, urban planning, often in the form of an interest in drains and sewers, the rearing of children, illness and its ethics, insanity ditto, the censorship of artists and suchlike riff-raff and anti-social elements, individual privacy and its invasion, the redefinition of language, and the administration of justice. If, that is, any such administration is needed. It is a characteristic of the extreme Utopia, at one end, and the extreme Dystopia at the other, that neither contains any lawyers. Extreme Utopias are communities of spirit, in which there cannot be any real disagreements among members because all are of like and right mind; extreme Dystopias are absolute tyrannies in which contention is not a possibility. In Utopia, then, no lawyers are needed; in Dystopia, no lawyers are allowed.

In between, however, is where most Utopia-Dystopias as well as most human societies fall, and here the composers of these fictions have shown remarkable fecundity. Relations between the sexes exhibit perhaps the widest range. Some Utopias go for a sort of healthy-minded communal sex, others, like W.H. Hudson's *Crystal Age*, for an ant-like arrangement in which most citizens are sexually neutral and only one pair per large country mansion actually breed, which is how they cut down on the birth rate. Still others, like Marge Piercey's, allow men to participate almost equally in child-rearing by allowing them to breast-feed via hormone injections, an option that may not rejoice your hearts but at least has the virtue of novelty. Then there are Huxley's ritualistic group sex and bottle babies, Skinner's boxes, and various minor science fictions, written by men I hasten to add, in which women devour their mates or paralyze them and lay eggs on them, *à la* spiders. Sexual relations in extreme Dystopias usually exhibit some form of slavery or, as in Orwell, extreme sexual repression.

The details, then, vary; but the Utopia-Dystopia as a form is a way of trying things out on paper first to see whether or not we might like them, should we ever have the chance to put them into actual practice. In addition, it challenges us to re-examine what we understand by the word ''human'', and above all what we intend by the word ''freedom''. For neither the Utopia or the Dystopia is open-ended. Utopia is an extreme example of the impulse to order: it's the word ''should'' run rampant. Dystopia, its nightmare mirror image, is the desire to squash dissent taken to inhuman and lunatic lengths. Neither are what you'd call tolerant, but both are necessary to the imagination: if we can't visualize the good, the ideal, if we can't formulate what we want, we'll get what we don't want, in spades. It's a sad commentary on our age that we find Dystopias a lot easier to believe in than Utopias: Utopias we can only imagine, Dystopias we've already got. But should we try too hard to enforce Utopia, Dystopia rapidly follows; because if enough people disagree with us we'll have to eliminate or suppress or terrorize or manipulate them, and then we've got 1984. As a rule, Utopia is only safe when it remains true to its name and stays nowhere. It's a nice place to visit, but do we really want to live there? Which may be the ultimate moral of such stories.

The word ''moral'' leads me to my third area of contemplation: the metaphysical. In the mimetic area, our emphasis was on lawyers as fictional characters; in the architectonic, on legal structures as compiled by the fictionalizing imagination; now we've come to justice as metaphor. The interface here is with secular society, true, but also with that whole set of religious concepts which attach, not only to the idea of the impersonality of justice - justice is blind, and so forth - but to its *personality*, to that bundle containing guilt and innocence, sin and redemption, crime and reparation. An eye for an eye, a tooth for a tooth, a pound of flesh - how much more personal, how much closer to body language can you get? The word *justice* is, not only for writers but for all of us, a loaded gun. It's noteworthy that in the Old Testament there's a Book of Judges but no book of lawyers, and that isn't merely a joke. To argue a case is one thing, to pronounce judgement quite another. A lawyer wins or loses, a judge does neither. A lawyer is supposed to be smart, a judge wise. A good lawyer, in the Book of Kings, might have got his client half a child; but a good judge, like Solomon, never would have awarded it. Judges, to conclude, exercise their judgement, whereas lawyers merely exercise.

Looming behind the concept of earthly justice is the heavenly or after-death variety, going back at least as far as the ancient Egyptians, for whom the soul of the departed was supposed to stand naked and trembling before the God Anubis - who, by the way, had the head of a jackal - to be weighed and rewarded or punished, according to its deeds while alive. In the Judaeo-Christian tradition, God is, among other things, a judge; an equation that some judges, having studied logic as undergraduates but having forgotten some of it, are inclined to reverse.

In literature, the assumed difference between divine justice and the human kind is that the human kind is - I hate to say this - fallible. The divine kind is on the other hand inscrutable, which was what led Milton to justify the ways of God toward men. In other words, what happens to us can often seem vastly unfair. One traditional way of coping with this is that of Job's comforters, who tried to convince Job that his skin diseases were his own fault, like herpes. But that didn't wash with Job, or with God either. The ways of God *can't* be justified to man, says the Book of Job, because man is too limited to understand them. Don't try reason, try faith.

It's from this double meaning of the word "justice" - from the gap between what man defines, by his petty man-made laws, as justice, and what God seems to do to him instead, that two of the finest literary constructions in this category have emerged. I refer of course to Dostoyevski's *Crime and Punishment* and Franz Kafka's *The Trial*. I mention them in passing, to indicate what kind of thing the literary imagination at its best is capable of producing from such material.

You may find the metaphysical side of the idea of justice dangerous, and it can be; witness Iran. But to equate "justice" with the more limited concept of "legality" can be equally dangerous. The massacre of the Jews under the Nazi regime was legal, but was it just? Apartheid is legal, but is it just? Closer to home - the confiscation of the property of Japanese Canadians and the unequal treaties made with Canadian Indians were sanctioned by "legal" documents, but were they just? Have women always been dealt with justly? A society whose members do not distinguish justice, used in this sense, from legality would be a society of termites. But I know here that I'm preaching to the converted. I hasten to add, too, that we don't need the idea of God to make this distinction, although that was where such a distinction originated.

Let me turn back to the literary tradition in its concrete form, and ask the seldomly-asked question: What is it that makes Perry Mason courtroom dramas at all interesting for non-specialists such as myself? Certainly not the verbal pyrotechnics. I think it's that the form itself is inherently dramatic, and engages our own fears about trial and judgment; and it is this, rather than the suits, that may account for my own terror in courtrooms. In fact, any trial - not only the kind in books - is, formally considered, a play, a morality play with set allegorical figures. The law, seen from one angle, is itself a literary form; for what is the giving of evidence but controlled story-telling, what is precedent but a batch of stories that have previously been told? For us, the readers or the audience, it's Everyman who stands in the dock - which is a symbolic structure meant to enclose possible evil and protect us from contamination - while God, represented by the judge, with his mysterious black clothing and magic thunderbolt hammer, sits in judgement. He wears black to suggest inscrutability and his connection with death; also incorruptibility and holiness, since priests too wear black. Why is Gardner's prosecuting attorney such a rat? Because, as a literary figure, he's descended from the Devil's Advocate, a stand-in for the Devil himself, who, in his few appearances in the Bible, always argues for condemnation.

The accused in such dramas is us. He or she is our sense of guilt and our hope for pardon, which is why Gardner always has the accused turn out to be innocent. It's the legal technicalities that interest Gardner, but it's the salvation that interests us. Think of Perry Mason losing and the accused turning out to be a mass murderer and you'll see what I mean. Kafka's *Trial*, on the other hand, is not what we hope for, but what we fear: that we are in fact guilty, and for no discernible reason. For some, the opposite of justice is injustice; for others its opposite is mercy, and I'd be willing to bet that most lawyers would choose the first definition and most writers the second. To lighten things up, I'll mention one more literary trial: the trial presided over by the Queen of Hearts in *Alice in Wonderland*. This is the legal process as it appears to the child in us: both frightening and ridiculous, founded on incomprehensible jargon, crazed unreason and the arbitrary power of the *status quo*, but capable of being overthrown by our own innocent child's-eye vision. ''You're nothing but a pack of cards'' is what we all want, at some time or other, to say to those who give us documents we can't read and subject us to legal procedures we don't understand. But this kind of freedom is available to us, alas, only in books, and children's books at that: mostly we find the law fearful. And why not, since it has such real power over our lives?

"Real power over our lives..." Perhaps this is what the difference between writing and the legal profession really boils down to. The law does have power over our lives, while writing has power only over our imaginations. But why do I say "only"?

For the law itself is a creature of the mind, and as such is limited to the categories of the human imagination itself. We can embody in the law only what we can first imagine as fully human beings; and the more stunted and repressive the imagination at work, the more harsh, punitive and intolerable will be the resulting laws.

How do my three categories apply to you and to what you think you're up to? If the legal system fails to think mimetically, to take reality-based satire of itself to heart - if it fails to think architectonically, to use such power as it has for the improvement of social structures - above all, if it convinces itself that law and justice are the same thing, and that its only job therefore is the enforcement of the *status quo* - it runs the risk of creating an unbridgeable gap between itself and the society it purports to serve. At such times it is in danger of being turned into a pack of cards indeed. Totalitarian regimes result from, among other things, a failure of the rule of law, as Dickens noted, and in them lawyers and judges get lined up against the wall right along with the labour leaders and, needless to say, the writers.

So you may think I'm - collectively - crazy and I may think you're - collectively - boring, but I at least have the sense to realize that we're in this together. All you may expect from me is a little fluff after the banquet, but I expect a good deal more from you. If you are judges, I expect prudence, wisdom, balance, flexibility and fairness. I expect you to take cognizance of the fact that the society you serve is not all white, all male or all middle-class. I expect you to stand up against panic, mob rule, and the kind of back-to-the-fold stampeding which is set off by our fears of what we think we can't control, such as each other's sex lives and the neutron bomb.

If you're lawyers, I expect you to clean up your language so I'll be able to understand what you're really saying to one another. I expect you to keep your buttons well done up, at least in public. I expect you to remember that, as little acorns into giant oak trees grow, so fares it with little lawyers: you may become judges one day, and you should therefore not close your minds as tidily as you close your cases.

And above all - for who is immune from subjectivity? - I as a writer expect the justice system to help create and maintain a social climate that will let a thousand flowers, and even a thousand bladders filled with dried peas, bloom.